Strategic Human Resource Management in the Public Arena

STRATEGIC HUMAN RESOURCE MANAGEMENT IN THE PUBLIC ARENA

A Managerial Perspective

J. Barton Cunningham

© J. Barton Cunningham 2016

All rights reserved. No reproduction, copy or transmission of this publication may be made without written permission.

No portion of this publication may be reproduced, copied or transmitted save with written permission or in accordance with the provisions of the Copyright, Designs and Patents Act 1988, or under the terms of any licence permitting limited copying issued by the Copyright Licensing Agency, Saffron House, 6–10 Kirby Street, London EC1N 8TS.

Any person who does any unauthorized act in relation to this publication may be liable to criminal prosecution and civil claims for damages.

The author has asserted his right to be identified as the author of this work in accordance with the Copyright, Designs and Patents Act 1988.

First published 2016 by
PALGRAVE

Palgrave in the UK is an imprint of Macmillan Publishers Limited, registered in England, company number 785998, of 4 Crinan Street, London N1 9XW.

Palgrave Macmillan in the US is a division of St Martin's Press LLC, 175 Fifth Avenue, New York, NY 10010.

Palgrave is a global imprint of the above companies and is represented throughout the world.

Palgrave® and Macmillan® are registered trademarks in the United States, the United Kingdom, Europe and other countries.
ISBN 978-1-137-43804-1   ISBN 978-1-137-43241-4 (eBook)
DOI 10.1007/978-1-137-43241-4

This book is printed on paper suitable for recycling and made from fully managed and sustained forest sources. Logging, pulping and manufacturing processes are expected to conform to the environmental regulations of the country of origin.

A catalogue record for this book is available from the British Library.

A catalog record for this book is available from the Library of Congress.

Short Contents

List of Figures	x
List of Tables	xi
Acknowledgements	xii
Preface	xiii

PART I: Putting Strategy into Human Resource Management in the Public Sector — 1
1. Human Resource Management's Strategic Pressures — 3
2. Using a SHRM Balanced Scorecard as a Strategic Framework — 25

PART II: Designing Customer-Focused Jobs — 47
3. Defining Competencies and Critical Requirements for a Job — 49
4. Engaging Employees in More Productive Ways of Working — 68
5. Workforce Forecasting and Planning — 89

PART III: Aligning Staffing and Performance Management Processes — 109
6. Recruiting a Diverse Workforce — 111
7. Aligning Selection Strategies — 135
8. Encouraging Employee Development in Reviewing Performance — 157

PART IV: Developing and Engaging Employees — 185
9. Encouraging Individually Directed Career Development — 187
10. Encouraging Competency-based Training and Development — 201
11. Reducing Stress and Improving Workplace Health and Safety — 214
12. Negotiating a Collective Agreement Using Positional and Interest-based Processes — 238
13. Developing a Positive Labour Relations Climate — 253

PART V: Compensating and Rewarding People — 271
14. Designing Compensation Systems to Respond to Equity Requirements — 273
15. Constructing Retirement and Benefits Plans — 289
16. Paying for Performance and Recognizing Employees — 305

References	318
Glossary	369
Index	389

Contents

List of Figures   x
List of Tables   xi
Acknowledgements   xii
Preface   xiii

PART I: Putting Strategy into Human Resource Management in the Public Sector   1

1 Human Resource Management's Strategic Pressures   3
    CHAPTER OBJECTIVES (COs)   3
    A DRIVING ISSUE FOCUSING MANAGERIAL ACTION: THE INCREASING IMPORTANCE OF INTANGIBLES IN PUBLIC SECTOR PERFORMANCE   3
    CO 1: STRATEGIC HUMAN RESOURCE MANAGEMENT (SHRM)   5
    CO 2: SOCIETAL FORCES OR PRESSURES SHAPING SHRM   9
    BEFORE APPLYING, LET'S REVIEW   21
    DISCUSSION AND REVIEW QUESTIONS   22

2 Using a SHRM Balanced Scorecard as a Strategic Framework   25
    CHAPTER OBJECTIVES (COs)   25
    A DRIVING ISSUE FOCUSING MANAGERIAL ACTION: NPM   25
    CO 1: DIFFERENT PERSPECTIVES DEFINING SHRM   27
    CO 2: THE BALANCED SCORECARD IN PUBLIC ORGANIZATIONS   31
    CO 3: THE SHRM BALANCED SCORECARD   34
    SHRM BSC TERMINOLOGY   41
    BEFORE APPLYING, LET'S REVIEW   42
    DISCUSSION AND REVIEW QUESTIONS   43

PART II: Designing Customer-Focused Jobs   47

3 Defining Competencies and Critical Requirements for a Job   49
    CHAPTER OBJECTIVES (COs)   49
    A DRIVING ISSUE FOCUSING MANAGERIAL ACTION: COMPETENCY-BASED MANAGEMENT (CBM)   49
    CO 1: IDENTIFYING ESSENTIAL JOB REQUIREMENTS AND COMPETENCIES IN THE JOB ANALYSIS PROCESS   51
    CO 2: COMPETENCY MODELS IN STRATEGIC MANAGEMENT   58
    CO 3: IDENTIFYING COMPETENCIES AND PERFORMANCE NORMS   62
    BEFORE APPLYING, LET'S REVIEW   64
    DISCUSSION AND REVIEW QUESTIONS   65

4 Engaging Employees in More Productive Ways of Working   68
    CHAPTER OBJECTIVES (COs)   68

	A DRIVING ISSUE FOCUSING MANAGERIAL ACTION: HOW PUBLIC SERVICE MOTIVATION (PSM) AFFECTS PUBLIC SERVICE ORGANIZATIONS	68
	CO 1: EMPLOYEE ENGAGEMENT AND JOB ENRICHMENT	70
	CO 2: QUALITY OF WORKING LIFE (QWL) AND TOTAL QUALITY MANAGEMENT (TQM)	76
	CO 3: EMERGING PERSPECTIVES ON JOB AND ORGANIZATIONAL DESIGN	81
	BEFORE APPLYING, LET'S REVIEW	85
	DISCUSSION AND REVIEW QUESTIONS	85
5	**Workforce Forecasting and Planning**	**89**
	CHAPTER OBJECTIVES (COs)	89
	A DRIVING ISSUE FOCUSING MANAGERIAL ACTION: RESPONDING TO THE CHANGING AGE PROFILE IN WORKFORCE PLANNING	89
	CO 1: WORKFORCE PLANNING IN THE PUBLIC SECTOR	91
	CO 2: TOOLS FOR FORECASTING DEMAND AND SUPPLY OF SKILLS	96
	CO 3: USING SCENARIOS IN PUBLIC SECTOR WORKFORCE PLANNING	101
	BEFORE APPLYING, LET'S REVIEW	104
	DISCUSSION AND REVIEW QUESTIONS	105
PART III: Aligning Staffing and Performance Management Processes		**109**
6	**Recruiting a Diverse Workforce**	**111**
	CHAPTER OBJECTIVES (COs)	111
	A DRIVING ISSUE FOCUSING MANAGERIAL ACTION: RECOGNIZING NEW PARADIGMS ON DIVERSITY	111
	CO 1: FOCUSING RECRUITMENT TO MEET DIVERSITY OBJECTIVES	113
	CO 2: THE RELEVANCE OF THREE RECRUITING STRATEGIES IN MEETING DIVERSITY OBJECTIVES	117
	CO 3: THE EMPLOYEE'S PERSPECTIVE – SEARCHING FOR A JOB	130
	BEFORE APPLYING, LET'S REVIEW	131
	DISCUSSION AND REVIEW QUESTIONS	132
7	**Aligning Selection Strategies**	**135**
	CHAPTER OBJECTIVES (COs)	135
	A DRIVING ISSUE FOCUSING MANAGERIAL ACTION: EMPLOYEE FITNESS IN THE STRATEGIC CONTEXT	135
	CO 1: APPLY THE TRIANGULATION PRINCIPLE IN PICKING SELECTION TOOLS TO RELIABLY AND VALIDLY MAKE SELECTION DECISIONS	137
	CO 2: TESTS AND INVENTORIES IN SELECTION	144
	CO 3: SELECTION INTERVIEWING	148
	BEFORE APPLYING, LET'S REVIEW	153
	DISCUSSION AND REVIEW QUESTIONS	154
8	**Encouraging Employee Development in Reviewing Performance**	**157**
	CHAPTER OBJECTIVES (COs)	157
	A DRIVING ISSUE FOCUSING MANAGERIAL ACTION: RESPONDING TO THE PROBLEMS WITH PERFORMANCE REVIEWS	157
	CO 1: GOAL SETTING IN THE STRATEGIC PROCESS	159

	CO 2: DIFFERENT APPROACHES TO MANAGING PERFORMANCE REVIEWS	161
	CO 3: FORMATIVE APPROACHES FOR ENCOURAGING FEEDBACK	169
	CO 4: CARRYING OUT A GOAL-SETTING PERFORMANCE REVIEW	171
	CO 5: CARRYING OUT DISCIPLINARY AND TERMINATION PROCEDURES	178
	BEFORE APPLYING, LET'S REVIEW	181
	DISCUSSION AND REVIEW QUESTIONS	182

PART IV: Developing and Engaging Employees — 185

9 Encouraging Individually Directed Career Development — 187

CHAPTER OBJECTIVES (COs)	187
A DRIVING ISSUE FOCUSING MANAGERIAL ACTION: RECOGNIZING HOW VOCATIONAL PREFERENCES SHAPE HOW PEOPLE FIT	187
CO 1: THE EMERGENCE OF A NEW CAREER CONTRACT	189
CO 2: ORGANIZATIONAL AND INDIVIDUALLY DIRECTED CAREER DEVELOPMENT	191
CO 3: CAREER DEVELOPMENT PLANNING FOR A BOUNDARY-LESS CAREER	195
BEFORE APPLYING, LET'S REVIEW	197
DISCUSSION AND REVIEW QUESTIONS	198

10 Encouraging Competency-based Training and Development — 201

CHAPTER OBJECTIVES (COs)	201
A DRIVING ISSUE FOCUSING MANAGERIAL ACTION: LINKING TRAINING TO APPLICATION	201
CO 1: COMPETENCY-BASED TRAINING IN MEETING TRAINING NEEDS	203
CO 2: APPLYING EXPERIENTIAL LEARNING IN TRAINING AND DEVELOPMENT	206
BEFORE APPLYING, LET'S REVIEW	211
DISCUSSION AND REVIEW QUESTIONS	211

11 Reducing Stress and Improving Workplace Health and Safety — 214

CHAPTER OBJECTIVES (COs)	214
A DRIVING ISSUE FOCUSING MANAGERIAL ACTION: RESPONDING TO THE NEW WORLD OF WORKPLACE SAFETY AND HEALTH	214
CO 1: WORKPLACE MENTAL HEALTH AND STRESS	216
CO 2: MANAGING ABSENTEEISM IN RETURNING PEOPLE TO WORK	224
CO 3: DEVELOPING A CULTURE SUPPORTING WORKPLACE SAFETY AND HEALTH	226
BEFORE APPLYING, LET'S REVIEW	233
DISCUSSION AND REVIEW QUESTIONS	233

12 Negotiating a Collective Agreement Using Positional and Interest-based Processes — 238

CHAPTER OBJECTIVES (COs)	238
A DRIVING ISSUE FOCUSING MANAGERIAL ACTION: RESPONDING TO THE WAY UNIONS HAVE CHANGED OVER THE YEARS	238
CO 1: NEGOTIATING A COLLECTIVE AGREEMENT IN THE PUBLIC SECTOR	240
CO 2: INTEGRATIVE OR INTEREST-BASED PROCESSES FOR RESOLVING DISPUTES	244
BEFORE APPLYING, LET'S REVIEW	249
DISCUSSION AND REVIEW QUESTIONS	250

13	**Developing a Positive Labour Relations Climate**	**253**
	CHAPTER OBJECTIVES (COs)	253
	A DRIVING ISSUE FOCUSING MANAGERIAL ACTION: WORKING WITH THE INTERNATIONAL FRAMEWORK OF LAWS FOR DEVELOPING A POSITIVE LABOUR RELATIONS CLIMATE	253
	CO 1: SHAPING AND INFLUENCING A POSITIVE LABOUR RELATIONS CLIMATE	255
	CO 2: INTEGRATIVE OR PROBLEM-SOLVING APPROACHES FOR RESOLVING DISPUTES	259
	CO 3: PROCEDURAL JUSTICE IN MAINTAINING A POSITIVE LABOUR RELATIONS CLIMATE	262
	BEFORE APPLYING, LET'S REVIEW	267
	DISCUSSION AND REVIEW QUESTIONS	267

PART V: Compensating and Rewarding People — 271

14	**Designing Compensation Systems to Respond to Equity Requirements**	**273**
	CHAPTER OBJECTIVES (COs)	273
	A DRIVING ISSUE FOCUSING MANAGERIAL ACTION: KNOWING WHAT IT IS ABOUT PAY THAT IS A SATISFIER	273
	CO 1: USING EQUITY OBJECTIVES TO DESIGN A COMPENSATION SYSTEM	275
	CO 2: TRADITIONAL APPROACHES FOR EVALUATING JOBS	277
	CO 3: DESIGNING AND APPLYING A POINT JOB EVALUATION APPROACH	279
	BEFORE APPLYING, LET'S REVIEW	286
	DISCUSSION AND REVIEW QUESTIONS	286

15	**Constructing Retirement and Benefits Plans**	**289**
	CHAPTER OBJECTIVES (COs)	289
	A DRIVING ISSUE FOCUSING MANAGERIAL ACTION: RECOGNIZING THAT DIFFERENT PEOPLE WANT DIFFERENT TYPES OF EMPLOYEE BENEFITS	289
	CO 1: THE NEW WORLD OF FUNDING PENSION BENEFITS	291
	CO 2: THE NEW WORLD OF FUNDING HEALTH CARE BENEFITS	295
	CO 3: THE NEW WORLD OF WORK–FAMILY BENEFITS	299
	BEFORE APPLYING, LET'S REVIEW	301
	DISCUSSION AND REVIEW QUESTIONS	302

16	**Paying for Performance and Recognizing Employees**	**305**
	CHAPTER OBJECTIVES (COs)	305
	A DRIVING ISSUE FOCUSING MANAGERIAL ACTION: SEEING HOW DIFFERENT COUNTRIES PLACE MORE EMPHASIS ON PAY FOR PERFORMANCE (PFP)	305
	CO 1: PFP IN PUBLIC ORGANIZATIONS	306
	CO 2: RECOGNIZING AND PROVIDING FEEDBACK ON EMPLOYEE CONTRIBUTIONS	313
	BEFORE APPLYING, LET'S REVIEW	315
	DISCUSSION AND REVIEW QUESTIONS	316

References — 318
Glossary — 369
Index — 389

List of Figures

1.1	Evolving roles and responsibilities of HRM	5
2.1	Linking resources to strategy	30
2.2	The organization's strategic framework within the BSC	33
2.3	The SHRM BSC in implementing the organization's strategic framework	35
2.4	Semi-causal chain linking objectives to vision and strategy	38
2.5	Cool Aid's strategy map linking HR strategic objectives to the organization's strategic themes	40
3.1	CAO competency scorecard	61
4.1	The factors defining motivation-hygiene theory	72
4.2	The job characteristics model (JCM) of job enrichment	74
4.3	Strategic theme: Improving the quality of life and productivity	86
5.1	Different scenarios reflecting unique economic and social environments	102
5.2	Strategy map for competencies in getting a good job	105
6.1	Three general recruiting strategies	117
6.2	Employee recruitment and selection – steps for external recruiting	118
6.3	Strategy map for improving diversity and inclusiveness in the workforce	133
7.1	Interview question yield hierarchy: The yield of different types of interview questions	151
9.1	How-why questions	196
9.2	How-why? process	198
10.1	Four phases of Kolb's learning model	207
11.1	The general adaptation syndrome	219
11.2	A framework for understanding some of the effects of stress	220
11.3	Enhancing workplace health and safety to the highest level	234
13.1	Strategy map for developing a positive labour relations climate	268
14.1	Pay structure for different groups of jobs	283

List of Tables

1.1	Pressures and Forces Shaping Society and the Way We Manage	10
1.2	Case – Societal Forces or Pressures Affecting HRM and How We Manage	24
2.1	Examples of Best Practices	29
3.1	Competency Clusters Illustrating Distinguishing (in Bold) and Threshold Competencies	50
3.2	Advantages and Disadvantages of Six Job Analysis Methods	57
3.3	Competencies	65
5.1	A General Workforce Planning Model	92
5.2	Quantitative Forecasting Techniques	97
5.3	Qualitative Forecasting Techniques	100
5.4	Initiatives and Measures for Implementing Strategic Objectives	106
6.1	Review of Recruiting Sources	120
6.2	Strategic Theme: Improving Diversity and Inclusiveness in the Workforce	133
7.1	Validity of Different Selection Methods	140
7.2	Application of Assessment Centre Exercises for Selecting Doctors for Postgraduate Training	144
7.3	Behavioural Questions for Selecting People with a 'Public Sector Motivation'	155
8.1	A Snapshot of Advantages and Disadvantages of Different Performance Review Approaches	162
8.2	Examples of a Graphic Rating Scale	164
8.3	Examples of Items in a Behavioural Checklist for Faculty Teaching Evaluation	165
8.4	BARS for the Dimension 'Ability to Absorb and Interpret Policies'	166
8.5	Example of a form for summarizing competencies	167
8.6	Examples of Critical Incident Descriptions of Teacher's Work	168
8.7	Example of a Form for 'One-Minute Goal Setting'	175
8.8	Example of a Form for a Performance Planning and Review Process – Work Plan	176
8.9	Skills Inventory Form	177
9.1	Strategic Objective: Taking Responsibility for Your Own Career Development	199
10.1	Evaluation Measures	212
11.1	General Occupational Stress Pressures and Those Resulting from New Public Management (NPM) Initiatives	218
12.1	Interest-based versus Positional Approaches to Bargaining	246
12.2	Tactics for Developing a Negotiation Plan from Either a Management or Union Perspective	250
14.1	Comparing Different Job Evaluation Methods	278
14.2	Factors and General Subfactors in CUPE's Job Evaluation Plan	280
14.3	Points Assigned to Factors and Subfactors in a Point Plan	282
14.4	Examples of Scores in a Point Job Evaluation Plan	282
14.5	Rating Different Jobs	288
15.1	Different Scheduling Options	303
15.2	Schedules Most Used in Various Health Organizations and Desired by Staff	303
16.1	The Pros and Cons of Individual, Team and Organizational Plans	310

Acknowledgements

I began working on this book in earnest in 2006 when I was on a sabbatical at Johannes Kepler University in Austria. I initially had a contract to write a book for the private sector context, but the chance to write a book for the public sector context was too attractive. This book benefited greatly from my work with Evelyne Glaser who provided valuable feedback to me when I was in Austria teaching international students. This book also builds on my experiences and teaching relationships in Austria, Canada, the United States, the United Kingdom, New Zealand, Czech Republic, Malaysia, Brunei, Macau and Singapore. This has involved interesting conversations with scholars such as Chester Newland, Gilbert Siegel, Alex McEachern, James MacGregor, Janice Ho, Mark Harcourt, Jarrod Haar, Ali Dastmalchian, Thea Vakil, Jenny Gibb, Linda Twiname, Newman Lam, Claudia Steinke and Jennifer Walinga.

There was also a cadre of senior public sector managers who played very active roles in shaping my ideas so that they were relevant for managers and for grounding public administration theories. Their experience in federal, provincial and local governments and not-for-profit organizations gave the book a practical perspective in helping me focus on problems they encountered in their work and made sure that what I was writing was useful to them. Most important among these people included James Kempling, Ken Strobl and John Farquharson who played very active roles in critiquing, editing, devising new charts and helping me step down from the ledge. Also important were Natasha Caverley, Greg Connor, Roy Emperingham and John Fryer.

In addition to the many Master's students who have helped me, there are three PhD students who helped bring my book to fruition. In particular, Jennifer Kroeker-Hall provided insightful review and editing. Her diligence and attention to detail, as well as her ability to grasp the big picture, brought fresh eyes to the text. Diana Campbell and Walter Lapore also contributed their time and energy to reviewing numerous chapters. And, a special thank you goes to my life partner, Donna, for her help over the decades.

Preface

> **Chapter Outline**
> - Chapter objectives (COs)   xiii
> - CO 1: Strategic Human Resource Management (SHRM) and the public arena   xiii
> - CO 2: A framework for SHRM in the public arena   xvii
> - Before applying, let's review   xx
> - Discussion and review questions   xxi

CHAPTER OBJECTIVES (COs)

After reading this chapter, you will be able to implement the following objectives:

CO 1: Understand the context affecting human resources (HR) in the public arena.

CO 2: Define a framework for strategic human resource management (SHRM) in the public arena.

> *STRATEGIC CONTEXT: HRM is where 'the rubber meets the road' in managing people. Almost every organizational strategic theme and objective that managers engage in involves some connection to HR processes such as those needed in defining job requirements, competencies and performance standards; setting goals and monitoring performance; and recruiting, selecting and compensating people.*
>
> *This book illustrates how HRM processes help an organization achieve its strategic objectives. Strategic Human Resource Management in the Public Arena offers a set of principles for managers in public sector organizations operating within an increasingly challenging environment that demands a balanced response to taxpayers, clients and a range of other stakeholders. This book's principles and tools are designed for students studying public organizations and the challenges they face which require them to be accountable to the public, businesses they regulate and other public organizations. It is also aimed at students studying business organizations engaged in providing public services. This chapter introduces a framework linking an organization's strategic themes and objectives so that they align with those of the HR system.*

CO 1: STRATEGIC HUMAN RESOURCE MANAGEMENT (SHRM) AND THE PUBLIC ARENA

What is generally thought of as the public sector includes organizations at the federal, provincial and local levels that provide services and programmes for the general public good. Organizations in the public arena carry out a wide variety of public-related tasks in providing social services (e.g. education, health care and social services), regulations (e.g. gaming, housing, transportation), safety and justice (e.g. police, courts, fire, military), common services (e.g. transportation, utilities) and in establishing planning guidelines (e.g. development, education, safety).

Private sector organizations are those for-profit businesses involved in the sale of goods or services, or both, to consumers. They include sole proprietorship, partnerships, larger corporations and consumer co-operatives, and involve activities such as farming, mining, financial services, manufacturing, real estate, retail services, transportation and utilities. However, like public organizations, some private organizations also work in the public arena, providing services for the general public good. Some business or private programmes operate hospitals, work with public organizations in public/private partnerships and act as philanthropic organizations contributing or managing programmes in the community.

The differentiation of what is public and private is confounded by several factors, including the growing involvement and regulation of business in all aspects of life – the operation of a business, the growth of the service economy where businesses carry out many governmental services and the adoption of business management practices in some public organizations. Public sector and private sector organizations are very interconnected. Observable processes include public/private partnerships (PPPs) involving co-operative arrangements in contracting, franchising or management of complex projects (such as those requiring infrastructure and technology).[1] In other cases, private organizations carry out traditional governmental services such as home care and highway maintenance under contracts from governmental organizations. In some of these cases, contracted private sector companies are so dependent on government contracts that they operate like governments immune from private market forces. In other cases, private organizations have so much market power (e.g. utilities) that they no longer operate like they are in a free enterprise market. It is also true that some of the differences related to managing people are more perceptual than factual, such as when people say that private sector employees work harder or public sector organizations are more bureaucratic. In the following chapters, this book provides examples and information relevant for SHRM in public organizations.

Is HRM in the public sector any different from that in the private sector? If not, why is it important to focus specifically on SHRM in public organizations rather than treat it as simply a generalist field relevant for all types of organization regardless of sector?

One of the most debated issues in management has been the extent to which managerial and HR processes and tools are applicable to a wide range of organizations. Can private sector practices be adopted to encourage strategic change in public organizations? In a review of the organizational theory history, there are several scholars who believe they can and should be. Indeed, Max Weber suggested that his view of bureaucracy was as relevant for private as for public organizations,[2] and Herbert Simon[3] and James D. Thompson[4] indicated that these sectors illustrated more commonalities than differences.

The private sector model has served as a guide for effective management in the public sector ever since public administration began and continues to be an important reference. The New Public Management (NPM), for example, is based on the conviction that the solution to improving government problems is to transfer, where possible, many government activities to the private sector through contracting out and privatization, or adopt business management practices to government.[5] Business ideas which have been transplanted to the public sector are of two types: mechanistic/rational and humanistic/organic. The more rational types of ideas include zero-based budgeting, management by objectives, performance measurement and accounting techniques and strategic management. Humanistic ideas which originated in the private sector include organic structures, humanistic management styles and empowerment.[6]

The assumptions underlying the transfer of a set of practices from one sector or one organization to another must be considered in various ways. First, are the organizational characteristics and environments similar? Secondly, are the resources similar and does the method of obtaining resources (e.g.

from profits vs. taxes) affect the way the practices are used? Thirdly, can issues in different sectors (e.g. incentives, labour relations) be solved with similar solutions?[7]

The theory and practice of public administration warns us to avoid making general conclusions or sharp distinctions between public and private organizations.[8] This book seeks to integrate the literature on SHRM with the research and practices in public sector organizations. Scholars in the field of psychology, sociology, management and organizational behaviour have provided a strong body of evidence on SHRM, just as political scientists, economists, public administration scholars and managers have enriched our understanding of policymaking and management in the public arena.

The difficulty of making distinctions between public and private organizations is partially linked to our different understanding of what we mean by public. Underlying the challenge is the fact that **public** means different things in different parts of the world. In some parts of Europe (e.g. France, Italy, Spain) and Latin America, services that are considered public (e.g. education, health) are provided free of charge. These are usually considered basic services that must be accessed independently of having the money to pay for it. Doing otherwise would imply the denial of civil rights.

Another challenge comes from the growth of organizational forms that are difficult to categorize using the traditional public versus private dichotomy. Examples of these blurred forms include research and development co-operatives, government contracted enterprises, defence contractors and public corporations. Given these hybrid forms, it might be appropriate to accept Barry Bozeman's suggestion that organizations might be placed on a dimension of publicness. As such, publicness is 'the degree to which the organization is affected by political authority'[9] and is public to the extent that it is constrained primarily by political authority, and private when constrained primarily by economic authority.

However, given these caveats, there is strong evidence that the nature of the public arena and the problems that managers face demand special attention.

Why is it important to focus on SHRM in the 'public arena'?

My comments on SHRM in the public arena are shaped by over 30 years of teaching and research in public organizations, in addition to nearly 10 years in business schools. The uniqueness is partially shaped by the raison d'être of public organization, the special role of public organizations in society, the people who work in public organizations and the prominence of public sector unions. Let me comment on each of these.

The raison d'être of public organizations. Public organizations have a unique purpose. At the national level, a state is a political organization that includes a territory, population and government. States and the public organizations within them have the responsibility for defining policies and making and administering rules, laws and guidelines. This general purpose in public organizations affects the tasks they do and goes beyond those performed by large high-profile profit organizations like Apple computers, Toyota, Airbus or Boeing.

The strategic context of public organizations is affected by the general purpose of public organizations. The raison d'être of public organizations can partially be illustrated in Dahl and Lindblom's legendary description of the relationship between political hierarchies and economic markets. In the political process, we see an array of contending interests and organizations that direct economic activities.[10] Although the price system in an economic market can facilitate production, marketing and allocation decisions, the political system can provide an inexpensive system for social controls. For example, it is cheaper to have people willingly pay taxes or not break the law rather than rely on ways to compensate or punish them for compliance. Because free markets are more flexible, they are often efficient in using resources, responding to changing consumer demands, and are less cumbersome.

Public organizations have a general responsibility to implement strategies and goals that serve the general public interest.[11] (i) Some strategies serve a general public interest and can more easily be provided for all of society. That is, although education and health services are sometimes provided by private organizations, public organizations often provide a majority of these services because they benefit everyone. (ii) Public organizations often provide regulatory functions because the individual actors do not have the information or incentives to do so. For example, governments regulate the behaviour of individuals in areas such as workplace safety, food and drug safety, and transportation. (iii) Public organizations also implement strategies to protect the public interest in areas where the free market economy cannot be remunerated, such as in making sure private individuals do not pollute the air or water when they manufacture their products.[12]

For some scholars, public organizations exist to regulate and respond to problems of a free market economy in redistributing income and providing stability to the market and implementing programmes that are too risky for private organizations. Several scholars argue for powerful governments to provide the rationality for a society that serves the general public good; others argue that markets will generally resolve many of the problems that government responds to. Within this reasoning, we can privatize many government services and operate them more efficiently.

Whether or not we agree with a strong government, the character of public organizational leadership is dramatically different from private organizations. In public organizations, we have two kinds of leaders who serve different but necessarily interdependent roles. Public organizations are led by political leaders who are elected by citizens and voters. They serve on school and community boards, municipal or regional councils, and provincial, state or national assemblies. Public organizations also have executives – the school superintendents, city managers and departmental heads – who act as policy leaders and managers. Their main function is to develop policies, regulations and guidelines and direct the organization and its programmes to reflect the needs of the organization as well as the will of the political leaders and electorates. They understand the realities and constraints from a managerial and organizational perspective, whereas their elected officials are more directly responsive in the political arena to citizens, interest groups and the media. The department leaders have the job of interfacing between elected officials and career managers who have more direct knowledge of the area they work in. The political leaders, theoretically, have a shorter tenure in some countries, and might be removed from office because of voter dissatisfaction, whereas career civil servants may work in these departments serving a variety of political perspectives throughout their careers.

Although people in public organizations often share private sector values such as efficiency and effectiveness, they are influenced by forces that are not as central to private organizations, such as accountability to elected officials, public demands and expectations, professional standards, interest groups and public scrutiny and criticism in a fish bowl-like environment. Managers face a wide range of expectations, and responding to all these stakeholders often calls for trading off efficiency for responsiveness to sensitive political needs.

The special value creating role of public organizations. A second observation on the uniqueness of public organizations is the role they play in nurturing society's values. Public sector managers and organizations act as agents in providing services and programmes which are value creating. They provide a model for others in society.

Managers model and nurture societal values by (i) using money, authority and resources to produce things that people value and (ii) establishing and using public institutions to do what people value.[13] 'A society's "public values" are those providing normative consensus about (a) the rights, benefits, and prerogatives to which citizens of society should (or should not) be entitled; (b) the obligations of citizens to society, the state, and to one another; and (c) the principles on which governments and policies should be based.'[14] Values are rooted in what people find important and not important. They reflect the preferences that individuals have, their rights, the benefits to which they are entitled and the obligations expected of citizens.[15] Individuals have their own individual values on these matters, but public organizations play an important role in defining and guiding the values of what people find important in society. They play a role in stretching out and being more responsive to the values of different cultural groups, diversity objectives and social and community priorities.

The people in public organizations. A third observation of the distinctive way in which public organizations operate is evident in how people in them respond to theories and ideas about management in general, and HRM in particular, a uniqueness which is supported with research evidence. People who work in public organizations have different interests and values. They observe different things and have different preconceptions or theories, different objectives, skills, habits and principles when they carry out their work. Some of these differences are partially shaped by demographic factors, in that public sector organizations need to be responsive to gender and ethnicity issues.[16] Some of these differences are shaped by an educational curriculum which teaches people in business about improving market share, profit and return on investment, whereas people in public administration are driven to develop policies and programmes to respond to societal problems related to crime, poverty and drug abuse. This is illustrated in the public sector motivational values of students who are concerned with policymaking and being responsive to public sector challenges like improving the environment and ending homelessness.

The prominence of public sector unions. A final observation of the uniqueness of public organizations relates to the need to work with unions. If you are a manager in a public sector organization, you will likely have to work with a union. Although there is a downward shift in the membership of private sector unions throughout the world, there is an increasing presence of public sector unions, a trend that began in the 1960s. The power of the union movement has changed since this time; public sector collective bargaining is unique in that the negotiations involve discussions between union leaders and management representatives who really are articulating the interests of the government. In the background, each party is bargaining and trying to sway the interests of the public.

HR's terms of reference and rules for assisting others revolve around helping managers interpret and manage within the collective agreement. In the same way, all the HR tools in this book cannot be implemented unilaterally, but rely on consultation with the union and developing a positive labour relations climate.

CO 2: A FRAMEWORK FOR SHRM IN THE PUBLIC ARENA

In theory, public organizations exist in a political rather than an economic system in establishing a framework to define and maintain laws and regulations that guide us. They provide the direction and goals for the nation as a whole and for community groups, and for our system of human rights, education, health, social justice and security. SHRM has an important role to play in this, as a partner in the planning and execution of public sector strategies. As such, HR[17] assists managers to achieve their strategic priorities by articulating the implementation framework – the culture, competencies, work designs and the underlying recruitment, selection, training, performance management and labour relations processes.

This book is not meant for specialists in HRM, but is focused to help practitioners and students who are generally involved in managing people. A key assumption is that all managers are responsible in some way for HR activities in the way that they organize the work for their employees, challenge them in their careers, and guide them in their performance. They are also responsible in terms of the quality of working life and employee relations.

This purpose of this book is to review the theory and practice of SHRM in a public arena. As a unifying theme, each chapter provides an overview of the public sector strategic context and performance metrics that have been used to chart progress in each area. Given the public sector strategic context, the different chapter objectives provide the reader with information to define strategic objectives and initiatives to implement a relevant SHRM theme. Although the book does not provide specific objectives and performance metrics for specific themes, it focuses the reader on key strategic themes and objectives relevant to each chapter in addition to reviewing studies that have illustrated various measures, markers or dependent variables relevant to chapter area. The end of chapter questions and cases help the reader implement various strategic objectives.

The first section of the book assesses the relevance of different approaches to strategic management before highlighting the Balanced Scorecard (BSC) and strategy maps[18] as a way to illustrate a semi-causal linkage between an organization's objectives and the strategic themes it is focusing on. The general Balanced Scorecard framework summarizes four perspectives – the customer/client, internal process, innovation and learning (learning and growth), and financial perspectives – arranged in a semi-causal chain. The framework asks you to develop strategic objectives in response to basic questions that summarize different perspectives important to the implementation of a strategic theme:

1. How do customers see us? – Client and Customer perspective.
2. What must we excel at? – Internal process perspective.
3. Can we continue to improve and create value? – Innovation and Learning perspective (or Learning and Growth).
4. How do we look to shareholders? – Financial perspective.[19]

The SHRM-Balanced Scorecard (SHRM BSC) builds on the BSC to show how various HR strategic objectives can be aligned to the organization's strategic objectives. The SHRM BSC framework is based on the assumption that HR strategic objectives are aligned to help line managers respond to the organizational strategic objectives. As such, strategies are initially aligned to respond to interests or needs of the line managers or the internal customers or clients that HR is responding to.

The customer orientation has ushered in a profound transformation in the way public services are designed, and particularly the way an organization's strategic HR objectives are linked to internal customers or clients (line managers). As in the general Balanced Scorecard framework, the SHRM BSC summarizes four perspectives arranged in a semi-causal chain and encourages HR to develop objectives and initiatives within each of the different perspectives. So, after articulating HR objectives to respond to internal clients, practitioners can define objectives within the internal process, learning and growth, and financial perspectives. Internal process objectives relate to internal efficiencies within HR and learning and growth objectives are those focused on improving motivation, general abilities, and empowerment in relation to service, and practices in recruitment, selection and training. Finally, the financial perspective articulates objectives for compensating and rewarding people.[20]

This framework is also used as a conceptual tool to assist managers and students see how various topic areas in the book are connected to each other in a semi-causal chain.

Part I – The HRM Strategic Context

The first part of this book reviews the need to manage more strategically in responding to the pressures HR managers are facing.

1. *Human Resource Management's Strategic Pressures*
2. *Using an SHRM Balanced Scorecard as a Strategic Framework*

Part II – Designing Customer-focused Jobs

This part of the book highlights the importance of keeping the customer in mind in designing jobs, developing competencies and forecasting workforce needs.

3. *Defining Competencies and Critical Requirements for a Job*
4. *Engaging Employees in More Productive Ways of Working*
5. *Workforce Forecasting and Planning*

Part III – Aligning Staffing and Performance Management Processes

One important client need is to efficiently design systems to create a positive environment where people feel 'included' and to use recruitment, selection and performance management in attracting and retaining diverse individuals into a culture that values their individuality.

6. *Recruiting a Diverse Workforce*
7. *Aligning Selection Strategies*
8. *Encouraging Employee Development in Reviewing Performance*

Part IV – Developing and Engaging Employees

These chapters focus on implementing objectives related to career development, training and development, health and well-being, and developing a positive labour relations climate.

9. *Encouraging Individually Directed Career Development*
10. *Encouraging Competency-based Training and Development*
11. *Reducing Stress and Improving Workplace Health and Safety*
12. *Negotiating a Collective Agreement Using Positional and Interest-based Processes*
13. *Developing a Positive Labour Relations Climate*

Part V – Compensating and Rewarding People

These chapters review four components of a compensation system – fixed salaries, pensions, benefits and incentives – and their relevance for public sector organizations.

14. *Designing Compensation Systems to Respond to Equity Requirements*
15. *Constructing Retirement and Benefits Plans*
16. *Paying for Performance and Recognizing Employees*

The SHRM BSC is used as a tool to pictorially illustrate how HR objectives and initiatives can be aligned within the strategic themes an organization is pursuing. The book highlights general performance measures or markers that can be used to calibrate the effectiveness of HR initiatives.[21] It also encourages HR managers to play a facilitative role in assisting managers in line departments to strategically focus their initiatives and activities in meeting the needs of external clients or customers.

Each chapter has the following distinguishing features:

- In keeping with the book's orientation in providing guidance for managers and students, each chapter opens with a broad outline, 'Chapter objectives', of the various content areas.

- Following the chapter outline is a review entitled 'A driving issue focusing managerial action.' Each driving issue summarizes research or new ideas shaping the field of HRM.
- Next, there is a short section that provides the strategic context for the chapter. It also highlights a strategic theme or objective that the reader might focus on in reading the chapter material.
- The content of each chapter is organized around chapter objectives that in some cases could be used as the foundation for one or more strategic objectives. The material is introduced so that the reader gets an appreciation of relevant research and ideas applicable for practice.
- Each chapter includes a short section called 'A relevant point of view' to summarize examples, experiences or research offering another perspective that should be considered. Some of the chapters include short quizzes that are meant to provoke the reader into thinking about key issues. The questions ask readers to offer their perceptions or predictions before turning to the website where they can compare their responses to research evidence.
- The book summarizes its key features in the sections: 'Managerial implications' and 'Before applying, let's review.' These should help the reader focus his or her application.
- The final sections of the book include 'Discussion and review questions' and a 'Case' that provides an opportunity to apply the material. In particular, the questions ask you to implement aspects of the SHRM BSC using the contents of the chapter, and the cases provide an opportunity to play the role of policy analyst or manager in applying some of the principles reviewed in the chapter.
- The book's website includes background material on cases. It also illustrates how the SHRM BSC can be applied.
- The reader should also be mindful that the website includes additional personal learning and experiential learning exercises and suggested ways to apply concepts.

Ultimately, the aim of each chapter is to encourage you to apply the theory and principles in resolving problems that challenge managers in public sector environments and to do so strategically.

> MANAGERIAL IMPLICATION: SHRM has a special role to play in assisting organizations in the public arena and public sector organizations. The SHRM Balanced Scorecard framework shows how various HR strategic objectives and processes can be aligned to the organization's strategic objectives. The SHRM Balanced Scorecard and the strategy maps used here provide a way to visualize how to align organizational and HR strategic objectives to unique competencies in recruitment and selection, in designing jobs which are motivating and rewarding, and in responding to a wide range of public sector labour relations issues.

BEFORE APPLYING, LET'S REVIEW

CO 1: Understand the context affecting human resources (HR) in the public arena.

Although it is dangerous to make oversimplified distinctions between public and private management, central to our understanding of the distinctiveness of public organizations is the nature of their goals and constraints. The strategic context affecting HR in public organizations is affected by the raison d'être of public organizations. Public organizations have a general responsibility to implement (i) strategies and goals that serve the general public interest and (ii) provide services and programmes that are value creating. The strategies and objectives of public organizations are influenced by forces that are not as central to private organizations, such as accountability to the public at large, responsiveness to public demands and being open to scrutiny and criticism in a fish bowl–like environment.

CO 2: Define a framework for strategic human resource management (SHRM) in the public arena.

HR can play a valuable partnership role in assisting managers achieve their strategic priorities by articulating the implementation framework – the culture, competencies, work designs and the underlying recruitment, selection, training, performance management and labour relations processes. The Balanced Scorecard provides a framework to show how various HR strategic objectives and processes can be aligned with an organization's strategic themes and goals. The general Balanced Scorecard framework summarizes four perspectives – the customer or client, internal process, financial, and innovation and learning (learning and growth) perspectives – arranged in a semi-causal chain. The chapters of the book are organized within this framework.

DISCUSSION AND REVIEW QUESTIONS

1. Think of an experience you have had or observed which describes a relationship with a public sector manager or employee in a public sector organization. Describe this experience and why it resonates with you.
2. Describe the Strategic Human Resource Balanced Scorecard and its four perspectives. What questions would you ask in defining objectives within each perspective?
3. What makes public organizations unique? Why might they be no different than other organizations?
4. Why might public organizations be more focused on managing constraints versus managing goals?
5. Identify some news issues that illustrate public and private sector managerial problems. What were the differences in terms of public reaction?

Part I: Putting Strategy into Human Resource Management in the Public Sector

Public sector human resource managers, as well as employees in the public sector, have been under siege and called upon, in recent years, to improve their delivery of services and 'do more with less'. Human resource managers, in particular, have taken a very active role in transforming human resource management (HRM) to improve performance and help managers meet their strategic objectives.

The human resource (HR) context in public organizations is different from what is found in private organizations. Although many public sectors are being called upon to introduce business-like practices and reforms such as the **new public management (NPM)**, these practices work differently in public sector organizations because the nature and composition of the public sector workforce differs from those found in the private sector:

- Workers in the public sector are generally older than those in the private sector.[1] They are more likely to stay with their employers for a longer period of time.
- The public sector throughout the world is a significant employer, making up approximately 20 per cent of the workforce in most countries.
- The gender balance varies in different countries, but in some OECD (Organisation for Economic Co-operation and Development) countries such as the United Kingdom and Canada, women represent the majority of employees. Even with their large numbers, they are underrepresented in senior positions. For instance, in the United States, women represent 44.2 per cent of employees, but only 29 per cent of executive positions. In Korea and Japan, women are represented in less than 10 per cent of the executive positions.[2]
- People in the public sector are more likely to have a degree compared to those in the private sector. More people are classified as professional, technical or administrative workers.
- Public sector workers are much more likely to be in a union, a factor which is relevant for negotiation of working conditions, compensation and benefits.
- Key issues for the future are the ageing workforce, the need for new skills to manage differently in public organizations and different job and career expectations of younger generations.

1 Human Resource Management's Strategic Pressures

Chapter Outline
- Chapter objectives (COs) 3
- A driving issue focusing managerial action: The increasing importance of intangibles in public sector performance 3
- CO 1: Strategic human resource management (SHRM) 5
- CO 2: Societal forces or pressures shaping SHRM 9
- Before applying, let's review 21
- Discussion and review questions 22
- Case: Defining some of the key societal pressures or forces facing HRM 23

CHAPTER OBJECTIVES (COs)

After reading this chapter, you will be able to implement the following objectives:

CO 1: Explain HRM and SHRM and illustrate the connection to effective management.

CO 2: Examine and prioritize the pressures and societal forces shaping HR managers and our ability to be strategic and effectively manage people.

A DRIVING ISSUE FOCUSING MANAGERIAL ACTION: THE INCREASING IMPORTANCE OF INTANGIBLES IN PUBLIC SECTOR PERFORMANCE

Public sector organizations, just like for-profit organizations, rely on tangible and intangible resources in delivering their services and products. Tangible resources include financial capital, materials and physical assets, whereas intangibles include the managerial capabilities, culture and other factors.

The importance of intangible assets, such as an organization's human capital, has increased significantly over the last 40 years in both the private and public sectors. In the for-profit sector, in 1978, nearly 80 per cent of the market value of a business could be attributed to tangible assets and only 20 per cent to intangibles. Twenty years later, at the turn of the century, the situation was reversed, and the intangible assets of the business defined 80 per cent of a corporation's value.[3] Today, the tangible assets are estimated to be as low as 15 per cent to 25 per cent, depending on the company.[4]

As one intangible, the term **human capital** became more prevalent in the strategic management and human resource literature in the mid-1990s, as interest grew in intellectual, social, relational and other types of capital that were useful in the knowledge society. Human capital was viewed as a part of intellectual capital – the intangible resources producing benefits for the organization. Organizations which make investments in people through formal and informal education and training increase their returns.[5] A defining feature of human capital theory is that it recognizes that it is held, or owned, by people.[6] As well, human capital may be relatively unique or rare, or it may be generic.[7] Human capital can be viewed as the knowledge, skills and abilities of employees as well as employee motivation in providing the direction and intensity of an employee's effort.[8] Examining ways to communicate and share information, motivate and engage employees, thus become greater considerations, as they affect whether organizations can benefit from their human capital.

The focus on improving **intangible assets** has become a primary strategic focus for many public organizations, particularly those providing knowledge-intensive services. In a study of local government organizations, research identified six key intangible assets: management capabilities, human capital, perceived organizational reputation, internal auditing, labour relations climate and organizational culture:[9]

- The managerial capabilities reflect the combined strengths of the management team in illustrating a combination of talents.
- The importance of human capital reflects the idea that the organization's members and their education and talents are the real source of energy and innovation for an organization's efficiency and effectiveness.
- The organization's perceived reputation is important because it can lead to relationships, contracts and decisions that clients and residents make in where they locate.
- An organization's internal auditing helps teach organizational members to better execute their jobs, enhances motivation, deters members from actions that might be damaging and increases the probability that appropriate actions are taken in relation to goals and accomplishments.
- A positive labour climate encourages employee commitment and the possibilities of better performance.
- The organizational culture describes the underlying values and beliefs and actions that influence and determine how the organization's members work together.

Researchers found that these intangibles were linked to effective performance of local governments and that organizational culture and an organization's perceived reputation were most important. The remaining four elements, in addition to the uncertainty of the environment and geographic location, were slightly less important. These elements seem to work together and reinforce each other. In this sense, the whole – the intangibles in combination – seems to be greater than the sum of the parts.

The results in this study are similar to other studies that illustrate that successful organizations in both the private and public sectors do not rely on one singular strategic element. Performance is due to several strategic elements (which can be termed **critical success factors**) working in a complementary fashion. Thus, while culture and reputation are important, so are other elements such as geographical location and environmental uncertainty. In addition to culture and reputation, four other success factors included labour relations, human capital, internal auditing and managerial capabilities.

> STRATEGIC CONTEXT: *The emphasis on improving intangible assets has become a primary strategic focus for many organizations, particularly those providing knowledge-intensive services. This is particularly true in public sector organizations which have a larger group of knowledge workers.*
>
> *As managers focus on achieving strategic objectives in responding to customers or clients, HR's purpose is to effectively use its tools to help managers attract, develop, reward, motivate, organize and retain talented staff. The challenge for HR managers is to understand the needs of employees in their jobs and the competencies they need to be effective and motivated in relationship to the organization's strategic objectives. This provides the foundation for developing a productive, well-managed workforce to respond to the challenges in their environments.*
>
> *However, there are pressures in public organizations that were amplified by the financial crisis that began in 2008 which required HR professionals to manage substantial change and, at the same time, downsize or outsource many of their own functions. This chapter reviews the current pressures facing HR in the public sector which require managers to be more focused in their work.*

CO 1: STRATEGIC HUMAN RESOURCE MANAGEMENT (SHRM)

The opening perspective in this chapter illustrates the increasing importance of intangibles in public sector performance. The importance of intangibles and the evolution towards a strategic approach to **human resource management (HRM)** did not appear until the founding of the modern field of HRM. This section provides a short snapshot of its history.[10]

The emergence of SHRM

In the history of HRM, there are no clear-cut junctures defining the 'traditional' public sector HRM model just as there is no real agreement on the timing and status of newer models of HRM. Given this caveat, the following paragraphs provide a snapshot[11] of the different responsibilities of HR over its history, as illustrated in Figure 1.1.

- *Labour/employment management:* The early history described the Labour or Employment Manager's administrative role in record keeping and handling enquiries. Key responsibilities included recruitment, selection and training.
- *Personnel management:* After World War II, until roughly 1980, Personnel's responsibilities also involved compensation, occupation health and safety, and collective bargaining, in addition to ensuring compliance with regulations, laws and collective agreements. The traditional public sector personnel system was highly centralized and run by central agencies responsible for hiring, setting employment policies and training and career development. Public sector employment was based on a 'career service' model of security and tenure based on lifelong employment.

Labour/Employment Manager → Traditional Personnel Management → Human Resource Manager → Strategic HRM Role

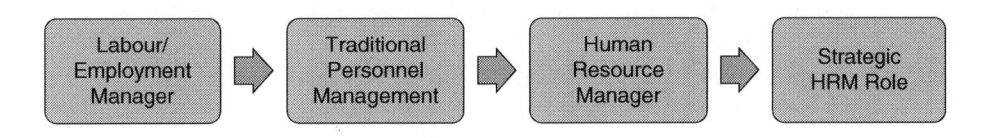

Figure 1.1 Evolving roles and responsibilities of HRM.

- *Human resource management (HRM):* Challenges created by increasing debt, high costs of services and the economic downturn of the early 1980s and 1990s combined to spawn calls for large-scale reform in government. HRM's role focused on delivering core activities such as training, recruitment, selection and classification in addition to technical expertise. HRM's role began to shift in recognizing employees as human resources. In the public sector, the centralized system came under pressure through the financial crisis in 2008, the criticisms of 'big government' and concerns regarding efficiency and the need to reduce government expenditures. The **new public management (NPM)** contributed to the implementation of ideas such as management by results, performance management, outsourcing, decentralization and devolution of activities, and risk management.
- *Strategic HRM:* **Strategic HRM** involves aligning and integrating HR's activities to support managers as they seek to achieve their strategic objectives. Today's public sector HRM is less centrally controlled with more empowerment of managers, and in some areas, there is evidence of a more strategic approach, restructured career paths, fewer seniority-based promotions, greater emphasis on performance and productivity measurement and removal of rigid employment categories. Central government agencies still retain a certain degree of control over policy and direction in areas such as management of the top level of civil servants, equal opportunities, health and safety and overarching themes such as being a 'model' employer as well as the general governing of issues related to codes of conduct, staff cuts and discipline.[12] In some countries, such as the United Kingdom, New Zealand, Denmark, Canada, Finland, the Netherlands and Sweden, there appears to be more devolution in areas of decision-making and planning, recruitment, mobility, flexible working conditions, job classification and pay.

Management guru Peter Drucker was the first to coin the term **human resource** in the seminal book *The Practice of Management*, published in 1954.[13] He defined the human resource as 'comparable to all other resources but for the fact that it is human' and has 'specific properties that are not present in other resources'.[14] Human resources have the ongoing ability to 'coordinate, to integrate, to judge and to imagine',[15] whereas other resources are consumed. Drucker encouraged managers to recognize the needs of people in motivating workers and creating jobs that challenge and develop them and in using people as a strategic resource by using tools such as job analysis, recruitment, selection, training, compensation and labour relations.

'To manage is to manage basic resources', according to Bakke's influential text *The Human Resources Function*. All managerial functions, whether sales, finance or engineering, evolve from 'the fact that the general job of management is to *use resources effectively for an organizational objective*'.[16] The basic resources to be managed are materials, money, market, ideas, nature and people. 'The function which is related to the understanding, maintenance, development, effective employment, and integration of the potential in the resource "people" I shall call simply *the human resources function*.'[17]

Miles' popular article *Human Relations or Human Resources*[18] coaches managers to pay attention to workers' welfare and happiness. The goal of the human resource model was a fuller utilization of employees as resources in making creative contributions. Even though the terms *HR* and *HRM* began to guide the field, the definitions in many important textbooks were, for a time, rooted in tradition and, though using the term *human resource*, authors used it as a synonym for *personnel management*. Although authors accepted the new terms, HRM was still 'personnel', or a list of technical activities carried out by personnel specialists.[19] For a brief period in the early 1980s under Prime Minister Thatcher, human resource management was a management-led philosophy for reducing costs and managing unions, although British managerial researchers generally disagreed with this orientation.[20]

The human resource model generally involves the 'acquisition, development, reward, and motivation maintenance and departure'[21] of employees, and includes planning, recruitment, selection, training and career development, performance management and compensation. HR is involved in the wide range of managerial activities in reorganizing people or creating team designs; assisting organizations to implement their plans; assigning, changing, enriching or enlarging jobs; developing incentive systems and guidelines for performance; and almost anything that relates to developing and motivating people.

Pressures of change. Over the last few decades, public sector organizations began facing increasing pressures to deliver a growing range of exceptional services and reduce costs. Some of these demands resulted from the general ageing in the population and the need for greater health care, law enforcement, mental health and educational services.[22]

In reducing costs to improve efficiency and effectiveness, there have been large reductions in government spending at the local, state and federal levels, resulting in job losses and a long series of reforms. When the NPM was introduced in the 1980s, there were calls for a much stronger focus on performance and efforts to change the way the public sector interacted with external organizations by introducing contracting out and competitive bidding.[23]

In responding to these pressures, HR has been called upon to play a primary role in shifting the operation of government by implementing changes involving decentralization, outsourcing, decreasing the number of people with special employment status, developing flexible career paths, changing the collective agreements and implementing equity procedures.[24] At the same time, HR is called upon to carry out work in modelling values of 'fairness, openness, transparency, equity and equality'[25] while working in an environment where HR managers are intensely scrutinized and monitored and have a broader range of stakeholders with a host of varied objectives.

Strategic human resource management. Newer models of HRM call for playing a more significant role in helping an organization improve its performance by aligning the HR system to the organization's strategic directions.[26] The general emphasis of SHRM argued for a more proactive role in linking HRM to an organization's strategic framework[27] to improve performance in achieving outcomes like commitment, competence, congruence and cost-effectiveness.[28]

For some professionals, SHRM is akin to human resource planning, which is broadly defined as seeking to shape personnel requirements to the demands of the organization's environment.[29] Several definitions of SHRM underline the importance of organizing HR activities and other activities affecting the behaviour of individuals so they 'fit' in a more strategic direction.[30] Other definitions point to the SHRM as a macro-organizational approach to coordinate HR activities for achieving organizational goals[31] and linking HR practices so that they are used by line managers.[32] Building on this history, we define SHRM as a process of aligning human resource objectives so that HR resources, activities and initiatives assist internal clients to achieve the organization's strategies and goals. Thus, SHRM seeks to assist the organization's line managers in their strategic management in implementing objectives related to external clients and customers.[33]

SHRM adds to the strategic management in focusing specifically on the HR system and how it links to the organizational system, and is different from traditional HR in two respects. First, SHRM focuses on organizational performance over individual performance in responding to pressures brought on by globalization and its continual demands for change and innovation. Early attempts to link HR activities to strategic management focused on each functional area. The result was separate areas called strategic selection, strategic recruitment, strategic appraisal and strategic compensation. There was little recognition of the interplay between various HR areas.[34]

Second, SHRM highlights the importance of 'HR management systems rather than individual HR practices in isolation'. The more recent emphasis is on a system of HR practices rather than the effects of single HR practices. Instead of implementing an HR best practice because it has been successful elsewhere, for example, SHRM means developing systems, practices, competencies and employee performance behaviours that 'align' the strategic objectives to the organization's human capital.[35] The focus is on linking HRM to the larger organization.

In responding to the strategic context in the public arena, the primary assets of public organizations are its intangible human assets. A strategic approach to HR links HR activities and processes to help line managers realize their department's strategic objectives and initiatives. It does this by adjusting the recruitment, selection and performance management processes to the competencies most relevant for line managers. In some cases, this involves competencies related to co-ordinating the work to be carried out in balancing how to use resources for achieving economic and social strategic objectives. In other cases, it involves designing retention strategies, training and career development, and competitive compensation and benefits practices. Because of the changing character of the problems in the public arena, a need also exists for continuously appraising and updating the HR processes to ensure they are connected to the plans and objectives of the public agency.

A RELEVANT POINT OF VIEW: FOUR ROLES FOR HR

One widely publicized view of HR is David Ulrich's 'A New Mandate for Human Resources', which describes four roles for HR, including being a strategic partner in strategy execution as well as being an administrative expert, change agent and employee champion.[36]

The strategic partner role involves HR in articulating a framework for how the organization should do its work and for conducting an audit in helping managers identify the components of the organization that need to change. Added to this is the responsibility for identifying methods for renovating the parts (e.g. job descriptions, health of the culture) and taking stock of its own priorities.

The administrative expert role is different from its old role of record keeper and includes the need to shed its image of being the rule-making police. In being an expert, HR needs to embrace the task of developing processes that are better, faster and cheaper. So, HR has to clean up its act and, for example, reduce the cycle time it takes to hire people. HR can also improve its value by illustrating how work can be more effectively carried out and by streamlining operations and increasing employee engagement.

The employee champion role asks HR to be accountable for engaging employees, a role which has increasing importance because of the changing and more demanding aspects of work in modern-day organizations. They are the voice for employees, but also the coach to assist managers in improving satisfaction and commitment in their units.

The change agent role is for helping employees respond to the forces of change in their environments and jobs. As a change agent, 'HR's role is to replace resistance with resolve, planning with results, and fear of change with excitement about its possibilities.'[37]

For most organizations, the new mandate is transformational, a radical departure from what it is doing now. The new mandate for HR in the 'public arena' requires HRM to be more connected to the organization and involved in helping managers attract, select, develop, engage and retain talented employees to help them achieve the organization's strategic objectives. 'Human' resources are now recognized as critical intellectual resources and have more value, in most cases, than an organization's capital assets.

The manager's roles. The manager, or more specifically 'line manager', has the direct responsibility for making decisions related to providing services to external stakeholders. In a traditional model of an organization, line managers had the responsibility for most, if not all, activities relating to managing employees. With the introduction of employment laws and regulations, many of the employee management activities were assigned to the personnel or human resource department, which took on other roles in keeping records, paying employees, managing compensation and benefits, and managing practices relating to recruitment, training, performance management and collective bargaining. Generally, HR became a service or 'staff function' that existed to advise and assist other managers, employees and the organization as a whole. Line managers had responsibility for job assignments and general performance while HR staff personnel played a significant role in advising and implementing the people decisions that many line managers made.

CO 2: SOCIETAL FORCES OR PRESSURES SHAPING SHRM

The global economic crisis beginning in 2008 imposed new expectations for public services around the world that called for 'doing more with less'. Many governments were asked to secure savings of 30 per cent over four years, while those in Greece, Italy, Portugal and Spain witnessed more serious cutbacks. HR professionals are being called upon to manage substantial change and at the same time downsize or outsource many of their own functions.

Given the various pressures and forces for reform, the starting point for most change in the public sector is HRM. These forces are like those that a sailor feels in a windstorm, which might knock a sailboat off course if the sailor is not prepared. In order to contextualize HR in the public sector, one initial task is to better understand the pressures that are most imminent at this point in time. Table 1.1 reviews 12 societal forces that require managers to be more strategic in their work. These pressures come from various arenas: the changing external environment; the increasing importance of human capital, culture and ethics; higher customer and employee requirements; and demands for organizing more efficiently and effectively.

The changing external environment

The external environment is reflected in a pace of change today which is dramatically more intense than it was 10 years ago, in addition to changes resulting from the Internet and the general requirement to adjust to new technologies in most facets of how we work.

Managing in a rapidly changing environment. In 1973, futurist Alvin Toffler wrote *Future Shock*, a bestseller that predicted a world becoming more and more stressed and disoriented by the pace of change. The changes he predicted would be more rapid and transformational, like the cultural shift of moving rapidly from communal to industrial or virtual societies. *Future shock* is like culture shock that leaves people disconnected because they are disoriented from what they know and value, because there is too much change in too short a period of time. Toffler suggested that the majority of the society's social problems – stress and disorientation from change – were symptoms of future shock.

Many organizational scientists today would agree that change is occurring more quickly, and as people and organizations experience future shock–like conditions, they have become more dependent on reacting strategically to their environment. In selecting a strategic objective of where one wants to be in the future, one only has to make good choices in selecting initiatives or actions which recognize the changing environment and the reactions of others.

Table 1.1 Pressures and Forces Shaping Society and the Way We Manage

Pressures	Main Effects
CHANGING EXTERNAL ENVIRONMENT	
1. Managing in a rapidly changing environment	Many problems are complex, and wicked problems require working with different specialized fields.
2. Changes from the rise of new communication technologies and the Internet	Organizational charts look less like hierarchies and more like networks of different intensities. Many relationships are virtual.
3. Changes requiring the use of technologies in implementing most organizational ideas	Information systems are key for implementing organization ideas.
IMPORTANCE OF AN ORGANIZATION'S SOCIAL SYSTEM	
4. The increasing importance and value of human and intellectual capital	Many more jobs involve tacit knowledge that is personal and context specific rather than transactional (scripted or programmed).
5. The need for employee involvement and engagement	Involvement and engagement increases employee feelings of ownership and commitment to improved service.
6. Organizations that are made up of a diversity of people, many different demographic groups, and many different national and group cultures	The different cultures illustrate cultures with different values, and there are possibilities for increased tensions as well as increasingly diverse methods.
7. Calls for more ethical and virtuous behaviour	An ethical culture has positive benefits in terms of motivation and a willingness to perform in a similar manner.
8. Calls for attention to human rights issues	In developed countries, issues of equity and equality drive the public agenda; in developing countries, the issues are related to freedoms and abuses.
9. Pressures for the more effective implementation of ideas	Many very useful and scientifically supported organizational ideas have a low implementation rate.
HIGHER QUALITY AND CUSTOMER REQUIREMENTS	
10. Higher expectations for quality services and products	Quality means refusing to accept error.
11. Higher expectations from customers	The customer focus has changed the metrics of performance of service delivery.
12. The need to outsource in reducing costs and gaining expertise	HR outsourcing and shared services models change the way that HR will be delivered.

The future shock-like environments are described as 'turbulent fields', where the ground is moving as people and organizations are choosing and implementing strategies.[38] Public organizations have to respond to the turbulence of major environmental events like earthquakes, floods and winter storms in addition to global threats from terrorism and local crises. Clearly, the strategies that an organization uses during turbulent times are not the same as those used during periods of greater stability.

In the public arena, many problems – like nutritional deficiencies, drug use, poverty and global warming – are complex and often irresolvable. Such **wicked** problems involve several stakeholders who have vested interests in seeing the problem addressed. Examples such as food shortages, drug use, poverty and global warming involve political, economic and environmental issues that are difficult to define, cannot be definitely solved and are intertwined with other challenges. Non-wicked problems are more discrete and can be resolved with conventional problem-solving processes. A wicked problem is a complex, tricky or thorny problem, often involving several different specialties. Wicked problems have no definitive solution and are sometimes so unique that there is no opportunity to learn by trial-and-error experiences. A wicked problem is often connected to other problems, and each problem is considered to be a symptom of another problem. The problems are not of a technical nature, and there is no definite formulation of any well-described set of potential solutions.[39]

Wicked problems affect more stakeholders, such as those concerned with the environment or world poverty, who are skilled at applying pressure through the media and politicians and at organizing interest groups. Such problem-solving requires political judgement, intellectual capital and negotiation skills rather than sound technical analysis. These skills are as important in creating solutions as they are in implementation. Implementation involves responding to multiple objectives and stakeholders. And even with the best-laid implementation plans, the co-ordinative strategies are complex, and divergent understandings of aims and means among participants are likely to exist.[40]

Changes from the rise of new communication technologies and the Internet. Although there are many factors driving change, one of the most significant changes is the rise of Internet (the Net) technologies. The Net and other technologies have led to transformational changes in the way we organize, communicate and work. Now, everyone in the organization – from the newly hired social worker to the executive director – has the ability to access mountains of information quickly.

The Internet allows greater access to information from a variety of sources and people located anywhere around the world. In the world before the World Wide Web, ideas took two or three weeks to move to another part of the world, whereas in the new Internet world, it takes only seconds to send an idea, question or answer around the world. The new world is the polar opposite of its predecessors.[41] Approximately 40 per cent of the world population, or over 3 billion people, had Internet in 2015, up from 1 per cent in 1995.[42]

Conventional technologies, like the telephone, recordings, film and television, are being redefined by the Internet, just as newspapers, books and the publishing industry have to adapt to new forms of communication such as blogs, websites, text messaging, Twitter and Flickr. The Internet consists of billions of public and private networks which are unconnected until they are linked for a purpose. The World Wide Web has dramatically changed the way public sector managers relate to citizens, customers and stakeholders as they have challenged centralized government organizations.

The twenty-first-century public organization differs in a number of ways from those in the previous century, ushering in changes in the way HR carries out its work. If we scan the readings on HR during the last century, we find terms such as **hierarchical organization, specialization, division of labour, unity of command, span of control** and **centralization of authority.** Today, we find that these traditional terms are disappearing and are replaced by words such as **boundary-less, temporary** and **virtual.** The full-time permanent job is disappearing as the growth of part-time and contract work increases. Part-time workers currently hold over 20 per cent of all jobs in Western organizations. The dominant model during the 1800s and early 1900s was a vertically integrated, centrally planned organization. The old organizational 'turf' of HR was the office building with large files of employment records.

Although hierarchical public organizations may still exist, the organizational charts of many twenty-first-century organizations are likely to look like a number of loosely connected strands or intricately woven lines connecting teams, partners, employees, contractors, clients and customers, and suppliers, working in collaborative relationships. In the extreme form, some might look like a virtual spider web rather than a hierarchical chart. Some twenty-first-century global organizations, connected virtually, will not have a central headquarters and will call on talent and resources around the world. Some **virtual public organizations,** such as ones dealing with public sector teams of specialists, come together – virtually – on projects like cybercrime and environmental sustainability and continue to work together on an ongoing basis.

Virtual workplaces where employees operate independently and remotely are becoming more common in the twenty-first century. These employees work at various times in cyberspace and in real time and connect by email, texting, faxes, teleconferencing and intranets (information networks within a company). Good reasons to work virtually include reduced office real estate costs, environmental impacts and travel costs as well as potential increases in productivity and customer service, as workers are more available during odd hours. Several jobs in fields such as consulting, marketing, teaching, sales and project management are ideally suited to the virtual workplace because they are customer focused. Project teams allow managers to take on special projects to focus on specific strategic objectives or projects, or to work on problems that cross divisional boundaries.

New technologies in implementing organizational ideas. The transformational changes in human resources go beyond the Internet. Almost every HR function, from job analysis to training, is being shaped by new information technologies. Just as tax departments use online tax forms and allow people to pay their taxes online, HR departments have used similar technologies to give their clients greater access. The workforce that HR is responsible for is managed within the rules administered by the software. Many of the previous mundane tasks related to filling in pension or benefits forms with the assistance of an HR staff member have been automated. Employees can print off or fill in forms related to travel and medical expenses and even have the reimbursements deposited directly into their bank account.

Those managing HR have recognized the substantial benefits of information technologies in improving access and communication, and a widespread use of a **human resource information system (HRIS)** has taken place. 'An *HRIS* is a systematic procedure for collecting, storing, maintaining, retrieving and validating the data needed by the organization for its human resources, personnel activities, and organization unit characteristics.'[43] An HRIS can be designed for different capabilities for data entry and tracking related to payroll, management and accounting.

Normally, an HRIS provides capabilities for managing, reporting and analysis of employee information. An HRIS can track attendance, pay raises and history, pay grades and positions held, performance management goals and ratings, training desired and received, disciplinary actions received, succession plans for key employees and applicant tracking and selection. It can be designed to provide information on almost everything an organization needs to track and analyse about current, former and potential employees. The challenge is to use this information for an organization's strategic requirements.

The increasing importance of an organization's social system

Part of an organization's social system includes the human component and the capabilities and competencies that people bring, the culture and diversity of people working together, their motivational energies and ethical behaviour.

The increasing value of human and intellectual capital. An organization's human capital defines the competencies – the knowledge, skills, abilities and other characteristics – that individuals gain through experience, education and innate talent.[44] It is now considered to be one of the most important factors defining an organization's success.[45] Adam Smith, in the *Wealth of Nations*, published in 1776, first pointed out the value of human capital in highlighting the importance of labour's abilities, or their skills, dexterity and judgement in producing wealth. He also indicated that the costs for acquiring these abilities through education, study and apprenticeship are capital investments in the individual.

Up until the 1950s and 1960s, economic textbooks defined four main factors of production: physical, capital, labour, land management.[46] But as a result of research in the early 1960s, it was discovered that these factors did not fully explain the dynamics of economic growth and development. Human capital was defined as a residual factor or missing link, as a person's learning capabilities are of comparable worth to other resources in the delivery of services and production of goods. Expenditures on education and training and on health of employees are capital investments. They produce 'human, not physical or financial, capital because you cannot separate a person from his or her knowledge, skills, health, or values, the way it is possible to move financial and physical assets while the owner stays put'.[47]

Human capital theory has had a significant influence in suggesting that an organization's success depends on its ability to attract, retain, develop and effectively organize the human capital of its employees. In the new public organizations which require greater linkages to stakeholders, strategies linked to an organization's human capital are now seen as more fruitful than capitalizing on traditional linkages to product and process technology, financial resources, economies of scale, management systems and protected niche markets.[48]

The value of human capital is enhanced when it is integrated with other intangible sources of capital. Human capital is a key component of an organization's general 'intellectual capital' that includes human capital (competencies), social capital (relationships and networks among people) and organizational capital (the structures, processes and culture of the organization).[49] Organizations which make investments in people through formal and informal education and training increase their returns.[50] A defining feature of human capital theory is that it recognizes that it is held, or owned, by people.[51] As well, human capital may be relatively unique or rare, or it may be generic.[52] Human capital can be viewed as the knowledge, skills and abilities of employees as well as employee motivation in providing the direction and intensity of an employee's effort.[53] Examining ways to communicate and share information and to motivate and engage employees thus become greater considerations, as they affect whether organizations can benefit from their human capital.

In these global web-like public organizations, the importance of intellectual capital is shaped by the fact that more jobs are more complex and involve a higher level of 'tacit knowledge' and judgement. Tacit knowledge is personal, context specific and difficult to program or universally apply to all settings. A new approach is required to designing training that improves performance, one which is context specific. For example, when teachers, nurses or software programmers relate to customers or clients, the knowledge they apply is personal, context specific and difficult to formalize or program. In contrast, 'transactional jobs' are those that can be scripted, automated or programmed, such as those of workers on a traditional assembly line. During the first part of the decade, the number of jobs emphasizing 'tacit interactions' has increased 2.5 times as fast as the number of transactional jobs, and three times as fast as employment in general. These jobs make up 40 per cent of the jobs in the developed economies and 70 per cent of the jobs created since 1998, a pattern which will be similar in developing countries as they get richer.[54]

The fact that more jobs are tacit in nature means that traditional HR has to change in response. Beyond the fact that these jobs are less programmable and less able to be defined rigidly in job descriptions, profound changes exist in how we fill jobs and in how we recruit and select new employees at all levels.

The need for employee involvement and engagement. The last 40 years has seen a renaissance of interest in improving employee involvement and engagement and in improving performance. **Involvement** implies consultation and input, whereas **engagement** suggests commitment in joint working relationship, active interchange and consensus. Employee involvement and engagement is seen as important for creating an environment in which people have an impact on decisions and actions that affect their jobs in order to contribute to the continuous improvement and performance of the organization.[55]

The mission of the HR function should be 'to increase the success of the organization by improving decisions that depend on or impact people'.[56] Enriched job designs, self-managed teams, career planning and customer-focused designs are just a few of the many ways that employees can be involved and engaged in organization activities. Involvement and engagement increase employee feelings of ownership and commitment or an employee's psychological attachment to the workplace. Engaged workers are more satisfied, motivated and committed[57] and are more likely to perform at a higher level. When employees are involved, they can more easily work cross-functionally with other departments and individuals, and the organization is more likely to capture their creativity, energy and ideas.

In public organizations, the ideas needed for improving service delivery and 'doing more with less' are driving the need for more employee involvement and engagement. In addition, public servants assume greater importance because many services, for example in the fields of health and social work, education and policing, rely on the relationship between employees and customer.

The most recent attention on performance management points to the importance of employee skills and knowledge, employee flexibility, positive labour relations and a variety of management tools such as development performance reviews, incentives and effectively designed jobs. The employee part of the equation in performance management became more prominent because of the feeling that technologies and economies of scale were less relevant because they are easier to imitate today.[58] Also, certain bundles of HRM practices related to employees are linked to higher performance, such as those related to staffing, performance management and remuneration, training and development, and communication. When HR managers report higher utilization of such practices, other managers perceive HR as having a higher strategic value.[59]

The changing diversity, demography and cultures in organizations. An increasingly diverse workforce is found in terms of race, gender, ethnicity, education levels and distinct 'generations'. In addition, a growing recognition exists of the changing demographics of our workforce, as projections are that by 2020, in most developed countries, one of every four people will be aged 65 or older. These changes are highlighted in other chapters.

The key assumption we live with today is that societal culture has a major impact on organizational forms and practices, leadership behaviours and the strategic behaviour of organizations. This is particularly true in public organizations which are called upon to model diversity and equality. **Culture** reflects the 'shared motives, values, beliefs, identities, and interpretations or meanings of significant events that result from common experiences or meanings of members of collectives and are transmitted a cross age and generations'.[60] Beyond being diverse and multi-generational, the workforce comprises different cultures consisting of a range of values, attitudes, traits and behaviours which lead to possibilities for increased tensions between groups and generations. A collective mental programming is what people have in common.[61] For example, many organizations are made up of groups of people who illustrate distinct national cultures, and each of these groups might illustrate key differences in some of the nine factors that have grown out of the GLOBE (Global Leadership and Organizational Behavior Effectiveness) research programme.

1. **Power Distance:** The degree to which powerful members of an organization and institutions (like the family) expect power to be distributed equally.
2. **Uncertainty Avoidance:** The degree to which a society (or group) relies on social norms to alleviate unpredictability in the future.
3. **Humane Orientation:** The degree to which people expect rewards to be fair, altruistic, generous, caring and kind to others.
4. **Collectivism I:** The degree to which institutional practices (i.e. public sector) encourage and reward collective distribution of resources and collective action.
5. **Collectivism II:** The expressions of pride, loyalty and cohesiveness in organizations and families.
6. **Assertiveness:** The demonstration of confrontation and aggressiveness in organizations and families.

7. **Gender Egalitarianism:** The degree to which society seeks to minimize gender inequality.
8. **Future Orientation:** The efforts to engage in future-oriented behaviours and delay gratification living for the present rather than investing in the future.
9. **Performance Orientation:** The efforts to reward and encourage performance improvement.[62]

In building on Hoftstede's classical framework,[63] the GLOBE research programme used nine factors for gathering information on culture from over 61 countries.[64] This research illustrates that different cultural factors have a major impact on organizational forms and practices, leadership behaviours and the strategic behaviour of organizations.

> **QUIZ 1.1 – ASSESSING DIFFERENT NATIONAL CULTURES**
>
> How would you rate the culture of different groups of countries (clusters) on the following dimensions: Institutional Collectivism, Uncertainty Avoidance and Gender Egalitarianism on a scale of 1 to 7, with 1 being low and 7 being high.
> Institutional Collectivism – Employees feel (or should feel) great loyalty towards this organization.
> Uncertainty Avoidance – Most people lead (should lead) highly structured lives with few unexpected events.
> Gender Egalitarianism – Boys are encouraged (should be encouraged) more than girls to attain higher education.
>
> | | Institutional Collectivism | Uncertainty Avoidance | Gender Egalitarianism |
> |---|---|---|---|
> | Confucian Asia | _____ | _____ | _____ |
> | Germanic Europe | _____ | _____ | _____ |
> | Anglo (outside Europe) | _____ | _____ | _____ |
> | Middle East | _____ | _____ | _____ |
>
> *Confucian Asia includes China, Hong Kong, Korea (Rep.), Singapore, Taiwan. Germanic Europe includes Austria, Germany, the Netherlands and Switzerland (German speaking). Anglo includes Australia, Canada (English speaking), the United States and New Zealand. Middle East includes Egypt, Arab Republic, Kuwait, Morocco, Qatar and Turkey.

Different national cultures might manifest differences in their expectations of obedience from followers (i.e. power distance), need for structure (i.e. uncertainty avoidance), feelings of gender equality (i.e. gender egalitarianism) and loyalty to groups or the organizations (i.e. collectivism). Picture a female manager trying to encourage team decision-making when one cultural group has a high need for structure and does not share a vision of gender equality. The challenge we live with today is that many public organizations include individuals who reflect different national cultures, which has a major impact on organizational forms and practices, leadership behaviours and the strategic behaviour of organizations.

Although an organization might seek to have its own unique organizational culture for relating to clients or working together, these values sometimes conflict with the values existing between generations and within the diversity of employee groups. Thus, the challenge is to create a culture recognizing the new demographics and the diversity in the different designated groups.

***Concerns for ethical and virtuous behaviour.* Ethical behaviour** has become a central concern to guide the conduct of individuals and organizations. High-profile cases of fraud and favouritism and inappropriate spending have elevated the concern for more transparency and accountability to guard against unethical behaviour. Calls have been made for reform, rules and standards to guide the ethical behaviour of individuals as they carry out their roles in organizations.

Some of the calls for more ethical behaviour are demonstrated in expectations for public organizations to be socially responsible and balance the dual interest of economic development in addition to quality of life of the workforce, families and the community at large. Although public organizations play a key role in providing incentives and regulations, one driving force encouraging social responsibility is underlined by the costs of being viewed as not socially responsible. Some of these costs are evident in some of the recent environmental disasters, particularly the Bhopal and Chernobyl disasters and the Exxon Valdez and Gulf of Mexico oil spills. The traditional view of what happens within the confines of the workplace is being challenged. Although major accidents have occurred before, the extent of current global coverage is having profound effects in demands for public and private organizations to be more socially responsible in their regulative and managerial roles. The most common social responsibility activities usually address problems related to the environment, such as pollution, poverty, health care, safety and environmental sustainability.[65]

Rules and standards for ethical behaviour of individuals and organizations are often seen to be avoiding harm and not engendering the values required in behaving ethically. For example, the lack of spirit for ethical behaviour can result when unions work to rule or when people follow the letter of law in accounting practices or environmental or ethical standards.

A key element driving ethical behaviour relates to the degree to which organizations support activities that encourage individuals to act in ethical and virtuous ways. These are reflected in cultures where people illustrate ethical behaviours, moral goodness and benefits to others. When fellow employees observe behaviours of ethical conduct and virtuousness such as loyalty, sharing and caring, this is known to foster positive behaviours.[66]

The importance of human rights issues related to equity and equality. The Universal Declaration of Human Rights[67] was adopted by the United Nations in December 1948 and reflected the intentions of people at the time to try to avoid the horrors they had just experienced in World War II. **Human rights** were then defined as rights concerning equity and equality, such as the right to life and liberty, freedom from slavery and torture, freedom of opinion and expression, the right to work and education and many more.

In most developed countries, the most obvious human rights issues have called for equal treatment of all people, regardless of gender, ethnicity, creed and ability, resulting in many organizational policies on accommodation such as statements of accommodation for people with disabilities, religious obligations and parental needs. Anti-racism protections and gender equity, sexual orientation equality and sexual harassment policies have been initiated in addition to special procedures for resolving complaints. Beyond these issues that continue to focus managers and public and private organizations, recent human rights abuses relate to the treatment of foreign workers, invasion of privacy and unfair wages paid to migrants.

Human rights issues in developing countries are more basic and include the rights of life and security and freedoms from torture and unlawful confinement, among other things. In some developing countries, the lack of equality for women and minorities and lack of freedom of expression are major issues.

Beyond the mountains of national and international legislation, public managers play a key role in changing expectations and providing safeguards in society regarding human rights. This role not only requires public managers to model exemplary human rights in public organizations but also to encourage private sector managers to recognize human rights principles when their organizations work in developing countries.[68]

Pressures for more effective implementation of organizational ideas. The pressure to increase performance is one of the cornerstones of successful organizations. In response, the organizational sciences have developed a range of tools and best practices to assist managers to introduce the most effective ideas. In many cases, HR professionals are responsible for acquiring and diffusing knowledge of organizational management throughout the organization.

Unfortunately, there are challenges in implementing scientific knowledge and best practices for practitioners, a topic that concerns most fields of study. In the organizational sciences and HRM, there is now considerable evidence suggesting that most organizations do not build on the most recent research. Although researchers in the last decade have been instrumental in showing the scientific value of specific HRM practices, practitioners lack this knowledge and use other tools and practices which they have deemed relevant for other reasons.

SHRM is being challenged by two implementation gaps in encouraging managers to (i) adopt many HR practices that are shown to be effective,[69] and (ii) strategically align HR functions, such as recruitment, selection and performance management.

Researchers often lament that managers in organizations do not implement HR practices that are shown to be scientifically supportive, such as in areas where managers do not recognize 'the importance of intelligence or general mental ability (GMA) for performance; the importance of goal setting and feedback for performance, and the validity of personality (of which integrity tests are one representation) for predicting performance'.[70] In some cases, managers disagree, whereas in others, they are simply not aware of new research. However, managerial beliefs about HRM practices reflect professional principles,[71] and most of the articles in HR practitioner magazines reflect 'interesting' practices rather than those that implement the latest scientific research.[72]

A second implementation gap concerns the degree to which organizations are strategic. Henry Mintzberg's *The Rise and Fall of Strategic Planning* offered a critique of strategic planning, indicating it should instead be called strategic programming because the process does little more than articulate strategies and visions that already exist. Strategic planning has been labelled a calculating style of management which does not engage people in the journey.[73] Kaplan and Norton's *Strategy Execution* suggests that a high percentage of organizations fail to execute strategies, don't link their budgets to strategies and don't link their HR or information technology (IT) departments to their strategies.[74]

QUIZ 1.2 – HOW SUCCESSFUL ARE CHANGE PROGRAMMES IN INSTILLING NEW PRACTICES?

Several high-profile change programmes implement various human resource ideas concerning strategic planning, decision-making, health, stress and physical fitness. How successful are these programmes in implementing their ideas and best practices?

Take a piece of paper and jot down your answers to the following questions. You are asked to indicate your best guess of the success of some change programmes in terms of getting people to accept the change.

HR-related organizational change programmes

1. Strategic planning has been a key organizational activity that managers have used to clarify their strategies and objectives. In terms of implementation, what percentage of effectively formulated strategies are implemented?

2. In a study of 400 decisions (in a variety of areas, from purchasing equipment to renovating space, to deciding on new services and products) made by top managers in private, public and non-profit organizations across the United States, Canada and Europe, what percentage of decisions ended in failure (that is, not used after two years)?
3. What percentage of re-engineering (core review) efforts are judged to be successful?

HR-related personal change programmes

4. Over the last 30 years, there have been many books and programmes that have sought to assist people to lose weight. We all know of various fad diets that never seem to work. Some of the best programmes are said to be those that help people change their habits and behaviours. What percentage of people reach their target weight after participating in one of our best programmes for health and diet?
5. What percentage of these people kept this weight off or maintained their target weight?
6. At a university recreational centre, organizers have a swimming programme where regular swimmers can 'swim across the country in the pool'. People who enter the programme are usually committed and goal oriented. You can swim at the beginner, intermediate or advanced levels and swim on a pro-rated basis (e.g. every kilometre = 5, 10 or 20 kilometres across the country). Of the 60 goal-oriented people who entered the programme two years ago, what percentage of people completed it?
7. What percentage of people quit smoking after their physicians counsel them to quit?
8. What percentage of people quit smoking and never start again after a major health event?

Higher quality and customer requirements

More than ever before, public and private organizations are expected to provide higher quality services and products in responding to their customers and clients.

Higher expectations for quality products and services. The emphasis on quality was vividly highlighted as an explanation for the resurgence of the Japanese economy after World War II and later became the new mantra for an organization's strategic orientation throughout the world. Before and immediately following the war, Japan had one of the worst reputations in the world for product quality, and up until the late 1960s, Japanese products were regarded as cheap, tacky and substandard. After the war, the commanding US General Douglas MacArthur asked his friend William Edward Deming to come to Japan and teach the Japanese his quality methods in rebuilding the war-devastated economy. Deming began his work in 1950 by teaching statistical quality control and the importance of quality methods to the heads of Japanese business. It was then that he made the famous prediction that if the Japanese learned and accepted his system of quality control, they would become a major exporting nation and would become known as a leading producer of high-quality goods and most-in-demand products. Today, in Japan, Deming's *Out of Crisis* is treated like a canonized guidebook for managers in the private and public sectors.[75]

Initially, the **quality movement** allowed for some errors. That is, Taylor's scientific management introduced rejection rates as an operational definition of quality. In terms of efficiency calculations, reducing the rejection rates and rates of return of goods and services improves efficiency and reduces costs. Efficiency measures focused on objectives like reducing rejection rates from 3 per cent to 2 per cent because of substantially lower costs.

The quality movement in all organizations now comes with new expectations that suggest rather bluntly, *'quality means refusing to accept error'*[76] in the products or services that the organization produces. Increasingly, the only acceptable quality level is 100 per cent, which means 0 per cent defects, complaints and rejections. New quality advocates warn us that even a 0.1 per cent rejection rate has serious implications in public organizations, such as in these cases:

- Of the approximately 547,500 babies born in a country during the year, we might accept that 547.5 of these would not be born successfully and perhaps not survive or be born with defects.
- 150 babies might be mistakenly put in the wrong cribs and end up with the wrong parents.
- Of the 4.85 million aircraft take-offs and landings in a country during a year, approximately 4,850 might crash.[77]
- Of the 600,000 pacemakers implanted each year worldwide, 600 would be implanted incorrectly.

Quality now means doing perfect work where rejection rates of 0.001 per cent are not acceptable.

Customer criteria will shape organizations and the way we respond. The Deming-inspired quality movement and **total quality management (TQM)** called for shaping organizational activities on meeting or exceeding customer expectations for products and services. The idea is to redesign the organization's entire service delivery and production system to meet customer needs.

In the private sector, because of the Internet and other technologies, customers have more choice in making comparisons and have been able to assert their preferences and demands for products and services. They are asking for custom-designed experiences, good service, fair prices and innovative offerings. If they don't get it from one company, they can more easily go elsewhere and can also tell others they are satisfied or dissatisfied with their experience.

In the public sector, the customer focus has driven new metrics on performance in improving the efficiency and effectiveness of service delivery. In attempts to be a more customer-centric public service, governments are reacting to higher expectations for faster service, more engagement of citizens, being responsive to needs, cost-effectiveness and choice. Citizens and the various customers of the public sector's organizations are more aware of their rights and have more access to information and much higher expectations for a positive customer experience.

Pressures to outsource to become more responsive and strategic. **Outsourcing** or contracting out specific functions of an organization – and sometimes entire divisions of an organization – is widely practiced. IT resources and services were once very commonly associated with the practice of outsourcing, due in large part to the rapid and radical evolution that occurred in IT during the latter part of the twenty-first century, which required an equally rapid and radical response on the part of business and industry. The practice has now become common in nearly all organizational divisions. India is the current outsourcing market leader, although other countries are close behind. The Chinese government has designated 20 cities as outsourcing hubs in an effort to attract more international investment, and the Philippine government has declared outsourcing a priority industry. Outsourcing within Western countries is projected to grow at an average of 10 per cent to 15 per cent annually.

HRM outsourcing is recognized as one of the fastest growing segments of the outsourcing sector.[78] The per cent of public organizations that outsource at least some of their human resource functions varies and range from lows of 53 to 62 per cent[79] to a high of 93 per cent.[80] The variance reported reflects differences in the type, scope and size of organization. Chapter 7 reviews HR's role in recruiting changes when production or service jobs are outsourced.

Comments on the reasons for HR outsourcing, and outsourcing generally, fall into two camps, either as a way of (i) reducing costs or (ii) gaining expertise and efficiencies.[81] The 'reducing costs' perspective suggests that an organization should outsource an activity when the cost of performing the activity is lower than doing it internally.[82] Cost savings from the possible greater efficiency that vendors offer is a driving force behind this perspective on outsourcing. Outsourced organizations can also enjoy economies of scale through specialization of a service for a number of clients, whereas client organizations would need to hire staff who may not have the same expertise or be fully employed performing the service. However, the decision to outsource services results in increased costs to monitor performance, although a vast majority of those outsourcing are looking to the overall cost advantage.[83]

Outsourcing is sometimes seen as a way of gaining expertise. This perspective suggests that HR capacities can be increased by exploiting expertise from those who have more experience in an area.[84] In implementing this strategy, core HR activities integral to implementing operational strategies are kept internal, and other activities are outsourced.[85] By outsourcing the *transactional* activities, for example, HR personnel are better able to focus their energies on issues that are of strategic importance to their organizations, like succession planning and skills development.[86]

The most common human resource administrative functions to be outsourced are those which are more transactional or peripheral in nature, like payroll services; benefits; employee assistance programmes (EAPs); pension plan administration; and training, recruitment and selection.[87] These functions tend to be non-core functions that are standard and routine across most organizations, and are often viewed as easily reproducible.[88] Unlike transactional activities, 'strategic' functions are often described as more core to the organization's strategic objectives[89] and are perceived to be 'valuable, rare, and difficult to imitate'.[90] These include career guidance and management, performance evaluation, internal communications,[91] labour relations and HR planning.[92] Some organizations consider training and development to be a strategic function, whereas others describe it as more transactional and peripheral.

The manner in which human resource functions and activities are outsourced varies greatly from one organization to the next. Small and medium organizations often outsource the human resource function in its entirety so that they can direct their already limited resources to more strategic functions. Large organizations are more likely to have more flexibility and can choose to outsource only specific HRM activities (e.g. administration of payroll) and particular functions (e.g. benefits and health care), or can contract out their entire HR division to the services of an external vendor or personnel employee organization:

- ***IT outsourcing or application service provider (ASP)*** occurs when only the human resource IT infrastructure is outsourced, and the ASP hosts the technology and is responsible for technical support, desktops, networks and software applications.
- ***Single-service or selective outsourcing*** involves transferring particular non-core functions like payroll services to a single provider; it is the simplest contracting out arrangement.
- ***Multiple-service solutions*** consist of transferring several non-core services.
- ***Transformational or comprehensive business process outsourcing*** involves solutions where HR's role and purpose is significantly changed and leveraged using technologies and approaches to improve performance.[93] This sort of outsourcing is the most dramatic and comprehensive in turning over the HR function to a third party. It is also the most infrequently used, as outsourcing becomes a total shifting or transformation of the HR function.

Like outsourcing, the shared services model has only recently gained prominence in the field of human resources. In its infancy, shared services was almost exclusively adopted by large organizations that had the resources and determination to overhaul their operations. More recently, it is estimated that close to 80 per cent of organizations (large and small, public and private sector) worldwide participate in some form of shared services. The prevalence of human resource shared services is currently estimated to be around 55 per cent.[94]

In its most basic form, the shared services model consolidates business services into a single unit. What differentiates shared services from centralization of services is the focus on the client. In a centralized organization, the corporate nucleus sets the direction, resources and policies for the field. In a shared services arrangement, it is the field – the internal customer or client – that sets the direction. Internal line managers articulate the needs of their unit, which dictate the type and level of services offered by the centre.[95]

When operating effectively, the shared services model is able to marry the cost savings and possible efficiencies of outsourcing or centralization with the customer satisfaction generated through decentralization. This, however, can only be achieved when shared services evolves through the vision of the client and operates in a manner that continues to satiate those needs.[96]

> MANAGERIAL IMPLICATION: We have reviewed 12 forces or pressures that come from various arenas: the changing external environment, the increasing importance of the organization's social system and from customer and quality requirements. In a traditional view of public organizations, the centralized organization would define strategies in setting and implementing a course of action, just like military generals are thought to do in setting forth a battle plan where they can control their environment. However, a more realistic view of today's political and managerial leaders is not that of a military commander, but that of a juggler. A juggler who is very good at manipulating a single ball is not interesting and will not be successful with an audience. It is only when the juggler can handle multiple balls at one time that his or her skill is respected.[97] The juggling act requires the balancing of many tasks such as outsourcing jobs for refocusing on core services in efforts to lower costs; or implementing quality circles, team processes or just-in-time production to improve efficiencies. It requires the ability to constantly assess and recalibrate important day-to-day initiatives in an environment that is rapidly changing. It is juggling when the ground is moving underneath you.
>
> In managing strategically, a municipal government might have a range of objectives related to strategic themes involving improving the environment, transportation, health, safety, economy and service. In working within any one of these themes, one must juggle conflicting priorities related to meeting the needs of citizens and employees, in addition to being financially prudent and efficient. Working to accomplish one set of objectives is hard enough, but it is more difficult to do in the context of socially challenging pressures and forces. Managers need a great deal of agility and ambidexterity in moving forward in implementing their programmes and initiatives.[98] HRM systems play a key role in encouraging organizational ambidexterity in shaping its workforce, through training, recruitment and selection practices that encourage innovation and adaptability.[99]

BEFORE APPLYING, LET'S REVIEW

CO 1: Explain HRM and SHRM and illustrate the connection to effective management.

Human resources are valuable resources in an organization and are like other resources such as materials and money. To manage is to manage basic resources, and human resource management grew to be a managerial function by finding innovative ways to more fully utilize people. As the general body of knowledge on human resource management developed, the challenge was to help align human resource processes to assist managers in implementing an organization's strategic plan. As managers focus on achieving strategies and objectives in responding to customers or clients, HR's purpose is to help them do this through four groups of tasks: planning and facilitating the strategic HRM process; designing jobs and staffing; linking performance to strategic goals and priorities through measuring and rewarding performance; and managing, developing and engaging employees.

CO 2: Examine and prioritize the pressures and societal forces shaping HR managers and our ability to be strategic and effectively management people.

While working to accomplish strategic objectives, HR managers and the organizations they work with have to respond to a range of pressures and forces that affect the process of managing. It is like juggling the requirements of different objectives while the (pressure) ground is moving underneath. The pressure arises from the fact that we live in an age of constant change and increasingly must recognize the importance of the human, cultural and ethical fabric in our organizations. Beyond this, we have stringent requirements for error-free performance and responsiveness to customers or clients. There are also increasingly pressures for efficiency and doing more with less.

DISCUSSION AND REVIEW QUESTIONS

1. Review the experiences you have had with HRM. The experiences that you and others have had with HRM provide a snapshot of what HRM is like and its importance to you. Describe examples of experiences you have had with an HR manager or the HRM system. These experiences might relate to (i) looking for a job, being interviewed and completing an application form; (ii) getting selected or terminated; (iii) being assigned job responsibilities in relation to the job description; (iv) getting trained for a job and being instructed on what to do; or (v) being evaluated or disciplined. Describe as many experiences as come to mind. What are the dominant themes? Share your experiences with others. Were the experiences mostly positive or negative? If they were positive, what made them positive? If they were not positive, why were they not positive?
2. When it comes to managing people, all managers are HR managers. Provide examples of shared relationships between managerial and HR responsibilities. Consider the statement that HRM processes are the way that we implement many managerial ideas on team management, service excellence and performance. What should managers do to help HRM? What can HR do to help managers?
3. Review the pressures and challenges that managers face, and identify those that are most important for managers to respond to. In entering the workforce, identify the pressures that are most important for you in your career. Develop a presentation that reviews some of the key forces affecting HR. Identify strategies for responding to these forces.
4. An organization's intangible assets are seen as increasingly important in developed economies. Why? Given that intangible assets are so important, why do you think that so many organizations engage in lay-offs, outsourcing and offshoring work to other countries?
5. Define human resource management and strategic human resource management.

CASE: DEFINING SOME OF THE KEY SOCIETAL PRESSURES OR FORCES FACING HRM

There is a stark new reality facing people entering the workforce. New facts suggest that it is very likely that you will face some turbulence in your career, including broad changes in your industry, organizational downsizing or even your desire to go in a different direction. The new reality: Career survival and progress is up to you, not the organization.

In the old human resource reality in Western organizations, lifetime employment was the ethos for people who worked for high-profile businesses and governments. Underlying this was an unwritten psychological contract where employers expected long-term commitment, trust and loyalty from their employees. In exchange, employees expected to have a career with promotions, recognition and benefits. Some organizations illustrated family-like values with commitment, connection, and parental-like benefits (like pensions and the expectation of lifetime employment) and financial security.

The new reality existing today is illustrated by two recent crises. First, there is the pension crisis and the fact that the retirement plans we created years ago might not be sustainable. A recent European Union (EU) report called for Europeans to work longer to keep receiving pension from increasingly cash-strapped governments. The recommendation is that the EU bloc would have to increase the normal retirement age from the current age of 60 to 70 by 2060 if workers are to continue supporting retirees at the current rate.

Then, there is the increasing cost of health benefits to employers because people are living longer and there are expensive improvements in diagnostic tests, drugs and treatments. Economically, health benefits are a significant cost item and a major percentage of the annual wage bill. When managers have to pay an extra 30 to 40 per cent of the wage bill for benefits, many have considered other options, including contracting out or shifting operations to other countries.

Which forces are more likely to have the greatest impact on HR, managers and on employees in their careers?

Task. In developing a better understanding of our future, you are asked to assess the possibility and the impact of various forces in the environment.

1. Rank the following list of 12 factors in Table 1.2 in order of their importance to you in the possible impact they will have on your career development. Place number 1 beside the item that you think will affect the way you work in organizations or the shape of HRM generally. Place number 2 beside the item that is next in importance to you or HRM, and so on, through number 12.
2. Break into small groups and together develop a single rank ordering by consensus, based on discussion with your group.

Share the ranking with others in your group, and discuss the differences in rankings. How did the rankings differ from individual scores to group scores? Did the composition of the group make a difference?

Table 1.2 Case – Societal forces or pressures affecting HRM and how we manage

Societal force or pressure	Your ranking	Group ranking
1. Managing in a rapidly changing environment.		
2. Changes from the rise of new communication technologies and the internet.		
3. Changes requiring the use of technologies in implementing most organizational ideas.		
4. The increasing importance and value of human and intellectual capital.		
5. The need for employee involvement and engagement.		
6. Organizations are made up of a increasing diversity of people, many different demographic groups, and many different national and group cultures.		
7. Calls for ethical and virtuous behaviour.		
8. Calls for attention to human rights issues.		
9. Pressures for the more effective implementation of ideas.		
10. High expectations for quality services and products.		
11. Customer criteria will shape organizations and the way we respond.		
12. Outsourcing in reducing costs and gaining expertise.		

2 Using a SHRM Balanced Scorecard as a Strategic Framework

Chapter Outline
- Chapter objectives (COs) 25
- A driving issue focusing managerial action: NPM 25
- CO 1: Different perspectives defining SHRM 27
- CO 2: The Balanced Scorecard in public organizations 31
- CO 3: The SHRM Balanced Scorecard 34
- SHRM BSC terminology 41
- Before applying, let's review 42
- Discussion and review questions 43
- Case: An HR Strategy Map for COOL AID 44

CHAPTER OBJECTIVES (COs)

After reading this chapter, you will be able to:

CO 1: Illustrate different perspectives defining SHRM.

CO 2: Apply the Balanced Scorecard Approach and its key perspectives in strategic planning.

CO 3: Assess the use of the SHRM Scorecard in linking HR objectives and initiatives to assist managers to implement their objectives.

A DRIVING ISSUE FOCUSING MANAGERIAL ACTION: NPM

New public management (NPM) *emerged in the 1990s at a time when the public had little faith in public institutions as a result of their inability to manage their finances. In part, NPM was a reaction to the traditional model of bureaucratic organizations and its monopolistic forms. NPM attempted to apply private sector, competitive-based strategies theories in developing public organizations in quasi-markets with clients or customers. The new vocabulary suggested that 'government organizations should be more businesslike'; 'citizens and stakeholders should be treated as customers'; and 'public servants should be more entrepreneurial'. Many of the reforms are premised on the belief that government operations, in particular, their efficiency and responsiveness,* can be significantly improved by streamlining procedures, empowering managers, focusing on results rather than process[1] and aligning operations to focus on customers or clients.[2]

Some of the impetus for what some people saw as a social movement came from Osborne and Gabler's Reinventing Government[3] and a later publication of Osborne and Plastrick's Banishing Bureaucracy.[4] The central themes underlying this view of reinventing government and performance management[5] suggest that political officials and executive managers set strategic goals and objectives and performance targets, and then secure resources for implementation of public programmes. Agencies and their managers should be empowered and held accountable for the results, and they should be given authority and broad limits to make certain the goals and objectives are achieved.[6]

NPM has had a significant impact in reforming or changing governments in Western countries and is often connected to Prime Minister Margaret Thatcher's programmes in the United Kingdom in the 1980s and later by political reforms in New Zealand and Australia. The reforms connected to NPM cover various government operations in redesigning services to better connect to citizens as customers of the administration. Among its goals was to break down the formal control structure, build an entrepreneurial and action-oriented bias in public organizations and provide explicit standards and measures of performance.[7] The intellectual footing for NPM is partially linked to Public Choice theory, which suggests that government services should be market based in using a business management approach to achieving productivity gains.

The majority of NPM reforms are in the public personnel management area and include decentralized and reorganized personnel structures which separate transaction and strategic functions, changes to classifications, recruitment, selection, incentives structures and greater concern for diversity and ethical issues, among other things.[8] NPM advocates claim that applying modern, researched human resource practices which have been successful in the private sector can make public organizations more businesslike, proactive and entrepreneurial.[9]

There has been some criticism of NPM and the 'reinventing government' movement, much of it connected to the fact that proponents seem to be working with the conviction that government is inefficient and that private sector management is superior in accomplishment. In being more efficient and clear on solid measures of performance, the focus is on being businesslike and market oriented and decreasing the size of government. The key reforms include privatization, downsizing, decentralization, de-bureaucratization and a managerial approach based on business protocols.[10] NPM encouraged differentiated pay and promotion based on performance in replacing seniority and a focus on individual accountability in the employment relationship. The reforms seek to bring about a cultural shift to a more entrepreneurial government embracing private sector vocabulary and terms such as: '"empowerment"; service to "clients" or "customers"; "responsiveness"; a shift from "process" to "performance"; and an emphasis on the need to "earn" rather than to "spend"'.[11]

Pundits might say that NPM overemphasized the appropriateness of the business model and, in some cases, a Tayloristic measurement approach. In assisting the future of SHRM, NPM has provoked some valuable discussion on the validity of measures of public sector performance. It has also helped recognize some of the advantages and disadvantages of the customer-centred approach to management and how to design HR activities to assist public managers to improve the delivery of services to citizens and clients.

Although NPM is a contested concept, there has been a convergence of views that it has challenged the traditional view of public organizations in encouraging a stronger focus on performance, efficiency and effectiveness. Some of the measures encourage more competition and foster a philosophy where the public sector would be more like the private sector. NPM encouraged managers to focus more on performance and, in some cases, to devolve strategy to local levels.

The challenge for HR managers is to define the place of NPM in a strategic approach to HR. Even though managers might not totally agree with the market-oriented philosophy, elements of NPM are here to stay in public organization. An emphasis on improving performance by strategically aligning HR and organizational objectives in responding to customer or client needs will continue. Strategic frameworks that seek to define how to gain a competitive advantage over others, however, may not be as relevant for public organizations that often have a monopoly over the services they provide. Getting more customers from competitors is not usually an issue, although police, fire and other public organizations are constantly under pressure to 'do more with less' and respond to different needs with fewer resources. Often, public sector programmes exist to fill the gap or provide something badly needed because the market does not or cannot provide it.[12]

> STRATEGIC CONTEXT: *Private sector approaches to* **strategic management** *focus on goals of being more effective in a competitive environment, such as improving profit, product quality, market share and customer satisfaction.*[13] *The strategic alternatives, according to a dominant paradigm are (i) lowering costs (cost leadership), (ii) differentiating an organization's strategies so that the products and services are unique or (iii) focusing efforts in a specialized way to a unique market.*[14]
>
> *Co-operative and co-ordinative strategies are relevant in all organizations but are particularly important in those public organizations whose strategic themes and initiatives are highly visible and which have to be tuned to the forces and pressures in society generally. In the public arena, a strategy helps to identify priorities and engage the community in addressing important policy problems, challenges or needs for change. It involves identifying strategic themes (those that an organization is pursuing in relation to its vision) in responding to pressures from various stakeholders or clients. In public organizations with social goals, strategy can be a tool for the activist manager in focusing his or her programme and engaging others in the cause.*[15]
>
> *In engaging and co-ordinating with others to secure resources to carry out their programme, public sector managers have to explain what they are doing and why they are doing it. They are asked to clarify their strategies, objectives, programmes or initiatives, outputs and outcomes in a very transparent way. This requires consultation and compromise in responding to divergent points of view.*
>
> *Implementation of strategies is a concern in any organization but is particularly relevant in public organizations, where there is a need for a co-operative definition of strategies. In this chapter, we outline different views of SHRM and the place of an SHRM Balanced Scorecard that is used to help identify different types of objectives and initiatives that are important to the implementation of strategy. This chapter introduces the SHRM Balanced Scorecard as a tool to help conceptualize how different strategic objectives are linked to an organization's strategic themes. The SHRM Balanced Scorecard links strategic themes, objectives and initiatives to the competencies that are needed for achieving them.*

CO 1: DIFFERENT PERSPECTIVES DEFINING SHRM

Those providing some of the original definitions of SHRM focused on responding to a range of questions on the contribution of human resources and HRM (practices) in relationship to the empirical world.[16] These questions attempted to provide a theoretical perspective to ground the field, such as these: How do certain HR practices 'fit' together and relate to an organization's strategy? What HR practices enhance performance and effectiveness? How do resources and competences contribute to effectively implementing strategies for different stakeholders? Basically, these and other questions encourage us to search for the theoretical logic defining strategy in HRM. This section assesses the relevance of four strategic perspectives shaping the direction of SHRM.

SHRM as 'Fit'. The business literature provides a review of how HRM components can be designed to fit an organization's strategies by (i) using known HR best practices to implement strategic objectives, (ii) aligning skills to strategic objectives or (iii) developing a culture which is in tune with the strategy.[17]

The **SHRM best practice fit** perspective suggests that there are complementary 'bundles' of 'high performance' – or 'high commitment' – oriented human resource practices that are more effective. In the private sector, HR practices in job design, employee appraisal and other areas affect the market value of the company by as much as 20 per cent, in addition to improving profits and reducing turnover.[18] Certain 'bundles' of HR best practices work well together in providing something extra in engaging people[19] to work smarter and accept more responsibility in developing their careers and in their contribution to the organization.[20]

The private sector has been the dominant context for studies of HR best practices, and most of these have been in US companies. One very popular view of the best practice perspective is reflected in Jeffrey Pfeffer's summary of seven best practices: employee security, selective hiring, self-managed teams, high pay contingent on performance, extensive training, reduction of status differences and sharing of information.[21] Table 2.1 summarizes best practices that focus on changes to the job's design, staffing and compensation, and the employees' relationship with the organization.[22]

A modern-day example of the best practice approach is the lean management and lean manufacturing systems practised and used by many consulting companies. These are management philosophies applied in public and private organizations that consider waste to be anything that does not directly create 'value' for customers.

The *SHRM best practice fit* perspective suggests that an organization might choose HRM 'best practices' that fit its chosen strategy.[23] The different versions of how these practices might fit together suggest that (i) there are 'bundles' which might be universally relevant for all situations; (ii) some practices might be more congruent with other organizational factors (e.g. life cycle); or (iii) a specific combination of best practices might be ideal for better performance.[24] That is, the type of organizational strategy (e.g. defender, prospector or analyser strategy types) might influence the set of HRM practices.[25]

A **strategy employee skills fit** perspective involves fitting HRM competencies or skills to the chosen strategies. Different strategies require people who have the unique competencies and specific motivations to implement them. The key questions are: What strategies are the organization trying to achieve? How can HR assist the management team in achieving their strategic themes by identifying relevant competencies, encouraging skilled and experienced employees to apply and selecting people who are most competent and motivated?[26] In the same way, attuning performance management and incentive systems has been shown to link with improved performance.[27]

A **strategy employee behaviour fit** perspective is making sure that HR strategies are horizontally congruent with the organization's culture and are implemented to improve efficiencies. Rather than picking HR high-performance practices as if they are on a convenient shopping list of things to do, the configuration of HR practices should fit well together and should fit the culture or context in the organization. Thus, the practices are designed to fit the desired relationship.[28] For example, empowerment practices are more likely to be useful if the job requires interactions and employees have a need and interest in taking on responsibilities. In the same way, reward systems and performance plans are not universally linked to high performance. A key in their successful implementation is the way the plan is designed and administered. The crucial questions are: How can HR align their practices so they effectively fit with other HR strategies and the organization's culture? What HR practices will improve efficiencies and quality of products and services?[29]

Table 2.1 Examples of Best Practices

Changes to the Job and Organization	Changes in Staffing and Compensation	Changes to the Employee Relationship with the Organization
Sharing knowledge about the organization.	Being selective in hiring.	Making a commitment to job security to recognize employee importance to the organization.
Flexible job descriptions which encourage movement between jobs and encourage people to take on challenging tasks where they can learn and develop their careers.	Using compensation arrangements to encourage and reward employees. Higher pay is often a commitment to attract better employees. Compensation can take many forms, including stock options, gain sharing, profit sharing and skill-based pay and team incentives.	Recognizing HR's role in improving the context for performance. This includes the *'lifespace,'* or context – of personal orientation, job stress, job design, supervisor-subordinate relationships and many other factors.
Self-managed teams replace hierarchical supervision with peer supervision and encourage people to feel more responsible and accountable for their work.		Being clear on the critical competencies and how to measure them. The competencies go beyond the job requirements and put a higher priority on attitudes, values and cultural fit, attributes that are linked to turnover and performance.
Reducing status distinctions by changing job titles (and replacing titles like 'secretary') and encouraging employees at all levels to feel valued and career oriented.		Developing broad career paths and promoting from within as a way of developing and preserving core competencies.
An open sharing of information – about salaries, financial performance and debt – promotes trust and eliminates conjectures and misinformation.		Making a commitment to training as an investment in improving an organization's competitive advantage. Training goes beyond specialist training and focuses on multi-skilling, improving the culture and higher-level learning.

The advantage of the strategic fit model in focusing SHRM in the public arena is that it recognizes that different types of HR practice might fit better with different types of public and private organizations and cultures.[30] Whereas the original research on strategic fit emerged in private sector organizations, the fit model is relevant in public sector organizations, and there is support for 'the overarching hypothesis that HR practices lead to superior organizational performance'.[31]

The resource-based view (RBV) of strategy. The resource-based view seeks to identify the resources and competencies needed to implement initiatives and programmes that are of strategic importance. There are two key assumptions of the resource-based view. One is that resources are scarce, and valuable resources are the only important factors capable of creating performance differences in successfully implementing strategies. In the business world, this is linked to competitive advantage. A second assumption is that rare resources, such as competencies and human capital, are not easy to imitate and cannot be easily replaced, or replicated by competitors.[32]

In the private sector, the RBV argues for developing resources that add value and that are unique.[33] This can be accomplished by developing and deploying physical, human and organizational resources in ways that are difficult for competitors to imitate.[34] In public organizations, the emphasis is more specifically on identifying and making use of distinctive human resources, especially distinctive competencies in implementing strategic themes and objectives. As such, the emphasis is on the role of managers in selecting, developing and deploying resources, rather than selecting a competitive position in an environment.

The resource-based view is particularly useful to public sector organizations that exist in an era of shifting resources, increased public scepticism and greater demands to provide greater value to citizens and stakeholders. A key to success is to use resources expertly in meeting strategic objectives.

For some researchers, the resource-based view has become the 'backdrop' for work in the SHRM area.[35] Historically, although resources have been useful in measures of efficiency (Efficiency = input/output), the resource-based view goes further and focuses on prioritizing resources and identifying core and distinctive competencies related to strategies. As illustrated in Figure 2.1, examples of strategic resources describe critical success factors related to the delivery of services, but most of all, they include the human capital and distinctive and core competencies.[36]

The appeal of the resource-based view is linked to the assumption that resources must be used strategically on higher priority objectives. The HR system is important in this regard because of its importance in recruiting, selecting, training and grooming human resources and in developing the intangible elements in an organization. The resource-based view provides a framework to identify and guide the pool of human resources and intangibles which best assist line managers to implement their strategies. In doing so, the resource-based view encourages managers to prioritize their strategies and objectives and to hone their human resources for these priorities.

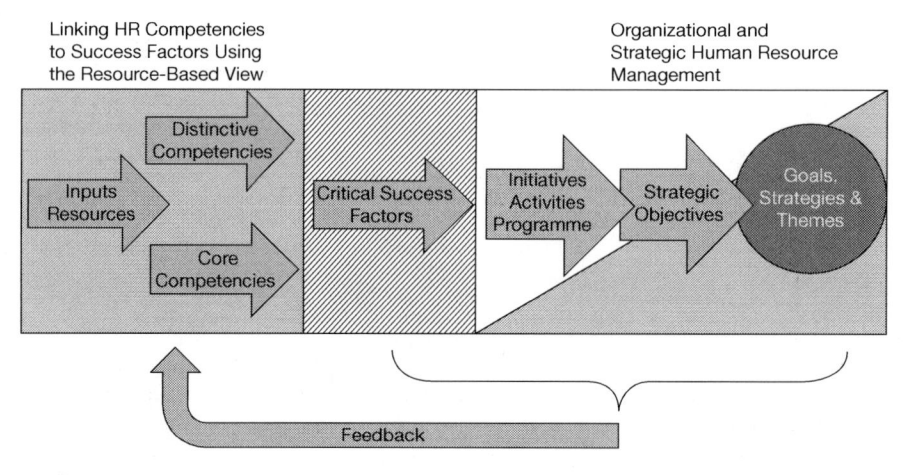

Figure 2.1 Linking resources to strategy.

CO 2: THE BALANCED SCORECARD IN PUBLIC ORGANIZATIONS

In seeking to balance various interests of multiple stakeholders, public sector organizations often find themselves doing a 'balancing act', of two public needs: the need for growth and economic development as well as social issues such as poverty, health care, education and environment. For example, the province of Upper Austria has economic strategies such as industrial production, energy, mobility and logistics and social strategies focused on improving health, responding to the needs of an ageing society and improving food and nutrition. In New South Wales, Australia, the strategic themes (goals) highlight the economic need to ensure a growing prosperity across the state (state and regional development). This is balanced with social strategic themes of providing better services (health, education, public transport and roads) and environment for living (environment, recreation and the arts). Other social-equity themes cover human rights, respect and responsibility (police, justice, anti-social behaviour, citizenship and volunteering) and fairness and opportunity (social justice and Aboriginal affairs).[37] In British Columbia, Canada, a key economic strategic goal relates to creating more jobs per capita than anywhere in Canada while social strategic themes point to improving education, health and fitness, support for persons with disabilities, special needs, children at risk and seniors, and assuring there is a sustainable environment of air, water quality and fisheries management.

An organization's strategic plan provides a way to conceptualize this 'balancing act' in illustrating how to align the organization's long-term visions, goals and strategies and align them with resources within a set of initiatives or programmes. John Bryson's *Strategic Planning for Public and Non-profit Organizations* describes strategic planning as a set of concepts, processes and tools for shaping and guiding 'what an organization (or other entity) is, what it does, and why'.[38] It is an aid to decision-making in providing a framework for focusing and charting an organization's progress in how it uses resources in development and implementation strategies and objectives. It provides a 'big picture' of the future and a way to communicate this picture in more specific terms to stakeholders.

The Balanced Scorecard (BSC) provides a framework for viewing the strategic themes, objectives and initiatives (use of resources) within different perspectives – customer, internal process, financial, and learning and growth – that need to be addressed in implementation. That is, given the customer-related objectives, we have to design efficient internal processes and define financial targets. Building on this, we have to design high-performance practices and train and motivate people to implement them. As emphasized by several researchers, the BSC is more than a measurement system; it is a management system to help facilitate the implementation of strategic objectives. An assumption is that organizations that are effective in implementing their strategies are able to align the various perspectives so that they illustrate a semi-causal relationship to facilitate implementation. In the public sector, the BSC is focused less on competition and profit than on implementing the mission and service relationship.[39]

In Kaplan and Norton's landmark book, *The Balanced Scorecard: Translating Strategy into Action*,[40] they ask us to imagine walking into the cockpit of a modern jet airplane which has one single measuring instrument for guiding the airplane. Even a pilot with exceptional talent relies on a variety of measurement instruments in piloting a plane, just as managers need a variety of measures for guiding an organization within the larger arena that these organizations relate to. Kaplan and Norton's idea of the BSC encourages us to recognize that we need measures that go beyond financial ones if we want to implement our objectives. Although the BSC retains financial measures, it includes others that calibrate the linkage to customer, internal process and employee and systems performance. In addition to being a way to assess progress, the BSC is considered a planning framework and communication tool that focuses on objectives and initiative, and measures within four areas or perspectives:[41]

1. Customer perspective: In achieving our vision, how do we appear to our stakeholders (or clients), and what is the distinct value we provide?
2. Internal process perspective: To satisfy our funders, clients and stakeholders, at what business processes should we excel?
3. Financial perspective: To satisfy our stakeholders, how do we add value in meeting tangible outcomes like economic value, cash flow or growth?
4. Learning and growth perspective: To achieve our internal process and client objectives, how do we design high-performance practices to improve our ability to learn and grow?

Although the initial implementations of the BSC framework were in for-profit organizations, there are now several examples of successful experiences in public and non-profit organizations.[42]

In other words, the BSC is simply a way of organizing strategic themes, objectives and initiatives (allocation of resources). The organization's mission provides a statement of its *raison d'être* and is often connected to a formal, legal or informal mandate for existence. The mission of many government agencies derives from legislation, but non-profit community groups often begin by identifying their social or political need they wish to fill in binding their stakeholders. Stakeholders' satisfaction in public organizations is critical. That is, people, groups or organizations can lay 'claim on an organization's attention, resources, or output' and completely derail a process if they are not satisfied.[43]

A **strategic planning** process often includes an analysis to identify the stakeholders and how it needs to respond to them and whether different aspects of the mission statement and strategies might be important to different groups. In a municipal organization, for example, some stakeholders might be calling for housing for senior citizens while others might prefer limited development.

An organization's **philosophy statement** identifies its core values and what it cherished, values which can be the cornerstone for strategic planning and its implementation. For example, the Cool Aid Society, a non-profit focusing on creating opportunities for people who are homeless or living in poverty, has 10 guiding principles in its philosophy statement, 3 of which are:

- We are committed to promoting fairness and equity within our organization.
- We support and value participation, build partnerships and encourage shared leadership in our community.
- We are action oriented and advocate for those we serve.

A strategic plan can also include a review of the organization's (S) strengths and (W) weaknesses, (O) opportunities and (T) threats, or a **SWOT analysis**. The review of the opportunities and threats provides a picture of the external environment while strengths and weaknesses are internally focused. A review of the internal environment provides a picture of the organization's strengths and weaknesses by summarizing the merits of how its resources are being used for achieving its objectives. At a broader level, a scanning of the **macro-environment** can provide an overview of the political, economic, social and demographic, technological, environmental or ecological, and legal forces that can affect an organization. **PESTEL** is an acronym for the (P) political, (E) economic, (S) social, (T) technological, (E) environmental and (L) legal factors.[44]

Figure 2.2 recognizes that all organizations have goals, whether explicitly defined or implicit.[45] **Goals** are long-term aims, whereas strategic themes are the main, high-level conceptual streams that are the basis for the organization's strategic framework. A **vision statement** illustrates a value-based sketch of the future, which pulls the organization in a certain direction. For example, The Victoria Cool Aid Society's vision is to *'act to end homelessness and improve our quality of life by working with others to build a community where: No one is forced to sleep on the street or go hungry. Everyone who needs supportive housing*

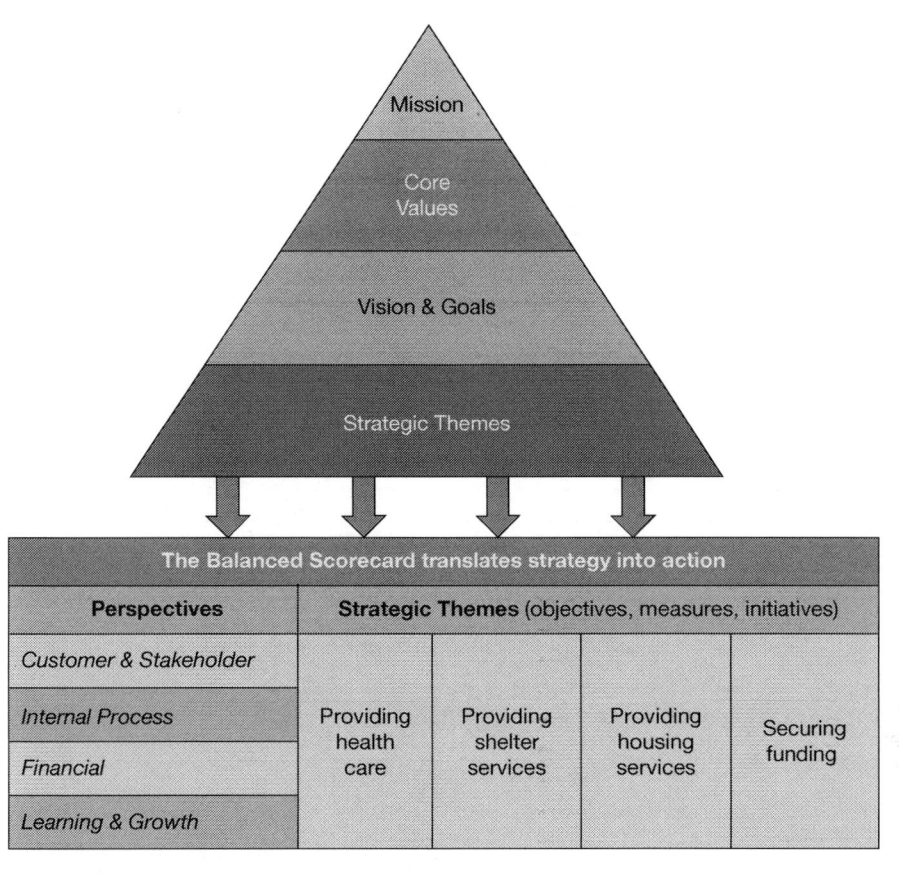

Figure 2.2 The organization's strategic framework within the BSC.

is getting it. Integrated health care service to treat illness and promote wellness is provided, and services are provided to those with mental health and addiction issues.'

Once people have agreed on the vision and philosophy for the organization (your picture of the future or desired future state), then it is possible to develop strategic themes, the high-level conceptual thrusts that the organization will pursue in achieving its vision. Each theme is defined so that strategic objectives are balanced within the four perspectives of the BSC (customer, internal process, finance and learning and growth). Whereas a **strategic objective** represents a result that a person or organization seeks to achieve within a time frame, **initiatives** define the change projects/programmes that are being used to implement the objective. Measures are the variables that can be used to assess progress, and targets are the desired values being sought.[46]

There are, of course, criticisms of the BSC. Yet, although there are criticisms of the rationale for the four perspectives, it is possible to change the logic linking the different perspectives or add perspectives that seem more relevant. In some settings, managers focus more on the measures and lose sight of the purpose of the BSC to encourage objectives and measures that relate to different parts of the implementation process. As a bottom line, the tool encourages us to expand our thinking about a range of perspectives that might be considered in implementing strategic themes and objectives.[48]

> ## A RELEVANT POINT OF VIEW: THREE APPROACHES FOR DEVELOPING STRATEGIC THEMES
>
> In developing strategic themes or directions to pursue, Bryson summarizes three approaches: the direction approach, the goals approach, or the visions of success approach.[47]
>
> The direction approach involves the identification of strategic themes after reviewing the environment (PESTEL analysis) and the organization's SWOT analysis (strengths, weaknesses, opportunities and threats). This approach is most appropriate where the organization's internal and external environments are changing, where there is no general agreement on goals, where there may be a high degree of conflict between actors and where interests are fragmented.
>
> The goals approach can be used in situations where there is already a commitment or understanding of the organization's general goals and needs it has to address. Police, fire and military organizations have broad general goals as do non-profit organizations – such as 'providing housing for people in need'.
>
> The visions of success approach can be used for moving from the way it is now to the way it will look and behave according to the 'vision' or picture of the future. Such an approach is appropriate where it is possible to mobilize people to work together with a common vision. The visions of success approach might be like an architect's vision when beginning the process of renovating an old heritage building. The architect begins with a vision and works within the constraints of the existing construction to 'focus' the vision and develop a model, sketches and an architectural plan. An architect's vision is adapted and refocused to the present construction, changing needs of the tenant and problems as they arise.

CO 3: THE SHRM BALANCED SCORECARD

This book adapts the Balanced Scorecard as a framework to assist HR managers to align HR processes and activities so that internal clients (line managers) can more effectively accomplish their strategic objectives. Although there are many ways to implement a strategic framework in HR, the Strategic Human Resource Balanced Scorecard (SHRM BSC) framework illustrates how HR strategic objectives are aligned to focus on implementing strategic HR themes that are important for assisting an organization to achieve its strategic goals and themes.

Figure 2.3 illustrates the SHRM BSC as a managerial framework for aligning the organization's mission with its strategic objectives and initiatives. For example, HR might assist line managers by defining and implementing objectives related to recruiting, selecting and training in attracting and developing people that are key in delivering specific strategic priorities. For most people doing HR work, the line managers are the customers or clients. As such, most HR relationships to external customers are indirect except in the case where HR relates directly to people for training, counselling and retirement services.

It is possible to add different perspectives or to change focus depending on the context of different organizations. For example, in one SHRM BSC application focusing on chief administrative officer performance in local government organizations, there were four perspectives: client, financial, administrative and HR processes, and strategic planning and leadership.[49] In a business management application,

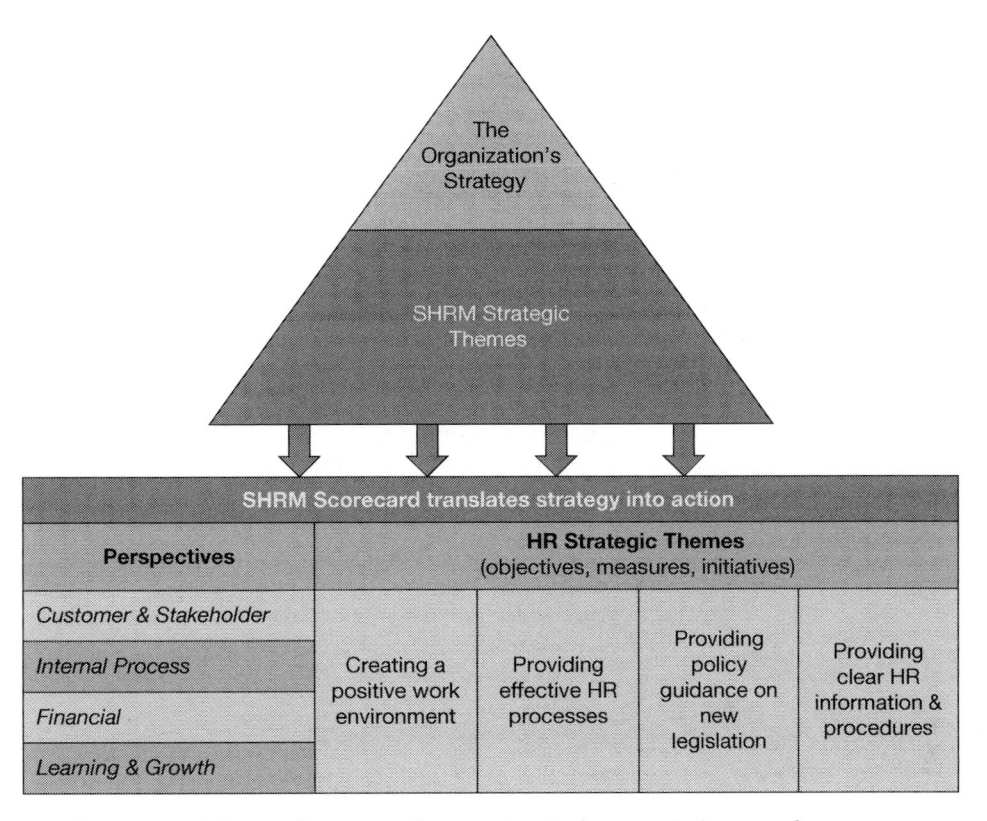

Figure 2.3 The SHRM BSC in implementing the organization's strategic framework.

Perspectives	HR Strategic Themes (objectives, measures, initiatives)			
Customer & Stakeholder	Creating a positive work environment	Providing effective HR processes	Providing policy guidance on new legislation	Providing clear HR information & procedures
Internal Process				
Financial				
Learning & Growth				

the scorecard development proceeds by focusing first on the financial perspective. In a public sector context, the semi-causal sequence usually begins by identifying with the needs and objectives of stakeholders, clients or customers.

The SHRM Balanced Scorecard uses the BSC–like framework in translating the organization's visions, mission and strategies (or the organization's BSC) into HR strategic objectives, initiatives and measures within four BSC perspectives linked in a semi-causal chain: Client and Customer, Internal Business Process, Learning and Growth, and Financial, as illustrated in Figure 2.3.

The client or customer perspective. Most organizations will say that they do serve their customers, and customers are important for feedback, in a general 'all things to customers' strategy'. In public organizations, there is a general strategy that says citizens are customers, and the general idea is to respond to them. In developing a more focused customer strategy, appropriate questions to ask are 'Who are our target customers?' and 'What is our value proposition in serving them?' The private sector mantras for developing a value proposition might come from providing value in quality, product leadership or customer intimacy.[50] In private organizations, a **customer service climate** is clearly linked to the profit chain as well as satisfying customers and developing customer loyalty to products and services. For employees, customer orientation is 'a set of beliefs that customer needs are a priority of an organization'.[51] The beliefs underlying customer orientation are reflected in the organizational culture and in developing a climate for service.[52]

In public service organizations, the customer value chain is more complex. For example, the customer in public organizations can be seen as the taxpayer. But, most public sector organizations have customers of different types with different needs. For example, in a penitentiary the customers include the citizens in the society at large, but they also include the inmates whose needs are important to recognize in the management of a prison. In addition, the victims of any crime might have different, more pronounced needs than the people in the general community.

The value propositions in public organizations often relate to service quality, customer satisfaction and providing value for costs. In public organizations, the customer orientation does not mean that the customers are the centre of the universe and have to be satisfied with a product in the same way as they do in a business organization. Rather, it suggests that services are provided to meet the customer needs in an optimum way. Although satisfaction with services might still be important, government organizations still have the responsibility for defining laws, policies and regulations; carrying out procedures; and making uncomfortable decisions often in an authoritative fashion.

HR's strategic role is to help managers provide services to external customers. In this regard, HR's role is to link directly to the line managers, the internal customers or clients. They do this by helping managers define their strategies and by defining HR processes to help managers provide quality and valued services. This might involve helping to facilitate the strategic management and planning process in clarifying the customer service goals and strategic themes. It also means defining competencies and other HR resources to help managers implement their customer-related objectives.

The internal process perspective. The internal process perspective of the BSC defines the key processes that we want to excel at in adding value to customers. For some public organizations, this has involved shifts not only in how to deliver good services but also in making sure services are most relevant to customers. In improving the internal processes in the knowledge-intensive public service organizations, one challenge is making the administrative apparatus less complex, costly, time-consuming and inflexible. Another challenge is to change the public service orientation from being one that is risk averse to one that focuses on innovative ways to co-ordinate the management of complex problems, service quality and results. One way to do this is to design internal processes that are more decentralized and nurture the workforce in using their skills in delivering the service.

HR's strategic role in linking directly to the line managers involves fostering a service orientation through operationalizing competencies and resources in efficiently and effectively designing jobs, recruitment, selection, training and performance management. This is done by using HR resources to assist managers to improve their capacities for innovation and service quality, and focusing on results.

The financial perspective. The financial perspective in strategic management generally provides a measure of the real costs of the programmes and initiatives in relationship to the value delivered. In the private sector, the value delivered is seen in the return on investment, whereas in the public sector the value delivered is partially calculated in relation to measures of health, safety and quality of life.

Although the general process involves determining the real costs of the services delivered, it is also suggested that HR calculate the added value of high-performance processes in services delivered and how they add value for dollars by what they do. HR's strategic role in the financial perspective also involves adding value through the way people are compensated and rewarded so that higher priority objectives and initiatives identified in other perspectives of the scorecard are successfully implemented. In some public service applications, the financial perspective is defined as the key enabler of the other three perspectives.

The learning and growth perspective. Within public service organizations, the learning and growth perspective facilitates our ability to efficiently and effectively provide valued services to clients and customers. The learning and growth perspective is often the enabler of the other three perspectives as it forms the foundation for how work is done. Though we might define clear service delivery and internal process objectives for improving efficiency, these will go nowhere unless people are trained and engaged in delivering that service.[53]

The financial, customer and internal-business-process objectives of the Balanced Scorecard usually reveal gaps between existing and needed capabilities of people, systems and procedures. Closing these gaps involves opportunities to encourage learning and growth of people.

HR's strategic role is to illustrate ways to add value by managing, developing and engaging employees. Some of the HR processes for doing this involve positive performance management, career development, workplace stress, health and safety and labour relations.

> ### QUIZ 2.1 – BARRIERS TO IMPLEMENTING STRATEGY
>
> There are a number of barriers to the implementation of strategy in organizations. Respond to the questions below in testing your assumptions about the implementation of a strategic approach. Then, compare your estimates against those from the research.
>
> 1. There is a general mantra that strategy is everyone's business. But what do respondents say? What percentage of respondents work within the belief that strategy is management's responsibility?
> 2. What percentage of managers who began the strategic process (at the top) stayed with it for the entire process?
> 3. Who are some of the key organizational actors in strategic management? Rank the following roles in terms of implementation: the CEO, Purchasing, Marketing, Research, Finance, Customers, Personnel, Trade Unions.
> 4. Assume three barriers to implementing strategy: employee understanding, management understanding and linkage to budget.
>   a. What percentage of the workforce understands the strategy?
>   b. What percentage of executive teams spend less than one hour per month discussing strategy?
>   c. What percentage of strategies are linked to budgets?
>
> Suggested answers to these questions are on the book's website.

The logic for using an SHRM BSC framework for strategy implementation

The SHRM BSC provides a template for what an organization should be emphasizing in 'balancing' its financial objectives with those that focus on responding to customers and stakeholders, being efficient in its internal processes, providing financial value and responding to the human aspects of an organization's needs for learning and growth. The SHRM system is aimed at helping an organization implement its strategic themes, objectives and initiatives.[54]

At least three reasons exist for using a framework like the BSC in balancing information from different perspectives. First, the use of a more comprehensive framework helps us get out of our single-mindedness and increases our choices. Our models and schools of thought have evolved over time and represent different perspectives or value statements of management. These schools – such as scientific management or industrial design, human relations, management and open systems theory – continue to evolve, and there is no one approach which can claim to have the all-encompassing view. They do not emerge exclusively from academic writers, new management practices or political movements, but more from a complex interaction among all these factors.[55] The models evolve as societal values change, and in some cases, organizations reflect the values of certain models over others. When people use one model, they are more sensitive to the type of information relevant to that model and, possibly, blind to others. The argument for using a comprehensive framework enriches our understanding and expands our choices.

A second argument for an SHRM BSC is that it encourages an understanding of different perspectives in the implementation of strategies and decisions. Within the BSC logic in Figure 2.4, the different perspectives illustrate a semi-causal chain of objectives that are important in implementing a vision and the strategic themes underlying it. After defining strategic objectives in relation to customers (clients or stakeholders), there is a need to consider financial objectives as well as internal process objectives related to efficiency and effective delivery. Then, we can define learning and growth objectives related to training and motivating people.

In using the BSC, we start by understanding the key strategic goals and themes that the organization wants to focus on. In the public sector, these are defined by different clients' or stakeholders' needs. We then proceed to consider the importance of different client needs in terms of the organization's mandate, before defining internal process, learning and growth, and financial objectives.

The scorecard recognizes that financial objectives and measures only provide a partial picture for guiding an organization in achieving all of its important strategies and goals. To be effective, an organization must also invest and measure its relationship to different clients, funders, employees, processes, technology and innovation. Some management analysts use one type of data over others, such as when financial people use accounting measures; engineers use efficiency measures; or human resource people rely only on statements of motivational needs from employees.

Recognizing some of the weaknesses and vagueness of previous management approaches, the BSC approach provides a clear prescription as to what an organization should measure in 'balancing' its financial goals with those that focus on responding to customers, internal processes and needs for learning and growth in the long run.

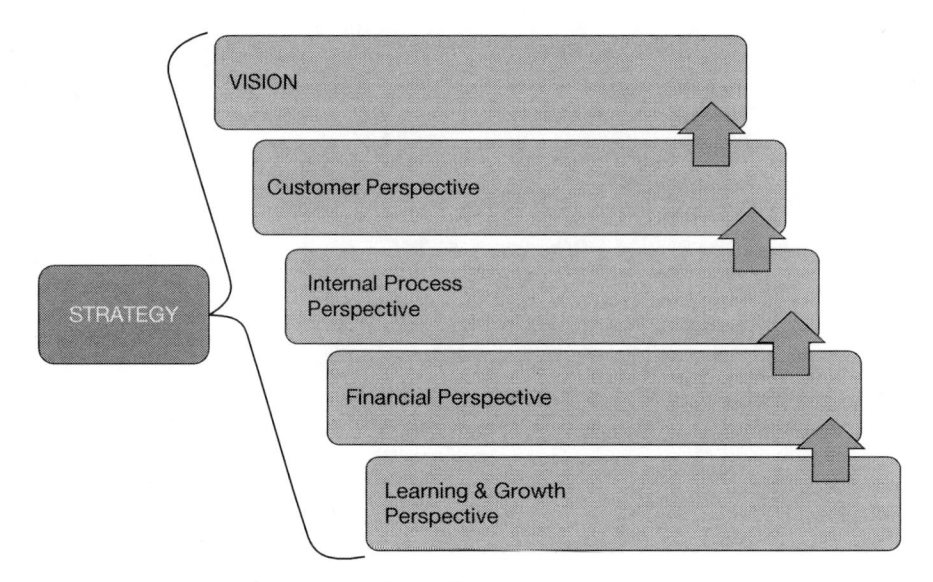

Figure 2.4 Semi-causal chain linking objectives to vision and strategy.

A third argument for an SHRM BSC is that it also represents a balance between external measures or criteria for success, with internal measures for measuring efficiency and learning growth. It also provides an opportunity to review and compare 'harder' efficiency and financial measures with 'softer' and more subjective measures of motivation and engagement.

Strategy mapping

A **strategy map** is a visual tool for representing the cause-and-effect relationship among the strategic objectives and other components of a strategy. In SHRM BSC terms, it illustrates a semi-causal connection between the overall strategic themes and the strategic objectives within each perspective.[56] Taken together, the visualization of this chain represents HR's strategic objectives in helping the organization achieve its vision and strategic themes.

It goes without saying that if you can't describe your strategy in a manner that everyone can clearly understand, you are unlikely to be successful. About 2,400 years ago, Sun-Tzu said those whose upper and lower ranks have the same idea will be victorious. A strategy map fills that gap by providing a simple method of describing a strategy and making explicit the cause-and-effect relationships that will lead to the fulfilment of the vision. It also provides a method of grouping major objectives by strategic theme and Balanced Scorecard perspective.

A strategy map in Figure 2.5 illustrates the relationship of strategic objectives within a strategic theme area.[57] In the strategy map developed for Cool Aid, for example,[58] we can identify a broad vision 'eliminating homelessness and improv[ing] the quality of life of our community' and four strategic themes related to enhancing (i) health care, (ii) shelter, (iii) housing and (iv) funding. These themes define the broad strategic directions that the Cool Aid Society envisioned as critical to its success.

In developing strategic objectives for each theme, managers responded to four questions that were aimed at each of the perspectives of the Balanced Scorecard:

- *Citizen or client perspective:* 'In working towards our vision, is the society delivering the services clients need and of value?'
- *Internal processes perspective:* 'How does Cool Aid improve its internal processes in adding value?'
- *Learning and Growth perspective:* 'How does Cool Aid give employees the tools and training to continually improve and respond to changing needs?'
- *Financial perspective:* 'Is Cool Aid managing resources wisely?'

Managers focused first on asking whether the society, in seeking to work within its vision of the future, is meeting the needs of clients. They asked several related questions such as 'What are our clients saying about us?' and 'What might we do to improve our service to clients?' The managers continued this line of questions to gather ideas and objectives for each of the other three perspectives of the BSC. This resulted in the strategy map in Figure 2.5 that illustrates 15 strategic objectives within each of four perspectives of the BSC. See a fuller description of Cool Aid in the case study below.

In developing their strategic plan, managers then identified initiatives which they would focus on in trying to meet the objectives. For example, the first strategic objective of 'developing quality care services', focused on delivering health care, working on addictions and providing mental health services in a fully integrated basis for meeting professional standards required for accreditation. They defined two initiatives to do this: The first called for tracking whether clients with complex needs had a well-developed care plan that was assigned to a case manager; the second initiative sought to reduce the number of shelter clients turned away, using measures of the average number of clients turned away each month from shelters and the number of people sleeping 'rough', as identified in the annual survey.

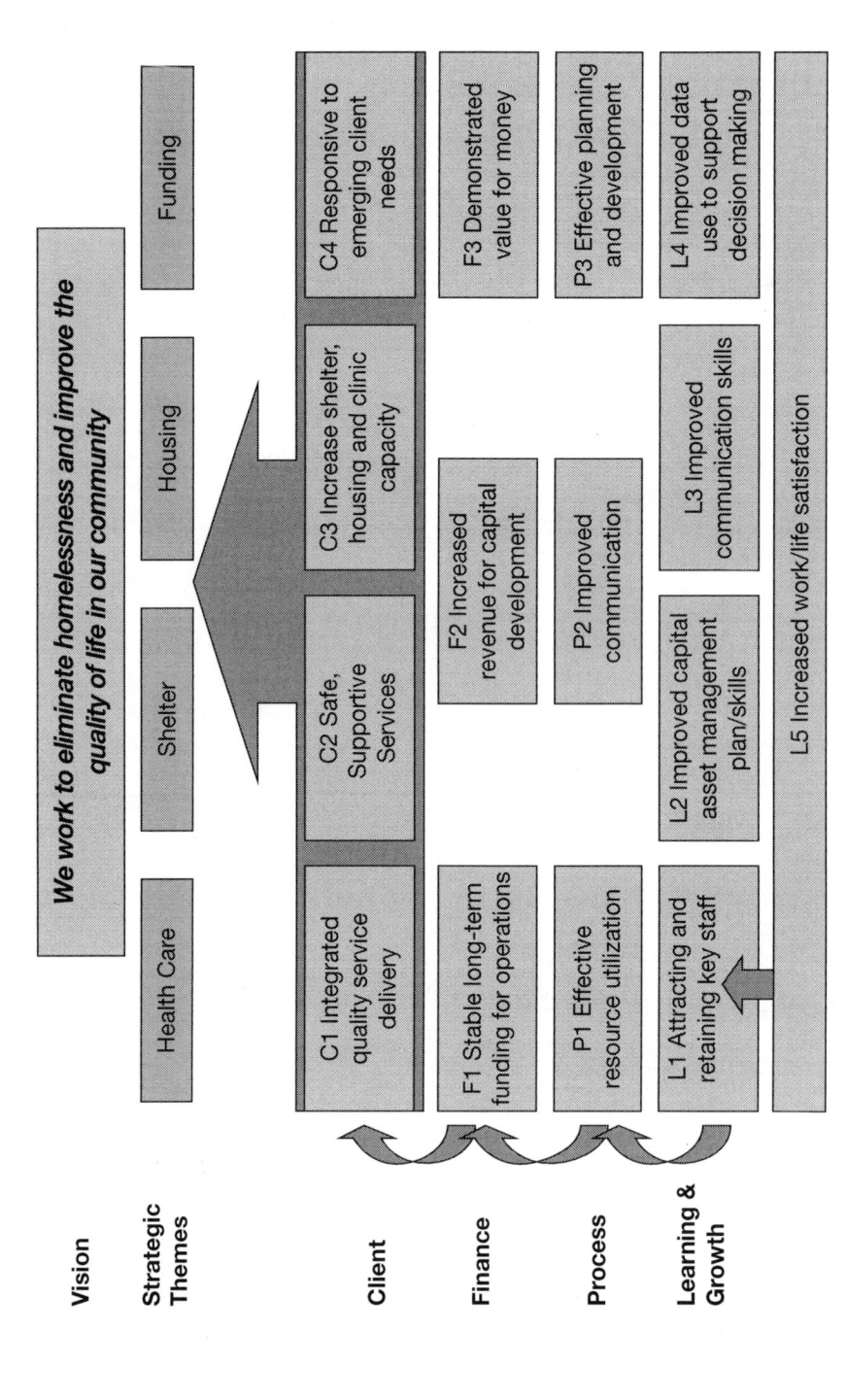

Vision: We work to eliminate homelessness and improve the quality of life in our community

Strategic Themes: Health Care | Shelter | Housing | Funding

Client:
- C1 Integrated quality service delivery
- C2 Safe, Supportive Services
- C3 Increase shelter, housing and clinic capacity
- C4 Responsive to emerging client needs

Finance:
- F1 Stable long-term funding for operations
- F2 Increased revenue for capital development
- F3 Demonstrated value for money

Process:
- P1 Effective resource utilization
- P2 Improved communication
- P3 Effective planning and development

Learning & Growth:
- L1 Attracting and retaining key staff
- L2 Improved capital asset management plan/skills
- L3 Improved communication skills
- L4 Improved data use to support decision making
- L5 Increased work/life satisfaction

Figure 2.5 Cool Aid's strategy map linking HR strategic objectives to the organization's strategic themes.

The strategy map is a graphic depiction of our strategy that helps us see how various objectives are linked together to achieve our vision. Learning and growth objectives support improved processes that deliver the improved client and financial outcomes necessary to achieve our vision. Starting with the Cool Aid Vision and the four strategic themes listed across the top of the strategy map above, the management team prepared our strategy map. The strategy map presently includes 15 strategic objectives, each addressing one or more of the four perspectives and linked to one or more strategic theme areas.

Based on Cool Aid's objectives and initiatives, the HR challenge is to develop an SHRM BSC and outline HR objectives, initiatives and markers to help managers implement their objectives.

SHRM BSC TERMINOLOGY

A highly debated topic is the use of the term **customer** in public sector organizations. 'Labels such as "customer", "consumer", "client", "user", "stakeholder", "citizen", "taxpayer", or "the public" are used in almost as many ways as there are writers about them.'[59] In public sector organizations, the customer or client relationship is not an economic exchange where a person buys a product for a price, but something that is enjoyed collectively, and the decisions about preferences are made in the democratic political process.[60]

Public administrators are continually asked to serve their customers, despite the conceptual and ethical problems in the use of the term for public organizations. Rather than responding to customers who might buy a product or service, the customer relationship in the public sector is a broader social exchange recognizing how governments have to respond to concerns of various publics or constituencies. Administrators often serve more than one constituency. It is a mistake to think of the public in the same way that we think of customers in the private sector. The customer relationship in public organizations can be professional (e.g. drug treatment), guardian (e.g. corrections officer), facilitator/ citizen (e.g. broking information) and regulator (e.g. environment protection). The role is often defined by legal, institutional and ethical norms.[61]

The BSC raises many issues in identifying customers as it recognizes that 'promoting public service values goes well beyond customer satisfaction' and requires understanding the relationship between what public providers do and what citizens want. It encourages administrators to seek to understand the public value that their programmes have to offer and what various publics need.[62]

External customers or clients are those constituencies to whom the organization seeks to respond. HR's role is to respond to an organization's internal customers or clients or the line managers who seek to implement an organization's strategic objectives. HR's job is to align the HR system so that it is responsive to an organization's **internal customers or clients**.

Strategic management. Whether in the private or public arena, strategic management's general purpose is to facilitate or enhance how an organization strategically responds successfully to its external environment in managing customer or client needs. 'A strategy describes the fundamental characteristics of the match that an organization achieves among its skills and resources and the opportunities and threats in its external environment that enables it to achieve its goals and objectives.'[63] A **strategy** provides a direction or intention to move an organization to a clearly defined future state. A strategy is articulated through goals, vision, strategic themes, objectives, initiatives, programmes or actions, decisions and skills as well as resource allocations, competencies and measures.

Goals. Goals are long-term aims, whereas strategic themes are the main, high-level plans that are the basis for the organization's strategic framework.

Vision. A vision is a value-based sketch of the future that pulls the organization in a certain direction.

Strategic themes. Strategic themes are the broad strategic thrusts or directions which the organization should excel in to achieve its vision.

Strategic objectives. Strategic objectives are specific things that need to be accomplished to execute a plan. They represent a result that a person or organization seeks to achieve within a time frame.

Goals and objectives. The literature is not consistent in its use of the terms **goals** and **objectives**. This inconsistency is illustrated in Chapter 8, 'Encouraging Employee Development in Reviewing Performance', which describes goal-setting theory and goal-directed behaviour. This literature suggests that objectives are ways to implement goals (rather than strategic themes).

Initiatives. Initiatives represent the activities, projects, programmes or actions that are being used to implement the objective.

Resources. Resources are the tangible and intangible assets used to implement initiatives.

Competency. A competency is 'an underlying characteristic of an individual which is causally related to effective or superior performance in a job'[64] and which illustrates the human resource talents which we need to implement our strategic objectives. A competency might be a 'motive, skill, aspect of a one's self-image or social role, or a body of knowledge which he or she uses'.[65]

Measures. These are the indicators used to assess or communicate progress in achieving initiatives. In using the SHRM BSC, there are different types of measures within each of the perspectives on the scorecard. **Customer service** measures respond to the question 'What value does this service offer, and what are the needs that must be addressed in providing this public value?' Key measures might relate to timing, quality, performance and type of service. **Internal processes** measures are generally efficiency measures. This encourages administrators to define the competencies and processes that create the higher public value. **Learning and Growth** measures relate to motivation, learning and improvement. In addition to motivational goals, other measures might relate to ways to improve the service. **Financial measures** relate to costs in providing a service and adding value, a challenge that the New Public Management advocates point to in encouraging public organizations to compare the costs of their services to having them outsourced.

> MANAGERIAL IMPLICATIONS: The Balanced Scorecard outlined here is a conceptual tool to illustrate the linkage between strategic objectives and initiatives within four perspectives as they relate to general strategic themes. Based on this organization's themes and objectives, HR's job is to develop an SHRM Balanced Scorecard to develop HR objectives and initiatives in order to help managers implement their objectives. The case study in this chapter illustrates an SHRM Balanced Scorecard which links to the strategy map described in Figure 2.5. For example, one way that HR can be helpful to managers is to recruit and select people to meet the competencies needed to accomplish objectives important to managers.
>
> The following three chapters focus HR on initial activities related to the customer or client perspective. These focus on designing jobs, competencies and workforce planning.

BEFORE APPLYING, LET'S REVIEW

CO 1: Apply the Balanced Scorecard Approach and its key perspectives in strategic planning.

Two different strategic perspectives or schools of thought include: HRM as fit and HRM as the strategic use of resources. The strategic fit model helps in understanding how to focus SHRM so that it recognizes that different HR types of practices might fit better with different types of public and private organizations and cultures. The open systems model illustrates that the HR subsystem is an essential function for survival and growth and that organizational and human resource systems are not directed by rational purposes, but its purposes and strategies are linked to the larger system needs and functions in relating to the environment. For some researchers, the RBV has become the 'backdrop' for work in the SHRM area. Historically, although resources have been useful in analysing organization efficiency (Efficiency = input/output), the RBV goes further by focusing on prioritizing resources and identifying core competencies related to strategies.

CO 2: Assess the use of the SHRM Scorecard in linking HR objectives and initiatives to assist managers to implement their objectives.

The Balanced Scorecard is a tool that encourages decision-makers to translate their strategic goals and themes into tangible objectives, initiatives and measures to represent different perspectives – customer, internal process, financial, and learning and growth – that need to be addressed in implementation. As such, the BSC is simply a way of organizing strategic themes, objectives and initiatives, and encourages us to recognize that performance goes beyond the financial perspective. The BSC assumes that each perspective is linked in a semi-causal way. In public sector organizations, we usually begin by recognizing customer objectives. Then we consider effective processes, in addition to effective financing. The learning and growth perspective recognizes that these objectives rely on a human component – motivation, training and the appropriate identification of competencies.

CO 3: Integrate a strategy map for linking a set of HR objectives within a strategic theme.

The Strategic Human Resource Balanced Scorecard (SHRM BSC) framework illustrates HR strategic objectives that are aligned to focus on implementing strategic HR themes. In linking to the organization's strategic framework, for example, HR might assist line managers by defining and implementing objectives related to recruiting, selecting and training in attracting and developing people that are key in delivering specific strategic priorities.

In SHRM Balanced Scorecard terms, a strategy map illustrates a semi-causal connection between the overall strategic themes and the strategic objectives within each perspective. It is a visual tool for representing the cause-and-effect relationship among the strategic objectives and other components of a strategy.

DISCUSSION AND REVIEW QUESTIONS

1. In implementing the BSC in private sector organizations, the perspective at the top of the scorecard is usually the financial perspective. Why is the customer perspective usually the first perspective in the public sector?
2. The Balanced Scorecard often includes four perspectives: customer, internal process, financial, and learning and growth. It is possible to add other perspectives if they are important in the causal chain or if there are other objectives and measures that are important. In the public sector, we might consider the political perspective and regulative perspective. Consider the relevance of other perspectives such as economic, social, technological and ecological. In what situations would these factors be relevant for a public organization?
3. One way to implement strategic HR is to develop an HR Balanced Scorecard that illustrates the linkage of strategic objectives within common theme areas. For example, the strategic theme 'Healthy Community' envisions a municipality where residents are physically and socially active and enjoying

various recreational, educational, social and cultural services. The strategic theme 'economic vibrancy' pictures a community that is connected to diverse economic opportunities ranging from technology to agriculture. The theme 'social well-being' illustrates a community which offers opportunities for different lifestyles. Using line managers as the internal client, define four to six objectives for the theme within the four perspectives of the scorecard by adapting the strategy map on the book's website. Note that it is not necessary to have objectives in each of the perspectives for all themes.[66]
4. Draw a personal strategy map to illustrate the objectives for the strategic theme 'improving your quality of working life' in living in a healthy community.
    - Customer perspective: In achieving your personal vision, what should you do to improve your quality of working life in being a healthy employee? What do you value? What are objectives related to this? How should we measure success?
    - Internal process perspective: What HR and personal processes should you and the organization excel at (e.g. occupational health and safety, performance management)? Objectives and initiatives? How should we measure success?
    - Financial perspective: To satisfy our internal clients, how do we add value in meeting tangible outcomes like reduced absenteeism, employee satisfaction and improved health? Objectives and initiatives? How should we measure success?
    - Learning and growth perspective: To achieve our HR internal process and client objectives, what HR and personal practices improve our ability to learn and grow? Objectives and initiatives? How should we measure success?

CASE: AN HR STRATEGY MAP FOR COOL AID

The Cool Aid Society is a community organization providing emergency shelter and other essential services such as food, medical care and psychiatric services to clients suffering from a multiplicity of problems, including chronic alcoholism, mental illness and drug abuse. Its history is traced to 10 June 1968, when it established an emergency shelter for transient youth who were travelling throughout the country.

Over the years, the shelter became a home for people at risk, and in various locations other programmes opened their doors, including a psychiatric group home, a free medical clinic, a day care centre, a youth emergency shelter, an outreach programme and a housing programme. In the early days, these combined programmes employed 100 staff and assisted over 300 people a day. The Cool Aid Society, sometimes written 'Kool Aid', was incorporated as the Cool Aid Society on 28 October 1976.

Streetlink was one of the best-known Cool Aid programmes and in 1989 evolved from a small dormitory-style shelter to serve a core of people downtown. In contrast to the warehouse-style dormitory shelter which had existed previously, the refurbished building has 55 emergency shelter beds in two- and three-bed rooms. The medical and dental clinic on the main floor and lower floors provided free confidential services. In addition, the building has 25 one-bedroom independent living apartments, and the rent is 30 per cent of a tenant's income. The tenants named it 'Swift House'.

In November 2010, Streetlink moved its shelter services. The old shelter was converted to 23 units of permanent, supportive housing for adults. It offers 84 permanent shelter spaces, 23 units of transitional housing and two units of family shelter. The main programmes which exist today include Streetlink's emergency shelter and a long-term shelter, a medical and dental clinic and housing for adults. Streetlink's beds are used to capacity, with over 99 per cent occupancy over the year. This provides 34,675 spaces per year and 110,000 hot meals to shelter and drop-in clients, in addition to 15,000 interventions per year (40 per day) on issues ranging from mental health to health, life skills, crisis intervention and housing.

The Cool Aid Society has an extensive housing programme that seeks to provide safe housing for people at risk. Building on the Swift House experience, the society has independent living locations and a downtown community centre that also includes the head office.

The Society also engages with other community organizations in providing cold and wet-weather shelter from September to April. It is involved with other shelter providers, faith groups, social service agencies and fire and police as member of a programme called Extreme Weather Protocol. These groups work together in providing shelter beds during periods of heavy wind, rain, snow and when temperatures are zero or lower. The shelter capacity increases to 370 emergency beds and mats (245).

The HR Context

At one time in the organization's history, the Society was philosophically divided between unionized and non-unionized employees, with one group being paid substantially more than others. Within its various programmes, the Cool Aid Society has 280 staff, of which 130 staff are non-union. The non-union staff work in the health area or are exempt managerial employees, and the union staff work in the emergency shelter.

The unionized workers were angry with managers, whom they viewed as right wing and anti-union. The bad relationships between managers and union leaders might have stemmed from several factors – polarized views, the labour scene at the time, lack of training or reluctance to work with the other party.

Over the Society's history, labour relations improved, and many management staff were replaced. To meet the needs of this large and diverse staff, the Cool Aid Society has two HR staff: the HR manager and the HR assistant manager. The general 'do it yourself' philosophy has served them well over the recent years as these two HR staff have helped develop a very positive HR climate.

Diana, the current HR director, started with Cool Aid in 2001 and was involved in Cool Aid's initial strategic planning, which identified four strategic themes: expanding supportive housing, expanding community shelter services, expanding holistic health services and ensuring secure long-term funding. The HR director now is the guiding force in facilitating this strategic planning, and although there were setbacks, the planning is still going on. The Society uses the Balanced Scorecard and has published an annual report which began in 2006 and continues.

In using the Balanced Scorecard, managers are interviewed and asked to identify their needs by answering five questions:

1. What key roles can HR best perform to help you achieve your objectives?
2. What are some positive ways that HR has helped you in the past? What are examples of these?
3. What are some functions or activities where you have needed HR to perform better? What are examples of times when you were frustrated with HR activities in this organization?
4. What are the roles you would like to see HR perform and the ideas you'd like to see it implement in the future, to help you achieve your objectives?

Answers to these questions helped Diana better understand the HR needs and develop an HR Scorecard for Cool Aid around these strategic themes:

1. Providing a positive work environment for managers and employees.
2. Delivering effective HR processes.
3. Providing policy guidance to managers.
4. Providing clear HR information and procedures.

The most recent strategic themes have focused on attracting and retaining qualified staff, expanding training and development, strengthening health and safety and improving employee engagement. The scorecard identified objectives within each of these four areas. In addition, Diana sought to undertake initiatives to measure their progress (see the book's website).

The Issue

One of Cool Aid's board members asked the managers whether the Cool Aid HR Balanced Scorecard illustrated in Figure 2.5 might better illustrate the link between the strategic objectives in each theme area. She asked if it was possible to draw lines illustrating how the strategic objectives might be linked to each theme. Also, she wanted some examples of initiatives and measures than might be used for some of the key objectives such as C1, C2 and L3, and P3.

Can you assist Diana, the HR director, in responding to this request?

Part II: Designing Customer-Focused Jobs

There are many ways to think of a job: 'I did a good job', 'I am trying to get a job', 'I'd like your job if I could get it', 'What are the qualifications for doing this job?'

For employees, a job provides money, a career, status and feelings of self-worth. For organizations, a job provides the mechanism through which work (and objectives) are accomplished and people are motivated to work.

The organizational challenge is to design jobs so that people work efficiently and effectively in adding value to customers or clients. In doing this, the next three chapters seek to answer three sets of questions. In Chapter 3, we address questions like 'What is the job and its critical requirements? What are the qualifications (competencies) and training for the job?' Then, in Chapter 4, we look at the big picture perspective and how we can design jobs that are both motivating and efficient. 'How do you measure performance and determine the worth of the job?' Finally, in Chapter 5, we ask, 'How do we forecast the demand and supply of competencies that are needed? How do we develop a workforce plan in an environment where there is a fair degree of economic and political turmoil?'

These chapters underline the fact that the public sector relationships with customers and clients are different from those in the private sector, where the customer has the ability to purchase a range of products or services. In the public sector, there are multiple publics, and the customer or client relationship involves adding value in responding to their needs by providing services such as health, education and safety.

3 Defining Competencies and Critical Requirements for a Job

Chapter Outline
- Chapter objectives (COs) 49
- A driving issue focusing managerial action: Competency-based management (CBM) 49
- CO 1: Identifying essential job requirements and competencies in the job analysis process 51
- CO 2: Competency models in strategic management 58
- CO 3: Identifying competencies and performance norms 62
- Before applying, let's review 64
- Discussion and review questions 65
- Case: Defining competencies of effective managers 66

CHAPTER OBJECTIVES (COs)

After reading this chapter, you will be able to implement the following objectives:

CO 1: Identify essential job requirements and competencies in the job analysis process.

CO 2: Describe competency modelling as a tool for implementing strategic objectives.

CO 3: Apply the critical incident interview and repertory grid technique in defining competencies for a job description.

A DRIVING ISSUE FOCUSING MANAGERIAL ACTION: COMPETENCY-BASED MANAGEMENT (CBM)

The performance of public organizations is a central topic for citizens, politicians and practitioners around the world. In an era of diminishing resources and increasing expectations, it has become increasingly difficult to fulfil the public purpose effectively and satisfy the needs of multiple stakeholders. In this context, traditional approaches to job analysis and determining efficient ways of working are being challenged amid requirements for newer HRM approaches.

Competency-based management (CBM) involves identifying a profile of competencies distinguishing high and average performers in various areas of organizational activity and using it as a framework for planning, work design, recruitment, selection, training and career development, and compensation.[1] Citing research that began in the 1970s, competency advocates point to David C. McClelland's classical research at the US State Department which sought to develop characteristics to replace traditional aptitude tests and exams which were unable to predict 'on the job' effectiveness of junior diplomats.

McClelland's methodology relied on the use of 'criterion' samples, or samples of job skills that predict proficiency on the job. Knowing how well a person drives a car (the criterion) involves administering a driver's test rather than a paper-and-pencil test on intelligence or ability to read a road map.[2] **Criterion testing** involves understanding the behaviours required, observing actual performance and comparing superior performers with less successful performers. In understanding the performance of people on a job – such as a policeman – we will need to make a careful behavioural analysis of what police do well and not so well in real life.

The experiment used a **behavioural event interview (BEI)**, which is a very focused, clinical-type, recorded interview that can take two to three hours to complete. The key step in the BEI, similar to the 'critical incident technique', is to elicit examples of behavioural events. The interview transcripts are analysed to distinguish between behaviours and intentions of superior performers, and are not identified by average performers. These thematic differences are translated into objective scores and coded by reliable experts.

McClelland was able to identify critical competencies predicting the performance of outstanding foreign service officers, predictors of performance that were significantly better than other attributes identified by experts through traditional job analysis methods.[3] As such, a **competency** is 'an underlying characteristic of an individual which is causally related to effective or superior performance in a job'[4] and which illustrates the human resource talents needed to implement strategic objectives. A competency might be a 'motive, skill, aspect of one's self-image or social role, or a body of knowledge which he or she uses.'[5]

The research provided a competency model and tests to administer to potential hires, although the new tests had a short tenure at the US State Department. This was partially due to resistance among those making hiring decisions who preferred using traditional instruments such as résumés which listed academic achievements.

Although the State Department did not fully use McClelland's work, his ideas gathered momentum among professionals and organizational psychologists. In addition, McClelland and colleagues used the BEI in their consulting work at McBer and Company during the late 1970s and 1980s. Based on this work, Richard Boyatzis compiled a competency framework, illustrated in Table 3.1, distinguishing effective and less effective public and private managers and threshold competencies (although essential to a manager, competencies are not causally related to superior performance).[6] The competency framework has been adapted to illustrate general managerial competencies displayed by outstanding performers.[7]

Table 3.1 Competency Clusters Illustrating Distinguishing (in Bold) and Threshold Competencies

- Goal and action orientation cluster: **efficiency orientation, proactivity, diagnostic use of concepts, concern with impact***.
- Leadership cluster: **self-confidence, use of oral presentations, conceptualization,** logical thought.
- HRM cluster: **use of socialized power, managing group processes,** positive regard, accurate self assessment.
- Directing subordinates cluster: Developing others, use of unilateral powers, spontaneity.
- Focus on others cluster: **self-control, personal objectivity, stamina and adaptability**.
- Specialized knowledge: specialized knowledge.

* Bolded items indicate that these are distinguishing competencies. Non-bolded items are threshold competencies.
* Distinguishing competencies are bolded.

With a newer appreciation of the importance of performance, many public organizations are moving rapidly to embrace CBM. The major difference between the competency and traditional approaches to improving performance is that the competency approach is centred on inputs, or the knowledge, skills and abilities for success, in addition to the personal qualities needed. CBM also provides the opportunity for employees to take responsibility in meeting objectives and career development while traditional approaches are more concerned with outputs and how best to perform on the job. The challenge for HR is to integrate CBM into the traditional approaches for analysing jobs.

> *STRATEGIC CONTEXT: Given an organization's vision, mission, strategic themes and objectives, next steps include defining the initiatives and jobs that need to be done, and the competencies of people who are needed to do the jobs. The traditional process of job analysis involved determining the tasks and then assigning responsibilities and duties to different people. CBM also provides the opportunity for employees to take responsibility in meeting objectives and career development, whereas traditional approaches are more concerned with outputs and how best to perform on the job. CBM is a way to link the human and non-human resources to an organization's strategic objectives. In knowledge-intensive public organizations, the emphasis is more specifically identifying and making use of distinctive human resources, especially distinctive competencies in implementing strategic themes and objectives. They provide a framework for managers in recruiting, selecting, developing and managing performance in relation to objectives.*
>
> *Although this chapter provides information on various job analysis approaches and the use of the critical incident process, an underlying key strategic objective relates to 'developing a competency framework to guide employee development'. After reading this chapter, you will be asked to identify competencies for implementing different strategic objectives and to define competencies to guide your development.*

CO 1: IDENTIFYING ESSENTIAL JOB REQUIREMENTS AND COMPETENCIES IN THE JOB ANALYSIS PROCESS

In developing an understanding of the job requirements and the competencies needed, the **job description** summarizes the information collected in a job analysis and provides an overall summary of the job's key requirements and specifications.

The most common picture that comes to mind when thinking about a **job analysis process** is of a job analyst interviewing an employee and observing people carrying out the work. It is common, in larger organizations, to seek information from groups that might include knowledgeable incumbents, supervisors, technical experts and others who interact or collaborate with those in the position being analysed. The analysis process gathers information about the job's tasks; responsibilities and duties; knowledge, skills and abilities (KSA) and performance expectations.

Although a conventional approach to job analysis focuses on knowledge, skills and abilities (KSA), interest in competencies includes a recognition of motives, traits and 'other' characteristics important in a job. Competencies and KSAs are intertwined, but they are distinguished in that competencies are more often used to focus on the future and more often linked to strategic objectives. They have been used in government-wide strategic HRM processes that attempt to align how individuals can contribute to an organization's performance. Also, competencies recognize that motivation, personality and other characteristics are important drivers of performance. Ideally, competencies can be used to develop performance guides distinguishing levels of performance, although this is not easily implemented, as managers often perceive other measures (such as credentials and years of experience) to be relevant in performance.[8] A job description summarizes the information collected in the job analysis process and is a way of documenting or formalizing the process.

The job description

A highly specific job description has often been linked to traditional principles of specialization and division of labour where the various functions of an organization are divided into different departments and jobs. Specific job descriptions define the responsibilities of one unique position, such as 'payroll clerk', and are written when a position has unique responsibilities that might be different from others in the organization. This highly specific (efficiency-centred) job design, as we know it today, was initiated by Frederick Taylor's scientific management. He sought to improve the efficiency and cost-effectiveness of the way products and services were delivered. His scientific approach attempted to reduce unnecessary work by establishing standardized procedures that have been tested using time-and-motion or industrial engineering studies. These designs often illustrated principles of job specialization, job simplification and division of labour, because workers could be quickly trained to perform simpler, more specified tasks.

In the past, most job descriptions were more specifically focused on job requirements and responsibilities, but more recently we have seen examples of generic job descriptions that might allow employees to grow in the position and carry out a variety of responsibilities. Generic job descriptions apply to a wide range of jobs and positions in various parts of the organization. For example, there might a generic job description for the position of administrative assistant throughout an entire government. **General** or **generic,** job descriptions are more flexible and easily kept up to date. They include a larger range of duties and responsibilities because employees have to continually adjust their tasks and activities in response to new initiatives, objectives or clients. Generic job descriptions define work expectations and accountabilities but do not describe the detail of the tasks to be performed. They focus on results, norms and expectations, and goals. Although some employees have complained that more generic job descriptions fail to provide a complete and accurate statement of job duties, judicial reviews are supportive of the change.

The strategic approach is often illustrated by **customer-centred job designs** focused on customer needs and designing and implementing services to achieve the organization's strategic objectives.[9] The customer-centred approach is the focal point of the total quality management (TQM),[10] re-engineering[11] and to some extent the New Public Management approaches that encourage customer service. When we focus on responding to customer needs, it is easier to identify essential job duties.[12]

Employee-centred job designs (eg. **job enrichment**) are used for improving effectiveness and productivity by improving employee satisfaction and commitment. This is accomplished by job design principles that encourage worker responsibility, learning, and empowerment. Job design approaches that illustrate this general approach include job enrichment, team development, and TQM.

Beyond efficiently and effectively designing a job and clarifying employee job requirements, job descriptions are used for classifying jobs and determining pay. In addition, job descriptions comply with governmental regulations and defend against possible allegations that they are using unfair hiring, promotion and pay practices. When there is a dispute or workplace accident, the first step is to see if the person had the qualifications identified in the job description or whether the job description identified the appropriate requirements. As such, a thorough job analysis should determine the bona fide job requirements (such as a special driver's licence or a medical certification) and the job level (the pay classification). The underlying purpose of this is to classify the job into a unique job category to establish fair and equitable pay, and to make certain that salary decisions are based upon the value of the job in meeting the organization's priorities and objectives.

Although a job description is thought to be important in guiding the HR process, it may not be a perfect tool. Many job descriptions do not accurately describe a person's job, and some employees say 'if I did only what was in the job description, nothing would get done,' or 'I saw my job description when I first started the job, but it is so out of date now that it is irrelevant.' In addition, job descriptions have been viewed as too confining and restrictive to encourage employee learning and development.

However, job analysis is central in large public organizations in articulating the organization's mandate and focusing a job's activities to achieve strategic goals and objectives. The process of writing the job description is as important as the job description itself as it helps in communicating the requirements of the position. After a job description is written, it is just as important to continue the managerial processes to make it work.

Although there is no standard format or structure for a job description, the following are examples of information which might be included: job identification, the reporting relationship, the job purpose and mission, duties and responsibilities, minimum requirements, job specifications and competencies, working conditions and performance norms and expectations.

Job identification. Job title, job code, job classification, location and other information.

Reporting relationships. Reporting relationship to supervisors and other staff, and connections to internal clients (other departments) and external clients (the key clients or customers outside the organization).

Job purpose or mission. How the job contributes to the overall mission of the organization and general duties in support of managerial and professional employees. This might also indicate the strategic objectives in a plan which are important to focus on.

Traditional job analysis. A traditional job analysis process begins by identifying the job requirements or necessary job tasks, activities or steps in performing a job in the workflow. Examples of key tasks for a building inspector might include meeting and greeting contractors, inspecting houses and contributing to a positive team environment in the public works or engineering department in a municipal government. In developing an understanding of their tasks, we might seek to understand their client and customer group (contractors and housing regulatory authorities) and what services (outputs and outcomes) are most important to them. We can then define the job requirements that are important to carrying out these tasks.

Moving beyond this, if we were to align HR with the needs of their internal clients (e.g. building inspectors and others) we would ask what job requirements (competencies, tasks, activities and steps) are essential to providing good services to help HR meet its objectives and meet customer needs. We might find that building inspectors and engineers might need better recruiting and selection tools for hiring building inspectors with customer relations and problem-solving skills, an understanding of building codes and other competencies.

Duties and responsibilities. An organization's strategic themes and objectives are implemented by the jobs that people perform. As such, each job has assigned duties and responsibilities that are important in implementing specific objectives as well as in contributing to the organization's general mandate. In a job description, the job's duties and responsibilities are written in an action-oriented style, usually with active verbs like *plan, direct, respond to, deliver, answer* and *implement*. Job duties and responsibilities explain what is done, how it is done and why it is done.

A responsibility describes the major purpose or reason that the job exists and is defined by a number of duties. A responsibility might consist of three or four essential tasks or duties that are significant in performing the job. For a building inspector, for example, a responsibility might relate to ensuring that contractors observe building codes and work within their building permit. This might be defined more specifically in terms of carrying out inspections, acting fairly and objectively in assessing the work of contractors and being responsive to the needs of the industry. In identifying the job responsibilities of building inspectors, for example, we can ask questions such as 'What is the prime purpose of the job? What are the key responsibilities and duties for external and internal customers, and clients and stakeholders?' In seeking to align HR's work to assist the building inspectors with their work, the challenge is to define job responsibilities and duties to the needs of the client groups or various stakeholders.

Competencies and job requirements. Each job has key requirements which can be defined by certifications, physical requirements, training and abilities to operate certain machines or tools or the competencies (**knowledge, skills, abilities and other characteristics [KSAOs]**) necessary to do the job. For guiding selection, training and performance management, this is one of the more important sections of the job description.

A competency framework is now commonly used in updating traditional job analysis to provide a statement of not only the KSAs (knowledge, skills and abilities) but also the 'other' aptitudes that are important to the job.[13] In a city manager's office, 'other' aptitudes might relate to a customer focus, leadership characteristics, ethics, integrity and conscientiousness, among other things. Research clearly indicates that personality constructs, such as the **'Big Five' personality factors** (openness, extraversion, conscientiousness, agreeableness and emotional stability) are linked to getting along and doing well in a job.[14] The competencies can be defined by seeking to understand: 'What are the knowledge, skills and abilities as well as the other aptitudes that are important in this job? When things go well, what competencies does this illustrate? When things go poorly, what competencies would improve this performance and link to an organization's strategic objectives?'

Core requirements. Core requirements define basic or threshold competencies or standards that job applicants must have to be considered for a job.

Working conditions. Job and employment security, physical conditions (related to safety and health), work character (work pace, workload and stress), working time (hours and shifts worked), opportunities for input and development, relationships at work and work–life balance.

Performance norms and expectations. Performance expectations are the norms and practices that are important to carry out the work effectively. In some organizations, there might be a physical requirement for lifting a specified weight or for driving a car. Performance expectations can also refer to expectations about working in a team or relating politely to customers. These can be defined by observing the task requirements of the job and by asking questions such as 'What are performance expectations relating to the key tasks and activities? What are examples of excellent performance in relating to customers and clients, carrying out the job's technical requirements and relating to co-workers, supervisors and managers?'

Linking to the strategic context

A point of view now emphasized in conventional job analysis methods is the importance of customer-centred job characteristics, or how the job might be assessed in relationship to an organization's strategic objectives. This means recognizing the importance of customers or clients and taking steps to assess their needs and how the job and the competencies can address these needs. In most cases in public organizations, we would ask, 'How do we appear to our stakeholders (or customer or clients), and what is the distinct value we should provide to meet their needs?' As a result, we might need to re-prioritize a position's competencies, duties and responsibilities, adding some and eliminating others.

As illustrated in the previous chapter, the most important attribute of the competency is to illustrate a link between the strategic objectives and what the job needs to accomplish and the value it adds. Competency models in the United Kingdom have been key in implementing SHRM processes in relation to staff development, appraisal of performance management and training.[15]

Performance metrics needed to validate competencies

The most important metric related to competencies is whether they accurately predict performance in implementing a strategic objective. A first step is to develop a job description that defines the job's critical requirements and the competencies needed; the next step is to try to validate whether the competencies predict performance.

Competency frameworks provide a way to validate the competencies important in performance and excellence. Establishing and validating this link, though challenging, takes time, and it is important to continually revisit the competencies to assure they are job related. As jobs are constantly changing, there is a continual need to reassess the job to maintain updated performance metrics.[16]

Gathering information on job requirements and competencies

Various methods are used to gather job analysis information, including questionnaires, interviews, diaries and observations. Using a number of these methods in combination helps obtain a complete picture of the tasks and their requirements.

1. **Questionnaires.** A typical technique is either an open-ended or structured questionnaire, which can be used in an interview-like fashion or as a survey to a number of incumbents and people knowledgeable about the job. Questionnaires can be either quite structured, asking respondents to rate the degree to which they carry out certain job activities, or they can be open-ended, asking for information about the job, the KSA requirements and responsibilities. The questionnaire is designed to identify behaviours such as communicating or using equipment. Tasks focus on *what* gets done in the job, whereas behaviours summarize *how* it is done. In the questionnaire, workers rate the degree to which tasks and behaviours are performed, and the rating provides a basis for scoring and developing a profile of the job requirements.
2. **Interviews.** Interviews can be structured or unstructured and might ask for information about work activities or critical incidents to illustrate key activities, skills and responsibilities. Interviews are often used where it is necessary to rely on the worker's description of a job. Structured questions allow interviewers to compare jobs on the same questions, although unstructured questions can be added to gather in-depth information.
3. **Critical Incidents.** Some organizations prefer to have more information about the kinds of behaviour that are critical or absolutely necessary for specific jobs. The critical incidents technique grew out of the studies of John Flanagan during World War II, one of which sought to identify the problems of combat leadership of bomber and tank crews. When interviewees were asked to describe what they thought made an effective leader, they responded with general terms such as *charismatic, assertive, knowledgeable*, and *ability to lead*. Researchers began to report specific incidents of effective and ineffective behaviour which were helpful or inadequate in accomplishing a mission. They asked, 'Describe the officer's action. What did he do?'[17] The incidents provided an entirely different

set of critical requirements of combat leadership. They described stories or vignettes (examples) of effective and ineffective work behaviour. During the critical incident process, employees describe verifiable incidents and behaviours as well as the feelings and perceptions of these experiences. A list of critical incidents experienced by employees provides a flavour of the issues and behaviour that are critical job requirements to employees. Such a pooling of shared experience provides a wider perspective of the variables underlying an event and is more inclusive than accumulating responses to general questions. Those interviewed describe their experiences and observations rather than expressing opinions or judgements of certain events.[18]

4. **Observations.** A well-known observation method is the time and motion study, a way of measuring the standard time involved in various work tasks. A time and motion study, although associated with Frederick Taylor's *Scientific Management*, is used to describe many work activities ranging from installing a fuel injection system on a car to decreasing the time required to issue a passport to a citizen. The analyst observes the employee or group of workers and records what, why and how the various parts of the job are performed.

5. **Diaries.** Instead of observing people performing a job, employees might be asked to keep a log or diary of their work activities.

6. **Job Performance.** An analyst performs the job under study to get first-hand knowledge of what it entails.

These job analysis methods are some of the more popular ones in use today. In reviewing the advantages and disadvantages of these methods in Table 3.2, we have to be mindful that the methods rely on the skills of the analyst in gathering and collating information about a job,[19] as incumbents tend to provide higher ratings of abilities needed than do supervisors or trained analysts.[20]

Different job analysis methods use different frameworks for classifying jobs. The frameworks illustrate more general norms, terms and standards and have a library of exemplary job descriptions. For example, the position analysis questionnaire (PAQ) measures 194 different items that are organized into six areas: information input (where and how the worker gets needed information), mental processes (reasoning and other processes that workers use), work output (physical activities and tools used to perform job), relationships with other persons (relationships required), job context (the physical and social contexts of work) and 'other' characteristics (other conditions and characteristics related to job).[21] The database is maintained by Purdue University. The framework for the Hay job analysis emphasizes know-how, problem-solving and accountability, whereas Fleishman's method emphasizes cognitive, psychomotor and physical skills.

The point of the job analysis is to develop a job description that helps an analyst organize jobs into general categories so that they can be classified. Many large government organizations have a standardized list of job descriptions that can be used as a reference point for writing a job description and classifying the job at a certain pay level.

O*NET (the Occupational Information Network) was developed by the US Department of Labor/Employment and Training Administration to serve as the primary source of occupational information in the United States. It provides comprehensive information on attributes and characteristics of occupations. O*NET includes 1,000 occupations. Occupational titles and codes are based on an updated taxonomy of jobs that is linked to other labour market information, such as wage and employment statistics.

The United Kingdom, Australia and New Zealand have similar lists of occupations used for job classification. Canada's NOC (National Occupational Classification), based on research by Human Resources and Skills Development Canada (HRSDC), provides information for writing job duties and employment requirements and a list of job titles. These provide occupational profiles that include information on

Table 3.2 *Advantages and Disadvantages of Six Job Analysis Methods*

Method	Advantages	Disadvantages
Questionnaires	Questionnaires are generally cheaper and quicker to administer, and with web-based questionnaires, implementation is easier. Questionnaires are most often used in larger organizations.	Given the general limitation that most methods have biases, it is useful to use more than one job analysis method. For example, questionnaires are often time consuming, and there is limited rapport between the analyst and respondent. As a result, response rates to questionnaires can be low. Also, different respondents offer different levels of detail.
Interviews	Although interviews can be useful for gathering information on standard jobs, they are more useful for gathering information on non-standard jobs involving mental work, working with others or gathering and processing complex information.	Interviews are time consuming, and although they provide a more intensive experience in understanding the job, they are often more biased than other methods. It is useful to supplement interviews with other job analysis methods.
Critical Incidents	The method asks for examples of positive (or effective) and not-so-positive (or less effective) examples of what people do in different situations (i.e. motivating others, resolving a conflict). The method encourages participants to reveal real examples rather than opinions or judgements.	Although the information gathered from critical incidents is generally highly valid, it takes time and skill to gather and categorize. Sometimes, participants have difficulty remembering. As a result, the method requires effective probing in assisting the interviewee.
Observations	Observations provide direct exposure to jobs and a more thorough understanding of the context and job requirements.	More useful for non-mental tasks which are difficult to observe. Also, it is always possible to observe some critical job requirements (such as handling an emergency).
Diaries	These are appropriate for understanding jobs where there is a great deal of variability such as the tasks of managers and the time they spend.	Diaries require a great deal of time to complete, and as a result, some people do a better job in completing them. Given the high degree of variability in the responses, it is useful to use an additional method (such as interviews).
Job Performance	Provides exposure to actual job tasks in understanding the mental, physical, environmental and social aspects of a job. It is more appropriate for jobs that do not require a great deal of time to learn the tasks.	This method is less appropriate for highly skilled jobs that require extensive training.

aptitudes, interests, involvement with data/people/things, physical activities, environmental conditions, education/training indicators, career progression and work settings. Canada's NOC also provides information for assisting employers link the job description to performance planning, job evaluation and selection.

One of HR's challenges is to move beyond these classifications in order to provide a competency framework linked to performance and excellence.[22]

CO 2: COMPETENCY MODELS IN STRATEGIC MANAGEMENT

In being strategic, competency models are a way to identify and link invisible assets, or the tangible, intangible, human and non-human resources, to an organization's strategic objectives.[23] Within a resource-based view (RBV) of strategy (described in Chapter 2), key resources are the KSAOs which are more rare and difficult to imitate. In knowledge-intensive public organizations, the emphasis is more specifically on identifying and making use of distinctive human resources, especially distinctive competencies in implementing strategic themes and objectives.

The distinctive or 'core' competence idea that emerged in the 1990s suggests that 'core' competencies are linked to success and uniqueness.[24] The US government, for example, has 28 competencies, six of which are the foundation for the Executive Core Qualifications. These include interpersonal skills, oral communication, integrity/honesty, written communication, continual learning, and public service motivation. These serve as the foundation for the 22 specific competencies defined within the functional areas: leading change, leading people, being results driven, attaining business acumen and building coalitions.[25]

Researchers point to different ways competencies are used in US and UK settings. The UK perspective has been described as an 'output-oriented' approach, possibly ignoring knowledge and theory and placing more emphasis on demonstrated skills. There are suggestions that the US approach emphasizes softer behavioural skills and 'inputs' that people bring to the job, a difference that might be seen as drivers of performance, different from the UK emphasis on standards in work. Given these differences, there is evidence of convergence and an internationalization of the competency movement and the need to develop common terminology.[26]

In current practice, competency modelling is not a substitute for using a conventional job analysis in developing a job description. In designing job descriptions, it is useful to gather information about various aspects of the job's tasks, responsibilities and duties, competencies required and performance expectations. For purposes of developing a training programme, it might be more important to focus more intensively on understanding job competencies required in the job, whereas the tasks, responsibilities and duties might be more important if the purpose was to gain information for job evaluation. Thus, any data gathering method – questionnaire or interview – must be adjusted to gain the information needed.

In competency modelling, we ask:

- What are the organization's strategic objectives?
- Who are the external and internal customers or clients that this position serves?
- What are the competencies needed to respond to customers' needs and strategic objectives?

Competencies describe the knowledge, skills and abilities and other characteristics (e.g. motives, attitudes, personality traits), or what are referred to as KSAOs, that an individual requires to be effective and efficient in achieving objectives and responding to clients.

- **Knowledge** is the 'know-how' and is the ability to understand and explain something. This might be defined by a degree or diploma.
- A **skill** is the 'can do' or the capability to practise. It is the expertise to practise and demonstrate and is sometimes illustrated in a person's ability to demonstrate or illustrate in practice.
- **Abilities** are the capabilities to do something, and represent the sum of one's expertise (knowledge) and skills working together. It illustrates a 'level' of mastery or talent in demonstrating your skill.

- The **'other' characteristics** important in a competency describe a range of hard-to-define characteristics such as motivation, attitude and ability to change. A large part of performance is related to a person's willingness and motivation to do something. For some managers, ability is 'what you're capable of doing, whereas motivation determines what you do and attitudes determine how well you do it'.

The most skilled people might not be the most competent to perform a task. We see this in sports, on the job or in classroom activities. In sports, for example, we often find that the best hockey team (based on individual statistics and overall team record) might not perform to expectations. On the job, we learn that some of the best performers are not necessarily those who are the most knowledgeable and skilled. As in hockey, where performance depends as much upon the motivation to win and confidence, the characteristics to do well go beyond skills and knowledge. Competence also depends on experience and the extent to which individuals can learn and adapt, but also on the desire to win.

The use of competencies to identify talented employees has become more widespread in HRM. Over the last 30 years, researchers and practitioners have advocated a wide range of competency models and competencies to improve recruitment, selection, training and development and performance management.[27] Competencies have also been used to help explain characteristics associated with executive career success and failure. For example, in interview studies with a large number of managers, researchers studied people who 'made it' and those who 'derailed' in their careers as a way to identify critical competencies. Four themes stand out, including problems with interpersonal relationships, failure to meet business objectives, failure to build and lead a team and inability to change or adapt during a transition. Although these results have been widely used to focus training programmes and numerous human resource initiatives, the competencies might not explain organizational performance. In some cases, those who were derailed in their careers might have performed well if not for these non-performance-related events.[28]

Posner and Kouzes' competency model[29] identified five important competencies – challenging the process, inspiring a vision, enabling others to act, modelling the way and encouraging the heart – and behaviours for implementing them. For example, the competency 'challenging the way' has associated behaviours of: (i) 'search out challenging opportunities to change, grow, innovate, and improve' and (ii) 'experiment, take risks, learn from the accompanying mistakes.'[30] The model has high construct validity based on evidence from their 30-item Leadership Practices Inventory in samples of 2,168 and 30,913. The measures of the competencies are highly reliable, and the authors report that those who are rated higher performers by their subordinates illustrate these competencies.

In a meta-analysis of 29 validated studies, researchers identified eight competencies that might be part of a generic framework predicting workplace performance.

1. 'Leading and deciding', or taking control in initiating action and taking responsibility.
2. 'Supporting and co-operating', or putting people first and behaving with clear values which complement the organization.
3. 'Interacting and presenting', or communicating and relating to others in persuading others in a confident, relaxed manner.
4. 'Analysing and interpreting', or showing evidence of analytical thinking in applying expertise to complex problems and issues.
5. 'Creating and conceptualizing', or being open to new ideas and thinking broadly and strategically.
6. 'Organizing and executing', or being able to plan ahead and focus on customer satisfaction and delivering quality services.

7. 'Adapting and coping', or adapting in responding to change and managing pressures effectively.
8. 'Enterprising and performing', or focusing on results and achieving work objectives.

This list of competencies[31] is consistent with other studies that highlight relationship and task competencies, those which emphasize context and task performance[32] and 'getting along' and 'getting ahead' competencies.[33]

In adding more theoretical understanding of the relationship of competencies in a strategic management framework, researchers illustrated that different groups of competencies are correlated with initial versus subsequent performance trends, whereas other competencies are related to other aspects of performance. Russell's study (2001) highlighted nine general managerial competencies: (i) understanding, analysing and setting direction for a business; (ii) staffing; (iii) short-term business execution; (iv) financial analysis; (v) communication and climate setting; (vi) strategic planning; (vii) customer and other external relations; (viii) product planning and development and (ix) organizational acumen.

Russell's findings suggest that certain competencies may be linked to initial performance, whereas others facilitated further key roles that an executive plays. For example, management relationships with employees or customers (e.g. staffing and customer interaction efforts) will take longer to see performance gains. Resource-problem-solving competencies – such as financial analysis, understanding the business and short-term business execution ratings – predict initial performance levels. Efforts to implement a new vision or mission, along with the necessary changes in trust, work values, corporate culture and vendor customer relations, do not occur quickly. People-related dimensions (staffing, climate setting, communications and customer interaction) contributed most to prediction of change in performance rather than actual performance.[34]

The implications of Russell's study are that we might rethink how to structure competency models so that some competencies are treated as enablers to others, and that measures of performance might be considered leading and lagging indicators. Similar logic is illustrated in the Balanced Scorecard framework, where organizational objectives and initiatives are arranged in the form of a logic model. To that end, the Balanced Scorecard encourages organizations to view performance holistically and in complement to one another, as opposed to in silos.

This competency model, shown in Figure 3.1, provides a perspective on using a Balanced Scorecard–like framework to describe chief administrative officers' (CAOs) performance.[35] Based on interviews with CAOs, it illustrates competencies within the four general areas of the Balanced Scorecard: responding to clients, financial management, internal (public sector administrative and HR) processes, and learning and growth (strategic planning and leadership). Although some of the management competencies were similar to those found by others,[36] this framework also highlighted additional financial competencies related to advocating for fiscally sustainable practices, acting as a steward of financial resources and building relationships of influence. The addition of these competencies might be explained by the financial pressures municipalities often face and the unique position they are in to ensure the municipality finds adequate financing and does not run a deficit.

The framework in Figure 3.1 highlights the importance of responding to clients (citizens, businesses, city council, etc.,) in being a successful CAO. Perhaps, because CAOs' work is performed under the supervision of elected officials, they are encouraged to build a customer service culture to ensure the public is satisfied with the level of service they receive for their tax dollars.

The competencies are grouped in a semi-causal way, where one set of competencies enables or is an input to others. Built on the idea of a Balanced Scorecard strategy map, where each box illustrates objectives to implement strategic themes, Figure 3.1 illustrates a CAO competency scorecard where the competencies are focused within strategic theme areas. For example, 'building and fostering

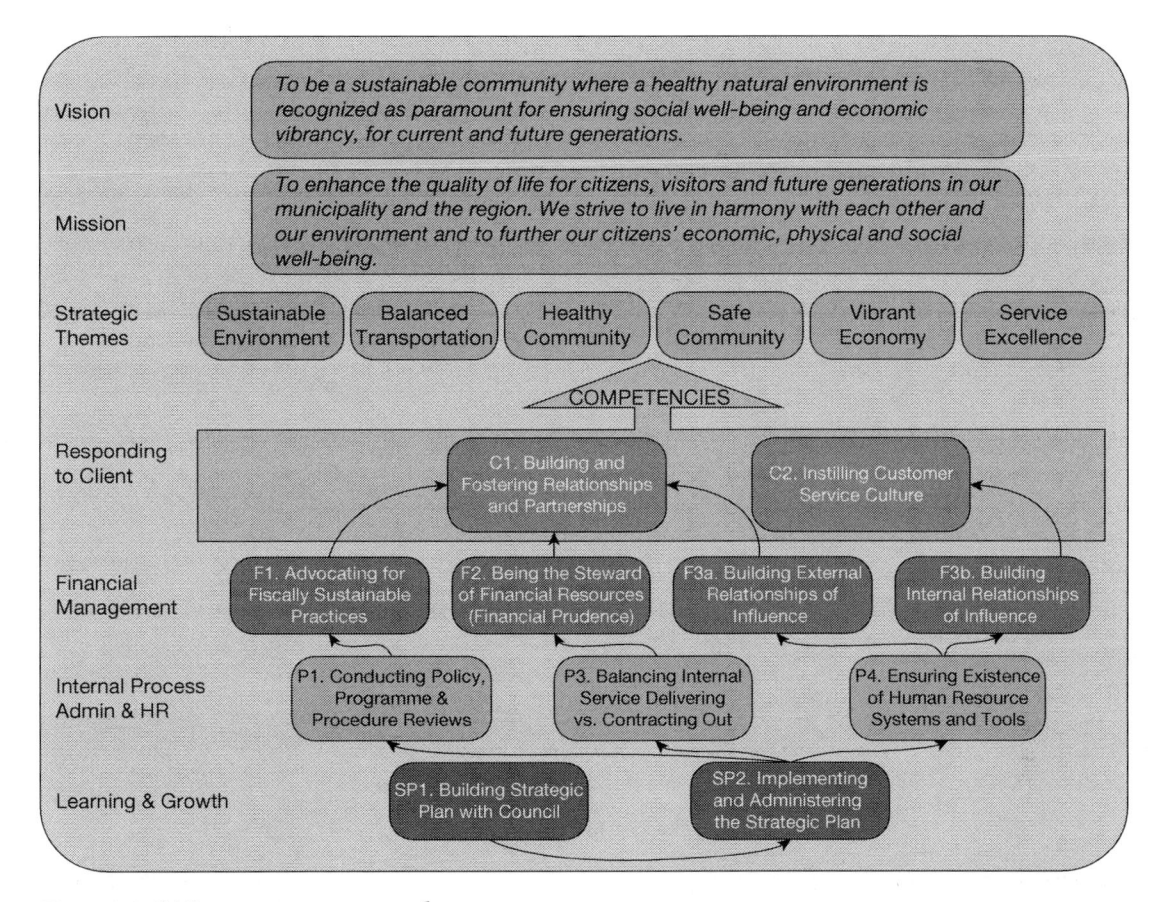

Figure 3.1 CAO competency scorecard.

relationships and partnerships' and 'instilling a customer service culture' are the key competencies that drive performance for CAOs in achieving the organization's vision and strategic themes. They are to respond to the service delivery needs of clients.

In the set of semi-causal links on the left, building and fostering relationships and partnership is enabled by three financial competencies that include advocating for sustainable practices, being a steward of financial resources and building external relationships of influence. In turn, these are enabled by internal administrative competencies related to conducting policy, programme and procedure reviews, instilling quality management procedures and balancing the efficiencies of delivering services internally with contracting out. In continuing this line of logic, these processes have more value if they implement the strategic plan and illustrate the competencies related to developing a vision and provide direction and guidance to employees and Council.

The semi-causal set of links on the right, focusing on instilling a customer service culture, rely on CAO competencies for building internal relationships of influence and build on competencies to implement and use internal HR systems and tools. They are also reliant on competencies related to implementing the strategic plan as well as those that implement the vision, guide employees, encourage training and develop an engaged culture. As with using the Balanced Scorecard for strategic planning, a next step in using the Competency Scorecard is to define the measures of performance and initiatives that are important for the CAO to work on.

CO 3: IDENTIFYING COMPETENCIES AND PERFORMANCE NORMS

Many organizations adapt competency frameworks from other organizations or from experts, a practice that might be questioned in terms of the long-term value. For example, in learning from other organizations, benchmarking is described as a process of exploring what others are doing and adapting and improving upon it. In the same way, experts can provide information on a job and save money and time in developing a competency framework.[37] However, the more popular scientific ways to develop a competency framework include the repertory grid, critical incident technique and the BEI.

Critical incident interviews. The critical incident interviewing process is an important job analysis method for understanding a job's critical requirements and the competencies that employees need to be effective and efficient in meeting strategic objectives. This technique has been used in a variety of settings to uncover the types of events that new employees see as critical in communicating an organization's culture,[38] understanding motivational characteristics,[39] discovering the training needs for youth[40] and identifying critical leadership competencies of manufacturing supervisors.[41]

Critical incidents are valuable for several reasons. They provide real examples of incidents, rather than opinions of effective and ineffective behaviour, and can be gathered from several perspectives, including that of the job holders, supervisor and client. The critical incident information, based on the words from respondents, lead directly to a clear behavioural description of competencies and performance norms.

The interviewer usually seeks critical incident examples that exemplify effective and ineffective behaviours or desirable and undesirable behaviours. The interviewer will probe for what happened and what led to the incident, who was involved, feelings and reactions and what resulted. The interviewer seeks examples of behaviour rather than evaluative comments. Incidents can be gathered through survey or interviews, although face-to-face interviews often provide richer information and provide the interviewer with an opportunity to probe for more depth or for other incidents.

Following are examples of critical incident questions that might be used in provoking information to identify competencies and performance norms and expectations on the job dimension client interpersonal relations.

Client interpersonal relations. The following questions illustrate examples of critical incident questions which seek to understand relationships with external clients (stakeholders other managers to report to). In answering these questions, can you describe some of the ways you engage with clients?

- We have all heard of problems and success stories in engaging with clients. Could you tell me about examples of the most satisfying relationship you had with a client when you felt you had accomplished something significant?
  Probes:
    - What did you do specifically for this client? What were the difficulties? What worked well and not so well?
    - I'd like to understand how you used some of these competencies. What KSAOs were most important?
    - Based on this, what might we expect other staff to do and not do? What might describe excellent performance? Unsatisfactory performance?
    - Can you give me another example?

- Could you give me an example of a difficult client relationship you encountered. What happened? Probes:
  - Why was this difficult? What were the difficulties?
  - How did you approach this differently?
  - Was there a key learning which would explain why this was so difficult?
  - I'd like to understand how you used some of these competencies that you relied on. What KSAOs were most important?
  - Based on this, what might we expect other staff to do and not do? What might describe excellent performance? Unsatisfactory performance?
  - Can you give me another example?
- Sometimes, you might have faced a situation where you were really angry with a client or the client got on your nerves. This might have been a situation where client expectations were unrealistic, or it might relate to particularly difficult clients. Tell me about a challenging client.
  - What led to the situation? What were the difficulties?
  - What did you say in response to the client? How did the client respond?
  - What was the outcome?
  - What are some of the competencies that you relied on? What KSAOs were most important?
  - Based on this, what might we expect other staff to do and not do? What might describe excellent performance? Unsatisfactory performance?
  - Can you give me another example?

These questions can provide a rich pool of incidents, feelings and perceptions, but the richness of the interviews often depends on the appropriate use of probes and encouraging interviewees to describe and reflect on their experiences. As respondents might have difficulty at times remembering examples, the probes provide a way to give people time to think about examples and provide details on them. The incidents are then analysed for content to define key job requirements and competencies.

Repertory grid interviews. In 1954, George Kelly offered a new theory of personality based on the idea that every individual characterizes his or her world through a series of constructs that are the basis by which an individual interprets the world. To help people order and define the constructs within their lives, Kelly developed what is known as the Role Construct Repertory Test, or RepGrid (Repertory Grid).[42] Even though the RepGrids were originally created as a way to help psychotherapists, they have since been adapted for a variety of studies, especially in identifying skills and characteristics of people and organizations.

The interviewee is asked to make a comparison of people, tasks, organizations or characteristics he or she is familiar with. The interview process encourages interviewees to define a set of constructs, concepts or terms and compare these with other cases. For example, in developing competencies of managers, the interviewee might be asked to identify six managers whom he or she is familiar with and can make a judgement about. The person is also asked to identify the worst and best (ideal) manager imaginable. This can be a real person or a general impression of what the worst or best would be like. Each of the eight names (or pseudo-names to protect confidentialities) can be written on notecards.[43] In other applications that identified skills in nursing, nurses were asked to recall six cases: two individuals who they viewed as effective in nursing, two that were ineffective, a nurse represented as 'self', and the nurse 'I want to become.'[44]

The interviewer then initiated a series of comparisons by choosing three notecards (on a systematic or random basis) and placed them in front of the interviewee. The interviewee was then asked to 'describe a characteristic that is common in two of the cases which is different in the third'. After the construct was identified, the interviewer probed to have it described more fully with questions such as 'What does this mean? Could you give me an example of this?' More than one characteristic might emerge from each set of comparisons.

The RepGrid style of questioning has been used in a wide variety of types of study identifying the skills of nurses,[45] measuring the change in how graduates perceived their environment after they left school and found employment,[46] or changes in self-image among a group of MBA students showing comparisons of the impact of courses.[47] It has also been compared to cognitive mapping as a research tool.[48] Its value in developing competencies is that it encourages participants to make comparisons of people who perform at different levels.

> MANAGERIAL IMPLICATIONS: This chapter is foundational, as it requires us to define the job's critical requirements and the competencies needed to implement different strategic objectives. Competencies are the basis for many HR processes. They focus the workforce planning, recruitment, selection and performance management, among other HR processes. They provide an avenue for effectively implementing the strategic objectives identified in any planning process. Within this book, we suggest that implementation of any strategic objectives requires people to illustrate the four types of competencies: (i) client or customer, (ii) internal processes focuses on efficiency, (iii) financial processes and (iv) learning and growth – represented by the different perspectives of the SHRM BSC.

BEFORE APPLYING, LET'S REVIEW

CO 1: Identify essential job requirements and competencies in the job analysis process.

An organization's strategic themes and objectives are implemented by the jobs that people perform. As such, each job has assigned duties and responsibilities and key requirements. Although the traditional approach to HRM focused on knowledge, skills and abilities (KSA), the focus on competencies expands the arena to include a recognition of motives, traits and other characteristics which are important in a job. The most important attribute of competency models is that they provide a nice link between the strategic objectives and the competencies needed to accomplish them. As such, they are key in implementing an SHRM process in that we focus in on recruiting, selecting, training and developing employees who have the competencies we need for our objectives.

CO 2: Describe competency modelling as a tool for implementing strategic objectives.

Competencies describe KSAOs employees need to be successful in the job. As such, competencies go beyond knowledge, skills and abilities and include motives, traits, aspects of one's self image and social roles that an employee utilizes in performing a job. More generally, they refer to the employee's capacity to meet (or exceed) a job's requirements. Key characteristics of a competency are listed here:

1. It is illustrated by a cluster of related knowledge, attitudes and skills that affect a major part of one's job.

2. It correlates with performance on the job.
3. It can be measured against well-accepted standards.

CO 3: Apply the critical incident and repertory grid interview in defining competencies for a job description.

A critical incident interview process encourages people to describe verifiable incidents and behaviours as well as the feelings and perceptions of these experiences. Interviewees describe their experiences and observations rather than expressing opinions or judgements of certain events. Interview questions ask people to describe positive and negative examples of incidents to understand motivation, communication, leadership or other competencies related to a job. The interview process relies on probing skills in continuing the line of questions in soliciting more examples and explanations. The RepGrid style of questioning has been used in a wide variety of studies and can be a valuable tool for defining competencies in that it encourages participants to make comparisons of people who perform at different levels.

DISCUSSION AND REVIEW QUESTIONS

1. Review the different approaches to job analysis and why one approach might be better than another. What are the advantages and disadvantages of the critical incident process?
2. Review the advantages and disadvantages of different types of job description: generic, highly specific, customer focused and employee focused.
3. Describe the similarities and differences between traditional job analysis and competency models.
4. Review the competencies presented in the various parts of this chapter. Using Table 3.3 below, add to the list of competencies for internal administrative officers (in a municipal government) who are focusing on the strategic objective of 'more effectively delivering services to the public'. Define competencies within each perspective of the SHRM BSC that you would emphasize in recruitment and training. Provide examples of KSAOs for each competency.

Table 3.3 Competencies

SHRM BSC Perspectives	Distinguishing, or Core, Competencies	Threshold Competency
Client or Customer Orientation	Concern with impact	
	Instilling customer service orientation	
Internal Business Process	Efficiency orientation	
	Developing a competency framework	
Finance	Demonstrating value for money	
Learning & Growth	Developing an engaged culture	

CASE: DEFINING COMPETENCIES OF EFFECTIVE MANAGERS

What are the competencies of effective managers?

Most of us have experienced working with or observing someone carrying out a managerial role. This might be a person you worked for in a summer job or career. The managers might have been carrying out tasks such as co-ordinating the work of a team or a group of volunteers. Or the manager might have been supervising the completing of a project. You are asked to develop a competency framework based on your experiences.

Task 1: The first part of this exercise asks you to describe two critical incidents of experiences you have had or observed which, for you, illustrate effective management and two which illustrate less than effective management.

A **critical incident** is a detailed example of an experience or incident that you have some experience with or knowledge about. A critical incident is a significant or an important (either positively or negatively) event or experience which you have experienced or observed.

In writing each incident, tell a story that describes an incident or experience which illustrates management. Pick a story which resonates with you. It may help to use the following structure when describing your critical incidents:

- Describe the event or incident. Why was it effective or ineffective?
- What led to the event?
- Who was involved?
- Describe your reactions and the reaction of others.
- Describe your feelings.
- What were the characteristics illustrated?
  - Knowledge
  - Skill
  - Ability
  - Other characteristics
- Describe the outcome. What was your learning?

Task 2: Meet with four or five other class members so that you have 16–20 incidents to work with. Team members begin by reading each incident to develop an understanding of the concepts or ideas that are being presented, perhaps making notes. They can highlight possible concepts and use labels such as incident description, knowledge, skill, abilities and personal characteristics. Cut up the summarized notes so that each idea and comment is identified on a separate piece of paper. Each message, statement, idea or concept should be separated from the rest so that it can be sorted and displayed in relationship to other categories. You will be left with a large pile of pieces of paper where each piece represents an idea, statement or concept. For this exercise, you might wish to carry out separate analyses for effective and less effective examples of management. You might also wish to identify one to three competencies for each incident and describe each competency by the KSAOs identified.

In future applications, you might wish to be more systematic in coding and indexing, which might help identify gender, level of management or some other category. Individuals can begin to sort pieces of paper into piles and begin to label the piles, recognizing effective versus ineffective examples. Individuals are first asked to group the responses together so that they have the same meaning. They are asked to take one piece of paper at a time and place it in a category by responding to the statement: 'This generally describes _____.' They would then place the response in a pile on the table representing that category. Some individuals might attach a general label (a sticker) to common piles. The most useful sorting process is to let the categories emerge rather naturally. In some cases, the researcher might decide to sort on the basis of predefined questions such as these: 'Why was this effective or ineffective? What led to the incident?' For each competency, individuals should describe the KSAOs. The decision on categorizing and interpretation is intuitive rather than logical. Sorting is a trial-and-error, iterative process of trying to understand how various items fit together. The sorters are not limited in the number of categories they are to develop and are simply given the information to arrange and asked to label the various interview statements into general categories. At some point, it is appropriate to begin arranging the various observations and ideas and to develop classes or categories.[49]

You should end up with themes describing each question. For example, there might be themes describing personal characteristics.

In summarizing this exercise, you are asked to define five or six of the top competencies that are each described by KSAOs.

4 Engaging Employees in More Productive Ways of Working

Chapter Outline
- Chapter objectives (COs)   68
- A driving issue focusing managerial action: How public service motivation (PSM) affects public service organizations   68
- CO 1: Employee engagement and job enrichment   70
- CO 2: Quality of Working Life (QWL) and Total Quality Management (TQM)   76
- CO 3: Emerging perspectives on job and organizational design   81
- Before applying, let's review   85
- Discussion and review questions   85
- Case: Daniel Boone at the Pensions Services Department   87

CHAPTER OBJECTIVES (COs)

After reading this chapter you will be able to implement the following objectives:

CO 1: Apply Herzberg's job enrichment and the job characteristics model (JCM) in a public sector context.

CO 2: Apply the principles of quality of working life (QWL) and total quality management (TQM) to public sector organizations.

CO 3: Devise new ideas on enriching public sector jobs.

A DRIVING ISSUE FOCUSING MANAGERIAL ACTION: HOW PUBLIC SERVICE MOTIVATION (PSM) AFFECTS PUBLIC SERVICE ORGANIZATIONS

Researchers suggest that if we ask people in public and private organizations about the values that drive them, people in the public sector are more likely to be concerned about intrinsically related work and meaningful assignments, whereas those in business are more likely to be driven by extrinsic rewards such as financial return and prestige. Public sector people have values of contributing to society, accomplishing meaningful assignments, making a difference, and serving their community, more so than people in private organizations. This does not suggest that people in public organizations are not interested in extrinsic rewards, but that they place a lower priority on them because of different beliefs, values and attitudes.[1]

Recruiters are being encouraged to recognize a **public service motivation (PSM)** or a unique predisposition that energizes and directs the people who are attracted to public service organizations.[2] It has been described as a 'motivational dimension that induces people to perform meaningful public service'[3] and 'an altruistic motivation to serve the interests of a community of people, a state, a nation, or humanity'.[4] It might be captured by 'the belief, values and attitudes that go beyond self-interest and organizational interest, that concern the interest of a larger political entity and that motivate individuals to act accordingly whenever appropriate'.[5]

PSM is defined by four core values: 'Attraction to public policy making and politics' describes the desire of public employees to get involved in politics and the policy process in making a difference. 'Commitment to the public interest' involves aspirations to improve the public good and public interest. 'Compassion' is illustrated in showing empathy for the welfare of others and being protective of their interests. 'Self-sacrifice' is related to a willingness to substitute service for others personal rewards.[6]

It is generally recognized that PSM is higher among people working in the public than in the private sector. PSM is associated with outcomes such as the willingness to participate in civic and other organizations and is now recognized as a key determinant of those who choose careers in public service. Those with PSM are more likely to be selected and have a longer retention than others. It is also associated with self-reports of individual and organizational performance.

Organizations are less likely to rely on extrinsic rewards for motivating people who illustrate PSM values and are more likely to rely on motivating people by providing intrinsically rewarding work. Research on PSM and its connections to performance and motivation is ongoing. One challenge is to connect PSM to other public service values and to better understand the conditions under which it can be encouraged.[7]

> STRATEGIC CONTEXT: This chapter focuses on the strategic theme of improving QWL and productivity in public sector organizations.
>
> The way a job is designed is a key driver in motivating people. That is, when jobs are designed so that participants experience a degree of challenge, autonomy and variety, they are more likely to be intrinsically motivated. Even though other factors such as administrative policy and administration as well as job security might reduce dissatisfaction, the job's **intrinsic characteristics** are more likely to provide long-term engagement or motivation.
>
> Job design is the foundation of the HR system as it shapes motivation and performance. An enriched job design is formalized in job descriptions that effectively assign people their duties and responsibilities, performance goals and the competencies. This chapter reviews various approaches to job design such as job enrichment, TQM and QWL. TQM approaches are important in public and private organizations because they provide a perspective on how customer-focused designs encourage employee engagement and performance. TQM and job enrichment approaches were initially applied in non-union, private sector organizations, whereas sociotechnical ideas originated in union settings and were often applied in public sector environments. The sociotechnical and QWL interventions are instructive in the use of a joint union-management steering committee guiding the implementation and illustrating the power of semi-autonomous work groups (and team management). Such a process that involves the organizational membership in the design of their own work can be useful for job enrichment and TQM ideas in the public arena.
>
> Each of the chapter objectives describes ways to implement different principles and models for designing jobs that are more engaging and productive. After reading this chapter, you might wish to design a strategy map to implement this strategy theme based on the ideas in each chapter objective.

CO 1: EMPLOYEE ENGAGEMENT AND JOB ENRICHMENT

Public sector reforms such as the New Public Management (NPM) are calling for an emphasis on more economic- and performance-oriented values, or values concerned with outputs and more effective use of resources. The design of public organizations concerned with cost control and goal achievement is very different from a design linked to other prominent public administration values related to equity, procedural justice and equity. The NPM principles seek to make government organizations more businesslike, market oriented, and customer focused while emphasizing more accountability and cost-effectiveness.[8] The paradigm has its roots in business concepts like customer service, TQM and public choice theory, which is a perspective on economics that views individuals as self-interested decision-makers who will act rationally to maximize their utility.[9]

A contrasting view, linked to PSM, is that individuals are drawn to their careers in public service by uniquely altruistic motives such as serving the public interest, effecting social change and shaping policies that affect society. Within this perspective, individuals are drawn to public sector employment and will flourish if we can 'engage' them in their work by designing tasks, responsibilities and roles to fully realize PSM values.

Linking to the strategic context for engaging employees

Kahn originally defined **employee engagement** as 'the harnessing of organization members' selves to their work roles: in engagement people employ and express themselves physically, cognitively, and emotionally during role performance'.[10] Whereas disengagement is withdrawal of selves from work, employee engagement captures how employees experience their work in being 'fully there'. This goes beyond **affective commitment**, or the emotional attachment based on shared values and interest (affective energy). It is also more than **job involvement**, which might be a facet of engagement (a cognitive energy). It reflects the 'passion' and willingness to embrace an organization's tasks, aspirations or assignments as one's own and has been found to be higher in some samples of public sector employees versus private sector employees and higher in public sector managers than their employees.[11]

Employee engagement is akin to the **internal motivation** which describes a self-directed or autonomous behaviour that manifests intrinsic or other higher-level needs or callings.[12] One way to improve employee engagement and respond to employees' PSM is to enrich their work so that it is intrinsically motivating and engaging. Practical suggestions for job enrichment can be found in Herzberg's Orthodox Job Enrichment and JCM. The proponents of these approaches would argue that the scientific management ideas of job design were based on the science and knowledge of the 1930s. A more up-to-date science would suggest newer principles of job design. **Job enrichment** is a way of vertically loading a job or giving it higher-level tasks and responsibilities which match the skills, knowledge and abilities of an employee. **Job enlargement** is a way of horizontally loading a job by increasing the number of tasks rather than the level of responsibility and skill required. It is useful in reducing some of the monotony associated with doing the same thing day-in and day-out.

Performance metrics in linking job characteristics to employee engagement

The early history of job design focused on designing jobs to illustrate the principles of specialization, division of labour and work simplification. Management theorists learned a great deal about specialization and division of labour from the military and leaders like Frederick the Great, who ruled Prussia from 1740 to 1786. The army he commanded was made up of unmotivated conscripts, criminals, paupers and foreign mercenaries. Fascinated with the workings of mechanical toys, and the practices of the Romans and the European armies of the sixteenth century, he developed many innovations which reduced his soldiers to robot-like automatons. His quest was to develop a reliable and efficient fighting force using principles of standardization of regulations, specialization of tasks, standardized equipment, a common language for communication and training to improve efficiency. Frederick the Great's vision of a mechanized army was elaborated by others, including the twentieth-century management theorist Frederick W. Taylor, who pioneered what became known as **scientific management**. The influence of scientific management in public administration was vivid in two of the field's initial textbooks: Leonard White's *Introduction to Public Administration* (1926) and W.F. Willoughby's *The Principles of Public Administration* (1927). Both authors argued for the application of scientific principles in governance to provide a performance guide to reform public administration.

The job design ideas described with job enrichment, QWL and TQM still argue for measuring the soundness of a job's design in delivering efficient and high-quality services. However, when jobs have more variety, challenge, autonomy and task significance, they are also more likely to encourage higher levels of engagement and motivation. This, in turn, will improve efficiency and service quality in the long term.

Herzberg's Orthodox Job Enrichment

Frederick Herzberg introduced Orthodox Job Enrichment in illustrating that factors that might reduce job dissatisfaction are very different from those motivating a person. He distinguished his theory from other motivational theories which is said were based on KITA principles, his acronym for 'kick in the a__', Herzberg's commentary on motivation theories is a 'tongue-in-cheek' summary of motivation, where he describes three types of KITA: (i) negative physical KITA, (ii) negative psychological KITA, and (iii) positive psychological KITA.[13]

Negative physical KITA. In this stereotypical example, we might imagine a manager motivating a person using physical force (a kick, slap or threat). Most types of KITA are inappropriate and possibly illegal in modern organizations, although we can imagine times in the past when whips and other forms of negative KITA were used.

Negative psychological KITA. Instead of physical force, we might imagine a manager using psychological pressures such as failing to communicate needed information, taking part in a chilly climate or negativity towards others, or socially ostracizing a person. The assumption is 'If you do this, I will be nice to you. If you don't, I will make you feel emotionally uncomfortable.' In Herzberg's description, instead of physical KITA, a manager is using psychological pressures to motivate.

Positive psychological KITA. Most of the motivational theories we saw in the 1950s and 1960s, according to Herzberg, are a form of 'positive psychological KITA'. This approach to motivation suggests: 'Do this for me, and in return I will give you a reward, recognition, more status or time off.' In motivating, the manager offers praise, feedback, more responsibility or a different alignment of responsibilities. Other examples include reducing time at work, increased wages, fringe benefits, human relations training, employee counselling, increasing job security and other 'rewards' and 'incentives' which are aimed at addressing grievances and complaints. In responding to employees, a manager offers incentives and other positive psychological encouragers. In order to keep motivating, the manager has to offer incentives that are more valuable than the ones previously given. Positive psychological KITA will only increase a person's motivation to get more encouragers rather than improving a person's internal motivation.

For Herzberg, motivation is an entirely different process, where the catalyst for action is within the person. **Motivation** is 'internal' to the individual and is a self-generated process that causes behaviour to be energized, directed and sustained. Rather than expecting managers or others to motivate people, the essence of motivation results from redesigning the job so it is motivating.

Herzberg's motivation-hygiene theory is based on research seeking to understand motivation and dissatisfaction where people identified critical incidents or stories of when they 'felt exceptionally good or bad about their job'.[14] Herzberg sorted these stories into two categories: those that result in satisfaction, which he called 'motivational factors', and those that lead to job dissatisfaction, called 'hygiene factors'. The **motivational factors** include achievement, recognition, work itself, responsibility, advancement and growth. The **dissatisfiers (hygiene factors)** include company policy and administration, supervision, interpersonal relations, working conditions, salary, status and security. The most important hygiene factor is company policy and administration, or the promotion of ineffectiveness or inefficiency within the organization, and the second most important is incompetent technical supervision. According to Herzberg, the job must fulfil certain hygiene, or maintenance, requirements, or employees will be dissatisfied.[15]

Motivation-hygiene theory suggests that the factors involved in producing motivation (job satisfaction) are different from those that lead to job dissatisfaction, each representing a unique continuum: one dealing with job satisfaction and one related to motivation.[16] This relationship is illustrated in Figure 4.1.

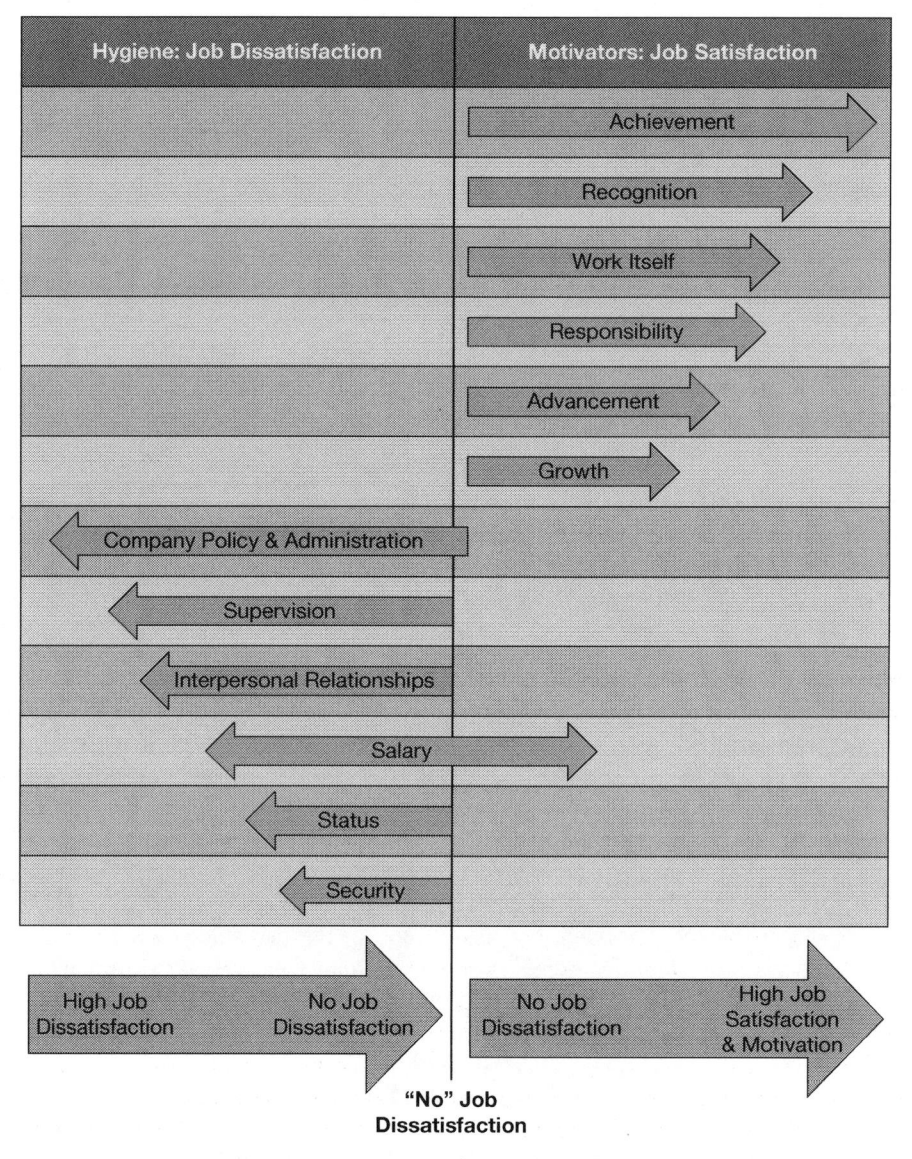

Figure 4.1 The factors defining motivation-hygiene theory.[17]

Trying to improve the hygiene factors or dissatisfiers in a job will not improve motivation, but will generally reduce the degree of dissatisfaction to no dissatisfaction. The key to motivation is in the design of the work itself. Herzberg suggests that the more long-term benefits are achieved by focusing on the motivators such as these:

- *Direct feedback*: The employee gets feedback directly from work performance (e.g. client feedback) rather than indirectly from a supervisor or other indirect means (provides 'recognition').
- *Client relationship*: The employee has a customer or client to serve (provides 'recognition').
- *New learning*: The employee has the opportunity to learn something purposeful and meaningful (provides 'growth').
- *Scheduling*: The employee is allowed to schedule the pace of the work and how it is organized (provides 'responsibility').
- *Unique expertise*: The employee is provided with aspects of the job that give him or her some personal uniqueness (provides 'achievement').
- *Control over resources*: The employee has discretion in the use of financial or other resources (provides 'responsibility').
- *Direct communications authority*: The employee is provided with new information to enable him or her to make decisions (provides 'recognition' and 'responsibility').
- *Personal accountability*: The employee is given control of and made accountable for the outcome of projects he or she is working on, rather than using rules and procedures to guard against error (provides 'recognition' and 'responsibility').[18]

Herzberg's theory has important implications for public sector HRM beyond contributing ideas for enriching jobs and changing the job's design and how we work. It offers a framework for understanding how pay, fringe benefits, time off and many of the other perks that we give employees may reduce satisfaction but might not enhance intrinsic motivation.

Implementing orthodox job enrichment. Herzberg argued that his job enrichment approach provided more updated scientific information, designing a job for improving productivity as well as responding to motivational issues. One aspect of the implementation involves developing a motivational profile of the organization by asking employees when they felt either exceptionally motivated or unmotivated in their work and the events which illustrated this. The profile provides a statement of the key motivations and dissatisfiers that may have to be dealt with before moving forward.

The process of job enrichment, according to Herzberg, could be directed by managers, supervisors or consultants. The initial step involves brainstorming ways to enrich the jobs, paying attention to asking how we would improve direct feedback, client relationship, new learning, scheduling, unique expertise, control over resources, direct communications authority and personal accountability. In making this relevant to the public sector context, it might be appropriate to add dimensions that have been used in public sector applications, such as designing opportunities to have a positive impact with recipients and having contact with citizens.[19] The framework can be easily adapted to include the values defined by PSM, such as being more involved in politics and the policy process, improving the public good and public interest, showing empathy for the welfare of others and focusing of service as a personal reward. It is also appropriate to introduce relational dimensions appropriate for jobs in the public sector.[20]

Subsequent steps of the implementation involve screening out suggestions that provide hygiene resolutions (e.g. provide more time off) and those which are too general (words like **responsibility, growth, achievement** and **challenge** are examples of vague words that need to be made more specific). It is also appropriate to eliminate horizontal-loading suggestions that focus on the same level of work and focus on higher-level tasks such as supervision or carrying out higher-level projects.

Herzberg's job enrichment approach is seminal in encouraging us to recognize the difference between internal motivation and hygiene factors. It is based on the assumption that we can improve a job's internal motivational dimensions by changing the design of the work.

The Job Characteristics Model (JCM)

The JCM has stimulated a great deal of discussion on ways to improve the design of work, and it is the inspiration for other theories of job design appropriate to public organizations.[21] The conceptual core behind the JCM is expectancy theory and the premise that people will perform well simply because it is intrinsically rewarding to do so. That is, motivation from rewards and supervisors is less relevant when the job's characteristics can be designed to make people feel good. When people feel positive about their work, they will experience high internal motivation.[22]

High internal motivation occurs when people exhibit three critical psychological states: (i) experienced meaningfulness, (ii) experienced responsibility and (iii) knowledge of results.[23]

i. *Experienced meaningfulness* – A person perceives his or her work as worthwhile or important and valued, and that what is done will 'count' and is not trivial.
ii. *Experienced responsibility* – A person may feel accountable for some work outcomes, and that their initiatives or efforts are important for achieving this.
iii. *Knowledge of results* – A person knows how well he or she is performing on a fairly regular basis.

Motivational and performance problems emerge if people experience little meaning, little responsibility for work outcomes or little information about how well they are performing.[24]

The model illustrated in Figure 4.2 summarizes five key characteristics or dimensions that contribute to the three psychological states.[25] They are skill variety, task identity, task significance, autonomy and feedback from the job:

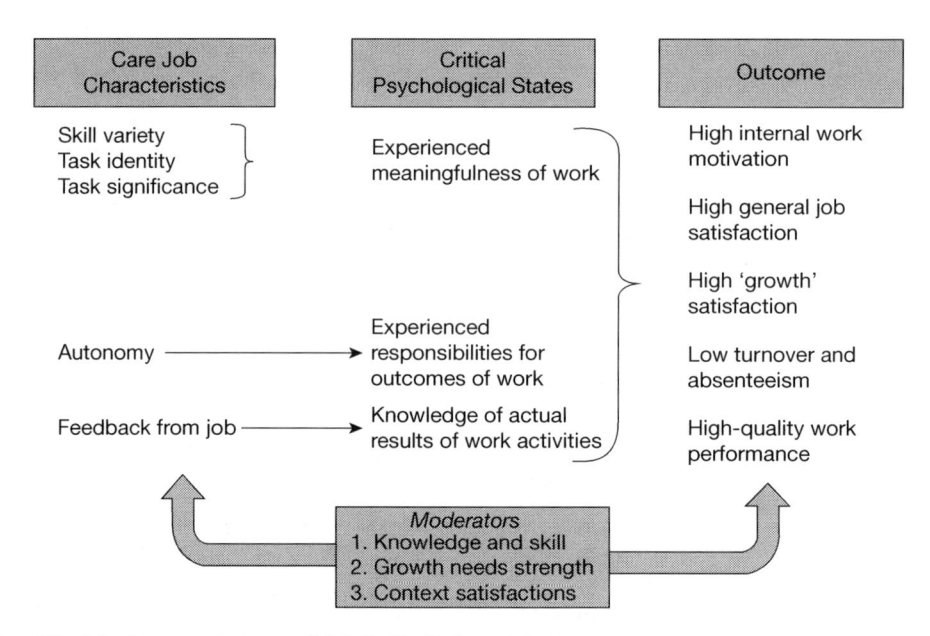

Figure 4.2 The job characteristics model (JCM) of job enrichment.

- Skill variety – doing different things, using unique abilities, talents and skills.
- Task identity – doing the whole job and the entire piece of work from beginning to end, rather than bits and pieces.
- Task significance – the degree to which the job has a meaningful impact on others and is important in the broader scheme of things.
- Autonomy – chances of using personal initiative and judgement; freedom to do the work, schedule and make decisions.
- Feedback – clear and direct information about the job and its outcomes; knowing whether you performed well after completing the job.

Three of the five job characteristics describe the experienced meaningfulness of the work; one connects to experienced responsibility; and one links to knowledge of results. The five characteristics can be summarized in a single index of the motivating potential score (MPS) of the job.

$$\text{MPS} = \left\{\frac{\text{Skill}}{\text{Variety}} + \frac{\text{Task}}{\text{Identity}} + \frac{\text{Task}}{\text{Significance}}\right\} \times \text{Autonomy} \times \text{Feedback}$$

Sometimes, the motivation problem might be moderated by something other than the job's characteristics, such as knowledge and skill, growth needs or context satisfaction. For example, an employee who has a higher need for growth might be more likely to respond positively to job enrichment.[26]

The JCM relies on a data collection instrument (the Job Diagnostic Survey, or JDS) which is intended to (1) diagnose the jobs prior to any change, and (2) evaluate the effects of changes made.[27] The instrument, in assessing the need for design, can be combined with other methods (interviews, observations by job incumbents, supervisors, staff members and outside consultants). It indicates the motivating potential of the job and the job characteristics on each of five core dimensions – skill variety, task identity, task significance, autonomy and feedback. The current levels of motivation, satisfaction and work performance are also assessed, in addition to satisfaction with pay, supervision and relationship with co-workers. This helps pinpoint the employees more likely to be responsive to a job enrichment programme.[28]

Five implementing concepts are part of the job characteristics approach:

- *Forming natural work units*: Work can be distributed so that a worker has more sense of responsibility for a body of work.
- *Combining tasks*: Existing and fragmented tasks can be grouped together to form larger bodies of work using a wider range of skills.
- *Establishing client relationships*: Encouraging people to establish direct relationships with the clients enhances skill variety, autonomy and feedback.
- *Vertical loading*: Responsibilities reserved for higher levels of management can be added to the job, giving an employee more discretion in setting schedules, checking on quality, granting additional authority, deciding when to start and stop work, troubleshooting and making crisis decisions, and establishing financial controls.
- *Opening feedback channels*: Feedback from the job is usually more immediate and accurate than that supplied by supervisors and increases a feeling of personal control over the work.

Although Herzberg's model might be seen as starting much of the debate on job design, the JCM became the dominant model in the for-profit sector and has been the subject of extensive reviews.[29] Later parts of this chapter describe new perspectives on job design which take into account the changing contexts of work and which focus on managers and professionals rather than front-line workers.

Implications of job enrichment and public sector motivation (PSM). In adding to the JCM, researchers have shown that jobs can be designed to foster prosocial motivation, a concept similar to PSM.[30] That is, jobs can be designed to encourage people to express their public sector values if we find opportunities for people to fulfil their values by interaction with service recipients. In building a model of job enrichment, Taylor[31] developed a model which built on two relational characteristics that Grant[32] suggested might motivate citizens to do good for their service recipients:

1. Opportunities to have a positive impact on recipients.[33]
2. Opportunities to have contact with citizens.[34]

In one local government setting, researchers found that people with a higher norm of performing public service work were more satisfied with their jobs because they felt they had more impact and that they could accomplish something worthwhile. However, the frequency of contacts with citizens, while important, did not significantly affect PSM, nor did it moderate the relationship between PSM and job satisfaction.[35] These results provide ideas for adapting the JCM because they indicate that establishing client relationship (one of the JCM implementing concepts) is not sufficient for improving internal motivation in that having meaningful impact in relationships with clients is more likely to enhance internal motivation.

CO 2: QUALITY OF WORKING LIFE (QWL) AND TOTAL QUALITY MANAGEMENT (TQM)

QWL and TQM go beyond job enrichment and focus on the entire organization. QWL was central in organizational studies as one of the first applications of semi-autonomous groups and team management and for illustrating a sociotechnical approach to organizational design. TQM inspired organizational theorists and practitioners to redesign their jobs and organizational systems to focus on responding to customer or client needs.

Quality of Working Life

QWL ideas expand the arena beyond the immediate job and its tasks to include the physical work environment as well as the social environment within the organization, the administrative system and the relationship between life on and off the job.[36]

The term **quality of working life (QWL)** was coined at an international conference in 1972 to summarize many experiments concerned with improving an organization's design. The factors in QWL designs evolve in response to the needs of the technology as well as the individuals in the social system. However, most designs involve the use of semi-autonomous work-group and sociotechnical principles and are linked to the idea of finding a balance in the work as well as more generally in life.

Following the influence of the British Tavistock Institute, there was a great deal of interest throughout the world. The applications in Norway and Sweden involved organization-wide experiences. In Norway, national organizations of labour and management sponsored experiments in 'industrial democracy' that were aimed at testing alternative forms of participative organization. Six individual needs guided the design work: challenge and variety, continued learning, personal decision-making and responsibility, social support and recognition, meaningful relation of work and social life, and relation of present job to future career. Although there were many other applications, two well-known Swedish experiments illustrating sociotechnical principles included the Saab-Scania plant at Sodertalje and the Volvo plant at Kalmar.[37] Canadian applications[38] illustrated similar design elements:

- *Technical systems changes*: The technical systems – equipment and facilities – might be modified for semi-autonomous group work, or close interaction between operating and maintenance personnel.
- *Job changes*: Job changes might encourage greater variety, greater discretion and more challenge and learning.
- *Participation and semi-autonomous groups:* The degree of direct participation might increase, and workers might have more direct and indirect input into the design and management of their work.
- *Pay/reward systems:* Pay and reward systems might be designed for rewarding employees on the basis of knowledge and skill as well as profit.
- *Compressed shift schedules:* Schedules can be modified to improve the relationship between an individual's work and social settings. In most cases, this meant the introduction of a 12-hour compressed shift schedule.
- *Training and recruitment:* Training programmes include team building, practical skills and setting objectives. The recruitment process emphasizes personal compatibility as well as technical competence.
- *Operating philosophy statement:* Explicit philosophy statements were developed to serve as an operating framework for how the design might proceed, as well as serving as a mechanism for developing a positive and co-operative work arrangement between union and management.
- *Collective agreement modification:* The development of a framework and set of guidelines for employees to work within might replace previous collective agreements which had many pages of legalistic requirements.[39]

QWL designs work where there is an open dialogue over the way the work is organized and managed. Individuals should be able to make judgements about what is desired and not desired. These choices related to improving wages, hours of work, job security, health safety and other conditions of work. The 'choices' can lead to the development of jobs and organizations that enable people to develop their abilities and to fulfil their needs. These jobs might have greater variety, challenge, responsibility and growth.

Implementing QWL. QWL made extensive inroads in public and private organizations based on a belief that workplace democracy has to be implemented in a participative process that allows individuals and groups to experience new and difficult challenges and to make choices governing the workplace. Participation has often meant that the process was jointly owned and controlled by various groups in the organization, and in many cases, joint union-management committees were involved in the implementation. In most organizations, union and management establish a joint body (often called a steering committee) to oversee and guide the process. The committee works by establishing a framework and defining design principles, objectives and conditions under which the change will proceed.

Part of any such QWL application is an underlying philosophy of change directed at understanding the needs of the organization's social and technical systems. This involves articulating a commitment to understanding the problems and issues and adapting theories and techniques to respond to them. There is also the recognition that individuals need to be involved in the process of designing the organizations they will be involved in. Any design will not be everlasting, as the process of redesign will need to continue to take into account the new technologies and changing individual needs and capacities.

The philosophy statement usually includes main sections recognizing the interrelationship between the social and technical systems, key considerations for the social system relating to communication and individual commitment, and implementation and maintenance of the philosophy statement. Key considerations for the social system relate to ensuring that (i) jobs are designed so they are reasonably demanding; (ii) individuals know what their job is and how to perform it; (iii) jobs have learning;

> ### A RELEVANT POINT OF VIEW: A SOCIOTECHNICAL PERSPECTIVE ON JOB DESIGN
>
> The way work is organized is often determined by the technology, as when employees process the applications for people who want to get a driver's licence or passport, or make a compensation claim. Often, when the work is organized by its technology (the tools, knowledge, techniques), it becomes specialized and routine, and employees end up doing the same type of tasks each day. The technology can put demands and limits on the way the work is organized, but the employees have social and psychological requirements of their own in any job. Major needs for people include closure, or a sense of finishing a meaningful unit of work; some control over these tasks; some challenge; and satisfactory relationships.
>
> Shortly after World War II, Tavistock researchers first illustrated that the work group could be a means in which social needs could be achieved in spite of the potential limitations of a technology.[40] In one of the projects, in a coal mining operation, they discovered an innovative work practice where workers exhibited high morale and low absenteeism and turnover in a mechanized coal mining operation. The new work practices involved autonomous groups supervising and regulating their own work and interchanging their roles and shifts. Group members were not organized according to the new highly mechanized 'longwall' mining technology, where work was broken into individual tasks and co-ordinated with the supervisor. Instead, the workers organized themselves into autonomous work groups and maintained their group cohesion in spite of the new, highly mechanized assembly-line system.[41] There was 'organization choice'.[42] Groups could design and choose a system that met their social requirements, as well as the requirements of the technology, rather than be constrained by the technology.
>
> This **sociotechnical perspective** on work design suggests that all organizations consist of both a social system (the people) and a technical system (the tools, knowledge, techniques) to provide services and goods that are of value to customers in the external environment. Also, it suggests that we need not be constrained by the imperatives of the technology and that we can find ways to design work, organizational and societal systems that complement between technological and social requirements.
>
> The sociotechnical perspective on design has stimulated new designs, work units, whole organizational systems and macrosocial systems in private and public organizations. The work is connected to applications in textile mills in India and in several applications in the United States, Canada and Europe.[43] There is also a conceptual linkage to the Norwegian industrial democracy application and the Swedish team assembly designs in Saab and Volvo.[44]

(iv) individuals have some discretion in decision-making; (v) individuals know they can rely on others for assistance; and (vi) individuals feel that the job leads to a desirable future in the organization.

The philosophy statement can include, among many other things, a statement of beliefs such as the following:

> [O]ur employees are responsible and trustworthy; individuals are capable of making proper decisions related to their spheres of responsibility, given the necessary information and training; groups of individuals can work effectively as members of a team with minimal supervision, collaborating on such matters as problem-solving (operational and personal training, 'hands-on' operations, maintenance, etc.[45]

Up until the late 1990s, QWL programmes using sociotechnical principles had been introduced in both the public and private sectors, providing innovative ideas for redesign in unionized environments. QWL is still alive and doing well, although it has changed and will continue to change. In some North American sectors, the term *QWL* has derived new meanings in relation to health and work–life balance, although this is not directly connected to its sociotechnical roots. Researchers have taken the sociotechnical framework in different directions with applications in health care, information systems and engineering. The main assumptions of these applications build on the work of the founders in illustrating the interface between technical and social systems.

In some European countries, such as Sweden and Denmark, policies on improving QWL gained ground with legislation and policies in the 1980s and 1990s for worker input and control in developing healthier work environments. For some scholars, these countries led the way as the programmes were judged to involve more improvements in the dimensions of work design such as variety, learning, participation, decision-making and career, although they are not judged to be further ahead than other European colleagues.[46] Various initiatives across Europe (e.g. Finland, Germany, Ireland, the United Kingdom, Belgium and the Netherlands) were shaped to improve performance.[47]

QWL has also been used as a measure of the health of the strategic human resource system. In Finnish municipalities, researchers suggested that there was a connection between the SHRM orientation and QWL. In municipalities where QWL is good, HRM is also doing something right. They could be strengthening the renewal potential, using high-involvement practices, and their employees have a generally high level of trust and collaboration.[48]

Total Quality Management (TQM)

After World War II in Japan, General MacArthur asked several leading American experts to offer advice on how to proceed with a programme for rebuilding industries. One of the visitors, Dr W. Edward Deming, observed that many Japanese companies were facing problems of morale and lack of investment funds, raw materials and components. He transformed traditional engineering ideas on statistical quality control into a management approach with an underlying philosophy, principles and practices. By the 1970s, Deming and his ideas were prominent among Japanese companies, most notably, Toyota Production System, which adopted quality ideas and **just-in-time (JIT) management**. Along with several other proponents such as Joseph Juran, Philip Crosby, Kaoru Ishikawa and others, he laid the foundations of **Total Quality Management (TQM)**.

TQM has received a great deal of prominence and is operationalized in a number of practices like QC circles, JIT management and statistical process control.[49] Quality management is also associated with quality ideas such as ISO 9000 standards and Six Sigma. Deming's method and TQM ideas are based on a philosophy of problem-solving, continuous improvement and employee involvement and are distinct from an engineering, scientific-management-type quality control philosophy in maintaining standards of efficiency.[50] Involvement implies consultation and is illustrated when people are given input on decisions or actions in improving the job design, delivery of services and ways to improve performance.

Deming's management method is articulated in 14 principles, and though many of these principles seem interrelated and overlapping, they might be grouped into seven key concept areas.[51]

1. *Visionary leadership:* Ability to establish, practise and realize a long-term vision related to changing customer requirements. This is demonstrated when leaders establish a clear vision and illustrate a participative, coaching-management style.
2. *Internal and external co-operation:* Capability to engage in co-operative activities with employees and suppliers. This is illustrated in organizational-supplier partnerships, collaborative relationships, teamwork and organization-wide involvement.

3. *Learning:* Ability to recognize and nurture skill development, abilities and knowledge. This is exemplified in organization-wide training, foundational and process knowledge, educational development, continuous improvement and managerial learning.
4. *Process management:* Capability to use practices for process management rather than results management. This is demonstrated in formative versus summative evaluation, prevention orientation, reduction of mass inspection, understanding variation, elimination of quotas, merit rating awards and management by objectives (MBO). It is demonstrated in motivated people, total cost accounting and stable employment practices.
5. *Continuous improvement:* Desire to pursue incremental and innovative improvements of processes, products and services. Continuous improvement and ongoing action learning demonstrate this.
6. *Employee fulfilment:* Degree to which employees perceive the organization satisfies their needs. This is illustrated in job satisfaction, job commitment and pride of workmanship.
7. *Customer satisfaction:* Degree to which customers feel that the organization's products and service meet their needs. A customer-driven focus is an illustration of this.[52]

Researchers have suggested that the concepts might be articulated in a semi-causal linkage between visionary leadership and customer satisfaction.[53] Deming's management approach and other Japanese management ideas are interwoven with a philosophy that treats the employees within 'family-like' norms. Among the norms of family life, **wa (harmony)** is the component most often emphasized in company philosophies. *Wa* expresses a 'quality of relationship', a form of teamwork or group consciousness of the employees. Individual employee action is not dominant in Japanese organizations and may be discouraged because of the competition and possible antagonisms it might generate among team members. There are a number of HR practices through which these ideas are realized, including lifetime employment guarantees, intensive socialization, job rotation within a non-specialized career path, intensive training and work group organization.[54]

Basic criteria for hiring are moderate views and harmonious personality, in addition to ability on the job. An intensive socialization process begins with a training programme geared to orienting new employees. The long-range experience-building programme encourages skill development in grooming people for future managerial positions by rotating people through various jobs so that they become immersed in the organization's philosophy and culture. Most of the rotations are lateral, but not all jobs at the same hierarchical level are equal in their importance to the organization's activities. As a result, some rotations provide more informal recognition and opportunities to learn skills required for future formal promotions.

Implementing TQM. Although QWL applications encourage a democratically guided process for improving work life and focus on finding a balance between social and technical requirements, TQM begins by recognizing a key external requirement – that of responding to customer needs. The inclusion of the customer criterion does not downgrade the importance of the organizational design, but simply suggests that design begins and ends in focusing on customers. This goes beyond the definition of a customer as purchaser and includes anyone to whom a person provides work, service or information.

TQM in the private sector provided a transformational new direction for improving services and linking them more closely to customer needs. Some of the TQM principles were adopted in the public sector as the NPM, whereas others were introduced in approaches to reorganize public services such as those proposed by Osborne and Gabler's Reinventing Government[55] and US Vice President Gore's Creating a Government That Works Better and Costs Less.[56] An essential idea underlying these applications is redesigning and invigorating governments by empowering employees and 'putting customers first'. While arguing that government cannot be run like a business, there were calls for mission-driven public organizations which allow employees to search for the most effective methods they can find to deliver services.

Implications of QWL and TQM. The customer emphasis is important and distinct from the 'making government run like a business' mantra of the NPM movement and has become a transformational shift in the way of organizing, different from a rational, production or managerial emphasis. Initially, many public sector scholars and practitioners rejected the word *customer*, and there was much debate about the relevance of using many business tools in public organizations. In some of the business literature, the concept of customer orientation was often seen as a synonym of market orientation. However, other perspectives see the customer orientation in responding to individual customer expectations and needs.

In the public sector, TQM's emphasis was on creating long-term success through customer satisfaction. Some of the original applications drew from Deming-like principles such as constancy of purpose, improving processes, instituting vigorous training and education and adopting a philosophy of quality improvement where everyone is involved.[57] The interest in TQM waned in practice and among researchers in the late 1990s, partially as a result of reduced funding for training and loss of interest as new trends focused on NPM, citizen satisfaction and quality improvement.[58] These newer approaches are not as tied to instilling the values and principles of TQM.

The job enrichment, QWL and TQM models planted the roots for the idea that work design is central in motivation and productivity. In addition to developing valuable theory and debate about design, we might conclude that these models have left us with key learnings in relation to motivation and productivity in public sector organizations.

- Internal motivation or engagement involves changing the design of work.
- Effective designs illustrate a balance between perspectives. In some cases, there might be a need to recognize sociotechnical-like principles in design. In other cases, designs might need to balance productive and social needs.
- The TQM history reveals that designs can be streamlined if they are more directly connected to customer requirements.
- All of these perspectives highlight that change is paramount and there is a need for continual adaptation, renewal and continuous improvement.

CO 3: EMERGING PERSPECTIVES ON JOB AND ORGANIZATIONAL DESIGN

The above job enrichment models left centre stage, in part because the nature of work changed. The decreased influence of these models partially illustrates the movement from the manufacturing economy where we produced tangible products in assembly-line type operations. In some cases, technology has reduced the need for assembly-line operations. Beyond this, there has been a global shift from a manufacturing economy to a knowledge and service economy. Organizational success increasingly emphasizes customers and clients. A large sector of our Western economies is in the service industries, including government and not-for profit organizations providing health, education, leisure, transportation and utilities. There are also for-profit organizations providing financial, professional and business, retail, hospitality and recreational services. The service sector also includes not-for-profits and First Nations organizations. In the United States, the service sector makes up over 60 per cent of the GDP and a growing share in India (40–49%) and China (30–39%). In Canada and the United Kingdom, the service sector employs nearly 75 per cent of the population and accounts for more than 70 per cent of the GDP.

The concept of 'job' is in flux, and though some people might have a defined job, there are changes in the relationships people have on the job, as some people telecommute rather than come to the office, while being responsible for several responsibilities beyond the job. Some are independent contractors working in different semi-permanent relationships, on project teams, with no single boss.[59]

Although the concept of the job is in flux, the issues that drove practitioners and researchers have not been. Worker dissatisfaction and motivation, absenteeism, presenteeism, turnover and shoddy work performance remain central issues in organizations. Although managers and other contextual factors play a part, the job design is still the main lever in developing high-performance organizations, much as it was when Trist, Herzberg and Deming began the discussions.

The changes in the new contexts of work, which are especially evident in public sector organizations, focus less on front-line workers and more on managers and professionals. In building on the JCM, researchers are recognizing that the knowledge characteristics of a job can affect its complexity, information requirements, ability to solve or address problems and need to work with other specialities. The Elaborated JCM summarizes several task characteristics, including autonomy, decision-making autonomy, work methods autonomy, task variety, task significance, task identity and feedback from the job. Knowledge characteristics include job complexity, information processing, problem-solving, skill variety and specialization, whereas social characteristics include social support, interdependence, interaction outside the organization and feedback from others. The model also summarizes the work context: ergonomics, physical demands, work conditions and equipment used. Their research points to the importance of the mental demands of the job as well as the social context.[60]

The Relational and Proactive Perspective

Despite the progress over the last 50 years in improving our models of job design, researchers are recognizing that the core characteristics of job go much beyond those described in the JCM or other models. In providing a broader perspective on work design, Grant and Parker's work points to the greater interdependence and uncertainty that organizations are facing. The interdependence of organizations reflects the fact that work roles are part of a much broader social system, and uncertainty describes the lack of predictability of the inputs, processes and outputs that are altered because of new ideas and customer needs. These two features point to the need for designing work to build on the (i) importance of relationships and (ii) to encourage people to be proactive when there are no set ways to respond. A relational perspective on work design recognizes the power of an organization's social system and builds on the Tavistock landmark studies in addition to elements of the JCM and other research highlighting the role of interpersonal relationships and social support. A proactive work design perspective gives more autonomy to employees rather than supervisors as many challenges and problems need to be addressed when they occur.[61]

Job design in teams: A relational perspective. In Hackman and Oldham's *Work Redesign*, they included two chapters on work design for teams, whereas the majority of the book and their research focused on enriching individual jobs. In applying the JCM to individual jobs, it is interesting to see how a job can be enriched by simply changing the design and asking people to work in groups, as most of the individual characteristics of the job will change, including the variety, feedback and autonomy.

Some of the evidence on team effectiveness has grown from the research on self-managed teams such as those proposed by Tavistock researchers.[62] Self-managed teams are recognized because they are correlated with high productivity, quality, better customer service and organizational commitment.[63] Self-managed teams have more freedom to set their work pace, conduct quality control and manage HR functions associated with recruiting and selecting team members and production functions related to scheduling work and fixing production or service problems. Such groups usually do not have a first-level supervisor, although the team might elect a person to fill this role.

Team concepts have also been used to improve the operation of non-self-managing teams such as temporary or long-standing committees, quality circles and project teams. In public organizations, the use of work or project teams has continued to grow in situations where complex tasks require the use of different specialities and the input of people with other talents.[64]

Teams are of various types and, in some cases, responsibility and authority rest within the groups, but in other cases, individual members are responsible. Here are some different types:

- *Surgical teams:* This type of team has a lead member and others there to assist.
- *Co-acting teams:* Individual members work independently and have responsibility. They are often formed to encourage teamwork, but there are times when there is little co-ordination.
- *Face-to-face teams:* Teams work together to supply a service, solve a problem or develop a product. Most of the 'team' research is on these types of teams.
- *Distributed teams:* These are sometimes called virtual teams.
- *Special teams:* Examples of special teams include leadership teams and a sand dune team. A leadership team includes a team of individuals who share responsibility for the organization. A sand dune team has a fluid rather than a fixed membership, and the size and composition varies just as sand dunes do.[65]

The type of team will affect the way it is designed. However, in developing a general notion of team design, Kirkman and Rosen use the term *empowered teams* to illustrate five dimensions which different teams might need to address: sense of potency, team meaningfulness, autonomy, impact or significance and goal clarity.[66]

i. *Sense of potency* – People believe that the 'team' can be effective.[67] Potency is similar to individual level competency or self-efficacy at the team level. Potency relates to team performance, whereas self-efficacy relates to individual performance.
   a. Positive experience. *I really felt we could win.*
   b. Not so positive experience. *No matter how we changed our tactics, it seemed like it was an impossible task.*
ii. *Team meaningfulness* – The team perceives its work as worthwhile, important and valuable, and that team members' experiences are meaningful to others.[68]
   a. Positive experience: *We really have a passion for what we are doing. People who work here are committed and want to make the world a better place.*
   b. Not so positive experience: *It's a job and the work we do might be important to someone in the organization, but in the scheme of life, what we do won't be missed if we quit tomorrow.*
iii. *Team autonomy* – The team experiences freedom and independence in making decisions that affect them. Decisions are made and executed by the team.
   a. Positive experience: *We know what we are doing and can make our own decisions.*
   b. Not so positive experience: *We get told what to do and can't question it.*
iv. *Impact or significance* – The team feels that they are accountable for some work outcomes and that their initiatives or efforts are important for achieving this.
   a. Positive experience: *We know that what we do has an impact on the organization's future.*
   b. Not so positive experience: *What we do is trivial and unimportant to anyone.*
v. *Goal clarity* – The team is clear on its goals and vision of success.
   a. Positive experience: *No matter what changes, we are always clear on what is important to do to be successful in our team.*
   b. Not so positive experience: *We didn't know what we were doing from one day to another. It was like playing a soccer game and not knowing where the goal posts were.*

Building on the JCM in the previous section, this team empowerment model suggests that motivational and performance problems emerge if teams experience little potency, meaning responsibility for work outcomes, information about their work and goal clarity. Enriched jobs for teams are similar to those for individuals and can be implemented by encouraging practices which allow the team to schedule or set its own work pace, clarify goals or change its way of organizing. For example, the team can be given wider responsibility for a number of its own managerial processes or for certain stages of production. The following design characteristics might enhance team empowerment:[69]

- *Delegating managerial and supervisorial responsibilities:* Teams might be given responsibility for certain managerial goals as well as specific tasks. In implementing this design factor, a first step is to train team members so they can perform the specific managerial tasks related to the strategies and priorities of the organization. Delegation means that they have the responsibility to participate and provide the logic and evidence for making organizational improvement in specific areas.
- *Delegating responsibilities for controlling the quality of production and service:* Effectively functioning teams often set their own production schedules, develop and train for quality improvement practices and take responsibility for specific projects or parts of the work process. This design factor suggests that teams be given responsibility to control the quality of products or services. Team members can also initiate actions to improve relationships with customers and clients. In implementing this design factor, it might be appropriate to set up structures which will gradually give teams more responsibility for managerial tasks such as streamlining the service, improving customer relationships and work scheduling.
- *Developing team-based HR policies:* Team HR policies relate to cross training, so team members can assist others; team rewards; and team input in recruiting and selecting team members. Cross training increases team flexibility, allowing team members to work in other jobs. Team-based rewards and incentives can also be a positive influence on the team, especially if team members see some value in the reward and if the reward is given in an objective and fair way. Rewards might be administrated by an impartial manager such as an employee-union committee.
- *Developing a team-based social structure:* Teams exist in a social structure where they will develop their own informal rules and procedures and norms for operating. Kurt Lewin's classical studies on changing of food habits and work production illustrate that it may be easier to change individuals who are part of a group.[70] The very fact that people work in a team encourages them to relate to others, give and receive feedback and take on a greater variety of responsibilities, ranging from doing the tasks to assuring their quality.

There are many frameworks for improving team effectiveness, most of which are based on anecdotal data. The key asset of Kirkman and Rosen's framework for empowered teams is that it illustrates five dimensions – sense of potency, team meaningfulness, autonomy, impact or significance, and goal clarity – which are generally supported by research on team effectiveness.

MANAGERIAL IMPLICATIONS: The design of work systems is considered to be the main lever in developing organization-wide high-performance systems, although we are encouraged to recognize that work today has changed and is more complex and relational. This calls for rethinking our concepts of design to emphasize relationships and the complex environments people are working in. When designing more interesting and productive jobs in the public sector, it is imperative that we do not lose sight of the fact that in most countries, work design is a result of a collaborative process between management and those responsible for collective bargaining. What appears to be a simple change, such as number of hours worked per day, requires not only a collaborative process but one that adapts the ideas of those involved in carrying out the work.

BEFORE APPLYING, LET'S REVIEW

CO 1: Apply Herzberg's job enrichment and the job characteristics model (JCM) in a public sector context.

Job enrichment approaches focus on changing the job's characteristics to provide an environment that is motivational. Job enrichment involves vertically loading a job, whereas job enlargement involves giving the job a variety of tasks at the same level. Herzberg's framework separates hygiene factors that will only reduce dissatisfaction from those that will attain a level of no dissatisfaction. Motivation results from designing an environment that captivates people. The power of the JCM is in linking job characteristics to what internally motivates people, taking into account that different individuals might have unique motivational needs.

CO 2: Apply the principles of QWL and TQM to public sector organizations.

QWL and TQM have unique origins, but both focus on changing the whole organizational system. Both approaches recognize the environment as important in organizational design, and both recognize the importance of working in groups, either semi-autonomous work groups or quality circles. The QWL perspective grew from sociotechnical researchers who were seeking to improve working conditions in coal mines and other industrial organizations, and TQM evolved from the efforts by Deming and others to improve productivity in post-war Japan. The lasting insight is in encouraging engineering and other designers to focus the design on customer requirements.

CO 3: Devise new ideas on enriching public sector jobs.

There are many changes in the way work is organized as technology has reduced the need for assembly-line operations in what has become known as a knowledge and service economy. These changes are most evident in public sector organizations and in the growth in the number of managerial, administrative and professional staff who have direct relationships with different stakeholders or publics. Tasks in government cannot be easily broken down in simpler specialized operations. Rather, they require connections between stakeholders in a much broader social system. Some of the new perspectives on job design build on the JCM and provide a wider set of characteristics in recognizing the changing context of work. These designs recognize the knowledge characteristics of jobs that have more complexity, information requirements, types of problems that are difficult to solve, ability to solve problems and need to work with other specialities. Many of these jobs have a relational component to them which could be implemented by working in teams.

DISCUSSION AND REVIEW QUESTIONS

1. The scientific management movement was criticized because it focused only on efficiently designing jobs that were highly specialized and required minimal skill requirements. The sociotechnical perspective suggests that designs that are effective in the long term respond to the social requirements in meeting individual needs as well as technical requirements for using technology appropriately. Think of two or three jobs you are familiar with, such as police officer or firefighter, and define technical requirements and social requirements of the job. How does the use of semi-autonomous teams help respond to both sets of requirements?
2. In illustrating Herzberg's motivation-hygiene theory, you are asked to focus on your experiences in relation to public sector organizations. Describe a situation that illustrates a critical incident when

you felt very dissatisfied (when you experienced a negative emotive state) in a job or a student experience, and one where you felt very satisfied when you experienced a positive emotive state. Try classifying your responses using the factors that Herzberg identified. Do the things that dissatisfied you correspond to Herzberg's dissatisfiers and do the things you found motivational relate to Herzberg's motivators? What are the differences between public and private sector organizations?
3. Outline the implementation process for enriching a job and improving QWL that you would use in a public sector union environment.
4. Use the strategy map outline in Figure 4.3 and use it for defining objectives and measures related to the theme of improving QWL and productivity in a public sector organization. Some of your customer or client objectives might focus on 'improving work–life balance and internal motivation (engagement)'. In the SHRM BSC, assume your internal client is one of the managers in a non-profit focusing on reducing homelessness. She is seeking to respond to external clients or customers (e.g. funders, local politicians, street people). How can you, in HR, help your internal clients? In forming objectives, recognize basic questions that are important to the implementation of a strategic theme:
  - How does the manager see us and how can we help him or her? How can we identify objectives to improve our ability to respond to the manager's needs which would add value? What are our measures of success? (Client or Customer perspective)

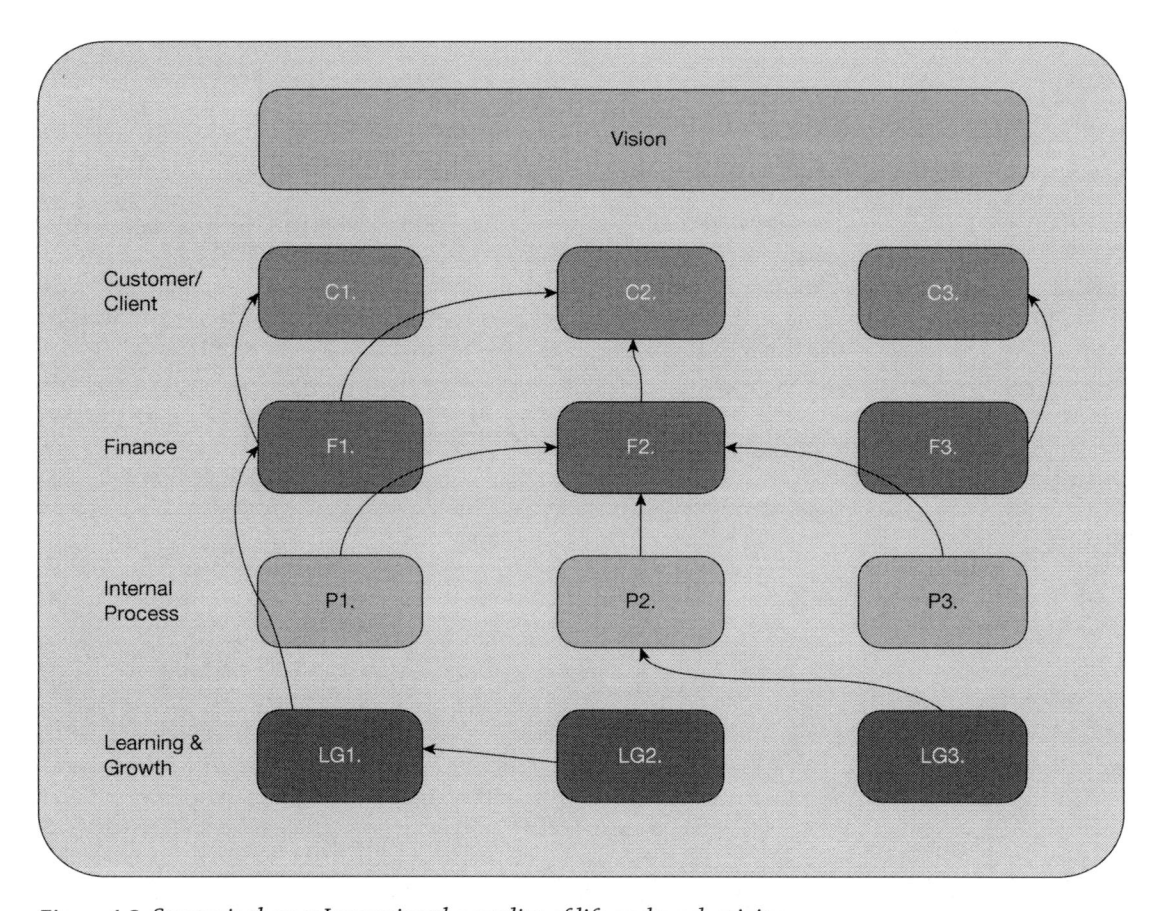

Figure 4.3 Strategic theme: Improving the quality of life and productivity.

- How do we look to shareholders or external funders, politicians and other stakeholders? How can we identify objectives to improve motivation and engagement, possibly by being more financially accountable? What are our measures of success? (Financial perspective)
- What must we excel at? How can we identify objectives to be more efficient in carrying out our work? What are out measures of success? (Internal process perspective)
- Can we continue to improve and create value? How can we identify objectives to improve motivation and engagement, possibly by changing the job's design? What are our measures of success? (Innovation and Learning perspective or Learning and Growth)

In reviewing the chapter for this task, you might define objectives such as improve engagement and internal motivation of staff and you might measure this through an assessment of PSM. Your productivity measures could be based on perceptions of service delivery and impact, in addition to objective measures of contact with client relations.

Based on these or other customer objectives, define objectives and measures within each of the perspectives of the strategy map.

CASE: DANIEL BOONE AT THE PENSIONS SERVICES DEPARTMENT

Over the last few years, the Pensions Service Department in the provincial government has become an increasingly difficult place to work, and managers complain of low productivity, abuse of sick leave privileges and low morale. Employees complain of stress and boredom, and are often frustrated by the demands of the job.

The department has 15 employees, nine women and six men, ranging in age from 45 to 59, and the most junior employee has just over nine years of service. Average sick leave in the department is 19.5 days per employee per year, compared to an average of nine days elsewhere in government. The number of grievances is very high, and the department has become a focal point for both union and management unrest and discord.

Over the last six years, the department has seen seven managers come and go, each one unable to change either the environment or the problems that seem to persist. Four of the managers who left cited low morale and employee unwillingness to change as the chief reason for their respective departures.

The physical layout of the office is confusing and chaotic, with desks everywhere and no clear or standard design apparent. The aisles are cluttered, file cabinets are scattered throughout, and a general sense of depression seems to fill the air.

Each employee has a specific set of assigned responsibilities and performs the same routine tasks over and over (e.g. one employee is responsible for the processing of all travel vouchers). The main function of two of the employees is auditing the work of their colleagues. There are three customer relations officers who respond to customers on the phone or in person and receive requests and applications, respond to complaints and deal with general customer questions.

Then, there are eight case managers, and each person usually engages five or so files each day. The job of the case worker consists of four of the five steps of the process: picking up the file, checking it for completeness, calculating years of service and salary, calculating the best five years and determining pension eligibility at various years of service.

Another four employees (case auditors) must check the file and complete similar steps. The file is then returned to the customer relations officers so he or she can notify the customers and deal with their questions. However, there are more difficult cases, and case auditors often pick the easier files for review. Sometimes, customers simply want estimates of their pension and confirmation of dates when they are eligible for retirement. Disputes arise when a customer disagrees with a calculation and claims that there is a mistake in the file.

There are several steps in the pension application case management process, depending on the request. The process is simple and there are three basic jobs: customer relations officers, case managers and case auditors.

Timelines for case processing have gone from 22 days to 37 days over the last four years, and a recent external review of the department indicated that relative to its size, the department had the highest staffing levels in the sector.

Any attempts at changing work processes or duties has been strongly resisted and even subverted in past efforts to address productivity issues. The department is becoming desperate to find a solution.

Daniel Boone is really discouraged with his department's performance. He knows that his employees have a very boring job, and the way the technological process is set up leaves little latitude for what he has learned about vertically loading the job through job enrichment. Yet he is convinced that there must be some way to make it more interesting. 'At least, I want to find out ways to make their jobs more satisfying and improve their performance,' he thinks.

Daniel has already tried a couple of things to improve performance. First, he decided to post each employee's performance on a daily basis and to reward the individuals with the highest performance by giving them a 'rubber duck' award that they can display at their workstations. This didn't work because the groups got angry when they didn't win and others won.

Then, Daniel asked the HR department (and Robin and Sabina) to get involved.

Task. You are asked to respond to the memo below and apply the JCM to help enrich the work in the Pensions Service Department described in the case (see the book's website for additional material).

Memo:
To: Sabrina Gerrard, Human Resources Manager
From: Robin Sykes, Human Resources Director
Re: Pensions Division
Sabrina, the Pensions Division has asked for some help.

Could I get you to review the issues in the Division (see case) and and get back to me with a plan on redesigning and enriching the jobs in the division so that they are more intrinsically motivating and productive?

Could you prepare a short report to illustrate how you would go about enriching the three key jobs? I would appreciate it if you would incorporate Hackman and Oldham's job enrichment model in your analysis.

Thanks, Robin

5 Workforce Forecasting and Planning

Chapter Outline
- Chapter objectives (COs) 89
- A driving issue focusing managerial action: Responding to the changing age profile in workforce planning 89
- CO 1: Workforce planning in the public sector 91
- CO 2: Tools for forecasting demand and supply of skills 96
- CO 3: Using scenarios in public sector workforce planning 101
- Before applying, let's review 104
- Discussion and review questions 105
- Case: Understanding the future job market using scenario planning 106

CHAPTER OBJECTIVES (COs)

After reading this chapter you will be able to implement the following objectives:

CO 1: Explain the purpose of workforce planning and identifying initiatives for its implementation.

CO 2: Examine the usefulness of different quantitative and qualitative forecasting tools.

CO 3: Apply a scenario building exercise in forecasting the future job market.

A DRIVING ISSUE FOCUSING MANAGERIAL ACTION: RESPONDING TO THE CHANGING AGE PROFILE IN WORKFORCE PLANNING

The public sector workforce in most countries is significantly older than those in the private sector. In OECD countries, the public sector workforces are ageing at a much faster rate than the rest of society, the largest cohort tending to be around 40–49 years old, and an important component being in the 50–54 and 55–59 age band. This suggests that the proportion of younger workers is smaller.[1]

Worldwide, we will be witnessing a significant increase of the number of older people (aged 60 and over), from 841 million in 2013 to 2 billion in 2050. The number of older people is projected to exceed the number of children for the first time in 2047. Other noteworthy facts are that the age profile is getting older as there is a growing share of people aged 80 or over, and this older population is predominantly female (as females live longer than males). The proportion of older people (aged 60 and over) grew from 9.2 per cent in 1990 to 11.7 per cent in 2013, and is expected to grow to 21.1 per cent by 2050.[2]

The effects of the ageing population are most vivid in the developed countries, effects which are just now unfolding in the least developed part of the world. In the developed world, the proportion of older people (60 and over) grew from 12 per cent in 1950 to 23 per cent in 2013, and is expected to reach 32 per cent in 2050.[3] Projections are that by 2020, in some developed countries one of every four people will be 65 or older. The largest proportions were in Japan (26.2 per cent) and Germany (21.6 per cent), although France (15.9 per cent), the United Kingdom (19.8 per cent), the United States (16.6 per cent), Australia (16.8 per cent), New Zealand (15.6 per cent) and Canada (18.2 per cent)[4] had a significant proportion of the population in that age group.[5]

Although some of the challenges of the ageing population point to the increasing demands on the health care system and declining government revenue, a more general challenge is finding talented people to work in organizations.[6] As the Baby Boomers – those born between the mid-1940s (post WWII) and the mid-1960s – reach retirement age, economic growth will slow. This is partially because fewer workers will be available to fill future job needs because of demographic changes in the workforce, as the population group immediately following the 'baby boomers', the 'baby busters' or 'Generation X', is dramatically smaller.[7] There are barely enough people entering the labour force to replace the number of people who retire at the age of 65. However, pressures still exist even though legislation in developed countries has allowed employees to work beyond age 65.

The more general issue about the ageing workforce is that, as the age profile of the public sector changes, we need a better understanding of people who reflect these new organizational profiles. The changing age profile is putting new pressures on our views of work motivation, career and retirement.[8]

Historically, we have paid more attention to engaging and motivating workers at their earlier stages of employment and worked with the assumption that older workers would be retiring. Given the fact that many older workers don't want to retire and want to work beyond the traditional retirement age, we have to develop an understanding of their motivational needs. In better understanding their later career, there is some evidence that older workers are different in that they value flexibility and that their priorities shift from financial benefits to lifestyle benefits. If older workers have more concern for work–life balance and employment flexibility, this might require changes in the way we design our jobs. The challenge might partially be in designing work for the mix of people who reflect different age profiles.[9]

Given that older workers are representing a significant proportion of the present and future workforce, one of the immediate challenges will be in adjusting to age-related stereotypes. Negative stereotypes are prevalent in recruiting and retaining older workers and in how younger workers perceive older workers. In addition, these stereotypes can affect the views and expectations that older workers have of themselves in terms of their intentions to stay with an organization and the roles they should take on. Common stereotypes are that they are poorer performers, less motivated, less willing to be trained, more resistant to change, less trusting, less healthy and more vulnerable to work–family imbalance. If we look at the evidence supporting these stereotypes, the only stereotype that has evidence underlying it is that older workers are more resistant to participating in training and career development activities. Although older workers want to work and are motivated to do so,[10] these stereotypes are likely to affect the recruitment and retention of older workers. Stereotypes often emerge from lack of understanding and contact with older workers and are difficult to dispel. Strategies include designing equity programmes, consciousness raising, multi-generational teams and more open discussions of the issue.[11] This suggests that the older public workforce is a new norm, and we need to align our public policies to reflect this.[12]

> STRATEGIC CONTEXT: *In the two previous chapters, we illustrated how competencies can be used to define the knowledge, skills, abilities and other characteristics (KSAOs) which are important for achieving strategic objectives. We also highlight the prominence of public sector motivation as a key characteristic that is important in a productive and engaged public sector workforce.*
>
> *This chapter reviews the workforce planning process in helping practitioners and students understand the trends affecting the demand and supply of workers in specific areas. The purpose of a workforce plan is to help align an organization's human capital with its strategic needs. The most basic workforce plan captures data about what jobs and competencies will be needed in the organization and the forces affecting whether they are available in the market. If we can do this, we should be able to develop sound strategies for recruiting and training and helping employees manage their careers. In the same sense, if practitioners and students understand these forces, they will better understand how to hone their competencies in responding to changes that might occur. The overall objective of the chapter is to help practitioners and students understand the job market they will face in the next five years given possible changes in the economic and social environment. Specifically, the chapter encourages you to develop objectives and initiatives to respond to different scenarios that might occur in the next five years. The scenarios will help in understanding the effects of changes such as the ageing workforce, in addition to other changes that are on the horizon.*
>
> *The workforce planning process provides a context for implementing strategic themes related to recruitment and selection in the next chapters. Based on the workforce plan, it is possible to define recruiting objectives targeted to attracting talented staff, reducing staff numbers or developing current staff. Given the difficulties of predicting, this chapter illustrates the advantages of a scenario planning process and applies it to forecasting the scenarios that students might face in their future job search.*

CO 1: WORKFORCE PLANNING IN THE PUBLIC SECTOR

The most critical issues affecting government workforces over the next few years are the ageing workforce, retirements in key managerial positions and finding ways to optimize the use of human resources.[13] Traditionally, most governments filled their management ranks from within, based on a public sector model that revolved around a centralized personnel agency which oversaw standardized employment practices relating to recruitment, promotion and tenure, based on merit. The central agency regulated the internal labour market where employees were centrally recruited and selected at a base grade level and promoted as they met certain qualifications during their careers.

Although **workforce planning (WFP)** has been a key part of the strategic human resource literature for several decades, it is only in the last 10 years that it has gained widespread acceptance.[14] The new HR model assumed that HR managers could perform a strategic role in planning and developing systems while the operational responsibilities were devolved to empowered local agencies. The ideal system would have a centralized database to meet the common workforce planning needs of the agencies. However, governments have faced several implementation problems, including the costs and time to construct reliable databases and the low level of attention of agencies to workforce planning because of other short-term priorities.[15]

Workforce planning seeks to forecast or predict future organizational and environmental demands affecting human resources and align an organization's human resources with the mission and strategic objectives of its strategic plan. Given the envisioned future, workforce planning seeks to ensure that the 'right people with the right skills are in the right place at the right time to help their organizations perform'.[16] When it is done well, HR has a greater strategic awareness of its staffing needs and whether it can effectively carry out its envisioned plans. The strategic emphasis involves aligning the workforce plan with the organization's strategic plan, targeting areas of the workforce that have the greatest impact and adjusting decisions on recruitment, training and career development.

Models of workforce planning include similar elements: supply analysis, demand analysis, gap analysis and solutions analysis. Building on the organization's strategic themes, the supply analysis identifies competencies in the current workforce, staff demographics and trends in the macro and internal environment. The demand analysis is a projection of future workforce activities and workloads and the competencies that will be needed. The gap analysis compares the supply and demand and identifies the gap between now and the future, and the solutions analysis defines initiatives for closing the gap in what exists and what is needed.[17] The underlying purpose is to achieve a balance between the organization's demand for people with certain competencies and the supply that can be developed in the organization or through recruitment. Based on the workforce plan, a human resources department can focus its recruitment, selection and training with the competencies required to meet future organizational objectives.[18] A workforce plan also needs to recognize the changing demographics, such as the ageing workforce and the shrinking pool of younger workers entering the workforce. It forecasts the macro environment and how the organization positions itself to respond.

Linking to the strategic context of attracting a competent workforce

The most basic workforce plan supports the SHRM BSC as it captures data about what jobs and competencies will be needed in the organization and the forces affecting whether they are available in the market. The planning is not an exact science, and it is even more challenging given the size and diversity of most public sectors. The link between education, competencies required for a job and the competencies that employees have is often tenuous, as the requirements of the job, in addition to an employee's competencies, are always changing. The analysis, illustrated in general terms in Table 5.1, starts with an estimate of the skills needed in various departments and organization wide. Then, it defines how much these skills are in demand today and in the future (in one to five years).

Once the gaps are identified for the current and future workforce, it is time to analyse and discuss what the organization plans to do about closing those gaps. This might mean hiring new talent, training the existing workforce, modifying the current job structure or changing the organization's recruitment strategy to meet the demands of the business. The model can tabulate the potential gaps based on retirements and turnover at a general level, and more refined calculations can identify the gaps within an occupation or skills area.

Table 5.1 A General Workforce Planning Model

Critical Skill		Supply	Demand	Gap	Strategy for Closing Gaps
	Now				
	1 yr				
	2 yr				
	5 yr				
	Now				
	1 yr				
	2 yr				
	5 yr				

A RELEVANT POINT OF VIEW: WORKFORCE PLANNING AT A NATIONAL LEVEL

Singapore real GDP grew by more than 22-fold while real per capita GDP expanded by more than 10-fold between 1960 and 1998. Singapore's success during this period was based on an efficient manufacturing sector where there was a skilled workforce and an infrastructure geared to support employers. As a result, Singapore became the head office for most multinational corporations in Asia and one of the largest shipping ports in the world.

During the latter 1990s, the 'writing was on the wall' that their monopoly of supplying cheap labour on the global market had stiff competition from larger Asian nations, particularly China and India. In May 1997, the Committee on Singapore's Competitiveness set out to propose appropriate strategies and policies, with a view to maintaining and strengthening Singapore's competitive position. They identified 'knowledge and skills' as key drivers of the global economic change in the early twenty-first century. The challenge was to turn the population at large into skilled, knowledgeable and competent workers for a knowledge-based economy.

In April 1999, Singapore's Ministry of Manpower developed a programme called the Manpower 21 Initiative. The vision was for Singapore to become a 'Talent Capital, a centre of ideas, innovation, and exchange'. It was to be the hub of continuous learning. Six strategies were part of this vision.

1. Improved workforce planning – to produce an enhanced information system to provide timely information about employee capabilities for policymakers, employers, training providers and individuals.
2. Implementation of the idea of 'Lifelong Learning for Lifelong Employability' – to support continuous learning and training of adult workers and enhance their lifelong employability. This involves a Skills Redevelopment Programme for enhancing employability and a National Skills Recognition System to develop skills standards and award recognition to persons acquiring training that meets the standards.
3. Augmentation of the talent pool – to implement an aggressive programme to recruit foreign talent.
4. Transforming the work environment – to improve the professionalism and image of domestic industries (e.g. the hotel industry) and improve worker attitudes. The goal is to upgrade the quality of workers and increase motivation through good HR practices.
5. Development of a vibrant manpower industry – to increase research and development to support a world-class workforce.
6. Redefining partnerships – to support labour-management initiatives, involving the Labour Management Partnership Programme.[19]

Common strategic themes in a workforce plan focus on attracting a diversified workforce, older or younger people or other groups who represent the community that the organization serves. Other examples of strategic themes could be improving productivity and delivery of services, providing better services for citizens or clients or improving employee health and wellness. Many workforce plans include initiatives to implement strategic objectives such as attracting staff during a time of labour shortage, reducing staff during times of restraint or developing staff for long-term careers in the organization.

Assuming a general strategic objective of augmenting the talent pool, such as Singapore identified several years ago in their national planning, a next step is to assess initiatives that would be used for implementation. These might include initiatives to attract new staff, to cut costs by reducing the number of staff in certain areas or to increase the competence of staff through training and development.

Workforce initiatives to attract talented staff. Several recruiting initiatives can assist in meeting the objective of attracting staff, such as targeting hard-to-get employees, developing programmes to attract people from the four designated groups and younger and older workers, and sourcing applicants from other countries or provinces. Short-term solutions might provide for overtime, hiring temporary workers or contracting out or outsourcing certain work responsibilities.

Workforce initiatives to reduce staff. Sometimes workforce objectives call for restraint or restructuring because of changes in the economy or reprioritization of the organization's strategic direction. There are several initiatives that managers use to cut costs and reduce staff, such as a **hiring freeze** that restricts hiring except for critical skill areas or occupations. The logic is that costs can be reduced through **attrition**, as the normal separation of people leaving through resignation, retirement and mortality can reduce the size of a workforce from 5 per cent to 10 per cent a year on average. Reducing staff through attrition has less traumatic effects on the workforce, although employers often have no control over the people who leave. And valuable employees are often the ones who are more likely to leave, as they are the ones that are most mobile.

Early retirement programmes. These can involve another set of initiatives to reduce staff and costs. In such programmes, employers offer incentives for people to leave by allowing them to retire earlier on full pension, in addition to receiving lump sum payments equal to some number of months' payment and a benefits package. For example, staff that are scheduled to retire at 55 might be encouraged to retire at 53 and still receive full pension and benefits. Although the advantages of such programmes are reducing the salary costs of many employees who are at the top of their wage scale, the programmes cost a great deal of money, and senior employees who leave are also the ones who have valuable experience, or 'institutional memory'.

Other initiatives for reducing costs include job sharing, part-time work, reduced workweeks, and work sharing. **Job sharing** involves taking the duties of one person and dividing them between two or more employees. For example, a schoolteacher's job might be shared between two teachers, with each teacher receiving half the salary. Although employers appreciate the energy and enthusiasm of having two people work one job, they often still have to pay benefit costs (dental, disability insurance, etc.) for two employees. Encouraging more *part-time workers* or *shorter hours* allows employers to hire workers for specific times or functions, such as when employers need more restaurant staff at peak hours. From the employee's standpoint, working part-time involves more discretionary free time; it also involves less pay. *Work sharing* is an initiative that avoids lay-offs, as employees work a three- or four-day week and receive employment insurance for the non-work days. The *reduced workweek* is similar to work sharing, without the employment insurance benefits, where employees work fewer hours per week for less pay.

Lay-offs and **terminations** are probably the most traumatic initiatives for reducing staff and costs. The word 'lay-off' can be seen as a temporary job loss, whereas a *termination* is thought of as being 'terminated without cause' or 'fired' because of poor performance or a disciplinary action. Some organizations use the terms *lay-off* or *permanent lay-off* when employees are displaced because of downturns in the economy or business or because of a change in the strategic direction. The lay-off usually involves identifying the people to be laid off on the basis of some criteria (such as seniority, performance or job type), consulting with employee representatives such as unions or professional associations and agreeing to the conditions of the lay-off. This can involve a severance package and agreement to pay for *outplacement assistance* to assist employees in finding employment elsewhere. Some lay-off initiatives are discussed in the chapter on labour relations.

Workforce initiatives to develop staff. Although external recruitment can provide new employees, internal staff development can reduce the need for relying on recruitment to fill vacancies as well as giving existing employees opportunities to be promoted. The initiatives for developing staff can be thought of within the general recruitment philosophy of internally developing employees for higher-level positions within the organization. The logic is that we can be much more effective in developing specialized training programmes to develop top-level managers and professionals who perform critical jobs than we could be if we tried to recruit people externally. Initiatives linked to internal career development include developing competency inventories to identify the skills and interests of employees; developing core and specialized competencies to guide employee development and training; and developing training programmes and job rotation experiences to help employees enhance their competencies.

Performance metrics in charting progress in workforce planning

Charting the progress of WFP has the challenge of balancing the need to implement initiatives (such as staff reduction) with the need to maintain the trust and open communication with employees and the union. In smaller local jurisdictions, like local governments, workforce planning has to illustrate visible benefits to justify its expenditures as well as gaining the confidence of employees. During the initial stages of implementation, managers might focus on staff development, addressing its staffing gaps or attracting people in the most difficult-to-hire positions. Tactics which have been helpful in encouraging the successful adoption of WFPs include initiatives for creating a larger pool of applicants, involving line management and developing training which links to employees' career paths.[20]

Measures of the progress of WFP might reflect activities necessary for success, as well as outcomes. Outcome measures might relate to the ability to fill talents and improvement in the delivery of services. In guiding the process, the RAND National Defense Research Institute suggests that WFP activities should seek to achieve the following goals:

- Determine the workforce characteristics needed to accomplish the organization's strategic intent and what is the desired distribution of characteristics.
- Determine the distribution of the current workforce and those needed in the future.
- Ascertain the future distribution given the current policies and programmes.
- Confirm HRM policies, practices and resource decisions which will eliminate the gaps.[21]

Useful outcome markers of progress include those used by the US Army, where they provided answers to questions like 'When do people retire?' 'What happens to retirements as the number of retirements eligible increase?' 'What do the retirement bubbles look like?' 'What are the key relationships between gains and losses needed to maintain workforce continuity?' and 'Have loss rates changed over time?'[22]

> **QUIZ 5.1 – HOW DO DIFFERENT GROUPS COMPARE TO GENERATION Y WORKERS?**
>
> The younger generation of employees now entering the job market is sometimes called Generation Y. Generation Y employees are those people born in the 1980s and are also known as millennials, echo boomers, and by other buzz terms. One older hospital supervisor lamented, 'They're self-absorbed and don't really care about their professional responsibility. We have to pay older nurses overtime because the younger nurses won't work night shifts on weekends.'

> Disparaging remarks about 'Yers' say that they were raised and coddled by baby boomer parents. They're fickle, spoiled, impatient and expect a lot. They're savvy about new technologies, much more than other workers, and can't live without cell phones, text messaging and online communications.
>
> Here are some sample statements that might be used to describe the Generation Y employee. Rate your perception of what Baby Boomers, Generation Xers[23] and Generation Yers are like on the following items on a 1 (strongly disagree) to 5 (strongly agree) scale.
>
> **Boomers   Xers   Yers**
>
> - _____ _____ _____ They are not engaged at work, and will probably job-hop a lot.
> - _____ _____ _____ They demand instant feedback, even when applying for a job.
> - _____ _____ _____ They are more techno-savvy than the older generation.[24]
> - _____ _____ _____ They multitask more than other workers.
> - _____ _____ _____ They are more obsessed with work–life balance.
> - _____ _____ _____ They are more self-absorbed.
> - _____ _____ _____ They are more collegial.[25]

CO 2: TOOLS FOR FORECASTING DEMAND AND SUPPLY OF SKILLS

Work planning models help us understand the future workforce pressures and make projections of the pressures on the workforce supply and future workforce demand. The models also permit managers and students to respond to various 'what if' questions.[26] That is, the manager might ask a question such as 'What would happen if retirements decreased because people feared that their pensions would be inadequate?' 'What would happen if the supply of workers was generally reduced because of competition from other organizations?'

Workforce planning tools illustrate the pressures within occupations impacting the supply and demand for skills. That is, market factors – such as higher than average growth in earnings, higher than average growth in employment or lower than average unemployment rate – summarize the demand and supply of workers in an occupation, or for the workforce in general. It is also possible to tabulate the annual rate of job growth and projected retirements.

Quantitative tools in forecasting. The quantitative forecasting tools in Table 5.2 provide useful answers to questions and project what might happen based on economic indicators. These techniques encourage decision-makers to base decisions on real information about what has happened previously in the organization or what might happen in the future.

These quantitative forecasting tools can be used to define an **external supply of candidates**, or the shortage or abundance of people with different skills as a reflection of the labour market. One source of data for some organizations includes the market indicators on employment vacancy, unemployment and wage growth. A *vacancy rate* is the ratio of vacancies in comparison with the percentage of all job openings (both filled and unfilled). A rising vacancy rate indicates that employers are having difficulty filling vacancies. Some employers track labour shortages by looking at the *unemployment rate*, which decreases as the pool of workers is employed. Another indicator of labour supply is **wage growth** as an upward trend in the average hourly rate as a possible indicator that the demand for labour exceeds the supply. The approaches provide a rough indication of labour supply based on past trends, but they might not provide projections for future demands as they are not sensitive to atypical occupations with higher than average turnover or frictional unemployment such as what exists in the Parks services during the winter.

Table 5.2 Quantitative Forecasting Techniques

Quantitative Techniques	Example
Trend analysis is a review of past workforce needs over a period of years to predict future needs.	A manager computes the number of employees in various positions (like management, administration and secretarial) to identify trends in the workforce during certain years or times in the year.
A **scatter plot** graphically shows the relationship between two variables (such as sales and staffing levels or number of beds and nurses required) over a period of time.	A hospital of 400 beds expects to expand to 1,000 beds in the next three years. In forecasting the number of registered nurses required for the increased number of patients, the human resource director contacts other hospitals in similar-sized regions to gather information about the number of registered nurses. This information is plotted in a graph with the number of nurses on one axis and number of beds on the other. If the points are related, then it should be easy to see that the number of nurses goes up in relation to the number of beds. It is possible to draw a line so that there is a minimum distance between the line and each plotted point.
Ratio analysis is a tool for making forecasts based on the historical ratio between causal factors (such as sales or demand for services) and the number of employees required.	An organization predicts the workforce needed by calculating historical ratios involving workforce size (such as comparing the ratio of citizens in the community to employees) and using the ratio to predict the future demand. An emergency room in a hospital defines staffing needs on the basis of demands for service and waiting time. A ratio analysis also can be linked to productivity measures. The number would be used to project the number or employees required for various services.
Simulation models are models of an actual or theoretical labour market within or outside the organization.	An organization designs a model of the internal labour market based on the existing demographics. Then managers ask 'what if': questions. For example, what if our ability to recruit in certain areas declined significantly? What if a significant number of employees decided to retire in the next two years?

Another source of information on labour supply can be obtained from employer-based surveys such as those carried out by governments or professional associations. Employer-based surveys provide information which comes directly from employers and reflects more current issues and trends, rather than those which might have been tabulated by market indicators.

A case illustrating the uncertainties of workforce planning

Forecasting demand is more difficult than supply because there are more uncertainties, such as in the domestic and global economic markets and the desire of people to work in certain areas. Other uncertainties exist in changes in technology; the vibrancy of local, national and international economies; or changes in government regulations. For example, new government regulations or taxes might open up new markets.

In 2008, a sudden and unexpected change in the economy drastically changed the demand for labour throughout the world. The subprime mortgage crisis that occurred was linked to US government policies and competitive pressures several years prior to the crisis. In the early 2000s, policies encouraged consumers to assume more loans and mortgages at low interest rates. However, as interest rates began to climb, borrowers were unable to find lenders to refinance with, and real estate prices dropped as a result of homes being put on the market or being foreclosed by lenders. Further, in July 2008, oil prices surged to £96 ($145) a barrel, but by November and December 2008, they had dropped to less than £33 ($50). The results of these economic factors caused widespread lay-offs.

In Ontario, Canada, for example, the projection for 2004–2009 was that most of the job creation would occur in the health care/social assistance (20.1%) and manufacturing (18.9%) sectors.[27] The projections indicated that certain occupational groups should grow in size. In the professional and technical occupations, there was a projected 24 per cent increase in jobs expected between 2004 and 2009.[28] These projections suggested that a range of workers would be needed, including engineers and information technology people to work in manufacturing organizations, in addition to other self-employed people (like lawyers and accountants) to assist. These jobs require college and university degrees, implying enrolments in these programmes would also need to increase.

These projections also revealed that manufacturing and processing would contribute about 10 per cent of new jobs, many of which would be entry-level jobs that do not require post-secondary degrees. Managers and health care workers were expected to account for over 9 per cent of new jobs, indicating that enrolments in these educational programmes will need to increase. Also, about 8 per cent of new jobs created would be in skilled trades in construction, manufacturing and the service sectors. The training of skilled trades workers combines college education and on-the-job training and experience. Some trades – like electricians, welders and plumbers – have apprenticeship programmes.

These projections were combined with projections of the replacement needs that are generated when workers retire, leaving job vacancies that must be filled. Given that baby boomers make up one-third of Ontario's population, there was projected to be an unusually large number of vacancies that need to be filled.

These projections did not predict the recession caused by the subprime mortgage crisis in the summer of 2008 that had major effects on the political environment of Canada and other countries. It resulted in major changes in the banking industry and turmoil in the political landscapes throughout the world, during which time Ontario lost 266,000 jobs. Although the economy has rebounded in recent years, job creation has not kept up with population growth. Long-term employment was the worst in the country in 2014, and there was a sharp rise in involuntary part-time employment. On average, each economic region has lost at least 18 per cent of the manufacturing jobs that existed 20 years earlier, and Ontario is no longer the manufacturing heartland of Canada. The economic crisis resulted in management demands for concessions in collective agreements in the auto sector in Ontario and the United States. General Motors and Chrysler promised to change their business model and emphasize more fuel-efficient cars in order to secure government financial assistance to avoid long-term bankruptcy. The federal government's 'Go Green' environmental goals were shelved in favour of goals related to creating employment. Forecasts of extreme labour shortages up until late 2008 had to be revised to reflect rising unemployment and surpluses in specific skill areas. And years of balancing the federal government budget gave way to deficit financing to generate jobs.

The clearest implication of the subprime crisis for HR was the shelving of the many forecasts of the looming labour shortages that existed before that time. In the years before the 2008 subprime crisis, we talked about a vibrant economy where it was hard to find a talented supply of employees and where those who could be found are more difficult to attract. In some regions in Canada, where there was a high demand for skilled trades and professional people, recruiters have had to be more creative. In Fort McMurray, for example, companies had to fly electricians and other trades people to the job site on a two-week-on and one-week-off schedule, while providing them with living quarters and meals. Incentives include overtime, paid travel, a higher hourly rate and away-from-home expenses. Fresh engineering graduates were given signing bonuses – in some cases as high as £39,539 ($60,000).

In late 2014 and early 2015, the world found itself in another crisis that was not clearly visible to most people before that time. An oil crisis saw oil prices drop from over £66 ($100) to a low of £30 ($45) a barrel because key countries (OPEC [Organization of the Petroleum Exporting Countries] and the United States) increased their production, and demand growth tailed off as the economies in China and Europe slowed. This was combined with the improved energy efficiencies in newer vehicles. Underlying the crisis was a scenario where US shale production increased as OPEC production grew, resulting in an oversupplied oil market.

The 2008 subprime crisis and the 2014 oil crisis seemed to catch the world by surprise. They illustrate the need to supplement quantitative forecasts and statistical projections with qualitative forecasting methods.

Qualitative forecasting

Given that there are often uncertainties in anticipating future demand for labour, qualitative tools such as those in Table 5.3 are available to supplement quantitative projections. Group techniques often use experts or participating groups in forecasting future events. Examples include scenario planning, the group consensus method, the nominal group technique and the Delphi method.

Scenario planning uses a set of contrasting scenarios to plan for the nature and impact of the driving forces affecting the future. Such techniques are used by public and private organizations to encourage managerial dialogue on current trends. The success of scenario planning is often linked to a case in 1973, when Royal Dutch Shell moved from one of the weakest of the seven large oil companies to second in size and number one in profitability at that time. During the planning, Royal Dutch Shell described scenarios of what might happen if there were depleting oil reserves and an oil crisis sparked by OPEC. The scenario helped managers think of things they would have to do if this scenario actually came true. In October 1973, the scenarios actually happened when the Yom Kippur war in the Middle East precipitated an oil price shock; of the major oil companies, Shell responded quickly and more effectively than other companies.

In its predictions in recent years, Shell developed two scenarios called 'Scramble' and 'Blue-prints'. In the Scramble scenario, planners suggest that there might be a mad dash by nations for the depleting energy resources, with policymakers paying little attention to energy consumption. It will be something of a 'zero-sum game' of competition for resources.

The Blue-prints scenario describes a world of political co-operation between governments, where there is agreement on efficiency standards and taxes. Policymakers will concentrate on developing emissions standards, and there will be pressure on local efforts to improve environmental performance in buildings.

The **group consensus method** pools the experience of managers or experts in making judgements. Normally, in applying this method, the group members list about 10–15 issues (in this instance, labour trends) they see as affecting the organization. They then seek to develop a consensus on the ranking of the importance of these trends and from there develop various strategies for responding to them. This method works well in encouraging vigorous debate in reviewing the issues and developing a consensus.

The **nominal group method** is a variant of the consensus method in that participants initially discuss the topic before they individually list the issues they each think are important. The general list of issues is developed from each individual listing before the total group begins a discussion. Members of the group then develop a consensus in the same way as they would in the group consensus method. The advantage of the nominal group is that it assures that each person individually identifies issues for discussion, whereas in the consensus method the initial list can result from one or two dominant personalities.

The **Delphi method** counters some of the potential problems of group methods where the opinions of one strong personality might sway the judgements of others. The Delphi group never meets together, and participants never know the opinions or logic used by other personalities. As a result, judgements are based on the logic of the argument presented rather than the persuasiveness of a personality. Input in a Delphi process consists of three or four questionnaires interspersed with a review of the logic about why people are forming their judgements.

A Delphi method for forecasting the issues that affect labour supply would start by asking each of the experts (possibly 7–15 people) to list issues and the logic for their list. The facilitator summarizes the list and the logic used, without revealing the individuals. In the second iteration, the experts are asked to rank the issues and provide their logic for their rankings. The information is again aggregated and returned to the experts for another anonymous ranking. The process continues through several rounds until experts agree on the issues and their importance.

All of these methods – scenarios, group consensus, nominal group and Delphi – encourage people to think 'outside of the box'. They are based on the assumption that past information cannot always help us manage in a very uncertain environment, and one of the best ways to do this is to tap intuition and thoughts of groups.

Forecasting includes summarizing data about the current workforce (such as headcount, turnover, competencies, age, retirement eligibility), projecting supply and demand over the next two to three years and reviewing the gap between supply and demand.

Table 5.3 Qualitative Forecasting Techniques

Qualitative Method	Example
Scenario planning uses a set of contrasting scenarios to create a dialogue about the nature and impact of the driving forces affecting the future.	Planners might use some worst- and best-case scenarios to assess the impact of demographic shifts in the number of workers entering the labour force. These scenarios could be refined to illustrate scenarios related to vibrant or slow economic growth and conflictive or non-conflictive relationships in society. The goal is to contrast the impact of a change (e.g. demographic changes or rising costs of oil) and view it from contrasting scenarios.
Group consensus is a method of decision-making that seeks to get agreement among participants by using the diversity of perspectives in coming up with insightful ideas or solutions.	In forecasting, when groups composed of people with different perspectives seek to solve a problem consensually, the opportunity exists for the diversity of perspectives to offer a perspective on the issues or chance to see problems in different ways. A group consensus method works well if the group seeks mutually agreeable solutions in responding to differences, rather than voting and compromising, to resolve mutually exclusive positions.
The **nominal group** combines individual generation of ideas with the group's consensual judgement of their implications.	In forecasting, a facilitator begins with a general introduction and discussion of the general problem of understanding the future issues affecting them. The participants in the group individually identify issues which they feel are important. The facilitator pools the issues from each member. Finally, members of the group seek to define a consensus on the most important issues affecting them.
The **Delphi Approach** is a series of questionnaires (three or more) to a panel of experts who are asked for anonymous comments or forecasts of future events. The group interaction in the Delphi is anonymous, as one of the goals of the approach is to guard against group biases or strong personalities when developing a consensus.	An organization wanting to forecast the impact of demographic changes on organizations asks experts to identify changes. Results are summarized and anonymously reported back to the experts, who are asked to assess and justify the likelihood of each change occurring. The process continues until there is a general consensus about which changes will occur.

Summarizing workforce data. A range of factors can affect the supply of skilled people, including technological changes requiring new skills sets, projected changes in budgets, projected turnover and intended retirements. Summarizing workforce data answers questions about how the workforce's composition is changing and is projected to change in the future. For example, workforce data can provide a profile of (i) the number of individuals performing different jobs; (ii) a breakdown of individuals by age, gender and other designated categories; and (iii) a summary of new hires, voluntary turnovers and retirements of employees by diversity groups, age and years of service. This information can be easily tabulated in a spreadsheet to answer questions such as 'What is the demographic profile of the organization? How many people are due to retire in the next five years? How will retirements affect people in different job classifications and skill levels? Which positions are more likely to be affected by retirement in the near future? What is the profile of people who are recently hired?'

A realistic way to project a public organization's future is to look at its internal supply of candidates, as many internal candidates can be groomed for higher-level positions. When employees are sought internally, the competency or skills inventory can be used to understand whether the competencies (KSAOs) are present within employees in the organization. It is also possible to develop succession plans or internal development programmes for grooming people from within, especially in senior and more critical jobs.

CO 3: USING SCENARIOS IN PUBLIC SECTOR WORKFORCE PLANNING

Workforce planning is difficult to do well given the even fundamental changes that are occurring in our society. The future might change because of an economic crisis, a conflict between countries, a political change or the invention of a new technology. The increasing frequency of such events is calling into question many of the mental maps and rational models we use to make sense of our world.

Scenario planning is based on the assumption that we are not trying to predict the future, but are outlining several possible stories of what the future might look like. A productive way to proceed is to develop alternative stories about the future while recognizing that there is more than one possible way that the future might unfold. Then, we can test our proposed plans or decisions against these alternative scenarios.[29]

Scenario planning became prominent in military planning and among futurists. For example, Herman Kahn became known for analysing the likelihood of nuclear war between the Soviet Union and the United States and for his recommendation on improving survivability. His major contributions were the strategies he developed during the Cold War to describe the unthinkable implications of a nuclear war. In 1967, Kahn and Wiener's book *The Year 2000: A Framework for Speculation on the Next Thirty-Three Years*[30] used scenarios for envisioning 'One Hundred Technical Innovations' that were likely to be developed during the last third of the twentieth century. The list included innovations such as multiple applications of lasers, super-performance fabrics and high-strength structural materials.

Scenarios can be used for different purposes such as detailing sequences of events that might occur in an economic or environment crisis or exploring situations that might lead to a more severe crisis. Other scenarios can be used to develop a picture of future development of the world and the skills that might be needed in different situations.[31] For example, the OECD used scenario planning in their 'Schooling for Tomorrow' programme to inform some of the challenges decision-makers face in education. They laid out six scenarios relating to four different perspectives:

- *The status quo* – bureaucratic school system continues scenario.
- *Diverse, dynamic schools or re-schooling after reform* – schools as focused learning organizations scenario and schools as core social centres scenario.

- *Alternatives to schools or de-schooling* – market model scenario and learning networks and network society scenario.
- *Disintegrate in a crisis* – system meltdown and teacher exodus.

Public health planners have defined different health care scenarios such as these: the present state of public health continuing as it is, a worst-case scenario of a health crisis and a best-case scenario where funding becomes available to deal with many of the world's public health issues. The scenarios allow participants to consider how the future will differ if funding priorities change and if new legislation is enacted.[32]

Scenario planning exercises usually define scenarios representing different points of view, best- and worst-case possibilities or different political or economic possibilities. In one scenario building workshop, two uncertainties – one economic and one social – provided the framework to pull together the various stories of how the future environment might be shaped.[33] The economic dimension describes the vibrancy of the economy. In a vibrant economic market, there is more money in the economy, and organizations are more willing to take risks, investing in new ideas and technology and opening more stores or offices. As a result, there are more jobs and more potential. However, at the polar end of this dimension is a no- or low-growth economy. Here, there are fewer jobs, reduced funding for programmes that are not doing well and businesses cutting back on less effective offices or stores cutting staff.

The second factor that affects our future is the degree of social consensus in society. In describing one polarity, we manage to find ways to construct a new social consensus and rebuild social cohesion, renewing the social contract in working with people who are less fortunate in society. At the other extreme, a lack of social consensus illustrates gaps in society between groups who have opposing ideas or abilities. Social fragmentation is continuing and accelerating. Although some groups of people live in nice homes, buy new cars and enjoy the increasingly prosperous world, there are also parts of society where there are shrinking opportunities and insecurity. There are gaps between 'haves' and 'have-nots' and a lack of social consensus.

In interrelating these two dimensions, the matrix in Figure 5.1 illustrates the possible workforce environments resulting from the interplay of different economic and social changes.

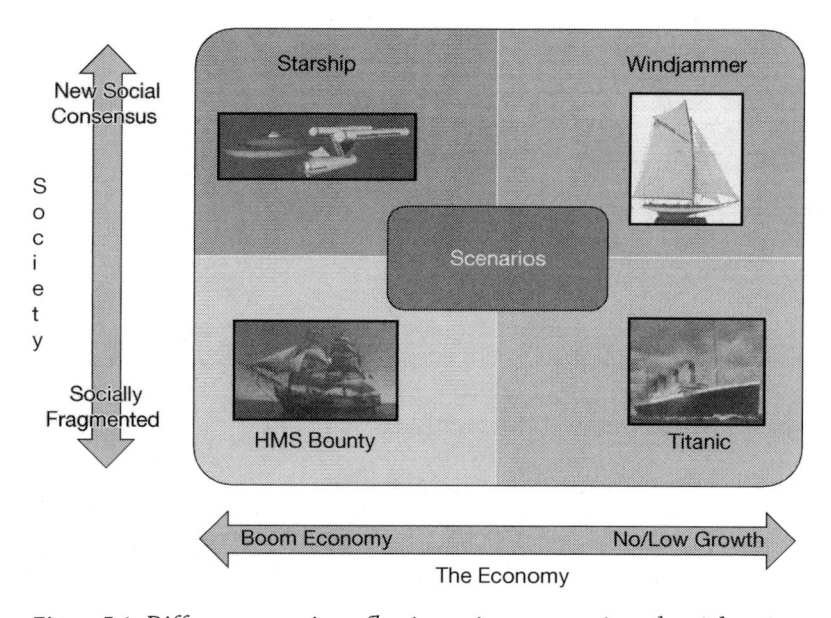

Figure 5.1 Different scenarios reflecting unique economic and social environments.

1. The *Starship* scenario envisions a world characterized by economic boom and the development of a positive social consensus. This is a metaphor of economic wealth and market-driven entrepreneurship in search of new opportunities. It is also a world of social tolerance, where people work and live in harmony. In this scenario, the public and private sectors work together to strengthen education and training, as they see it as essential for a healthy society.
2. The *Titanic* scenario is the other extreme, with low or no economic growth, coupled with social fragmentation. This is the sinking ship metaphor, where there are no high-paying jobs replacing those being lost, and institutions are responding defensively, cutting jobs and sending work offshore. There is social intolerance, alienation in work and society, and social anxiety. In this scenario, both public and private institutions are unable to cope with the demands placed upon them, and there is a lack of understanding that the economy has fundamentally changed to a knowledge economy. Governments and private organizations are waiting for a recovery to happen, but the economy does not produce enough high-paying jobs to replace those that have been lost. High unemployment persists, with little or no growth.
3. The *Bounty* scenario combines an economic boom and a fragmented, polarized and less positive social environment. The Bounty metaphor comes from the famous historical incident and the classic book and movie *Mutiny on the Bounty*. The mutineers in 1789, according to historical accounts, were attracted to the possibilities of an 'idyllic' life in Tahiti, motivated by Captain Bligh's harsh treatment of them. So, they set the captain off in a small boat with 22 crew members who were loyal to him. The scenario describes a booming economy with lots of jobs, but it is a society where all people are not participating equally, and there is polarization between the rich and the poor, or between those who have jobs and those who do not.
4. The *Windjammer* scenario envisions low or no economic growth and a new and positive social environment. The Windjammer metaphor relates to a type of sailboat that is very efficient in sailing windward. Although there is no economic growth, in this scenario, there is a collective will to work together through tough times and to respect the diversity of people.

A general issue in strategically managing a public service organization is to better understand the future social and economic environment of each of these scenarios. The assumption is that if we have a better understanding of this environment, we should be more capable of effectively responding. Practitioners and students have a similar issue in figuring out how to develop and focus their skills given the changing job market:

- Will the labour market exist in its current form in the next five years?
- What competencies will be in demand? What competencies are in good supply?
- How will critical events – economic issues such as a recession, terrorists' threats and other issues – affect the job market?
- Will the economy sustain the social safety nets that exist now?

Answers to questions like these are impossible to predict with certainty, but it is possible to identify different scenarios that illustrate what might happen and, as a result, gain a powerful understanding of the forces shaping our future. In the case of students, they can construct a picture of the different scenarios where they will need different types of skills.

The story within each scenario might respond to specific questions or detail key elements such as the labour market supply and demand, the competencies needed and critical events that might occur. Other key elements might describe the changing cultural or age demographics, gender balance, education or impact of unions.

It is also a useful exercise to define the likelihood of a certain scenario or combination of scenarios which might occur. Although the goal of a scenario exercise is to identify forces that we need to respond to rather than predict the future, the definition of a most likely scenario provokes discussion that is of value.

A key step in the scenario planning exercise is to identify strategies for responding. So, within each scenario, what are relevant strategic themes and objectives, initiatives that would implement the objectives, competencies and measures or markers of progress. Alternatively, it might be useful to test out the appropriateness of different strategic objectives and initiatives. That is, how successful would different strategic objectives and initiatives be within different scenarios?

> MANAGERIAL IMPLICATION: The workforce plan provides data about what jobs and competencies will be needed in an organization and the changes affecting whether they are available in the market. In developing the workforce plan, there are a variety of quantitative and qualitative tools to assist the planners.
>
> This chapter suggests that it is difficult to predict the impact of changes that might happen in the next five years. Given this difficulty, this chapter encourages you to develop objectives and initiatives to respond to different scenarios that might occur in the next five years. The scenarios will help in understanding the affects of changes such as the ageing workforce, in addition to other changes that are on the horizon.

BEFORE APPLYING, LET'S REVIEW

CO 1: Explain the purpose of workforce planning and identify initiatives for its implementation.

The workforce plan helps align an organization's human capital with its strategic needs. A workforce plan recognizes changing demographics, such as the impact of a shrinking pool of younger workers entering the workforce, in focusing its recruitment, selection and training within the competencies required to meet future organizational objectives. The workforce plan develops a number of workforce strategic themes, objectives and initiatives to meet the organization's priorities and environmental context. A strategic theme could cover an employment equity policy which defines the organization's commitment to equity in employment and workplace practices. The plan will identify initiatives (or programmes or activities) to implement strategic objectives such as attracting staff during a time of labour shortage, reducing staff during times of restraint or developing staff for long-term careers in the organization.

CO 2: Examine the usefulness of different quantitative and qualitative forecasting tools.

Trend analysis, scatter plots, ratio analysis and simulation models are some of the quantitative tools that can be used in forecasting. These can be combined with qualitative tools such as scenarios, group consensus, nominal group and Delphi that encourage people to think 'outside of the box'.

CO 3: Apply a scenario building exercise in forecasting the future job market.

Predicting the future is very difficult to do, particularly in the midst of fundamental changes in our society. In helping us understand our future, scenario planning is based on the assumption that we should not try to predict things that are generally unpredictable. Instead, a productive way to proceed is to develop alternative stories about the future while recognizing that there is more than one possible way that the future might unfold. Then, we can test our proposed plans or decisions against these alternative scenarios.

DISCUSSION AND REVIEW QUESTIONS

1. Using a search engine, type in the words 'population pyramid', and you will find programmes that illustrate how the age profile is changing. The website http://populationpyramid.net/world/2100/ gives a population pyramid of the world population growth, and http://www.footwork.com/pyramids.asp shows one for Canada.
2. Review the advantages of quantitative and qualitative approaches for forecasting the demand and supply of skills. What factors might occur which affect the accuracy of our forecasts?
3. In adding to the following strategy map, identify activities or initiatives and markers for each of the objectives in Figure 5.2 and Table 5.4.

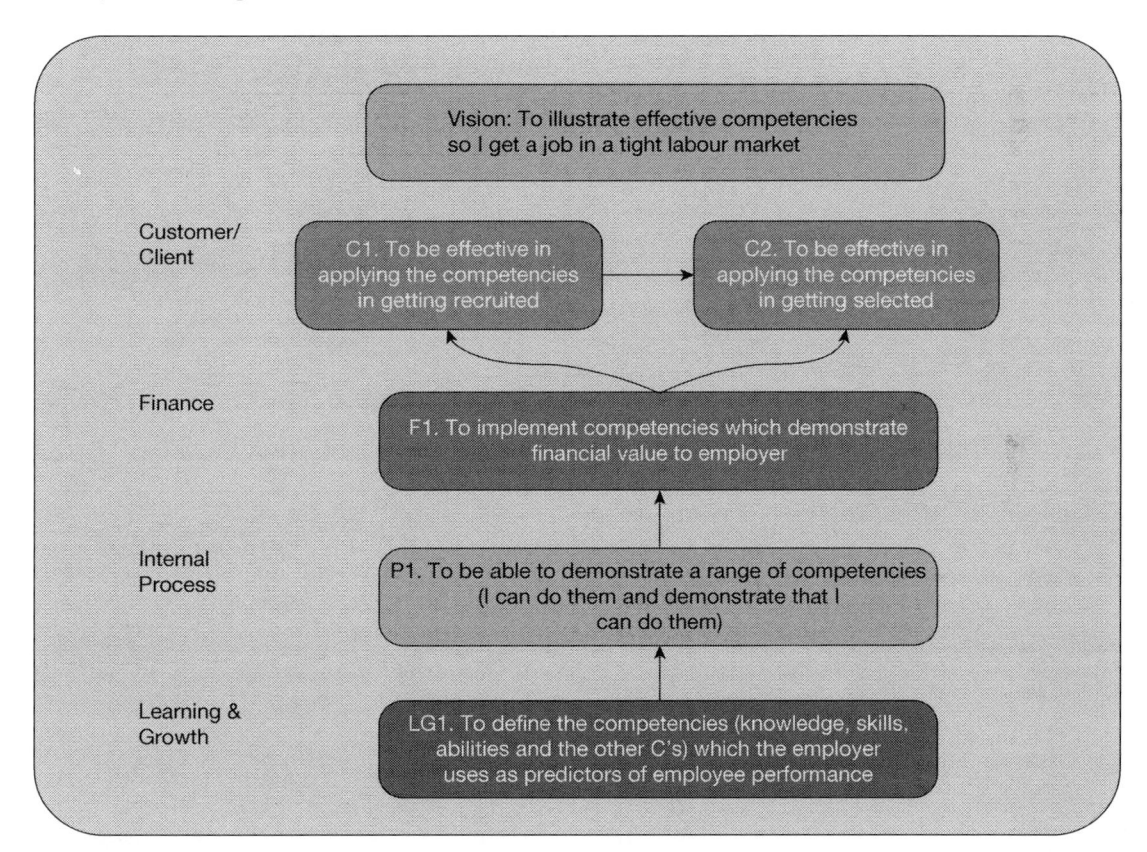

Figure 5.2 Strategy map for competencies in getting a good job.

Table 5.4 *Initiatives and Measures for Implementing Strategic Objectives*

Strategy: To get a job in…			
Objective	Activity or Initiative	Measures or Markers	Date
CUSTOMER OR CLIENT OBJECTIVES			
Objective 1:	1.		
	2.		
	3.		
	4.		
Objective 2: Be effective in applying the competencies in getting selected	1. Practise interviewing in simulated situations		
	2. Update CV		
	3.		
	4.		
FINANCIAL OBJECTIVES			
Objective 1.	1.		
	2.		
	3.		
BUSINESS PROCESS OBJECTIVES			
Objective 1: Demonstrate a competency in report writing	1. Practise writing reports in classes		
	2. Develop a résumé of different types of reports		
	3.		
LEARNING AND GROWTH OBJECTIVES			
Objective 1. Learn report writing skills	1. Define competencies related to report writing		
	2.		
	3.		

CASE: UNDERSTANDING THE FUTURE JOB MARKET USING SCENARIO PLANNING

In the following exercise on scenario planning, you are encouraged to define possible scenarios that might affect your employability over the next five years and the skills and strategies you will need to be effective in getting a job. The different scenarios are perspectives on the future that can affect the labour market.

The different scenarios – Starship, Titanic, Bounty and Windjammer – are perspectives on the future that can affect the labour market. In this exercise, construct a story around each scenario, describing what the labour force will look like. Start with the Starship and then repeat the process for the Titanic, Bounty and Windjammer scenarios. The goal is to understand each environment and define the competencies and strategies needed in responding. With each scenario, ask questions about the characteristics of the environment.

- What are the characteristics of this economic environment? What are examples?
- What are the characteristics of the social environment? What are examples to describe this?
- What will the labour force look like? What is the employment rate?
- In arriving at this scenario, what has occurred? How is it maintained?

What are forces that will create positive or negative change (market forces, corruption and ethics, terrorism, competitiveness, environment, poor management) in each scenario?

- Identify which scenario is most likely to happen.
- Rate the likelihood (1–5) of each scenario occurring in the next five years. Which combination of scenarios is most likely? Why?
- Within each scenario:
  - What is your vision of this future?
  - What strategic themes, objectives, initiatives and measures of progress are important?
  - What competencies will be most useful in responding?
  - What steps and initiatives would you use to be attractive to an organization?
  - When considering your personal plan, are there things you need to change?
  - Are there things you should keep forever?

Part III: Aligning Staffing and Performance Management Processes

These chapters focus on effectively aligning staffing and performance management so that they help line managers achieve their strategic objectives in adding value to clients or customers. Underlying these chapters is the need to improve workplace diversity and inclusiveness so that the workforce better represents society. When addressing workplace diversity, emphasis is on responding to groups of people that, for historical, cultural and systemic reasons, have faced barriers that have inhibited their full participation in the workforce. Diversity research is aimed at attacking problems connected with diversity, such as discrimination, inequity, bias and lack of representation.

The challenge for practitioners and scholars is how to distinguish the concept of diversity from employment equity, affirmative action or other programmes aimed at improving workplace representation. In most countries, under-represented groups include women; members of visible minorities; persons with disabilities; Aboriginal peoples; and lesbian, gay, bisexual and transgendered/transsexual (LGBT) peoples.

More recent discussions of diversity include not only people in designated groups but also people who are diverse because of age, culture, religion, politics, beliefs, abilities, skills and interests. This broader perspective on managing diversity involves creating a positive environment where people feel 'included' and using recruitment, selection and performance management in attracting and retaining diverse individuals into a culture that values their individuality.[1] This view of diversity contributes to organization decision-making, effectiveness and responsiveness, because diversity brings with it unique insights, values and knowledge to address problems and meet the needs of a diverse community.

6 Recruiting a Diverse Workforce

Chapter Outline
- Chapter objectives (COs)   111
- A driving issue focusing managerial action: Recognizing new paradigms on diversity   111
- CO 1: Focusing recruitment to meet diversity objectives   113
- CO 2: The relevance of three recruiting strategies in meeting diversity objectives   117
- CO 3: The employee's perspective – searching for a job   130
- Before applying, let's review   131
- Discussion and review questions   132
- Case: Recruiting more women in policing   134

CHAPTER OBJECTIVES (COs)

After reading this chapter, you will be able to implement the following objectives:

CO 1: Focus recruitment to meet diversity objectives.

CO 2: Compare the advantages and disadvantages of external recruiting, internal recruiting and outsourcing for attracting and retaining employees.

CO 3: Demonstrate the set of steps for undertaking the job search.

A DRIVING ISSUE FOCUSING MANAGERIAL ACTION: RECOGNIZING NEW PARADIGMS ON DIVERSITY

Because of the changing labour force demographics, practitioners and scholars have shifted their goals to focus on a broader definition of workplace diversity which challenges the conventional paradigm or set of assumptions defining diversity. In doing this, Thomas and Ely[2] suggest that one conventional set of assumptions in improving diversity has been to comply with legal requirements in implementing diversity goals (a discrimination and fairness paradigm). Another perspective in implementing diversity is to be representative of society so that we have better access and legitimacy with key constituents (an access and legitimacy paradigm). The learning and effectiveness paradigm for diversity requires defining values of diversity based on learning, involving all members in active participation (and not just representation), carefully designing jobs to more fully utilize the diversity of talents, encouraging debate and constructive conflict, making people feel valued, reflecting the culture in the vision and mission statements and encouraging an egalitarian structure which is welcoming of the exchange of ideas and values.[3] Selden and Selden's fourth paradigm, creating a multicultural organization by valuing and integrating, emphasizes processes of acculturation where non-dominant cultures can exist within a dominant culture.[4]

Discrimination and fairness paradigm (Paradigm 1). *Public organizations pursuing diversity using the discrimination and fairness lens focus on equal opportunity, compliance, fairness and recruitment that respects human rights legislation. Although progress using this paradigm can be measured by how well an organization achieves its recruitment and retention goals and how well it is representative of the designated groups, key mechanisms are those that assure fairness and due process. Managerial processes should encourage the fair treatment of people and groups and provide safeguards so that no one has an unfair advantage over another.*

The access and legitimacy paradigm (Paradigm 2). *As the discrimination and fairness paradigm (Paradigm 1) encourages assimilation and racial and gender blindness, the access and legitimacy paradigm (Paradigm 2) is based on the belief that we should accept our differences and design an organizational profile so that its unique demographic characteristics match that in society. The value of diversity is that it allows people to get better access and services to the constituents, because they have more legitimacy with these constituents. Given the multicultural richness of a country, its workforce should be demographically diverse in order to gain access to these ethnic groups. Organizations should have multicultural skills if they are to effectively understand and serve the rich variety of customers and clients. Diversity is more than fairness. It makes good business sense. Organizations that operate in this environment are those that have diverse customers and labour.*

The learning and effectiveness paradigm (Paradigm 3). *This paradigm encourages people to internalize their differences among employees so that they can learn from them. Any team is made up of people who represent separate points of view and perspectives. This diversity allows public organizations to expand their options for understanding issues and reframe them in creative ways which would not have been possible from groups made up of one ethnic group (e.g. an all-white male group). One of the advantages of the learning and effectiveness paradigm is that it encourages creative problem-solving, learning, change and the avoidance of mental blind spots. It also encourages integration where people with diverse perspectives are able to frame issues and devise creative solutions more effectively.*

Valuing and integrating in creating a multicultural organization (Paradigm 4). *Paradigm 4 suggests that organizations that seek to value cultural diversity should support and foster acculturation in environments where non-dominant cultures can exist within a dominant culture. This paradigm builds on the other paradigms and the values of access, democratization, effectiveness and service to stakeholders. Organizations using this paradigm should be more effective not only in recruiting but also in retaining people because this paradigm responds better to the needs of diverse individuals. In Paradigm 4, there is a recognition that the organization's dominant culture is influenced by less dominant cultures of its members. As such, the culture is multicultural in reflecting a totality of the 'ideals, beliefs, skills, tools, customs and institutions into which each member is born.'[5] The non-dominant culture remains intact rather than being absorbed.*

Changing our paradigm of diversity will affect the way we carry out recruitment, selection and performance management. That is, rather than solely targeting individuals because they represent designated groups, we need to recognize the value of designated and other groups within a larger organizational culture. This suggests that we need to go beyond the conventional recruitment, selection and performance management activities and take steps needed to orient and support new people in the culture and connect them with relevant people and projects. It also involves using their diversity in relationships and in solving problems.

STRATEGIC CONTEXT: *In building on the opening vignette which illustrates four diversity paradigms, this chapter suggests that improving the representativeness of employees will enhance an employee's perceptions of feeling included in the workforce. Representativeness might be the first step in developing a workplace which is inclusive of all individuals.*

> *Inclusion goes beyond diversity management programmes that, in the past, sought to improve the diversity of employees in specific designated groups. Diversity management might be a first step, whereas an inclusionary approach puts a value on differences in individuals and leverages this in supporting people for their differences.*
>
> *In assisting line managers to meet their strategic themes and objectives within the SHRM BSC framework, you might keep in mind the strategic theme of improving diversity and inclusiveness of different people in a public organization so that you focus on objectives and initiatives related to external and internal requirements.*

CO 1: FOCUSING RECRUITMENT TO MEET DIVERSITY OBJECTIVES

Recruitment is the process of attracting an adequate pool of qualified candidates to sustain qualified and talented staff for specific job requirements now and in the future. When there is a large supply of people in the labour pool, employers don't need to be as strategic to attract a reasonable pool of applicants. Not-for-profit managers, such as those who manage emergency shelters, recognize that they cannot count on the applications they receive from placing a poster in a community if they want to find talented people with special skills.

Two reasons we need to be especially strategic in recruiting relate to (i) the projected skills shortage in certain areas and (ii) the need to adjust our workforce to reflect a more diverse culture. The increased interest in the topic of recruitment is partially a result of projected labour shortages but is also due to skill shortages in key specializations and locations or in finding people representing designated groups.[6] Skills shortages do not mean general labour shortages. Rather, they relate to finding people in specialized areas. The 'hot skills' most in demand now include those in information technology, finance, leadership positions and other professional and technical occupations (e.g. engineering and technical trades).

A second recruiting challenge is locating, attracting and retaining people that reflect a community's diversity. In some cases, this means finding people in different designated groups such as those representing (i) women; (ii) members of visible minorities; (iii) persons with disabilities; (iv) Aboriginal peoples; and (v) lesbian, gay, bisexual and transgendered/transsexual (LGBT) peoples. It also means trying to attract people by developing an organizational profile that illustrates diverse interests and cultures, among other things.

If there are too few people representing groups that an organization designates as important to represent, managers might feel compelled to hire people simply to meet a quota. This often results from the failure to locate and induce capable, competent people to apply for a job. The result is a smaller pool of potential applicants. As a result, diversity gets a bad name simply because the recruitment process did not attract enough qualified applicants in a designated diversity group.

A **strategic recruiting perspective** calls for managers to be creative in attracting an external or internal pool of qualified applicants in a changing economic and social environment. This also involves shaping recruitment initiatives to achieve strategic objectives that have a higher value to an organization.

Within the recruitment area, strategic recruiting can be shaped by objectives related to improving workplace diversity and implementing initiatives for accommodating people who are different, who have disabilities, or who need assistance during the interview process. In going further, a diversity perspective seeks to provide a supportive environment for employees and for helping all employees fit. This recognizes the importance of fit – interests, motivations, goals, career aspirations – in attracting and retaining talented employees.[7] Some organizations make a commitment to career-based hiring practices and training practices to develop people in a career path within the organization. This can also be implemented with recruitment practices which illustrate values related to hiring on the basis of merit, providing broad access and demonstrating a commitment to values of trust, fairness, diversity, excellence, creativity, collaboration, efficiency and responsiveness. As such, the diversity perspective is a useful framework for recruiting.

Linking to the strategic context and the evolving definition of diversity

Public sector organizations have taken a leading role in modelling ideas for encouraging workplace diversity, and in the last few decades, the composition of their workforce has become much more diverse; managers are under pressure to attract not only talented people who have specialized skills but those who reflect the same societal diversity. They have provided training that focuses on valuing differences in ethnicity, gender, race, religion, disabilities and sexual orientation in addition to implementing diversity management through mentoring, coaching, legislation and policy changes, discipline and alternative work arrangements.[8]

In responding to several legislative requirements, diversity management programmes were designed to provide training and policies to foster equal opportunity, compliance, and fairness in the recruitment process. Progress usually is measured by how well an organization achieves its recruitment and retention goals and how well it is representative of the designated groups.[9]

One of the original intents of many affirmative action or equity programmes was to establish an organization with a diversity of gender cultures, races, ethnicities and age groups, where the diversity in the organization was in the same proportion as in the general population. The argument was that such a version of the public organization would be responsive to the general public interests based on a theory of representative democracy.[10] As such, representation ensures our ability to achieve broad social goals in education and health that are important to its different groups of citizens (e.g. women, older people). This chapter suggests that improving the representativeness of employees will enhance an employee's perceptions of feeling included in the workforce.[11] Given that peoples' values are strong determinants of individual interests, if a public organization has a diversity of backgrounds, there is a greater possibility that the policies and ideas leading our society will more truly represent the values and interests of society.[12] In addition, political scientists argue that providing a more diverse public sector is a symbolic commitment to equal access to power.[13]

Many public organizations have been in a leadership role in implementing diversity programmes, and an ongoing debate still exists as to the best approach. In some cases, public organizations have found it necessary to implement hard quotas and schedules, some of which have been met with criticism, cynicism and legal action. To say the least, diversity is still a hot topic, and the approaches to implementation often create a great deal of conflict and mistrust in organizations. Many of the implementations have backfired and divided workplaces.

Although diversity management programmes often increase demographic diversity and fair treatment on the surface, they are not always viewed as meeting their objectives. For example, employees taking advantage of alternative work arrangements report backlash because they feel singled out for preferential treatment. Although improved performance often results from varied perspectives that diverse employees bring to solving problems, such heterogeneous groups may take longer to come together and resolve conflicting ideas.[14] In the same way, people who belong to a diverse group can be excluded from the central culture or from those making decisions.[15]

The workplace today is much more diverse than it was 20 years ago, as reflected in the greater numbers of women, people with disabilities and other designated groups such as, in some countries, Aboriginal peoples.[16] For example, in terms of gender composition, the picture varies in different countries. In the United Kingdom, there are almost twice as many women employed in public service, whereas the opposite is true in the private sector.[17] In Canada, over 55 per cent of federal employees are women, up from 42 per cent in 1983.[18] In other countries, such as the United States, Portugal, Ireland and New Zealand, women represent less than 50 per cent of public employees.[19]

In most countries of the world, women are under-represented at the senior levels and do not hold over 40 per cent of the senior positions in any country. In the United States, for example, women hold 29 per cent of the senior positions but represent 44.2 of employees; and in Australia, they make up 57 per cent of the workforce, but only 40 per cent of the senior positions.[20] In Japan, Switzerland and Korea, women hold fewer than 10 per cent of the senior positions.[21] The picture is generally more bleak in private sector organizations as government organizations have been in the leadership role in redressing gender imbalances.

Becoming more attractive as an 'employer of choice'

The 'employer of choice' idea is relevant for thinking of ways to design workplaces so they are attractive to people in different designated groups. It also encourages a supportive, inclusive culture for women as well as other designated groups. A supportive workplace culture is defined by beliefs, values and norms that describe appropriate and inappropriate behaviour. A workplace culture that is supportive and inclusive of designated groups is likely to be an attractive place to work for all groups. Such a workplace culture recognizes what people value and need in their work. These needs point towards a supportive work environment, a challenging job, a good fit between life on and off the job, adequate compensation, working in an organization that has high values and having the opportunity for high achievement.[22] There might be slight differences among some individuals and groups, but it is safe to assume that these needs are essential for motivating and committing all people at work and for attracting applicants. In the competition for competent staff, workplaces that welcome all segments of the workforce are being recognized as 'employers of choice.'

The term **employer of choice** describes a workplace which people find attractive because people are respected for their diversity. Such employment practices are good for the organization's bottom line in improving retention, attendance, safety and performance and work quality. Diverse and inclusive workplaces are often more innovative in that team members create a wider range of solutions to problems.[23]

Some groups face barriers when entering a non-traditional workplace, including:

- Discrimination and stereotyping in hiring practices (where some groups of people are viewed as more capable of carrying out the job).
- Unfriendly workplaces because groups of workers are discriminated against, isolated or harassed.
- Lack of understanding and training in diversity.
- A focus on seniority systems defined in collective agreements, making it difficult to be eligible for promotion based on skill and competence.
- Lack of flexibility in responding to family needs, religious practices or health issues.
- Traditional attitudes that say certain occupations are performed by certain groups (race, gender, disability, Aboriginals).
- Lack of role models.
- Lack of access to training.

These barriers can exist for women, Aboriginal people, people with disabilities, visible minorities, younger and older workers and other groups of people who might not fit into the dominant workplace culture. In some workplaces, rewards and promotions might be tied to people working long hours and time spent socializing after work. Although this cultural characteristic of a workplace affects all groups equally, it might have a negative impact on people with family responsibilities and could create a greater barrier for women.[24]

Several OECD public services have embraced the vision of being an 'employer of choice' in undertaking renewal programmes to improve the efficiency and effectiveness of their public services by designing services which are responsive to citizens and employees needs. Some countries have used the term *employer of choice* to indicate their vision of being an ideal employer in order to be more attractive to designated groups, including older and younger workers.[25] Given that all applicants make choices, they will choose employers who are attractive in meeting their needs. Public and private organizations on Canada's Top 100 'Employers of Choice' were selected based on initiatives in the following areas: (1) Physical Workplace; (2) Work Atmosphere & Social; (3) Health, Financial & Family Benefits; (4) Vacation & Time Off; (5) Employee Communications; (6) Performance Management; (7) Training & Skills Development; and (8) Community Involvement.[26] The 'employer of choice' idea is like a brand, an image we have of an organization as a great place to work in the minds of current employees and key stakeholders.

Developing an inclusive model of diversity

It is not always clear whether inclusiveness in the workforce, though it is the heart of a 'learning and effectiveness' paradigm, is achieved through diversity management programmes. With inclusiveness, individuals feel part of the critical organizational processes and can influence decision-making. They feel valued, utilized and welcome in being partnered with others, and they feel safe when expressing their ideas.[27]

Diversity management might be a first step, but an inclusionary approach puts a value on differences in individuals and leverages this in supporting people for their differences. Inclusion is the opposite end of the continuum from an exclusive workplace that has pre-established norms which dictate who is involved in different networks and how decisions are made. Although diversity programmes seek to achieve equality goals, inclusion highlights the removal of barriers for all employees.

Accepting inclusion as the objective in managing diversity would change performance metrics to focus on improving voice in decision-making, team relationships, inclusion in the organization's culture and support from co-workers and leaders. Inclusiveness means feeling valued, safe, involved and engaged in the work. For example, there is some interest in developing a better understanding of the relationship between the representation of women and other designated groups and the degree to which they feel included in the workforce. In a sample of 325,119 employees in the UK public service, researchers sought to better understand whether gender and minority representation had any effect on perceptions of workplace inclusion. The results point out that, though inclusiveness might be a broader definition of diversity, it was encouraged by policies that promoted representativeness. 'Public organizations that more closely resemble the population they serve are perceived by their employees to be more inclusive environments in which to work.'[28]

Performance metrics in illustrating diversity

Measures of the effectiveness of recruitment processes might focus on assessing different recruiting methods in developing a pool of diverse, talented applicants. The most important measures relate to types of sources used and whether they result in a larger pool of applicants. Other measures relate to how well an organization develops and promotes internal employees rather than attracting new recruits from the external market. An organization that is committed to developing internal candidates often operates with a belief system that the best employees can be developed from within and that this increases employee commitment and productivity.[29] Measures of activities related to internal recruitment include training and learning activities focused on developing employees.

Outcome measures of the implementation of diversity objectives often chart the representativeness of various groups and the degree to which they mirror the profile in society. Inclusion is defined by the degree that employees feel 'accepted and treated as an insider by others in a system'[30] and involves a stronger commitment to the depth or quality of the social relationship.[31] Gender and minority representation is a measure of the proportion of employees who were women and of ethnic origin and how closely it mirrored that of the UK population. Inclusiveness can be measured using a scale of items describing feeling fairly treated, valued and respected for individual differences.[32]

CO 2: THE RELEVANCE OF THREE RECRUITING STRATEGIES IN MEETING DIVERSITY OBJECTIVES

Three general recruiting approaches can be used to achieve diversity objectives. The external recruiting process encourages managers to look outside the organization in identifying qualified people. Outsourcing offers another perspective as it implies that it is more efficient and cost-effective to contract out for services the organization needs. Each of the approaches in Figure 6.1 is illustrated in the following sections.

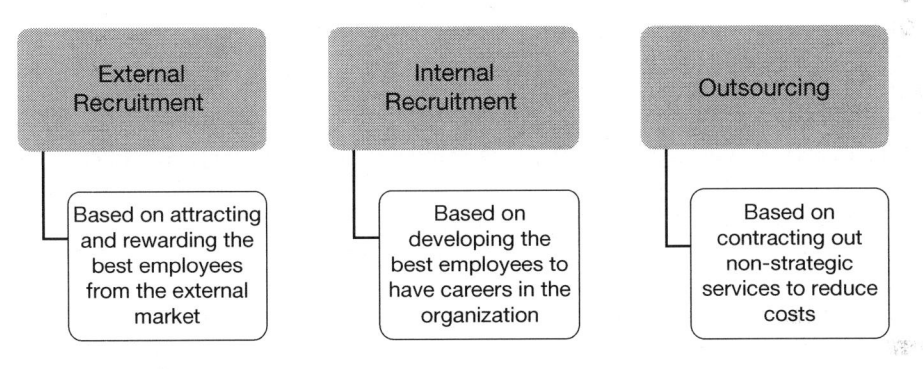

Figure 6.1 Three general recruiting strategies.

I External recruiting with a diversity model

Recruitment begins with specifying human resource requirements and competencies needed for different jobs or job openings. The initial steps summarized in Figure 6.2 begin with the job analysis and workforce planning described in Chapters 3 and 5. Larger public organizations will have plans including competency inventories for various positions, promotion ladders and the recruiting priorities for the next few years. The plans might also indicate recruitment needs to meet attrition or retirements, or how the workforce needs might change because of new technologies or a shift in direction. It can also highlight the organization's diversity goals and initiatives. Examples include taking steps to ensure a balanced workforce, strengthening the organization's ability to attract a diverse workforce in positively responding to employee suggestions and becoming an 'employer of choice'.

Job Analysis and Specifying Job Requirements and Competencies → Identifying Key Sources for Developing a Pool of Good Applicants → Being Creative in Using Different Sources to Develop a Larger Pool of Diverse Applicants → Using Online Sources → Designing the Application Process to Meet Diversity Requirements

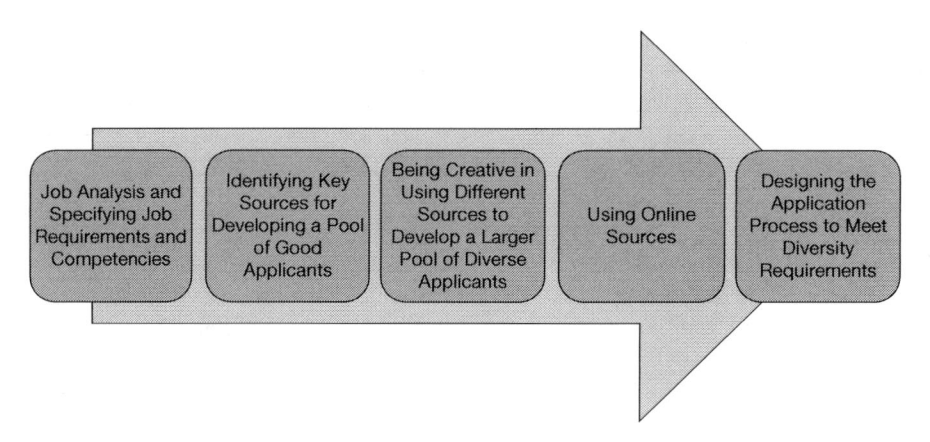

Figure 6.2 Employee recruitment and selection – steps for external recruiting.

The actual recruitment process can begin in earnest when there is a clear understanding of the competencies needed, the number of people needed at that competency level, and the time frame when they are needed. Four initiatives are helpful in moving the recruiting process beyond the job analysis and planning process: (i) identifying key sources for developing a pool of applicants, (ii) being creative in using different sources to develop a larger pool of diverse applicants, (iii) using on-line sources and (iv) designing the application process to meet diversity requirements.

Identifying key sources for developing a pool of good applicants

The importance of the strategic recruiting function becomes painfully obvious if we find ourselves on a selection panel where only three applicants responded to the advertisements and none of the applicants were highly qualified. This might occur because recruitment was not focused in the right places or because the job advertisement was not worded in a way that was attractive to the applicants or because we are searching in a highly competitive pool where good applicants are scarce.

The recruiter's job in sourcing is like the marketer's task of capturing a market niche for a product or service. This involves identifying niche markets for finding targeted groups of employees, including designated groups and older and younger workers, and then using the appropriate sources for getting people to apply.

Identifying 'niche' markets for recruiting. The 'first stop' in recruitment is understanding the job and the competencies needed; however, it is also helpful to define the special characteristics sought in meeting diversity objectives. For example, in indicating the special characteristics of employees they are seeking, the New Zealand Police articulated their organization's vision and set of values describing integrity, professionalism, respect and commitment to Māori and the Treaty of Waitangi. For this police organization, diversity is essential to serve the needs of New Zealand's communities.[33]

Both the public and private sectors emphasize social skills, but the evidence is that the public sector recruiters are focused on communication and collaborative skills, whereas the private sector recruiters are interested in personal characteristics such as dynamism, creativity and strategic thinking. The inference is that in the public sector, developing consensus, encouraging input and influence are more important in a highly political process.[34]

Although the unique features of the public sector are important, we also have to be cognizant of what attracts people. Most traditional job recruiting exercises assume that people make rational decisions about jobs, and as a result, recruiters sometimes place a heavy emphasis on pay and what the person does on the job. However, people often make emotional choices based on location, values and interests of people who work in the organization. For example, we might ask: (i) 'Who are the employees in our niche and what do they like to do?' (ii) 'What are their work and life values?' (iii) 'What are their educational and career goals?' These questions help recognize that even though applicants are attracted to a job in an organization, they also are attracted by non-job-related factors.

Generally, younger millennial workers seem to place a high value on goals related to balancing personal life and career, pursuing further education, building a sound financial base, contributing to society and working internationally. For those who wanted to work in the public sector, the leading characteristics were balancing personal life and career, pursuing further education and contributing to society. Public sector aspirants wanted employers who illustrated high ethical standards, social responsibility and progressive work environment and who value a diverse workforce and environmental consciousness. The most desirable job characteristic for all people was flexible working conditions. Those desiring public sector positions were more interested in secure employment and sponsorship of education, whereas those interested in the private sector were likely to indicate clear advancement and competitive compensation. Those preferring private sector employment indicated the importance of building a sound financial future as a key career goal. Rather than accept that all millennials are the same, the purpose is to encourage us to gear our recruiting strategies to the interests, goals and values of the people we are seeking to attract.[35]

Assessing the value of different recruiting sources. Sources for recruiting include advertisements or job postings using local newspapers, trade journals, radio, television, bulletin boards, posters, email, websites, and through the use of social media. We can also advertise in storefronts or office windows and at trade schools, universities or union halls. As recognition of the importance of recruitment has increased substantially over the last few years, a great deal of research and interest has focused on effectiveness of various sources (e.g. advertising, referrals) and how the appropriateness of the sources can enhance the recruitment process.[36] Table 6.1 reviews a range of recruiting sources and issues related to their use.

Each of these sources for recruiting people has advantages and disadvantages in identifying talented people who represent diversity objectives.[37] Advantages of external recruiting include attracting new people with backgrounds or sets of skills that are unique and highly specialized. For example, in the IT sector, it is sometimes necessary to recruit software developers with highly specialized programming skills that differ depending on upcoming projects. In a police department, staff with uniquely specialized computer forensics skills might be hard to recruit.

In assessing the different sourcing options, key criteria relate to the effectiveness of the sources in finding applicants who stay with the organization for a period of time and who perform well. Certain sources are better than others, according to research. Generally, applicants who are referred by current employees were more successful than others recruited from sources like employment agencies and advertising. Inside sources (e.g. employee referrals and rehires) provide a candidate with an inside track in getting jobs and provide informal information about how to fit in.[38] Although this presents a selection bias, others argue that these inside referrals act as a prescreen, assuming that only the best are referred.[39] One implication of this research is that if you are an employer or employee searching for a job, don't underestimate the role referrals, informal sources and social media play.[40]

Being creative in using sources to develop a larger pool of diverse applicants

There are usually significant costs associated with external recruitment, which include the cost of advertising and staff time in preparing material and sourcing candidates. More importantly, if an

Table 6.1 Review of Recruiting Sources

Source	Description	Review	Disadvantages
Print advertisements	A well-written advertisement is sent to a broad audience. This is the most common method of attracting applicants, even with the advent of online recruiting.	- Well-written ads can highlight the assets of the position. - They can be more effective if the ad is creatively designed. - They can be more effective if ads are directed at carefully selected newspapers, posters or trade journals, or other select audiences.	- Advertisements may not reach people who do not read or view certain media. - Competent people who are already employed may not be searching job advertisements. - Large numbers of people who are not appropriate might apply if ads are not carefully worded.
Internet job boards	Organizations can post a job opening online for a fee. General website examples include Eluta (Eluta.ca), Monster (www.monster.ca), Nicejob (www.nicejob.ca), Workopolis (www.workopolis.ca).	- Job boards are fast and convenient to use and can be customized with the organizational logo. - Job seekers can search and apply online through the jobs by title, type and location. - Job boards are popular among job applicants who are comfortable with using this medium. - An easy link to the website provides information about why the organization is a great place to work.	- Internet job boards may attract large numbers of candidates who do not have the KSAOs. - They may not reach people who are not connected. - They may not reach competent people who are employed elsewhere.
Organization job boards	Job boards on organizational websites promote the organization and educate the applicant about the organization.	- Organizational job boards can reduce time and costs. - Most software allows recruiters to track candidates through the entire recruitment and selection process. - Organizations can keep an active pool of applicants. - Candidates can track progress of their application. - It is possible to cope with the volume by sending applicants automatic replies acknowledging receipt of application.	- These may attract large numbers of candidates who do not have the KSAOs. - Organization job boards may not reach people who are not connected. - They may not reach competent people who are employed elsewhere.
Walk-in and write-in	Individuals visit the organization in person with a referral or invitation.	- Individuals use this method to introduce themselves to the organization. - A positive response to a walk-in visit is a valuable way to advertise the organization. - Walk-ins are a common way of recruiting in smaller organizations.	- Applicants who visit the organization represent a select audience of people with select skills, or people not comfortable with other recruiting strategies.

Outsourced recruiters and employment agencies	Specialized consulting services are available to recruit executive, highly skilled people or hard-to-recruit jobs. They attempt to match applicants with specific needs of organizations.	– Recruiting agencies often specialize in different areas such as university, executive, sales, scientific, secretarial and middle management. – They know and understand the market and have networks of appropriate people, including internationally.	– These are expensive. The cost has to be balanced against time saved and people recruited. – Recruiters are sales oriented in pushing selected applicants. – Managers become insulated from the recruiting process.
Employee referrals	Applicants are encouraged by using a network of friends and associates.	– Managers are interested in referrals, feeling that trusted referrals can validly judge the applicant quality. – Given the high biases that might result from referrals, it is often appropriate to develop norms guarding against conflict of interest, and not hiring protégés or family members. Norms might include 'standing down' from a particular recruitment and selection search.	– There is a potential for **nepotism** and lack of diversity, which could result in future morale problems. – There are considerable biases associated with hiring referrals. – The method might result in systemic discrimination. It feels good to hire someone who has been referred.
Professional organizations, union halls and temporary agencies	Listing and placement services are available for those in the profession or union. A placement service is sometimes established at conventions and conferences.	– Placement services at conventions and union meetings provide a way to review a large number of candidates hunting for jobs. – Unions can be the principal meeting ground for blue collar and trade workers.	– Placement services are restricted to those involved with professional organization or union and those who have paid their annual dues.
Educational institutions	Universities, colleges, technical skills, and high schools are a source of trained applicants.	– Educational institutions are good sources of new applicants for technical and managerial personnel.	– Employers are competing with one another for the same pool of entry-level recruits.

inappropriate person is hired, the costs of replacement are expensive. Estimates of costs for hiring are complicated, and some approximations range up to 200 percent of the position's annual salary for executive positions when the figure includes housing allowances, moving expenses and third party fees. Many costs – such as understaffing because of turnover, customer service disruption, decreased morale or poor performance of the person to be replaced – are hard to quantify. As a result, in a competitive environment, identification of good sources for finding candidates helps in guaranteeing a sufficient number of applicants with the unique skills needed.

Using general, unfocused sources for recruiting applicants is like trying to fish without first trying to find out where the fish are most likely to be. Some fishing holes are better than others, and some are a waste of time. In the same way, some recruitment sources are more effective because they reach applicants from new and diverse population groups.[41]

The effectiveness of recruitment practices can partially be explained by the information provided and the employer's reputation.[42] Informal sources are generally more effective than formal sources in recruiting applicants,[43] but recruiters can improve their effectiveness of job advertisements and other formal sources by providing useful and reliable information to applicants. High information recruitment practices enhance an employer's reputation and the job information an applicant has for making a decision.[44]

Recruiting to locate people who meet diversity objectives. The recruitment sources identified can be used to attract designated group members just as easily as other candidates. However, unless we are creative in applying them in unique ways, we might not fulfil the objectives we hoped to achieve in an equity policy. In each case, we must ask, 'Is this source the best way to attract people within the designated group?'

One objective that some public and private agencies may be more successful in using to attract people from designated groups is that they have implemented initiatives to become 'employers of choice' – that is, they have implemented practices and a culture that makes them attractive to different designated groups. For example, Canada's Best Diversity Employers are recognized for exceptional workplace diversity and initiatives in including programmes for five major designated groups: (i) women; (ii) members of visible minorities; (iii) persons with disabilities; (iv) Aboriginal peoples; and (e) lesbian, gay, bisexual and transgendered/transsexual (LGBT) people. Many of the 50 organizations selected are public organizations, including hydro companies, colleges and universities, cities, provincial and federal departments, hospitals and non-profits. The reasons they are more successful vary and include implementing initiatives to improve workplace diversity, establishing an immigrant employee support network and maintaining a community fund for projects related to equity, diversity and inclusion.[45]

ETHICAL QUESTION: IS IT FAIR TO USE YOUR FRIENDS OR RELATIVES TO HELP YOU GET A JOB?

Employers often rely on employee referrals as a good source of talented applicants, and many applicants have learned to believe that this is a useful strategy to get linked up with employers. Some organizations encourage applications from relatives and friends of employees. There are disadvantages, including nepotism, inbreeding and discrimination against people from other groups. There are also advantages in that the organization hires people who other people like, and these people might have common values. What do you think? What are the advantages and disadvantages?

There is much more to the recruitment process beyond advertising jobs and encouraging candidates to join an organization. A process designed to be successful in the long term links recruitment to the organization's strategies, focusing on current and future workforce needs while defining the specific requirements, competencies and special characteristics needed in the job. Beyond finding competent people, it seeks to attract people who 'fit' within the workplace culture. These people are more likely to be engaged in their work and committed to a career with the organization. Posting an advertisement without understanding the advantages of different sources is like beginning a research paper without thinking clearly about the topic you are interested in studying. As in marketing, broad advertisements that are unfocused may not connect to the right people. Instead, the best strategies for sourcing involve targeted advertising and recruitment efforts appropriate to the population, where there is a greater chance of getting highly qualified applicants.[46]

Identifying niche sources of younger and older workers. A workplace culture that is supportive and inclusive of designated groups is likely to be an attractive place to work for all groups, including younger and older workers. Recruiting younger and older workers demands the same level of strategic focus as recruiting from any designated groups. As a first step, the Internet and universities, colleges and high schools can be useful points. Adding to this, employers can use an online application process and interactive ways to communicate to applicants and provide feedback during the application process.[47] They can be more proactive by funding internships and co-operative education experiences. Career fairs, presentations to student groups, and research projects are also ways to engage students in recruiting. As an example of being proactive, one non-profit organization involved the work team in the recruitment and selection process, and when applicants were selected, team members were involved in an orientation process that gave new applicants a head start on their jobs.

'Employer of choice' awards illustrate organizations that exemplify inclusive workplace cultures illustrating diverse beliefs, values and norms. One 'Top Employers for Young People' award recognizes public and private employers for their apprentice programmes, paid internship, conferences for younger people and mentor programmes, among other things.[48] Their programmes to attract and retain younger people include tuition assistance, co-op and work–study programmes, training programmes, benefits such as bonuses for completing a professional designation, career programmes and workforce management inventories that help younger people advance faster in the organization. Canada has a similar top employer award for older workers.[49]

The sources for recruiting older workers might be more traditional, given that this generation of workers is more likely to read the classified columns in the newspapers than communicate through social networking sites.[50] The employers on the 'Employers of Choice for Older Workers' list offer more generous pension plans or registered savings plan contributions, and sometimes both. They often extend health coverage to their retired employees and assist older employees with retirement and succession planning. They also create opportunities for their retirees to stay socially connected to former co-workers through organized social activities and volunteering, and offer mentorship and phased-in retirement to ease the emotional challenges of retirement and ensure older employees' skill sets are transferred to the next generation.

Using online recruiting ideas and tools

Job advertising and searching is simplified by using online resources. The online environment has changed the world of recruiting. Not only is online recruiting faster, but the cost of online recruiting is about 1/20th of that of traditional recruiting.[55] From an employer's standpoint, online recruiting can be linked to an organization's marketing efforts in selling the organization as an 'employer of choice.' The organizational home page, linked to an easily accessible jobs page, can prominently advertise added

> **QUIZ 6.1 – ASSESSING YOUR VIEWS: WHAT DO MALES AND FEMALES WANT FROM THEIR WORK?**
>
> Do men and women have dissimilar values in what is important in their work? A common theory is that men and women are as different as Mars and Venus.[51] Some people suggest that women might not advance in their jobs because they are more apt to leave the workplace, driven by values and goals that differ from those of men. Rank-order your perception of what men and women value in their work, with 1 being the highest and 6 being the lowest.
>
> | Men | Women | |
> |---|---|---|
> | ___ | ___ | A supportive work environment |
> | ___ | ___ | A challenging job |
> | ___ | ___ | A good fit between life on and off the job |
> | ___ | ___ | Being well compensated |
> | ___ | ___ | Working in an organization that has high values |
> | ___ | ___ | Having the opportunity for high achievement. |
>
> Research on the differences between what men and women want in their work offer conflicting results. Some researchers suggest that women are more likely to value social interactions[52] and attachment to work, financial security and self-interest.[53] However, other studies suggest that any differences in gender attitudes are more likely to be explained by age, education and occupation, and other socio-economic variables.[54] How would you rank what men and women want? Compare your responses to those on the book's website.

benefits of working for the organization – diversity, employee benefits and work–life balance. Online recruitment also provides an environment where recruiters can reach out and possibly contact people who might not be actively engaged in job hunting, but who might be excellent candidates.

Although technology has opened up new opportunities for reaching out to students, it's still worthwhile for employers to have a personal, face-to-face presence in informal networks and organized events. Career fairs, on-campus information sessions with free food, trade shows held by schools, sponsorship of scholarships or events, or even physical spaces on campus, internships or co-op work experience programmes and industry panel discussions, are all commonplace at today's universities and colleges.

From a job hunter's standpoint, the Internet presents several opportunities to simplify the job search and application process. However, advisers remind students that it still requires a lot of legwork on their part to get a job that meets their needs. That means doing research, networking and preparing a strong résumé and portfolio package that highlights how their degree translates into in-demand skills for any given employer.

The employer and potential employees have many interesting recruiting sources and opportunities. It is easy for job seekers to fire off hundreds of résumés without a lot of work. Just as employers are more strategic when they target applicants that fit their strategies, it is probably more fruitful for potential job applicants to hone their résumés to organizations that are important to their interests and objectives.

Designing the application process to meet human rights requirements

All employers are guided by international, national, provincial or state human rights and equity legislation that prohibits intentional and unintentional discrimination in employment.[56] Human rights

> **QUIZ 6.2 – THINKING ABOUT GETTING RECRUITED?**
>
> Most individuals, at some stage in their life, will be looking for a job and will rely on various sources such as job advertisements in newspapers, web advertisements and ideas from friends or mentors. In finding a job, some sources are better than others.
>
> In order of usage, recruiters in public organizations are more likely to say they post positions by using newspapers (33%), college recruiters (17%), professional journals (12%), employment agencies (13%), employee referrals (13%), walk-ins (25%), help-wanted signs (19%) and computer résumé services (3%).[57]
>
> How would you rank these sources as to their effectiveness for you in terms of your success in getting a job for an entry-level position?
>
> _____ *College hiring*
> _____ *Employee referrals*
> _____ *Career sites*
> _____ *Search firm*
> _____ *Walk-ins*
> _____ *Newspaper ad*
>
> Compare your responses to those on the book's website.

legislation is based on the principle that an applicant's ability to do the job is the most important job requirement or qualification. As a result, employers are advised to design competency-based recruitment and selection procedures to guard against other factors that might intentionally or unintentionally discriminate in the workplace.

Human rights commissions are set up to investigate, promote and protect human rights. International human rights commissions exist within the United Nations, representing various continents.[58] They provide guidelines for wording job advertisements and application forms, in addition to setting out important principles of hiring. That is, generally, we cannot ask for information on race, ancestry, place of origin, colour, ethnic origin, citizenship, creed, gender, sexual orientation, age, record of offences, marital status, family status or handicaps. Job requirements should be reasonable and directly related to the job. For example, it might be reasonable to expect a receptionist to speak clear, intelligible English. It is not acceptable to ask for 'unaccented English.' The guidelines are intended to ensure equal opportunity and non-discrimination in organizations, assisting employers in wording the competencies they are seeking in applicants.

Writing the application form. The application form (digital or non-digital) is used as the prescreening device for identifying an appropriate pool of applicants. When online applications were initially introduced, recruiters found themselves buried in stacks of electronic résumés besides the stacks of résumés that were submitted in the mail, in person or by fax. Standardized online application forms were cumbersome and often did not provide information related to the objectives of the organization or the hiring process. Thanks to sophisticated software programs, many online applications can be tailored to relate to the organization's strategic needs and the objectives of the hiring process and designed to gather information on the experiences and competencies needed in the job and related information on education and career progress.

> ## A RELEVANT POINT OF VIEW: CAREER-BASED OR POSITION-BASED RECRUITMENT SYSTEMS AND AUTONOMY
>
> Career-based and position-based recruiting systems have unique objectives and methods for attracting and retaining employees. According to an OECD report on central government recruitment systems, which reviewed the type of recruitment systems used in 25 countries, Japan was similar to Ireland and France and a few other countries who emphasized a career-based recruitment system.[59] **Career-based systems** such as these have a competitive selection process early in the public servant's career, and higher-level posting is connected to the career path. One key advantage of such systems is the nourishment of a cross-government set of values and experiences, and a long-term commitment to the employee's career within the organization. In a **position-based system**, job aspirants apply for specific jobs that are open to internal and external candidates.
>
> The OECD report illustrates an index that rates the career-based and position-based systems. In countries like the United Kingdom, Finland, the Netherlands, New Zealand, Sweden and Switzerland, all positions below senior management (and some senior management and all diplomatic positions) are open to external recruitment. In France and Japan, where career-based systems exist, employees are recruited almost exclusively at lower levels and groomed to take on higher-level posts later in their careers. However, in some career-based systems (Belgium, Mexico, Ireland, Japan, Germany, Korea, Luxemburg, Portugal), there are still opportunities for external recruitment of top managers and special top-level experts.
>
> The OECD report shows an interesting relationship where countries with more position-based recruitment systems seem to allow their line ministries more autonomy to make HRM decisions. For example, managers appear to have more flexibility in hiring in Australia, New Zealand and Sweden. However, there are exceptions, as Japan and the Netherlands seem to allow a similar level of discretion, and Japan illustrates a career-based system, whereas the Netherlands illustrates a position-based system.

In complying with human rights legislation, there are a number of things to be aware of in developing application forms:

Education. Dates of attendance and graduation from various schools – academic, professional or vocational – can indicate a person's age. These questions might not comply with the legislation.

Arrest record. Questions about arrest records are generally not permissible. It is permissible for an employer to ask whether an applicant has been convicted of a criminal offence for which a pardon has not been granted. If a job requires that a person be bonded or have a criminal record check completed, an employer may ask if the applicant is eligible.

Memberships. Application forms may ask a person to list memberships in clubs, organizations and societies, and offices held. If this question is asked, employers should include instructions not to include organizations that reveal a person's religion, race, physical handicaps, marital status, political affiliations or ancestry.

Persons to notify in an emergency. The employer can ask for the name, address and phone number of the person to notify in an emergency. However, asking the relationship of this person to the applicant could indicate marital status or relationship and therefore might not be seen as appropriate.

Marital status. The application should not ask for information on marital status, whether a person is single, divorced or living with someone. It is also not appropriate to ask the names, occupations and ages of the applicant's spouse or children.

Housing. It is not appropriate to ask whether a person owns, rents or leases a house, as this could be discriminatory.

Health and physical handicaps. It is not appropriate to ask about the applicant's health or handicaps unless the application also asks for those illnesses or handicaps that might interfere with job performance (e.g. a pilot might need a certain standard of vision). It is also not appropriate to ask whether an employee has previously received workers' compensation.

External recruitment allows managers to reach out and enrich their competencies and experiences that other organizations have developed, as well as provides an opportunity to change the organization's diversity profile. However, an overemphasis on external recruiting can be demoralizing for some employees if they feel that they have fewer chances of promotion because their organization gets all its top talent externally. Also, there are more chances to make mistakes in external recruitment, especially if the people don't fit in with the culture.

II Internal recruitment and succession planning

Managers have a choice in developing and promoting internal employees or trying to attract new recruits from the external market. An organization that is committed to developing internal candidates often operates with a belief system that the best employees can be developed from within and that this increases employee commitment and productivity.[60]

An internal recruitment philosophy. This entails more than simply posting job openings and distributing them throughout the organization so that employees are aware of them. The real emphasis of internal recruitment is a commitment to training and development of employees for a career in the organization. Internal recruitment is most critical for developing higher-level or specialized jobs in rounding out an employee's tacit and contextual knowledge.[61]

The development of a competency inventory for various positions serves the dual purpose of guiding the organization's development and prioritizing its competencies in implementing strategic objectives. It also sends a signal to employees on the competencies they should use in guiding their development for key positions. Finally, it connects training and skill development to competencies that the organization values.

There are advantages and disadvantages of picking people who are seen as having more potential versus having a general policy of 'come one, come all'. When certain employees are groomed for higher-level positions, they get greater attention and mentorship as well as opportunities to work in different areas as part of their preparation. In the interest of fairness, there is an argument to give all employees equal treatment and access to similar opportunities related to staffing. Equal access might not mean that all employees are trained equally. Rather, it encourages open access so that all people can compete in a fair way. This provides for development of a process where employees trust the process and see it as fair.[62]

In identifying and grooming suitable employees for future roles, **succession planning** can be a useful tool to guide the internal recruitment model in managing the development of competencies from one set of employees to another. The planning recognizes the timing of when positions will need replacing, identifying the initial competencies, designing developmental opportunities, developing and maintaining a talent pool and reassessing the progress in meeting competencies and placement. The development activities include plan involvement in team projects, rotational assignments, briefings of key issues, management development training, coaching and mentoring, and a placement process.[63] The plan also includes contingencies to find external candidates if internal candidates are not interested or available.

Internal recruiting and succession planning puts the onus on the organization to develop training opportunities to develop all employees as well as those who want to work in key positions. These include defining how university programmes, in-house training programmes, action learning experiences, mentoring and job rotations can be focused on developing employees for the specific needs of the organization. For example, an employee taking post-secondary courses could be encouraged to focus class assignments and reports on topics that are important to the organization.

Internal recruitment, or promoting from within, is a model of employee development focused on organizational fitness versus job fitness. It can be helpful in developing people within an organization to meet diversity objectives as well as developing qualified people for specific jobs. Promoting and developing people from within an organization is a policy that changes the recruitment dynamics and encourages managers and recruiters to recognize how an employee might eventually fit into the organization in higher-level jobs. It also means that employees should be shaped for higher-level positions and that external recruitment should begin only when there are no qualified internal candidates.[64]

Using internal recruitment strategies might allow the organization to achieve the following objectives:

- Groom or develop employees so they have specific skills required for higher-level jobs.
- Gain from the life history and experience of people who have worked in the organization for a longer period of time.
- Be more certain of the reliability of recruitment and selections made, as they are based on years of experience with that organization.

The internal recruitment model assumes that employees are being recruited for a career with the organization. This means that the organization has a commitment to human resource and career planning for employees and is aware of the competencies that will be needed for other positions. It also means that the organization is committed to training employees and to providing them with experiences that develop their careers. The internal recruitment model encourages longer tenure with an organization and more commitment to its long-range goals, and for this reason, there is generally more job security and loyalty.

The downside of internal recruitment is that there is the possibility of inbreeding, where the entire management team has been trained in a similar way and might have a similar philosophy. Internal candidates can become competitive and attempt to manoeuvre their way into certain positions ahead of their colleagues, as there is also the likelihood that some team members might not be willing to be managed by a person who was one of the team.

III Outsourcing as a recruitment strategy

Outsourcing, contracting out or shifting operational jobs to an outside third party has become a central issue in public organizations as a way to respond to the challenge of finding the best way to deliver public services.[65] From a transactional or economics perspective, the process of *outsourcing* or contracting out services has been seen as a means of focusing on objectives related to co-ordination, motivation and minimizing transaction costs. A contract can specify the requirements (where, when and how) in 'co-ordinating' what is done, define obligations to 'motivate' the vendor and 'minimize costs'. Although advocates claim reduced costs, some critiques suggest outsourcing cannot neglect the changes that take place in the culture and relationship of people in an organization.[66] Outsourcing is viewed as potentially disruptive to an organization's culture and employee–management relations as there is a perception that its main goal is to downsize the number of staff or reduce the significance of the union.[67] Employees who remain with the organization after outsourcing may feel that the change was unjustified and may resist.[68]

Information technology (IT) resources and services were once very commonly associated with the practice of outsourcing, due in large part to the rapid and radical evolution that occurred in IT during the latter part of the twenty-first century. The practice has now become common in nearly all organizational divisions. India is the current outsourcing market leader, although other countries are close behind. The Chinese government has designated 20 cities as outsourcing hubs in an effort to attract more international investment, and the Philippine government has declared outsourcing a priority industry. Outsourcing within Western countries is projected to grow at an average of 10–15 per cent annually.[69]

As an alternative to the transactional perspective, outsourcing can be viewed as a model for contracting out specific competencies that can be done elsewhere or from a resource-based perspective of securing needed resources from contractors.[70] From a recruitment perspective, contracting out involves searching for competencies or a range of services from an outside vendor, rather than recruiting individuals. Experienced outsourcing providers might be able to carry out the work more effectively, and perhaps with greater quality, because they have specialized competencies with a range of organizations and are up to date with the latest ideas and best practices. In assessing the feasibility, outsourcing only adds value if it provides a better alternative to internal delivery, at a cost advantage, with greater expertise and on demand. In making the decision of what should be outsourced, most people accept the general principle that core business activities or those activities essential to an organization's strategic advantage should not be outsourced.[71]

Competencies can be viewed as a resource, and over the last several decades, the landscape of public organizations has changed as governments increasingly rely on a complex web of employee relationships. Recruiting for competencies and services allows an organization to more flexibly engage higher-level services that may not currently reside or be easily developed within the host organization, something which can reduce liability and risk because the vendor has the specialists who are current on experiences. It can allow the organization to focus its resources on strategic and core competencies related to policymaking and engaging with clients. For example, non-core tasks such as IT maintenance and payroll processing can consume a great deal of time. If they can be outsourced, executives can potentially be reoriented to more strategic issues.

Outsourcing has its share of associated risks and challenges related to costs, performance management and the loss of a culture of accountability. Often, the price of the outsourcing contract may seem more attractive, but it does not take into account the time taken in providing the same services in-house. Transactional costs – costs associated with negotiating, monitoring and maintaining relationships, and correcting poor or non-performance – need to be considered. Negotiations with the union are required, and concessions may have to be made to get union agreement. Contracting out can involve unseen transaction costs to a point where it might be more affordable and less onerous to perform the services in-house.[72]

Outsourcing puts a new face on performance management, as some competencies related to some services are not easily definable. In particular, when contracting out social services and education, government contractors might be defining performance measures that might not be easily measured. Given an emphasis on performance measures and the need to identify results, the system of monitoring and evaluation might be difficult to administer.[73] A vendor's poor performance can affect a client's satisfaction with the organization. With more and more outsourcing, the organization loses its core competencies as it is made up of contractors, partnerships and consortia. The organization may no longer have the potential to develop expertise and competencies that are needed for future innovative products and services in that area.

Recruiting and selecting outsourcing suppliers. With the growing reliance on outsourcing, there are increasing challenges for recruiting and selecting vendors, and the practices vary in different countries. Some public agencies encourage the hiring of their former employees who work as private contractors, whereas others have restrictive provisions in their ethical codes (not hiring for periods of six months up to two years). Hiring vendors who have former employees on staff is seen as an advantage because these employees have inside knowledge of issues, culture, personnel, procedures and goals of the agency. In this respect, prior relationships and reputation are almost as important as qualifications.

There is a perception that 'the revolving door from public agency to contractor is driven by relational and insider factors', and many public agencies are viewed as a supplier of experienced and trained people who later take work as contractors in privatized companies. The research evidence does not substantiate that this sort of favouritism is widespread. However, agency managers seem to have a preference for people familiar with the culture, rules and practices over those who are not, and hire strategically to ensure the work is completed and to minimize transaction costs. The implication is that relationships and knowledge of procedures are important in recruiting and selecting contractors, just as it is a key element when recruiters hire external candidates in a regular recruiting process.[74]

CO 3: THE EMPLOYEE'S PERSPECTIVE – SEARCHING FOR A JOB

Just as organizations take steps in recruiting the most attractive and talented employees, job aspirants need to take similar steps when searching for an appealing job. This is the other side of recruitment – being more strategic than other students in searching for a highly valued job. These steps are relevant for new students entering the job market or for mid-career employees who have been downsized or restructured or who want to locate jobs to implement their career plans.

As illustrated in other sections of this book, recruitment is a bit of a mating game in which organizations are looking for attractive talent and employees are searching for attractive organizations. Just as personal contacts are important for organizations to find good people, the best way to locate an attractive job is through personal contacts, referrals and networks rather than cold calls or sending your résumé to the HR office. And, you are much more likely to get an interview and a job from a referral than from a résumé.[75]

In searching for a job, here are some questions to consider in developing a plan:

1. Who are the 'employers of choice' that you would like to work for? What are your values compared to other job aspirants, and do they correspond to the 'employers of choice' that you are targeting?
2. What are the general core competencies that your choice organizations are requiring?
3. What are your general and specific competencies, and what is your plan to develop them? What are your strengths and weaknesses? What are your valued experiences that are relevant to potential employers?
4. Does your résumé nicely display your competencies and experiences?
5. Given your 'employers of choice,' what are the advantages and disadvantages of different recruiting sources? Which sources are most useful and what steps should you take in implementing them?

The job search requires a great deal of personal fortitude and goal clarity. Existing research suggests a 'hobo syndrome' in that some individuals might be more prone to movement. In building on personality research – which is based on the Big Five factors (openness, extraversion, conscientiousness,

> MANAGERIAL IMPLICATIONS: This recruitment process sets the stage for the selection process described in the next chapter. If the recruiting process was effectively carried out, we will have a rich pool of talented applicants who represent a diversity of perspectives and groups. As such, it will be easier to carry out the selection process.
>
> A strategic theme important in this chapter is improving the diversity and inclusiveness of staff. Seeking to address this strategic theme helps in providing a diversity of staff that mirrors the profile in society. The general recruitment framework for improving diversity and inclusiveness is a framework that responds to all individuals and encourages their involvement in organizations.

agreeableness and emotional stability) – those who are more agreeable (trusting, compliant, caring), neurotic (anxious, insecure), and open to experience (imaginative, autonomous) are more likely to engage in a job search.[76] Younger people who had a higher level of confidence in themselves (self-efficacy) and who are driven by a learning-related goal orientation are more likely to be more assertive in career planning and exploration and have higher career aspirations.[77] The challenge is to recognize how your personality and goal orientation contribute to the job search.

BEFORE APPLYING, LET'S REVIEW

CO 1: Focus recruitment to meet diversity objectives.

Workplace diversity programmes encourage an inclusive culture for women, Aboriginal peoples, people with disabilities and those with visible minorities. Most diversity perspectives encourage 'adherence to legislation' and 'providing a more level platform' so that everyone has equal access. A diversity perspective that encourages inclusion and goes beyond may be more supportive and inclusive as an attractive place to work for all designated groups. It also makes it attractive for younger and older workers and respects all people rather than just people in designated groups.

CO 2: Compare the advantages and disadvantages of external recruiting, internal recruiting and outsourcing for attracting and retaining employees.

The external recruiting and outsourcing processes rely on the external market for finding talented employees, whereas the internal recruitment perspective is based on a promotion-from-within, developmental philosophy. Given the competencies sought, there are advantages of different sources and niche markets for designated groups and for older and younger workers. Even though recruiting is made easier and more efficient through information technology, managers place a great deal of reliance on referrals and networking in finding talented employees.

CO 3: Demonstrate the set of steps for undertaking the job search.

Personal contacts, referrals and networks are just as important for an applicant's job search as they are for employers in finding attractive candidates. Given that recruitment is a bit of a mating game, useful steps in developing a plan include matching your competencies and values to your 'employers of choice' and then using the appropriate recruitment sources.

DISCUSSION AND REVIEW QUESTIONS

1. Identify key changes in the recruitment environment, describing the increasing importance of being strategic in recruiting.
2. Review different paradigms on workplace diversity, describing discrimination and fairness, access and legitimacy paradigm, learning and effective multiculturalism. Your task is to review each paradigm's strengths and weaknesses and then define a statement of values and norms for making your workplace more inclusive of diverse groups of people.
3. Identify the barriers, values and norms that groups might face in entering the workplace and how you would overcome them. Useful questions in defining the values and norms for diverse groups of people include these: (i) 'What are some of the barriers that diverse groups of people might perceive in a traditional workplace?' (ii) 'What are values and norms for developing a positive, inclusive culture?' (iii) 'What ideas or recommendations might you have for overcoming these barriers and helping this group realize its values in the workplace?' Summarize your findings in a report using the following structure: (i) barriers, (ii) values and (iii) recommendations for responding to these barriers.
4. In recruitment and selection, the SHRM BSC encourages you to link competencies to the organization's strategic objectives in responding to customer or client needs. Assume your internal client is one of the managers in a local government department who is seeking to respond to diversity and inclusiveness of staff. In forming objectives, the framework addresses basic questions that are important to the implementation of a strategic theme:

    - How does the manager see us and how can we help him or her? How can we identify objectives to improve our ability to respond to the manager's needs? What are our measures of success? (Client or Customer perspective)
    - How do we look to shareholders or external funders, politicians and other stakeholders? How do we identify objectives to improve motivation and engagement, possibly by changing or being more financially accountable? What are our measures of success? (Financial perspective)
    - What must we excel at? How do we identify objectives to be more efficient in carrying out our work? What are our measures of success? (Internal process perspective)
    - Can we continue to improve and create value? How do we identify objectives to be improve motivation and engagement, possibly by changing the job's design? (What are our measures of success? (Innovation and Learning perspective or Learning and Growth)

    In the following tasks, you are asked to define recruitment objectives, initiatives and measures for each of the two following customer objectives.
    Strategic objective 1: Improve staff inclusiveness
    Initiatives: _____
    Markers: _____
    Strategic objective 2: Develop internal recruitment activities open to all employees, but targeted to groups
    Initiatives: _____
    Markers: _____

5. In adding details to the strategy map in Figure 6.3 and Table 6.2, identify HR activities or initiatives and markers for each of the objectives. That is, what should HR do to help managers achieve these strategic objectives?

Recruiting a Diverse Workforce   133

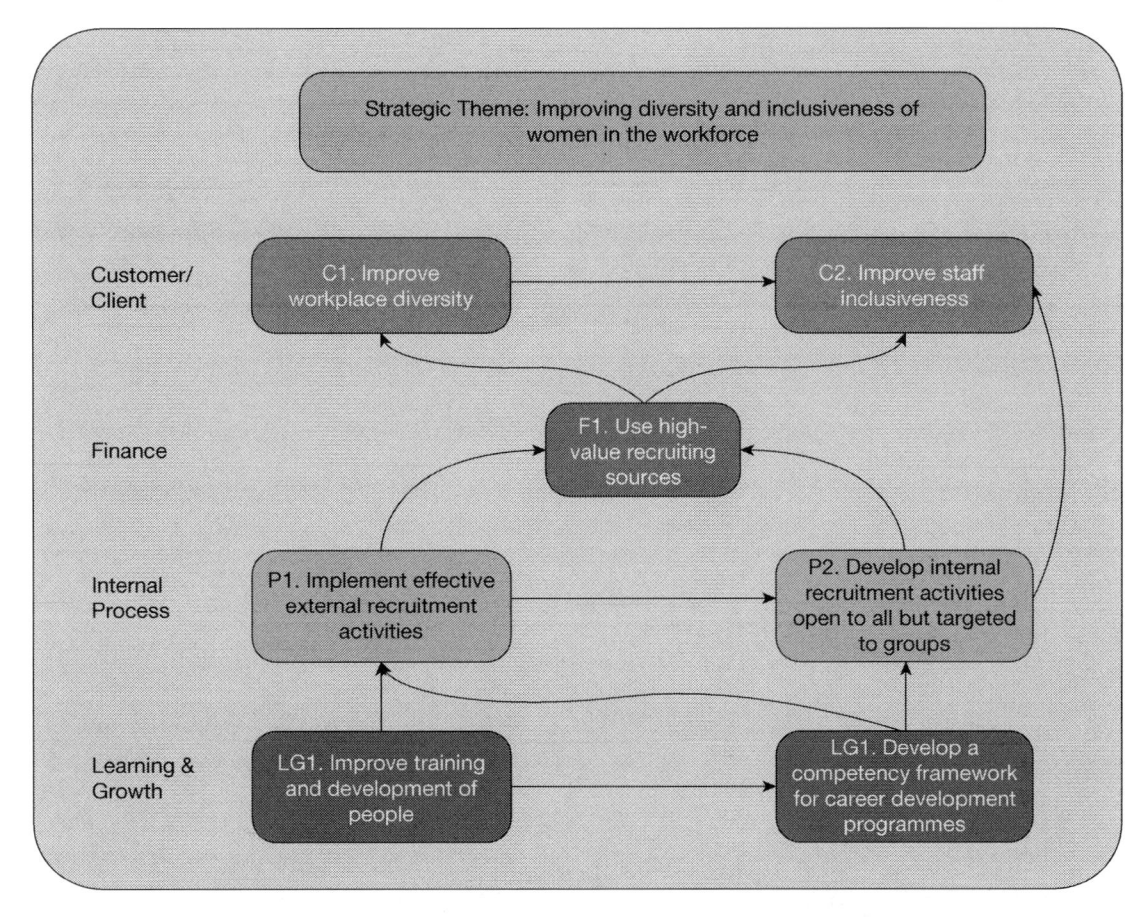

Figure 6.3 Strategy map for improving diversity and inclusiveness in the workforce.

Table 6.2 Strategic Theme: Improving Diversity and Inclusiveness in the Workforce

Objective	Initiatives	Markers or Measures	Time Period
CUSTOMER OR CLIENT PERSPECTIVE			
Objective 1	1. 2.		
Objective 2	1. 2.		
Objective 3	1. 2.		
FINANCIAL			
Objective 4	1. 2.		
Objective 5	1. 2.		

INTERNAL PROCESS	
Objective 6	1.
	2
Objective 7	1.
	2.
LEARNING & GROWTH	
Objective 8	1.
	2.
Objective 9	1.
	2.

You might also identify initiatives and markers (measures of progress) for the other objectives in the strategy map. In describing the 'dates', you might define the number of months (or whether it is ongoing) that the initiative is expected to take.

CASE: RECRUITING MORE WOMEN IN POLICING

Commissioner Green looked at the Fitzgerald Inquiry report in front of him and said, 'They say there's a lack of progress on recruiting women in policing. And, they want to know what we can do about it.' Four men and one woman sat across from Commissioner Green, all seasoned veterans in the Queensland Police Force. They were gathered together to prepare a report updating progress and identifying goals and initiatives for removing barriers and improving the recruitment and promotion of women in policing.

The Fitzgerald Inquiry in Australia, over 20 years ago, found a web of corruption and abuse of power perpetuated by a male culture of policing where physical strength and authority ruled.[78] The report pointed to a culture of policing predicated on an unwritten police code of silence that ensured that criminal activities were unquestioned and immune from scrutiny. Using the code, police took advantage of opportunities to steal seized or forfeited property; use informants to dispose of illegally acquired property; and accept money, property and sexual favours in exchange for information and warnings that police can provide.

Discussion. You might wish to discuss whether or not a 50/50 gender balance is realistic for an equity programme in policing in Queensland. Should the equity goals seek to establish an organizational profile that illustrates equal representation for men and women? Is there a difference between employment equity and equality? Which equity groups should be recognized, and how do you balance the needs of equity and equality? How should programmes put higher priority on recruitment and promotion?

Task. Develop strategic objectives, initiatives and measures that will address the equity imbalance and improve the inclusiveness of all staff. The book's website has additional background information relevant to this case.

7 Aligning Selection Strategies

Chapter Outline
- Chapter objectives (COs)   135
- A driving issue focusing managerial action: Employee fitness in the strategic context   135
- CO 1: Apply the triangulation principle in picking selection tools to reliably and validly make selection decisions   137
- CO 2: Tests and inventories in selection   144
- CO 3: Selection interviewing   148
- Before applying, let's review   153
- Discussion and review questions   154
- Case: Selecting an HR manager   155

CHAPTER OBJECTIVES (COs)

After reading this chapter, you will be able to implement the following objectives:

CO 1: Apply the triangulation principle in picking selection tools to reliably and validly make selection decisions.

CO 2: Assess the usefulness of different selection tests and inventories.

CO 3: Design and administer an interview guide using behavioural description and situational questions for assessing competencies important to strategic objectives.

A DRIVING ISSUE FOCUSING MANAGERIAL ACTION: EMPLOYEE FITNESS IN THE STRATEGIC CONTEXT

The cartoon character Popeye said, 'I y'am what I y'am', suggesting his personal traits defined him.[1] In following this logic, some HR practitioners suggest that a person's personal traits endure and need to be recognized in selection, in addition to an applicant's knowledge, skills and abilities. While recognizing technical competencies, Japanese organizations place a heavy emphasis on 'other' characteristics such as social background, temperament, motivation and character, as they are key drivers in performance.[2]

In the public sector, one 'other' characteristic important in selection is a person's public sector motivation, a defining set of characteristics which predicts people who are more likely to 'fit' best in public service organizations. The underlying assumption of this research is that people who are attracted and motivated to work in the public sector are those who find a fit between the character of a public service organization and their own personal characteristics.[3] People tend to stay with organizations when their values, motives and needs 'fit' with those of the organization, and tend to leave when there are differences.[4] Also, fit is a strong predictor of motivation and job performance.[5] Person–organizational (P–O) fit is the degree to which individuals (their values, skills and needs) match those of the workplace.[6] Person–job (P–J) fit is the match between a person's growth needs (e.g. need for challenge, job security) and the job's ability to meet these needs,[7] and person–group (P–G) fit is the match between individuals and work groups (i.e. co-workers, team and supervisors).[8]

Your 'fitness' depends most on your values

Drawing on research in anthropology and sociology, researchers point to values, needs and preferences as the defining elements of an organization's culture. Values, as the defining agents around an organization's culture, are illustrated in different ways. Rokeach's definition of values argued that there are two general types of values, and people hold to them in different degrees. **Instrumental values** are the standards of conduct that we might have for attaining a goal or methods for attaining an end. There are two types of instrumental values: morality (behaving appropriately or being honest) and competence (being logical, obedient or helpful).[9]

Terminal values describe outcomes or goals for an individual. According to Rokeach, there are few of these, but they are easier to identify in society. They are either personal (e.g. desire for peace of mind, happiness or excitement) or social (e.g. equality, security, national security, world peace).[10]

Different groups of people illustrate different values. Compared to a general population, managers place a higher value on sense of accomplishment, self-respect and a comfortable life. Ambition is the highest instrumental value for managers, and sense of accomplishment is the most important terminal value. These values can explain why managers might be rather impatient with a lack of career progress.

Values are the starting point for understanding how people interact, and they illustrate why some organizations are more or less attractive for different groups of people. The congruence in values between an individual and an organization is most likely to result in positive organizational interactions as well as a higher likelihood that a person will stay in the organization.[11] The value congruence between interviewers and applicant is also important in whether you get a job. Interviewers who liked the applicants were more likely to think that their interviewees would 'fit' as an employee.[12]

An organization's culture describes the 'shared basic assumptions that the group learned as it solved its problems of external adaptation and internal integration, that has worked well enough to be considered valid and, therefore, to be taught to new members as the correct way to perceive, think, and feel in relation to those problems'. Culture is present at different levels: visible artefacts which can be easily discerned, espoused beliefs and values which are conscious strategies and goals, and basic assumptions that people share (these are the core unconscious assumptions which are difficult to discern and which are often taken for granted as beliefs and values.[13] In public organizations, the values illustrating a public service motivation are partially described in the following questions.

- I am very interested in what is going on in my community. (Commitment to public interest)
- The give and take of public policymaking and politics appeals to me. (Attraction to policymaking)
- I often think of the welfare of people in distress. (Compassion)
- Making a difference in society means more to me than personal or financial achievements. (Self-sacrifice)[14]

If you responded positively to the above questions, you are likely to 'fit' well in the character of public service organizations.

> STRATEGIC CONTEXT: *Competencies are defined by knowledge, skills, abilities, and other characteristics (KSAO). Given the requirements needed to achieve an organization's strategic themes, most Western organizations use selection tools that focus on knowledge, skills and abilities, while Japanese organizations pay more attention to the other characteristics that define how well people fit in to the organization. While encouraging the use of tools that assess the total KSAOs, this chapter reviews testing and behavioural and situational interview questions in selection. These tools can be honed to capture 'other' characteristics important in selection, in addition to KSAs.*
>
> *Strategic themes relevant for this chapter relate to: selecting people who are motivated and fit in public sector organizations and selecting people to illustrate competencies relevant to the organization's success. These themes encourage you to use selection methods that help you predict job success and longevity in public service organizations. The implementation of these themes is based on the ability to use the appropriate selection tools. This chapter also provides an opportunity for practitioners and students to learn how to respond to different types of interview question.*

CO 1: APPLY THE TRIANGULATION PRINCIPLE IN PICKING SELECTION TOOLS TO RELIABLY AND VALIDLY MAKE SELECTION DECISIONS

Historically, over part of their history, public sector organizations were guided by principles of a career service that governed staff selection, principles which were designed to assure that staff selection was based on merit rather than patronage that existed in earlier times. In this sense, public organizations were distinctly different from private organizations in that central personnel authorities exerted a high degree of control over ministries and departments. They guided the recruitment and selection based on open, competitive examinations and provided for central mechanism for safeguarding merit.

Merit has been defined in different ways in different countries and during different periods of time. Merit generally means that people who are hired and promoted with the public service must possess certain competencies (merit) rather than political connections.[15] However, discussions of merit have encountered several debates as to what should count as criteria of merit, and in some cases, the way in which 'equity and merit have been pursued have differed over time depending on which group controlled staff selection'.[16] In some cases, merit was based on seniority, and in other cases it has been defined to benefit groups with certain educational qualifications and experience.

Public sector workers have, over their history, enjoyed a special status as 'public servants' that offered unique privileges, rights and conditions of work which were centrally determined by central personnel agencies. More recent changes in the form and structure of government have resulted in some changes to this special status in some countries, illustrated in a shift from 'career-based' systems and a greater emphasis on external recruitment, reduced job security and short-term employment contracts. Added to this, New Public Management (NPM) ideas and other reforms have resulted in greater discretion, as exemplified in individualized pay determination, performance-related pay systems and promotion based on performance.[17] There is evidence of transfer of responsibilities from central personnel bodies to ministries and departments, a general simplification of rules and procedures, and the development of more flexible policies. However, central governments still retain control over policy development and strategic directions, although common areas of devolution are recruitment and selection, job classification and pay.[18]

There are different variations in the degree of strategic choice that the HR department has from the more central agencies. At the national and state or provincial levels, central agencies often define the strategic directions in HR in areas such as diversity in hiring or attracting talented and motivated employees, while local ministries and departments have a great degree of choice and influence in implementing selection practices.

Linking selection to the strategic context defining the competencies needed

The strategic planning process helps focus selection decisions by ensuring that the competencies (KSAOs) of the selection process link the organization's strategic themes and objectives. Most HR departments have a degree of influence in operationalizing the general strategic themes in innovative ways. Within the broad outline of the centralized strategic themes, managers and HR professionals have to continually make adaptations and adjustments in the way they address strategic themes and objectives.

The challenge of using the SHRM BSC in addressing strategic themes highlighted in this chapter is to reliably and validly use selection tools – including interview guides and tests – for selecting the right employees to help achieve an organization's strategic objectives. Good selection decisions help us choose the best person who illustrates competencies we have defined as important in public service motivation and job performance. Poor choices can have disastrous consequences.[19] Everyone is happy when the right decision is made, as the organization gains a motivated and capable person who effectively performs the job, and the new hire is a positive addition to the team. We see this in sports, where successful managers are able to find and attract good talent while less successful managers are not as capable at attracting top people.

Selection errors have tremendous costs and are of two types. The **'false positive error'** occurs when an employer hires a person who does not perform as expected or does not fit with the public sector culture. There are costs associated with hiring an under-performer, including loss of production, placement and replacement costs and team conflicts. The motivational and production costs are easier to see in inefficiencies, rework or supervision costs, and the greater possibility of accidents or absenteeism. Replacement and placement costs relate to hiring, training and terminating an employee and then initiating additional expenses to find a new person. Team ineffectiveness costs are harder to measure but are illustrated by team members not wanting to work with others or feeling angry because they have to correct the mistakes made by less capable co-workers.

A **'false-negative error'** occurs when an employer rejects a person who would have been a talented staff member. Most false-negative decisions go unnoticed except when the rejected applicant excels with one of the organization's competitors. In some cases, a 'false-negative' error is illustrated when an applicant files a complaint that they were discriminated against even though they were qualified for the job. False positive and false negative errors are typical in many selection decisions in life. In professional sports, a team manager might draft a player who does not live up to potential (false positive) or reject a player who later becomes a star with another team (false negative).

Selection, as one of the most important decisions for managers to make, is the process of choosing the best applicants among individuals who have been recruited for existing jobs or projected vacancies. During the selection process, both the candidate and the interviewer are trying to make themselves attractive to each other. In the selection process, both the employer and the candidate are involved in the act of decision-making. Employers are trying to sell the organization as an attractive place to work and at the same time trying to assess whether the candidate might be a good employee. In the same way, employees are trying to sell themselves to the organization in addition to making judgements about whether this is the best place to work. Therefore, there is a chance that expectations can be misrepresented or become unclear.

Performance metrics in improving the reliability and validity of selection tools

When we cannot rely on our selection tools, or if they are not valid indicators of the competencies or personal characteristics we want, there are tremendous consequences. Just as we rely on the accuracy of our digital watches in consistently giving us the correct time, the goal of selection tools is to accurately gather information on knowledge, skills, abilities and other characteristics (KSAOs) related to the competencies we are seeking in implementing our strategic themes and objectives. If the selection tools are not reliable and valid, the decisions made on the basis of them can have costly implications including poor hiring choices and possible grievances or law suits.

Reliability is the degree to which an interview, test or other selection procedure gives consistent results over a period of time, under equivalent conditions. Just as a thermometer is reliable when we are confident that it is calibrated correctly, reliability in selection is the consistency of our measurement device. Reliability is also concerned with the consistency of different interviewers in producing the same ratings of applicants. For example, testing tools or measures are reliable if applicants provide similar responses over different periods of time (assuming no changes have occurred). In the same way, interview questions (or an equivalent version of the questions) are reliable when they produce similar results at different times assuming nothing else has changed during that time.

Generally, **validity** is the degree to which the characteristics measured in a test are related to the requirements of some aspect of the job performed.[20] Because a goal in using a selection test is to determine a person's potential motivation or performance, the validity of a test or interview is the extent to which the information gathered corresponds to actual motivation or job performance. Selection tools that are not valid may present legal problems as the relevance (validity) of a selection tool is a critical piece of evidence when assessing complaints.

In addition to reliability and validity, there are different reasons that managers and HR practitioners might use a selection tool, including costs in development and costs in administration. Although the overall effectiveness of a selection programme depends on the manager's ability to interpret the responses he or she generates, this job is much easier if the manager can be assured that the tools being used have some level of validity.

In Table 7.1, it is interesting to note that years of experience, years of education and age have the lowest validity in predicting job performance. Table 7.1 also indicates that some of the most valid selection tools in predictive performance are those that are more closely linked to behaviours on the job. These include work samples, job knowledge tests, peer ratings and structured interviews. Assessment centres might also be included in this group, even though their validity is slightly lower, possibly because their validity is an average of a variety of selection tools used.

The **realistic job preview (RJP)** is a way of providing realistic information about job demands, expectations, the customer environment and strategic objectives of the organization.[21] RJPs can be designed in different ways. The information can be presented orally (on the telephone or in person) by the manager or HR staff member. It can be presented electronically through a tour of the organization, working conditions and other facilities.

Those who advocate the use of a formal or informal RJP process argue that new candidates are less likely to be disappointed because their expectations are not met or they encounter conditions they were not prepared for. After an RJP, it is also possible for employers to make changes to the job to meet employee expectations. Although there is evidence to suggest a link between RJP and reduced turnover, it is not clear that more realistic or lowered expectations will result in improved job satisfaction. It is possible that the impact of an RJP results more from an improved ability to cope with the job conditions or because of the creation of an atmosphere of greater openness and honesty.[22]

Table 7.1 Validity of Different Selection Methods

Selection Tool	Validity[23]	Costs for Development/Administration[24]
Application forms seek information on employment status, experience and general biographical data. **Weighted application forms** give more importance to certain questions.	Weighted forms validities (0.25–0.50)[25]	High/low
Years of experience refers to the number of years of experience on the same or a similar job.	0.18	Low/low
Biographical information measures a variety of characteristics through questions about past life experience in family and high school, and with hobbies and interests.	0.35	Low/low
Letters of recommendation and references can provide information about the applicant's education and employment history, competencies, interpersonal skills and personal character, and work ethic.	Moderate validity if focused on specific questions	Low/low
Years of education is an indication of level of education achieved.	0.10	
Age is chronological age.	−0.01	
GMA tests (also called general cognitive ability and general intelligence) measures mental abilities such as logic, reading comprehension, verbal, or mathematical reasoning ability, and perceptual ability, typically with paper-and-pencil or computer-based instruments.	0.51	Low/low
Job knowledge tests measure the knowledge required for a job, usually through a paper-and-pencil test. For example, tests are available to test the job knowledge of machinists and electricians.	0.48	High/low
Conscientiousness measures the personal trait 'conscientiousness', or the care, thoroughness and character of a person.	0.31	Low/low
Integrity tests measure attitudes and propensities to behaviour that is counterproductive such as drinking on the job and stealing from the employer; they also measure behavioural characteristics such as a person's honesty, dependability, trustworthiness and reliability, typically with multiple-choice or true/false formats.	0.41	Low/low
Situational judgement tests are paper-and-pencil tests designed to measure judgement in a work situation. Applicants are presented with short scenarios (either in written or video format) and asked to respond in an open-ended or multiple-choice format.	0.34	High/low
Structured employment interviews use questions which follow a structured format so that each applicant gets the same questions and probes. The questions are usually formed after a careful analysis of the job.	0.51	Low/high

Unstructured interviews have no fixed format and measure non-cognitive skills and abilities (e.g. ability to work in a team, interpersonal relations, ability to meet objectives, etc.) using questions that vary from candidate to candidate, and interview to interview, for the same job. Often there is no fixed format for evaluating (or rating) the applicant.	0.31	Low/high
Work samples (like realistic job previews) are hands-on simulations of all or part of the job. A job applicant might be asked to perform a job such as wiring a circuit or repairing an electric motor. Work samples are often used to hire electricians, welders, carpenters and other skilled workers.	0.54	High/high
Peer ratings are evaluations of the potential or actual performance made by peers or co-workers.	0.49	
Assessment centres measure knowledge, skills and abilities through a series of work samples/exercises that reflect job content and types of problems faced on the job, cognitive ability tests, personality inventories and/or job knowledge tests.	0.37	High/high
Reference checks provide information about an applicant's past performance or measure the accuracy of an applicant's statements on the résumé or in interviews by asking individuals who have previous experience with a job candidate to provide an evaluation.	0.26	Low/low

Checking references. Many managers are sceptical of the value of letters of recommendation and references, as most are positive and often general. When applicants ask a person to be a reference, most people are cautious in picking only those who will be positive. So, from a manager's viewpoint, what good are references that are likely to be biased and undiscerning? This scepticism of the lack of candour and questionable value of references is more pronounced in situations where employees have access to this information under freedom of information legislation. However, even with this scepticism, managers find that the process can provide useful information.[26]

The validity of letters of recommendation and references can be increased if the employer takes a more proactive approach in asking the referee to focus the reference letter or comments on key competencies or needs of the organization. Instead of simply asking for a reference on the candidate's skills and abilities, the employer can ask for specific examples of the applicant's ability to work, for example with customers; ability to direct a sales force; or willingness to work on team projects. In the same way, in requesting verbal or written references, it is useful to ask for job- or organization-related information and both positive and negative examples of performance relating to job competencies. In some highly sensitive positions, a more thorough review of references from different perspectives might be necessary. In key managerial positions, you might ask for references from supervisors, peers and subordinates; in hiring an engineer to supervise construction projects at a university, you might seek references from former employers, customers or clients, building inspectors, planners and subcontractors who have worked with the engineer.

Background and reference checks. Background checks, depending on the job opening, can include criminal background checks, driving history, immigration status checks or verification of academic achievement. A background check is one way to confirm a candidate's experience or status and helps avoid lawsuits on negligent hiring practices. The need for background checks is underscored by the frequency with which misinformation is submitted by job applicants on résumés. A surprisingly high percentage of job applicants lie on their résumé, and education was one of the most frequently falsified qualifications. One background checking company found that 45 per cent of the 453,320 education, employment and/or reference checks made revealed discrepancies. In one well-publicized example, the dean of Admissions at the Massachusetts Institute of Technology (MIT) resigned after it was discovered that she had misrepresented her education 28 years before. At various times, she had reported having degrees which she did not have.[27]

Many organizations ask for references or letters of recommendation, even though they are not highly correlated with job performance.[28] Most letters of recommendation are highly positive, as most applicants are more likely to ask people who will provide positive comments. Managers and HR practitioners can improve the validity of reference letters if they are proactive in asking referees to respond to certain questions. Instead of asking a referee broad questions, for example 'Could you provide comments on the applicant over the years he or she has worked in your organization?', ask specific questions that relate to the competencies required in the job, that is, 'Could you provide examples of how this person has demonstrated specific skills in building and working in teams, assisting fellow co-workers and carrying out projects within specific guidelines? We would appreciate both positive examples as well as examples of times when this person has had difficulty demonstrating these skills.'

It is also possible to increase the validity of references by paying more attention to the examples or the traits described rather than the positivity of the responses. Although two applicants might receive positive responses, one referee might comment on the applicant's interpersonal characteristics in relating to others while other referees might describe the second person as a detail-oriented person. The job to be filled usually requires one set of skills over another. For example, a job that requires teamwork needs good interpersonal skills, whereas an accountant might need to be better at details.[29]

Drug testing. Many countries do not have mandatory drug testing of employees, although people working in the United States may be asked to respect US legislation for performing drug tests. The US legislation is supported by research such as that done in the US Postal Service, which found that employees who tested positive for drugs are absent 41 per cent more often and fired 38 per cent more often than employees who did not test positive.[30] Those who argue for compulsory employee drug testing suggest that it is a means of ensuring a drug- and alcohol-free workplace. They argue that it generally improves safety, security and productivity, and that persons who test positively for drugs and alcohol are absent more often, do not perform as well on the job, and pose a safety threat to the workplace. Those who oppose drug testing argue that it is invasive and an infringement of a person's right to privacy.

Using the triangulation principle

The goal of any selection process is to identify the best applicants on the basis of the competencies identified as being important to job or organizational performance. However, risks exist of making mistakes in selecting a candidate who should have been rejected (acceptance error) or rejecting someone who should have been accepted (erroneous rejection).

All selection tools are biased to some degree. A person's résumé and reference letters provide only a positive statement of the candidate, and interviews often favour those people who are better able to answer questions, for example, those who are more socially adept and conversational, characteristics that might only partially fulfil a job's requirements.

The use of multiple selection tools illustrates a principle of **triangulation**, or gaining data and information from a variety of perspectives and viewpoints. Triangulation in social science research involves using a combination of methodologies in the study of the same phenomena and is analogous to navigation and military practices where multiple reference points are used to pinpoint a ship's location.[31]

One way to improve the selection process is to use a variety of methods to validate the results of an assessment of an applicant's competencies. Some organizations use a **multiple-hurdle strategy** that involves a series of steps, or hurdles (prescreening, testing, interviewing, background reference checks). Applicants who are successful during the initial selection steps go on to the next step. In a similar way, while résumés, application forms, and written tests are also relied on, large Japanese public organizations use **multi-rater sequential interviewing**. In this interviewing style, potential applicants participate in several interviews with different people who assess applicants at different stages of the process.

Police and military organizations use an **assessment centre process** which consists of a variety of techniques – job-related simulations, interviews, psychological tests, group exercises and in-basket problems – to allow prospective candidates to illustrate a wider variety of competencies under different conditions. Assessment centres can consist of small or large numbers of exercises, depending on the goals of the selection process. In some police or military organizations, the assessment centres involve three or four days of interviews, role plays, oral presentations and other exercises. In the selection of university faculty, the assessment centre concept is applied over one or two days and involves research and teaching presentations, interviews and student discussion.

Assessment centres usually are designed so that they include some sort of in-basket exercise whose contents are similar to those that are found in the actual tasks involved in the job being tested for. Other possibilities include oral exercises, counselling simulations, problem analysis exercises, interview simulations, role-play exercises, written report/analysis exercises and leaderless group exercises. Assessment centres allow candidates to demonstrate more of their skills through a number of job-relevant situations.

In an example of an assessment centre selecting doctors for postgraduate training in paediatrics, assessors defined 14 competency domains: (i) professional integrity and respect for others, (ii) empathy and sensitivity, (iii) personal attributes (such as flexibility and sense of humour), (iv) communication skills, (v) teamwork, (vi) learning and personal development, (vii) coping with pressure, (viii) personal organization and administration skills, (ix) vigilance and situational awareness, (x) clinical/technical knowledge and expertise, (xi) conceptual thinking, problem-solving and decision-making, (xii) legal, ethical and political awareness, (xiii) managing others and (xiv) teaching.[32] The competencies illustrated in Table 7.2 were developed from critical incident interviews asking patients and doctors to indicate examples of good performance and past performance. The competencies were then rated in terms of their importance in the job.

The assessment centre exercises were developed by three consultants in paediatrics and included two group exercises, two written exercises and three simulated consultations (two consultations with parents and one with a child and parent). Various trained assessors participated in the rating of the 27 candidates (for 10 possible positions). A panel of three assessors carried out the interviews, each person asking one question, and all assessors scoring each question on a scale of 1–10 (total score = 90). Assessors observed the candidate, recorded factual information on behaviours, classified the observations as positive or negative behaviours and evaluated performance. The overall rating was based on a total of the 14 competency scores. A score of 1–4 was then given to the person's performance on the overall exercise.

Table 7.2 Application of Assessment Centre Exercises for Selecting Doctors for Postgraduate Training[1]

Assessment Centre Approach	Application for Selection of Doctors	Competency Domains
In role-playing exercises candidates assume a role and deal with another person in a job-related situation. A trained role-player responds 'in character' to the actions of the candidate. Performance is assessed by observing raters.	In the role plays, the applicant consults with a concerned parent (played by a trained medical actor) of a 2-year-old child.	Professional integrity and respect for others. Empathy and sensitivity. Communication skills. Coping with pressure, clinical/technical knowledge and expertise. Conceptual thinking, problem-solving and decision-making.
In-basket-type exercises can be carried out by groups or individuals. The tasks in the exercise correspond to those the job holder might experience in a job or organization.	Applicant has to discuss and prioritize 11 competing administrative tasks, as well as clinical tasks, and to hold discussions with patients, parents and colleagues.	Professional integrity and respect for others. Communication skills. Team work. Personal organization and administration skills. Conceptual thinking, problem-solving and decision-making.
Group exercises may ask individuals to prioritize various tasks or problems or discuss a case. Individual test exercises can be combined with group exercises that ask individuals to reflect on their experience.	Applicants are asked to work in a group to prioritize various tasks and provide their reasoning.	Professional integrity and respect for others. Communication skills. Learning and personal development. Personal organization and administration skills. Conceptual thinking, problem-solving and decision-making.
Interviews can consist of different types of questions: technical, situational and behavioural description.	Candidates are asked three situational questions relating to their CV, each question designed to assess 2 or 3 competencies: one question deals with a risk management problem in paediatrics, and one relates to how to respond to a particular situation in his or her medical career.	Empathy and sensitivity. Communication skills. Team work. Coping with pressure. Vigilance and situational awareness. Legal, ethical and political awareness.

CO 2: TESTS AND INVENTORIES IN SELECTION

The need to classify and select large numbers of military recruits in the early 1940s provided a great deal of impetus for the field of testing.[39] 'Efforts to develop and create tests to assist managers with personnel selection have ranged from the absurd to the hopeful and into the stage of continued refinement and growing efficiency.'[40] Tests and inventories are now becoming more common in both selection and promotions,. partially because they have illustrated how they can help managers predict performance and guard against future work problems.

An overwhelming number of tests and instruments are available for assessment, and the primary task of an HR manager is to recognize the different attributes they assess and the validity of the tests, or

A RELEVANT POINT OF VIEW: SELECTION CRITERIA IN JAPANESE ORGANIZATIONS

Selection criteria and procedures in Japanese organizations focus on general employability characteristics and include personal characteristics such as conscientiousness and general intelligence.[33] In a survey conducted by the Japanese Institute of Labour, 80 per cent of the managers who responded indicated that 'motivation and personality' were more important than 'knowledge and abilities' in selecting applicants. Other characteristics which they thought important were a candidate's general knowledge and agreeableness.[34]

The uniqueness of the Japanese model of person–organizational fit is that it describes the compatibility between the individual and organization, and encourages employee participation, learning and career development. HR plays a key role in facilitating this.[35] Job classifications are broad and flexibly defined, and employees are expected to accept frequent changes in assignments. Employees are required to work in various quality circles, cross-functional teams or problem-solving teams (which are central to the kaizen, a continuous improvement process).[36]

Selection criteria are usually broadly defined and in many cases are not focused on selecting people for specific jobs. Employees are expected to hold multiple jobs in their long-term careers, and most knowledge, skills and abilities (KSAs) can be developed or trained internally. Selection focuses less on person–job fit as new employees are not expected to have specific KSAs for specific jobs. Even in selecting white-collar technical employees, less emphasis is put on technical expertise.

Japanese recruitment and selection activities are keyed to broad job categories: blue collar, white-collar administrative and white-collar technical. When hiring college graduates, the emphasis is on white-collar generalists (sogo-shoku), staff employees (ippan-shoku), and white-collar technical employees (gijutsu-shoku). White-collar generalists and white-collar technical employees are core employees expected to advance into management. The KSAOs within these broad categories emphasize different jobs focused on developing an employee's career.[37] The selection process in Japanese organizations puts a heavy emphasis on interviewing which is focused on assessing the match between applicant attitudes and needs and those of the organization.

To what degree do public sector organizations in other countries emphasize 'other' characteristics? In a study of recruitment advertising in the United Kingdom, Germany and France, researchers found the German and French managers put a higher emphasis on technical qualifications. UK managers stressed personal characteristics such as social, political and putative leadership skills.[38]

If Western organizations wanted to implement Japanese-type person–organizational fit ideas in selecting and retaining employees, what actions might they have to encourage in training, learning and employee development?

the degree to which the characteristics measured in the tests are related to some important requirement of what is being sought in the job.[41] Recent research illustrates tests – describing personality characteristics, cognitive abilities, and integrity and social behaviours – that provide different information in selecting applicants who are more likely to perform better on the job.

Personality. Although personality testing was widely criticized in the past, there is a renewed interest in its potential. Some researchers suggest that these tests might be used in conjunction with the more valid cognitive tests, and others illustrate how psychometric tests have enhanced their value. Although there has been confusion about how personality is defined, one more recent approach has focused on the Big Five personality factors:[42]

1. **Extroversion** describes the degree to which a person is active, assertive, gregarious, sociable and talkative. Extroverts are people who energize themselves in the presence of others. Introverts need time alone.
2. **Emotional stability** is the degree to which a person is emotionally capable, secure and positive. It is the opposite of instability, which describes a person who is angry, anxious, depressed, emotional, insecure or worried. Abraham Lincoln said, 'Most people are just about as happy as they choose to be.' Most of us would agree with Abraham Lincoln's statement about happiness because it implies that a person's outlook plays a big part, more so than the circumstances around us. Psychologists might rephrase this statement to say, 'Most people are just as happy as their level of emotional stability leads them to be.'[43]
3. **Agreeableness** summarizes attributes related to being co-operative, courteous, flexible, good-natured, tolerant and trusting. The other side of this dimension is being prickly, hard to get along with, abrasive and corrosive.
4. **Conscientiousness** is an indication of whether a person is achievement oriented, organized, persevering, responsible and thorough. People who are conscientious are engaged and feel accountable. They are more likely to accept responsibility and want to accomplish things. They are proactive rather than reactive.
5. **Openness to experience** describes attributes describing the degree to which the individual is artistically sensitive, broad-minded, cultured, curious and original. People who are open to experience are more likely to want to find new ways to do things.

Why are the Big Five factors important? First, they provide a consensus in defining personality and help us focus the hundreds of general attributes such as kindness, sociability, enthusiasm and loyalty by combining these to indicate that they really describe five general factors.

Second, researchers selected 117 studies to better understand how these five predictors affected training and performance for given groups: professionals, police officers, managers, salespersons and skilled and semiskilled employees in a wide range of occupations. The results suggest that conscientiousness predicted job performance in each of the five occupations; and conscientiousness also predicted training performance, although openness to new experiences and extroversion were also important in some cases.[44] Practically, conscientiousness is also related to characteristics that help an organization achieve other objectives. For example, conscientious people are more likely to pay attention to safety regulations and tend to have fewer accidents.[45]

The Big Five factors help bring a consensus in defining personality factors relevant to the workplace. Although the research illustrates that conscientiousness is an extremely important personality characteristic, other personality factors might be valid predictors of job performance for some specific jobs. For example, agreeableness and working well with others might be important for client-oriented jobs or working in teams which demand close relationships with others. Though some measures might be important in jobs that require teamwork and flexibility, they might be less important in assembly-line jobs, where the pace of work depends on the technology.

Cognitive ability tests. Tests in this category measure a range of **general mental abilities (GMAs)**, from verbal and quantitative skills to aptitude. Cognitive ability is different from cognitive style. **Cognitive style** is generally described as the way people think, gather, remember and use information in problem-solving; **cognitive ability** is a description of a person's intelligence or aptitude. Such tests have been widely used in public service organizations to assess reasoning and problem-solving ability as well as judgement in solving problems in work-related situations.

General intelligence tests. These tests provide a measure of a person's intellectual ability, based on a number of abilities including memory, verbal ability, vocabulary and numerical ability. Originally, an IQ test was a quotient measuring a child's mental age (using an intelligence test), divided by the child's chronological age and then multiplied by 100. If a girl of 10 years old answered questions that a 12-year-old might, her IQ would be 12 divided by 10 multiplied by 100, so her IQ would be 120. For an adult, dividing mental age by chronological age does not make a lot of sense, because a 50-year-old person might not be more intelligent than a 23-year-old. Therefore, an adult's IQ score is a measure of the extent to which a person is above or below the intelligence of an 'average' adult.

For some people, IQ or GMA is important in making selection decisions. Bill Gates, founder of Microsoft, illustrates this bias. Intelligence or smartness is valued over other attributes, and Microsoft recruiters seek high-IQ candidates and train them for specific jobs after they are hired.[46]

In defining intelligence, each human being has a mixture of different intelligences: deductive, inductive, mechanical, memory, numerical, perceptual, reasoning, verbal and vocabulary.[47] Others argue that these specific types of intelligence are really measures of a single human ability called 'general intelligence', or 'g'. There is consistent evidence that 'g' predicts performance in a wide range of jobs, not just those which require people to do a lot of thinking.[48] Although a solid predictor of performance, most people agree that it is more highly correlated with job knowledge, which enhances job performance.[49]

Aptitude tests. These tests measure the applicant's aptitude to do a job, or the person's potential to do the job after being properly trained. The Royal Canadian Mounted Police tests applicants on aptitudes related to composition, comprehension, memory, judgement, observation, logic and computation. For example, in one section of the test, applicants are asked to memorize the pictorial and textual materials of a picture. That is, four mug shots of individuals are presented, along with names, descriptions and crimes for which these people are wanted. The test also gives descriptions of six vehicles, including the make, colour, licence plate and, occasionally, a crime in which the vehicle was involved. The applicant's task is to memorize this information.[50]

Other aptitude tests measure a person's understanding of mechanical principles important for certain jobs like a machinist or engineer. Aptitude tests screen for aptitudes needed in specialized positions – such as medical and legal workers – requiring knowledge of technical terminology and procedures. Under the supervision of an attorney, legal assistants use this knowledge to prepare correspondence and legal papers such as motions, subpoenas and complaints. Medical secretaries require knowledge to transcribe dictation and assist physicians or allied health professionals with reports. They need to be able to record simple medical histories and arrange hospitalization for patients, and they have to be familiar with hospital and laboratory procedures. In addition, general aptitude tests show a high degree of validity in measuring competencies related to software technologies, call centre listening and keying, keyboard and secretarial skills related to filing and office management, as well as literacy and numeracy.

Integrity tests. There are two types of integrity test. In overt integrity tests, the purpose is clear in assessing attitudes related to dishonest behaviour. A second type involves the use of personality-based measures aimed at predicting a broad range of deviant behaviours related to disciplinary behaviours, excessive absenteeism, drug use and violence on the job.

The evidence, based on an accumulation of research across studies, suggests that the average validity coefficient of integrity tests is 0.41 when predicting supervisory ratings of job performance. This value is constant across settings, and overt and covert tests produce similar validities. Overt integrity tests seem to better predict counterproductive behaviours – such as theft, absenteeism or violence – than do personality-based tests.[51]

Should tests be used in selection? Whether or not HR practitioners use tests, the research in this area has highlighted that certain personal characteristics (beyond knowledge and skills) are relevant for predicting job performance. These include conscientiousness and personal integrity as well as cognitive abilities. When using tests, human resource practitioners should consider two issues: (i) Applicants do alter their responses and might not provide the most honest answers to integrity tests. Most of the current scales in use do not contain ways to detect distorted responses. (ii) Some tests (e.g. integrity tests) provide more accurate measures than others. A person with low moral behaviour might 'get it right' after a period of time, but it is less likely that a person who demonstrates low intelligence will 'get smart'. This suggests that people with a shady past who have truly reformed may get low scores. Thus, we should be cautious about unverified conclusions made from integrity tests.

A RELEVANT POINT OF VIEW: WHAT IS WRONG WITH THE USE OF THESE QUESTIONS IN SOME SELECTION INTERVIEWS?

In the past, many selection interviews included a number of questions relating to your goals, qualifications, strengths and weaknesses and your skills. What is wrong with these questions?

- Why do you want to work for this organization?
- What qualifications do you have that make you feel you will be successful in this job?
- This position involves a lot of contact with the public. How do you feel about your skills in dealing with people?
- This position involves working closely with others. How did you get along with others in your previous employment? Have you ever had any problems getting along with co-workers in the past?
- What are your goals and visions of what you would like to do in the next few years?
- What are some of your strengths and weaknesses?
- If you had to try to get the co-operation of someone, how would you do it?
- If you had to deal with a member of the public who was angry, what would you do?

Most people who are applying for a job will prepare for these questions. They are classic, textbook questions that indicate the job applicant was prepared for the interview. However, they often reveal very little about a person's competencies. For instance, a person's goals and visions are just his or her aspirations and do not tell you anything about how the person works on a day-to-day basis. Hypothetical questions about gaining co-operation and handling difficult people may only illustrate that this person is up to date with the most recent management literature, rather than whether he or she will be successful on the job in gaining co-operation or in handling difficult people. And do we honestly expect people to tell us about their real weaknesses? Would we expect a person to tell us about being unethical or being fired for incompetence in a previous organization? No, of course not. These people would rephrase their answers to reveal their most positive side.

CO 3: SELECTION INTERVIEWING

Well-designed interviews can gather information on competencies that are difficult to assess in other ways. For example, interviews can tap social and motivational competencies much better than other selection tools. Social and motivational competencies relate to the dependability of the applicant and his or her work habits, responsibilities taken for different jobs, ability to work with others, sincerity of interest in the job, ability to be adaptable, goals in relation to the opportunities which the organization can provide, manner and appearance and a general view of the applicant's qualification in relation to work performance.

In practice, selection interviews focus on certain characteristics more than others. In a review of 388 characteristics that were rated in 47 actual interview situations, researchers indicated that personality traits and applied social skills were rated more often than other characteristics. Examples of personality traits rated included responsibility, dependability and persistence, all of which are related to conscientiousness in carrying out work. Applied social skills rated were interpersonal relations, social skills and ability to work in a team. This suggests that interviews can be appropriately used, alone or in conjunction with other tools, to gather information relevant to future job performance.[52]

The interview continues to be one of the most popular selection tools and is often used as the only selection tool in organizations.[53] This popularity might partially be explained by a belief that in order to make a good judgement, it is important to have a personal conversation with a candidate.

Although the interview is probably the most popular selection tool, it has been widely criticized. Several studies have shown that interviewers do not agree with one another on their assessment of a candidate.[54] An early Canadian study suggested that most interviewers made decisions on the candidate in the first two to five minutes of the interview.[55]

A major criticism of traditional open-ended interviews is that candidates might be asked different questions with no set structure, and the information provided from the different candidates would be hard to judge consistently. For instance, one interviewer might begin with a question such as 'Tell us about your past experience,' and then continue with questions based on the initial answer. Other interviewees might be asked different questions, depending on their response.

Dissatisfaction with this form of open-ended, informal interview led to a structured form of interview based directly on job analysis. The traditional **structured interview** applied a series of job-related questions with predetermined answers across all interviews for a particular job. The traditional structured interview, although more reliable and valid, was very restrictive, and many interviewers rejected it because it was too confining and stressful for the candidate. A review of the research on interviewing illustrates six principles for effectively structuring the selection interviewing process.[56]

1. *Defining the purpose of the job and competencies required.* When job analysis information is used, interviewers are less likely to develop interview questions based on mistaken beliefs about what the person is expected to do on the job.[57] Although job analysis information encourages interviewers to ask job-related questions, it is also appropriate to develop interview questions that go beyond the job and relate to a person's job fitness and organizational fitness.
2. *Establishing fair practices and procedures so that all people are treated equally.* Interviewers can reduce bias in interviewing by treating candidates uniformly and granting all applicants an equal chance to illustrate their qualifications by using (i) standardized interview protocols and (ii) standardized rating scales.[58]
3. *Implementing behavioural-based questions.* In eliminating ambiguity and subjectivity in making employment decisions, effective interviews involve two types of *behavioural-based questions*.[59] **Situational** questions ask interviewees what they would do in a hypothetical situation that is similar to ones they will experience in the position they are being interviewed for,[60] for example 'What would you do if...?' Such questions are based on the assumption that a person's expressed behavioural intentions are related to subsequent behaviour.
    - **Behavioural description** questions ask candidates to describe how they actually behaved in past situations that are similar to situations they might encounter in the job they are being

interviewed for.[61] An example would be 'Can you describe an example of incident where you ... ?' This type of question is based on the assumption that a good indicator of future behaviour is what a person did in the past in a similar situation. Instead of asking, 'How would you motivate an employee?', the interviewer would ask, 'Give me an example of a time when you had to motivate a person. What actions did you take and what was the result?'

4. **Training interviewers so they are aware of conventions.** Training and guidance on how to conduct interviews helps interviewers become aware of the conventions they need to observe by not asking illegal questions that might contravene human rights acts.[62]
5. **Gathering usable information so that good decisions can be made.** There is little information on an appropriate way to take notes, but HR practitioners use a variety of note-taking styles. Many interviewers take 'summary' notes (52.8%) or 'verbatim' notes (31.9%). Content notes can be taken throughout the interview as the candidate is speaking (61.5%), at the end before doing anything else (22.6%) or at the end of the candidate's response to each question (11.6%).
6. **Involving others to verify information gathering and decision-making.** Multiple interviewers are recommended to share perceptions in grounding inferences, thus reducing the possibility of bias and encouraging the recall of points made by the interviewee. In addition to gathering reliable information for making a decision, these principles for structuring the interview process provide protection against discrimination in hiring.[63]

Developing behavioural description interview questions

Behavioural description interviewing is based on the often quoted principle *'The best predictor of future behaviour or performance is past behaviour or performance in similar circumstances.'*[64] This is based on the assumption that behaviour in a previous situation usually predicts behaviour in a similar situation later on. The idea is that by asking detailed questions about your thoughts, feelings and actions in past situations, an employer can look for clear evidence as to whether you possess the qualities the organization is seeking. The principle is illustrated in everyday life situations. Banks lend money to people who have a proven financial record of repaying their loans. If you wanted to bet on a sports team winning during the playoffs, one of the best ways to make a prediction would be to review the team's record during the past season.

Janz, Hellervick and Gilmore, in their book *Behaviour Description Interviewing*, suggest two corollaries in recognizing that people can change and are not always wedded to what they did in the past.

- *Corollary 1:* The more recent the past behaviour, the greater its predictive power.
- *Corollary 2:* The more longstanding the behaviour, the greater its predictive power.[65]

The first corollary encourages interviewers to focus more on recent behaviour, although still recognizing behaviour in the distant past. The second corollary suggests that we should seek more than one sample of past behaviour in similar circumstances, rather than rely on just one instance.

A third corollary is also important in recognizing that past behaviours might not be the only useful information for assessing a candidate. That is, we might want to know about a person's goals, aspirations and vision, in addition to what happened in the past.

- *Corollary 3:* An applicant's goals, aspirations and vision can also have predictive power and should be assessed in relation to past behaviour. That is, information about a person's past is one perspective in predicting future job performance; other perspectives are also appropriate.

Information from interviews might provide information on attitudes (how people feel about an attitude object such as a person, idea or institution), beliefs (what people believe to be true), behaviour (what people actually do or have done), attributes (characteristics such as sex, age, background and income)[66] and special skills, and certifications.[67] In any interview, the questions we use and the information we seek are of different value. Some information and interview questions might be **low yield** in that the information has low predictive power. For example, though all information has some relevance, a question such as 'What sport teams do you like?' would provide 'low-yield' information.[68]

Figure 7.1 illustrates an **interview question yield hierarchy** summarizing the potential yield of different interview questions.[69] The questions at the top of the hierarchy might provide more-specific information on age, specializations and degrees, information which might be gained from other sources than interviews. The information from these questions has less predictive value in terms of predicting performance because it requires a large inferential leap in understanding future behaviour or because it can be judgemental, opinionated and unsubstantiated.

For example, questions on a person's age, background, history and experience may not be the best predictor of how a person will perform in the future, because performance is based on skill and other characteristics. In the same way, just because people have a degree or certification, there is no guarantee that they have the competence to perform certain job functions. Similarly, questions asking about a person's specialized knowledge and skills might ascertain that a person might have some understanding of certain functions, such as reading a financial statement or performing a medical procedure, but such questions do not predict the person's proficiency.

Much of the information at this top part of the hierarchy is usually difficult or cumbersome to ask in interviews and can usually be gathered through other methods. For example, a person's degrees, certificates, diplomas and other achievements might be found in a curriculum vitae or from a reference check.

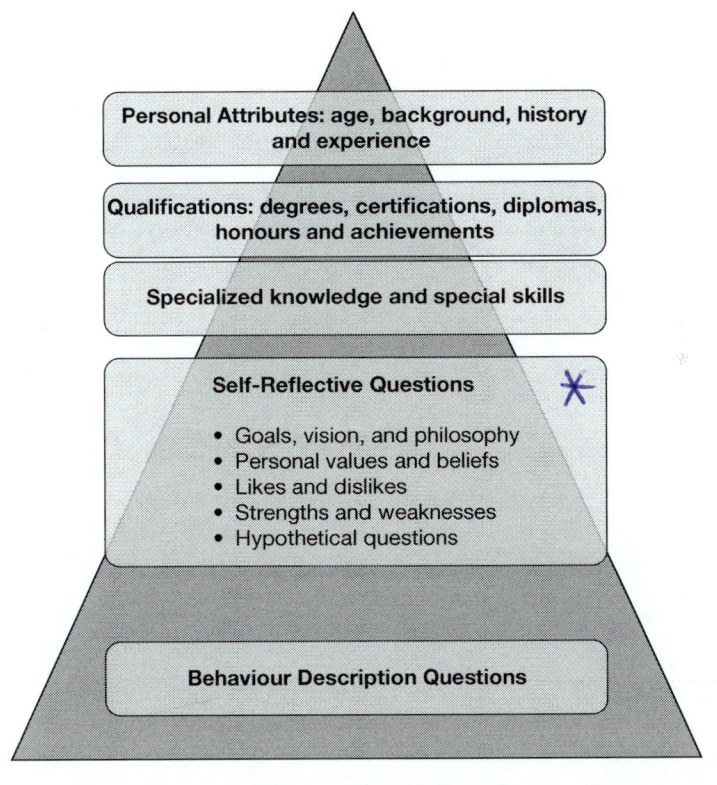

Figure 7.1 Interview question yield hierarchy: The yield of different types of interview questions.

The middle part of the information hierarchy points to *self-reflective* information about a person's attitudes, values and beliefs; likes and dislikes; strengths and weaknesses; and goals, and comments on what a person might do in a specific situation.

Attitudes, values and beliefs. Interviewers often seek information on a person's attitudes, values and beliefs with questions like 'What are your thoughts and beliefs about how we deal with a difficult union?' or 'What is most important to you in managing?'

Likes and dislikes. Questions on likes and dislikes seek to get at feelings about what the individual finds enjoyable and motivating or not enjoyable and punishing. Typical types of question are 'What do you like most about your job?', 'What do you like least about your job?' and 'What is your favourite job activity?'

Strengths and weaknesses. Questions on strength and weaknesses assume the interviewee's own interpretation is a relevant indicator of future behaviour. These might be questions such as 'What are your personal strengths (weaknesses)?'

Goals and vision. Goals provide an indication of what a person might be directed towards or what the organization might be directed towards. Questions might be 'What do you plan to do in the future?' and 'How do your goals tie in to the goals of this organization?'

Hypothetical questions. These questions ask how a person would respond in a certain situation. For instance: 'If you were required to terminate an employee, how would you carry it out?'

Although information from these self-reflective questions is relevant, people who answer these questions well in interviews are more likely to be people who are more verbally adept and comfortable in conversational situations.

Behavioural description questions. In responding to the potential low yield of many conventional interview questions, the goal of behaviour description questions is to provide information about what actually happens, based on the assumption that answers to these questions are a better indication of future behaviour. The behavioural question is a form of critical incident question asking applicants to identify examples of incidents that reflect on selected behaviours. These questions can focus on specific aspects such as planning, responding to performance issues, helping others and leadership.

1. Describe a project you accomplished which best illustrated your approach to planning. Where did the idea come from? How did you plan it? How did you implement the plan, and how did you deal with some of the major obstacles? What did you learn? What would you do differently now?
2. Give me an example of a situation where an employee you were responsible for was not performing well. Describe the situation and how you dealt with it. What did you say to the individual? Were you pleased with the outcome? Why or why not?
3. Give me an example of a project you completed that you think best demonstrates your leadership ability. Why did it demonstrate good leadership?

These types of questions, when they are followed with further behavioural description probes, can provide approximations of a person's past behaviour and performance. Behavioural description probes are questions that ask for more detail, for example 'How did others react?' or 'What happened then?' They encourage the individual to describe his or her exact behaviour in a particular work setting.

Behavioural description interview questions set up a format so that individuals will describe 'extreme' cases. These types of questions will help you uncover those things that individuals view as the most and least important, the best and worst, or the easiest and toughest. In this sense, they are more realistic than questions relating to opinions and commonsense truths. Examples of 'extreme case' questions would be:

1. 'Give me an example of a time when you felt you did a very good job of motivating an employee.' As the interviewer, you would follow up this question with appropriate probes, such as 'How do you know you were successful?'
2. 'Give me an example of a time when you felt you did a very bad job of motivating an employee.' Again, follow up with probes, such as 'What caused you to fail in this example? How would you do things differently now?'

Questions about past behaviours are also useful for understanding organizations, as they describe observable events and acts. In principle, it should be easy to get good information from these types of questions because they simply ask a person to summarize an event or experience.

Janz, Hellervik and Gilmore's classic book on behavioural description interviewing (1986) includes a number of questions within each competency. For example, in assessing the competency Ability to Meet Objectives, we might use one general question and two extreme case questions (which ask for positive and negative critical incidents) in addition to two other questions.

There are some limitations to these types of question. The interviewer must recognize difficulties with the reliability of the job applicant's information – because of memory loss, because he or she remembers less significant events or highlights the most recent ones, or because some answers might be threatening or confidential. However, behavioural description questions remain valuable because the answers they elicit are both observable and verifiable and, as a result, are a more reliable guide to people's past behaviour and performance than the opinions and beliefs that are usually drawn out by more traditional questions.

> MANAGERIAL IMPLICATIONS: The selection process assumes a rational model where we define the competencies that are important to the job and organization and then use different selection tools to gather information on the various candidates who have applied. Selection is probably the most important decision a manager or group of people can make. As HRM is increasingly recognized as a vital factor in an organization's survival and success, selection takes on an important role.[70] The SHRM BSC framework encourages you to align needed competencies to specific objectives and use the best selection methods to predict job success and longevity in the organization.
>
> As competencies are important in guiding the recruitment and selection process, they are also key to guiding the performance management process described in the next chapter.

BEFORE APPLYING, LET'S REVIEW

CO 1: Apply the triangulation principle in picking selection tools to reliably and validly make selection decisions.

The selection process begins with an understanding of an organization's strategic theme, such as selecting people who fit in public service organizations. Some selection tools are more reliable and valid than others. An updated understanding of the job – and the KSAOs – focuses the design of selection tools that are shown to be reliable and valid, based on the needs of the job and job analysis information.

CO 2: Assess the usefulness of different selection tests and inventories.

Certain tests – describing personality characteristics, cognitive abilities, and integrity and social behaviours – provide useful information in selecting applicants who are more likely to perform better on the job. Even though some tests have a high degree of reliability, people are sceptical of their value, and it is prudent to use other information to verify test results.

CO 3: Design and administer an interview guide using behavioural description and situational questions for assessing competencies important to strategic objectives.

Structured interviews that include behavioural description and situational questions tend to produce the best results. Examples of behavioural questions include 'Tell me about a time you were very successful in dealing with a difficult problem' or 'Give me an example of a time when you got something accomplished with a person who was difficult to get along with and tell me about some of the things that you did to make it work.' There is only one correct answer to this question, and that is what really happened – remember that a referee could be asked to substantiate your answer. The best preparation is to consider answers for behavioural description questions that are likely to arise. Here are some examples of situational questions: 'Imagine your spouse is away on a business trip and you are preparing to be at work for 7:00 a.m. in preparation for a 9:00 a.m. presentation to a team of managers. Whoops! Your ailing mother from across town phones and tells you she really feels ill. What do you do?' Behavioural questions are more valid as they tap into what people actually did in the past rather than what they think they will do. Situational questions provide another perspective on what people might do if they were faced with that particular situation.

DISCUSSION AND REVIEW QUESTIONS

1. Selection errors are of two types. We could select a person who should have been rejected (selection error). Or we could reject a person who should have been accepted (rejection error). Which errors are more serious?
2. In a simple model of selection for hiring a life guard or recreation staff at the community or university swimming pool, it would be easy to define and select potential applicants on the basis of job competencies related to pool supervision, responding to an emergency, aquatic rescue techniques, health and safety, customer service and civil defence. Select the best applicants on the basis of job fit, and whether they have the competencies required for the job. How would you select a person to recognize people–culture fit?
3. Review various selection tools, and assess their advantages and disadvantages in terms of entry-level, operational or managerial employees. Identify a battery of selection tools you would use that best implements the strategic theme of selecting highly motivated public service employees who 'fit' in the character of public service organizations.
4. Review the advantages and disadvantages of behavioural and situational interview questions in Table 7.3.
5. 'Public service motivation' is a unique predisposition that energizes and directs the people who are attracted to public service organizations[71] and, as such, is very important to the implementation of an organization's strategic objectives. It is described by four core values: attraction to public policy-making, commitment to public interest, compassion and self-sacrifice.[72] Develop a set of behavioural interview questions to select people illustrating these competencies in Table 7.3.

Table 7.3 Behavioural Questions for Selecting People with a 'Public Sector Motivation'

	Behavioral Question Worksheet
Public policymaking	Positive question:
	Not-so-positive question:
	Situational:
	Other:
Commitment to public interest	Positive question:
	Not-so-positive question:
	Situational:
	Other:
Compassion	Positive question:
	Not-so-positive question:
	Situational:
	Other:
Self-sacrifice	Positive question:
	Not-so-positive question:
	Situational:
	Other:

CASE: SELECTING AN HR MANAGER

The Human Resources Department is heading into a period of great stress and change with the implementation of a new performance management programme, an organization-wide succession plan and preparation for an upcoming round of bargaining with support staff. Finding the right person to come in and 'hit the ground running' has become a critical need for the department.

The current selection model for the human resource manager, which has been in use for nine years, consists of a panel interview and reference checks. The interview is focused on tasks and knowledge of human resources, and candidates are graded on a set of criteria developed for each question. There is a question on each functional area of human resources, including labour relations, compensation, classification, occupational safety and health, and recruitment and retention.

Task. In this task, you will develop and apply an interview guide for selecting an HR manager. The class will be divided into groups of four, and each group should prepare an interview guide which includes general questions, behaviour questions and situational questions. After completing the interview guide, participants should test it on themselves and practice answering some of the questions. Then, participate in a role play by responding to questions posed.

- *Step 1:* Review the job description on the book's website to gain more information on the job, types of questions you might use and other information relevant to the case. Develop Behavioural Description and Situational Interview Questions (60 minutes). You are asked to develop an interview guide that includes examples of behavioural and situational questions for selecting an HR manager. You are encouraged to include one positive and one negative behavioural description and one or two situational questions for at least three of the following six competencies: (i) interpersonal relations, (ii) meeting business objectives, (iii) building and leading a team, (iv) ability to change or adapt during a transition, (v) integrity and (vi) planning and organizing. You may wish to use different competencies than those listed.
- *Step 2:* Prepare answers for behavioural, situational and other types of questions (15 minutes). Before beginning the role play, prepare answers to questions you might be asked in an interview. As a first step, how would you answer the questions you prepared? You might also prepare answers to conventional questions about your strengths and weaknesses and goals. Also, review some of the information on the book's website about how to answer questions.
- *Step 3:* Participate in role-play interview (30 minutes). Each individual in the group should interview one person in another group. Then, switch roles so that each person gets the chance to be an interviewer and a job applicant.

8 Encouraging Employee Development in Reviewing Performance

Chapter Outline
- Chapter objectives (COs)   157
- A driving issue focusing managerial action: Responding to the problems with performance reviews   157
- CO 1: Goal setting in the strategic process   159
- CO 2: Different approaches to managing performance reviews   161
- CO 3: Formative approaches for encouraging feedback   169
- CO 4: Carrying out a goal-setting performance review   171
- CO 5: Carrying out disciplinary and termination procedures   178
- Before applying, let's review   181
- Discussion and review questions   182
- Case: Defining goals to resolve a performance problem   183

CHAPTER OBJECTIVES (COs)

After reading this chapter you will be able to implement the following objectives:

CO 1: Review the relevance of performance management in focusing an organization on strategic themes and objectives.

CO 2: Review approaches that have been used in assessing different aspects of performance.

CO 3: Apply formative review processes in encouraging employee development.

CO 4: Implement a goal-setting approach in linking to strategic themes and objectives.

CO 5: Implement disciplinary procedures.

A DRIVING ISSUE FOCUSING MANAGERIAL ACTION: RESPONDING TO THE PROBLEMS WITH PERFORMANCE REVIEWS

Badly executed performance reviews (PR) have the potential to cause significant damage to an organization and the people within it:

- *They hurt the relationship between employees and managers, sometimes creating an acidic relationship.*

- *They might even encourage non-effective skills and behaviours.*
- *Managers lose credibility when their judgements don't accurately reflect the total situation.*
- *Performance reviews take time. If they don't add value and improve performance, they are unnecessary costs.*
- *Poor performance review forms and processes make the field of HR and managers in HR look bad. When the forms and processes are not useful, managers will participate reluctantly, and employees will not take the process seriously.*

Many well-respected researchers and managers have questioned whether performance reviews are worth the effort. Employees, the recipients of performance feedback, are often very dissatisfied with the performance review process and reject it and the feedback they receive. In a survey of almost 50,000 organizational respondents, an international consulting firm found that only 13 per cent of employees and managers, and 6 per cent of CEOs, felt that their performance management systems were useful.[1] The perception is that performance reviews do not improve performance, nor do they motivate or guide personal development.[2] The possible conflicts created between supervisors and employees as a result of a performance review are sometimes long-lasting.[3]

The good news is that there are excellent examples of organizations which carry out effective performance review practices, such as reviewing previously stated goals and benchmarks; using the performance review to discuss development as well as compensation or promotions; and using the performance review as a progress report rather than an evaluation.[4] Effective practices fall into two areas: the way the process is designed and its implementation.[5]

Effective design characteristics:

- *The content of the PR is based on job analysis or is closely linked to job and subject matter experts (current job holders) have input into performance objectives or dimensions used.*
- *The PR is based on objectives and observable job behaviours where possible rather than on traits or personality characteristics.*
- *The PR is standardized (using forms and clear procedures)*

Effective implementation characteristics:

- *The PR is aligned with the organization's goals and objectives, and the timing is spread over a number of intervals (not too many and not too few).*
- *The review is an independent process, and people are trained to carry it out.*
- *The performance expectations are clearly communicated to employees; employee participation is encouraged in the PR process (e.g. setting goals, providing input into performance); and the PR also encourages employee development (e.g. indicates how to improve).*

STRATEGIC CONTEXT: This chapter's introductory perspective summarizes some of the problems with performance reviews and the difficulties in getting employees to improve their performance or commit themselves to new objectives.

Within the chapter, the underlying theme of the SHRM BSC framework is motivating employees to work together towards agreed strategic objectives. In doing this, a critical part of the process is encouraging individual goal or objective setting in performance management. The chapter illustrates how goals and objectives are an integrating process linking individual and organizational goals and objectives. More importantly, if done effectively in a problem-solving way, setting goals and objectives encourages motivation and commitment.

CO 1: GOAL SETTING IN THE STRATEGIC PROCESS

The term **performance management** is broadly defined at the strategic level to describe 'any managerial process that involves collecting, interpreting and/or utilizing performance information – whether for budgeting, programme management, performance contracting, or personnel management'.[6] At the supervisor and employee level, performance management is implemented by working with employees in developing performance plans, appraising performance, motivating employees to perform at a higher level and setting goals and objectives.

Performance management has been a central theme in public organizations for years, and its importance was further emphasized by public sector reforms such as the New Public Management (NPM). Reforms in OECD countries have reoriented performance management and appraisal systems to centre on targets and objectives.[7] For organizations, these reoriented performance reviews provide an opportunity to align employee work plans with the organization's strategic themes and objectives in addition to motivating people to improve their performance in certain areas. For individuals, performance reviews provide an opportunity to improve their skills and abilities.[8] Focusing on personal development improves an employee's capability to do a job and can prepare him or her for future jobs in an organization. It can help employees recognize the importance of ongoing skill development for higher-level positions within the organization. The developmental purpose of a performance review supports and encourages training and grooming of staff. In this way, it can help establish objectives for training programmes.

The performance review is usually a face-to-face meeting between the manager and employee for the purpose of solving personal and organizational problems, linking performance to organization performance organization priorities and encouraging employee learning, development and motivation to improve. The term **performance review**, unlike terms such as **performance appraisal** and **evaluation**, suggests that managers and employees are jointly involved in reviewing performance and encouraging development and improvement.

Linking to the strategic context

The strategic context surrounding goal achievement in public organizations is very much defined by the character of public service goals and motivations of public sector workers. The performance review process using the SHRM BSC is an opportunity to motivate employees and align their goals with those of the organization.

Government organizations tend to have multiple, conflicting and ambiguous goals, partially due to potential political interference, competing demands from stakeholders, conflicting values (e.g. preservation of the environment vs. development of natural resources) and lack of clear measures of performance (e.g. profit).[9] Ambiguous goals arise for several reasons in public organizations. As profitability is the ultimate criterion for success in private organizations, managers and employees have goals that can be more concrete and specific to responding to customers.[10] Employees in public sector organizations have multiple goals, obtain funding from an appropriation process and are susceptive to a political process requiring them to be responsive to multiple constituencies or clients. The culture of public organization has conflicting values where political considerations may take priority over operational efficiency or rationality. Often, in government organizations there is a need to shift the emphases because of a shift in a political priority or reaction to public opinion.[11]

Some authors have pointed to the positive aspects of goal ambiguity in increasing managerial discretion by reducing the controls of central authorities. When goals are complex, the potential exists for more meaningful communication among stakeholder groups to develop more clarity and understanding.[12]

In focusing performance management and reviews on public sector workers, there is also a need to recognize the fast-growing literature on public sector motivation (PSM) which suggests that people who 'fit' in public service organizations have unique incentives relating to their public interests, attraction to policymaking, compassion for those in need and desire to make a difference. In going further, some scholars have studied the relationship between PSM and work motivation and have clearly illustrated that intrinsic motivators are central, whereas extrinsic work motivators are not related to PSM or are not important.[13] This supports other research that indicates that public service workers are likely to be interested in intrinsic motivators more so than their private sector counterparts.[14]

Performance review processes focusing on defining and reviewing employee goals and objectives are most in tune with the unique context of public sector organizations. The organization's strategic themes and objectives can provide the framework for guiding employee objective setting and skill development. Goal-setting theory suggests that goals can be used to enhance individual performance, job satisfaction and organizational performance.[15] The theory seeks to illustrate how organizational goals, strategic themes and objectives can be cascaded to the individual level in performance plans.[16]

Performance metrics underlying goal setting in performance reviews

Most performance review tools are **summative tools** for assessing performance in reaching goals and outputs. Such performance measures are prone to the same errors of measurement as we might find in the selection process relating to reliability, validity and fairness of the performance criteria. Are the measures reliable and an accurate yardstick that does not change over time? Are the measures a valid measure of job performance in describing the most important aspects of performance? Do they describe a useful perspective on performance? Is the process fair in that employees feel that the last review was fair and valuable in improving their performance? Will employees accept the review and implement the results?

The most noted critic of performance and merit reviews was W. Edward Deming, one of the proponents of TQM and one of the most influential managerial thinkers. He indicated that it might be alluring to evaluate people in order to improve their performance, and even give merit or pay increases based on these evaluations, but performance reviews do not lead to such performance improvement. Instead, the evaluations leave 'people bitter, despondent, dejected, some even depressed, all unfit for work for weeks after receipt of rating, unable to comprehend why they are inferior. It is unfair, as it ascribes to the people in a group differences that may be caused totally by the system they work in.'[17] He argued that many systemic factors – such as training, communication, tools and supervision – are beyond the control of the employee and account for 90 to 95 per cent of performance. Continuing to use performance appraisals can have unintended consequences. Employees can be very creative in looking good before a performance appraisal interview just for the sake of getting a better review. For example, employees might encourage customers or clients to send in complementary letters or change their work behaviour just to get a higher evaluation.

Systemic rater errors. Managers might have a tendency to believe they are accurate and fair in their reviews, whereas employees might tend to be overly optimistic about what the ratings should be. **Systemic rater errors** are biases of the performance review process – unclear benchmarks, halo effect, recency effect, leniency tendencies and societal stereotypes – which produce reviews or ratings that are consistently too high or low in relation to performance.

1. *Unclear benchmarks or performance measures:* The MBO (Management by Observation) and BARS (Behavioural Anchored Rating Scales) systems provide clearer benchmarks, whereas a graphic rating scale focused on general employee characteristics might be more open to interpretation as different supervisors could differ on their views of the quality and quantity of the work.
2. *Halo effect:* Sometimes a rating on one characteristic (such as problem-solving ability) can bias the perception of other characteristics (such as service orientation).[18]

3. *Recency effect:* Sometimes recent events or experiences can skew an evaluation. When appraisals are not done on a regular basis and occur only once a year, there is a tendency to forget performance events months earlier.
4. *Leniency or strictness tendency:* Different supervisors have a tendency to be more lenient or strict than others. Students know this in the classes they take. Some instructors are tough graders, and others are more generous with their grades.
5. *Societal stereotypes in rating:* Human rights legislation has been created in an effort to guard against discrimination based on designated groups and age. However, some societal stereotypes do exist and are fairly entrenched in our culture. In a study of discriminatory attitudes towards older workers, researchers found that selection interviewers often view older job applicants as more difficult to train, more resistant to change and less suitable for promotion.[19]

Difficulties in assessing progress in meeting goals and objectives. A dilemma that is particularly relevant in public organizations is that priorities and objectives shift often because of changing political needs or citizen complaints or requests. This calls for supervisors to play an active role in continually reviewing progress and redefining and fine-tuning objectives. This chapter describes how supervisors can use the goal- and objective-setting process in an environment where priorities and objectives shift.

Ambiguous goals and objectives are often based solely on individual perceptions of what needs to be done, whereas clear and specific goals provide tangible conditions or examples of what is to be achieved.[20] When employees perceive that their goals and objectives are clear and specific as a result of their performance reviews, they are more likely to identify with their work.

Goal and motivational theorists highlight the importance of motivational aspects of goals or tasks in improving motivation and productivity. A public organization's strategic framework can be operationalized using the SHRM BSC. This provides a statement of the vision, mission, strategic themes and objectives that shape how an organization's members perceive and think about their work.

CO 2: DIFFERENT APPROACHES TO MANAGING PERFORMANCE REVIEWS

Different performance review approaches make unique assumptions about how to review performance and might be appropriate for different jobs or organizational needs. The overriding purpose of performance reviews within an SHRM BSC framework is to align individual objectives and plans with the organization's strategic themes and objectives.

A central stream of the performance management and performance appraisal literature focuses on performance measurement of (i) personal characteristics and attitudes, (ii) competencies potentially describing what a person brings to the job and (iii) behaviours, (iv) the quality of the outputs and (v) goals and objectives. Much of the performance appraisal literature focuses on measurement and quality of the evaluations, but ignores the overall purpose of motivation and improving goal alignment. Table 8.1 reviews key approaches and their advantages and disadvantages within different performance areas.

Performance management, in an ideal world, could recognize each aspect of performance rather than focusing on a single dimension. However, proponents of the results-based approaches point to the importance of goal alignment for increasing performance, especially in the public sector.[21] This involves aligning the organization's strategic themes and objectives to an individual's goals and work plans, using approaches such as MBO and performance planning and review.

Setting goals and objectives for personal and organizational development

Goals and objectives are important for all performance reviews, especially for a strategic perspective, but they are particularly relevant for focus on specific projects or initiatives that are part of a strategic plan. Goals and objectives can describe targets that a person might seek to accomplish over a defined period

Table 8.1 A Snapshot of Advantages and Disadvantages of Different Performance Review Approaches

Setting Goals and Objectives for Personal and Organizational Development

Management by Objectives (MBO): Valuable in linking individual work to an organization's strategic plan and objectives, although managers find it cumbersome and time consuming. Difficult to compare employees who have different goals. Sometimes, goals and objectives change quickly, making the original goal less relevant. Many goals are not within the control of employees.

Performance Planning and Review: Valuable in encouraging employees to focus on results and performance. Although linkage to strategic planning is important, the job and department's priorities are more central. Like Management by Objectives, it can be cumbersome and time consuming, but encourages employees and supervisors to focus on job-related results. Difficult to compare employees, as people are asked to focus on different results.

Focusing on Person-oriented and Behaviour-oriented Measures for Improvement

Ranking and Paired Comparison Method: Useful for making comparisons. It is important to clearly define and hold to the criteria for ranking. Less useful for development and feedback. Does not encourage team development.

Forced Distribution: Useful for making comparisons. Forces raters to make comparisons, but it might not be fair if the group is made up of high performers (or low performers). Does not encourage team development.

Graphic Rating Scales: Easy to use, less time consuming to fill out and easy to administer. It is possible to compare people overall or on one or more performance measures. Managers like graphic scales because they are standardized and they allow comparisons of employees in different parts of the organization. Graphic scales often do not clearly define dimensions of performance.

Behavioural checklists: Easy to use. Linked to job behaviours if measures are validly developed. Allow for comparison between employees. Less emphasis on employee feedback and development.

Behavioural Anchored Rating Scales (BARS): Very useful for providing feedback for individual development in addition to allowing comparisons between employees. Time consuming to develop, but dimensions and job behaviours are useful benchmarks of performance. Performs as a tool for making forecasts based on the historical ratio between causal factors (such as sales or demand for services) and the number of employees required.

Assessing Competencies to Perform

Competency-based Narratives: Useful as a development approach when attached to competencies. Difficult to compare people.

Assessment Centres and Simulations: Very useful for certification and for assessing competencies in real-life conditions. Difficult to develop. Allows for comparisons.

Focusing on Results-Oriented Performance Reviews

The Critical Incident Performance Review: Focuses on critical incidents and allows an in-depth review of the incident to determine what was effective and ineffective. It is useful for developing other measures (in BARS and behavioural checklists), but it is difficult to compare people.

Review of Outputs and Outcomes: The focus on specific organizational outputs and outcomes might discourage performance in other areas.

---

of time in responding to identified problems or improving a competency. Prominent examples of this perspective include management by objectives (MBO) and a performance planning and review approach.

Often, goals and objectives in performance reviews are used interchangeably to describe the same thing. Goals are usually broad statements of how an organization seeks to attain its vision. Within the broad goals of a municipal government, for example, we might have strategic themes such as 'a safe community', and 'economic vibrancy'. Within each of these strategic themes might be objectives such as 'enhancing public safety' and 'continuing community engagement'. In performance reviews, the organization's goals and strategic themes are the basis for employee goals and objectives.

Management by objectives. Peter Drucker's classic book The Practice of Management[22] outlined **management by objectives** as an approach for defining objectives so that employees can compare their performance against objectives that are important for the organization. For Drucker, objective setting helps managers avoid an 'activity trap' where they react to day-to-day activities and do not prioritize their work and focus on organizational objectives.

A manager would implement the MBO system by jointly setting goals, defining employee responsibilities in relation to results expected and using measures to guide, assess and provide feedback on the progress of the employee's accomplishments.[23] As such, an MBO performance review is not focused on employee behaviours, but on how an employee contributes to the organization's goals and objectives. In most MBO programmes, managers and employees are more aware of the organization's goals and priorities and have set more specific goals, objectives and initiatives connected to the organizational goals. Advantages include the ability to focus on agreed priorities, better resource utilization and more communication and understanding among employees and managers. A key potential positive feature relates to helping employees focus on objectives and on linking personal and organizational objectives.[24]

There is a resurgence of interest in the role of goals and objectives in helping managers and employees improve performance[25] and linking to an organization's strategic themes.[26] Researchers suggest that goals affect performance by focusing attention on goal-related activities, energizing people, increasing persistence and encouraging problem-solving and creativity.[27] Employees also find goal-setting reviews useful and acceptable when managers support them and assist them to achieve these goals.[28] However, a most positive feature of a goal-setting programme is linked to the mutual participation and problem-solving between employees and supervisors, rather than on an emphasis where superiors play a dominant role in setting and evaluating progress on objectives.[29]

Person-oriented and behaviour-oriented measures for improvement

Many performance reviews focus a person's **characteristics** in doing the job. Personal characteristics are relevant to many public sector jobs where people are working with other people. However, these reviews are more helpful when the assessment of the characteristics is also linked to the objectives which need to be achieved.

Personal characteristics and attitudes and behaviours are also important as performance dimensions, although it is harder to make the link to strategic objectives. For example, attitudes and interpersonal characteristics describe conscientiousness, reliability, customer orientation, leadership ability and team attitude. These dimensions are often thought to be difficult to measure, and many managers have sought to replace them with behavioural dimensions. That is, instead of rating a person's leadership ability, the measure would focus on whether the person exhibited specific personal characteristics or behaviours, for example assisting staff in solving a problem and encouraging team building.

Forced distribution systems. Many organizations have experimented with forced comparison methods such as ranking, paired comparisons and forced distributions. It is possible for managers to rank employees on a competency or performance measure by using a ranking method where all employees are ranked from the highest to lowest, as when real estate or car sales people are often ranked each month on the basis of sales made. In a paired-comparison method, each employee is compared with other employees on the basis of different criteria, and for each characteristic the manager compares all the employees against each other, rating each as higher or lower. The forced distribution system operates like the bell-curve grading system at school, which suggests only a certain number of employees can be rated as As while a certain number are classified as lower performers.

Over the years, many organizations, including universities and police organizations, have used forced comparison systems that encourage managers to rank employees against each other. Some organizations still use them. Comparison methods are intuitive in being able to identify the top people. If the criterion being ranked can be reliably and validly measured, as well as agreeable to employees, it can be a useful method. The idea of a forced distribution system seems appealing because managers can jolt employees out of complacency and discourage artificially high performance ratings. With the rankings, managers can identify top performers and those they view as holding the company back. Hopefully, if these lower performers voluntarily resign, they can be replaced with more qualified performers. However, the downside is that managers can easily make mistakes in ranking a potentially competent employee as mediocre because of the quotas within each part of the distribution system.

Most universities and school systems no longer use the forced distribution system for grading students, and most governments are moving to using goals and objectives as the basis for performance reviews. Critics suggest that forced distribution systems create an overly competitive culture that is cut-throat and discourages employees from giving help to their colleagues.

The graphic rating scale. The graphic rating scale has been a popular scale for rating employees on the basis of defined attitudes or characteristics. For the list of characteristics identified (knowledge of job, ability to plan work, accuracy in work performance), the supervisor is asked to rate the employee on a range of values such as excellent, above average, satisfactory, below average and needing improvement. See Table 8.2.

The scores can be tallied up for various categories of performance or to summarize a total score for all performance characteristics. Such scales which focus on personal characteristics are viewed as being very subjective and not clearly linked to actual performance.

Using the graphic rating scale, it is possible to add subjective narrative comments and identify employee strengths. The graphic rating scales can also be adjusted to assist the evaluation. (i) Some scales vary as to the extent to which the rating values are defined by providing the evaluator with norms for what above average or below average means. (ii) Also, some scales are more precise in their definition of the performance characteristic so that it is directly related to the work being carried out or to specific behaviours.

Behavioural checklists. The graphic rating scale has also been used to rate behavioural statements that describe job-related behaviours important to performance. This sort of scale can be used for performance reviews but has also been applied to rate behaviours such as customer service in organizations as well as teaching effectiveness. In these cases, the raters are not supervisors, but consumers, students or other people who might or might not have observed the job behaviour.

Table 8.3 summarizes an example of a behavioural student rating form. It illustrates a number of teaching behaviours such as being organized, being knowledgeable about the course and being approachable and respectful. Such behaviours are likely to be more reliable and valid when they are based on behaviours that the student feels are important and valued.[30] For each statement, the student might not be asked for an evaluation or judgement of satisfaction or effectiveness. Rather, the student could be asked to rate how often he or she observed the behaviours: never, occasionally, fairly often, very often,

Table 8.2 Examples of a Graphic Rating Scale

	Excellent	Above Average	Satisfactory	Below average	Needing Improvement
Ability to plan work					
Ability to complete work on time					

*Table 8.3 Examples of Items in a Behavioural Checklist for Faculty Teaching Evaluation**

A. The Instructor	Always	Very Often	Fairly Often	Occasionally	Never
1. The instructor was organized and prepared for the course.					
2. The instructor was knowledgeable about course content.					
3. The instructor was approachable and respectful.					
4. The instructor's feedback on my assignments helped me to improve my work.					
B. The Course					
1. The activities and assignments appropriately related to the content of the course.					
2. The activities and assignments were relevant to the real world.					
3. This course furthers my career goals.					

* The rater checks the responses that best describes the instructor's behaviour. It is possible to compute a total score under instructor or course measures or on the total course experience.

always. The student checks the response which best describes the person being observed. The categories can be weighted, where 'never' is given a 1 and 'always' a 5 to summarize an overall rating.

Behavioural Anchored Rating Scales (BARS). The BARS method combines elements of behavioural checklists and the critical incidents method described in Chapter 3. The first step is to define the critical job dimensions or performance areas. Thus, in performing the job, participants are asked to identify critical incidents that, in the recent past, stand out in illustrating effective and ineffective job performance. For example, in the teaching environment we might ask teachers to think of critical incidents that made them feel good about their performance. We might also ask them to identify critical incidents that made them feel that they performed poorly in their job. From interviews using these questions, we might develop an understanding of the areas that teachers consider to be important in their job. These could possibly define performance areas such as commitment to students, professional development and teamwork in the school and community. The BARS might include 6–12 performance areas, such as the example that follows.

In evaluating interviewers and claims deputies who provided employment services for clients, supervisors were asked to write examples of effective and ineffective incidents and to describe behaviours rather than traits that were illustrated. Six performance dimensions were agreed:

1. **Ability to absorb and interpret policies** – learns new policies and procedures with a minimum of instruction; serves as a source of information on new and changed policies.
2. **Adaptability** – can adjust to new or modified situations; adjusts to diversity of situations and/or tasks; functions effectively in unstable conditions.
3. **Effective use of resources** – plans effective use of own time and equipment; organizes work and appropriately assigns priorities; anticipates and plans for unusual situations.

4. **Interpersonal relationships** – behaves in a manner appropriate to the situation and individuals involved; is sensitive to and understands behaviour of others; does not complicate difficult emotional and social situations.
5. **Job involvement** – fulfils responsibilities and carries out work assignments; is reliable in carrying out required tasks and maintains high standards of performance.
6. **Knowledge and judgement** – is familiar with, understands and can apply information needed for employment.[31]

Table 8.4 illustrates one behavioural anchored rating scale for the performance dimension *Ability to absorb and interpret policies.*

The scale illustrates different job behaviours ranging from more effective to less effective behaviour. The job behaviours reflect what a person actually does on a day-to-day basis rather than what a person plans to do. They reflect mannerisms and skills that a person might bring to bear in solving a problem effectively or ineffectively.

The process of developing the BARS encourages staff to develop a range of effective, acceptable and less acceptable behaviours around performance areas that are thought to be critical to effective performance. As such, employees can be involved in defining examples of specific behaviours at various levels of effectiveness and then validating them.

Table 8.4 BARS for the Dimension 'Ability to Absorb and Interpret Policies'[32]

Interviewers and claims deputies must keep abreast of current changes and interpret and apply new information. Some can absorb and interpret new policy guides and procedures quickly with a minimum of explanation. Others seem unable to learn even after repeated explanations and practice. They have difficulty learning and following new policies. When making this rating, disregard job knowledge and experience, and evaluate ability to learn on the job.

Very Positive	9	This interviewer could be expected to serve as an information source concerning new and changed policies for others in the office.
	8	This interviewer could be expected to be quickly aware of programme changes and explain these changes to employers.
	7	This interviewer could be expected to reconcile conflicting policies and procedures correctly to meet immediate job needs.
Positive	6	This interviewer could be expected to recognize the need for additional information to gain better understanding of policy changes.
	5	After receiving instruction on completing ESAR forms, this interviewer could be expected to complete the forms correctly.
	4	This interviewer could be expected to require some help and practice in mastering new policies and procedures.
Improvement required	3	This interviewer could be expected to know that there is a problem, but might go down many blind alleys before realizing they are wrong.
	2	This interviewer could be expected to incorrectly interpret programme guidelines, thereby referring an unqualified person.
	1	Even after repeated explanations, this interviewer could be expected to be unable to learn new procedures.

The purpose of behavioural feedback is to focus a positive, constructive and actionable dialogue about job behaviours. BARS replace numerical and adjectival anchors with descriptions of actual job behaviours that reflect varying levels of effectiveness on the performance dimension under consideration.

Assessing competencies in job performance

Some performance reviews focus more on a person's competencies in doing the job, especially if it is difficult to measure outputs or outcomes. For example, airline pilots are assessed on their competencies in flight simulators, and police officers undergo assessment centre evaluations when they leave police college and at certain stages of their career. In a similar way, many schools identify a range of competencies related to commitment to pupils and pupil learning, professional knowledge, professional practice, learning in learning communities and ongoing professional development. Competencies are relevant to many public sector jobs because they are ways to operationalize what is needed to accomplish strategic objectives. They are also useful where it is difficult to reliably measure outputs and outcomes or where other systemic factors might affect whether they are achieved. For example, outputs such as high scores among students depend partially on the teacher's competence, but they are also affected by the composition of the classroom and the interest and assistance of the parents, as well as by the school and its setting.

Competency-based narratives. The narrative method, in its simplest form, can be described as an essay that outlines a person's strengths, weaknesses, potential and plan for improvement. The narratives can be focused on 8–10 competency areas – such as service orientation and problem-solving – deemed to be important for the job. Each description of a person's strengths and weaknesses can be backed up with examples. See Table 8.5.

Managers can offer candid statements (narrative descriptions) of an employee's competencies in various areas: service orientation, strategic orientation, problem-solving, interpersonal abilities, empowerment, teamwork and ability to meet objectives. Such narratives don't allow managers to rank employees, and the essays often provide unique descriptions that focus on unique strengths and potential. Although a key disadvantage of such narratives is that they do not allow managers to make comparisons with others, their key advantage is that they can provide specific and personalized information to help the employee develop and improve.

Assessment centres and simulations. Assessment centres and simulations are often used for testing and certifying employees' performance capability. They are based on the rule of thumb that how a person performs in a simulated situation is a good indicator of performance in real situations. Assessment centres or simulated tasks can be a requirement in reviewing performance and certifying that people are capable to perform. For example, police officers, firefighters, military personnel and airplane pilots have to perform effectively in a simulation in order to work.

Police officers undergo training simulations where they have to make quick decisions in life-and-death situations. The simulations include interactive video displays where officers are presented with

Table 8.5 Example of a form for summarizing competencies

Competency Areas	Review of Strengths and Weaknesses (provide examples)	Improvement Plan
Service Orientation: Desire to identify and serve clients and customers (internal and external). Discovering and meeting needs of clients and customers.		

simulated real-life scenarios, such as needing to use pepper spray to diffuse a situation, to fire a gun in self-defence or to navigate a car in snowy conditions while under pressure.

Medicine is an area where simulations are used more often. Medical simulations can mimic situations where a surgeon has to place a stent in a coronary artery, or they can create a medical procedure room in its fullest detail. Most recently, medical boards are actively evaluating simulations as a tool to assess proficiency in performing procedures.[33]

Focusing on outputs or outcomes in performance reviews

Outputs can also be a very useful dimension for measuring performance. **Outputs** refer to completed work and among a staff of accountants might describe the number of expense claims handled or cheque requisitions issued. Outputs might be described by the quantity of the reports and the quality (error-free) with which they were performed. These outputs might be important for the department in achieving **outcomes** like improved accounting services and customer satisfaction, which might enhance the organization's long range outcomes of improving its customer base.

The critical incident performance review. The **critical incident technique (CIT)** was originally developed for examining crew selection, readiness and performance[34] and has been used for carrying out a systematic performance audit or review of practices. The critical incident method can be used as a general anecdotal report on performance. Supervisors can log employee behaviours that are particularly effective or ineffective in accomplishing specific tasks. For example, a principal might review the performance of a teacher by observing behaviours related to dealing with students. After several observations, the principal would describe examples of critical incidents and meet with the teacher, using the incidents as examples to improve ways to relate to customers. See Table 8.6.

Table 8.6 Examples of Critical Incident Descriptions of Teacher's Work

On May 1, an observation of class took place. This lesson focused on reading and writing. Mrs T., using appropriate questioning techniques, was able to determine the learners' understanding of the objectives of the lesson, which were stated verbally and visually using the chart paper in the classroom. The tasks at hand in reading and writing were time sensitive, and Mrs T. effectively used the magnetic timepiece located on the whiteboard. As the lesson progressed, it was evident that Mrs T. had a clear and detailed plan for the lesson, moving the students towards accomplishing the tasks. With improved pacing of the lesson and clear expectations on students' deportment, students will be able to move on to the tasks even more effectively. As discussed with Mrs T. in the post-conference, it will be important for her to focus on developing strategies in classroom management and on her expectations for the class, which should be consistent and clear for students.
On May 26, an observation took place with the topic of journal writing. This was an activity which was based on a previous lesson taught with a kindergarten class on caterpillars. Mrs T. successfully used student examples of this type of sentence writing required for the task. Through effective questioning and the use of samples on the chart paper, all students were enabled to clearly understand the objective set out for them. In addition, the concrete use of the chart paper, with the day and date displayed, was a good visual check for the students to ensure their writing reflected one of the objectives set out for the journal writing. The use of the sentence strips was a useful tool for students of this age group to begin to develop appropriate writing skills. An improvement has occurred in Mrs T.'s classroom management skills, as evidenced by her setting the stage for her expectations before the class moved on to their task. Students demonstrated a better understanding of Mrs T.'s behavioural expectations, and they are asking appropriately for assistance when needed, enabling Mrs T. to focus on the learning needs of students requiring more of her attention.

These anecdotal examples force attention on actual incidents and on the situation that illustrates behaviours and the way a person performed. They can illustrate what a person did effectively and less effectively. The real advantages of critical incidents are that they encourage supervisors to fully describe the incidents, providing examples in full detail, rather than simply to make judgements.

The critical incident method as an anecdotal performance appraisal method is most useful in supplementing other performance appraisal methods, as many supervisors find it onerous to record incidents on a regular basis. CIT is particularly useful in developing job performance dimensions or examples of job behaviours (e.g. in the BARS method). A recording of incidents may only provide a partial picture of job performance and is probably more useful in providing examples of behaviour to supplement other performance review methods that provide a wider view of the employee's performance.

Review of actual performance outputs. Production records are often seen as a rather neat, uncomplicated and unbiased way to evaluate an individual's performance. Although production records may have some drawbacks, they are an indication of the employee's ability to perform the job.

Periodic tests measuring outputs are designed to measure the efficiency at one or more specific times. Instead of asking employees to set their own performance goals, many organizations have measures of daily, weekly or yearly output. Examples include these:

- Social workers – cases handled, types of cases.
- Management – meeting citizen needs, accomplishing strategic objectives, achieving budget objectives, grievances or turnovers.
- Police personnel – arrests, traffic offence notices.
- Scientists – publications, patents, studies completed.

Output measures vary with different jobs but are generally a reliable measure of performance as they can be consistently measured from one time period to another.

The question to be asked about measuring organizational outputs is 'Do they validly provide a useful perspective on performance, and are the measures important components of the job's performance?' For example, police might argue that the number of traffic offence notices (or speeding tickets) is a poor measure of performance because a police person might target places where it is easy to catch speeders, rather than locations where there is a need to enforce traffic regulations (e.g. in school zones or areas where there are more accidents) but where it might be more difficult to catch speeders. Similar questions can be raised about any performance output measure, which suggests that these measures should be combined with other performance review approaches rather than used on their own.

CO 3: FORMATIVE APPROACHES FOR ENCOURAGING FEEDBACK

Whereas summative performance reviews focus more directly on performance, **formative assessments** seek to provide feedback to help people change and develop. The goal with formative assessments is to get beyond the summative assessments and encourage feedback from peer groups, clients or customers.

Peer ratings. In some jobs that involve teamwork, it makes sense to involve peers or co-workers in reviewing performance and providing feedback. In addition, the judgement of team members can provide a different perspective on performance than a supervisor's perspective or actual performance measures. Peers often have more opportunities to witness performance of their co-workers and provide a useful perspective in predicting performance and promotions.[35] In addition, peer ratings are increasingly recognized because they are a reliable, valid and useful form for reviewing performance and providing feedback.[36]

The increased popularity of peer ratings[37] is partially linked to flatter (less hierarchical), team and project-based organizational structures,[38] and the perceived usefulness of receiving feedback from a variety of sources.[39] The peer review process in assessing individual or team performance is similar to the one scientific journals, editors and granting agencies rely on for anonymously assessing a book or grant proposals.[40] In business and sports organizations, where there is intense pressure to improve the effectiveness of some characteristic or characteristics of the group performance, the input of peers is also extremely important.[41]

Peer ratings are valuable in feedback because they provide information from different people who offer various perspectives. However, in order to overcome the potential of friendship or negative biases, it is important to be specific about what peers should evaluate and how to evaluate specific indicators, through training exercises.[42] Peers are better at rating those things they have a perspective on, such as the quality of help received in responding to problems. Members have to be capable to perceive and interpret the salient aspects of each other's behaviour objectively, using standard measurements.[43] Asking peers for both positive and negative comments, pooling information and holding face-to-face discussions are ways to increase the acceptability, reliability and validity of feedback.[44]

Subordinates' ratings. Some organizations use feedback or input from subordinates for providing supervisors or managers with information on their performance.[45] When used for providing information on supervisorial leadership development, subordinate information is extremely helpful as subordinates have a useful perspective on leadership qualities, for example how well the supervisor delegates, communicates, meets objectives and organizes meetings.[46] What managers do with the feedback from subordinates relates to the benefit of the feedback in improving their performance. Those who were more positive and met with subordinates to discuss the feedback were more likely to improve performance.[47]

Customer ratings. Some organizations use measures from internal and external customers to help improve their performance. In using customer service measures, public managers might focus on citizens and hope to understand their needs in order to better focus services. In some cases, certain departments in the organization will assess the satisfaction of internal customers, or the people or groups inside the organization who depend on their services. For example, HR departments or accounting departments might ask line departments about how their services could be more useful to them. This feedback, in the case of HR, might help them design or redesign training programmes or focus recruitment efforts.[48]

Self-appraisals. Employees can be asked to evaluate themselves. In a self-appraisal process, employees are asked to complete their own evaluation before meeting with supervisors. This can be implemented by giving employees an opportunity to think about their own strengths and weaknesses and to identify issues that they want to talk about with their supervisors. During the performance review discussion, the supervisor and the employee can focus in on issues they think are important.

Researchers suggest that employees can be harder on themselves and are likely to be more critical in a self-appraisal situation. However, critics of self-appraisals indicate that employees are likely to be too lenient or that they will present themselves too positively. Also, the fear exists that self-ratings will moderate a supervisor's evaluation of poor performers.[49] Self-appraisals work well when supervisors and employees jointly define objectives or initiatives to improve performance or to assist employees. They are extremely useful when used with other measures or when employers are using them for developmental purposes.[50]

360-degree feedback or multi-rater reviews. The 360-degree feedback process has gained a great deal of popularity in providing feedback to assist managers and other employees. The process goes beyond a traditional supervisorial review or appraisal process and enlists multi-constituencies, including supervisors, peers, co-workers, internal and external clients and citizens. The constituent is expected to evaluate the person's performance on various behaviour dimensions. The person being rated is encouraged to carry out his or her self-appraisal and use the feedback to respond to the needs of the group. Such a blend of an individual perception of performance with the relevant constituents fits well with the needs of a more team-oriented and customer-focused workplace.[51]

Another characteristic of the 360-degree feedback process is that the feedback is given anonymously. Feedback given anonymously is more honest and closer to what the rater actually feels about the person. On the other hand, raters who are known by the recipient are more likely to give higher ratings than anonymous raters.[52]

The benefits of a 360-degree feedback process as a collaborative, developmental tool are substantial. Changes in behaviour from the feedback tend to be immediate and dramatic.[53] Given that millions of dollars are spent each year in training and development initiatives, the 360-degree feedback process is a cost-effective way to encourage employee development.[54]

The 360-degree feedback has typically been used in managerial settings, based on a survey of the members of the Society of Human Resource Managers. In organizations using 360-degree feedback, 35 per cent of the applications were used for executives and 37 per cent for upper middle managers. It was used for middle and first-level managers in 23 per cent and 18 per cent of the applications, respectively.[55]

It is difficult to argue against the logic of using multi-raters in providing feedback, given the fact that all employees have to respond to multiple constituents and diverse perspectives. For example, the performance of an employee in a police department is viewed from different perspectives. The supervisor has one perspective on performance, and co-workers provide others, as do other stakeholders. For policing, it is also relevant to understand how the police person deals with citizens in enforcing the law and in general community relations. Given the potential biases of using information from any one source, this logic of the 360-degree feedback process is compelling.

However, there are some issues in using the 360-degree feedback process, many of which are similar to other performance review processes. For example, different raters (bosses, peers, subordinates, self and customers) often focus on unique aspects of a person's performance, but some raters can only comment from a limited perspective.[56] The 360-degree feedback process is more likely to be effective if raters provide comments related to the person's ability to complete tasks or goals and less likely to be useful when focused on a personal level.[57]

CO 4: CARRYING OUT A GOAL-SETTING PERFORMANCE REVIEW

Goal-setting approaches can be linked to early applications of management by objectives, and the experimental work by Latham and Locke has provided solid evidence that 'specific, high (hard) goals lead to a higher level of task performance than do easy goals or vague, abstract goals' such as suggestions like 'Do your best' or 'Try hard'.

Many theories of motivation, beginning with Lewin and Tolman,[64] focused on goal-directed behaviour and the extent to which people initiate and persist when they believe that goals will lead to desired outcomes.[65] Research over the last four decades has supported the hypothesis that conscious goals affect how people behave and that higher and more difficult goals produce higher levels of effort and performance.[66] That is, specific and challenging goals lead to higher levels of performance

A RELEVANT POINT OF VIEW: THE PYGMALION EFFECT IN PERFORMANCE REVIEWS

The Pygmalion effect is a type of self-fulfilling prophecy where a person or group of people internalize higher expectations placed on them and act in ways to fulfil these expectations. Researchers, in demonstrating this theory, tested the IQs of students in 18 classrooms of an elementary school and then randomly labelled 20 per cent of the students in each class as 'intellectual bloomers'. Teachers were told that these 'intellectual bloomers' would show significantly more improvements compared with other students. When the students were tested eight months later, the 'intellectual bloomers' had indeed improved significantly, an improvement that occurred in spite of the fact that there was no difference between the 'intellectual bloomers' and other students, except in the 'teacher's mind'.[58]

The *Pygmalion* effect is dramatized in the play and movie *My Fair Lady*, based on George Bernard Shaw's work, *Pygmalion*. It is the story of Professor Henry Higgins, who makes a wager with his friend that he can teach speech and refine the manners of Cockney flower girl Eliza Doolittle, who illustrates her expectations when she says in the play: 'You see, really and truly, apart from things anyone can pick up (the dressing and the proper way of speaking and so on), the difference between a lady and flower girl is not how she behaves, but how she's treated. I shall always be a flower girl to Professor Higgins, and always will be, but know I can be a lady to you, because you always treat me as a lady, and always will.'[59]

The Golem effect is the negative or dark side of Pygmalion, where low or negative expectations lower subordinates' performance. The term Golem originates in Hasidic mythology. In one version of the tale, the Golem is a monster created by Rabbi Loew of Prague during the sixteenth century. Life is infused into a clay creature so that it can be a servant of its creator. Unfortunately, on the Sabbath, the Golem needs to be shut down or it will become destructive. But on one Sabbath, the Rabbi forgets to shut the Golem down, and it runs amok. There is the belief that if it continues to exist, there will be destruction. So, it must be destroyed.[60] In management, the Golem effect describes the destructive and performance-restricting effects of supervisors with low expectations of a person's performance. If we have low expectations, we are likely to get what we expect.

The Pygmalion effect has been demonstrated in a variety of work settings, including factories, retail stores, universities and the military.[61] For example, the Defence Forces had a special programme to meet the needs of inductees who were unable to meet normal qualifications for service. The programme was something of a boot camp where superiors predicted that certain inductees would not be able to succeed in basic training. In one particular case, there were too many possible inductees for the special training programme that was to be offered, and individuals who were to be placed in the programme were sent on the regular basic training. To avoid stigmatization, instructors were not told of the inductees' special problems. The result was that when instructors treated them as regular inductees, their performance, as well as their dropout rates, disciplinary problems and proficiency levels, were no different from that of the regular inductees.[62]

Managers play Pygmalion-like roles in carrying out performance reviews, developing their employees and in stimulating performance. Some managers develop relationships and treat their subordinates in ways that lead to superior performance while others treat their people in ways which result in much lower performance than they are capable of. The scientific research[63] illustrates that a manager's Pygmalion role has an impact on performance.

The question we must ask is 'How can we use the Pygmalion effect in treating employees by having positive expectations of them?'

than easy, unclear (e.g. 'Do your best') or no goals. Four things happen when we set specific and challenging goals:

1. **Goals direct attention**. Goals help focus attention on related activities and away from those activities that are less relevant. For example, students' learning objectives help focus on activities that are relevant and away from those activities that are less relevant.
2. **Goals can energize people**. When people set goals related to exercising and dieting, they are energized to accomplish these goals in the same way that subjective goals energize people to take action.
3. **Goals affect persistence**. When goals are set, people are more likely to be persistent in trying to accomplish them. It is possible to work faster and more intensely in a short time period or to work more slowly over a long time period to achieve a goal.
4. **Goals encourage discovery**. Goals can indirectly encourage people to discover new solutions to problems. People draw on their skills and knowledge for the achievement of routine goals, but they also draw on a larger repertoire of skills for more complex tasks. Goal setting is affected by planning, training, goal specificity, encouragement and personal self-efficacy.[67]

According to Latham and Locke, improving performance by setting goals and objectives is more likely if we recognize certain moderators, which are things we can do to improve our chances.[68]

Commitment. Commitment enhances performance and is most important when goals are more difficult to achieve. Factors linked to commitment are (i) the importance of the outcome expected and (ii) the belief that a goal or outcome can be achieved. Commitment is generated when employees are involved in the goal-setting process and are given support and assistance for achieving goals.

Feedback. Feedback provides progress reports on how well people are doing as they carry out their goals. When people know they are on target, they can increase their efforts to achieve their goals, or adjust their direction if they are not on target.

Task complexity. Higher levels of skills are required as the complexity of a task increases, and as a result, the achievement of the goal depends on employee skills, assistance they receive, or on the effectiveness of strategies used.

Encouraging a problem-solving relationship in goal setting

Effective performance reviews depend on the quality of the dialogue between the manager and the employee, and the ability to unite the manager and employee in a common purpose of improving performance.[69] Over five decades ago, Norman Maier's classic experiments compared the dialogues that develop in three different performance review relationships that he called tell and sell, tell and listen, and problem-solving.[70]

Norman Maier likened the tell-and-sell perspective on performance reviews as involving telling the employee what needed to be improved and then selling him or her through skills of persuasive communication, logic and knowledge of possible ideas and incentives to motivate the employee to improve performance. The tell-and-listen approach looks very much like the tell-and-sell approach when the manager communicates the evaluation. But in the second part of the performance review, the manager reverts to a non-directive counsellor, listening and attending to the employee's feelings.

A third perspective on performance reviews is called 'problem-solving,' which can also be called a 'collaborative employee development' approach. The problem-solving approach takes the manager out of the role of judge and encourages the manager and employee to jointly discuss problems and develop solutions. Problem-solving strategies start with the assumption that certain alternatives are not yet apparent and can best be discovered through combined efforts.

In examining the effectiveness of different supervisorial relationships in motivating employees to improve, Maier compared supervisors who were more 'tell and sell', and 'tell and listen', in their approach with those using a problem-solving approach. In experimental and field settings, he illustrated that the collaborative, problem-solving approach was more likely to generate mutual understanding between employees and supervisors and had a better chance of improving performance and developing employees. Since that time, several studies have enlarged this body of research and highlighted the effects of supervisorial relationships, and the social context of the review, in conducting effective performance reviews.[71]

An important characteristic of supervisors and employees in tell-and-sell interviews was a relationship where the nature of the communication was more confrontational, negative and directive. In the problem-solving relationship, the supervisor is more willing to attend and respond to employee needs and provide needed resources. Employees tend to reciprocate. They perform at a higher level, trust their supervisors and have positive attitudes towards them. The investment of time and energy for both parties is established before the performance review and will continue afterwards.[72]

The relationship is akin to a healthy leader–member exchange (LMX) and a willingness to respond helpfully and constructively in working together. This is characterized by three factors: respect, trust and obligation in a working relationship. Respect is illustrated in the respect that one person has for the capabilities of other people and is not an indication of personal friendship or liking. Trust is defined by ability, benevolence and integrity.[73] In a performance review, if an 'employee believes a supervisor has the skills to properly appraise, has the interests of the employee at heart, and believes the supervisor upholds standards and values, the employee is likely to trust that supervisor'.[74] Obligation is the 'expectation that interacting obligation will grow over time as career-oriented social exchanges blossom into a partnership'.[75]

The once-a-year performance review or meeting with employees has questionable value in developing a positive relationship. The relationship begins long before the interview and includes the pre-existing and ongoing relationship between supervisor and employee (leader–member).[76] Feedback is much more effective in an interview if employees have a relatively accurate perception of performance before the interview.[77] The problem-solving relationship is enhanced by ongoing communication and feedback. Positive feedback is part of a positive leader–member relationship that encourages respect, trust and obligation. On the other hand, negative communication reduces the desire to engage in future relationships and has long-term negative effects in achieving self-set goals and improving self-confidence.[78]

Implementing goal theory in performance reviews

Goal theory has been used effectively in the performance review process as a way to focus employee efforts and encourage development. Sometimes, HR departments develop a common form for goal setting, such as the one used in the planning and review process in Table 8.8, and use a problem-solving relationship in implementing it, such as the one described in the previous section.

Maier's problem-solving process is legendary in encouraging acceptance of the performance review results and a commitment to action.[79] As suggested in the previous section, managers will get an entirely different result if they change from a tell-and-sell script to one where they guide the process by asking questions that encourage problem-solving.

The working rules in this process suggest that we should try not to 'tell people what to do', but should instead ask questions to assist their problem-solving, goal setting and actions. The focus is more on reviewing rather than evaluating performance, by helping employees solve problems and motivating them to take action. The guiding 'mantra' is 'What are the goals we (supervisor and employees) want to achieve in resolving the problems or issues we face?'

The idea of using questions in encouraging learning can be linked to the dialectic method of inquiry (also known as the Socratic method or method of elenchus), which Socrates used in examining moral concepts such as 'good' and 'justice'. Plato first described this method in the *Socratic Dialogues*. Problems were broken down into a series of questions seeking clarification, probing assumptions, probing reasons and evidence, seeking different viewpoints and perspectives, probing implications and consequences, and questions on the relevance of the question.

There are difficulties in using motivation and goal-setting theory, and researchers like Latham and Locke recognize them. That is, organizational goals can conflict with individual goals, and some individuals might be rather risky and ambitious in setting goals while others might be risk averse. Goals can change and should change, and the process needs to reflect this.

One-minute goal setting. Given the overall purpose that goal-setting theory is to encourage purposeful behaviour in organizations and in the individuals who work for them, one of the best ways to respond to these and other difficulties is to see goal setting as a dynamic process. Problems occur, opportunities arise and there is a constant need for upgrading and refocusing for focusing goals. Ken Blanchard and Spencer Johnson's popular book *The One Minute Manager* highlights this by suggesting that the most important aspect of goal setting is taking a few minutes to engage employees in an ongoing way. That is, problems occur on a regular basis and as they do, they can be resolved in discussions in quick one-minute meetings. In the meeting, the issue and the facts underlying it are defined. Then, a goal is agreed to be used to implement the ideas in the discussion. The trick is to write it down in less than 250 words (on a sheet of paper or a form such as the one in Table 8.7) that describes the issue, goals and measures of the goals, and then to check later to see whether the results match the goal. This goal setting adds or revises the goals already set in the performance review process. An important part of this one-minute goal-setting process is a relationship which provides ongoing, honest feedback on a continual basis.[80]

Table 8.7 Example of a Form for 'One-Minute Goal Setting'

Issue:		
Goal:		
Strategic Theme Area: _____ Relationship to Strategic Objective: _____		
Goal Stated as a SMART Goal:		
Actions to Take	Actions Steps 1. 2. 3.	Dates Which This Might Be Accomplished
Potential Obstacles:		
Support Needed:		

Performance planning and review. The performance planning and review process now practised in many public organizations builds on many of the assumptions of MBO and other goal-setting approaches. In the process, employees develop their annual plan including organizational and personal goals and objectives. They might also define personal development goals and objectives related to the competencies for the job, values, skills identified for the role as well as any goals to support personal well-being and life balance. Examples of forms which might be used in this process are shown in Tables 8.8 and 8.9.[81]

Table 8.8 Example of a Form for a Performance Planning and Review Process – Work Plan

Employee name	Supervisor name

The performance plan is an agreement between the employee and the supervisor. Both must be committed to its success, and both are accountable for the results achieved. It is expected that there will be some risk in any plan. Both parties are responsible for managing that risk and, where necessary, modifying the plan to reflect changed circumstances. In addition to the formal review at the end of the reporting period, informal reviews will take place on a regular basis.

Plan objectives during the review period	How will performance be measured?

Employee Signature   *Date*   *Supervisor Signature*   *Date*

What additional support may be required to achieve the desired results?

Informal meeting to discuss progress and refine the plan was held on the following dates:

Performance Review (to be completed at the end of the review period)

Describe measured results	Describe major achievements

Employee Signature   *Date*   *Supervisor Signature*   *Date*

Employee's copy ☐   Supervisor's copy ☐

The process links organizational strategic themes and objectives to work and personal development goals and objectives. A dialogue between the employee and the supervisor facilitates identification of strengths, areas for further development and discussions of issues or concerns. Feedback and self-reflection in the performance review process provide further input for development goals for the following year. In the first year of the performance review, an individual's annual plan will focus on key accomplishments rather than measurement of performance against goals.

Table 8.9 Skills Inventory Form

Skills Inventory Form

Last Name	First Name	Date of Birth	Tel #	email
Position	Section	Department	Supervisor	

Education

Degree/Diploma/ Certificate	Subject or Course	University/ College School	Year

Other Skills and Training Including Language Skills

Skill	Certificate, If Any	Skill	Certificate, If Any

Work Experience

Position	Employer	Years	Comment

Career Development Interests

What other types of positions are you interested in?

What type of training do you want to improve your performance in your present position or advance?

Position Flexibility

Are you willing to consider:		Comments or Limitations	
A lateral move?			
A move to another location?			
Weekend work?			
Evening work?			
Part time work?			

Employee Number		**Date Completed**	

A critical part of performance development is the feedback and coaching aimed at recognizing positive contributions and providing direction and support when required. This should be an ongoing process to support progress towards objectives and to identify and address problems, issues or barriers as they arise. This ongoing dialogue should eliminate any surprises during progress reviews or performance reviews. Keeping a 'Dialogue Log' or summarizing new goals set during the year (see 'One-Minute Goal Setting' in Table 8.7) may be useful in keeping records about topics and activities throughout the year.

This information is mutually beneficial for progress reviews and the performance review. Learning opportunities to enhance the skills and competencies related to responsibilities of the employee's role can be supported through a variety of venues both on-site and off-site.

A periodic review of progress towards goals allows for identification of adjustments that may be required to the plan within the context of changing conditions and priorities within the work area, programme or department, the organization and the external environment. This also maintains focus and mutual understanding of the status of each goal and ensures that there are no 'surprises' in the performance review. Progress reviews are usually recommended every three months and should be documented on the individual plan.

The actual performance review is an opportunity to review performance against goals, to provide feedback and to plan for the next year of activity, learning and development. The approach should be a collaborative process initiated by the supervisor and as much as possible directed by the employee. The review should include targeted third-party feedback, reflective self-evaluation and evaluation by the supervisor.[82]

CO 5: CARRYING OUT DISCIPLINARY AND TERMINATION PROCEDURES

The 'management rights' clause in the collective agreement gives managers the authority to use reasonable rules to guide workplace conduct and discipline an employee when there is **'just cause'**. This usually requires employers to be 'just', make fair judgements and provide evidence to illustrate an employee's liability and negligence. Other requirements include warning the employee, giving the employee a fair hearing and being fair and reasonable in making sure the rules are enforced evenly and without discrimination. Just-cause dismissals involve cases such as theft, sexual harassment, fraud and dishonesty, intoxication and wilful disobedience. The norms in implementing suggest that the rules should be uniformly applied, clearly publicized and reasonable.

Due process involves using fair means to determine employee wrongdoings so that employee rights are maintained. Employee rights to due process are usually based on the collective bargaining agreement, legislative procedures and procedures that organizations use. In union organizations, due process is illustrated in employee rights to the grievance and arbitration procedures, and other mechanisms.

In most cases, employees work very hard and conduct themselves in ways that are acceptable to their employers and their fellow workers. Occasionally, managers will have to deal with problems relating to poor work performance, absenteeism or unacceptable behaviour. These problems go beyond those that can be corrected through feedback, supportive communication and goal setting.

In exceptional cases, formal discipline may be necessary and beneficial in clearly signalling the need for change[83] and to correct the errant behaviour. Managers may fail to take action for various reasons: (i) lack of awareness of the rules, (ii) fear of losing the employee's friendship or respect, (iii) lack of support from other managers, (iv) fear of a complaint or a grievance or (v) a belief that nothing will change. Some managers share a belief that implementing disciplinary procedures might alienate employees or make them even more unwilling to change, as people who are disciplined often receive support and positive reinforcement from peers and co-workers.[84]

The best approach to discipline is a form of **self-discipline** where managers encourage people to take responsibility for problems or unproductive work behaviours. In exceptional cases, more formal discipline may be necessary and beneficial in that it clearly signals the need for change.[85] Failure to administer discipline in a timely manner can be seen as accepting, or at least not disapproving, of the behaviour and may make it even more difficult to deal with the problem later.

Several organizations follow two approaches to discipline: positive discipline and progressive discipline. **Positive discipline** is a participatory process which encourages the employee to recognize his or her deficiencies, take responsibility for improving and recommit to the organization's goals and mission.

It is an attempt to avoid entering a formal disciplinary process and yet encourage an employee to address the need for change. Although it encourages communication and goal setting, it also requires supervisors to develop and apply these skills effectively. For some unions, positive discipline is no more than a dressed-up version of a disciplinary process, although its intent is to encourage a softer approach where employees receive a 'reminder' rather than a 'reprimand'.[86]

Progressive discipline follows a four-step progression of verbal warning, written warning, suspension and dismissal. It is a process where increasingly severe disciplinary measures are applied with the objective of ensuring that employees understand the errant behaviour and have a reasonable time period to improve their performance.[87]

Progressive discipline focuses on unacceptable, **culpable actions** which are within an employee's control. These are actions where the employee knows or can be expected to know what is required, is capable of carrying out what is required and chooses to perform in a manner that is inconsistent with this. Non-culpable conduct is performance which the employee is not able to control, such as poor performance because of lack of aptitude or absenteeism because of illness.

The advantage of a progressive discipline approach is that it impresses on employees the seriousness of repeated violations while encouraging employees to change. However, one of the disadvantages is that it can put management in an adversarial relationship with employees by focusing on addressing mistakes rather than recommitting to proper performance. Also, managers may be reluctant to perform a disciplinary role, and some managers might be more willing to tolerate poor performance rather than assuming an adversarial role.

Progressive discipline focuses on past events and the needs for improvement, whereas positive discipline focuses on trying to create a responsible employee through mutual problem-solving and continuous improvement. A key difference between the two approaches is that the positive discipline approach recognizes that the employee has to make a choice of either recommitting or resigning. Otherwise, positive discipline reduces the chances of wrongful dismissal because its goal is to not enter into an adversarial approach in ensuring compliance. The goal is to develop responsibility in the employee through problem-solving.

The employee has the right to request union representation during any disciplinary meeting, and the role of the union is to ensure disciplinary action is based on just cause. Managers today are responsible for taking the extra step in rejuvenating a problem employee, and clearly illustrating that this step has been taken will prevent any legal action based on wrongful discharge or discrimination.

Carrying out a termination interview

No one wants to terminate an employee as it is one of the most difficult things that a manager might have to do. For those terminated, there are perceptions of procedural injustice, unfairness and stress. There are possible expensive legal repercussions for not doing this correctly.

There are generally three types of termination. A **non-misconduct termination** results for reasons such as lack of work and is not the fault of an employee. A **disciplinary discharge** results from a gross breach of conduct such as fighting, theft, fraud or wilful destruction of property. A **progressive discharge** results from more minor breaches of conduct or negligence such as problems in performance, violation of work rules, disobeying a supervisor and general personal behaviour.[88]

Terminations can be as traumatic for the manager as for the employee. Even the most seasoned managers get the jitters when using words such as 'Your services are no longer required by our organization,' or 'Times are tough and we have to let you go.'

Several terms are used to describe employee termination, such as being 'let go', 'discharged', 'fired', or 'permanently laid off'.[89] Termination severs the employee's contract with an organization, due to bankruptcy or insolvency, temporary lay-off or constructive dismissal.

How should terminations be handled? Certainly not the way some organizations do this. At 4:00 p.m. Ken was called in the HR director's office, where he was informed of his dismissal: 'This is nothing personal, Ken, but the organization is going in a different direction.' After a brief conversation, a consultant knocked on the door, and Ken was escorted past other employees, down to his office, where he was given 10 minutes to take any personal effects. He was asked to return his office keys and cell phone, and his email account became immediately inaccessible. Ken was escorted out of the building, and he arranged to return that evening to pick up any other personal effects that were in his office. Ken is still bitter 14 years later.

Employees express a wide range of emotions when faced with losing their jobs, whether the reason is a constructive dismissal or lay-off. These emotions that might exist during a lay-off as a result of the organization's acquisition by another and include the following:

- *Loss of identity:* Employees often experience 'shock, anger, disbelief, depression and helplessness' and feel a loss of identity as if an anchor has been taken from them.
- *Lack of information and anxiety:* There is a shortage of accurate information and a person's world is a mass of information and misinformation as if 'drifting in the wind, with no direction, but a lot of information to worry about'.
- *Survival becoming an obsession:* Self-survival becomes an obsession as people try to protect themselves from changes which might harm them and a sense of a need to preserve one's 'status, prestige, power and career'.
- *Lost talent:* Many people who left felt angry and vindictive. Those who observed others losing their jobs also felt anger.
- *Family repercussions:* When someone is terminated, the family's economic status is threatened, and feelings of guilt and loss of self-esteem affect interactions with family members.[90]

In a perfect world, there would be little need for terminations or job loss, and employees would never feel inclined to sue their employees for breaching the employer–employee contract.

Concerns on whether a termination was conducted properly involve whether (i) a progressive discipline procedure was followed; (ii) a well-executed grievance procedure was observed; and (iii) the termination responded to current legislation and ways to deal with protected employees.

Employers have the responsibility for implementing progressive discipline procedures when employees are terminated for performance problems or for misconduct. The courts are more lenient when terminating an employee for inappropriate work behaviours such as theft or gross misconduct. In other cases, managers are often called on to cut staff because the organization is experiencing financial difficulties or during economic downturns. The general rules in terminations for misconduct are to use due diligence in identifying the reasons for the termination, documenting the case; employ progressive discipline when appropriate; and if necessary, suspend an employee while an investigation is carried out. For terminations due to lay-offs, be aware of employees who might be 'protected' by legislation and review contractual obligations related to the lay-off.[91]

MANAGERIAL IMPLICATION: Based on this chapter, one underlying theme of the SHRM BSC framework emphasizes 'motivating employees to work together toward agreed strategic objectives'. Solid empirical evidence underlies goal-setting theory. It is the basis of all things we do in HR, in defining an organization's purpose and strategic focus, in aligning HR processes and in aligning individual goals and objectives to those of the organization. Goal and objective setting is also

> crucial for employee motivation, learning and development and in encouraging positive actions. It is implemented by asking employees to identify the goals they want to achieve in resolving the issues or problems they face.
>
> The effectiveness of any performance review system is directly related to what the organization does with the results. A beautiful system will produce nothing if participation is spotty, the results end up in a dusty file and nothing happens. Even a mediocre system that results in meaningful conversations between supervisors and employees and has significant consequences within the organization can produce good results.

BEFORE APPLYING, LET'S REVIEW

CO 1: Review the strategic relevance of performance management in focusing an organization on strategic themes and objectives.

Performance reviews serve different purposes: (i) linking organizational goals to employee goals, (ii) facilitating feedback and career development, (iii) encouraging managers and employees to engage in mutual problem-solving and (iv) providing legal justification for administrative actions (promotions, lay-offs, termination and compensation).

CO 2: Assess approaches that have been used in assessing different aspects of performance.

Various performance review perspectives include goals and objectives, attitudes and interpersonal characteristics and behaviours, competencies and outputs. Different performance management approaches make unique assumptions about how to encourage performance and might be appropriate for different jobs or organizational needs. Goals and objectives can describe targets which the person might seek to accomplish over the next period of time, whereas attitudes and interpersonal characteristics and behaviours describe competencies like conscientiousness, reliability, customer orientation, leadership ability and team attitude. For some organizations, it is also important to recognize a person's competencies in doing the job, especially if it is difficult to measure outputs or outcomes. Outputs, outcomes and satisfied customers are useful dimensions for measuring performance. Each of these performance dimensions offers a partial perspective on performance, and some perspectives are more useful for different jobs. Performance management, in an ideal world, would recognize each aspect of performance rather than focusing on a single dimension. Goals and objectives can be a key integrating mechanism in helping an organization be more strategic in achieving its strategic themes.

CO 3: Apply formative review processes in encouraging employee development.

Formative approaches focus on providing feedback to encourage change and employee development, and they are less concerned in evaluating performance in a summative sense. The formative review is based on the assumption that feedback encourages learning and change and that this will, in the long run, improve actual performance. Different approaches include involving peers, subordinates, customers, self-appraisals and multiple raters in the 360-degree feedback process. The different perspectives are valuable in that they encourage a more balanced process, one which employees can be more involved in.

CO 4: Implementing a goal-setting approach in linking to strategic themes and objectives.

Research over the last four decades has supported the hypothesis that specific and challenging goals lead to higher levels of performance than easy, unclear (e.g. 'Do your best') goals or no goals. Goals direct attention and energize people. When goals are set, people are more likely to be persistent in trying to accomplish them and will likely be more creative in drawing on a larger repertoire of skills. Maier's problem-solving process is helpful in linking goal setting in the performance review process in reviewing rather than evaluating performance by helping employees solve problems and motivating them to take action. The question is 'How do we (supervisors and employees) resolve the work and career issues we face in positively meeting work and career goals?'

CO 5: Implementing disciplinary procedures.

Occasionally managers will face problems relating to poor work performance, absenteeism or unacceptable behaviour and may have to discipline employees. Positive discipline encourages the employee to recognize his or her deficiencies and jointly work with the manager in addressing any problems and improving performance. Progressive discipline involves increasingly severe disciplinary measures in ensuring that an employee understands the errant behaviour and improves performance within a reasonable time period.

DISCUSSION AND REVIEW QUESTIONS

1. Performance reviews can be used for providing feedback for employee development (and improving performance) and assessing people for merit awards and promotion. Should performance reviews that focus on developing employees and improving performance be separated from performance reviews that focus on merit or salary considerations?
2. Review the advantages and disadvantages of the four different systems to reviewing performance: management by objectives (MBO), graphic rating scales, a behavioural checklist and critical incidents. Define what each approach might look like before you review the strengths and weaknesses. Would certain approaches be more useful for managerial jobs? For operational jobs? Why?
3. How can managers or supervisors avoid errors and biases such as the halo effect, the recency effect, and leniency, strictness, and central tendency errors in ratings?
4. Review the purposes, skills and assumptions of the problem-solving, tell-and-sell and tell-and-listen approaches. How would you design a problem-solving performance review process for implementing a goal-setting approach? Develop an interview guide.
5. One of the challenges in implementing an organization's strategic objectives in the SHRM BSC is linking them to an individual's objectives in a performance management process or in a general discussion between a manager and employee. In the previous chapters, we identified three strategic objectives: (i) improving customer or client service delivery, (ii) developing managers' competencies on mentoring, training and career guidance and (iii) developing managers' competencies in improving workplace satisfaction and health. Identify individual objectives that an employee might define for each of these strategic objectives. Then, using the performance planning and review process described in this chapter and the form suggested, meet with another class member to develop objectives in this area. Define objectives within each perspective on the SHRM BSC. You can adapt the interview guide from the book's website. As a working rule, using the problem-solving approach rather than a tell-and-sell approach.

6. The collective agreement provides a framework of policies and procedures for managing and disciplining employees. For some managers, implementing disciplinary procedures might alienate employees or make them even more unwilling to change. What do you think? What advice would you give a manager who was about to terminate an employee?
7. As an HR professional, one of your managers has asked for your assistance in motivating and disciplining employees. You are asked to review three approaches: positive performance management (see Chapter 9), positive discipline and progressive discipline. Develop a table that outlines the strengths and weaknesses of each approach. Your review responds to the following issue: Four of the supervisors reported on problem employees who are unwilling to improve their performance. For example, one supervisor reported that she has an administrative assistant who is unwilling to improve her performance. She is consistently late to work, takes longer times for coffee and lunch breaks and has a poor work attitude. This supervisor says she has tried everything, including problem-solving interviews and offers of training, flex scheduling and new job responsibilities. The employee is not interested. She comes to work and does very little. When she is asked to take on responsibilities such as typing up a new schedule, she takes a very long time to do it, and it is usually full of mistakes.

CASE: DEFINING GOALS TO RESOLVE A PERFORMANCE PROBLEM

To test the effectiveness of two interview approaches – tell-and-sell and problem-solving – you are asked to participate in a role play of a performance review. You are asked to begin the process with a tell-and-sell style. Then, try it with a problem-solving approach using the goal-setting form in Table 8.7. Adapt the interview guide on the book's website.

Case A: Employee with a performance problem

Manager Role (Your Employee is Tom)

You (Emily) have taken over as the manager of the City Information Centre. You have been in the job for three weeks and are just getting to know the five employees working in the centre. A few hours ago, you recognized one of the long-time employees sitting around and staring out the window while he could have been doing things, like updating the brochures, restocking some of the art prints or other items and generally rearranging things. You asked to have a short meeting, just to check in.

Employee
- Six years to go to retirement, a highly valuable employee in the past.
- Has been with the organization for many years – worked his way in a steady job and a reliable employee.
- Not much formal education, but is very skilled from many years on the job.

Present Situation. Six months ago he applied for a job that would have meant a promotion because it would have given him/her the opportunity to learn some new things about wildlife and the ecosystem. He would have provided tourists with mini-lectures and guided tours, in addition to other duties.

It was given to a younger fast-tracker with much more formal education and much less practical experience.

He seems to do his work and that's about it – no more helping anyone else, no talking with co-workers at coffee or lunch. You've heard through the grapevine that he's doing the pub scene.

Employee Role (Tom)

You have been with the City Information Centre for many years and have worked your way up one step at a time. You have six years to go to retirement. You have been a highly valuable employee, and although you have no formal education, you are very skilled in what you do.

Present Situation. Six months ago you applied for a job that would have meant a bit of a promotion in that you would have been given the opportunity to learn some new things about wildlife and the eco system. You would have been able to provide tourists with mini-lectures and guided tours, in addition to other duties.

It was given to a younger fast-tracker with more formal education and much less practical experience.

You told your previous boss that you accepted the decision, but frankly, you are really ticked off. For the past six weeks, you have been on a bit of a downer, thinking of your options.

You've come to the conclusion that you are not going to go the 'extra' mile anymore. You're going to do your own work, and that's it – no more helping anyone else, no more going to lunch or coffee to discuss work.

You've picked up with some old friends and are starting to do some of the things you did before, like going out to pubs, fishing and other fun things.

This afternoon your new boss saw you sitting around, staring out the window. She wants to have a short meeting, and you are not sure what it will be about.

Part IV Developing and Engaging Employees

In Chapter 4, we suggested that one way to improve employee engagement and respond to employees' public sector motivation is to enrich their work so that it is intrinsically motivating and engaging. In the next five chapters, we illustrate strategic objectives for developing and engaging employees by focusing their career development, developing training and development programmes to enhance their competencies, improve their health and well-being and develop a positive labour relations climate.

9 Encouraging Individually Directed Career Development

Chapter Outline
- Chapter objectives (COs)   187
- A driving issue focusing managerial action: Recognizing how vocational preferences shape how people fit   187
- CO 1: The emergence of a new career contract   189
- CO 2: Organizational and individually directed career development   191
- CO 3: Career development planning for a boundary-less career   195
- Before applying, let's review   197
- Discussion and review questions   198
- Case: 'Come one, come all' in training for career development   200

CHAPTER OBJECTIVES (COs)

After reading this chapter, you will be able to implement the following objectives:

CO 1: Examine the new boundary-less career where employees have no set career path.

CO 2: Compare organizational and individually directed career development.

CO 3: Apply a career development planning perspective for a boundary-less career.

A DRIVING ISSUE FOCUSING MANAGERIAL ACTION: RECOGNIZING HOW VOCATIONAL PREFERENCES SHAPE HOW PEOPLE FIT

According to Richard Nelson Bolles, author of What Color Is Your Parachute?, *individuals often make poor career choices because they rely too much on perceived competencies.*[1] *They became lawyers because of the profession's status and their passion for social justice issues. Unfortunately, when they began working as a lawyer, they found that much of their paid work involved drafting letters, preparing wills and assisting unemployed workers obtain unemployment benefits. As many as half the people* polled in the United States and other parts of the world, and more than one-third of those polled in Canada, say they chose the wrong career.[2] The occupation they chose was very different to what they thought it would be.

Holland's congruence theory suggests that when people choose an occupation that is consistent with their vocational preferences, they are more likely to be satisfied and successful in that occupation.[3] Congruence theory is relevant, not only because it is one of the most influential approaches to improving choices in the jobs we pick, but also because it recognizes that individuals have unique preferences which may fit with the character of the job.[4] Person–organizational (P–O) fit describes the fit between an individual's values and skills and those in an organization.[5]

Individuals can be described with six vocational types – realistic, investigative, artistic, social, enterprising and conventional. Most work settings and occupations can be summarized within similar categories. To help define your vocational preferences, rank the following statements from 1–6, inserting a '1' next to the statement that reflects the tasks you prefer to perform.

_____ My values are practical, productive and concrete; I am comfortable with manual and mechanical tasks. (Realistic)
_____ I am analytical, sceptical and value the acquisition of knowledge through scholarship or investigation. I tend to be logical and analytical. (Investigative)
_____ I am open to experience innovative, intellectual and artistic activities. I like tasks where I can use my imagination and creativity. (Artistic)
_____ I am empathic, patient and have concerns for the welfare of others. I will sacrifice my personal goals for the sake of the organization. (Social)
_____ I have the ability to be persuasive and enjoy influencing others and selling. (Enterprising)
_____ I have technical skills for business or producing things. I am practical, structured, orderly and efficient, and I enjoy physical activities, possibly with machines and tools. (Conventional)

In a practical illustration of the typology, researchers had high school students work in simulated occupational environments where each environment required people to perform tasks and solve a problem of a different character. In the experiment, they found that a person's vocational interests paralleled the problems and task he or she liked to perform. That is, those with artistic interests felt more adept at solving artistic-type problems.[6] On the other hand, when incongruence occurs, people tend to be more dissatisfied, instable in their career path and lower performers.[7]

Holland's 'social' vocational preference describes a concern for the welfare of others which might be similar to public sector motivational (PSM)[8] values and beliefs related to being focused on the public good and being protective of the public's interests. In addition to PSM, New Public Management (NPM) ideas describe another view of P–O fit by encouraging making public organizations more enterprising and connected to the public, with higher standards of service quality. Prominent values which stand out in NPM are (i) responsiveness to citizen needs, (ii) transparency, (iii) innovativeness and reinvention, and (iv) a goal-achievement orientation that is performance based.[9] Scholars have independently demonstrated that PSM and NPM values are good predictors of commitment, job satisfaction and public service climate. Whether these values can exist simultaneously is not fully understood.

These two perspectives are in agreement that P–O fit congruence is an influential element in the quest for improving performance and job satisfaction in public organizations. Individuals who do not fit in are more likely to perceive the organization more negatively.

> STRATEGIC CONTEXT: *In the old HR reality, people were likely to work for an organization for their entire careers, and the organization would guide them through the career path. As a result of reforms in government and changes in society at large, fewer people are working for one organization for their entire career. Historians suggest that a new psychological contract or set of expectations has evolved, where individuals are encouraged to be more proactive in their career development and are empowered to assume responsibility for developing their careers through experiences inside and outside of organizations. As job security fades, employees will rely on their ability to be employable and learn new competencies that are in demand as they adapt and change in a protean-style career. This requires employees to have a clear understanding of the competencies that are important for their career development and then to use individually directed career development initiatives – such as mentors and job rotations – in furthering their development. It also encourages employees to be proactive in setting and meeting self-development goals.*
>
> *A key strategic objective underlying this chapter relates to 'developing a career development plan to guide your career growth'. In responding to this strategic objective, you might develop your own* **Leadership Action Plan (LAP)** *using the format described in CO 3 (see the book's website for examples). The LAP encourages you to define performance and learning goals in implementing a career plan that is based on your initiative. It relies on your motivation and willingness to learn, and much of this depends on a person's ability to focus on competencies which fit into relevant career goals. Your LAP can be informed by different scenarios which might occur in the future and might require a range of different competencies (see Chapter 5).*
>
> *We encourage you to use the SHRM BSC framework to align your personal competencies to your career objectives. You might develop an LAP to define these competencies and set out a plan for their implementation. Within the SHRM BSC framework, we suggest you identify formal and informal training and development initiatives that are relevant for your LAP.*

CO 1: THE EMERGENCE OF A NEW CAREER CONTRACT

When people are asked to use the word career in a free association test, they offer a range of responses. 'She is a career woman or a career civil servant.' 'She just made a career-limiting move and just kissed her career goodbye.' 'You are making a career of doing as little as possible in that job.' 'In that organization, you have a career for life.' 'He quickly moved up the career ladder.' 'You need career counselling.' 'We are involved in a career-planning exercise.' 'Those are interesting career dynamics.' The conclusion we draw from these statements is that the word is connected to many different meanings.

A public service career was generally thought to be composed of people who spent, or planned to spend, more of their careers in government, and even with a change of government, they are viewed as permanent employees appointed on the basis of merit rather than political affiliation.[10] One's career was akin to a ladder or a sequence of promotions, moves or transfers to more responsible or prestigious positions.[11] Underlying this view was an unwritten psychological contract where employers expected long-term commitment, trust and loyalty from their employees.[12] In exchange, employees expected to have a career path with promotions, recognition and benefits. Scholars pointed to the prominence of a public service motivation that committed public sector workers to the type of work they did.[13] In addition, in public organizations there was an expectation of lifetime employment, attractive pension and benefits packages and family-like values with commitment, connections and financial security. If you had a job in government, it was a job for life, with expectations for training for assignments to meet your career goals.[14]

A strategic shift in the concept of career

During the 1980s, a new reality began to evolve, with increased job mobility and lay-offs, as many organizations were put in a painful position of not being able to supply career opportunities that their employees had learned to expect. Several events combined to change the nature of careers, such as reductions in the level of supervision, changes in organization demographics, growth in the number of temporary workers, reductions in the size of the public sector and reductions in services offered by governments.[15] In the private sector, trendsetting organizations like IBM and AT&T changed their job security policies, and employees were let go. Coinciding with NPM and other changes, British Prime Minister Margaret Thatcher's reforms in downsizing and privatizing services resulted in a 30 per cent reduction in staff over the 15 years she was in power. New Zealand, Australia and Canada also underwent radical staff reductions.[16] In one year, during 1985, the Canadian government introduced plans to reduce the size of its workforce by some 15,000 workers using slogans like 'Doing more with less' in efforts to control the size of the debt.[17] Being 'lean and mean' was seen by some decision-makers as the way to be as competitive as business organizations.[18]

Historians argue that a new psychological contract or set of expectations evolved during this period, one that shifted from an organizationally directed career to one where individuals needed to direct their own careers. For Douglas Hall, 'The career of the 21st century will be **protean**, a career that is driven by the person, not the organization, and that will be reinvented by the person from time to time, as the person and the environment change'.[19] The metaphor is based on Proteus, a mythical sea-god and one of the several deities described in Homer's *Odyssey*, who had the power of assuming different shapes and being flexible, versatile and adaptable.

The new contract illustrates a **boundary-less career** with no set career path. Careers do not unfold in one organization, but result from less structured sequences of jobs across different occupational, organizational and geographical boundaries.[20] The individual's role requires more 'self-direction in the pursuit of psychological success in one's work'.[21] As the job and organization become less dominant in people's lives, a career is no longer based on lifetime employment with an organization, but is a 'boundary-less' career that includes both subjective and objective reference points.

The objective definitions of career recognize the effects of job mobility and insecurity, and that an individual's career illustrates a lifelong sequence of jobs, life experiences and the different roles that people play.[22] Regardless of the job, a career might be the sequence of jobs performed over the course of a lifetime.

A subjective view of a career, reflecting a person's perceptions and aspirations, is the way we experience the jobs, roles, experiences and challenges in our work history.[23] A career reflects a person's vision or direction in life and work, and personal needs, values, talent and abilities. A career might even go beyond work and refer to other non-paying roles and activities in life such as homemaker and community volunteer. A career describes where the person is going in life and work, and reflects a person's (i) unique vision and perspective, (ii) talents and abilities, (iii) values and (iv) career motives and needs.[24]

With NPM, boundary-less careers are expected to offer new career perspectives. Rather than a career being driven by the organization, individuals are expected to steer their careers and take advantage of organizational and non-organizational opportunities for achieving their vision. Organizations can play a role in communicating their direction and the competencies they will need, and employees can use this information to direct their career initiatives.

Performance metrics defining career success

The goal of the traditional career was climbing the career ladder; however, the boundary-less career is more individually focused on psychological success, or 'the feeling of pride and personal accomplishment that comes from achieving one's most important goals in life, be they achievement, family happiness, inner peace, or something else'.[25] Connected to the principle that individuals have control of their career is the idea that they have control of their measures of success. Success is personal, reflecting one's own career interests and goals rather than external criteria held by employers, parents, colleagues or friends. If individuals really want to control their careers, they must also be empowered to define their standards of success.

Within an **individually directed perspective of career development**, individuals are encouraged to be more proactive in their career development and to assume responsibility for developing their careers through experiences inside and outside of organizations. A strategy is key. As job security fades, employees must rely on their ability to be employable and learn new skills that are in demand as they adapt and change in a protean-style career. Although this approach to career management and development consists of recognizing that employees have responsibility for their careers, management helps employees by clarifying the directions and competencies that they will need in the organization, providing opportunities for the employee and organizationally initiated continuous learning and encouraging an atmosphere which supports learning and career self-reliance.

Career success is the outcome of one's career experiences, defined either in subjective or objective terms. Subjective success is a personal assessment across dimensions important to the individual, such as progression, income, access to learning and general career satisfaction.[26] **Career satisfaction** describes one's perceptions of success in career, progress in meeting career goals, success in meeting income goals, advancement and development of new skills.[27] In contrast, objective career success is usually defined from an external perspective and is often connected to status, official position or job level. Career dissatisfaction involves frustration in the way the work is managed or designed, on-the-job nuisances, people problems or other issues related to overwork, low pay, lack of promotion or insufficient recognition.

CO 2: ORGANIZATIONAL AND INDIVIDUALLY DIRECTED CAREER DEVELOPMENT

If a career relates to a person's lifelong experiences, **career development** describes the way people manage and structure their career paths within and outside organizations, and 'who develops whom, when and how'. In the organizationally directed idea of career development, managers focused and directed employee career paths as a logical, planned progression of development for higher-level positions. A person might start work as a research assistant before moving to a policy advisor position, then to a project manager, and then on to other positions. Such organizationally directed careers are more likely to work well in stable environments where there is intra-organizational focus, and in larger organizations where there are likely to be some vacancies and mobility.[28]

Organizationally directed career development often target training for high-potential or managerial employees within a **career path** guiding a employee through different experiences. This involves careful screening, identified career path, career counselling, performance reviews, focused training and development opportunities, mentorships, transfers, rotations and promotions. By investing in a few key employees, the organization can prepare certain people to take on specific roles and responsibilities. From a cost-benefit perspective, choosing to support high potential employees makes sense as it aligns with the logic that it is more cost-effective to focus in on those thought to be most valuable.[29] However, being less restrictive in developing all employees has the advantage of improving the general HR capabilities of the organization's membership. In addition, as learning and career development are important to most individuals, a more open employee career development philosophy enhances motivation and commitment.

The *traditional organizationally directed career* is nicely exemplified in military and police services, where officers have carefully planned and controlled career assignments to develop those who will finally achieve high ranks in the inner nucleus of decision-makers. Opportunities within the services are largely for training and increased responsibilities. In the Canadian Military, non-commissioned members have five developmental processes, and an officer has four. In addition, military personnel enlarge their repertoires through development opportunities offered by increased levels of 'accountability, responsibility, authority, competency, military leadership ability, and knowledge of operations and war'.[30]

Organizationally directed careers are also prominently exemplified in many major Japanese organizations, where careful screening of potential employees and planned career progression is the basis of lifetime employment systems. Large cohorts of newly recruited employees are trained to work in various jobs and rotated to various responsibilities. The first few years involve intense training where HR managers extensively monitor and evaluate employees every few months. The recruit spends the first few years training and rotating in multiple jobs where consistent performance enhances opportunities for career progression, in addition to developing networks of peers and superiors who assist the employee's career progress.[31]

The boundary-less perspective encourages individuals to direct their own careers and draw on resources and initiatives that they can access inside and outside the organization. Such **career-related continuous learning (CRCL)** is 'characterized as a self-initiated, discretionary, planned, and proactive pattern of formal (e.g., institutional) and informal activities' focused on applying knowledge for career development.[32] The following range of activities relies on being interested in learning and being proactive in one's self-development.[33]

- *Mentor-protégé relationships:* Mentoring has long been viewed as a process to assist employee development. The word **mentor** is connected to Greek legend and appears in Homer's *The Odyssey*.[34] Mentor is really the goddess Athena in disguise, who counsels or teaches Odysseus' son, Telemachus. Her role as teacher is in encouraging and guiding. Historically, there are many examples of the mentor–protégé relationship. A mentor is someone who serves as a career model and who actively advises, guides and promotes another's career and training in a relationship of trust.[35] Terms such as *role model, guide, guru, counsellor, confidante, teacher* and *adviser* are also used in connection with mentoring. Some of these unique terms might reflect those used in specific professional fields; nurses use 'role model' where there exists a formal, educational relationship in which experienced nurses act as guides, or role models, to student nurses.[36] The mentoring process can also be an informal relationship when a mentor and protégé connect. Mentoring can also occur in relationships with bosses, subordinates and peers.[37] The logic underlying the importance of mentorship is based on evidence that many successful managers indicate that mentors were important in their development. Those who had mentors earned higher incomes and more promotions and were more satisfied with their careers than executives who did not have a mentor. Career mentoring was positively related to career outcomes, as those who had mentors followed a more definite career path and were more willing to serve as mentors for others.[38]
- *Peer mentoring relationships:* Individuals can gain many of the advantages of mentoring relationships in establishing peer relationships to guide a career development when they focus on (i) sharing and confirmation of values and beliefs; (ii) emotional support; (iii) learning about leadership style, how they affect others and balancing work and family; and (iv) friendship. **Peer mentoring relationships** focusing on career guidance have many of the same advantages of mentoring in addition to offering a degree of mutuality, where both peers are givers and takers. There are different types of peer relationship:
    - *Informational peer:* This role involves the exchange of information about work and the organization. 'We exchange technical ideas. We talk about work and technical problems. His problems and mine. I contribute ideas to him and he contributes to me.'[39]

- *Collegial peer:* An information-sharing role is combined with increasing levels of emotional support, feedback and confirmation. 'We talk about all sorts of things . . . from business to personal. It is always helpful to talk about those with someone you can trust.'[40]
- *Special peer:* This role involves greater openness and self-expression as well as a deeper connection to each other. 'We're pretty open and trustful of one another, and we'll give a valued judgement, even if it's wrong. I think the other is willing to accept that.'[41]
- **Coaching:** Employees can seek ongoing coaching and advice about jobs or careers from managers or seek assistance from professional coaches. Employee coaching can consist of regular meetings between supervisors or managers and employees to discuss career needs and development. Coaching can be job specific and involve formal training in day-to-day practice from supervisors, colleagues, HR staff or mentors. The coaching emphasis is linked to the sports metaphor of being a good coach to develop a winning team, and it differs from the traditional metaphor of manager as director or boss providing answers, pointing out weaknesses, diagnosing and solving problems. The value given to coaching encourages managers and employees to work in a 'problem-solving' relationship. There are several services and programmes for providing employee coaching.
- **Job rotations:** People in the same field of work (e.g. HR) can exchange responsibilities for a set period of time, thus providing employees with wider job experience and encouraging them to acquire a wide range of skills.
- **Temporary assignments:** Individuals can jump-start their careers by engaging in temporary assignments which help get a person's career started or provide opportunities to experience new challenges or experiences.
- **Cross training:** Cross training in sport refers to combining various exercises to work various parts of the body because one particular exercise only emphasizes one muscle group. Similarly, this training uses many of the principles of job rotations and refers to training one employee to do another's work.
- **Internships or co-op experiences:** Students can get involved in internships as part of their university or college programme. These temporary positions or on-the-job training are similar to apprenticeships and range from paid to unpaid on-the-job experiences which allow employees to gain experience and applicable knowledge. Internships are common in medicine, accounting, engineering, teaching and law as a certification requirement. A co-operative education experience, similar to an internship, has the goal of combining classroom teaching with practical work experience.
- **Projects and development assignments:** Individuals can get involved on projects that respond to their development needs in providing useful skills, contacts or experiences which employees find valuable.
- **Diplomas and certificates:** Individuals can access a wide range of specialized skills through university and college diploma and certificate programmes. Examples include project management, public relations and HR certifications. In some locations, diplomas are awarded by colleges of applied arts and technology; however, in some jurisdictions, diplomas and certificates are dependent on entrance requirements and course requirements.

There are several advantages to the boundary-less career for public sector workers in encouraging mobility and skill development, fostering co-operation between other units or departments and breaking down organizational silos. With the decline of the traditional career and the move to the boundary-less career, we can expect changes in career satisfaction. Although greater empowerment is likely to encourage greater career satisfaction, employees are still very satisfied with the traditional career model. The boundary-less career is not yet the norm for all organizations and people, but this is changing. It is likely that people in a boundary-less career who illustrate a greater degree of change and mobility are more successful in earnings in the long run, although the greatest benefits are in terms of psychological success.[42] It is likely that only employees who are willing to invest in their own careers and networks and those who are more highly educated report having the values associated with the boundary-less career.[43]

A RELEVANT POINT OF VIEW: THE POWER OF INFORMAL LEARNING

There is a growing recognition of the role of informal learning in adult education and employee development.[44] Studies of informal learning in adults suggest that people are constantly picking up additional skills, knowledge and ideas in informal settings. Suggestions are that the majority of learning in the workplace (more than 70%) is informal, even though organizations spend billions of dollars each year on formal learning. A startling fact is that training and development programmes are not the prime method of transferring learning and represent only 20 per cent of the ways that people learn.

Informal learning goes beyond formal classroom courses, structured on-the-job programmes, workshops, seminars, instructional CD-ROMs and online courses, and takes place without an externally imposed curriculum. It can take place during ad hoc problem-solving, incidental conversations, coaching and mentoring, group problem-solving, lunch-and-learns and communities of practice.

In one public service organization, informal learning resulted from three key activities:

- Learning through relationships such as formal mentoring, informal mentoring and mentoring in peer relationships (representing 38.9% of activities).
- Learning opportunities generated from temporary job changes, cross training and stretch assignments (representing 29.5% of activities).
- Learning opportunities from enriched jobs involving acting management opportunities, full-time temporary assignments and on-the-job learning contacts or meetings (representing 31.6% of the activities).

Also important to informal learning was the process by which it was carried out. This included:

- Planning and organizational processes for assisting others in goal setting and scheduling, matching employee talents with jobs and reviewing progress and expectations (16.5% of activities).
- Providing feedback and support in modelling, developing supportive relationships and recognizing positive behaviours (44.6% of activities).
- Processes which encouraged positive relationships, clear communication, trust, respect and developing positive connections among participants (12.6% of activities).
- Processes which were application oriented, connected to an organization's long-term planning and performance appraisal process and grounded in an individual's daily work (26.4 per cent of activities).

Informal learning may have many possibilities for motivating people to learn because it engages people in learning activities that are more relevant for them and, possibly, connected to their careers. Because individuals learn best with those they trust, they are more likely to feel safe and supported than they would in a classroom.

CO 3: CAREER DEVELOPMENT PLANNING FOR A BOUNDARY-LESS CAREER

The boundary-less career has encouraged public sector managers and professionals to take more responsibility for their own career planning. In response, most government websites offer templates of career planning that include self-analysis, research, goal setting and planning.

The psychological process associated with self-directed behaviour can be linked to social cognitive career theory (SCCT),[45] which builds on social cognitive theory.[46] Within this body of theory, three cognitive mechanisms are especially relevant for career development: self-efficacy beliefs, outcome expectations and goal representations. This theory suggests that self-regulated learners set challenging goals for themselves, apply appropriate initiatives to achieve these goals and enlist self-regulating influences to motivate and guide their development. Self-regulated learners have a high degree of self-efficacy in their capabilities and a commitment to fulfil their challenges.[47] What is crucial in the process is whether an individual views the activities to implement a goal as worthwhile and can overcome the barriers to being successful.

The LAP is a career-planning template for implementing SCCT in linking a person's goals in a meaningful way to encourage commitment and self-efficacy. The LAP structure includes (i) an introduction, (ii) personal needs assessment (PNA), (iii) vision and goals, competencies and principles, (iv) action strategies and (v) conclusion. It encourages you to review your personal needs, values and beliefs; articulate your vision, goals and principles; and identify a plan for implementation.

Personal needs assessment. Building on the introduction which provides the background and purpose, the PNA provides a description of your perceived strengths and weaknesses, and personal style, including cognitive style, values and beliefs, and general disposition (attitudes, self-efficacy and ability to handle stress). This part of the LAP builds on self-assessment instruments (like the Big Five described in Chapter 7) and feedback received from others. The basis of this PNA should highlight how your personal style will drive your career plan.

Vision, goals and competencies. This section of the LAP provides a direction for your career plan as setting career goals and objectives can be viewed as a way for improving performance and energizing you to work towards goal-related activities. People who set goals and adopt higher goals are more likely to be successful and perform at a higher level.[48] Goals which are challenging can encourage you to stretch yourself to better utilize your existing knowledge, in addition to encouraging you to acquire new and needed knowledge.[49]

A goal is described 'as an aim that one is committed to that serves to guide future behaviour'.[50] An important aspect of goals is a person's **goal orientation** which describes 'one's dispositional or situational preferences in achievement situations'.[51] In the 1960s, Professor David C. McClelland and his colleagues were interested in why certain individuals expressed their preference for certain outcomes. He used the term **high need for achievement** (N-Ach) to describe individuals who had a tendency to be more goal oriented and take on moderately difficult tasks. The need for achievement describes a person's desire or motive for success. Individuals with a high need for achievement seek more challenging assignments and are persistent in their need to accomplish them. High achievers found that their most satisfying reward was the recognition of their achievements as an illustration of their competence and effort. They sought moderately challenging and realistic goals rather than highly risky or easy-to-accomplish goals.[52]

An individual's goal orientation has also been described by learning and performance dimensions.[53] **Learning goals** relate to task learning or improvement, skill development or competence (learning a new competency or skill such as becoming competent at problem-solving).[54] Learning goals are generally intrinsically motivating and are articulated in a **competency framework** defining ongoing learning and development. **Performance goals** focus on outcomes (solving the problem; getting a job, degree, good grade; making money) rather than the achievement process. Performance goals focus on the end result, whereas learning goals put more emphasis on the process or means for achievement.[55]

Both learning and performance goals are relevant. Performance goals are more clearly linked to performance improvement, and learning goals are correlated with intrinsic motivation. There are cases when avoiding poor performance rather than improving performance can inhibit motivation. But positive performance and learning goals linked to intrinsic motivation are important to your career. As such, it is logical to encourage a balanced approach to goal setting.[56] Goals in focusing career development should emphasize improving performance as well as learning goals, which are intrinsically motivating and link to an individual's values, needs, drives and other desired standards.[57] Examples include having a desire to learn, develop and explore in providing intrinsic motivation and having the desire to understand your environment and to develop necessary skills.

According to motivated action theory (MAT),[58] goals are hierarchically structured such that higher-order goals provide a rationale or overall purpose (the 'why') of action, and lower-level goals apply increasingly more specific principles and actions (the 'how'). It is possible to think of different levels of goals, such as visionary goals, self-goals and action goals. Higher-level visions are general goals; self-goals are fundamental personal outcomes that people desire; and learning goals concern being fulfilled, healthy and getting ahead. Lower-level action goals reflect strategies, pathways or tactics for achieving desired goals. There are several possible action goals, such as getting feedback to improve learning, working with others, and prioritizing and balancing tasks, which have short- and long-term implications.

One part of this section of the LAP defines these by using the 'how-why' process in Figure 9.1 to articulate a hierarchy of goals, beginning with a personal vision statement, self-goals and action goals, and taking into account both performance and learning goals in each area. A second part of this section articulates competencies and principles for implementing learning goals. For example, a learning goal might be to improve your competence work and lead in a team, whereas principles might include 'using goal setting to improve team work', 'empowering team members by linking their work to personal goals', and 'providing time for task- and relationship-oriented activities'. For each set of competencies and principles, you might define the empirical and anecdotal logic supporting them.

Action strategies. Each set of performance and learning goals should be accompanied by a set of action strategies that are specific activities which will be used to guide the implementation. This section should also include benchmarks for assessing the progress in implementing the plan. The LAP also includes a conclusion that highlights the important parts of each section and the steps that are needed for regularly reviewing progress.

Figure 9.1 *How-why questions.*

An important managerial task is to help a person develop a career plan for implementing performance and learning goals, and there is much that a manager can do to be helpful to employees and colleagues. Setting goals is a first step. Beyond that, managers can be helpful to employees in encouraging them to be more goal oriented and recognize that goals are causally linked in a hierarchy. Not only can managers be helpful in this process, but so can colleagues and friends.

> MANAGERIAL IMPLICATIONS: In responding to the strategic objective 'developing a career development plan to guide employee development', you might develop your own LAP using the format described in CO 3 (see website for examples). The LAP encourages you to define performance and learning goals in implementing an individually directed career plan. It relies on your motivation and willingness to learn and depends on your ability to focus on competencies which fit into relevant career goals. Your LAP can be informed by different scenarios that might occur in the future and which might require unique competencies (see Chapter 5).

BEFORE APPLYING, LET'S REVIEW

CO 1: Examine the new boundary-less career where employees have no set career path.

As employers contracted out their services and reduced the size of their workforces to reduce costs, a new set of expectations or psychological contract emerged, where employees could no longer expect to work in one organization for their whole career. The new contract suggested that individuals had to be responsible for their careers and that the career involves a less structured sequence of jobs across different occupational, organizational and geographical boundaries. If a *career* articulates a person's unique vision and sense of self-worth, *career development* describes that way people manage and structure their career paths within and outside organizations.

CO 2: Compare organizational and individually directed career development.

Career-related continuous learning (CRCL) encourages you to be proactive in setting self-development goals and engaging in development activities. Mentor–protégé and peer relationships can assist career development by focusing on sharing and confirmation of values and beliefs, emotional support, learning about leadership style, how the employee affects others and balancing work, family and friendship. The design of this relationship hinges on the mutual respect and positive expectations of those involved, as well as their commitment to make the process work.

CO 3: Apply a career development planning perspective for a boundary-less career.

Social cognitive career theory (SCCT) suggests that self-regulated learners set challenging goals for themselves, apply appropriate initiatives to achieve these goals and enlist self-regulating influences to motivate and guide their development. The LAP is a career-planning template for implementing SCCT in linking a person's goals to encourage commitment and self-efficacy. The LAP structure encourages people to review their personal needs, values and beliefs; articulate their vision, goals, and principles; and identify a plan for implementation.

DISCUSSION AND REVIEW QUESTIONS

1. Complete some of the instruments describing your personality, cognitive styles, values and career anchors. Go online and search 'Holland vocational preference inventory' and 'Schein's career anchors' to find online tests. Also, locate a short version of Schein's anchors.[59] You might also use other personal assessment instruments that assess your personality preferences[60] and review the Big Five inventory.[61] What do these instruments say about the type of career you might fit best in?
2. A manager you are working for wants you to review the literature on vocational fitness and competencies in relationship to job performance and turnover. In your short report, define various perspectives on personal fitness and the advantages and disadvantages of using it for career development.
3. The majority of learning in organization is informal, characterized as unplanned or spontaneous interactions between employees, colleagues and supervisors which affect the completion of tasks and the work. What things can be done to leverage and support informal learning (e.g. meeting rooms, whiteboards)?
4. Develop a LAP which includes three sections: (i) personal needs assessment (review of your personal style, strengths and weaknesses), (ii) vision and goals (including competencies and principles to implement learning goals), (iii) action strategies implementation plan (strategies and benchmarks, obstacles and schedule for implementation). See the Web for an example of an LAP.
5. How do organizations help develop careers in this new reality? For example, mentor–protégé and peer relationships can be a useful way to guide your career. What steps might you take in beginning and maintaining such a relationship?
6. There is more to goal setting than stating a goal to improve your skills or performance. Most of us know this based on experiences such as setting goals in New Year's resolutions that are often forgotten or never implemented. If goal setting is to be effective, short-term goals must be connected in a causal way to higher-level goals defining an overall purpose.
    - For the performance goal getting promoted, identify higher- and lower-level goals for each by asking the questions 'Why?' and 'How?' Then, focus on a key learning goal such as building competencies in a certain area. Ask why you are doing this. Then ask, 'How might I do this? What action goals implement my higher-level achievement goals and improve working relationships?' Adapt the goals in the How-Why process in Figure 9.2.

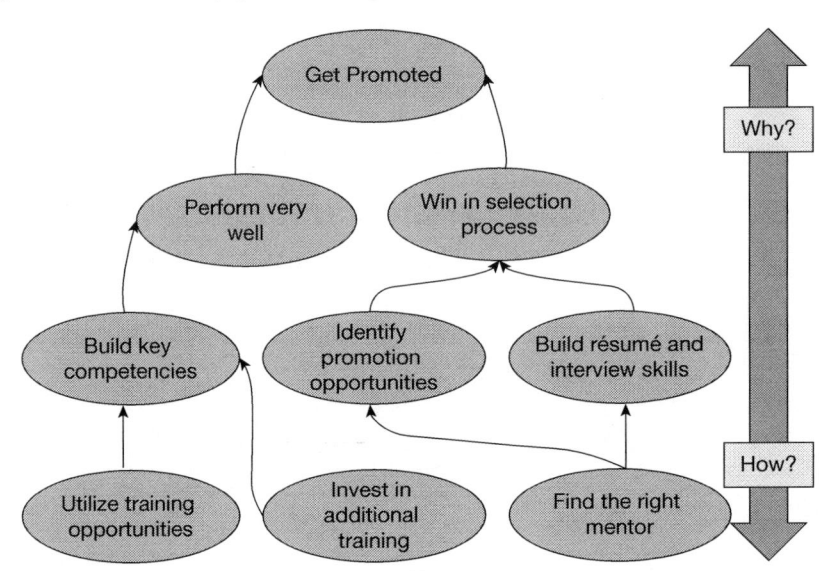

Figure 9.2 How-why? process

7. Build on the SHRM BSC framework in Table 9.1 to define strategic competencies and initiatives that are important for implementing the strategic objective that illustrates your responsibility for your own career management. In forming competencies and initiatives, the framework asks you to recognize basic questions that are important to the implementation:
   - How do customers or clients (employers) who might hire me see me, and what value do I offer which is unique? Which competencies are important, and what are initiatives for implementing them? (Client or Customer perspective)
   - What must I excel at? Which competencies are important and what are initiatives for implementing them? (Internal process perspective)
   - How do I provide added financial value to clients? Which competencies are important and what are initiatives for implementing them? (Financial perspective)
   - What initiatives can I use to continue to improve and create value? Which competencies are important, and what are initiatives for implementing them? (Innovation and Learning perspective, or Learning and Growth)

Table 9.1 Strategic Objective: Taking Responsibility for Your Own Career Development

Competencies	Initiatives	Markers or Measures	Time Period
CUSTOMER OR CLIENT PERSPECTIVE			
Competency 1	1. 2.		
Competency 2	1. 2.		
Competency 3	1. 2.		
FINANCIAL			
Competency 4	1. 2.		
Competency 5	1. 2.		
INTERNAL PROCESS			
Competency 6	1. 2.		
Competency 7	1. 2.		

LEARNING & GROWTH			
Competency 8	1. 2.		
Competency 9	1. 2.		

CASE: 'COME ONE, COME ALL' IN TRAINING FOR CAREER DEVELOPMENT

Jenny Poole's letter on behalf of the union included several high-pitched words like 'favouritism', 'backward style of management favouring the old guard', 'lack of consideration for merit and competencies of employees', 'discrimination in picking people who were management's favourites'. The union has asked for a meeting with management, and they wished to debate the merits of the policy of hand-picking a number of high-potential employees and training them for higher-level positions.

Task. Should organizational training and career development be reserved for people who the organization feels are high potential or should it be provided on a 'come one, come all' basis? You (Jenny Poole) have asked a team of your researchers to write a briefing note defining and reviewing the strengths and weaknesses of each career development option and presenting your recommendation. The briefing note structure includes (i) definition of the issue and purpose, (ii) criteria on which to base the decision, (iii) definition of each option, (iv) review of the strengths and weaknesses of each option and (v) a recommendation illustrating the criteria which are most important. See website for additional background material.

10 Encouraging Competency-based Training and Development

> **Chapter Outline**
> - Chapter objectives (COs)   201
> - A driving issue focusing managerial action: Linking training to application   201
> - CO 1: Competency-based training in meeting training needs   203
> - CO 2: Applying experiential learning in training and development   206
> - Before applying, let's review   211
> - Discussion and review questions   211
> - Case: Why train them for a career if they're just going to leave?   213

CHAPTER OBJECTIVES (COs)

After reading this chapter, you will be able to implement the following objectives:

CO 1: Apply competency-based training in meeting training needs.

CO 2: Illustrate how experiential learning principles can be used to enhance training and development.

A DRIVING ISSUE FOCUSING MANAGERIAL ACTION: LINKING TRAINING TO APPLICATION

Training and development is a multi-billion-dollar industry, with over £93 billion ($141 billion) spent in North America and £261 billion ($396 billion) globally in 2013, a growth of 5.2 per cent over the previous year.[1]

Training and development means different things in public organizations, ranging from providing information on procedures to developing an employee's competencies. Some training programmes are used to communicate procedures and protect organizations from potential litigation by providing information about controversial topics and laws relating to sexual harassment, pay equity, employment equity, occupational health and safety or new administrative processes, technical processes, technology and customer requirements. For others, training is about developing employee competencies so they can be more effective in working towards an organization's strategic objectives. Given that there are many meanings of training, labelling everything as 'training' might send a foggy message to employees.[2]

The success of any training and development programme often is based on its ability to encourage participants to use and apply relevant information. As such, training and development of competencies is more effective if it is viewed as an experiential process that involves information exchange and application of the concepts alongside opportunities to observe others and reflect on the learning. Whether the purpose is to learn how to ride a bike, sail a boat or improve one's conflict resolution skills, this definition of training and development involves experientially applying competencies to meet defined needs.

Training and development methods can be classified into four general categories: information presentation, simulation methods, on-the-job methods and action learning. As we move down in the listing, participants are more involved experientially in applying the concepts or ideas.

- **Information presentation techniques** consist of lectures and presentations, conferences, video or compact disks, web links on the Internet or intranet, distance learning, interactive media and tutoring.
- **Simulation methods** include in-basket exercises, role playing, interactive simulations, case methods and management or business simulations.
- **On-the-job training techniques** include orientation, apprenticeships or training by mentors on the job, job rotation, project assignments, coaching or mentorship, and performance feedback and management.
- In **action learning**, participants learn through experience in solving real-life problems. In action learning, projects become the central learning experience, where participants, working in groups, are charged with developing a solution for an important organizational task. After initial training, the participants manage the project in carrying out a diagnosis and developing a solution that they present to management.[3]

Although lectures and most classroom experiences provide an opportunity to review the fundamental concepts for understanding the real world (through the eyes of the lecturer and the textbooks), they do not provide real-world opportunities to experientially apply and utilize the information. In the same way, bicycle riders can gain numerous ideas from a book, but the book does not provide an opportunity to experience and apply the learning. 'Taking in information is only distantly related to real learning. It would be nonsensical to say, "I just read a great book about bicycle riding – I now learned that."'[4]

> STRATEGIC CONTEXT: Before beginning this chapter, describe a situation when you experienced a most inspirational and transformational learning. Chances are that your response will likely suggest a real-life experience that involved you experientially and which emphasized your learning needs. Some of this learning was not planned.
>
> As in the previous chapter on career development, a competency framework can be a useful guide for training and development. In this chapter, you might focus on defining initiatives and activities for implementing an experiential model of learning and experiential principles in training and development. A competency framework is key for assessing training needs, evaluating the success of training experience and orienting new employees.

CO 1: COMPETENCY-BASED TRAINING IN MEETING TRAINING NEEDS

Competency-based training aims to develop employees' knowledge, skills, abilities and other characteristics (KSAOs) and also to improve performance in achieving an organization's strategic objectives.[5] The training requires employees to demonstrate their ability to perform tasks and is often measured against behavioural objectives.[6] It places greater responsibility on the learner for taking initiative in gaining knowledge and skills and demonstrating their use.[7]

As competency-based training emphasizes developing employees, it is generally an investment in their career and long-term contribution.[8] Employee development increases an individual's employability and value to an organization generally, and it also enhances a person's self-worth. Employability training is a statement of a commitment to the employee and to developing 'a workforce that is multi-skilled, adaptable, and with a broad conceptual knowledge'.[9] When training is linked to the organization's mission and vision and its strategic objectives, employees are more aware of the organization's priorities and practices that are valued.[10] The training not only helps to clarify strategic objectives, but it is also often a type of training which is more intrinsically motivational because the problem-solving skills and competencies being trained are relevant in helping employees learn and develop in their work and careers.[11]

The effectiveness of any training is often related to an individual's motivation, willingness to learn and involvement in the design of the programme.[12] Personal attributes related to motivation to learn include conscientiousness (related to setting high performance standards and challenging goals), an internal locus of control (a belief in being a master of one's own destiny), self-efficacy and openness to change.[13] The motivation to learn is also related to the way the training is framed, such as when it is linked to preparing people for management.[14]

An effective way to tap into a person's willingness and motivation to learn is by linking competency training to personal and career goals.[15] These findings suggest certain practices:

- Begin by asking participants to identify examples of training where they were motivated and those where they were not motivated. Based on this, summarize a set of principles to guide the training workshop. Clearly communicate the goals and objectives of the training programme at the beginning.
- Encourage participants to set personal goals and objectives to challenge themselves and that link to their learning needs or career development.
- Clearly link the objectives to competencies that the organization identifies for achieving strategic objectives.

Linking to the strategic context by identifying training needs

When training is linked to an organization's strategic objectives and priorities in job performance, it is more likely to be relevant to those being trained.[16] In doing this, a training needs analysis is used to identify gaps between the current work performance and desired performance.

Most methodologies on identifying training needs seek to gather employee input in identifying 'felt needs', such as asking employees to rank training courses they thought would help them improve their performance.[17] However, there are calls to be more comprehensive in carrying out a performance-based needs assessment, one that recognizes the organization's performance in meeting its objectives, the processes underlying the performance, and the performance of individuals. In larger organizations, this is a challenging task that requires a substantial outlay of resources as such methodologies seem to 'assume that assessment is being carried out within a limited domain of jobs or individuals, or that assessors have enough time to conduct needs analysis through multiple stages'.[18]

The vast majority of training programmes are designed based on input from field or line managers (63%) rather than an assessment of training needs (28%).[19] A landmark text[20] on training needs in the early 1960s referred to these early approaches as 'armchair cerebration' while arguing for a three-faceted approach that reviewed organizational, operational and personal needs for training. These facets illustrate an attempt to define 'real training needs' as opposed to 'felt needs'.

The **organizational analysis** assesses the strategic capabilities needs and the training which should occur in an organization as it seeks to achieve its strategic themes. This is aimed at the objectives and initiatives that an organization is using to achieve its strategic themes, in order to find out if the proper objectives and initiatives are being used.

The **operational analysis or task analysis** focuses on the performance gaps and is used to decide what the training should consist of. This involves a study of what a person should be taught in performing the tasks effectively and in pinpointing the capabilities needed to improve performance. This analysis focuses on the job description and job requirements, and reviews whether the job is effectively designed and the appropriateness of the tasks to be performed.

The **employee needs analysis (ENA)** focuses on the competency gaps (in separating learning from non-learning needs) and determines who needs to be trained and the competencies that should be focused on in the training. It identifies performance objectives, benchmarks and the competencies needed.

Implementing this three-faceted approach involves reviewing the organizational objectives, what employees should be taught in performing a job and how well they are performing their jobs.[21] This framework is still regarded as seminal despite the fact that it was published in 1961.

The comprehensive needs assessment methodology has been adapted in larger government organizations such as in the Louisiana state government of 72,000 employees. Researchers recognized it would take years and millions of dollars to implement a fully comprehensive assessment, because employees worked in various locations and held several job categories throughout the state. The training needs assessment therefore sought to identify and prioritize the gaps between what was and what should be in the goals and results achieved. In the first phase, researchers carried out a top-down strategic needs assessment in identifying high-level organizational goals and training intervention to support them. The second phase involved a bottom-up strategy designed with employees involved in identifying the tasks and training needed to improve performance. The results from these phases were prioritized in developing training tied to what employees perceived as important to their performance, in addition to linking training to organizational goals. Although this needs assessment does fully implement a more comprehensive needs assessment called for in the present literature, it was viewed as a major step in moving 'from curriculum-based to performance-based training'.[22]

Critical incident questions. Using critical incident questions is a good way to implement the training needs assessment by identifying the gaps at the organizational, operational and employee level. The questions can be designed into an interview or questionnaire to gather examples, best practices and unique competencies that employees, supervisors, experts and others have learned or observed in their work experience.

In Chapter 3, we pointed to McClelland's work in using critical incidents, which predicted the performance of outstanding foreign service officers,[23] and discussed how this work led to the development of a managerial job competency modelling which revolutionized traditional job analysis.[24] The use of critical incident questions for training purposes is relevant because it is (i) specific to the planned training, (ii) responsive to changing strategic objectives, (iii) focused specifically on critical requirements and (iv) responsive to recognized gaps in performance or to new client priorities. Most importantly, the needs assessment provides a way to verify the competencies to demonstrate the job's critical requirements. The information gained in assessing training needs and defining objectives provides a blueprint for a training programme and the measures of success.[25]

Performance metrics in assessing training

In assessing training, evaluators usually pose one of two questions: (i) whether training objectives are achieved (learning issues) or (ii) whether the accomplishment of the training objectives enhanced job performance or helped the organization achieve its strategic objectives (transfer issues).[26] Though recognizing the importance of the second question, most training evaluations in public organizations focus on training objectives or learning issues because of the difficulty of linking training to strategic objectives, outcomes and results.[27]

Historically, the most widely recognized evaluation model in the training field, proposed by Kirkpatrick, provided a first step in the development of guidelines for the assessment of learning outcomes. The guidelines examine the extent to which trainees have acquired principles, facts and learning and skills, as illustrated in changes in the trainee's behaviour assessed by multiple-choice tests. Learning is assessed at four levels: (i) reaction of learners, (ii) learning, (iii) behaviour and (iv) results.[28]

- **Reaction of learners:** 'What did you think or feel about the training?' This evaluation taps into initial participant reactions and feelings about the training experience through in-session feedback or post-training surveys. It focuses on participant perceptions of satisfaction, relevance, degree of participation, effort and practicality. The evaluations are easy to administer and analyse, and provide useful information to gauge participants' feelings.
- **Learning:** 'Did the training result in increased knowledge or capability?' Learning can be evaluated by testing individuals before and after the training, using measures which are linked to the goals of the training. This information can be gained through interviews or observations. An assessment of learning asks whether participants learned what was intended and whether skills and capabilities actually changed. Although it is harder to develop measures for assessing new behaviours and skills, they are very relevant as they provide information on the goals of the training programmes.
- **Behaviours:** 'Has the training resulted in measurable improvements or changes in behaviour and capability?' If the new skills and behaviours are relevant, participants should use them and keep using them. For this reason, it is relevant to assess the impact of training over several months and on an ongoing basis. Evaluating behaviours helps to determine whether the trainees implemented their learning, whether they used the new skills and behaviours and whether there was a measurable change in activity and performance back on the job. This form of assessment is extremely important because it goes beyond participants' reactions and learning, and focuses on the impact of the training in the work setting.
- **Results:** 'Did the improved performance have an effect on the organization and its environment?' This is the acid test of training as it asks whether training has had an effect on organizational performance measures such as increased work quality, performance, satisfaction or turnover. Many of these measures are already collected by organizations, but it is most important to identify which measures relate to the training and to the trainee's impact. Also, external factors – such as changing market conditions and increased competition – can affect performance. Where these measures are useful is in establishing broad goals or long-range outcomes for training. To be useful as an assessment of training, it is important to identify areas where trainees can have an impact.

Although the power of Kirkpatrick's framework is helping people define a framework and criteria for evaluation, the greatest shortcoming is the lack of clarity on the specific outcomes that might be expected as a result of the training or learning event and the challenge of identifying the appropriate assessment tools. Kirkpatrick has been challenged on his assumption that each level is connected in a semi-causal hierarchy, and whether each level is correlated with the next level. That is, reactions in level 1 might be unrelated to learning and outcomes. Reactions in training events are sought because it is relatively easy to ask participants to complete a post-session evaluation. However, most studies do not focus only on reactions alone, and though many evaluations in practice might focus on reactions, evaluation results reported in journals have provided measures of learning, behaviour and outcomes.[29]

In adding to Kirkpatrick's framework, different types of outcome are useful in validating whether a training programme accomplishes its learning objectives. Objectives might focus on different learning outcomes: cognitive, skill-based and affective. Cognitive outcomes include verbal skills, knowledge and cognitive strategies, and relate to the trainee's knowledge acquisition and application; skill-based outcomes relate to both the compiling and the processing of technical and motor skills. Affective outcomes include key attitudinal and motivational outcomes, such as disposition, self-efficacy and goal setting.[30]

Also, rather than assuming that there is a semi-causal link between Kirkpatrick's levels of training, it might be appropriate to assess four target areas: training content and design, changes in the learners' competencies, changes in the organization (results and transfer)[31] and meeting client needs.

- *Training content and design:* Was the content relevant for learning needs? Did the design of the training assist learning? How might this be improved in future training designs?
- *Changes in the learner's competencies:* What skills, knowledge or capabilities did trainees find useful in this training? How will they use the skills, knowledge and capabilities gained in the training? What specifically will they do differently? How might this be improved in future training designs?
- *Results and transfer:* Is the training positively connected to the organization's goals and requirements? How can it be better connected? How can the training be improved to have an impact on performance? What measures are appropriate to understand this? How can we improve the effect on the organization and its environment?
- *Meeting client needs:* One noticeable outcome of the NPM emphasis is that government agencies are encouraged to think of customer or client satisfaction as a key measure of performance.[32] Although it is hard to link any direct effects of training in meeting long-term outcomes such as customer service and in addressing citizen needs, customer measures highlight how training evaluation can be used to respond to strategic objectives and to support employees in implementing the competencies they have learned.

CO 2: APPLYING EXPERIENTIAL LEARNING IN TRAINING AND DEVELOPMENT

Experiential learning theory draws on the work of several early scholars such as John Dewey, Kurt Lewin, Jean Paiget, Carl Jung and others. Inspired by this original work, David Kolb's experiential learning model, shown in Figure 10.1, includes four phases:[33]

1. *Concrete experience (CE):* Taking in information from tangible, *concrete experiences*, or having the inclination to want to learn from those things which are more concrete; which can be felt and touched; or getting a chance to be immersed in the situation.
2. *Reflective observation (RO):* Observing, scrutinizing the information and reflecting on it.
3. *Abstract conceptualization (AC):* Developing concepts, principles or ways to generalize.
4. *Active experimentation (AE):* Engaging, testing out new information and experimenting, and then forming hypotheses to explain how they act.

Kolb illustrates four different learning styles: accommodator, diverger, converger and assimilator. People illustrating the *accommodator* style are good at carrying out plans and tasks and involving

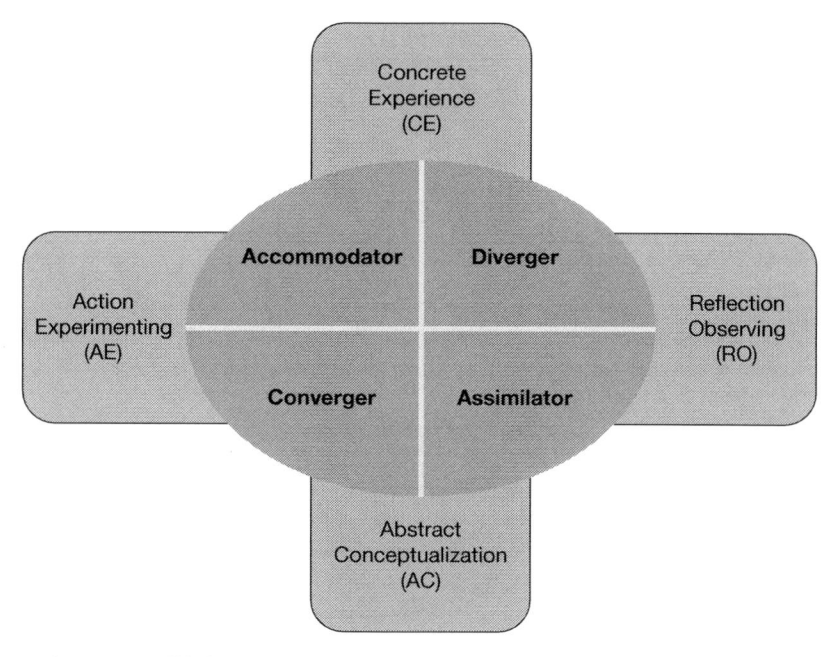

Figure 10.1 Four phases of Kolb's learning model.

themselves in new experiences. They prefer to solve problems in a trial-and-error manner, relying on their intuition or other people. *Divergers* are best at carrying out imaginative tasks and view things from a variety of perspectives. They perform best in situations that call for generating ideas, brainstorming and innovative applications. *Convergers* are best in situations where they can practically apply their ideas in problem-solving and decision-making. They are less focused on people and more concerned with ideas and abstract concepts. The strengths of *assimilators* lie in their inductive reasoning and ability to assimilate disparate observations into an integrated explanation. They are best in situations where they can reflect on their environment and create theories about it.

At the strategic level, feedback allows people to see the connections and interrelationships between the environment, training events and their integration in organization practices. Here, learners gain feedback from their concrete experience, reflect on that experience, devise new concepts (as well as use available ones) to understand their experience and, finally, develop an action plan to respond to the situation.

Implementing experiential learning in training and development

Experiential learning encourages a continuous cycle involving concrete experience, observations and reflections, the development of principles, concepts and generalizations, and the application and integration with real-life practices.[36] Kolb's experiential model can be integrated within conventional steps of training and development focused on the **transfer** of training from the classroom experience to the job so that it can be easily practised over a long period of time.[37]

In using experiential principles, a trainer might begin a workshop or training experience by highlighting the learning objectives focusing on key competencies, concepts and information. A first step is to develop an understanding of the concepts or competencies that are to be learned and how they help people in solving problems or improving their practice.

A RELEVANT POINT OF VIEW: EXPERIENTIAL LEARNING IN THE ACQUISITION OF TACIT KNOWLEDGE

Scholars argue that there is a difference between explicit and tacit knowledge. Explicit knowledge is easily identified as the competencies relevant to a job or for meeting specific strategic objectives. Tacit knowledge is believed to be a product of learning from experience that affects performance in real-life situations but which is less definable and measurable, and which differentiates successful from less successful individuals. It is described as knowledge which is personal, profound and non-scientific, and derives from experience and analogical reasoning, and which forms intuitions and instincts.[34]

Tacit knowledge is said to be determined by the variety of an individual's experiences and involvement in the context of a situation and is said to be linked to a person's learning style, or their way of responding to and using ideas in their learning.

In a study of 356 Malaysian public sector employees from 19 different units, researchers compared the learning styles of expert/successful managers who were expected to respond differently than novices due to their tacit knowledge. The managers identified as expert and successful were those nominated as exemplary managers, who had received a prestigious public service award within the last three years and who had scored high on three years of annual appraisal.

The research found that managerial tacit knowledge was higher in expert/successful managers compared to other groups. This knowledge was not related to the length of a person's work experience, but to how people learn from experience. Based on Kolb's learning style inventory, people with an accommodating learning style are likely to excel at learning tasks which help build tacit knowledge because people with this style are more likely to excel in situations that lack structure, require commitment to objective, and require skills involving dealing with people and exploiting opportunities. In addition, people who scored high on all four styles illustrated higher levels of tacit knowledge.

The study concludes by asking the question 'How do we facilitate the acquisition of management tacit knowledge as one of the most important factors distinguishing successful managers from others?' Given that most tacit knowledge comes from the job, management educators and trainers can involve learners in experiential approaches that encourage informal learning, real life applications and action learning.[35]

Transfer of training is more likely when employees know the training content is based on a needs analysis or skills requirement, when training includes opportunities to practise, when criteria are attached to the training content and when employees know that their managers have taken the same training.[38] Transfer is illustrated by the following principles for presenting concepts and information:

- Provide an overview of the material and learning objectives, how each segment of the programme is related and how it contributes to the overall objectives of the organization or the issues or problems which need addressing.
- Use questions and practical anecdotes to engage the learner, and examples to help present the material so that it is relevant to the learner.
- Present material in segments so that simpler parts support larger bodies of knowledge.
- Summarize concepts into simpler actionable principles, rules or practices.

A key second step in an experiential model is to provide participants with a real-life experience, a case, role play or simulation that allows people to understand a problem and to reflect on it.

A third step is to encourage participants to reflect on the experience and catalogue their observations and their feelings and reactions.

Participants are then encouraged to reflect on the competencies, concepts and practices which are derived from the experience and observations, and then distil actionable principles to apply the competencies in future practice.

A fifth step involves creating opportunities to practise or apply the skills or actionable principles. Transfer is encouraged when people have the opportunity to practise through active practice, overlearning and longer practice sessions.[39]

- ***Active practice:*** Active practice involves having individuals perform job-related skills or tasks during training. This involves giving individuals a chance to demonstrate them in a simulated or applied task. This is similar to attending a lecture on tennis or golf, followed by an opportunity to practise with the guidance of an instructor.
- ***Overlearning:*** The more a trainee has an opportunity to practise in a variety of simulated settings, the better the chance that skill will become second nature. **Overlearning** is the deliberate overtraining of a task beyond a set criterion.[40] Overlearning might be more important for certain tasks such as training a pilot to land an airplane or training for the Olympic competitions in pairs figure skating. These are usually critical or exceptional tasks. For other more routine tasks – repairing an automobile or installing an electrical switch – overlearning might be less important because the individual practises the skills on a daily basis.
- ***Spacing the practice sessions:*** Spaced practice is superior to mass practice conditions in a variety of situations. **Mass practice** conditions are when individuals practise a task continuously without rest, whereas **spaced practices** are those in which individuals are given rest intervals during the training. For example, imagine that you need to memorize lines for an audition, and during the next week, you have only 14 hours to practise. How do you set up a practice schedule? In mass practice conditions, you might practise 7 hours during the last 2 days of the week. In a spaced practice, you would practise 2 hours a day for each day of the week. Which set of conditions is likely to be more effective? The evidence is clear: spaced or distributed practice is likely to achieve better results.[41]

A final step in the process involves providing feedback to trainees during and after practices. Transfer is more likely when there is feedback on what is learned and how trainees might improve. In training, we might recognize two types of feedback: reinforcing and balancing.

- ***Reinforcing feedback*** is positive feedback given to trainees when they perform something correctly. 'Your report is very well done because it solves the problem and is well structured.'[42] The emphasis should be on identifying when things are done correctly so that trainees are not reinforced in other ways.
- ***Balancing (or stabilizing)*** feedback provides 'correction' and is more useful when it provides a correction to a clear goal or objective. Rather than providing negative feedback in training, balancing feedback is more effective because it is corrective in helping people adjust their progress in reaching the objective.

To have the greatest impact, feedback should occur as soon as possible after the trainee demonstration and should be given by people (such as trainers, supervisors or peers) whom the trainee trusts and feels are competent.

In encouraging transfer, one of the easiest things that supervisors can do is to involve trained employees and peers in setting objectives to assist the application of the new learning.[43] Transfer is more likely when the training is supported by supervisors and peers. There is nothing more rewarding than returning to a workplace to find that others want to learn and use the skills you have learned. Supervisors and peers are like gatekeepers who can block or reinforce transfer of learning. If they do not support the new skills, either by ignoring or discouraging, there is very little chance that the training will have impact on job performance.[44]

Using experiential principles with E-technology

New training ideas are introduced every year. Some are based on solid learning theory and demonstrate better ways to transfer information, skills and behaviours (e.g. action learning). Others involve new ways to transfer information through new technologies (e.g. interactive e-technology, e-training, presentation software, computer animation).

Technology-assisted learning has existed for years and has grown in use as new technologies have developed. Early innovations included televisions and videos to enhance classroom activities. Today, we not only have computers with incomprehensible speed and broadband technologies, but there is a range of tools. There are many ways to use technology, from television (distance education) and DVD to computer Internet systems (distributive education). International, national, regional and video teleconferences use large-screen television satellites with telephone outlets to facilitate distance-learning experiences.

Engaging experientially in distance learning. Distance learning has been around for decades. Early versions were generally a correspondence course allowing students the flexibility to pace their learning as they worked at home. In the early version, there was little interaction between students and teachers, and teachers 'poured' knowledge into students in the same way they did in the classroom. A second wave of distance education added video and audiotapes to provide more human contact. This allowed more interaction using email, mail and fax, but the direction of the interaction was still one way. Generally, many early Internet classes tried to create an environment similar to the one which existed in face-to-face classrooms.

A newer version of distance education using the Internet began in 1985 and provided opportunities for instructors and students to engage experientially in an interaction.[45] A **community of practice** is a group of people who are bound by a shared practice and who have a context for learning from each other.[46] The instructor seeks to overcome student isolation through discussion formats offered on the e-learning site. It is possible to use discussion formats where students can present their ideas at the same time or at different times. For example, as in a traditional classroom, e-learning sites offer chat rooms and videoconferencing, where students can engage at a common time. Or students might choose to 'attend class' when they want to set aside time, a type of connection which is suited to situations where class members live in different time zones or for students who want the flexibility to 'attend' as their schedule permits. Instructors can upload lectures to the e-learning site, specify assignment due dates and co-ordinate the class activities.[47]

Over the last 30 years, technology has moved us from verbal to visual, to virtual training environments.[48] As the virtual world can encourage individual activity, instructors can focus training students on assignments which are meaningful to learning objectives. In making content connections, the Web can be used as a vehicle for answering problem-solving and, as in classroom environments, one of the best ways to do this is through the application of games and simulations. The assumption is that learners develop interpretations, principles and solutions through discussions, conversations and tasks where they work with others. In virtual reality, people may never meet. However, there are many ways to engage people experientially in online discussions and group work. The difficulty is that although learners may be accustomed to Web chatting, they may not be well schooled on solving problems. For example, a Web discussion might begin when the instructor poses a question or a problem and then students are asked to review the problem and define a set of principles from the textbook that might be appropriate to solve it. They might have three days to make a decision and post their response on the Web, without being able to see others' responses. At the end of day three, the instructor would open up the discussion by first allowing all participants to read and comment on others' responses. Then the instructor would begin a discussion by posing another question, perhaps asking students to focus in on implementing a strategy or assessing the implications of a certain decision. The instructor can review the dominant themes presented and discussed during the session and conclude by offering other examples or guiding principles.

> MANAGERIAL IMPLICATIONS: In defining initiatives and activities for implementing an experiential model of learning and experiential principles in training and development, you might focus on one of the following objectives: ability to work in a team, ability to set and meet objectives, ability to work in and lead a team, or interpersonal competence.[49] These competencies were identified as key causes of executive derailment in an international study.

BEFORE APPLYING, LET'S REVIEW

CO 1: Apply competency-based training and development in meeting training needs.

A comprehensive assessment of training needs involves reviewing organizational, operational and personal needs for training. The organizational analysis assesses whether the proper objectives and initiatives are being focused on, and the operational analysis reviews the tasks and performance gaps in improving performance. The employee analysis identifies the competencies that should be focused on in training. As such, a training needs assessment is used to identify gaps between the current organizational, operational and employee-level performance and desired performance.

CO 2: Illustrate how experiential learning principles can be used to enhance training and development.

Experiential learning principles suggest that learning is a cyclical process that includes the following steps: (i) developing a need to understand the concepts or learn certain competencies either by recognition of problems that need to be solved or by demonstrating this need; (ii) participating in a real-life experience, a case, a role play or a simulation that allows people to understand a problem and to reflect on it; (iii) reflecting on the experience and cataloguing observations, feelings and reactions; (iv) distilling the competencies, concepts and practices that are derived from the experience and observations, and then developing actionable principles to apply the competencies in future practice; (v) creating opportunities to practise or apply the skills or actionable principles; (vi) providing feedback to trainees during and after practices. Transfer is more likely when there is systemic feedback.

DISCUSSION AND REVIEW QUESTIONS

1. Review the phases of the experiential learning model. Identify questions you might ask at each phase of the learning model, and ask yourself how you would apply these phases in developing a lecture on career e-learning or orientation.

Table 10.1 Evaluation Measures

Level		What are measures for each level of evaluation?
1	Response	How can you improve your satisfaction in the training and learning you are now experiencing in classes?
2	Learning	How can you improve what you are learning?
3	Performance	How can you make sure your learning is better connected to performance in class and other activities?
4	Results	How can your learning affect your performance and abilities in your future work and career?

2. Review Kirkpatrick four evaluation measures in Table 10.1: (i) reaction of learners, (ii) learning, (iii) behaviour and (iv) results. What are the advantages of paying more attention to the reactions of learners in comparison to evaluation measures? Please consider this framework in reviewing your current class by responding to the following questions.
3. Training is a function that is often outsourced. What are the strategic implications of outsourcing training?
4. As an HR department, you are asked to develop a set of strategic objectives to respond to the issue of the department's downsizing; 50 current employees must be laid off or reassigned within government. You have six months' lead time, and you are directed to minimize the cost of payout estimated at six months' wages for those involved, or £23,064 ($35,000). However, if you can retrain and retain people for less than £23,064 ($35,000) on average, you can save government money and hopefully keep good employees. Your strategy map of strategic objectives should include the four BSC perspectives. Your internal process objectives might relate to developing a skills inventory, carrying out a needs assessment and developing a training and transition plan to move people to new positions.
5. Assess your learning style by accessing Kolb's learning style inventory on the book's website.
6. In building on the SHRM BSC framework, define objectives, initiatives and competencies that are important for attracting and retaining younger workers. In forming objectives, the framework asks you to recognize basic questions that are important to the implementation.
    - How do customers and clients who might hire millennial workers see them? What objectives, competencies and initiatives are important? (Client or Customer perspective)
    - What objectives, competencies and initiatives illustrate their efficiency and effectiveness? (Internal process perspective)
    - How do they provide added financial value to clients? What objectives, competencies and initiatives are important for helping them add value? (Financial perspective)
    - What objectives, initiatives and competencies are useful and should be improved so the employee can create value and stay with the organization?
7. Define learning initiatives and activities to implement a strategic objective of experientially involving managers in training to enhance their career. First, define key competencies you want to train for, such as ability to work in a team, ability to set and meet objectives, ability to work in and lead a team, or interpersonal competence. Or you might focus on implementing the diversity objective: ability to work well with people with diverse skills and values.
    a   *Learning objective* – developing a need to understand the concepts or learn certain competencies either by recognition of problems that need to be solved or by demonstrating this need.
        Training initiative or activity: _____

b *Learning objective* – participating in a real-life experience, a case, role play or simulation that allows people to understand a problem and to reflect on it.
   Training initiative or activity: _____
c *Learning objective* – reflecting on the experience and cataloguing observations, feelings and reactions.
   Training initiative or activity: _____
d *Learning objective* – distilling the competencies, concepts and practices that are derived from the experience and observations and then develop actionable principles to apply the competencies in future practice.
   Training initiative or activity: _____
e *Learning objective* – creating opportunities to practise or apply the skills or actionable principles.
   Training initiative or activity: _____
f *Learning objective* – providing feedback to trainees during and after practices.
   Training initiative or activity: _____

CASE: WHY TRAIN THEM FOR A CAREER IF THEY'RE JUST GOING TO LEAVE?

Sharlene looked at the letter of resignation on her desk from one of the bright prospects that she had hired a year ago to respond to the wave of retirements and the loss of experienced workers that the federal government was facing.

Dan Shipley, her HR director, sitting across from her, had just joined her and wanted to talk about the costs of training new employees who ended up quitting and going elsewhere. 'We spent a major part of our training budget on people who did not stay with government. So, we have trained people who are poached by other organizations.'

Attracting and keeping younger workers makes good sense, especially as the so-called millennials – those born between 1981 and 2000 – move into the workforce and older workers move out of the workforce. But based on a major study which pinpoints the problems, there is high turnover of this group of workers. Although 40 per cent of millennials say they expect to stay in their first job for at least five years, an estimated 70 per cent leave their first position in the first two years. Employers face a 'leaky bucket' of turnover which is costly because many of these workers have received training and are much more valuable than when they were hired.

One of the reasons identified for leaving is the lack of mentorship, and 81 per cent of millennials say they want to be connected with an experienced mentor and have opportunities for career development. They also say they are concerned about work–life balance, want to be heard, value feedback and like to work in a fun environment.

Task. Some managers might not see the value in hiring and training younger workers, only to watch them depart for new opportunities, but there is an argument to be made for having them on staff. They are more comfortable with new technology, have lots of energy, offer a fresh perspective on issues and are expressive in offering their ideas.

There's a huge appetite for understanding these generational differences and how we can train younger workers and reduce their turnover.

Sharlene has asked Dan to offer his recommendations and prepare a briefing note defining and reviewing the strengths and weaknesses of different training and mentoring options for attracting and keeping younger workers.

11 Reducing Stress and Improving Workplace Health and Safety

Chapter Outline
- Chapter objectives (COs)   214
- A driving issue focusing managerial action: Responding to the new world of workplace safety and health   214
- CO 1: Workplace mental health and stress   216
- CO 2: Managing absenteeism in returning people to work   224
- CO 3: Developing a culture supporting workplace safety and health   226
- Before applying, let's review   233
- Discussion and review questions   233
- Case: Returning to work   235

CHAPTER OBJECTIVES (COs)

After reading this chapter, you will be able to implement the following objectives:

CO 1: Identify factors defining organizational stress and their impact on individuals.

CO 2: Apply return-to-work practices to respond to absenteeism and disability issues.

CO 3: Assess the facets important in preventing accidents and developing a culture of workplace safety.

A DRIVING ISSUE FOCUSING MANAGERIAL ACTION: RESPONDING TO THE NEW WORLD OF WORKPLACE SAFETY AND HEALTH

Go back a hundred years in the workplace safety area, and you will find many dodgy practices that we would not do today. Take, for example, a practice that underground miners used to test if there was a risk of an explosion from methane gas. 'Before the miners would go down, they'd send a couple of guys down, and they'd have a candle on the end of a long stick. They'd go to the place where they thought methane would collect, and they'd put the candle on the end of the stick and light the candle and get back as far as the stick would allow. If there was a small amount of methane gas, the candle would get rid of it. If there was a major concentration, there would be an explosion.'[1]

The good news for government regulators is that workplace injuries have been declining in many industrialized countries, but the bad news is that this has been offset by a shift of dangerous work in manufacturing, construction, mining and agriculture to developing countries, particularly Asia.

Although there have been clear safety gains in industrialized countries through regulation, prevention and the application of best practices, work-related health issues are still a top concern. Globally, 2.3 million occupational deaths take place annually according to International Labour Organization (ILO) estimates, and of these, 318,000 are occupational injuries and 2,022,000 are due to work-related diseases.

The World Health Organization's definition of health as contained in its constitution states: 'Health is a state of complete physical, mental and social well-being and not merely the absence of disease or infirmity.' Mental health is one part of a person's overall health and is a state of well-being which allows people to realize their potential and cope with the stresses of life in being able to work productively and fruitfully in contributing to his or her community.[2] A person suffering from mental health issues may face depression, stress, anxiety, relationship problems, addiction, learning disabilities, mood disorders or other psychological concerns.

In terms of health and safety, the major causes of workplace death are from cancer (32%) and work-related circulatory diseases (23%), cardiovascular diseases and strokes, communicable diseases (17%, more often in developing countries and farming) and occupational accidents (18%).[3] These statistics do not take into account mental health issues connected to stress and depression, nor do they consider issues of workplace violence and substance use. The economic burden of mental health exceeds the burden in the four other major categories of non-communicable disease: diabetes, cardiovascular, respiratory and cancer.

Major depressive disorder is the second largest contributor of years lived with disability (YLD).[4] Other behavioural disorders, such as anxiety disorders, drug-use and alcohol-use disorders, schizophrenia, bipolar disorder and dysthymia, rank among the 20 conditions contributing to the largest global share of YLDs. Taken together, mental and behavioural disorders contribute to 22.7 per cent of global burden of YLD, which is higher than that resulting from any other disease category.[5]

The World Health Organization (WHO) describes depression as a mental disorder that has symptoms of 'depressed mood, loss of interest or pleasure, feelings of guilt or low self-worth, disturbed sleep or appetite, low energy, and poor concentration'. If the problems become chronic and recurrent, depression can lead to impairment of the individual's ability to carry out his or her work and, at its worst, can lead to suicide, which currently accounts for 850,000 deaths worldwide each year.[6]

Workplace safety appears to be very different from workplace mental health, and the professionals in these areas often have different goals, backgrounds and unique philosophies for solving problems. Workplace safety relates to injuries and violence, whereas workplace health is concerned with mental health, stress and physical health. However, the areas are very connected because people who suffer a physical injury are much more likely (more than six times) to have mental health problems and feel more stress because of dealing with an injury. In addition, people who suffer from mental health issues such as depression are much more likely to be involved in a workplace injury and might be more prone to workplace violence.[7]

As public and private employees continue to face changes as a result of delayering, downsizing and restructuring, workplace mental health and stress has become an increasing concern.[8] Although stress is high in both public and private organizations, it is most evident in public organizations, which experience almost twice as much turbulence as private sector organizations.[9] The turbulence comes from normal organizational work pressures in addition to those associated with performance-based reforms such as the New Public Management (NPM)[10] and higher expectations for quality service.[11] In some public service jobs, such as police work, nursing and social services, the stresses are connected to the emotionally taxing interactions with citizens or clients as well as ethical and moral distress.[12]

Workplace safety and health is also a policy issue for government managers who oversee agreements to work in a global setting. The seriousness of the policy issue on safety for government managers is underlined in World

Health Organization reports that highlight that accidents in many developing countries are 30 to 100 times those of Western countries. Others point out that many of these workers are children. They are challenged by proponents of free trade and globalization who argue that the factories benefit people who would otherwise not be employed. Workplace mental health is also more serious in developing countries, where as many as 75 per cent of the people are not treated.[13]

> STRATEGIC CONTEXT: Building on the above perspective, workplace health and safety is a large and important area that public sector governments and managers need to respond to. Mental health is one important aspect of health that is a growing concern in public sector workplaces and in the workplaces governments are responsible for.
>
> Within the general theme of this chapter, we concentrate more specifically on the workplace stress connection, as it is an area where public sector managers can make a significant contribution. As such, workplace stress and job strain are important determinants of mental health. This linkage is illustrated in studies linking stress to measures of psychological health[14] and meta-analysis research connecting stress to depression and other mental health disorders.[15]
>
> Implementing strategic objectives related to reducing workplace stress can make a significant influence on mental health. Other tangible things managers can do relate to 'encouraging health and wellness' and 'developing a culture for health and safety'.
>
> Within the SHRM BSC, this chapter discusses initiatives related to strategic objectives of reducing workplace stress, reducing absenteeism and returning people to work, preventing workplace accidents and developing a culture of safety.

CO 1: WORKPLACE MENTAL HEALTH AND STRESS

Virtually all models of workplace mental health and well-being point to the prominence of job stress and the resulting strain it produces. Understanding stress begins with Lazarus and Folkman's description of how our interactions may generate emotions that lead to stress responses. Through primary appraisal, a person evaluates the potential effects of a stressor (e.g. of having too much work) to decide whether it will cause harm or a threat. The secondary appraisal (the emotional response) takes place as the person asks, 'What can I do?' and evaluates his or her capability for coping or finding the resources (time, assistance, confidence) to reduce the stress.[16] How much personal control a person thinks he or she has is a major factor in coping, as most people experience more stress in uncontrollable situations. Because personal control is a cognitive process, the more one feels in control, the better he or she will feel about being able to cope with the stress.

Two prominent models explaining the impact of stress are the Demand/Control and Effort/Reward models. In the **Demand/Control Model**, an individual's stress results from the demands in the job and the tension stress creates, a result of the person's perception of how able he or she is to control the demands.[17] A high-stress environment is one where there is high demand and little opportunity to control the demands.[18] Individuals can better handle stressors if they think they can control the environment causing them and can make decisions on how to respond. Social support at work from supervisors or co-workers can help employees reduce the stresses of not having control. An important study illustrating this model, the Whitehall study, was carried out in the British civil service. Researchers found that people who had little control within their jobs were 50 per cent more likely to suffer from heart disease, and this was a higher risk factor than low physical activity or smoking.[19]

The **Effort/Reward Model** suggests that stress is related to the balance between the degree of effort you put into the job and the level of reward resulting from that effort.[20] This makes the assumption that stressors are less harmful if there are rewards and pleasures associated with them. Researchers suggest that individuals experiencing extremely high effort with low reward had more than triple the rate of cardiovascular problems, in addition to significantly higher incidences of anxiety and depression compared to those who experienced high levels of effort with high rewards.[21]

These models overlap in pointing to how stressors impact personal and work behaviours. They explain evidence such as this:

- High job demands and stressful environments are correlated with various physical effects, such as increases in smoking, blood pressure, hypertension, blood lipids levels (particularly LDL cholesterol), alcohol consumption and substance use.[22]
- High job demands and stress environments are correlated with various organizational impacts, such as burnout, work disengagement and intention to quit, turnover, lower productivity, absenteeism and sickness **presenteeism** (coming to work despite having an illness that justifies an absence).[23]

These models illustrate that there is not always a correlation between high job demands and stressful environments and impacts on personal and work behaviours. Stress might have different impacts, depending on an individual's personal style in appraising the stressors involved. In other words, a person's primary appraisal provides information about the stressors or the problems he or she might face. In a secondary appraisal, the person will react emotionally depending on his or her perception and personality. For example, those who are more anxious or aggressive may be more likely to experience stress. In addition to personal style, stress will be different if the person can control the surrounding environment and if he or she finds the job environment rewarding. Although it might not be possible to say that public and private workers experience different levels of stress, we can predict stress by the demands of the work and the degree of control that workers experience in their environments.[24]

Linking to the strategic context of workplace stress

The Demand/Control model has been used in reviewing the stresses and health issues that people are experiencing as a result of the increased work pressures attributed to performance-based reforms such as the New Public Management (NPM). People report higher job expectations and increased job stress resulting from increased workloads and reduced resources,[25] and increased health issues, absenteeism and presenteeism.[26]

Although anything in the external and internal environment can be a stressor, a useful framework for defining workplace stress is the one developed by Cary Cooper and his colleagues in their research of health care workers.[27] The original Occupational Stress Indicator (OSI) model suggested that stress can be caused by pressure from workload, relationships, lack of recognition, organizational climate, personal responsibility, managerial responsibilities or lack of opportunity, home and work balance and daily hassles, although the researchers revised and renamed the instrument as the Pressure Management Indicator (PMI).[28] Since its development, it has been used in several primary, secondary and tertiary health care organizations and is appropriate for the public sector generally. As illustrated in Table 11.1, the application of NPM in government illustrates similar pressures or job demands that are increasing the perception of stress relating to (i) unfair treatment from more senior staff, (ii) lack of recognition for good work, (iii) lack of feedback, (iv) lack of opportunity to take on more senior roles[29] (v) work pressure, (vi) emotional demands, (vii) physical demands, (viii) conflict with home life[30] and (ix) red tape in doing the job.[31]

Table 11.1 General Occupational Stress Pressures and Those Resulting from New Public Management (NPM) Initiatives

	General Occupational Stress Pressures Identified in Occupational Stress Indicator (OSI)	Pressures Identified in New Public Management (NPM) Literature
Workload	Difficulty of work	Physical demands of job
Relationships	Getting along with people in and outside the organization	Unfair treatment from more senior staff
Recognition	Feeling of need to be recognized	Lack of feedback
Organizational climate	The 'feel' or 'atmosphere' within the workplace	Emotional demands
Personal responsibility	For actions and decisions	Work pressure
Managerial role	For managing and supervising people	Lack of opportunity to take on more senior roles
Home and work balance	Being able to 'switch off' from the pressures of work	Conflict with home life
Daily hassles	Day-to-day irritants	Red tape in doing the job

The demands causing occupational stress

Dr Hans Selye, an endocrinologist at the University of Montreal, is frequently referred to as the 'Father of Stress'. He introduced the term **stress** as a **general adaptation syndrome**, as essentially the body's nonspecific response to the demands placed on it.[32] **Stressors** are the outside forces or agents acting on an organism which can potentially wear it down. A stressor is any stimulus or condition that has the potential to be appraised as challenging, threatening or harmful.

Dr Hans Selye divided demands into three categories of stressors: distressors, eustressors and neutrals.

Distressors. These are negative stressors which can have long- and short-term effects in the form of absenteeism, withdrawal from others and illness. Examples of negative stressors might be an imminent deadline or fears that a person might do poorly in a job interview. Distress occurs when the negative stress becomes unbearable or overly taxes our capability to respond.

Eustressors. Positive stressors can motivate and inspire a person to do things that he or she would not normally be able to do, for example, completing a race or improving grades to get into graduate school. Although eustressors are usually motivating, being overly motivated can push you too hard, like running so hard in a race that you have a heart attack. That is, there might be a positive stress from running, but overdoing it can cause harm.

Neutrals. Most of the stressors we encounter have neither a negative nor a positive effect. The effects are neutral, until the stress is perceived as a negative distressor or a positive eustressor.

The stress reaction. The theory underlying individual differences is based on Selye's review of how the body's entire stress system is activated when it encounters a threat or stressor. As a result of a person's appraisal of the situation as being potentially harmful or threatening, the body mobilizes its forces as it adapts to defend itself. Some of these responses are clearly visible (e.g. blushing and perspiring). Three distinct phases of the stress response, illustrated in Figure 11.1, include alarm, resistance and exhaustion.

The alarm stage occurs when a threat or stress is encountered, exciting the body's entire stress system. During the alarm stage, the body's energy reserves are activated. Adrenaline acts on the muscles and fat tissues, causing them to release the various chemicals they store. The brain registers emotions like fear or anger,

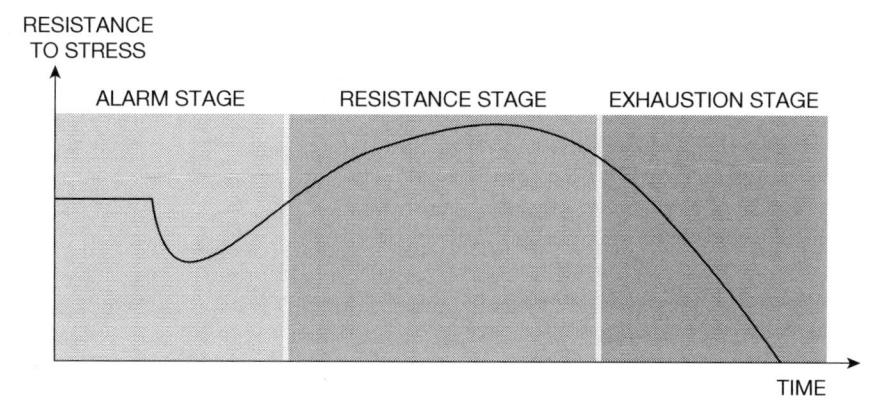

Figure 11.1 The general adaptation syndrome.

and breathing rates speed up, enabling more oxygen and nutrients to be released to the muscles for a fight-or-flight response. This mobilization draws on the body's energy reserves, and digestive processes decrease while blood is diverted to the needed areas. Common feelings during this stage are anger, panic, hurt or sadness as the person tries to respond. The alarm stage can be very exciting, as a person feels challenged and excited.

During the resistance stage, a person can become frustrated and full of anger. As the stressor persists and the energy resources of the body are gradually being depleted, the body attempts to cope in adjusting to the overload. As the stress and other events become taxing or overwhelming, a person might become more anxious and pressured. Eventually, he or she could feel run down or tired, possibly displaying bouts of irritation and erratic behaviour, forgetting and overreacting. Often, sleep patterns are disrupted.

The final stage is exhaustion, where prolonged and continued exposure to a range of stressors might eventually use up the adaptive energy available. Over a prolonged period of time of encountering the stressors and reacting to them, the body's resources are eventually depleted or exhausted. The body is unable to maintain a normal functioning. Initial stress reactions, like sweating and raised heart rate, may reappear. If this stage is extended, long-term damage might occur because the glands (especially the adrenal gland) and the immune system are exhausted. This is when the person feels burned out, exhausted or lacks enthusiasm to work and even to get up in the morning. It is possible that this is when psychosomatic diseases emerge, such as emotional exhaustion, elevated blood pressure, weight loss or gain and insomnia.

Our instinctive fight-or-flight response evolved over our human history, beginning with Stone Age living, when the readiness for fight-or-flight was necessary for survival. Today, threats like a rampaging bear very rarely occur. Most of our stresses are psychological, and we don't have to react physically. Yet we respond to the psychological threats in the same way that the Stone Age humans did, because the body's response has been constructed and fine-tuned over millions of years of evolution.[33]

Performance metrics in understanding the effects of stress

Figure 11.2 illustrates how the pressures at work and outside of work affect a person in the short and long term. In addition to the pressures from work, pressures outside of work include family problems, personal life crises (e.g. illness), potential financial difficulties and lifestyle issues.[34] Given that stress affects individuals in different ways, stress might be higher for those who are more prone to stress. That is, a person's unique cognitive style, including perceptions and judgement, triggers the way a person interprets a stressor. Some people are anxious and prone to interpret a meeting with a supervisor as threatening, whereas others might see the meeting as an opportunity. We learned a great deal about the relationship between personality and appraisal from the pioneering work by researchers Meyer

220

Work Pressures

Job related: Stressful physical conditions, safety, working conditions, ergonomics, shiftwork

Job demands: Work load, time pressure, risk, danger, too much responsibility, major changes

Role related: Conflict, lack of role clarity, responsibility for staff, disputes resolution issues

Career related: Lack of job security, lack of career opportunity, frustrated ambition, under valued

Working relationships: Conflict with supervisors, difficult relationships with colleagues or subordinates

Climate related: Office politics, lack of trust, negativity, bullying, discrimination

Non-work Pressures

Family problems: Problems with spouse or partner and children, conflicts with in-laws

Personal life crises: Health issues, job problems, deaths, divorce

Financial difficulties: Major debts or mortgages, difficulty making ends meet

Stressful lifestyle: Demanding social life, personal commitments in community, stressful social relationships

Sedentary lifestyle: Lack of exercise, non-healthy diet and lifestyle, social isolation

Individual Characteristics
Modifying Responses

Personal Disposition:
Type A or B behaviour
Level of anxiety
Low self-esteem
Ability to tolerate Ambiguity

Personal Characteristics:
Genetic factors
Gender
Age

Initial Stress Effects

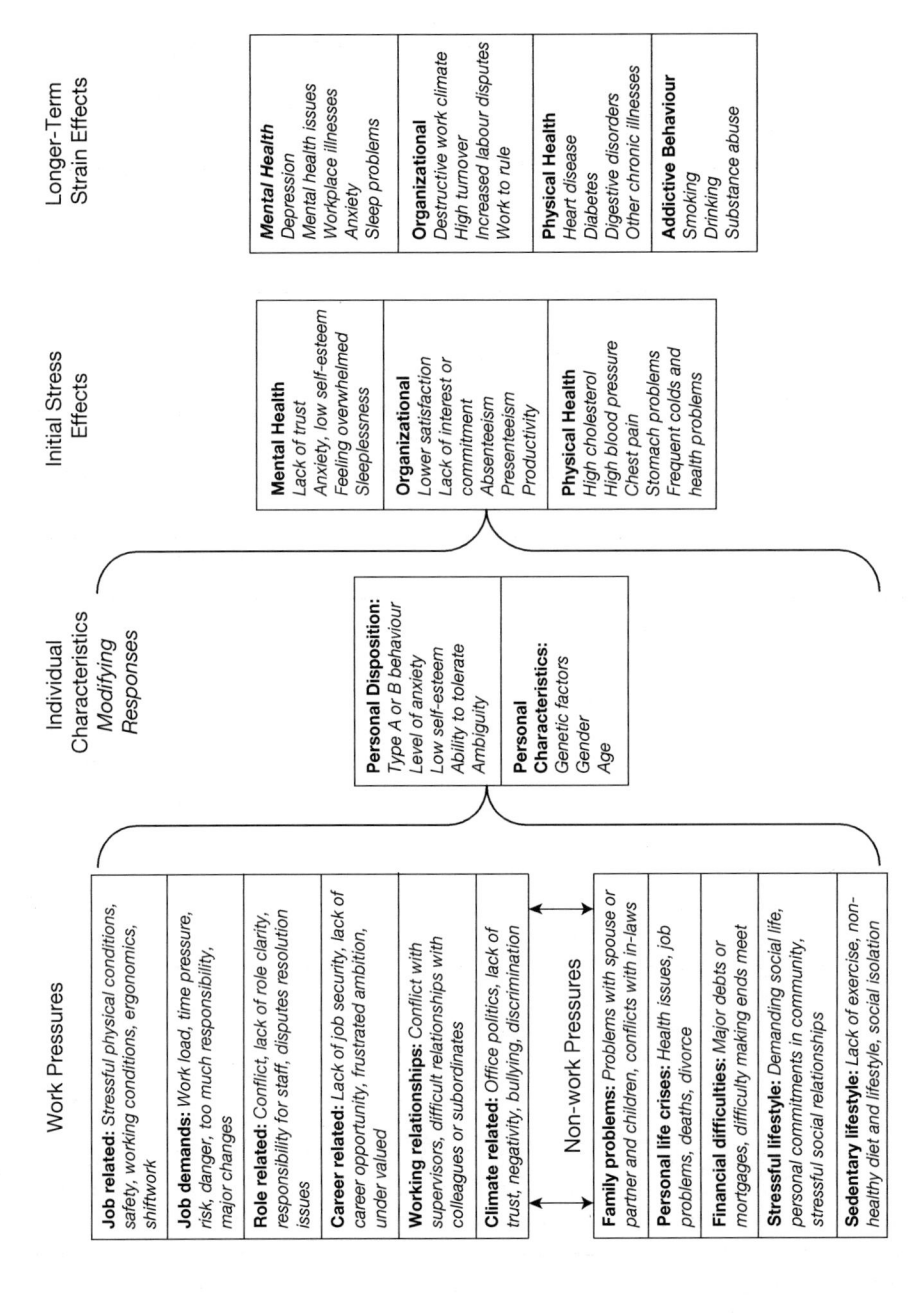

Mental Health
Lack of trust
Anxiety, low self-esteem
Feeling overwhelmed
Sleeplessness

Organizational
Lower satisfaction
Lack of interest or commitment
Absenteeism
Presenteeism
Productivity

Physical Health
High cholesterol
High blood pressure
Chest pain
Stomach problems
Frequent colds and health problems

Longer-Term Strain Effects

Mental Health
Depression
Mental health issues
Workplace illnesses
Anxiety
Sleep problems

Organizational
Destructive work climate
High turnover
Increased labour disputes
Work to rule

Physical Health
Heart disease
Diabetes
Digestive disorders
Other chronic illnesses

Addictive Behaviour
Smoking
Drinking
Substance abuse

Figure 11.2 A framework for understanding some of the effects of stress.

Friedman and Ray Rosenman, authors of *Type A Behavior and Your Heart*. Most of the medical journals at the time reported that heart attacks were most certainly linked to dietary indulgence, cigarette smoking and lack of exercise. Beyond these key factors, they observed that patients in their medical practices had common personality characteristics like a sense of time urgency and an excessively competitive drive. Some patients showed some hostility.

Friedman and Rosenman found that, among accountants, serum cholesterol levels increased each year during the months before the tax deadline when they had to work long hours to meet their reporting deadlines. In May and June, after the tax season ended, the serum cholesterol fell. In one of their studies, they compared Type A individuals (whom they classified as being competitive with a free-floating hostility) with a control group of Type B people (who felt no sense of time urgency and exhibited no excessive competitive drive or free-floating hostility). The Type B individual had much lower serum cholesterol levels than the Type A individual, and 28 per cent of the Type A sample already had coronary heart disease, which was seven times higher than those in the Type B group. This type of research illustrates how a person's personality affects his or her reactions to stressors and increases the chances of succumbing to coronary heart disease. As such, stress may be higher for those who have more of a Type A personality, who tend to feel that they have less control of a situation and who do not have effective coping strategies. Other personality characteristics – patience, locus of control and degree of confidence, personal influence, problem focus and work–life balance – have also been recognized as important in understanding how we respond to stress and might be indicators of a stress-prone personality.[35]

ASSESSING YOUR PERSONAL STYLE: HOW TYPE A ARE YOU?[36]

For each statement, place a number from 1 to 4 on the line to the left of the item. The numbers mean:

1	2	3	4
Very Untrue	Somewhat Untrue	Somewhat True	Very True

_____ 1. Whenever I undertake a task, I try to work as quickly as I can in completing it.
_____ 2. I seem to never have time to enjoy some of the things that I have accomplished.
_____ 3. Even though I may not show it, I like to win.
_____ 4. I tend to be undertaking a number of tasks or assignments at the same time.

If you scored more than 10, you are more likely to be Type A than Type B. Take a look at some of the tests on the book's website.

The pressures from work and non-work can have personal, organizational and physical health effects. Initial personal effects include increased distrust, anxiety and low self-esteem, and organizational effects may result in lower levels of job satisfaction and interest in work as well as increased absenteeism and presenteeism. These feelings may also manifest themselves in physical health effects such as higher cholesterol, blood pressure and stomach problems because of changes in a person's state of mind, resilience, confidence and feelings of calmness.[37] Over the long term, there are possible strain effects such as depression and other mental health problems, higher job dissatisfaction and workplace problems, absenteeism, presenteeism and turnover. The strain effects can result in more chronic physical health problems such as heart disease and other chronic health issues, in addition to increased drinking and substance use.[38]

The strategic interests in improving workplace safety and health relate to reducing costs, improving health and reducing stress. Other effects are lost time at work and lower productivity. Absenteeism is rising worldwide, partially due to rising levels of work stress, although other factors are also responsible – an ageing workforce, a higher proportion of women in the workforce who have multiple responsibilities (e.g. child care) and liberal leave policies used to recruit and retain today's workers. Predictions are that sick leave costs and short-term disability might surpass the costs of long-term disabilities.

Added to the cost of absenteeism is the hidden cost of presenteeism, or the average number of days employees attend work even though they are ill or injured. Sickness presenteeism is associated with tension headaches, migraines, allergies, depression, gastrointestinal problems and asthma/breathing difficulties, or benign illnesses that reduce a person's productivity but do not force a person to stay away from work. Employees might be substituting sickness presenteeism for sickness absence. Presenteeism is common in jobs where employees feel a sense of responsibility towards clients and in occupations where work accumulates if a person is absent because co-workers have their own responsibilities and are not able to fill in. Increasing levels of presenteeism are connected to higher levels of overtime, increased job insecurity, decreases in career opportunities and eroded levels of trust and supervisory support.[39]

Early diagnosis

Is there any way to diagnose the problems of stress before they result in chronic outcomes? In most cases, many of these conditions are the result of acute depression or exhaustion from extreme stress, or burnout.

Pre-burnout. Hans Selye's second stage of stress, the resistance stage, is really a pre-burnout stage. Early warning signs during the pre-burnout stage include minor mental lapses, such as the inability to concentrate, reduced attention span and impaired decision-making abilities. For other people, the behavioural effects to workplace stressors might be fatigue, loss of sleep, inability to relax and a loss of confidence.

> **QUIZ 11.1 – PRE-BURNOUT**
>
> Answer yes or no.
> _____ 1. Have you recently felt insecure about life and work?
> _____ 2. Have you recently lost sleep because of worry?
> If you answered yes, these may be some examples of symptoms of pre-burnout.

Burnout. Burnout is a stage of exhaustion or overload, and typifies Hans Seyle's third stage, where continuing exposure to the stressors may eventually overtax various organs in the body.

Burnout can later manifest itself as depression that can affect a person's appetite, sleep and self-esteem. People who manifest signs of burnout may exhibit one of the following profiles:

- Unassertive, timid and submissive, anxious and irritable; may feel sad or lonely and may have lost interest in many of life's activities.
- Impatient and intolerant, easily angered and frustrated.
- Lacking confidence and self-esteem and having no desire for autonomy or control.
- Authoritarian, an excessive need for control, a tendency to want to do it all, inability to delegate and overload oneself.

People experiencing burnout may wake up often in the early hours of the morning; have difficulty concentrating; withdraw from others; feel lonely, worthless and helpless; and perhaps turn to alcohol or drugs. Burnout has been associated with greater work stress and may be causally related to job satisfaction. Burnout is also likely to affect a person's physiological health, as it is a generalized state characterized by a depletion of energy and significantly lessened personal effectiveness. When a person is less effective than he or she used to be and has less energy available, the individual is, to some degree, burnt out.

Burnout may feel very much like a cold or lack of sleep, at first. A person might feel more easily tired or weary. He or she might feel frustrated and have minor hostile reactions. This short-term burnout may go completely unnoticed, and people will go to work as if everything was normal, although feeling slightly 'under the weather'.

> ### SIDEBAR TEST: BURNOUT
>
> Answer yes or no.
>
> _____ 1. I feel like quitting.
> _____ 2. I feel like withdrawing from people lately.
>
> If you answered yes, these may be some indicators of burnout.
> See the book's website for other measures.

Stress and depression. High stress is associated with depression for both male and female workers, and mental health workers were most vulnerable.[40] Based on an Australian study, job strain, and the stresses from an environment where there is bullying, together comprise about 37 per cent of the causes of worker compensation claims for mental stress.[41] Although there are many risk factors of depression, such as older age, illness, low family income and lack of education, it is most often linked to job satisfaction and stress.[42] Stress and depression are associated with physical health problems such as chronic fatigue syndrome, gastrointestinal ulcers, chronic bronchitis, migraine headaches, high blood pressure, arthritis and back problems. People who suffer these problems are more likely to take time off and are more likely to be treated for mental health as well as other health problems. People experiencing major depressive episodes are more prone to injury, just as injuries increase the likelihood of major depressive episodes.[43]

Damaged relationships. Positive relationships and social support are extremely important in helping people deal with stress and depression.[44] People who experience stress and depression are more likely to have problems with relationships. They are more frequently widowed, divorced or separated, and being single is commonly associated with chronic depression. Those depressed had a greater number of psychiatric conditions overall, and life-time suicide attempts were significantly more common. People with chronic depression were more frequently unemployed.[45]

Substance abuse. Substance use includes the use of controlled substances, alcohol and other drugs. Depression is the most common mental disorder in the general population, and substance abuse is the second major disorder, followed by social phobia and panic disorder. This pattern is true for low-income and non-low-income populations, although the prevalence rates are significantly higher in non-low-income groups.[46]

Unfortunately, substance abuse also creates other problems for family, friends and fellow workers, the very people who might be able to help and provide support for people who encounter stress. Substance abuse is linked to a range of problems in organizations, including poor performance, accidents, violence, lateness, absenteeism, theft and harassment. Alcohol and other drugs can affect a worker's judgement in a number of ways, such as missing a day of work or arriving late for work. Several workers report losing concentration, missing a deadline, making errors in judgement they would not normally make, using time to make a lot of personal phone calls related to the problem and forgetting safety and security procedures. This impacts not only their own safety but also the safety of those around them. For example, healthcare workers who use narcotics may steal from patients who are experiencing pain.

Given that experts suggest that 5 to 15 per cent of the employees in a workforce are likely to have a substance abuse problem (alcohol or drugs) serious enough to raise concerns about health and safety, what is an appropriate policy to adopt? The hard-line approach is a zero-tolerance policy, which many argue might drive the problem underground. This would mean firing workers who test positive and not offering any treatment or rehabilitation. The softer approach is to rehabilitate the person and possibly steer him or her into non-strategic positions for health and safety reasons.

CO 2: MANAGING ABSENTEEISM IN RETURNING PEOPLE TO WORK

Globally, employers are becoming increasingly concerned about the effects of mental health and stress as well as the rise of workplace absenteeism and the costs associated with it. One of the challenges of managing absenteeism is that far too few organizations track absenteeism rates to identify the reasons for absenteeism or the costs. Among those that do track the direct costs, estimations in Canada and the United Kingdom are that the costs are 0.08 to 5 per cent of payroll, whereas those in the United States are about 6 per cent (considering labour expenses plus net lost productivity value). On average, workers in the private sector are absent 5.4 days per year, and public sector workers miss 7.9, or an additional 2.5 days, each year. The difficulty in tracking often relates to lack of line manager interest or motivation. Public sector organizations and union organizations seem to take a more active role in tracking absences, and those in the private sector were more likely to take a disciplinary stance.[47]

A majority of the 255 organizations surveyed in a Canadian report distinguished among casual absences, short-term disability and long-term disability. Casual absences, usually involve incidental or non-consecutive absences of up to nine days, and nearly all organizations surveyed manage these by direct communication between managers and employees. In this study, an overwhelming majority (92%) do not provide attendance incentives. The lack of interest in incentive programmes to encourage attendance relates to the increased costs associated with it, unintended consequences of encouraging presenteeism, and the possibility that such programmes might contravene collective agreements.[48] During the survey period, 9 per cent of the employees were on short-term disability leave that allowed for 84 per cent of salary coverage for up to 22 weeks. On average 2.5 per cent of employees were on long-term disability that covered an average of 67 per cent of salary until the age of 65.[49] These are substantial costs for the organization. Beyond developing a programme to track absenteeism, the higher level of absenteeism in public sector organizations has led to a number of recommendations for improving absence management, such as (i) health promotion, (ii) assisting employees through employee assistance programmes (EAPs) and (iii) return to work (RTW) programmes.

Health promotion in reducing absenteeism. Employers are showing an increased interest in health promotion and wellness as a way to reduce the costs of health-related benefits and to assist employees in improving their health, easing stress and promoting healthier behaviour like being more physically active or quitting smoking. Those who participate in such programmes tend to be healthier and absent less often.

A most important facet of health and wellness programmes is the link to an organization's strategies and objectives, mission and values.[50] Such programmes are sometimes seen as less important than other safety programmes where it is easier to measure accident statistics, but there is growing evidence that these programmes are about more than just being nice to employees. The programmes respond to the organization's strategic interests in reducing absenteeism and improving job satisfaction and employee commitment, as expressed in employees being more responsible in working towards an organization's goals and interests. Public organizations, by addressing health and lifestyle needs of employees, can be seen as 'employers of choice' for employees who are seeking a better quality of life at work.

Health and wellness programmes are thought to reduce stress by improving the health of employees and teaching people how to cope with work stress.[51] In defining the business case for the employee health and wellness programme in the private sector, Sears was one of the first organizations to quantify the relationship between employee and customer satisfaction. For every five-unit increase in employee satisfaction in a business quarter, there was a two-unit increase in customer satisfaction in the next quarter and a 0.5 per cent increase in revenues above the national average for the following quarter.[52] In the public sector, the business case is possibly connected to the fact that people in such programmes are more satisfied, committed to the organization and more willing to take responsibility in working towards an organization's strategic objectives.[53]

Assisting employees through employee assistance programmes. Employee assistance programmes, or EAPs, are the most common health and wellness programme offered by organizations.[54] Programmes offer professional counselling, referral and other services for employees and their family members to help with emotional, family, stress and substance abuse problems that might ultimately impact work performance and health.[55] Family problems and emotional issues are often the most prevalent issues, and estimates suggest that services range from family difficulties (25%), stress (23%) and depression (21%) to substance abuse (16%) and work conflicts (9%).[56] Other difficulties are those related to legal, financial and career issues.

EAP services vary significantly across different work sectors. These services were significantly more likely to exist in governmental organizations (87%) rather than retail trade (48%) and construction organizations (20%). Worksites which have EAPs are significantly more likely to be unionized. A small percentage of worksites have EAP committees (28.1%), and several provide training to help supervisors detect symptoms of problems such as depression or substance abuse (52.8%).[57] One of the goals of offering EAPs is to lower medical costs and reduce absenteeism and job accidents,[58] in addition to reducing turnover and improving employee well-being and performance.

Return-to-work (RTW) programmes. The workers' compensation systems in most OECD countries require facilitating the process of returning people to work after a long-term or short-term disability absence. The duty to accommodate is a legal obligation to take steps to eliminate disadvantages that result from a rule, practice or physical barrier that has or may have an adverse impact on individuals or groups protected. In an Australian study of 14 worksites in the health sector, researchers highlighted the importance of RTW co-ordinators in helping workers return to work, resulting in shorter absences and lower costs for employers.[59]

The RTW co-ordinators' roles required a knowledge of the workers' compensation system and its rules as well as an understanding of how to structure suitable duties in arranging early RTW. This involved negotiations with managers and other stakeholders in creatively finding ways to modify work to accommodate the needs of the returning workers. This often involved reduced workloads or time at work but also the redesign of work facilities or activities that allowed workers to feel they were contributing and giving them self-worth. Co-ordinators also pointed to their abilities to communicate with injured workers, 'coupled with broad shoulders capable of carrying the emotional outpourings of people who are distressed and in pain'.[60] The role of the RTW co-ordinators also involved dealing with different degrees of conflict, as the role must balance advocacy and support for ill or injured workers with legitimate requirements of the employer and insurer.

Beyond the facilitation of the RTW co-ordinator, other research demonstrates the need for supportive conditions at work for increasing work ability. Examples of supportive conditions include providing work where people have some influence, degree of freedom, meaning, satisfaction, possibilities for development, positive relations with leaders, social support, sense of community and feeling of being welcomed back at work.[61]

There is growing evidence of the impact of RTW programmes in that the benefits are clearly greater than the costs of the programme. That is, given that the costs of administering the programme, in addition to any adjustments in the work or reduced work, are substantial, there are gains from having people back to work sooner.[62] In a controlled study involving people with severe mental illness, researchers compared traditional vocational rehabilitation with a supportive employment programme which included a job coach. Although costs were similar, participants in the supported programme had fewer hospital admissions, a better self-rated quality of life, greater client earnings and overall longer return of investment.[63] These and other results demonstrate the cost and social benefits of programmes that support people returning to work by finding creative ways to help people integrate.

QUIZ 11.2 – BELIEFS ABOUT THE GROUPS WHO CAUSE ACCIDENTS

Over the last decade, compensation claims for lost work days because of injuries have declined in North America and Europe, partially because the economies are increasingly characterized by brainpower rather brawn-power jobs.[64] Even though these declines are encouraging, improvements are not noted for all workers. Most safety people know that certain unsafe acts – like lifting improperly, using unsafe procedures in working or acting without thinking – are more likely to cause accidents. In addition, there are suspicions that individuals and groups are more likely to have certain types of accidents. In your mind, which group is more likely to have an accident?

1. Do men have more accidents?
2. Are younger workers safe workers?
3. Are older workers less safe?
4. Are certain people more accident prone?

See the book's website for research answering these questions.

CO 3: DEVELOPING A CULTURE SUPPORTING WORKPLACE SAFETY AND HEALTH

Government's role, in addition to managing its own workforce, is to serve the general society by developing and monitoring safety regulations and to develop a culture supporting workplace health and safety. Over the last number of years, managers throughout the world have had to respond to safety problems and industrial accidents which have had international repercussions.

The impact of an industrial accident can be costly and can tie up governments and companies in court action for years. For example, on 20 April 2010, an explosion occurred on the Deepwater Horizon drilling rig, killing 11 platform workers and injuring 17 of their colleagues. The oil leak that caused the explosion spewed about 4.9 million barrels of crude oil into the Gulf of Mexico for five months before it was capped, creating one of largest industrial marine accidents in the petroleum industry and causing extensive damage to marine and wildlife habitats and the Gulf's fishing and tourist industries. British Petroleum had leased the drilling rig and was the responsible party under the Oil Spill Pollution Act of 1990. 'Are they negligent?' 'Does their behavior warrant punitive damages?' A BP report concluded that decisions made by 'multiple companies and work teams' contributed to the accident which it says arose from 'a complex and interlinked series of mechanical failures, human judgments, engineering design, operational implementation and team interfaces'. BP's bill for containing and cleaning up the oil spill had reached £6.6 billion ($10 billion) as of September 2010, and they have set up a £13.2 billion ($20 billion) compensation fund to help. In 2015, BP agreed to pay £12.3 billion ($18.7 billion) in fines over the next 15 years to the US federal government and state governments of Alabama, Florida, Louisiana, Mississippi and Texas.

As this example makes clear, occupational health and safety accidents can have severe international repercussions for a company's bottom line and reputation, in addition to the costs of life and possible environmental damage. Such examples call into question government's role in managing occupational health and safety at a societal level.

What causes accidents?

To improve workplace safety, we have to ask, 'What causes accidents?' Consider this question, and list the five reasons for certain types of accident (e.g. industrial or offshore oil exploration) from the most important cause (1) to the least important cause (5).

I believe the top five causes of accidents in the workplace are:

1.
2.
3.
4.
5.

Example of responses to the question 'What causes accidents?' often include:

- Personal error, carelessness and not paying attention
- Alcohol
- Trying to do too much in a hurry
- Low skill/poor training
- Unsafe procedures

Many of the responses to this question point to the 'individual' as the major cause of accidents, either because of error, substance use, lack of training, carelessness or other mental health-related issues. When workplace accidents occur, 'analysts' typically focus on identifying the incident and what individuals or an individual did wrong, rather than the systemic characteristics surrounding the accident. In one study, for example, analysts attributed 60–80 per cent of industrial accidents to the individual errors made. However, under closer examination, the estimate should have been as low as 30–40 per cent.[65]

When trying to understand the cause of accidents, there are two possible attribution errors at work. The **fundamental attribution error** describes the tendency of an investigator to blame, overestimate or use as a scapegoat the individuals who are closest to the accident and to underestimate the influence of the context or the behaviour of others. At the worker level, the **defensive attribution error** is the tendency to empathize with the victim and to attribute the accidents to external factors. Each attribution error magnifies the differences between investigators' and workers' perception of the causes of accidents.[66] Workers are more likely to find external blame, whereas the investigators who write the reports are more likely to hone in on individual causes.[67]

A useful approach is to conduct a risk assessment that identifies the types of hazards in the workplace that might cause harm for you, your employees or members of the public. In hazard identification and assessment, analysts often use a risk analysis procedure for assessing the health and safety risks of critical tasks, machines and working conditions. For example, they would review a job by breaking it down into its various tasks and then identify the hazards and risks under different conditions. *A risk* is calculated based on the probability or likelihood of the harm being realized and the severity of the consequences, expressed mathematically in the formula: Risk = Probability × Severity. For example, in preparing for your wedding, consider the risk of rain during your outdoor ceremony and party. Estimate the probability of rain during August and the severity or harm created if it did rain. Using a scale ranging from 0 to 100, you might estimate that the probability is unlikely (estimate is 20% probability), and the severity or harm to be minimal (estimate of 20%). Based on this calculation, you might feel that there is a low risk (20% × 20%) of holding the wedding outside. This common-sense calculation helps analysts recognize the hazards and risks associated with different marine and industrial jobs such as docking ships during storms or gales or abandoning the ship during an emergency.

Underlying causes of accidents

When we step back and review accidents systematically, we often find larger organizational practices affect why a safe procedure is breached and the attribution that people make of the causes. Some of the larger organizational practices include organizational pressures to complete work quickly, taking excessive risks, ineffective communication and safety concerns. Four key practices stand out as contributing to accident reduction: (i) reducing role overload and pressure to perform, (ii) developing a climate and culture encouraging safety, (iii) making a commitment to joint management and communicating safety values and (iv) communicating and reinforcing safety norms.

Reducing pressures to perform. When people are under pressure because they do not have enough time, training and resources, they are more likely to be involved in unsafe acts. This is consistent with the view that as workload increases, people are more likely to adopt a shortcut which might be unsafe.[68] The pressure to perform is consistent with safety studies of fatal accidents of offshore oil workers in the North Sea, BP's oil disaster in the Gulf of Mexico and the sinking of the Ocean Ranger drilling platform in a Valentine's Day storm off the coast of Newfoundland in 1984, which killed 84 people. One major theme was the pressure to complete the work as quickly as possible, looking for shortcuts, even at the expense of safety.[69] Best practices are not always followed, and regulations allow companies to cut corners.[70]

The pressure to perform in response to workload pressures is also present in the field of nursing. As a result of staffing shortages and health care budget cuts, nurses are feeling the pressure to perform more work because there are fewer colleagues to share the load. In addition, they have a wider range of tasks including delivering and retrieving food trays, housekeeping, transporting patients, ordering, co-ordinating and performing ancillary services. The consequences include higher turnover and a greater likelihood that medical errors will be made.[71]

The pressure to perform is most notable in sports, where we hear it is commonplace for top athletes to take performance-enhancing drugs, even when these drugs have severe health consequences. A famous case was that of Lance Armstrong, who won the Tour de France a record seven consecutive times before he was disqualified and banned for doping offences. Another case of illicit drug use was Canadian Ben Johnson's winning of the 100-metre race in the 1988 Summer Olympics in South Korea, only to be later stripped of his medal when he tested positive for drug use. Ironically, Carl Lewis, the US runner, who placed second in the race, was eventually given the gold medal only to be exposed when 2003 investigations revealed that Lewis and some 100 other US athletes were also involved in drugs and should not have been able to compete in the 1988 Olympics. Carl Lewis later broke his silence on the issue, saying that he benefited from a cover-up. Several athletes later indicated the difficulty in standing up against group pressures which were pushing in another direction. Many athletes later spoke against the cover-up they knew was going on but could do nothing about.

The pressure to perform is similar to a group think[72] or group pressures to seek consensus and adopt a course of action while discounting the warnings of others. These pressures are said to have been prominent when the space shuttle *Challenger* exploded in mid-air on 28 January 1986. The review of the incident concluded that although technical problems caused the explosion, a serious problem was the flawed decision-making process, where managers discounted the warnings of their engineers to cancel the launch. Yes, managers felt compelled to go ahead because of pressures to meet their goals and flight schedules.

Another example of pressures to conform were those applied to Dr Frances Kelsey as a medical officer in the US Food and Drug Administration in Washington nearly 50 years ago. She held her ground and refused to approve the drug thalidomide for distribution to the US market, even though it was said to be a 'wonder' drug for expectant mothers to cure anxiety, insomnia and tension. The drug, developed and manufactured in Germany, was approved in Canada and other countries. Dr Kelsey's decision to hold the line spared thousands of American lives from tragedy as the drug has resulted in thousands of deaths and deformities for those exposed to it while in the womb. Throughout the world in 46 countries, thalidomide has been implicated in thousands of deformities such as missing or deformed limbs, missing appendices and shortening of upper limbs. This example underscores the pressures that public policymakers and managers are subject to as they carry out their work.[73]

Developing a climate and culture encouraging safety. People engage in safer work behaviour when they perceive that their work climate or environment encourages safety. Where there was a positive safety-related climate, team members would 'take personal ownership in safety activities, develop strong norms regarding the performance of tasks in a safe manner and, therefore, engage in fewer unsafe behaviors'.[74]

Key elements of the safety climate include management's commitment to safety, the priority of safety, co-worker safety behaviour, general safety policies, procedures and practices, safety training, safety communication, safety reporting and employee safety involvement. However, there is much support for the fact that management's commitment to a safety climate is clearly the most robust predictor of injuries.[75] The term **safety climate**, which developed from the field of social psychology, describes the perceptions, behaviours and expressions of feelings by organizational members and the relationships with management. It is a snapshot of the safety culture and subject to change.

The term **safety culture** reflects the enduring attitudes, beliefs, perceptions and values that employees share in relation to safety. The term was possibly first introduced by the International Nuclear Safety Advisory Group (INSAG) report on the Chernobyl nuclear meltdown, where 2 plant workers died immediately and another 28 died two weeks later because of acute radiation poisoning. The incident occurred on 26 April 1986, following two explosions that blew the 1,000-tonne concrete cap off the Chernobyl-4 reactor. The release of molten core fragments into the immediate vicinity, and fission products into the atmosphere, marked the worst accident in the history of commercial nuclear power generation. In addition to the lives lost, the accident contaminated over 400 square miles surrounding the Ukrainian plant and significantly increased the risk of cancer deaths over a wide area of Scandinavia and Western Europe.[76]

Some organizational indicators of a safety culture include organizational commitment of managers to demonstrate positive attitudes towards safety, management involvement and participation in risk identification and training, employee empowerment or voice in safety decisions, reward systems which recognize safe practices, and reporting systems identifying the weaknesses and vulnerabilities in safety management.[77] These broader contextual indicators assist in thinking of ways to redesign jobs to encourage a culture of people who are safety minded.

Making a commitment to joint management and communication. The most effective policies define workplace safety and violence in precise, concrete language, the organization's statutory requirement, and provide clear examples of unacceptable behaviour and working conditions. The trick is to state these in clear terms so that organizational members understand them and the consequences. The policies should encourage the reporting of accidents and incidents of violence and should outline the confidential process by which employees can report incidents and to whom. Clear policies are also needed in outlining the procedures for investigating and resolving complaints, describing how information about risks of potential accidents and violence will be communicated to employees and statements of commitment of support services to victims of accidents and violence, confidential employee assistance programmes (EAPs) and training to prevent accidents and violence.

Commitment goes beyond words and phrases echoing policies and procedures for increasing safety and reducing violence. Commitment is illustrated when top managers and key employees are directly involved in joint management committees. Joint Health and Safety Committees encourage organizational representatives to develop responsibility for preventing work-related injuries and diseases and violence. The committees are required in some countries in organizations with a minimum number of employees, usually between 10 and 20. The committee works in a non-adversarial environment and acts as an advisory committee in identifying hazards, recommending corrections and participating in accident investigations and workplace inspections. In union environments, at least one management and union representative should be certified and have training which includes committee responsibilities, safety laws, principles and accident causation, hazard recognition, job safety analysis, hygiene, raising safety awareness, inspections, accident investigation and effective oral communication.

Many workplaces find that joint worker/employer safety and health committees are an excellent means of consultation and can help identify responsibilities, establish positive attitudes and assist the employer with reducing or eliminating workplace injuries or diseases. The committee has the general responsibility for workplace inspections, identifying potential health and safety hazards and making recommendations and implementing solutions. They are also responsible for investigating health and safety complaints.

Communicating and reinforcing positive safety norms and behaviours. The safety-related norms and behaviours of a work group define how the group members work together in helping each other and communicating openly about safety-related issues. In some groups, team members talk about safety on an ongoing basis. The group process includes activities that encourage safety, including the ease with which individuals participate, ask questions and monitor each other's safety. When members do not feel they can easily communicate with others, norms of not questioning or even hiding errors are more likely to occur. A different group process is involved when people own up to their mistakes and are willing to offer suggestions to others so they can learn from the mistakes.

Effective communication and co-ordination is often more important than technical knowledge and is often illustrated in a team process where individuals (i) monitor each others' performance in making sure procedures are followed and the work is completed in a timely way, (ii) freely and openly offer feedback, (iii) efficiently communicate in exchanging information and (iv) assist team members when they need help.[78]

The supervisor is the most important person in creating a group process that encourages people to communicate effectively around safety issues. According to most legislation, a supervisor is anyone who has either charge of a workplace or authority over a worker. Beyond developing an effective group process, the supervisor is responsible for implementing the provisions of the safety related legislation.

Managers are advised to exercise 'due diligence', which requires employers to make sure all reasonable precautions are taken to ensure health and safety. This could mean taking an aggressive employee aside to address the conflict or making employees aware of issues that might affect their safety. This also means taking precautions and developing a culture of appropriate communications. To do this, the employer has the responsibility to implement a plan to identify possible workplace hazards and design the workplace to prevent accidents from occurring. This involves developing written workplace health and safety policies and training in developing a culture that recognizes occupational health and safety legislation and issues such as control of toxic substances, substance abuse, workplace smoking and general health and safety.

Workers also have responsibilities to ensure their own safety and the safety of their co-workers. Employees in most countries have three basic rights within the provisions of the joint responsibility model: the right to refuse work which is unsafe, the right to participate in the workplace health and safety process through joint health and safety committees and the right to know or be informed of actual or potential dangers in the workplace. The right to refuse unsafe work is based on the assumption that there is a 'reasonable cause' to believe that the work is unsafe. This usually means that a safety problem puts a worker in danger or that a complaint has not been resolved. Some of the circumstances considered to be reasonable cause include unsafe vehicles or scaffolding. Even police, firefighters, workers employed in correctional institutions and health workers have the right to refuse unsafe work. For example, although a police officer does not have the right to refuse to intervene in a robbery, the officer could, at the beginning of a shift, refuse to ride in a vehicle that had defective brakes. In addition, safe procedures for police officers involve asking for assistance. Similarly, although firefighters cannot refuse to perform a dangerous task in an emergency, they can refuse to test for an infectious virus where the proper protective clothing and safety equipment is not available.

A RELEVANT POINT OF VIEW: UNSAFE WORKPLACES WHERE THERE IS VIOLENCE AND BULLYING

Nearly one in five incidents of violent victimization, including physical and sexual assault, occurred in the victim's workplace, and a high proportion of these crimes were against those working in social assistance or health care services such as hospitals, nursing or residential care facilities. A high proportion was also reported in accommodation or food services, retail or wholesale trade, and educational services sectors.[79] People who work in premises where alcohol is served are more likely to encounter incidents, and workplace violence is more likely to occur in situations where people are interacting with the public or carrying out inspection or enforcement (such as municipal housing inspectors, public works employees, police, corrections officers or security officers). When violence occurs in the workplace, it has repercussions on others, as in nearly 9 in 10 incidents, the victims of workplace violence told another co-worker; two-thirds told their family; and two-thirds told friends and neighbours.

Millions of people work in public administration, and many of these people are on the front line and have to present a calm demeanour to demanding customers. Public sector workers, such as police, social workers, teachers and nurses, are required to maintain their poise. With good reason, workplace violence is a safety issue concerning many employers, who carry a legal obligation. In many countries, responsibilities include (i) assessing the risks of workplace violence and implementing changes to minimize them; (ii) developing and posting workplace violence and harassment policies; (iii) establishing workplace violence and harassment programmes for implementing procedures for reporting incidences of violence and harassment, and investigating and dealing with complaints; and (iv) providing training for workers. Employers are required to take every reasonable precaution to protect workers from domestic violence. If employers are aware of a person's history of violent behaviour, they may be obligated to protect other workers who might be exposed.

There are many faces of violence: threats, intimidation, verbal abuse, emotional or psychological abuse[80] and actions and incidents that hurt, threaten, humiliate or injure persons while they carry out their professional responsibilities.[81] Physical assaults are more traumatic and observable. But violence is more than pushing a person against a wall or delivering a belt on the chin, and a growing literature has used terms such as *bullying, mobbing, harassment, incivility* and *misbehaviour*. The hard-hitting, macho-style executive who gets results by intimidating employees is seen by some people as effective. On the other hand, physical acts of violence and sexual harassment by touching, leering and making bad jokes are clearly inappropriate behaviours. **Bullying**, as a form of violence, is hard to identify as it 'occurs when one employee creates a hostile work environment for another, through verbal and non-verbal behaviors'. Victims and witnesses to bullying quit or are driven away in 75 per cent of the cases.[82] **Mobbing** is more sophisticated than bullying as it involves cliques of people working collectively to control others. Many of these faces of violence fly under the radar in organizations because people are unclear of what constitutes violence, and it can be said that what is considered inappropriate to one person might not be to another.

Workplace bullying can be seen as similar to aggression, where people with higher needs for control want to rule over others. Other explanations point to organizational structures and norms which enable and do not discourage violence, such as those where managers assert themselves in performance management procedures. Bullying has also been seen as corruption where alliances and people in various positions are vying for power.

Australian researchers have linked the implications of stress from bullying to depression. Within the Job-Demand-Control model of work stress, job strain is illustrated when there are a combination of high job demands and low job control. If policies and norms for bullying are lacking, this may serve as a reinforcement for bullying behaviour. Job strain and bullying are two factors that are linked to depression and mental stress claims made to the workers' compensation system.[83]

In this chapter, we suggest that employers have clear roles to play in discouraging workplace violence and bullying by enacting rules of behaviour and developing a positive culture. In addition, employees also have the responsibility to firmly tell employees that offensive behaviour is not acceptable. Keeping factual records, including dates, times and witnesses and reporting the harassment to the person identified in your workplace policy (e.g. your supervisor) is everyone's responsibility. If they don't listen, proceed to the next level of management.

MANAGERIAL IMPLICATIONS: This chapter concentrates more specifically on the workplace stress connection to improving mental health and reducing absenteeism. It provides information in support of strategic objectives like reducing workplace stress, reducing absenteeism and returning people to work, preventing workplace accidents and developing a culture of safety. Although other objectives are certainly important in improving mental health, physical health and safety, these objectives are a first step within the strategic theme of improving workplace health and safety.

BEFORE APPLYING, LET'S REVIEW

CO 1: Identify factors defining organizational stress and their impact on individuals.

In an organization, the key sources of stress result from: the tensions of family/social life, lack of career and achievement, safety problems, the problems of managing others and relationships with others, the physical environment at the workplace, living environment, managerial reponsibilities, ergonomics, shift work and organizational structure. However, much stress depends on how a person reacts to a stressful incident. That is, certain personality characteristics affect a person's reaction to stressors and increase the chance of succumbing to heart disease and other ill health effects. We are seeing the emergence of many health-related injuries (such as depression) which are harder to diagnose and deal with. In responding to the mental health problems people are increasingly experiencing in work, we are also seeing a linkage between workplace stress and mental health problems. Stress can hinder a person's ability to cope and perform, and depression is one of the more serious manifestations of this. Stress and depression have a variety of effects in the workplace and may result in damaged relationships, substance and alcohol abuse and general ill health.

CO 2: Apply return-to-work practices to respond to absenteeism and disability issues.

The costs of workplace absenteeism have led to a number of recommendations for improving absence management such as: (i) health promotion, (ii) assisting employees through Employee Assistance Programmes (EAPs) and (iii) return to work (RTW) programmes. The research demonstrates that programmes that provide supportive conditions at work are effective in reducing absenteeism costs.

CO 3: Assess the facets important to preventing accidents and developing a culture of workplace safety.

Preventing accidents from happening, encouraging due diligence, setting up a joint committee, communication, training and education, enforcement and developing a safety culture are key components to a safer workplace. The safety culture underlying prevention encourages workers to pay more attention to safety issues. In some cases, group members don't effectively communicate about safety issues, or the group culture might encourage people to take risks rather than act safely. It is helpful to keep these broader contextual influences in mind when thinking of ways to redesign jobs and improve team performance by developing better communication processes and a culture of people who are safety minded.

DISCUSSION AND REVIEW QUESTIONS

1. Mental health problems might be related to many other factors than those found in a workplace. There might be pressures in the home, and in some cases, genetic factors might be the cause. Does the employer still have a responsibility to deal with these problems? Why? What occupational pressures are more prominent in public sector organizations?
2. Improving health and safety in the workplace often depends on group practices – pressures to perform, group process and safety culture. What are some of the resistances you might expect in changing these practices in a work group to be more conscious of health and safety? What steps would you take in trying to develop a positive culture of workplace health and safety?
3. What are the differences and similarities in the roles and responsibilities of employers, supervisors and employees?

4. Employee health and wellness is often thought of as very different from employee safety, representing different disciplines and professions. What are the similarities and differences in each area, and how might you approach each area? Would you approach each area in the same way?
5. Studies indicate that jurisdictions that force cyclists to wear helmets have the highest helmet use. Safety experts and medical professionals say that helmet use is linked to a reduction in head injuries, but others say that wearing helmets inhibits the freedom to choose and might even discourage bicycle use. Should you legislate helmet use? Divide the class into groups of three or four students. Half of the groups will defend the position that helmet use should be mandatory for all ages. The other group will take the stance that helmets should not be mandatory, as they affect a person's freedom to choose. Each group should defend its position against a group that is taking a different stance. Each group should have five minutes to articulate their position, four minutes for the rebuttal and two minutes for concluding statements. All members of each group should have the opportunity to speak.
6. Develop a strategy map template in Figure 11.3 for the strategic theme of 'enhancing workplace health and safety to the highest level'. You should identify strategic objectives and examples of initiatives to implement them within each of the perspectives of the SHRM BSC.

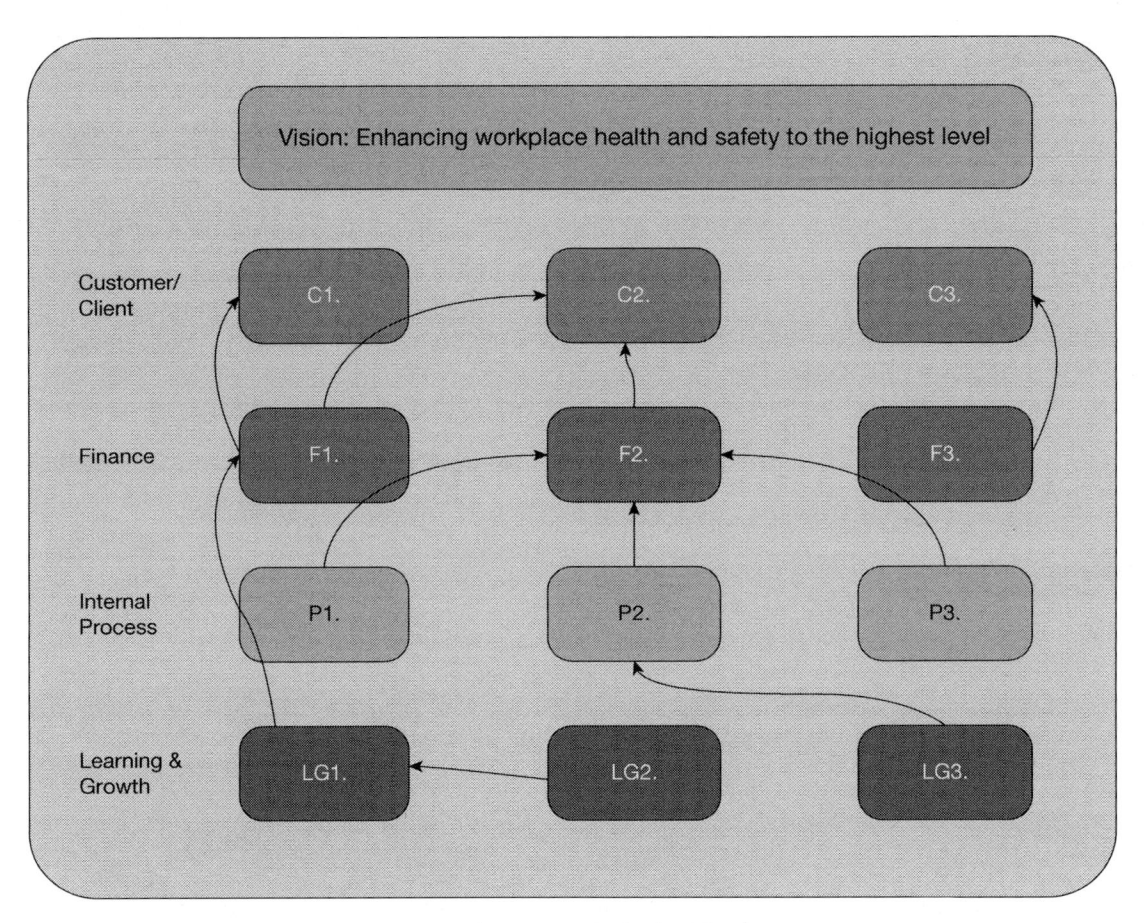

Figure 11.3 Enhancing workplace health and safety to the highest level.

CASE: RETURNING TO WORK

Tara Sandhu is 42, married and has a six-year-old boy and a 4-year-old girl. She has an MPA degree with undergraduate expertise in political science and policy analysis. She was a great student when she completed her MPA two years ago and won the award for the best thesis/managerial report. She was active in sports, including swimming, sailing, biking and hiking.

After graduation, Tara began working for the Streettohome Foundation, a programme aimed at feeding and housing homeless people in Brisbane, Australia. In addition to meeting with clients who might provide funding, she spent two days a week supervising a programme for feeding street people and locating shelters for them. For Tara, this was a fun part of her job, a chance to work directly with homeless people and get a real feel for their needs. The Foundation is a non-profit organization whose mission is to end homelessness in the community by bringing in new money (private sector), innovative ideas and opportunities for collaboration to solve homelessness. Tara expected to be promoted to the position of manager because the current job incumbent was slated to move up in the organization to a recently vacated vice-presidential position. She had been told that she was a strong candidate for the job.

Tara was involved in a near fatal accident while returning home late from work. She was hit by a car which lost control on a slippery road. Her body bounced off the car, which skidded into another car, overturning on impact. When she awoke from a coma two days later, she was unable to move her legs as she had broken her lower back. For the next year, she went through a lengthy physiotherapy programme, and with the support of her husband and friends, she learned to move about in a wheelchair. She was able to resume some sports and was able to rig up a sailboat to accommodate her disability and was working on learning how to ride a bike propelled with her hands.

After over a year at home, Tara sought to return to work. She was getting bored at home and wanted the challenge of a job, the social activities in the office and the chance to work with homeless people again. When she called up her old boss, she discovered that he had left for another job, and a new person, Terri Connor, was in charge.

Tara sent an email to Terri and copied it to the HR manager.

> *Dear Ms. Conway,*
>
> *I'd be interested in returning to work in my previous job, where I worked in a supervisory capacity in feeding and housing some of the homeless people on the city's west side.*
>
> *Over a year ago, I had a serious car accident while walking home from work, but I have recovered and feel I am able to return to work. You will see from my records that I had an exemplary record with Streetohome and feel I can continue working at that level on my return.*
>
> *I'd be interested in meeting with you at your earliest convenience.*
>
> *Sincerely,*
> *Tara Sandhu*

A week after sending the email, Tara popped into her old building and was able to meet with Terri.

Terri: Great to finally meet you. I've heard so much about you.
Tara: Yes ... thank you. And nice to meet you.

>**Terri:** I am sorry to hear about your accident, and I can only imagine the time you spent rehabilitating. ... How are things with you now?
>**Tara:** Fine. ... I am looking forward to returning to work.
>**Terri:** You know the old job required quite a bit of movement to and from various locations, and you were on your feet a lot. And we have somebody doing your old job now. ... I didn't know you were still in a wheelchair when I got your email.
>**Tara:** Is that still important?
>**Terri:** Well, I just need to know what you can and cannot do. Can you work regular hours?
>**Tara:** Sure, I'm fine.
>**Terri:** Some of our facilities are very hard to get in and out of, you know. That is, we don't have wheelchair access in some of our locations. And, some of the doors are hard to open.
>**Tara:** I am sure we can get by. It is probably possible to build a ramp here and there and I know that there is government money to help do this. As for the door, I am sure we can get a door that has a button which we can press to open it. Besides, this will help other disabled people.
>**Terri:** And, the washroom?
>**Tara:** I looked at it ... Yes, it could be easily changed for wheelchair access.

From Terri's questions, Tara felt that there was not a high level of enthusiasm about her returning to work. Terri promised that she would be in touch soon on possibilities and walked Tara to the door and assisted her out and down the stairs.

Three weeks later, Tara had still not received a response. So, she called Terri who answered her phone and apologized for not responding sooner, as she had been really busy. 'It was that time of year and she had to get the budget approved and was away for a bit at a conference.' Terri said that Tara's old position had been filled, and she had been trying to find other work for her. The following letter arrived a few days later.

Dear Ms. Tara Sandhu,

Thank you for your interest in returning to work at the Streettohome Foundation. We regret that we cannot find a place for you at this time, and as you know, your old job has been filled by another person.

We recognize the difficulty of accommodating people with a wheelchair in our facilities because we have to contract with private agencies for the use of some of their facilities, many of which are substandard. There would have to be substantial modifications made to our facilities, which go beyond our present budget, but as you point out, there is probably government money to help do this.

We hope you understand that we cannot presently accommodate you but will keep your application on file and see what we can do in the near future.

Sincerely,
Terri Connor

Two months later, Tara heard from some of her former colleagues that Terri had hired another staff member, and wondered why she was not given the chance to apply for that position. When she called, Terri said it was just an entry position and that Tara was overqualified.

But at least this entry-level position would have given her a job.

Tara was angry and thought of complaining to the Human Rights Commission because she felt the employer had the duty to accommodate people in their return to work. On the other hand, she was sure that Terri would say that employers need only accommodate a physically less able person if it does not impose a hardship on the organization. Tara's friends warned her that if she won an appeal, she would likely face an unfriendly work environment, and Terri would make it a miserable work experience.

Task. Review the situation and advise Tara of the strengths and weaknesses of her case if she presented it to a Human Rights Commission.

12 Negotiating a Collective Agreement Using Positional and Interest-based Processes

Chapter Outline
- Chapter objectives (COs) 238
- A driving issue focusing managerial action: Responding to the way unions have changed over the years 238
- CO 1: Negotiating a collective agreement in the public sector 240
- CO 2: Integrative or interest-based processes for resolving disputes 244
- Before applying, let's review 249
- Discussion and review questions 250
- Case: Negotiating a collective agreement with teachers 251

CHAPTER OBJECTIVES (COs)

After reading this chapter, you will be able to implement the following objectives:

CO 1: Understand the dynamics of negotiating a collective bargaining agreement.

CO 2: Implement integrative and interest-based processes in a negotiating environment.

A DRIVING ISSUE FOCUSING MANAGERIAL ACTION: RESPONDING TO THE WAY UNIONS HAVE CHANGED OVER THE YEARS

Union membership is changing throughout the world in both the public and private sectors. The biggest and most transformational shifts have been increases in the number of women and more representation in public sector organizations. As manufacturing companies have shifted offshore in attempts to reduce costs, jobs in the service sector, small business, contract workers, knowledge workers and part-time work has grown.

The biggest shift in union membership is the number of women, which was a mere 10 to 15 per cent in the late 1970s. Now, women represent more than 50 per cent of the membership in most industrialized countries. In the UK and Canada, the average trade unionist is a young, educated female working in a profession.[1]

Another big shift is the overall growth of public sector unions, beginning during the 1960s.[2] *In terms of density, the rate of public sector unionization is about 70 to 80 per cent in countries like Canada, Finland, the United Kingdom, and Australia and New Zealand as well as in European countries, whereas union density in the private sector is less than 20 per cent in many countries. In the United States, there are now more people in public sector unions than in private ones. In 2013, 35.3 per cent of the public sector workforce was unionized, up significantly from 10.6 per cent in 1958.*[3]

There has been a downwards shift in trade union membership in private sector organizations in many industrialized countries, a trend that is evident in the United States, Australia and Germany. Even in Great Britain, where unions were very strong, similar declines in union membership have occurred. Membership declined in the United States from about 35 per cent in the 1950s to 25 per cent in 1970, to 13 per cent in 1999, and then 11 per cent in 2013; Australian membership declined from 25 per cent in 1999 to 17 per cent in 2013; in the same period, Canadian members declined from 28 per cent to 27 per cent; UK members from 30 per cent to 25 per cent; New Zealand from 21 per cent to 19 per cent; Sweden from 80 per cent to 67 per cent; Germany from 25 per cent to 17 per cent; Denmark from 74 per cent to 66 per cent; Netherlands from 24 per cent to 17 per cent. Membership is highest in Belgium at 55 per cent, Denmark at 66 per cent, Sweden at 67 per cent, Norway at 54 per cent and Iceland at 83 per cent.[4]

Those who are critical of unions might suggest that one of the reasons for the decline is because many employees no longer feel they need unions to get good wages and benefits. Research does not support this, as unionized workers are paid significantly higher than non-union workers and also work fewer hours. Also, women who are in unions are more likely to have equitable pay, as the wage gap for women was much larger for non-union women workers.

Most labour movements are being challenged to respond to shifts in workforce demographics, political shifts in society, labour laws and the declining influence of international unions. The shifts also include the feminization of the labour movement, which partially reflects the increasing prominence of unions in public sector organizations.[5] *The union movement continues to play a key role in government organizations, and if you are a manager in a public sector organization, you will likely have to work with a union.*

STRATEGIC CONTEXT: *For many HR managers in the public sector, the collective agreement is the framework for managing. Most HR processes – such as procedures for job analysis and design, staffing, compensation and training – are defined by language in the collective agreement. For example, if HR managers want to change a job or outsource certain jobs, they will have to respond to terms that are defined in the collective agreement.*

This chapter reviews the nature of collective bargaining process that can be approached in an adversarial or integrative way. In using the SHRM BSC in this chapter, you might focus on this strategic objective: 'managing effectively in negotiating and administering a collective agreement'. Creating a negotiating plan could be part of this objective. The next chapter adds information on another relevant strategic objective: developing a positive labour relations climate.

CO 1: NEGOTIATING A COLLECTIVE AGREEMENT IN THE PUBLIC SECTOR

Collective bargaining is the process of negotiating a formal collective agreement or contract on issues such as wages and benefits, hours of work, working conditions, health and safety, overtime, grievance mechanisms and the right to participate in workplace decisions. Dynamics often conflict because as unions are seeking more job and income security, employers want to increase flexibility and reduce labour costs. Overt displays of conflict involve strikes and lockouts. However, each party has common goals such as sustaining the organization and assuring workplace health and safety.

Negotiation usually involves one of two positions: win–lose and win–win. In win–lose, or what is known as distributive bargaining, the assumption is that the goals of each party are different and irreconcilable and that there is a limited, controlled amount of resources. The win–lose posture suggests that there is a 'fixed pie' and what one party will gain, the other will lose. Such adversarial, win–lose games, are like a game of poker.[6] Like being effective in poker, negotiating skills and theatrics are critical in demonstrating one's position as each party tries to figure out the other party's position; some people may even go to great lengths to dramatize the power of their own hand. Negotiators resort to a range of theatrics to demonstrate their position. For example, when Canada's Air Traffic controllers were bargaining for their first contract after they were privatized, the union felt they needed to demonstrate that their members were solidly behind the negotiation team. The employer did not believe the union could pull the employees together. So, the union orchestrated a day when every union member across the country came in proudly displaying a white T-shirt with the Union logo on it. When the union appeared at the bargaining table the next day, the employer understood the message that the employees were solidly behind them.

The theatrics are also demonstrated in the protocols at the bargaining table. Usually, there is one spokesperson for each party in a carefully orchestrated show of solidarity. The spokesperson states the position as clearly as possible while other team members illustrate their agreement, nodding their heads keenly to show their complete support. The other team, of course, will display less positive emotions. After the presentation of proposals and their arguments, team members caucus before convening to offer counterproposals and rebuttals to the other team's proposals on the issue being discussed.

For many head negotiators, the bargaining goes beyond what occurs at the bargaining table. Many head negotiators will meet outside the scheduled meetings to seek ways to get an agreement. Both parties know that some issues are more important than others. In one example in a public sector negotiation where the union had won the right to a 35-hour week in a previous collective agreement, the employer wanted to re-introduce a 37½ week. 'No way!' said the union, who walked out of the bargaining for two weeks before the head negotiators agreed to meet over coffee to discuss the issue. The union knew they would get no sympathy from the public if they went on strike for this issue. But the employer agreed to take the issue off the bargaining agenda so that negotiating could commence on other issues.

Being involved in collective bargaining means the employer is required to meet with employee representations, receive proposals, discuss them, bargain in good faith and make reasonable effort to enter into a collective agreement. This means that employers and union negotiators must make a sincere effort to reach an agreement through reasonable compromise, and regularly meet and engage in a discussion with a willingness to reach an agreement. It also requires that proposals and counterproposals be realistic and that parties make concessions or agree on proposals. On the other hand, bad faith bargaining might involve actions such as these:

- Failing to meet by refusing to meet once a notice to begin bargaining has been served, missing procedural steps such as identifying people authorized to bargain or not signing the agreement, refusing to attend meetings and attending meetings unprepared to bargain.

- Undermining the union by not recognizing the union's statutory role as the bargaining agent.
- Surface bargaining or conducting oneself in a way that is inconsistent with the intent of entering a collective agreement. Complaints related to surface bargaining include reactivating proposals that have been signed off, adding new proposals later in the dispute (also called receding horizon bargaining) or stalling.
- Illegal bargaining proposals including proposals which are in conflict with the Labour Relations Code (such as proposals which contravene employment standards) or proposals which are in conflict with terms already agreed.[7]

Linking to the evolving strategic context

Skilled negotiators illustrate certain behaviours. In one study, 48 skilled negotiators were rated on the basis of their effectiveness, track record and low implementation failures by both labour and management. The behaviour of the skilled negotiators was compared with 'average' negotiators. Six areas stand out for effective negotiating behaviour:[8]

1. *Planning time:* Effective negotiators spent more time planning.
2. *Exploration of options:* Skilled negotiators considered more options for action (5.1 vs. 2.6 for average negotiators).
3. *Common ground:* Effective negotiators spent more attention looking for areas of common ground where there are possible integrative solutions (three times more attention than average negotiators).
4. *Long-term versus short-term orientation:* Skilled people made more than twice the number of comments related to looking at the long term.
5. *Setting limits:* Skilled negotiators are more likely to plan in terms of upper and lower limits, whereas average negotiators set fixed targets (e.g. we want a raise of 10 per cent pay).
6. *Sequence and planning of issues:* Skilled negotiators tend to view issues as independent and not as part of a sequence or tied to other issues. As a result, they are more flexible.

The behaviours illustrate the importance of planning, looking for common ground, being flexible and being willing to look for integrative solutions. Adding to the importance of the bargaining strategy, at least in a municipal context, is the history. That is, past relationships of what has occurred in previous exchanges, in addition to what is presently going on in the negotiation, are important determinants of success. These might be more vital than the style or strategy of the negotiators or their context. 'In short, what one does, is more important to the negotiation process than who you are or the environment in which one operates.'[9]

Based on their strategic priorities, negotiators often work with a carefully thought-out plan which highlights the proposals to be made, reasonable arguments which support their positions and rebuttal arguments to possible positions given by the other party. This plan is often informal and unwritten. For management, the organization's strategic themes and objectives set the direction in collective bargaining and include objectives related to improving efficiencies, reducing costs, changing job requirements, reducing absenteeism costs and maintaining a healthy labour relations climate.

The strategic priorities for the union are often shaped by goals relating to improving wages, hours of work, working conditions and job security. Collective bargaining gives unions the opportunity to influence workplace rules and influence decision-making in the workplace. Pay and working conditions have been traditional driving forces, but now public sector unions have to respond to new issues such as performance pay, contracting out, mental health of workers and pensions and benefits. Examples of the range of issues that might appear on the bargaining agenda are listed here:

- Wages and overtime rates, incentive pay, insurance, deductions from wages, pensions.
- Regular hours of work, work schedule, overtime work hours, vacations, holidays.
- Paid annual holidays as well as special holidays that vary for different cultures and countries.
- Benefits against financial hardship related to sickness, accident, bereavement, unemployment, maternity and other areas.
- Security of employment, reasonable period of notice if person is dismissed for reasons other than serious misconduct, and payments in the event of redundancy.
- Working environment, occupational health and safety, identification of hazards and prevention of accidents.

A RELEVANT POINT OF VIEW: FOUR TYPES OF BARGAINING

Bargaining involves more than negotiations between managers and unions to develop a collective agreement. Walton and McKersie's classic book *A Behavioral Theory of Labor Negotiations* suggests that collective bargaining involves four different types of activities, each of which includes different negotiation strategies and tactics. These different bargaining activities – distributive, integrative, attitudinal structuring and intra-organizational bargaining – occur at different times during the course of negotiating a collective bargaining contract.[10]

Distributive bargaining functions to resolve pure conflicts of interest and often involves arguing over the distribution of wages, salaries and bonuses; it tends to be positional in nature and also competitive, as when the union and management are in conflict in 'dividing up the pie'.

Integrative bargaining involves activities focused on attaining objectives that are not fundamentally in conflict, where the parties can work together on a common concern or problem. Parties can work integratively on all issues; however, there is more potential to do so where a solution can clearly benefit both parties, such as training and safety issues.

Attitudinal structuring describes the bargaining activities that are involved in shaping and influencing relationships between the parties in relation to friendship or hostility and trust or distrust. Whereas distributive and integrative bargaining describe the content of negotiations, attitudinal structuring describes tactics for shaping attitudes so that parties share common motivations, beliefs about the other's legitimacy, and illustrate trust and friendliness. In bargaining, negotiators can shape the other party's attitudes in focusing on relationship issues in addition to substantive issues. This involves not taking advantage of a power position, being respectful during the negotiation and when speaking about the other party, and showing an interest in building a working relationship.

Intra-organizational bargaining. Ultimately, the solutions agreed to at the bargaining table must satisfy the principals and persuade their constituents that they got the best solution possible. Intra-organizational bargaining describes the activities that bring the expectations of the principals (the members of the Board and the trade union members) into line with those of the negotiators.

Collective bargaining is not one set of bargaining activities to achieve a strategy, but comprises different types of bargaining, each with different strategies and tactics, during any collective bargaining experience or during the management of the collective agreement. These different bargaining activities are unique in the public sector because the parties are also trying to shape the opinion of the public to maximize their advantages (e.g. Intra-organizational bargaining).

Performance metric in the process of negotiating a fair agreement

In the eyes of the union, the best possible settlement is one that reflects the priorities of the membership. Union leaders spend a great deal of time working with their membership in defining or shaping the issues that will be addressed in the bargaining. The union meeting has traditionally been the heart of democratic action for unions, as this was the place where union leaders could learn from their members and discuss issues and problems and develop a culture of unity and solidarity. Union leaders are led by the strategic priorities which reflect their reading of what is possible, what the central union wants to push (e.g. disability benefits), what they have successfully negotiated in other settings, in addition to responding to the defined interests of their members. Union leaders are using other tools, including employee surveys, blogs, email communications and focus groups, to connect to their membership and to define the positions they feel are important.

The strategic priorities for the union have been shaped by goals relating to improving wages, hours of work, working conditions and job security. Beyond this, the trade union movement's strategic priorities are being challenged as their membership has been declining and they have been forced to recognize new priorities. Collective bargaining gives unions the opportunity to influence workplace rules and gives unions and their members opportunities to influence decision-making in the workplace.

In the eyes of management, a good settlement responds to the organization's strategic objectives while not damaging political and economic objectives.

The process of negotiating a collective agreement

The negotiating plan can define the bargaining team's strategies, tactics, proposals and the arguments they need to make, in addition to counterarguments for proposals they expect from other team members. Strategies in a negotiation plan outline the direction negotiators take in responding to specific issues. Tactics are the devices used, the way that changes are made in implementing the strategy. These include inflating initial demands, setting preconditions, using intimidation and exaggerating the importance of certain information, as well as feinting (apparent move in one direction to divert attention from another) and blanketing (e.g. shotgun coverage of a large area to achieve a breakthrough in one area).[11] A strategy for the union might be to ask for a 5 per cent increase in pay but be willing to compromise. The tactic will be to emphasize the 5 per cent objective but be willing to compromise if management backs off on their ideas for a performance pay. The strategies and tactics are confidential to each bargaining team.

During the initial stages of the negotiation, the union's positions are likely to be inflated while management's positions are deflated. Both sides exaggerate their positions and needs. In addition, each side tries to avoid giving up things or conceding positions they have gained in previous negotiations. The union knows it has a lower limit, beyond which it is prepared to go on strike, and management also has an upper limit it will not exceed. In the process of negotiation, management and the union are each trying to estimate and stretch the real limits of the other's bottom line or walk-away position.

As both sides exaggerate their positions, they are trying to establish a zone of possible agreement (ZOPA), or the bargaining zone where an agreement between the two parties is possible.[12] The ZOPA is the intellectual zone or range where an agreement can be met which is satisfactory for both parties. Outside this zone, an agreement is not possible in the negotiation. For example, if management's bottom line is a 2 per cent salary increase and the union's is 4 per cent, a possible agreement is outside the ZOPA.

The controversy in distributive negotiations is whether to engage in hard-line or soft-line bargaining. That is, does the negotiator carry out competitive hard-line strategies such as making extreme first offers and/or minimizing willingness to concede? Or does a negotiator introduce soft-line strategies aimed at creating a co-operative context by conceding on some points and demonstrating responsiveness to the other's interests?

In a meta-analysis of studies illustrating these two strategies, hard-line strategies lead to potentially higher economic outcomes while soft-line strategies lead to higher socio-economic outcomes. The advantages of hard-line versus soft-line strategies is based on aspiration theory, which suggests that receiving an aggressive first offer with minimal concessions communicates an unwillingness to give up any more than necessary. As a result, the opposing party will need to concede to get an agreement. A problem with this line of negotiation is that if each party takes the same stance, there might be a deadlock.

The rationale for soft-line strategies is that they reduce tension and develop an atmosphere of give-and-take. The model communicates one's co-operative intentions and avoids competitive and aggressive tactics in favour of a more problem-solving orientation. Soft-line strategies work well in achieving high economic outcomes when both parties act in the same way, but they do not prevail when there is a risk of an impasse.[13]

The initial stages of the negotiation also establish the list of issues that the parties plan to discuss, and though different proposals might be presented during the later stages of bargaining, they are within the agenda of issues that have been agreed. The union often presents its initial demands first, and then management initiates its own proposals in areas beyond the union's proposals. After this initial exchange of positions, the bargaining agenda becomes evident to each team, and usually there will be more issues on the agenda than either negotiating team expects to resolve. Through the negotiations, the long agenda of demands may be gradually whittled down as each team gains an understanding of the other's real positions and the issues to focus on.[14]

Once this core bargaining agenda becomes clear, the parties will work on one issue, presenting proposals and counterproposals. Often, the committee will see some degree of agreement and put the issue aside, or encourage a subcommittee to study the issue further. The committee then begins working on another issue and, when there is some agreement, might also set this aside or assign it to a subcommittee pending the resolution of other issues.

Negotiators in public sector collective bargaining know that, for political and economic reasons, they will not achieve all of their objectives. There are issues that each side feels it must achieve and others that are important on which the party hopes to gain some ground. A third level of importance are the less important issues the negotiators are putting on the table, which the party uses in bartering, as 'If you can agree on this, I will agree on that.' In the discussions, the negotiators are trying to get a sense of how important an issue really is to the other side.

A most important part of the context for bargaining is the labour relations climate that exists between management and the union. Barring unusual situations, the past is a good predictor of what might happen in the future. If there have been good relationships in the past, they are likely to continue. However, if the union has been abrasive and aggressive in the past, its representatives are unlikely to change their behaviour unless management does something different. In the same way, the context might suggest certain issues will surface in the bargaining, such as the costs of benefits, pensions and performance.

CO 2: INTEGRATIVE OR INTEREST-BASED PROCESSES FOR RESOLVING DISPUTES

Collective bargaining is often grounded in the assumption that labour and management have fundamentally different and conflicting interests. As summarized in Table 12.1, this approach has been called positional bargaining or distributive bargaining. It is often assumed to be a 'zero-sum' negotiating

A RELEVANT POINT OF VIEW: UNION STRENGTH IS TRIGGERED BY A SENSE OF INJUSTICE

During the early days, before unions, if you were an unskilled, uneducated worker, you were on your own. There were no wage standards or labour codes to protect you from unfair labour practices. Employers could pay you what they wanted and could dismiss you if you refused to do what might be considered unsafe work. Employers were known for their 'yellow dog' contracts, where employees had to promise not to join unions. They also hired strike-breakers, or goons, and blacklisted those who joined the union. After craft unions began to form in the latter part of the nineteenth century, strikes were often used to achieve their objectives. Workers who crossed the picket line and continued to work were called 'scabs' and were shunned by other union members, who refused to work with them or even interact with them socially.

At the start of the nineteenth century, unions thought more about wages and working conditions than they did about anything else. In most cases, such as in the United Kingdom, Canada, Australia, New Zealand, the United States and various countries in Europe, unions did their job and, currently on average, full-time union workers are paid almost 20 per cent more per hour than non-union workers, and part-time workers make greater than 35 per cent more an hour than non-union counterparts. Union members are more likely to have scheduled work. They work more hours, which results in a higher overall wage. Women in unionized jobs are more likely to meet pay equity objectives. Their wages average 94 per cent of union full-time men's average. The wage gap for non-union female workers was 81 per cent of male counterparts.[15]

Although the union advantage can be seen in wages, the reason that people join unions goes beyond wages. In fact, on a strictly cost-benefit analysis, which includes income lost during strikes and jobs lost as a result of the contract, the overall benefits might not be very pronounced.[16]

In the end, union members are likely to support their union because it ensures their rights as workers and gives them a voice in the workplace. According to the executive director of a Confederation of Faculty Associations, unionizing is a way of addressing a power imbalance during bargaining by certifying, everything is on the bargaining table. That includes workloads, tenure and curriculum. Unionization is not about salaries. Rather, it's about equalizing this power and finding a way in which everybody moves forward. As opposed to this imbalance where management is just dictating things.'[17]

Managers who fail to treat workers with respect or involve them invite collective action. More than anything else, labour relationships are affected by employees' dissatisfaction, frustration and alienation with the job. Employees who are dissatisfied are more likely to demand union representation and express their disenchantment towards management or what is happening in an organization.[18]

Also, positive attitudes towards unions are linked to attitudes, predispositions or identification with the union movement and its goals. Beyond the employee's family, people who join a union are often influenced by their work group, and positive managerial attitudes towards unions are connected to higher unionization.[19] According to mobilization theory,[20] unionization is more likely to be triggered by a sense of injustice and breaches in what are assumed to be employee rights. These rights might reflect procedural issues, such as fair procedures for determining classroom size for teachers. Or they might reflect substantive issues such as fair pay increments.[21]

Given that public sector workers are more likely to be professional workers, adversarial tactics might be deemed to be less successful. However, this does not appear to be born out in practice as there seems to be more similarities than differences among various groups of workers as to their reasons for organizing.[22] A new pressure for unions in the public sector is reforms such as the NPM and other initiatives that are seeking to reduce the workforce by 'doing more with less'.[23]

Table 12.1 Interest-based versus Positional Approaches to Bargaining

Interest-based Bargaining	**Positional Bargaining**
Integrative in nature based on win–win assumptions where it is possible for each party to win or resolve the problem so that mutual interests are satisfied	Distributive in nature, based on the win–lose assumption that what one party wins, another will have to give up something
Treats conflict as finding a creative solution in a problem-solving process	Treats conflict as an adversarial process where a solution results from debate
Steps include clearly defining the issue and then identifying mutual interests in resolving it	Steps involve stating one's position, hearing rebuttals, compromise and agreement to respond to one party's best interest
Works to develop a joint relationship where each party has joint responsibility in problem-solving	Works to reinforce separate relationships in problem-solving
Uses skills for creative problem-solving and research	Uses skills of debate and negotiating
Focuses on the problem	Focuses on adversary
Associated with terms such as **mutual gains, integrative, principled negotiations, win–win approaches** and **non-zero sum negotiating**	Associated with terms such as **adversarial, distributive, win–lose approaches** and **zero sum negotiating**

situation; when one side gains a concession (wins), the other must make a concession (loses). Each party tries to gain an advantage and be viewed by their key stakeholders as the winner. Often described as a 'hard bargaining model', distributive bargaining is a competitive, position-based approach where negotiators are viewed as adversaries who reach agreement by conceding on some issues in an effort to reach a compromise.

Interest-based, or mutual gains, bargaining is based on co-operative, 'non-zero sum' assumptions. That is, both parties can be winners by working together and responding to mutually common interests. One party's success does not occur at the expense of the other party, as in positional or distributive bargaining.[24]

The history of integrative bargaining goes back to Mary Parker Follett, who talked about a win–win philosophy as an approach to conflict which focuses on developing integrative solutions rather than compromising to get an agreement.[25] Walter and McKersie linked it to the labour and management field as a co-operative, win–win, or mutual gains, approach based on the idea that there is no fixed pie, but that we use our resources in a creative way so that both parties can achieve their interests.[26]

Fisher and Ury's best-selling book *Getting to Yes*[27] used the term **interest-based bargaining** in describing how focusing on each party's interests can be a useful process for getting beyond strongly held positions. Interest-based bargaining has also been called principled negotiations, integrative bargaining, mutual gains bargaining or consensus bargaining[28] in which parties collaborate in finding a solution where both parties can win. Rather than having the negotiation process that begins when both labour and management overstate their real positions (followed by a series of offers and counterproposals), negotiators jointly engage in a problem-solving process focused on resolving the problems they need to address. The integrative process is generally defined by steps: (i) identifying the issue and trying to separate the personal issues from the real issues; (ii) identifying interests, not positions, and recognizing a working rule to set aside background feelings and ideological differences; (iii) recognizing mutual interests and developing a range of options where there can be mutual gain; and (iv) using objective criteria to assess and select the best alternative.

Separating the people from the problem. Integrative problem-solving begins by defining the problem or issue and identifying all the facts and feelings that describe the problem in objective terms. In distributive bargaining, negotiators are like poker players or personal adversaries who are trying to win as much as they can, using tactics such as deceptions, threats, bluffs, stalling and pressuring. The term *separating the people from the problem* is used to suggest that negotiators need to get beyond being adversaries and begin working together collaboratively to understand the issue and find an integrative solution to resolving it. This involves paying attention to the people side of negotiations and recognizing the importance of 'face-saving' solutions so that each party enjoys some level of self-esteem. It also involves using 'I' messages rather than 'you' messages, such as saying, 'I am frustrated' rather than 'You are dishonest'.

Focusing on common interests, not positions. In distributive bargaining, parties start by stating their more desired positions and then working towards agreement by giving small concessions. Underlying each position are interests tied to basic needs such as self-actualization, esteem, recognition, security or physiological needs. Interests can be unearthed by asking 'why?' questions or 'What are your needs here?' For example, 'Why do you need that?' or 'What are your interests or needs underlying your position?' For each issue, identify the interests each party has and then those interests that the parties have in common.

Taking positions in resolving conflict results in win–lose or lose–lose outcomes. The longer the negotiation continues, the more committed people become to their initial positions and the less psychologically willing they are to back down.

Identifying options for mutual gain. There are many conflicts where people may be willing to work together but are unable to see a creative solution. That is, they may be locked into seeing the resolution to the problem in traditional ways. Creating a novel resolution to a dispute often requires a shift in paradigms or an ability to restructure one's thinking in order to see the problem in a different light. The creative process might be enhanced by (i) separating the act of inventing options from the act of judging them (e.g. through brainstorming); (ii) broadening the range of options on the table rather than looking for a single answer (i.e. looking at the problem through the eyes of different experts, such as an accountant, an educator, a psychiatrist, etc.), and (iii) looking for mutual gain (i.e. by indicating how a particular solution will meet the interests of both parties and by forming it in a way that is easy to implement).

Using objective criteria. Often, the best way to judge a creative solution is to use objective criteria that are mutually agreed beforehand.

Interest-based problem-solving is more than a set of steps. It is based on the assumption that there is a need to shift from an adversarial, distributive-like approach to an integrative problem-solving approach. Thus, an initial goal is to create a climate for planning and problem-solving where ideas are encouraged and valued and for developing a culture where each party is jointly responsible for assessing the issues and interests and then looking for solutions. This can be initiated by answering the question 'What principles do we agree to in working together to take joint responsibility for solving our problems?' Fisher and Ury encourage negotiators to use a (best alternative to a negotiated agreement) BATNA or the standard against which the proposed agreement will be judged.

It is the standard that prevents a negotiator from accepting something which is unfavourable. The BATNA is more than a person's walk-away point or bottom line, as it is an alternative option which is real and valued. The BATNA is a safety net and increases the negotiator's leverage.

In many applications, management and union negotiations teams begin their work by attending a joint training session so they are both familiar with the approach and have practised it in simulated situations.[29] The core competencies are the knowledge, skills, attitudes and behaviours associated with effectively facilitating co-operation within the area of dispute resolution. Some of the common competencies for negotiators to enhance problem-solving include the following:

- Willingness and ability to listen actively and question effectively.
- Ability to work in a group and to work towards a consensus.
- Identifying issues and the facts and feelings defining the issues.
- Framing the issues for resolution or decision-making.
- Brainstorming and ability to think of solutions in different ways.
- Ability to assess the solutions using objective criteria.
- Awareness of one's negotiation style.

The ability to define the issues in an integrative problem-solving arena often relies on practice and the recognition that some issues might be inherently more difficult to work with. Team members might gain experience by beginning with issues that are easier to resolve in an integrative way. However, many issues brought forth in collective bargaining, such as wages and job security, are clearly distributive in nature. Although experience is crucial for applying interest-based negotiations in resolving these issues, it is also realistic to recognize that some of these issues might have to be settled with a little bit of compromise and debate.

Instead of beginning a collective bargaining session by defining initial positions, parties are encouraged to focus on issues that are important to resolve. Such issues might relate to pay, working conditions, safety and contract wording. But instead of presenting positions, the goal is to begin to jointly understand the issues and common interests in resolving it. Fisher and Ury urge us to get beyond the personalities and delve into defining the issues.

> Emotions typically become entangled with the objective merits of the problem. Taking positions just makes this worse because people's egos become identified in their positions. Hence, before working on the substantive problem, the 'people problem' should be disentangled from it and dealt with separately. Figuratively if not literally, the participants should come to see themselves as working side-by-side, attacking the problem, not each other. Hence, the first proposition: Separate the people from the problem.[30]

An interest-based bargaining process seeks to realize mutual interests of both parties and can be facilitated by questions like 'What are some of the facts and evidence describing this issue?' Facts include hard information and evidence on how people feel about the issue. Each party might have positions, suggested solutions or goals for what to do, but problem-solving is best served when people are jointly engaged in activities of mutual interest. In this sense, problem-solving is more likely to occur if initial discussions provide information on problems or issues to be discussed. Although both parties have clear positions or suggested solutions and know what they want to achieve, the best solutions are realized when we focus on mutual interests of both parties in achieving any goals. But underlying each position, each party will have interests. Interests might be seen as needs and can be surfaced by asking the question 'Why?' So, for example, beneath one party's position for changing the safety procedures, there are fundamental interests or needs such as safety or addressing employee fears. The working rule is to define the interests underlying each problem and then brainstorm possible solutions which respond to the mutual interests of both parties.

The general mutual interests of both parties include resolving the problems, improving performance, encouraging performance and, possibly, improving satisfaction. In developing a solution, put aside other individual interests for the moment and focus on mutual interests. This process does not discourage employees and managers from reviewing organizational goals, reasonable targets, requirements to be more competitive or changes necessary in order to better serve new customers. It simply suggests that the best way to achieve change is through realizing the mutual interests of the manager and employee.[31]

People who have used interest-based bargaining are more likely to report increased flexibility in the final contract language, work rules and pay arrangements, although they do not report any observable outcomes related to wage and benefits increases, wage reductions or health and safety issues. While proponents claim interest-based bargaining can be used for settling distributive issues relating to wages, benefits or threats of outsourcing, the approach has not changed the face of collective bargaining difficult issues. Proponents seem more willing to adopt the approach if there is a sense of urgency generated by failure of previous acrimonious negotiations or pressures in the industry generally. Interest-based bargaining is likely to gain further acceptance only if it can deliver on the promise of responding to mutual interests of both parties. However, one of the significant roadblocks is the perception that it is a soft approach and that better gains can be achieved through hard bargaining.[32]

> MANAGERIAL IMPLICATIONS: This chapter describes the nature of the collective bargaining process that can be approached in either an adversarial or integrative way. Although the collective bargaining process is potentially adversarial, HR can encourage managers to recognize that issues can be approached in an integrative way, and in doing so, this has the potential for developing a more positive labour relations climate.
>
> In focusing on the strategic theme 'managing effectively in negotiating and administering a collective agreement', it might be useful to focus on an objectives such as 'defining a negotiation plan' for working with the union while including initiatives that are inherently distributive and those that can be approached in an integrative way. The next chapter adds information on another relevant strategic objective: developing a positive labour relations climate.

BEFORE APPLYING, LET'S REVIEW

CO 1: Understand the dynamics of negotiating a collective bargaining agreement.

Despite its limitations and risks, negotiating a collective agreement is an indispensable process for realizing common interests between managers and employees on issues such as health and safety while compromising on conflicting interests such as the size of wage settlement. Negotiating a collective agreement is often seen as an adversarial, win–lose game like a game of poker. Being involved in collective bargaining means the employer is required to meet with employee representatives, receive and discuss proposals, bargain in good faith and make a reasonable effort to enter into a collective agreement. This means than employers and union negotiators must make a sincere effort to reach an agreement through reasonable compromise, and regularly meet and engage in a discussion with a willingness to reach an agreement.

CO 2: Implement integrative and interest-based processes in a negotiating environment.

Rather than a negotiation process that begins when both labour and management overstate their real positions (followed by a series of offers and counterproposals), the integrative process is generally defined by steps: (i) identifying the issue and trying to separate the personal issues from the real issues; (ii) identifying interests, not positions, and recognizing a working rule to separate the personality issues from the problems discussed, or setting aside background feelings and ideological differences; (iii) recognizing mutual interests and developing a range of options where there can be mutual gain; and (iv) using objective criteria to assess and select the best alternative.

DISCUSSION AND REVIEW QUESTIONS

1. Identify why people join a union. What are the advantages and disadvantages of unions for public sector managers?
2. Use the poker metaphor to guide you, from a management and union standpoint, in planning how you would negotiate a collective agreement. Change the metaphor and review the steps: If you were a union management team which openly shared all information, how could you use a win–win approach?
3. If you, as a manager, wanted to encourage your management and union to begin a process of interest-based bargaining, what steps would you take?
4. In working towards the theme 'managing effectively in negotiating and administering a collective agreement', develop a negotiating plan for management for the case at the end of this chapter. Identify your bargaining objectives, and respond to how each objective meets the needs of your client and the other party's client, and how its adds value from a financial, efficiency and learning and growth perspective. This is based on the assumption that objectives are more clearly stated when they respond to each of the perspectives of SHRM BSC.

Using Table 12.2, for each objective, define the tactics and possible counter positions that you might expect.

Table 12.2 Tactics for Developing a Negotiation Plan from Either a Management or Union Perspective

Objectives	Tactic	Expected Counter-position	Rebuttal
Objective 1	1. 2.		
Objective 2	1. 2.		
Objective 3	1. 2.		
Objective 4	1. 2.		
Objective 5	1. 2.		
Objective 6	1. 2.		
Objective 7	1. 2.		
Objective 8	1. 2.		
Objective 9	1. 2.		

CASE: NEGOTIATING A COLLECTIVE AGREEMENT WITH TEACHERS

You have agreed to meet to resume the negotiation of a collective agreement in response to mounting public pressure from parents (see the book's website for more background material).

It is 15 September, two weeks into the school year. Beginning in early February, the province's 40,000 teachers carried out an escalating series of job actions that ended when the teachers called a strike on 15 June, with two weeks left before the summer recess. There was little negotiation during the summer, as each side blamed the other for not wanting to come to the bargaining table. The province's 540,000 students waited, and parents vented their anger at both the government and the teachers. The premier has promised to pay parents £26.30 ($40) a day for child care services while the strike goes on, money that the teachers say could be used for settling the contract and for funding educational assistants.

Preparation and assignment

Divide the class into bargaining teams representing the Provincial Teachers' Federation (PTF) and the Public School Employers' Association (PSEA). Each team should prepare for the negotiation by constructing arguments for and against the positions on the table. The bargaining of the collective agreement should take place over one 3-hour time period (or various sessions depending on the class). During this time, teams will present the positions, caucus among themselves and then reconvene for as many face-to-face bargaining sessions as necessary.

All bargaining is to be limited to the issues identified. Assume that the negotiations are taking place in real time. Teams reaching agreement must submit the terms of their settlement to the instructor, and the only acceptable evidence that an agreement has been reached is the submission to the instructor of a memorandum of agreement signed by both parties. During the course of bargaining, the instructor will be available to all teams to respond to questions and to discuss bargaining strategy.

There are nine outstanding issues that require resolution for the union and nine for management. In beginning your discussion with your colleagues, you might first prioritize the issues before you start.

1. In preparation, each team should prepare a bargaining plan. Prioritize the nine outstanding issues with number 1 being the most important and number 9 being the least important.
2. The bargaining plan document should also contain: (i) your target goal on each issue and (ii) your resistance point. The **target goal** is what you want to achieve and would regard as a 'win'. The **resistance position** (or bottom line) is your absolute minimally acceptable position, where you might be willing to strike or lock out before you will concede anything further.
3. Each team should have enough space to meet separately without interruptions and should prepare their positions and possible counterproposals.
4. When management and union teams meet with each other at the bargaining table, a team spokesperson will present the team's position and the logic for its position. After the presentation, the opposing team might ask questions for clarification before caucusing and then returning to present counterproposals. There will likely be five or six such presentations.
5. The meetings at the bargaining table are carefully planned. There is some formality at the meeting, which is led by the team leaders. Each team will have a spokesperson for presenting the proposal and counterproposals. Other team members do not speak out of turn and are there to illustrate their support.

6. During the course of the bargaining and caucusing, the instructor will be available to all teams to respond to questions and consult on bargaining strategy or legal interpretations.
7. When teams reach an agreement, they must sign and submit the terms of their settlement to the instructor. The only acceptable evidence that an agreement has been reached is the submission to the instructor of a memorandum of agreement signed by both parties.

Issues

1. Terms of contract: Union agrees to a five-year contract, whereas management wants a seven-year contract.
2. Class size and composition: The union wants to establish a new Workload Fund, but management does not want to negotiate on this issue, pending the court appeal.
3. Education fund.
4. Grievance fund: Union wants £148.3 million ($225 million), and management suggests £69.1 million ($105 million).
5. Wage increase: Union wants a 10 per cent salary increase over five years, and management wants 7 per cent over five years.
6. Benefits: Union wants improvements to the extended health benefits plan; management has not added any details on proposals.
7. The union wants a signing bonus of £3,295 ($5,000); the employer is offering £792 ($1,200).
8. Union has asked for pregnancy/parental supplemental employment benefits, but management has not given a proposal.
9. Preparation time: The PTF has proposed increases to preparation time to 120 minutes a week this year, 150 minutes next year and 180 minutes in 2016.
10. The union wants the employer to pay premiums for the medical, dental and extended health care plans, and the employer wants to set up a joint committee to discuss this.
11. The employer wants changes to the performance appraisal system.

13 Developing a Positive Labour Relations Climate

Chapter Outline
- Chapter objectives (COs)   253
- A driving issue focusing managerial action: Working with the international framework of laws for developing a positive labour relations climate   253
- CO 1: Shaping and influencing a positive labour relations climate   255
- CO 2: Integrative or problem-solving approaches for resolving disputes   259
- CO 3: Procedural justice in maintaining a positive labour relations climate   262
- Before applying, let's review   267
- Discussion and review questions   267
- Case: Resolving issues of working with older nurses   269

CHAPTER OBJECTIVES (COs)

After reading this chapter, you will be able to implement the following objectives:

CO 1: Apply principles related to developing a positive labour relations climate.

CO 2: Review alternative models for improving the labour relations climate in the public sector.

CO 3: Identify various ways of providing procedural justice to improve the labour relations climate.

A DRIVING ISSUE FOCUSING MANAGERIAL ACTION: WORKING WITH THE INTERNATIONAL FRAMEWORK OF LAWS FOR DEVELOPING A POSITIVE LABOUR RELATIONS CLIMATE

The fundamentals of labour relations law in every country are connected to general international agreements or laws which require managers to take certain steps such as meeting and conferring with elected union representatives on decisions relating to working conditions, pay and hours of work. When union members are not satisfied with certain decisions, managers might face a grievance, or the union may take labour action, including the possibility of a strike.

Certain fundamental human rights, such as freedom of association and the right to free collective bargaining, are well established in a number of international documents originating in the United Nations and the International Labour Organization (ILO), which was established in 1919. Twenty-five years later, in 1944, on the eve of the end of World War II, the Declaration of Philadelphia redefined the purposes of the ILO and set out some guiding principles for its work: (i) labour is not a commodity; (ii) freedom of expression and of association are essential to sustained progress; (iii) poverty anywhere constitutes a danger to prosperity anywhere; and (iv) all human beings, irrespective of race, creed or sex, have the right to pursue both their material well-being and their spiritual development in conditions of freedom and dignity, of economic security and equal opportunity.

In stating that labour is not a commodity, the ILO indicated that labour is not like buying a car or other inanimate product that can be negotiated at higher and lower prices. As work is part of everyone's life and part of a person's dignity and self-worth, economic development should also focus on creation of jobs and improving working conditions so that people exist in freedom, safety and dignity. That is, economic development should not be undertaken for its own sake as it has other purposes.

The ILO's governing body has identified 189 conventions, 203 recommendations and six protocols, some of these dating back to 1919. Some of the more fundamental conventions cover topics such as freedom of association, the right to organize, abolition of forced labour, minimum age, child labour, equal remuneration and discrimination. In 1948, the ILO Convention No. 87 provided the right of all workers to form and join unions of their choice; it also laid out a series of guarantees for free operations without interference with the public authorities, as well as the right to engage in collective bargaining.[1] These principles are also covered in the ILO's Declaration of Fundamental Principles and Rights at Work (1998). This reaffirmed a commitment 'to respect, to promote and to realize in good faith' the rights of workers in eliminating discrimination in employment. Fundamental rights include freedom of association and the effective recognition of the right of collective bargaining, elimination of all forms of forced or compulsory labour, abolition of child labour and elimination of discrimination in respect of employment and occupation.[2]

A 1978 Convention (No. 151) promoted collective bargaining for public employees in addition to promoting ways that they could be involved in determining their conditions of employment. The convention also provides mechanisms for resolving disputes, including negotiation, mediation, conciliation and arbitration.

The ILO conventions represent an international consensus among government, employers and workers on how labour problems should be tackled. The standards provided by the ILO are written in such a way that countries can apply them directly in their national legal system. In several countries, the laws automatically apply when the ILO treaties are ratified. As such, the courts are able to apply international standards to national cases or to adapt accepted definitions such as those on forced labour, child labour and equality of opportunity and treatment regardless of sex, skin colour, ethnicity or beliefs, without regard to capabilities and skills.

STRATEGIC CONTEXT: In implementing the strategic objective 'managing effectively in negotiating and administering a collective agreement', the previous chapter encourages you to develop a negotiation plan to respond to management and employee needs. A strategic theme important to this chapter relates to 'developing a positive labour relations climate' that is illustrated in the positivity and the quality of relationships among employees, their unions and management. It reflects the workplace norms and attitudes perceived by management and employees (and their representatives). After defining this concept, this chapter encourages you to define objectives and initiatives to implement each perspective

> *of the SHRM BSC. For example, in beginning with the client or customer perspective, what might we do so that unions and managers feel that there is a positive labour relations climate? What objectives and initiatives would help us implement this?*

CO 1: SHAPING AND INFLUENCING A POSITIVE LABOUR RELATIONS CLIMATE

Working with the framework of international and national laws and standards described in the introductory perspective, the character or general tempo of the relationships that management and workers have in working together defines its **labour relations climate**. Labour relationships are usually positive if managers and employees work well together and if employees are generally satisfied. In certain contexts, some employees might be strongly identified with the union movement and committed to its activities. Positive labour relationships are more likely if managers recognize employee needs, give them input into policies that affect their jobs and treat them fairly. This is an environment where the union and its employees work closely with management in solving common problems. If employees feel they lack influence, they are more likely to be supportive of acrimonious union activities in solving problems or improving their well-being.[3]

In describing a labour relations climate, there is a long-standing labour-relations adage that 'bosses get the union they deserve'. If managers want to deal with a union that is trustworthy, capable of jointly solving problems and prepared to listen, they need to behave in the same way. On the other hand, if managers are more comfortable with unilateral decision-making and confrontation, they should not be surprised if the union and their employees will respond in kind.

This adage goes both ways, as there are examples where unions have been unreasonable in their demands and unnecessarily confrontational, resulting in adversarial managerial reactions.

Linking strategies on improved performance to a positive labour relations climate

Given the pressure to improve performance in public sector organizations, there has been increasing interest among practitioners and scholars on how management and organized labour might more effectively co-exist and work more collaboratively. Some commentators have suggested that unions might consider adopting new approaches to collective bargaining that were more integrative in encouraging unions and managers to focus on common interests[4] or be more concerned with helping management enhance productivity.[5]

The relationship between the union and management has long been seen as connected to improved performance. A harmonious climate has also been associated with enhanced employee relations outcomes, organizational commitment and union loyalty. In addition, a positive labour relations climate increases employee commitment and client/customer satisfaction, reduces absenteeism and turnover and supports a better quality of working life. As a result, there has been a growing interest in the ways in which unions and managers can work together.

There are reports of how union and management officials can be instrumental in facilitating such a climate by their action in setting the tone during contract negotiations and in employing a joint problem-solving rather than adversarial approach. Co-operative relationships have been linked to improved production and service delivery processes, reductions in overhead and waste and improved use of equipment.[6] The downside of co-operative arrangements is that the union can be accused of being co-opted or 'in bed' with management and to have given up its traditional role of standing up for the rights of workers and forcefully seeking to improve working conditions.

In seeking to change the labour relations climate, the Trades Union Congress (TUC) in the 1990s in the UK began a process of recruiting and training union organizers to promote more co-operative forms of industrial relations as a way to build support for unions in public and private sector organizations. In 2001, the TUC established the Partnership Institute to promote co-operative labour relations within six partnership principles: commitment to the success of the organization, recognition of legitimate interests, commitment to employment security, focus on the quality of working life, transparency and mutual gains.[7]

The argument for partnership strategies in providing a more positive labour relations environment is based on the assumption that unions can no longer engage in heavy-handed adversarial approaches to collective bargaining, nor can workers take wages and conditions for granted. Such partnerships ensure a more direct form of employee voice[8] and increase union membership and influence.[9] In the UK, about two-thirds of the partnership projects have been in public service, and there are indications that these projects are associated with positive outcomes such as greater employee participation; more union influence on policies relating to outsourcing, protection of terms and conditions over whom is transferred to privately funded initiatives and greater influence over pay, training and flexibility reforms initiated by government.[10]

Those who are critical of partnerships point out that they might have less than positive effects on union organizations and worker interests, as people who join the union do so because of a sense of injustice and an assertion of worker rights on issues related to pay, health and safety.[11] On the other hand, partnership in working closely with management might improve employment-related matters and provide better access to information, issues which might appeal to the people who join and support their union.

In studies conducted in a large governmental utility in Melbourne, Australia, researchers pointed out that there is unlikely to be a dual commitment to both the union and the employer. Guided by role theory, this research suggests that in a hostile climate, unions and managers have different and incompatible goals. As a result, there are possibly different factors associated with organization versus union commitment, whereas a co-operative labour relations climate might enhance commitment to an organization but might have adverse effects on union commitment.[12]

However, other research reports increased organizational commitment and union loyalty when there is a positive labour relations climate.[13] Higher commitment and performance seem to be more likely when management is seen as being instrumental in providing employees with valued outcomes. This might mean designing jobs with greater autonomy and variety, and more promotional opportunities. Dual allegiance might be more likely when management and union relations go beyond co-operation to involve designing and implementing initiatives and jobs which are of value to union members.[14]

Performance metrics linked to a positive labour relations climate

Over two decades ago, Ali Dastmalchian and colleagues began a series of studies in public and private organizations in Canada, Australia and the United Kingdom, defining the labour relations climate and its importance in contributing to productivity and performance.[15] The climate is described in terms of the degree of positivity and the quality of relationships among employees, their unions and management. It reflects 'the workplace norms and attitudes perceived by management and employees (and their representatives) about the industrial relations and the nature of union-management relationships in an organization'.[16] After several rounds of testing in various countries, the concept of labour relations climate was refined to include five general dimensions: fairness, union-management consultation, mutual regard, member support and union legitimacy.

- *Fairness:* Employees generally view their collective agreement and dealings with management as fair. There is an atmosphere of good faith surrounding negotiations; parties keep their word and generally feel that work conditions are fair and grievances are settled promptly.
- *Union-management consultation:* Parties make sincere efforts to solve common problems. Management seeks input from the union before initiating changes and exchanges information freely. Union and management illustrate concern for other parties, use joint management committees in implementing important changes in conditions, and collaborate to make the organization a better place to work.
- *Mutual regard:* There is a general sense of fairness associated with management dealings. Parties in the organization keep their word and express a degree of concern for the other party's point of view in the union-management relationship.
- *Member support:* There is general membership interest in the quality of union-management relationship and support of the union by its members.
- *Union legitimacy:* Unions are felt to make a positive contribution to the organization. There is respect for shop stewards in that they play a helpful role and encourage members to get involved with the union.[17]

There are several behaviours that illustrate how the five labour relations climate dimensions might be implemented to encourage a dual allegiance. But let's focus on one: union-management consultation. It suggests that parties such as the nurses, union members, hospital managers and government administrators would be better served if they worked to create an environment designed to solve common problems. There are many common problems, including safety and occupational health, where the parties could work on solutions in an integrative problem-solving, non-partisan manner. Other problems might include absenteeism and an environment that could be healthier, plus ways to encourage health and wellness among nurses.

In such an environment, management would seek input from the union and its members before initiating changes; freely exchange information; illustrate concern for other parties; and use joint management committees to help implement proposed changes to working conditions. It would be a co-operative effort to make the organization a better place to work and, in so doing, help nurses deliver first-rate health care.

Co-operative labour relations practices include anything from quality of work programmes to gain sharing, to union-management committees. When the union is seen to be working with management in solving problems, this partnership seems to result in higher attendance and lower absenteeism. Also, when the union is working to deliver programmes for work-life improvements, there are possible productivity gains. Practices for ensuring good relationships – such as those that encourage individuals to accept responsibility in developing a good union management relationship – are also associated with improved union loyalty and reduced absenteeism.[18]

The results of research in this area should not be overstated. However, they point managers in a direction that certain managerial, union and individually focused practices are important in improving the co-operative labour relations climate and productivity, quality of service and lower absenteeism. The interesting aspect of research in this area is that it nicely illustrates that a co-operative labour relations climate and improved performance can be enhanced by the behaviours of managers, union leaders and employees that focus on initiatives which are of value to members or which involve union members in achieving valued goals.[19]

A RELEVANT POINT OF VIEW: INDUSTRIAL DEMOCRACY AND ITS LEGACY IN IMPROVING LABOUR CLIMATE

A long-standing topic in labour relations is the varying degrees and forms of industrial democracy – or various forms of social partnership, democracy or participation – that should exist between managers and workers in governing the workplace. The term industrial democracy (ID) has varied meanings, depending on the country, from workers' direct participation in the work setting in worker councils and shop-floor programmes, to worker's participation and co-management at the management and board level, to worker's self-governance as semi-autonomous work groups. It is an organizational model for involving employees in managing and operating the workplace.[20]

Industrial democracy existed in different forms in different countries and is often connected with a political undertone in involving workers and unions in management. Some of the impetus came from the Yugoslavian model in the 1950s and 1960s, but other legendary ideas on industrial democracy grew out of an eight-year-long experimentation programme in Norway which was jointly sponsored by employer associations, unions and government. The first phase of the research illustrated the value of employee representation on the board of directors in improving decision-making, reducing resistance to change and reducing the chance of decisions that might be unpopular with employees. The second phase, involving four experiments, illustrated the positive impacts of organizational changes such as work groups with considerable autonomy, job changes to provide more enriching work experiences, bonus systems and adjustments of technologies within socio technical principles.[21] Some of the lead researchers in Norway were later involved in Australia. They helped stir the interest of the Labour Ministry and trade unions in South Australia, leading to an Industrial Democracy Unit advocating for worker participation.[22]

Swedish legislation in the 1970s increased worker representation in worker councils, on corporate boards, in joint labour-management health and safety committees and in other areas. Sweden also passed laws encouraging co-determination and the establishment of the Centre for Working Life. 'No country in the world produced more materials in English for the international audience and the impact worldwide since the 1970s has been huge.'[23] The Centre's research programme led to other legislation and information improving the work environment in areas such as occupational health, ergonomics, technology and work, and workplace democracy.[24]

In Germany, a legal structure still exists that allows for a system of dual representation where union and employers participate in collective bargaining at the organizational level. The German system of co-determination provides two channels of employee input as representatives on worker councils at the organizational level and as employee representatives on the board of directors. The primary goals of a co-determination system are to improve labour relations and engage workers in taking responsibility for joint management.[25]

Industrial democracy is very different today, as both governmental and industrial unions have declined in significance. For example, union membership has declined in the private sector in many developed countries, including heavily unionized countries like Sweden, Norway and Denmark. In addition, in the public sector, the political landscape changed under Thatcherism, Reaganism and the loss of labour governments in Sweden, Norway, New Zealand and Australia. Other changes were the fall of the Berlin Wall in 1989, the breakup of Yugoslavia and the creation of the European Union.[26] Moreover, there are few people who hold onto the long-standing belief that employees have the 'right' to be co-managers in an organization.

Within today's public sector efficiency mantra, workplace democracy ideals persist because of their importance for attracting union members in addition to responding to unemployment and organizational performance issues. The organizing model of involving employees in the management and operation of the workforce continues to be important for unions. Industrial democracy ideals are illustrated in tripartite negotiations between governments, unions and private organizations on wage and tax issues, public sector employment and job creation. Progressive unions, in Finland for example, have 'an interest in questions like renewing the work organizations, quality of working life, types of management, co-determination and the quality of products and service delivered'.[27] Other examples include worker co-operatives and self-managing teams.[28] In this chapter, we suggest this organizing model can be enhanced in a positive labour relations climate.

Although there has been increasing prominence of unions in the public sector in most countries, public sector industrial democracy initiatives are overshadowed by drives for private sector efficiency reform and concerns for job losses.[29] The previous chapter reviewed the traditional collective bargaining process that underlines most of the public sector negotiations. In this chapter, we review ideas pertaining to industrial democracy for increasing union involvement and membership voice in the management and operation of an organization.

CO 2: INTEGRATIVE OR PROBLEM-SOLVING APPROACHES FOR RESOLVING DISPUTES

Public sector labour relations has undergone a momentous change in the number of strikes and lockouts in the public sector over the last 10 years, down significantly from the early days when public sector unions first got the right to strike. Unions have had to confront New Public Management reforms focused on improved efficiencies, performance management, downsizing and contracting out, while salary increases and other worker improvements have been relatively modest. What has changed is the political background surrounding the labour relations climate where governments are more than willing to invoke legislation and other measures to temper free collective bargaining.[30]

The traditional strike and lockout model. The 'strike and lockout' model of labour relations was based on legislation giving basic rights to private sector employees to organize into trade unions, engage in collective bargaining for better terms and conditions at work and take collective action, including striking if necessary.[31] A **strike** is described as a cessation or refusal to work or a slowdown of work activities on the part of employees in an effort to restrict or limit output, whereas a lockout describes the closing of a place of employment or suspension of work by an employer to compel employees to agree to conditions of employment. Initially, public sector workers were forbidden to strike, as was the case when Franklin Roosevelt, during the Great Depression, likened a strike by public employees as an intention to obstruct the operations of government and said that such action was unthinkable by those who were at the same time sworn to support it. As late as 1959, George Meany, the head of the AFL-CIO, agreed that bargaining with a government is impossible.

When public sector unions first got the right to strike, strikes and lockouts were viewed as legitimate ways to compel or persuade 'the other side' to agree to terms and conditions of employment. In the US, public sector unionization began when New York's mayor Robert Wagner gave public employees the right to bargain collectively and the right to strike in 1958. President Kennedy, in looking to mobilize public sector workers as a way of finding new Democratic support, issued an executive order in 1962 giving federal workers the right to organize and to strike. Public service workers in most Western countries gained the right to strike in the decade between 1967 and 1977, but in the three decades that followed, there were many restrictions imposed on bargaining rights. Some of the legislation forced workers back to work, and laws imposed settlements or limited the issues for bargaining.[32] When hard bargaining did not work, governments resorted to legislation to require workers to return to work, or required conciliation or mediation before a legal work stoppage. Governments also passed laws to set wage restraints, prescribe wage guidelines, roll back wages and extend collective agreements. Other laws were used to weaken job security by allowing for contracting out or privatization, restraining the right to strike and suspending the access to interest arbitration or modifying criteria for appointing arbitrators.[33] In other cases, police and fire workers have been deemed to provide essential services, and though most jurisdictions give hospital workers and teachers the right to strike, others have considered their work to be essential services.[34] Another example of tinkering is the Wisconsin reform law that limits public sector collective bargaining to wages only (excluding benefits, work rules and pensions) and ends the right to strike.

This general strike and lockout model operates very differently in the public sector, where the cessation of the delivery of needed public services mostly impacts the public in different ways than in the private sector. The provision of public education, health care and a host of other critical public services have very little in common with the production of a particular brand of automobile or other product, where so many alternatives are so readily available in the event of a work stoppage.

Steering around the impact of the strike and lockout model. Strikes and lockouts have had adverse effects on the labour relations climate and the relationships of public organizations to their citizens. In trying to steer around the power of the strike and lockout model in affecting the public, legislators have designated certain services as essential during a strike. When certain employees or a percentage of employees are deemed as essential during a strike or are prohibited from striking, the power of the union to strike is preserved, and essential public services are guaranteed. The challenge in the designation model is to come to an agreement on what is considered essential, which can be resolved through bargaining or by referring the decision to an impartial industrial labour relations board. If too high a number of employees is designated as essential, the power of the strike option is limited; if too low a number is defined, then essential services are not delivered. Over the years, there seem to have been dramatic rises in the number of people or groups designated, as tribunals and labour relations boards tended to defer on the side of safety.[35]

Another mechanism for negotiating strikes and lockouts in the public sector is the use of an arbitration body, which serves like an independent commission in providing impartial recommendations. Such a body, which might be called a public interest disputes commission (PIDC), could go beyond the terms of reference of an arbitration and take into account the public interest and examine issues as an impartial institution, independent of government. In adjudicating disputes, it would have access to a range of established dispute-settlement techniques, such as fact finding and mediation. The commission would exist as an independent body and would report directly to a legislative body rather than a department head or minister of government. As an independent agency of the political legislature, the PIDC's recommendations for settlement of a dispute would be released simultaneously to both the elected representatives and the public as well as to the parties directly at odds.[36]

Third-party dispute settlement processes

Several third-party dispute settlement processes, such as mediation, interactive problem-solving, fact finding and interest arbitration, are available to practitioners to help settle disputes.

Mediation. Mediation is a process by which a neutral third party assists the two parties to come to an agreement on the issues that divide them. The mediator does not act as a judge to decide how the conflict should be resolved, but is involved in persuading, using open communication, looking for common ground and making suggestions. Mediators are involved by invitation of the two parties, and any advice they give is only suggestive. However, mediation has the advantage in that the mediator can encourage parties to make concessions and agreements beyond the bargaining table.

Mediation is attractive in that it addresses many of the weaknesses of conventional dispute resolution in allowing direct involvement of parties. It also produces results at a lower cost than courts or arbitrations. Public sector mediation relies on the skills of the mediator, and these reflect various backgrounds and operating styles, but most mediators have gained some experience in the collective bargaining arena.

One view of a mediator is that of a neutral third party or facilitator who arranges meetings, gathers information, tenders proposals and magically finds a middle ground. In the international arena, Henry Kissinger was recognized for his shuttle diplomacy in the 1973 Israeli-Arab war, where he feigned neutrality to the Arabs while secretly pushing his objectives. His approach illustrates a range of roles that go much beyond a neutral facilitator or catalyst and include (i) controlling communication between parties, (ii) persuading parties to make concessions, (iii) being a scapegoat to allow parties to express their anger to him or her rather than to each other, (iv) co-ordinating the exchange of concessions and masking the strengths of the other party, (v) manufacturing his or her own proposals and (vi) creating and maintaining the momentum of the negotiations. These roles are said to be similar to those public sector labour relations where the choices have substantial spillovers that go far beyond the immediate two parties. Thus, mediators in public sector disputes have to be responsive to the broader public interest and the effects of the decisions on other parties.[37]

Interactive problem-solving. As a form of third-party consultation, interactive problem-solving, or informal mediation, has been used to resolve conflicts in the international arena, such as in the Middle East, Cyprus, Rhodesia, Sri Lanka and Northern Ireland.[38] The process emphasizes analytical dialogue and joint problem-solving and is designed to go deeper in researching the problems or issues driving the conflict. This involves exploration of underlying motivations, needs, values and fears.

Interactive problem-solving begins with a review of political needs of the different parties and a discussion of the constraints they face. The purpose is to help parties see the conflict as a problem that needs to be resolved jointly, rather than through back and forth debates. This involves improving the openness of communication, clarifying expectations, seeking to define mutual motivations and, ultimately, building a stronger working relationship.

Fact finding. This is another neutral third-party mechanism commonly used in the public sector to resolve an impasse. In this process, each party submits whatever information it thinks is relevant to the resolution of the dispute. The neutral fact finder provides a report that might provide pressure to induce the parties to resolve the dispute in a certain way. The term **fact finder** is probably a misnomer as fact finders often have statutory authority and render a public recommendation.

Interest arbitration. In meeting the public interest, interest arbitration has often been considered and adapted in various ways. Mediation is used in helping parties reach their own agreement; in an arbitration decision, a binding settlement is based on the positions of each party and the facts surrounding the case. Arbitration usually dictates a settlement, whereas fact finding recommends a settlement.

Mainly used in the public sector, the arbitration process has been seen to protect the public interest in that it results in fewer strikes. In interest arbitration, both sides agree on an independent, neutral adjudicator to resolve the dispute by objectively considering the positions of both the employer and the union. Arbitrators also consider contract provisions for employees doing similar work, impact on service and the employer's ability to pay. However, governments have not readily agreed to use arbitrators, partially because of a fear that arbitrated settlements will be higher than what might be negotiated at the bargaining table, something which is particularly concerning during times of retrenchment when there are desires to downsize and/or reduce spending. Arbitrations often take much longer – in some jurisdictions, three times as long as negotiation in the private sector and twice as long as in the public sector. There are cases where a highly constrained arbitration system actually exacerbates conflict and inhibits genuine bargaining and negotiation on issues that really need to be worked through, such as class size and composition in schools.[39]

The strengths and weaknesses of these processes might be assessed not only in relation to their ability to resolve disputes effectively but also in terms of maintaining a positive labour relations climate. In reviewing essential services disputes, researchers have used criteria such as the ability to ensure (i) the provision of essential services such as health and education, (ii) the integrity of the collective bargaining so that there are no delays in the settlement, (iii) agreements that are peaceful and voluntary rather than forced through legislation and (iv) agreements that are acceptable for employers, employees and the public.[40] Stacked up against these criteria, no process is totally effective, although the designation of an essential services model might provide the best overall results. Researchers point out that although a disputes commission model might seem like a logical alternative, a political reality suggests that governments are unlikely to grant a commission independence to insulate public sector bargaining from political interference. 'Major revisions to the status quo appear unlikely.'[41]

Many dispute resolution scholars favour the use of mediation as a way of saving governments money by resolving disputes rather than having them enter the court system. The cost-effectiveness of mediation has been assessed in various areas related to civil cases, family mediation, motor vehicle accident claims, workplace conflict and labour relations. Estimates in the US say that workplace mediation can save approximately £236.6 billion ($359 billion) a year in avoiding the losses from lost productivity, absenteeism, employee turnover and failed projects.[42] In a study of 449 disputes (i.e. contract, personal injury, construction and property damage disputes) by four major service providers in the US, mediation was able to settle 78 per cent of the cases, took less time and was judged to be a highly satisfactory process. The average cost was £1,818 ($2,759), compared to arbitration average of £7,776 ($11,800). In addition to cost, mediation participants are more satisfied with the process, outcomes and the effect on the relationships than with the people involved in an arbitration case. There did not appear to be any advantage between an interest-based and an advisory opinion type of mediation process, although settlements were more likely when the two types of processes were combined.[43] For managers negotiating in the public arena, one key benefit of a mediation process is that it has the potential to contribute to developing a positive labour climate.

CO 3: PROCEDURAL JUSTICE IN MAINTAINING A POSITIVE LABOUR RELATIONS CLIMATE

The collective agreement is a guiding framework for managing employees, and it exists to support the organization in achieving its strategic objectives as well as in defining the responsibilities of employees to work towards these objectives.

Occasionally, during the life of a collective agreement, disputes arise about the interpretation of a clause, or there might be a potential violation of management's responsibility, such as conditions of work that might be considered unsafe. Employee complaints often indicate dissatisfaction and can cause problems between employees and management. They affect the general tone of the labour relations climate and the way that the organization manages its employees in assuring their rights and due process.

'Just' procedures and systems provide the foundation for resolving conflicts and maintaining a positive labour relations climate. Procedures are fair when they are consistent over time, free from bias, based on accurate information, representative of those concerned and correctable, and when they illustrate an ethical standard. Conflict or disagreements relating to **procedural injustices** describe an employee's perception of the fairness of procedures – whether they are perceived to be biased or as not recognizing any prevailing ethical and moral codes.[44] When just procedures exist, employees are more likely to be supportive of organizational planning processes, trusting of their leaders and committed to their employers.[45]

Fairness is a driving criterion for judging procedural justice in public organizations, and its importance is underlined in many decisions, for example those relating to merit pay, promotion and performance appraisal. 'Was the decision fair?' This question, important in all organizations, is nested in the DNA of public organizations that are governed by high ethical standards and the norms and values they profess for society relating to honesty, equality and equity.[46] The question is even more important in conducting the administration of the collective agreements that guide most public organizations. Taking steps to improve procedural justice and fairness is linked to (i) higher levels of trust and commitment; (ii) improved job performance, where employees more effectively discharge their job duties; (iii) organizational citizenship behaviour where employees go beyond the call of duty; and (iv) greater client/customer loyalty.[47]

Fair treatment is linked to reduced stress[48] and increased health. The stress experienced from perceptions of unfair treatment is contagious; an individual's perception of fairness often affects others, as they express their concerns to fellow employees and to their union. Special health problems as a result of stress include insomnia, coronary heart disease and mental well-being.[49] When procedural justice does not exist, employees are more likely to pursue litigation in trying to resolve disputes.

Components of procedural justice also include interpersonal and informational justice. **Interpersonal justice** describes the quality of the interpersonal treatment among employees and between employees and their supervisor. A positive interpersonal climate is one which is free from public harassment and humiliation, criticism and abusive action by supervisors and co-workers. It might be described by a positive leader–member exchange and typically illustrates three factors: respect, trust and obligation. **Respect** is the mutual respect that one person has for the capabilities of other people and is not an indication of personal friendship or liking. **Trust** is defined by ability, benevolence and integrity. **Obligation** is the 'expectation that interacting obligation will grow over time as career-oriented social exchanges blossom into a partnership'.[50] When there is a positive relationship, the supervisor is more willing to attend and respond to employee needs and provide needed resources. Employees tend to reciprocate.[51]

Interpersonal justice is provided where there are positive co-worker relations, as illustrated in environments where there is social support and enjoyment of one's work and commitment to an organization. A supportive environment can aid in helping a person feel appreciated and cared for by co-workers and can have a positive effect on one's work attitude and mental health.

Informational justice describes a person's feeling about the information supplied and whether it is truthful, accurate and adequate when things don't go well, as when a person is receiving feedback on why he or she did not get promoted.

The best way to think about interpersonal and informational justice is to think about your experiences and how you felt when decisions were made concerning a change. Were the procedures fair? How did supervisors and fellow employees react? Did you have the opportunity to voice your concerns and change the situation? The components of a procedurally just system might be used as criteria to assess the health of the labour relations climate, just as much as they represent a foundation upon which a healthy climate might depend.

Using voice systems to improve procedural justice

One very practical set of suggestions for ensuring procedural justice is to provide employees with a voice so they can communicate and seek ways to resolve the issues that affect them. The procedural justice literature suggests that 'voice' is a procedural mechanism for attaining justice. The term **voice** is generally used to describe how employees are able and willing to have a say in work activities and in the way they work.[52] Organizations might introduce voice systems as a way to increase employee perceptions of fairness.[53] The following are examples of voice systems.

- *Client engagement* – focus groups, citizen survey, public forums, task forces and commissions of inquiry.
- *Voice for the organization* – surveys of employees' needs and attitudes; focus groups, strategic planning workshops, suggestion systems, complaint procedures allowing employees a formal, internal review of decisions.
- *Voice to managers and supervisors* – employee meetings with managers and supervisors: open-door policies by which employees can approach a supervisor or manager on problems or suggestions; participative committees that encourage employee involvement in decision-making; senior management or supervisor check-in or on-site visits.
- *Voice within work groups* – employees in self-directed teams or semi-autonomous groups who manage schedules and monitor attendance, health and safety issues and work processes; employees working in problem-solving groups, workforce meetings, team briefings.
- *Voice in union-management relations* – employee involvement on worker councils and on board of directors, joint committees on safety and health, collective bargaining, grievance and arbitration procedures.

The existence of these practices is no guarantee that they will provide the benefit of employees believing and having confidence in being heard or being treated fairly. Employees must have a degree of confidence in these mechanisms and be willing and able to use them. A person's perception of voice is moderated by their degree of engagement and whether they (i) communicate and exchange their views, (ii) involve themselves in solving problems, (iii) represent themselves as a group, (iv) feel they can express themselves to management in an open and supportive manner and (v) believe they have a 'say' on the issues and that change will result.[54]

Voice systems can have positive effects in relation to job satisfaction and job attitudes and encourage greater commitment and attachment to the organization and its values. As such, commitment is illustrated in an employee's beliefs and acceptance of the organization and its values and their willingness to exert effort to be a positive organizational member.[55] In addition, when people feel detached from their organization, they are less willing to improve their organization and engage in a positive manner. Employees who are more satisfied with the supervision, work and promotional opportunities, when confronted with adverse conditions, are more likely to voice their concerns informally in a considerate way. Those that are dissatisfied will more likely voice their concern informally in an aggressive and inconsiderate way.[56]

Researchers draw a distinction between prosocial and justice-centred voice. Although prosocial voice can benefit an organization in improving its processes, justice-centred voice often stems from mistreatment or perceived inequities. Justice-focused voice calls attention to a questionable decision. **Prosocial voice** is seen as a form of citizen behaviour and allows individuals to show their value to their managers is more likely to be linked to job satisfaction and commitment.[57]

In several instances, justice-centred and prosocial voice are linked. As such, some justice-centred grievances on performance management might be motivated to improve the way performance appraisals are conducted in the future. On the other hand, when prosocial voice systems are working well, there might be less need for justice-centred voice systems.

Using procedural justice procedures to guard employee rights

Beyond improving the positivity of the general labour relations climate, an organization's grievance and arbitration procedures are a check on the procedural justice systems in the workplace. Although management generally has the right to impose reasonable and fair rules for conducting business and for disciplining employees, employees have the right to challenge these decisions. Management rights are frequently challenged in grievances and in the courts, and individual managers can be held liable when hirings, promotions and dismissals have not been compliant with non-discriminatory practices.

The grievance. Conflicts arise in even the most progressive workplaces. Even if they don't arise, the procedures for resolving conflicts provide guidelines just in case a person feels unfairly treated, harassed, overlooked in promotion or wrongfully evaluated in a performance review. Employee complaints might indicate dissatisfaction, but a **grievance** is a written complaint against action or inactions relating to terms and conditions of employment as part of the collective bargaining process. For many, grievances are the day-to-day operations of the collective agreement. There are various types of grievance. **Individual grievances** concern the complaint of one individual, whereas **group grievances** are concerns of the work team or group. That is, complaints about a supervisor's lack of fairness in the performance review process might be either an individual or group grievance. A **policy grievance** can be filed against management because of a misapplication or misinterpretation of the collective agreement on a range of issues like scheduling or overtime payments. The number of complaints and grievances in any organization is a gauge of the labour relations climate and a measure of potential problems and employee concerns. Complaints provide an indication of the need for change and additions to the collective agreement.

In the first step, the employee and the union representative meet to review the issue and the facts underlying it and to determine if the employee's rights have been violated and if a grievance exists. They then meet with the supervisor to try to resolve the conflict informally before filing a grievance. Even after the grievance is filed, the union representative will meet with the supervisor in trying to find a solution in order to put the grievance aside. Underlying this step is the belief that a grievance should be resolved closest to where the dispute originates, under the assumption that communication will correct misunderstandings. If the disagreement cannot be resolved informally within a set time period (possibly 30 days), it goes to step 2.

In step 2, the employee and the union representative meet with the supervisor's manager and try to resolve the grievance. Before this meeting, the union representative works with the employee to discuss how the issue or problem faced has breached the labour code or collective agreement. The union will also be aware of arbitration law and how arbitrators have ruled on similar cases. For example, in cases of unsatisfactory performance reviews, the union might try to focus the grievance around issues such as fairness of procedures, potential biases in the methods, or the way they were applied because of recent arbitrator's decisions in those areas. Managers usually like to support their supervisor's decisions and many grievances move to the next step.

The grievance is usually out of the employee's hands during step 3 as the union is trying to bargain with HR, the managers and the supervisor in finding a solution. Typically, the union and the managers are trying to avoid moving to arbitration as both the union and the organization will have to hire lawyers and share the costs of paying for an arbitrator. However, in some cases, the union might want to make a point and push for the arbitration as they have done on issues assuring workplace equity and eliminating biases in selection and job evaluation. Often, the grievances are resolved through negotiations where management might try to find a way to settle the dispute without stepping on the manager. Neither party wants to admit it is wrong, but they are both looking for a solution. For example, in one case of an unsatisfactory performance appraisal, the employee moved to another department and received a satisfactory performance assessment. If the grievance is not solved, it goes to arbitration.

Arbitration. The arbitration process comes into effect when informal bargaining to settle the grievance has not been effective, and the steps to the grievance process have been systematically followed without satisfaction. Although arbitration panels are sometimes used, the usual practice is to use a single ad hoc arbitrator who has been mutually agreed to by both parties.

The principal responsibilities of the arbitrator are to ensure a fair hearing. To do this, arbitrators work within rules where all parties (i) must receive notice of time and place of the hearing and the opportunity to attend; (ii) are allowed to introduce evidence, present witnesses, and have the opportunity to cross-examine witnesses; (iii) can make concluding arguments to summarize the thrust of their evidence; and (iv) can file a written, post-hearing brief. In the arbitration process, witnesses are not permitted in the hearing until they are called, under the assumption that their views will likely be influenced by others' testimony.[58]

When the arbitration begins, the side bearing the burden of proof (the griever) makes the opening statement and sets forth the issue in dispute, the facts and what the party expects from the arbitrator. The opposing party is also allowed an opening statement. The exception is for cases involving discipline or discharge where the employer and the griever are only required to establish that there is a collective agreement and that the person was employed and then disciplined or discharged. After this, the burden of proof shifts to the employer. After the employer has made the prima facie case of just cause, the burden of proof moves to the employee, who has the responsibility of presenting a defence.

Taking the dispute before an arbitrator is expensive as the two parties share the costs of the proceedings, which include the arbitrator's fees, fees for hotel rooms where the arbitration is held and other costs such as expenses to bring in witnesses. Some organizations have experimented with **expedited arbitration** as a way of reducing the time and costs of the traditional arbitration process. If parties choose this option, a grievance commissioner is appointed and proceeds in an informal way. The commissioner works within a two-step process which calls for (i) submission of written information on the nature of the grievance and evidence to support the case and (ii) a hearing solely to clarify facts. Usually, witnesses are not called, and the commissioner renders a decision within seven days of the hearing.[59]

> MANAGERIAL IMPLICATIONS: Given this potentially adversarial process, HR will be called upon by management to interpret the collective agreement and to assist management in dealing with employees' issues and possible grievances. Underlying the collective bargaining process is the labour relations climate and the general relationship between managers and their employees and union leaders.
>
> This chapter provides information for developing initiatives for implementing the strategic objective 'developing a positive labour relations climate'. A key to implementing this objective is to begin with the customer or client perspective and ask what we do so that unions and managers feel that there is a positive labour relations climate. What objectives and initiatives would help us implement this? The next steps involve asking similar questions relating to other perspectives of the SHRM BSC such as these: What might we do so that managers and union people feel that we are effective and efficient in responding to union and management issues in encouraging positive labour relations? What might we do to enhance the learning and growth perspective in encouraging motivation and innovation to developing a positive labour relations climate? Finally, what might we do to illustrate the financial value of a positive labour relations climate to our managers and union members?

BEFORE APPLYING, LET'S REVIEW

CO 1: Apply principles related to developing a positive labour relations climate.

Positive labour relationships are more likely if there is a positive labour relations climate where the union and its employees work closely with management in solving common problems. The labour relations climate can be defined by five dimensions: fairness, union-management consultation, mutual regard, member support and union legitimacy. Co-operative labour relations practices include anything from quality of work life programmes, gain sharing and union–management committees. When the union is seen to be working with management in solving problems, this partnership seems to result in higher attendance and lower absenteeism.

CO 2: Review alternative models for improving the labour relations climate.

The framework for negotiating a collective agreement in the public arena is guided by different models: the strike and lockout model and various third-party interventions (fact finding, mediation, arbitration, public disputes commission) and designation of essential services. The general strike and lockout model operates very differently in the public sector, where the cessation of the delivery of needed public services mostly impacts the public in different ways than in the private sector. No model is totally effective, although the designation model might provide the best overall results. The disputes commission model shows promise but might be unlikely within a political reality where governments are unlikely to grant a commission independence to insulate public sector bargaining from political interferences.

CO 3: Identify various ways of providing procedural justice to improve the labour relations climate.

Occasionally during the life of a collective agreement, disputes arise about the interpretation of a clause, or there might be a potential violation of management's responsibility, such as conditions of work that might be considered unsafe. One very practical set of suggestions for ensuring procedural justice is to provide employees with a voice so they communicate and seek ways to resolve the issues that affect them. Researchers draw a distinction between a prosocial and a justice-centred voice. Although a prosocial voice can benefit an organization in improving its processes, a justice-centred voice often stems from mistreatment or perceived inequities. A justice-focused voice calls attention to a questionable decision. When prosocial voice systems are working well, there may be less need for justice-centred voice systems.

DISCUSSION AND REVIEW QUESTIONS

1. Link to the ILO's Declaration of Fundamental Principles and Rights at Work (1998) on the Internet. Identify the most important fundamental rights of workers.
2. Review the strengths and weaknesses of strike, essential service, arbitration and commission models. What are the criteria for assessing the appropriateness of these models?
3. Discuss the difference between procedural, distributive and interpersonal justice. How can you develop voice systems for responding to prosocial and procedural justice issues?
4. In establishing initiatives for developing and implementing a positive labour relations climate, managers have to discuss and debate certain policy questions. You are asked to play the role of an executive committee and define a set of HR labour relations guidelines for your organization. Following is a list of questions that you might use in defining your approach to labour relations:

- How do we work with the union in developing a positive labour relations climate? In what committees or processes in HR do you want union involvement? Consider processes such as job analysis and design, recruitment and selection, performance management, employment equity, training and career development, occupational health and safety, strategic planning, compensation and incentives. What level of involvement would you advise?
- In many labour relations negotiations, union and management agree to a 'gag' rule, where they will not bargain in public. However, as managers, you might want to communicate directly to employees rather than waiting for everything to get resolved before communicating. What is your advice on this?
- Employee voice is considered to be an important element in communicating to employees. How would you implement this?
- In implementing a strategic objective for 'developing a positive labour relations climate', what initiatives are important to do this? What are key measures or markers?
- What is our policy for training? Do we train everyone for all potential jobs or focus our training on employees whom we regard as having higher potential?

Answers to these and other questions provide a set of working assumptions underlying how you will develop a positive labour relations climate.

5. The concept of positive labour relations climate was refined to include five general dimensions: fairness, union–management consultation, mutual regard, member support and union legitimacy. Use the strategy map in Figure 13.1 to summarize objectives within each of the perspectives on the SHRM BSC for the strategic theme 'developing a positive labour relationship with the union'.

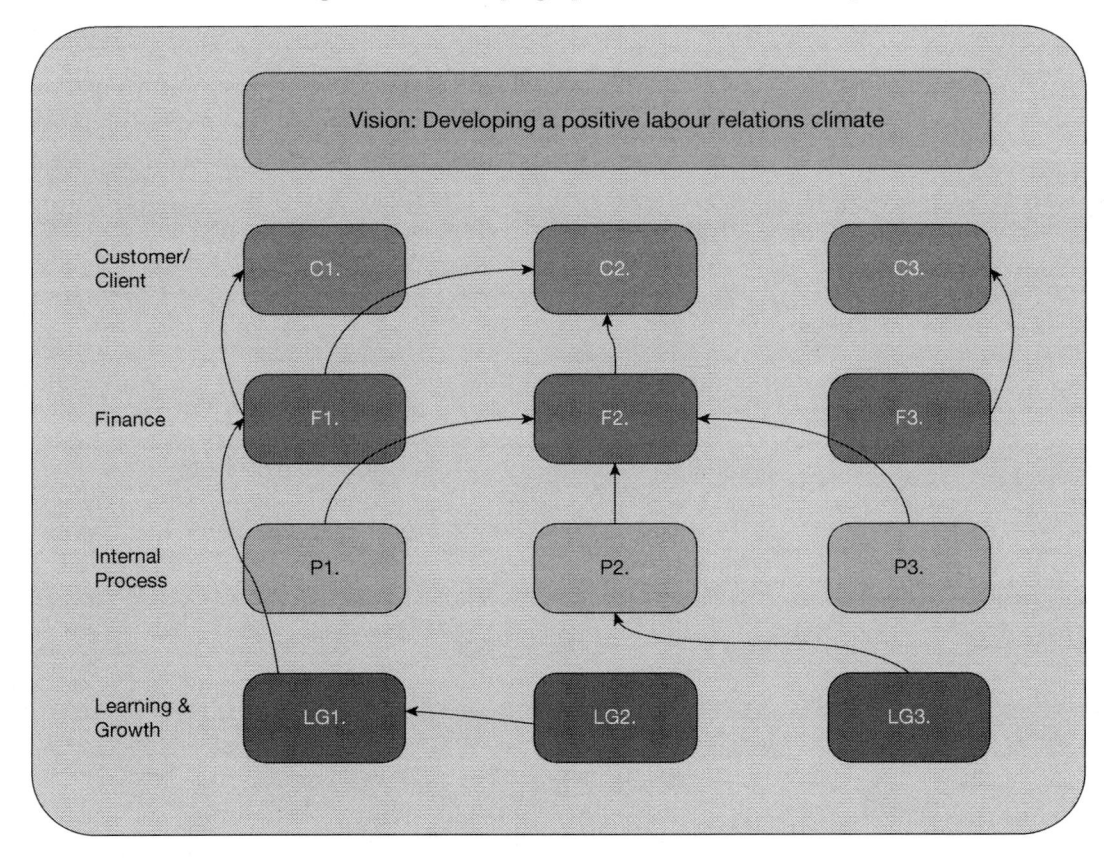

Figure 13.1 Strategy map for developing a positive labour relations climate.

CASE: RESOLVING ISSUES OF WORKING WITH OLDER NURSES

During the last 10 years at Waikato County Hospital in Hamilton, New Zealand, there has been an increased need for paediatric nurses, resulting from community growth and more births. Just five years ago, human rights legislation changed the mandatory retirement rules, and people no longer have to retire at the age of 65. Therefore, during the past 10 years many new people have been hired, and now about 40 new nurses work in the Paediatrics Ward, doubling its size. As a result, there are approximately 10 nurses over 65 years old and 30 between the ages of 55 and 65. The rest of the nurses are between the ages of 25 and 40. Thus, there is a fairly large group of old-timers and newcomers. The two groups do not get along very well. The younger group often refers to the old-timers as 'old biddies', 'old maids' and 'sour pusses', and use names such as 'Nurse Ratched' and 'Major Houlihan', whereas the old group refers to the younger group as 'jazz kids', 'dumb bunnies', 'the entitled generation' and 'airheads'. The older nurses say that the younger generation of mothers are 'too posh to push' and would rather have a caesarean birth. The hospital administration has recognized the problem, and it is common for them to think in stereotypical terms of 'old' and 'young' people.

Ms Heather Campbell, from Human Resources, has been responsible for all the hiring in the last 15 years and is generally responsible for all HR activities, such as transfers, changes in pay rates, etc. She is in a staff position and relates to the Paediatrics Ward and two other nursing units in the hospital.

Ms Diana Fawkes is the head nurse in charge of Paediatrics. There are four nurse supervisors who report to her, and her position in the organization is comparable to Ms Campbell's. Because both of these women report to different directors, neither has authority over the other.

Ms Campbell has asked Ms Fawkes to see her to discuss a problem in connection with the 'old people'. Ms Fawkes is about to enter Campbell's office.

Before beginning the role play, Ms Campbell might tell the instructor what she wishes to accomplish and should refer to the material on the book's website.

Task. The purpose of this case is to illustrate how persons with different attitudes may disagree even when they both have the same facts. The role playing may be terminated when it has become apparent that the two people have resolved the issue or have agreed that nothing will be done. The instructor may check with you to determine whether your pair of role players has ceased introducing additional factual material.

Ms Campbell's task is to try to encourage Ms Fawkes to be more responsive to the needs of older workers and to take steps to build a better team in her department. Ms Campbell has read about the integrative negotiation conflict resolution process and is attempting to use it in her discussion with Ms Fawkes.

Ms Fawkes's task is to play the role of a person who generally is not receptive to older workers.

In carrying out this task, Ms Campbell might consider a mediation process where she acts as a facilitator and assists in developing an agreement between the parties. The mediator's job is to facilitate in defining the issues, opening communication, looking for common ground and making suggestions. She might consider using the interest-based process, which is generally described in the previous chapter and outlined on the book's website.

Part V: Compensating and Rewarding People

The chapters in Part V review four components of a compensation system: fixed salaries, pensions, benefits and incentives. Chapter 14 illustrates how to design and implement a point job evaluation system that meets pay equity objectives, and Chapter 15 reviews how the financial crisis put pressure on public organizations to review their pension and benefits plans to improve their sustainability. In responding to pressure to reform governmental services, Chapter 16 reviews the relevance of pay for performance and recognition ideas for public sector organizations.

14 Designing Compensation Systems to Respond to Equity Requirements

> **Chapter Outline**
> - Chapter objectives (COs) 273
> - A driving issue focusing managerial action: Knowing what it is about pay that is a satisfier 273
> - CO 1: Using equity objectives to design a compensation system 275
> - CO 2: Traditional approaches for evaluating jobs 277
> - CO 3: Designing and applying a point job evaluation approach 279
> - Before applying, let's review 286
> - Discussion and review questions 286
> - Case: Resolving equity issues with a point evaluation plan 287

CHAPTER OBJECTIVES (COs)

After reading this chapter, you will be able to implement the following objectives:

CO 1: Define how inequities in women's versus men's pay helped shape the design of a fairer way to evaluate jobs.

CO 2: Illustrate the advantages and disadvantages of four different job evaluation approaches – ranking, job classification, factor comparison and the point system.

CO 3: Demonstrate how to design and implement a point job evaluation system that meets pay equity objectives.

A DRIVING ISSUE FOCUSING MANAGERIAL ACTION: KNOWING WHAT IT IS ABOUT PAY THAT IS A SATISFIER

Employee compensation is the most costly budgetary item in any organization and can be as high as 60 per cent of total costs in some manufacturing organizations and much higher (70 to 80 per cent) in service organizations. When researchers ask people to rate the importance of pay in comparison to other factors, pay often rates lower than other motivators.[1] In general polls, it has been ranked as low as 14th and is often ranked lower than learning and development, creativity, corporate culture. However, there are other studies and anecdotal evidence supporting the proposition that pay is a very important satisfier for people.[2]

Why are there so many discrepancies in our research on pay? One explanation is 'social desirability' or the tendency to say that certain motivators (e.g. achievement and career) are more important and that pay is not really that important. Social desirability occurs when people are not open or when they do not have the self-insight to reflect on their preferences.[3] There might be social norms that view the pursuit of money as a less honourable source of motivation than interesting work or contributing to one's organization or society.[4]

What is it about pay that makes it a motivator?

Even though employees say that other factors – such as challenging work, using one's skills and abilities, relationships with supervisor and meeting career goals – are more important motivators, pay remains a key driver because it is seen as a form of recognition for our place in life. This might explain why 25 per cent of employees say they would quit their present jobs for a 10 per cent pay increase and more than 55 per cent would depart for income of 20 per cent more or greater.[5]

People are often motivated to increase their pay. They may see it as a marker of their well-being. Depending on those who respond, or the economic conditions they face, money can be ranked much higher than other factors. In a meta-analysis of various scientific studies on the importance of pay, people tended to place it around fifth (ranging from second to eighth) in comparison with other motivators such as interesting work, career opportunities, appreciation, company, management, co-workers and job security.[6]

Wanting higher pay and the desire to be the highest paid is a strong motivator in sports and business. **Pay satisfaction** is an attitude about one's pay compared with what others are paid.[7] Because a person's attitudes are linked to behaviours, pay dissatisfaction can lead to overall job dissatisfaction and the desire to leave an organization.[8] More pay and increases in pay lead to even higher expectations about the future, as we tend to be happier when we keep improving, but not when we do not improve as much as we learn to expect.[9]

For some people, the size of the pay cheque is important. However, what people find satisfying depends on who they are (their age and background, for example) and the stage in their careers, among many other factors. This partially explains why pay satisfaction for one person might be linked to the amount of money received, whereas others see the benefits package or the pension as important.

Pay satisfaction might be defined by four factors:[10]

1. *Pay level:* Satisfaction with take-home pay and overall level of pay.
2. *Benefits:* Satisfaction with the number and value of the benefits received, the total benefits package, and the contributions made by the organization.
3. *Raises:* Satisfaction with recent raise and raises received in the past, influence of supervisor in the decision, and how the raises are determined.
4. *Structure and administration:* Satisfaction with the organization's pay structure and its fairness, and information given about pay issues, pay of other jobs, the consistency of pay policies, differences in pay among jobs and the administration of pay.

Employees also attach a fair degree of importance to the raises they receive, possibly because this is a form of recognition for their work from supervisors. A raise or a bonus might be a marker of success or a form of recognition.

STRATEGIC CONTEXT: An employee's total compensation has four components: fixed salaries, pensions, benefits and incentives. The compensation mix is the relative proportion of compensation and varies from organization to organization. The direct forms of compensation include the fixed salaries *a person receives as an hourly, weekly or monthly wage and any pay incentives designed to reward employees for good performance. An employee's pensions and benefits, often called indirect forms of compensation, include pension benefits, health care and dental plans and paid holidays. Most employees undervalue these indirect forms of compensation or benefits, which can cost up to 30 per cent of the total compensation.[11] Underlying the whole area of pay is the consistency and fairness of the pay system and its administration.*

This chapter focuses specifically on designing a compensation plan to meet strategic objectives related to fixed salaries and to meet the strategic theme of 'designing compensation systems which are fair and meet employment equity objectives'. The following two chapters focus on strategic objectives related to pensions and benefits and incentives and performance pay.

CO 1: USING EQUITY OBJECTIVES TO DESIGN A COMPENSATION SYSTEM

This chapter's opening vignette illustrates the many facets of pay satisfaction and points to the structure and administration of equitable pay systems. One basic hallmark for a well-designed pay system is its 'fairness' and acceptability to employees. Unless the compensation system is perceived to be fair, the system will breed mistrust and scepticism among employees. Few instruments of management evoke more powerful and complex emotions in an organization's membership than the fairness of an organization's compensation policy. Perceptions of inequity evoke dissatisfaction, especially if people feel that others are getting the same pay when they seem to be doing less work. Such has been the case in the inequities in what women and men have been paid throughout the world.

Traditionally, compensation systems are designed to attract, retain and reward people, and in improving performance, compensation was a way of aligning a person's worth with the organization's strategic objectives and priorities. A person's worth or value to an organization is, theoretically, defined by his or her competence and value. In many cases, the process of determining worth has been the subject of much debate. For example, in our early history in Western societies, men and women working side by side, doing exactly the same jobs, were paid different wages. In some cases, help wanted signs listed different rates for women and men.

Linking to the strategic context surrounding pay equity

Since the 1970s, the public has become more conscious of the pay equity issues between men and women that have been smouldering for years. For example, the rate of pay appeared to be unfairly depressed in jobs where women dominated the occupational groups, or what is known as **segregated occupations**, where at least 70 or 80 per cent of the workers are of one sex. As examples, for a number of years, the number of women working in craft and production jobs declined while the percentage of men increased. Women seemed relegated to secretarial jobs, sales positions, health occupations (predominantly nursing) and teaching.[12]

In some cases, women did not achieve pay parity with men because their personal qualifications did not match those of men. But this was less the case as women became more equally represented in the workforce, and today more than half of those attending university and earning a degree are women.

Although the gender-wage gap decreased during the 1980s, the rate of change has not been sustained in the present century, although the public sector treats women more fairly than do private sector organizations.[13] In Europe, Australia, New Zealand and South Africa, substantial differences exist across countries and between public and private sectors. Although scholars agree that there is currently a gender-wage gap, which is sometimes less pronounced in the public sector, there is little agreement on key reasons for it or ways to resolve it.[14]

The pay equity issues were partially vocalized in debates about 'job segregation' and 'pay discrimination' and a 'glass ceiling' for women. Women's rights groups, the courts, government agencies and unions became active in identifying and resolving the gap in wages for women in health, education, clerical work and other segregated occupations.[15] Internationally, the United Nations Convention on the Elimination of All Forms of Discrimination Against Women is described as the bill of rights for women, and the International Labour Organization's Equal Remuneration Convention, which adopted the principle of equal remuneration for men and women.[16]

The primary legislation in the United Kingdom is the Equality Act 2010, which prevents discrimination and requires equal treatment in access to employment regardless of personal characteristics of age, disability, gender reassignment, marriage or civil partnership, race, religion or belief, sex and sexual orientation. In Canada, equity legislation can be linked to the 1982 Charter of Rights and Freedoms goals of improving the conditions of disadvantaged groups and preventing discrimination on similar personal characteristics.[17] Canadian legislation used the term **employment equity** while encouraging special measures and accommodation of differences, distinguishing it from how the United States and Australia use the term **affirmative action** by promoting equal treatment.[18]

Employers have the responsibility for (i) identifying male- and female-dominated job classes, (ii) determining the value of the jobs using a gender neutral job evaluation plan and comparing male and female job classes, (iii) determining whether any pay differences exist and (iv) preparing an equity plan to remedy the differences (if they cannot be justified).

Performance metrics in relation to pay equity

The increased interest and international attention on the issues of pay equity, job segregation and pay discrimination has led to a corollary increased interest in the way that professionals evaluate jobs for purposes of establishing pay level. Professionals put job evaluation methods for determining pay under the microscope and began to ask whether the methods were helpful in understanding the key characteristics of the job and how the job should be paid. Possibly, the methods had inherent biases and have been masking hidden attitudes or forces which have undervalued the work traditionally carried out by women, resulting in lower wages paid for that work. That is, they might illustrate a **systemic discrimination**, a practice that appears, on the surface, to be fair and neutral and applied equally to all individuals, but which results in one group being treated in a different way. Some of these attitudes are manifest in occupational segregation and stereotypical assumptions about the work women perform. For example, there is a conventional wisdom that women are better teachers and care givers; or we assume they wouldn't like blue-collar work. Addressing the systemic discrimination issues related to pay inequity involves working with two principles:

Providing equal pay for equal work. This concerns the more overt wage discrimination between men and women, cases where both sexes are doing basically the same job and it is possible to directly compare their wages. For example, when two accountants are doing the same work, using the same skills and abilities, they should be paid the same.

Providing equal pay for work of equal value. Equal pay for work of equal value has a broader application as it attempts to address wage discrimination that exists where women perform work which is different from what men perform, but which has equal value. The equal pay principle prohibits wage discrimination where employees are performing work of equal or comparable value. The pay equity legislation underlying the principles of equal pay for work of equal value requires employers to identify and eliminate discrimination in compensation.

One goal of pay equity is to recognize that all jobs should be paid on the basis of their value rather than because these jobs have historically been performed by either women or men. Although it was easy to pinpoint discriminatory cases where men were paid more for doing the same work, the issue of **comparable worth** is concerned with how we validly and accurately make comparisons between dissimilar jobs.[19] The job's worth is defined by its requirement for certain skills, effort, responsibilities and working conditions. Important in this discussion is the recognition that pay equity makes good business sense. Pay equity reduces social costs as it provides full employment benefits to a wider sector of workers and thereby reduces costs for social assistance and unemployment insurance. In addition, removing barriers to employment encourages a greater number and diversity of candidates.[20]

Achieving pay equity objectives. In addressing equity objectives, the organization will undoubtedly have to strike a balance between internal, external and employee equity. Internal equity is related to the internal consistency among jobs (in terms of job worth) in the organization's pay structure and the relative value that each job contributes to the organization's objectives. External equity relates to the external market and perceived consistency of the pay structure compared to what similar organizations pay. Employee (individual) equity relates to comparisons among individuals doing the same or similar job and whether people are paid more for such factors as their background, experience and seniority.

In some cases, longer serving people within an organization are paid lower salaries than new recruits, as when the organization has to offer higher salaries for new engineers and technology graduates in order to attract them. Some employers may offer a one-time signing bonus to attract people, and this will affect internal equity. The question that managers have to ask is whether they should seek to adjust the internal equity balance. In addition, some organizations have a policy of paying above-market rates to attract people, whereas others pay below the market rate because they feel that their working environment or locations are superior.

CO 2: TRADITIONAL APPROACHES FOR EVALUATING JOBS

Pay equity legislation has encouraged professionals to be more systematic in assessing the value of work traditionally performed by men and women to address possible inequities. In doing this, they have improved **job evaluation** methods for establishing the worth of a job or position with respect to its value or worth to the organization, in order to meet equity objectives. Thus, we should examine jobs traditionally performed by women – clerical work, teaching and nursing – and those performed by men – police work, firefighting and operating equipment – and assess the comparable worth of these jobs using gender-neutral criteria.

Job evaluation approaches are both non-quantitative and quantitative in nature. The non-quantitative methods include ranking whole jobs from highest to lowest and job classification methods which put jobs into classes or grades of professional, technical, managerial, clerical and sales without understanding the skills and abilities these jobs required. Quantitative methods include the factor comparison method – a variation of the ranking and point method – where evaluators rank jobs within specific factors. In the point system, evaluators rate jobs and assign points to factors which are weighted in terms of their importance. Each method has unique advantages and disadvantages which are illustrated in Table 14.1. However, the debates over pay equity encouraged professionals to move towards quantitative plans that allowed for comparisons of the characteristics of the job and their value for the organization.

Table 14.1 Comparing Different Job Evaluation Methods

Method of Comparison	Unit of Comparison	
	Evaluate the Whole Job	**Evaluate Factors of the Job**
	Job Ranking	**Factor Comparison**
Compare job vs. job	• Rank jobs on their value or worth to the organization relative to other jobs. • The method is simple and easy to understand. • The method is subjective, and not as useful in larger organizations.	• Rank jobs relative to others within compensable factors which are important for the organization. • Like ranking, it is easy to explain and understand. • The method requires regular updating and the general importance of factors to all jobs is often assumed.
	Job Classification	**Point Method**
Classifies jobs into grades by classification or point values	• Jobs are assigned to job grades or classifications which represent a class of jobs. • Applicable to a large number of varied jobs; easy to understand and adjust. • Might reinforce jobs within certain class designations; time consuming to administer.	• Jobs are rated on the degree to which they require certain compensable factors (skills, responsibilities, effort, or working conditions). • The method is easy to understand and administer; understandable for employees to understand how to aspire to higher levels. • Time consuming to develop; lack of universal applicability of compensable factors to all jobs.

Non-quantitative job evaluation plans

Ranking is a basic and rudimentary job evaluation technique where jobs are evaluated and ordinally ranked by 'order of importance'. By comparing sets of jobs, evaluators subjectively rank the least and/or most valued or important jobs(s) in an organization.

Ranking has the advantage of being simple to administer, easy to explain to raters, flexible, inexpensive and fast. Raters must know all or many of the jobs well, and they are ranking based on whole job comparisons, often without the assistance of a predetermined scale or criteria. There is also no assurance of equal-interval ranks, and the method might only be practical with ranking a small number of jobs. The major flaw with ranking is its extreme subjectivity, as the evaluations are often a reflection of individuals' norms and broader biases. So, if a judge has a preconception that outside work is of more importance to the organization, the work of labourers would be ranked higher than that of inside workers like secretaries and file clerks.

The **job classification method**, the once dominant plan in governmental organizations, involves fitting jobs into established job classifications, or a hierarchy of classes and grades. Each classification describes a group of jobs, and each grade defines different levels of difficulty, responsibility and education required. For example, in the class from administrative workers, grade one might contain those jobs in which people perform tasks under constant supervision and requires a high school diploma, whereas jobs in grade three might be performed with no supervision while requiring a vocational degree and some knowledge of word processing and spreadsheets. The higher the grade, the more education, skill and ability required.

Classifications are designed to define groups of occupational families, or 'classes', such as administrative workers, clerks, engineers, managers and technicians. The classifications are often based on pre-existing norms of which job is more valuable. And although the classification system is simple and inexpensive, it is difficult to change, as evaluators are more likely to clarify current jobs within older classifications rather than changing the classifications to reflect new norms or equity requirements.

Quantitative job evaluation plans

The quantitative methods are unique in that evaluators rank or rate each job on the basis of common factors. Evaluators using the **factor comparison** plan compare or rank each job relative to the others, on the basis of a set of compensable factors like job knowledge, mental effort, physical effort, working conditions, supervision and responsibility. After ranking the job on each factor, money values are assigned to each level on each factor. Given its complexity, there is a great deal of subjectivity in weighting of factors and assigning pay rates.

The point method is the most frequently used job evaluation technique and involves defining the jobs by several compensable factors, giving each job a numerical score on each of the factors and summing the scores to obtain the value of the job. The rating scales are carefully worded and include a definition of the compensable factor, several divisions or degrees of each factor carefully outlined and a point score for each degree. Evaluators assign a numerical value for each factor. Assessments using the point method involve the conversion of the sum of all the points to a predetermined money value, rather than the usual practice of setting up pay grades of equal point spread.

The major advantage of the point system is that it has been a key instrument in providing a more valid system for comparing a wide range of jobs and in establishing new gender-neutral norms for evaluation. Once developed, the systems are quite stable, and even though jobs may change, the system has enough flexibility to respond. However, in developing the point method, defining and weighting the factors, defining the degrees to factors and subfactors, and developing a job evaluation manual takes a great deal of time and effort. A second disadvantage is that organizations using the point system often end up with pay grades or classes, even though they sought to eliminate them in a point method. That is, an organization with a 1,200-point pay plan might end up with 12 grades with 100 points in each grade or classification. Sceptics might ask, 'Why go through the point evaluation process if the organization eventually reverts back to job classifications at the end of it.' Overall, the process establishes a system which is defensible and based on logic. It replaces systems of classification and ranking where it was hard to justify a person's pay on the basis of what organizational members agree to be important for achieving their objectives.[21]

A key disadvantage of all formal systems of job evaluation is that they can encourage more rigidity in job and pay structures, and align pay with internal equity rather than performance goals.[22] These disadvantages, in most cases, can be reckoned with and minimized. For example, it is possible to define compensable factors that are linked to achieving strategic objectives and performance goals.

CO 3: DESIGNING AND APPLYING A POINT JOB EVALUATION APPROACH

The **point job evaluation system** allows evaluators to rate jobs on a factor-by-factor basis, weighting each compensable factor (e.g. knowledge, skills) for comparisons to different kinds of jobs. It has been an extremely important plan in governmental organizations in providing a defensible structure to compare jobs and attempting to eliminate many of the biases as to what constitutes male and female jobs.

The factors chosen in a point job evaluation system are those deemed to be important in rewarding work and distinguishing among jobs. The **factors** are the yardstick for measuring jobs and the heart of the point method of job evaluation. They describe broad category job features like skills, content and qualifications, which can be used to group jobs (e.g. education, mental demands, physical demands, responsibility and working conditions).

There are two ways to select and define compensable factors to use in a point job evaluation plan: (i) customizing the plan from the ground up and (ii) adapting an existing plan. Most applications fall between the two and involve adapting an existing plan while including subfactors that are unique to the organization. For example, some unions have a broad set of factors in defining a 'gender-neutral' job evaluation plan and allow different municipalities to adapt the factors in their standard plan and to include new factors.[23]

It is theoretically possible that an organization can construct one point job evaluation system for evaluating all the jobs. In practice, HR people find it useful to define unique factors for specific groups of jobs or for developing unique plans for clerical, operational, technical and managerial groups. There are pragmatic reasons for this in that it is difficult to develop one set of comparable factors for all jobs. For example, while working conditions such as coldness or danger in the job environment might be important for some labour jobs, it might not be as useful as a compensable factor for managerial or office jobs. A second reason is that the factors describing different jobs have unique meanings and terminology for the job holders, as one plan might use the term *disagreeable conditions* and another might use the term *surroundings* to describe similar things. Because job holders should easily understand factor definitions, different plans often reflect unique terminology and operational definitions. In government organizations, it is common to find different plans for blue-collar workers, and non-exempt clerical, technical or service positions.[24]

A well-known managerial job evaluation system used in government and private industry throughout the world is the plan developed by the Hay Consulting Group.[25] Its plan is based on three compensable factors: know-how, problem-solving and accountability.

The Canadian Union of Public Employees (CUPE) Plan has four broad factors: (i) the skills required in the job, (ii) the effort needed for the job, (iii) the job's responsibilities and (iv) the working conditions under which the job is done. Each factor in Table 14.2 is defined by measurable subfactors. The definitions of the subfactors may change depending on the application.

The CUPE job evaluation plan is non-copyrighted and is provided free of cost to interested organizations, mainly municipal governments. The key characteristics of the plan are its use of gender-neutral

Table 14.2 Factors and General Subfactors in CUPE's Job Evaluation Plan

Skills	Responsibility	Effort	Working Conditions
Measures the degree with which employees need to know or do in performing job	**Measures responsibility for people, ideas and things**	**Measures the mental and physical exertion required**	**Measures the physical and psychological conditions of work and the potential effects on the health of employees**
• Job content knowledge application • Contextual knowledge • Communication • Motor and sensory skills	• Information for the use of others • Well-being of individuals • Leadership of human resources • Money • Physical assets and products • Ensuring compliance	• Intellectual effort • Sustained attention • Psychological/ emotional effort • Physical effort	• Work environment • Risk to health

terminology, how it encourages a balance of participation from women and men, and its being flexible enough to be adapted to unique factors that an organization might wish to focus on. CUPE will train people to adapt this general plan and administer the job evaluation process.

In order to be useful in comparisons, job factors must possess certain characteristics. First, they have to exist in all the different jobs so that evaluators can differentiate the worth of each job. Each factor or subfactor should be measurable and should not overlap with another, and each should be weighted on the basis of its importance to the organization. Finally, factors should be acceptable to employers, employees and the union in that their viewpoints should be reflected in the factors chosen. Factors should also be gender neutral and apply to all jobs regardless of gender dominance.

In most job evaluation applications, such as CUPE's, a committee is selected to design or adapt the plan and administer it in evaluating jobs. In the CUPE process, the goal is to have a balance of representation from union and management members, and of men and women.

The job evaluation committee picks **benchmark jobs** which serve to anchor the job evaluation plan and against which other jobs can be compared. In large organizations, a sample of 20–25 jobs is chosen to represent different job types and levels. An ideal benchmark job is one that is stable in the organization and common enough to be found in wage and salary surveys.[26] These benchmark jobs could be jobs that managers would hold across organizations and are key jobs that represent what the organization does.

The benchmark jobs are used for three purposes in developing a compensation plan: (i) By using them, it is possible to see the wage profile or hierarchy of what one key job is paid in relationship to others in the organization; (ii) these key jobs can be compared to other jobs in other organizations in helping managers establish external equity; (iii) the training in evaluating benchmark jobs can also be valuable to the committee for developing norms and working principles about how to evaluate jobs.

The job evaluation committee decides on the number of points that will be used to differentiate the importance of each factor and subfactor, using a working rule that the number of total points in a plan will be sufficient to differentiate among the various jobs being evaluated.[27] The committee then allocates the points among the factors and subfactors (elements). Assigning points to factors is the same thing as weighting the factors in terms of what the organization considers most important. For example, skills required might receive 45 per cent weight, responsibility 30 per cent, effort required 15 per cent and working conditions 10 per cent. Although some plans use statistical procedures, such as regression, to determine which factors best predict performance, many plans encourage decision-makers to use their judgement in weighting the factors and subfactors and distributing points among them. As an example, one organization divided 1,200 total points among the various factors: skills, 540; responsibility, 360; effort, 180; and working conditions, 120. Then, it distributed these points among the subfactors.

Each subfactor is described by various levels or degrees. For example, there may be 10 'degrees', or levels, of the subfactor job knowledge. Degree 8 could require an understanding of the theory of the trade, craft or technical area. The relative worth of each degree is designated in points, with the highest number of points given to the highest degree. Degree 5 of job content knowledge may be worth 240 points, whereas degree 4 is given only 220 points because it might not require as complete an understanding of the theory of the trade, craft or technical area. Table 14.3 illustrates the allocation of points among the four subfactors in the skill factor.

In the final analysis, the primary purpose of identifying compensable factors in the evaluation process is to establish an internally equitable base pay for each job within the organization. By identifying and defining each factor, it is easier to evaluate each one relative to all the others. Thus, it is easier to rate each job.[28] The importance or weight given to each factor and subfactor, therefore, reflects the priorities of the organization.

Table 14.3 Points Assigned to Factors and Subfactors in a Point Plan

Factors & Subfactors			Degrees			Total
Points	1	2	3	4	5	
Skill Factor (max 540) Weight 45%						
Job content knowledge	160	180	200	220	240	
Contextual knowledge	120	140	160	180	200	
Communication	40	45	50	55	60	
Motor & sensory skills	20	25	30	35	40	
Total						

Ensuring internal equity. Job descriptions are relied on for assisting the steering committee to rate each job. However, before evaluating jobs, the committee might discover that the information it has in current job descriptions is insufficient, outdated and written for other purposes. For this reason it may have to update the job descriptions by asking job holders to provide information which committee members need on each of the factors in the plan.

The point system requires evaluators to rate jobs on a factor-by-factor basis. Evaluators rate the jobs on the basis of each factor by defining the number of points (a rating of the job's worth). Each job's relative value in the organization is a measure of the total number of points assigned to it, and this locates the job in the pay structure. For example, Table 14.4 illustrates the point allocation for the jobs of customer service and liaison payroll assistant.

The committee usually begins its work after members receive training in how to apply the plan in rating different types of jobs. Committee members often begin by evaluating benchmark jobs. One practice for improving decision-making is to encourage members to make their ratings independently before meeting as a whole committee. In some cases, the chairperson can use a Delphi-like process in pooling independent ratings so that dominant personalities do not have more influence.[29] The quality of decision-making is often a reflection of the chairperson's ability to encourage independence of thought in developing a consensus among group members.

The above steps do not establish what the salary should be. The outcome is a numeric score (total points) of what that job is worth in relation to others. As such, the process only establishes the relative position of a job in relation to others. The final pay range may be adjusted depending on what the job is paid in other organizations.

Ensuring external equity. The procedure for determining external equity is similar to the one for defining internal equity, except that we survey the external market to determine what other organizations are paying. We collect information externally – through surveys, interviews and professional wage summaries – on key benchmark jobs to identify pay, benefits, pensions and performance pay. One

Table 14.4 Examples of Scores in a Point Job Evaluation Plan

Job	Skill Score	Effort Score	Responsibility Effort Score	Working Conditions Score	Total Value (Points)	Yearly Wage Range
Customer Service Liaison	150	100	180	20	450	£23,986–27,600 ($36,400–42,000)
Payroll Assistant	85	65	145	20	315	£16,790–20,560 ($25,480–31,200)

important purpose of the market survey is to understand market changes and trends, for example new pay packages or incentives that other employers are using.[30]

The pay level for each position reflects the results of a combination of data taken from the job evaluation process, reviewing the internal equity of the jobs and the market data that illustrate what jobs are paid in other organizations.

Figure 14.1 illustrates different pay grades from I (A, B, C) to VI (P, Q, R) and the actual minimum and maximum pay levels defined by the salary survey. Each dot in Figure 14.1 represents the intersection between the market survey information that determines the pay rate of these jobs in other organizations and the point value from the job evaluation process. A wage policy line (WPL) charts the wage rates and corresponding point values for each position in an organization. This policy line is drawn up after first identifying the internal wage policy line and comparing it with market rates. The line is a reference point to guide the pay structure.

Most positions fall within the guidelines for their assigned wage group or pay grade. In some cases, there might be a few positions that are much higher than the policy range. If there are no legitimate reasons for this, these positions might be red circled to indicate that they land above the policy line and might not receive any annual increases until they are within the policy range. **Green-circled positions** are those paid below the policy line. In these cases, it may be appropriate to increase the annual adjustments until they fall within guidelines.

Constructing the pay range is a bit of a balancing act, or an iterative process where the analyst tries to respond to internal policy objectives about what people should be paid at different levels and whether there is a belief that the organization should lead the market in pay rates. Some analysts average the salary data from the survey to arrive at a midpoint.

The employer's decisions in establishing a WPL reflect whether it believes higher pay is important in attracting and retaining employees and rewarding people with different levels of skills. Once the

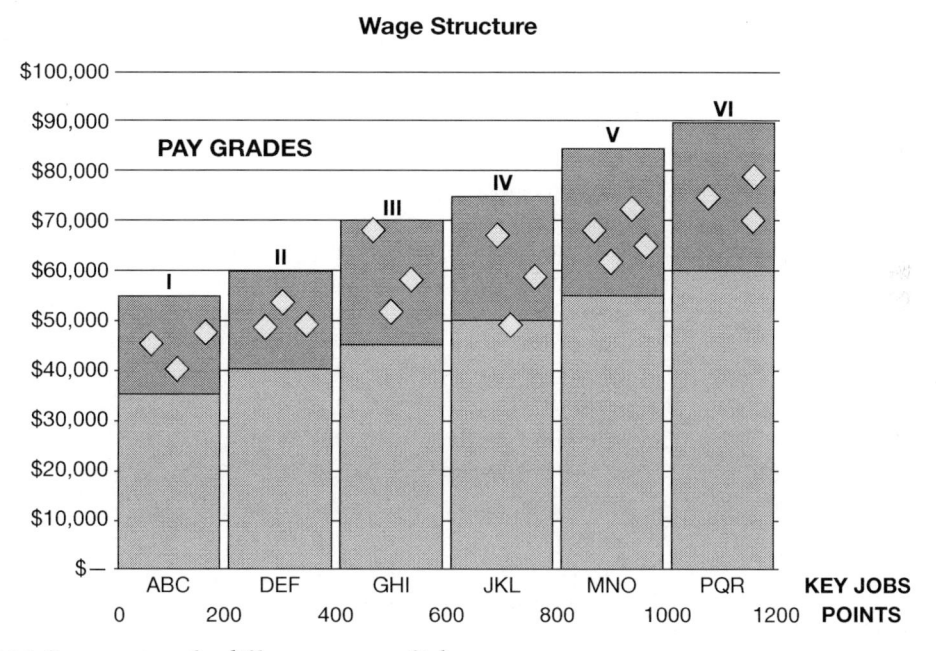

Figure 14.1 Pay structure for different groups of jobs.

WPL is established, the organization has to decide how to make adjustments upwards or downwards in responding to the market.

It is a common practice to establish pay grades in an organization by grouping jobs together which have similar points. This makes the pay plan simpler. Compensation systems with 20 grades, or 'bands', might end up with as few as five grades, a process call **broad banding**. This reduces or collapses salary grades or levels into a few bands, each containing a relatively wide range of job and salary levels. Constructing pay grades involves creating a **job hierarchy** or listing of the relative assessed value of jobs from highest to lowest. If a job evaluation plan has a total number of 1,200 points, it is not likely that any position will have more than 1,000 points or less than 200. Possibly, jobs with 200 and 300 points might be in grade 1, and jobs with 300 to 400 might be in grade 2.

A RELEVANT POINT OF VIEW: MOVING FROM A KNOWLEDGE-BASED TO SKILL-BASED PAY

Most job evaluation plans, and pay plans in general, are job rather than skill based. Pay relates to the evaluation of the job rather than skills people have, as the job, not the person, is the unit of analysis. This means that a PhD in mechanical engineering who accepts a job as a mechanic will not get paid any more because of the PhD. The person might do a superior job and organize the company's way of doing business, but the person's credentials have nothing to do with the job's requirements. The only way the person can get more pay would be from a higher-level position.

Managers might decide to emphasize individual skills, abilities, potential and flexibility in being able to perform different tasks. **Skill-based** or **knowledge-based (competency-based)** pay plans pay people according to the skills they possess rather than just the skills they perform. For example, teachers are paid more because they have more education, and welders receive more income if they have higher qualifications. As such, employees who are more competent should have a better understanding of the position and the needs of the organization. Because the pay is determined by the skills the person has rather than the job or the supervisor's rating of performance, there is less competition between workers. In addition, workers are motivated to improve their skills and possibly become more responsible for learning skills for a wider set of jobs.[31]

Skill-based pay plans are based on the principle that employees should be paid for the skills rather than for the jobs they do. This encourages employees to be actively involved in learning and career development, and helps organizations to more fully utilize employee skills in a wider variety of situations, including management. Key features of skill-based pay plans include the following:

1. *Competence testing*. Under job-based plans, competence might affect performance, but not base pay. Under a skill-based plan, pay is attached to the employee's skills. The employee must be certified as competent to perform the skills specified by the job to receive pay increases.
2. *Pay does not change with job changes*. When an employee receives a new job, pay will not change because of the job. Pay will change when employees are certified to perform new skills.
3. *Seniority and other factors*. Skill-based plans are based on skills and not seniority. Employees must be certified. However, seniority might be used as a criterion to determine which employees have first access to training.
4. *Wider opportunities*. Theoretically, there are more possibilities for advancement in skill-based programmes. Essentially, employees can develop the skills for a wider sector of jobs, and employees are more versatile and flexible to take on new jobs.[32]

The most obvious advantage of a skill-based system is flexibility. Individuals can perform multiple tasks, and organizations can quickly refocus and retool to adjust to new priorities.[33] Beyond being able to take on a greater variety of tasks, skill-based systems allow employees to perform higher-level and more sophisticated tasks. Employees' jobs are more enriched, and they can ebb and flow between operational and managerial tasks. The greater knowledge that employees have increases a manager's ability to use them in a variety of assignments and to enrich and enlarge their work. This encourages more generic job descriptions and more flexible organizational designs where people can quickly reassign employees depending on priorities.

A skill-based system provides a number of advantages: (i) Employees are encouraged to learn skills for problem-solving and improving the organization's operations. (ii) Employees have a greater sense of commitment when they are part of the larger organization. They are more able to connect their work to what clients or customers might need and work in a larger number of jobs. (iii) Skill-based programmes encourage a participative culture where career development is important. Skill-based systems motivate employees to improve their capabilities and skills to enhance their careers generally. (iv) Employees are more likely to be self-managing and better able to take responsibility for their own work. This can lead to fewer levels of management and more teams and self-managing groups.[34]

Even though skill-based systems have distinct advantages, they have potential downsides. As everyone has the opportunity to learn new skills, there is a larger investment in training, and production time losses occur when training is carried out. Skill assessment can also raise challenges similar to those faced in performance appraisals, relating to defining skills and accurately assessing them in a valid and fair way. It is possible for a person to 'top out', and learn all the skills and have nowhere to go. If people move too rapidly between jobs, they might not be as productive, and it is rarely possible for employees to keep their skills honed. Other difficulties relate to keeping up-to-date skills inventories and establishing external equity.[35]

The real upside of a job evaluation system using the point system is responding to pay equity issues, not only in paying women more fairly in comparison with men but also in providing a fair pay system generally. The motivational value of pay in this case relates to perception of fairness. People make comparisons with others, and they compare their inputs (effort and perceived contribution) and their outcomes (pay, incentives, recognition). If people feel their pay is unfair, they are likely to change their behaviour in various ways (voicing their dissatisfaction, putting more time in and working harder, or working less).[36]

MANAGERIAL IMPLICATIONS: The job evaluation process is aimed at designing a compensation system within the principles of providing equal pay for equal work and providing equal pay for work of equal value. These principles generally recognize that all jobs should be paid on the basis of their value rather than because women or men have historically performed these jobs. The job evaluation process builds on the job analysis process in that it relies on an understanding of the job requirements and skills and the importance of these jobs in achieving the organization's strategic plan and objectives. The job evaluation process assesses jobs, not people, and generally only focuses on motivation to the extent that it seeks to design a fair compensation system. It provides information for the strategic theme 'designing compensation systems which are fair and meet employment equity objectives'.

BEFORE APPLYING, LET'S REVIEW

CO 1: Define how inequities in women's versus men's pay helped shape the design of a fairer way to evaluate jobs.

Since the 1970s, the public has become more conscious of the pay equity issues between men and women that had been smouldering for years. The pay equity issues were partially vocalized in debates about 'job segregation' and 'pay discrimination' and a 'glass ceiling' for women. In responding, government organizations played a key role in initiating legislation for employment equity and setting an example as a workforce that implemented principles related to providing (i) equal pay for equal work and (ii) more pay for more important work.

CO 2: Illustrate the advantages and disadvantages of four different job evaluation approaches – ranking, job classification, factor comparison and the point system.

In reviewing different job evaluation approaches – ranking, job classification, factor comparison and the point system – how useful are these approaches to fairly rating the worth of each job and determining the level of pay? The non-quantitative methods include ranking whole jobs from highest to lowest and job classification methods where analysts slot jobs into classes, or grades, of professional, technical, managerial, clerical and sales. Quantitative methods include the factor comparison method and the point method. With the factor comparison approach, evaluators rank jobs within specific compensable factors. Using the point system, evaluators rate jobs by assigning points for specific compensable factors, each factor being weighted in terms of its importance.

CO 3: Demonstrate how to design and implement a point job evaluation system that meets pay equity objectives.

This chapter demonstrates how to design and implement a point job evaluation system in implementing pay equity objectives. This involves defining competencies which act as standards for comparing the different jobs. Each job, as described in the job description and job specification, is rated, one factor at a time, within various competency areas. After assigning point values to each job, a wage rate is then given to the job. Point job evaluation plans became popular as organizations responded to internal equity objectives.

DISCUSSION AND REVIEW QUESTIONS

1. In carrying out job evaluations, employers have the responsibility to show that their plans are gender neutral. In response, point job evaluation plans have been implemented to fairly judge each job, using the same factors or criteria. However, some pundits have suggested that there might be systemic biases in such plans in awarding more points to jobs held by men because of the choice and weighting of each factor. They suggest that the factor 'supervisory responsibility' put more weight on jobs more likely to be performed by men. In response, they suggest putting more weight on other factors. Do you agree?
2. In some applications of the point system, blue-collar work traditionally performed by men (ditch digging, cutting trees, driving trucks) has been re-evaluated in favour of the skills required in clerical and administrative work (operating office equipment and being proficient in running computer software). However, it might be that our weighting has changed because it is more acceptable to put

weight on other factors. Generally, what factors and components of jobs traditionally performed by men have been given higher value or weight than components of jobs traditionally thought of as women's?
3. Four different job evaluation plans – ranking, job classification, factor comparison and the point system – are based on different objectives and assumptions about internal equity. Define the uniqueness of each type of plan and its advantages and disadvantages.
4. A manager you are working for wants you to develop compensable factors under the general headings skill, effort, responsibility and working conditions. You might use some of the subfactors described in this chapter. Choose a recent job experience. In your short report, define subfactors within each of the factor areas. Assign a weight to each of the subfactors by distributing 100 points among the subfactors. Conclude with a recommendation for how you would implement such a plan in an organization.
5. In building on the SHRM BSC framework, define objectives, initiatives and markers that are important for 'designing compensation systems which are fair and meet employment equity objectives'. In forming one to three objectives within each of the areas, the framework asks you to respond to questions like the following:
    - How do we want customers and clients (different employee groups) to see us?
    - What processes (e.g. job analysis, job evaluation, communication) must we excel at?
    - For the learning and growth perspective, how do we design a compensation system to enhance motivation and growth (e.g. fairness, job progression)?
    - How do we want to look to shareholders (e.g. citizens, politicians)?

CASE: RESOLVING EQUITY ISSUES WITH A POINT EVALUATION PLAN

Working with a partner, your task as consultants is to assess whether a point job evaluation plan (like CUPE's gender-neutral plan) might be useful for resolving internal equity issues for your client. Go to the website to find out what points and wages are recommended by evaluators.

Your client, a local government organization, has asked you to review two job descriptions: a Custodian II job which traditionally has been performed by men, and a Clerk IV job which historically has been held by women. One of the goals of pay equity is to encourage equal pay for work of equal value and to reduce any wage differences in jobs where pay reflects the fact that they are male- or female-dominated jobs.

In the previous job classification plan, these positions were paid about the same hourly rate. Your client has asked you to use CUPE's job evaluation plan.

Clerk IV Responsible for clerical work under supervision. The work involves preparation and maintenance of records, preparation and input of data to the electronic data processing system and checking the results for validity, posting adjustments, maintaining files and providing and obtaining information relative to the field of work. The work is checked for quality and quantity, and problems involving interpretation of procedures or concerning policy decisions are referred to the supervisor. The work is differentiated from that of Clerk III by the greater complexity of tasks and the degree of independent action allowed.

Custodian II Responsible for custodial work, which involves cleaning and maintaining offices and buildings, carrying out repairs to interior and exterior of the buildings, maintaining and repairing machines, making and maintaining ice, maintaining correct water and chlorine levels, attending functions and maintaining security of various buildings. Specific duties assigned vary according to the type and function of facilities the employee is assigned to. The work is routine and repetitive, involves the supervision of a small group and is differentiated from that of a Custodian I level by the additional supervisory duties and the independence of action allowed in the setting of work duties.

1. Connect to CUPE's job evaluation manual by inserting the CUPE job evaluation in the web browser.
2. Review the job descriptions below.
3. CUPE's job evaluation manual lists a number of factors on which each job is to be rated and then breaks each factor down into a number of degrees. In Table 14.5, for each factor pick the degree level which describes each job. You might want to rate each job before referring to the following table, which reviews the points for the various levels.

Table 14.5 Rating Different Jobs

Subfactor	Clerk IV Degree Level	Points	Custodian II Degree Level	Points
Knowledge				
Experience				
Judgement				
Mental effort				
Physical activity				
Dexterity				
Accountability				

4. In being fair in establishing general equity, how should the weighting of the factors be adjusted in the degree table?

15 Constructing Retirement and Benefits Plans

Chapter Outline
- Chapter objectives (COs)   289
- A driving issue focusing managerial action: Recognizing that different people want different types of employee benefits   289
- CO 1: The new world of funding pension benefits   291
- CO 2: The new world of funding health care benefits   295
- CO 3: The new world of work–family benefits   299
- Before applying, let's review   301
- Discussion and review questions   302
- Case: Changing a work schedule at Provincial Health   302

CHAPTER OBJECTIVES (COs)

After reading this chapter, you will be able to implement the following objectives:

CO 1: Review the new world of employee retirement plans.

CO 2: Review the new world of health benefits provided by the government and employers.

CO 3: Illustrate the new world of family-friendly organizational practices.

A DRIVING ISSUE FOCUSING MANAGERIAL ACTION: RECOGNIZING THAT DIFFERENT PEOPLE WANT DIFFERENT TYPES OF EMPLOYEE BENEFITS

In the early 1990s, when everything seemed to be going right economically, experts suggested that employers needed to be more generous in developing benefit packages to attract and retain the declining pool of talented workers. Most organizations offer **retirement benefits** *to support employees when they are no longer earning income from employment. Then, there are basic* **health care benefits**, *and* **social benefits** *such as unemployment insurance and social assistance provided by federal, provincial, state and territorial laws. Some health benefits protect employees and their families when they are ill or injured, and others encourage preventative health, dental and optical health.*

Beyond basic retirement and health benefits, employers began offering a range of **work–family benefits** *that provide flexibility in balancing work and non-work and in supporting employees in their personal development. These include benefits such as flextime, compressed workweeks, job sharing, part-time work, seasonal schedules, telecommuting, paid time-off plans, personal leave of absence or respite, child care benefits, work–family benefits and educational benefits.[1] Some of these benefits provide scheduling changes which allow people to better balance their work and non-work lives, and others allow for relaxation and time off from work in holidays and family support. Other benefits provide training and educational development to support employees in learning new skills.*

Benifit plans are part of the total pay package that goes beyond pay for time spent at work or incentives. Benifit plans can be seen in two ways: (i) they provide financial protections during retirement or from risks during ill health in addition to providing ways to reduce work–family conflict; and (ii) they attract or encourage overall satisfaction with an organization, promote loyalty and discourage people from leaving.[2]

The desire for particular benefits is related to work values and preferences, which are linked closely to demographics such as marital status, number of dependants, employment status and age. Although some people clearly have strong preferences, most people seem to have the greatest interest in flexible packages because of the increased choice and control they offer. Older workers prefer time off and schedule flexibility over cash compensation.[3] They are also more likely to prefer a flexible lifestyle and training and education benefits. Single workers prefer 'financial advancement' and 'work–life balance' over family supportive benefits, and those who have partners and young families pick 'opportunities for skill building and professional growth' as being of greatest value to them. Gender, age and number of dependants are also related to the perceived importance of family-supportive programmes.[4] Women are more interested in child care benefits over flextime, telecommuting, and eldercare[5] and single parents want both child care and parental leave. Families with two working parents often end up with certain benefits duplicated.[6] People with a strong public service motivation have a lower preference for bonus-type rewards and a stronger preference for health care packages.[7]

QUIZ 15.1 – WHAT ARE THE MOST IMPORTANT BENEFITS FOR YOU?

If your employer could not provide an increase in wages, what increase in benefits, if any, would be the most important to you in order to keep you satisfied? Rank from most important (1) to least important as applicable.

1. Automobile and motor vehicle allowance
2. Organizational pension plan
3. Disability-related employment benefits
4. Employer-paid group life insurance premiums
5. Gifts and awards
6. Medical expenses
7. Professional membership dues
8. Provincial or state health care premiums
9. Registered retirement savings plan (RRSP) or other retirement premiums (e.g. US 401(k) plan)
10. Social events
11. Tuition fees
12. Sick time
13. Vacation

STRATEGIC CONTEXT: This chapter reviews the second and third components of the total compensation package: pensions and benefits. A strategic theme relevant to this chapter relates to providing sustainable pensions and benefits programmes which attract and retain employees. This chapter should encourage you to think of objectives and initiatives that balance the financial needs of the organization and the social and financial needs of employees.

Performance metrics of different benefits. *The introductory perspective summarizes benefits that organizations provide relating to retirement, protection from health issues and creating a supportive work–family relationship. In one study, benefit plans represent 22.5 per cent of the basic wage paid to some public sector workers compared to 18.8 per cent in the private sector,[8] although in some cases they can cost up to 30 per cent.[9] The biggest components are paid time-off programmes (vacations, statutory holidays, maternity leave), mandatory benefits and legally required payments for government pension plans, employment insurance and workers' compensation. This makes up nearly 75 per cent of the total benefits costs.*

The financial crisis provoked a great deal of discussion about the ability to pay for these benefits, a discussion which has put pressure on public organizations because of the significant differences between their offerings and those in private organizations. These benefit programmes will not motivate a person on a daily basis, but they have been used to attract and retain employees. In labour negotiations, managers face increasing pressures to adjust the benefit plans so they are more sustainable and so that they meet both financial and employee objectives. In building on the introductory perspective, a first task is to recognize the challenges that organizations and employees face in this area.

CO 1: THE NEW WORLD OF FUNDING PENSION BENEFITS

Pension issues for public and private sector workers became much more salient as a result of the financial crisis of 2007–2008, and fears that retirement plans that were created years before might not be sustainable because people are living longer, thus drawing more money from the pension system. The seeds of the crisis were sown years earlier when, to avoid recession, the US Federal Reserve lowered the interest rate from 6.5 to 1.75 per cent in December 2001, and to 1.0 per cent in June 2003. This created a flood of cheap money and overzealous bankers who provided funds for homes to people who had few assets or jobs. As more homes were purchased with more buyers, prices appreciated. Troubles started when the US Federal Reserve started to raise interest rates, and by 2006, the interest rate was 5.25 per cent. With lower demand for houses, prices fell, and there was a 40 per cent decline in prices during 2006. Many subprime borrowers could not pay these higher interest rates and began defaulting on their loans. With the defaults, many banks filed for bankruptcy.

The 'big bang' that sounded the alarm about the viability of the pension system occurred during the global financial meltdown beginning in the summer of 2008. Pension fund investments in the stock market lost 20 per cent of their value, and it became evident that they did not have funds to support their liabilities. But even with a modest recovery a year later, the average pension plan is 20 per cent short of the assets it needs to fund its obligations. As an example, in the Netherlands, average pension assets exceeded liabilities by 44 per cent before the crisis, but at the end of 2008, assets were 5 per cent lower than liabilities. About 60 per cent of the OECD pension assets are in defined benefits and similar plans that offer guaranteed returns. The 'big bang' has encouraged us to ask questions about the pension system and other benefits offered to employees.[10]

The 'big bang' was an awakening for most of the industrial world, especially because most of the pension funds were invested in stocks rather than bonds. The crisis encouraged defined benefit plan sponsors to begin reviewing the longevity estimates (actuarial tables) they employed, as people were living longer and would be demanding support for a longer term. Simply put, pensions were designed to be supported by contributions from the current workforce and money set aside from the operating budgets and returns on investing these funds.

The strategic alternatives: Different pension plans for government workers

There is often a debate on the relevance of different types of pension plan – defined benefit (DB), defined contribution (DC) and hybrid plans – and whether they should complement a country's social security system.

Defined benefit plans. There are significant differences between public and private sector pension plans and benefit packages generally. Defined benefit plans give employees guaranteed benefits based on years of service, salary earned and age at retirement. The benefit promise is fixed, depending on age and years of service. It is based on a formula such as a percentage of the best average three to five years of annual earnings. For example, in one DB plan, the retirement salary is a percentage of the best five years' average earnings. If your best five years of salary was an average of £65,898 ($100,000) over five years, you would calculate your pension by multiplying by 2 per cent (or another agreed on percentage like 1.5%) and by the years of service. For example, if Jackie and Karl had an average salary of £65,898 ($100,000) for five years, and Jackie worked 35 years and Karl 10 years, then Jackie's retirement income would be £46,129 ($70,000) and Karl's, £13,180 ($20,000).

- Jackie's calculation: £65,898 ($100,000) × 2% × 35 years = £46,129 ($70,000)
- Karl's calculation: £65,898 ($100,000) × 2% × 10 years = £13,180 ($20,000)

DB plans are generally employer initiated or sponsored. That is, even though unions and employees may participate in administering the plan, it is the employer's responsibility to fund and provide the benefits. The employer must manage contributions, benefits and investments in order to have enough funds in the plan to provide the promised benefit. The risk sits with the employer. Pension promises for government workers are a major policy challenge because the large pension commitments made have to be supported by other means if a plan is not sustainable. In some cases, employers seek to reduce the benefits paid by changing the formula. Also, most government plans are of a DB nature and tend to be rather generous compared to private sector plans.

DB plans were very popular with employers in the early 1950s because they were seen as inexpensive ways of rewarding employees for long-term service. The plans encouraged employees to stay with one organization. In the 1970s and 1980s, that fitted well with a belief that working within one organization for life was a good way to have a successful career.

One downside of DB plans is that they have been slow in making adjustments to actuarial assumptions that recognize that people are living much longer.[11] For example, the average age at death in one OECD country rose from 70.9 in 1991 to 74.2 in 2005, to 80.4 in 2008. The extra costs created by having to support plan members for longer periods of time were compounded because of the decline in long-term interest rates and the corresponding devaluation of pension assets. Pension fund managers, who traditionally used the bond market to fund the plans, began searching for higher returns in the stock market. The stock market, being more prone to ups and downs, collapsed in 2008, and several pension funds lost a large percentage of their assets.

In the emerging landscape following the financial crisis, many DB plans have been terminated or adjusted to include defined contribution components (e.g. Chile, Denmark, Hungary, Mexico and Poland).[12] In other cases, public sector workers have been included in the main public pension plans (e.g. Austria, Chile, Czech Republic, Greece, Hungary, Mexico, Poland, Spain and the United States). Some countries have lowered the payments to pension holders to bring the plans in line with others in the private sector (e.g. Finland, France, Germany, Italy, Portugal and Sweden).

Traditionally, most OECD governments offered special DB plans for public sector workers. For example, in Canada, 84 per cent of public service workers have pensions, and 78 per cent of these are DB plans. In the private sector, 26 per cent of the employees have pension plans, and 16 per cent are DB plans. Sixty per cent of Canada's workers have no pension at all, and 45 per cent have no pension or registered retirement savings.[13] The fiscal burden of government pension plans is considerable as the pension benefits are guaranteed and future benefits are often paid for directly from government revenues (pay as you go) because many pension plans have tended to be underfunded.[14]

Defined contribution plans. Defined contribution (DC) plans, also called money purchase plans (MPPs), rely on employer and employee yearly contributions to the plan. Instead of paying into a DB plan, the employee and employer contributions are part of a fund where the benefits accrue from the contributions and the earnings (interest) of investing them. The rewards of watching these contributions accumulate in a bull market, and the risks of losing money in a bear market rest solely with the employee.

A defined contribution plan is like an employee's private pension fund. The funds belong to the employees who have input into the decisions on the level of investment conservatism or aggressiveness. In that the risks and rewards rest with the employees and the soundness of investments, employees cannot count on the level of income they will receive when they retire. The employer is insulated from the risks of adverse returns.

The contributions to a defined contribution plan are based on a percentage of an employee's earnings. On retirement, the pension holder has various options, one of which is to buy a life annuity or what is called a life income fund (LIF). If the pension holder has approximately £988,469 ($1,500,000) in the account, the money could draw 4 per cent a year, or £39,539 ($60,000). The money belongs to the pension holder, who can draw into the principal to enhance his or her annual pension. Some jurisdictions allow plan members to choose the types of investment they wish to participate in. For example, in the Saskatchewan public service plan, older employees can select a more conservative approach, and younger employees can choose a more risky strategy of higher risk or, possibly, higher return investments. Employees can even contribute more in their careers and participate in a range of financial counselling services to support their decisions.[15]

One advantage of defined contribution plans is that the money in the account belongs to the employee or the estate and does not disappear when you or your spouse pass on (as in a defined benefit plan which may not return to the estate the full invested value of your account). These plans, in contrast to the defined benefit plan, are simpler to administer and are more realistic in that plan members are more accountable for some of the costs, risks and benefits of the plan.

For the pension holder, there is more uncertainty as the returns are not guaranteed and depend on contributions and investment returns, which ebb and flow with the market and depend on the soundness of the decisions in managing the fund. Bad investment decisions have an effect on returns, whereas the benefits in a defined benefit plan are guaranteed. During the subprime crisis, many pension accounts lost 20–30 per cent of their value. That is, an account holder with £790,775 ($1,200,000) in a pension account might have seen this value diminish to £626,030 or £658,979 ($950,000 or $1,000,000) in eight months. In most cases, these funds recovered after two years. However, many financial institutions went bankrupt, and many people lost a great deal of their pension assets.

Hybrid pension plans. Most hybrid plans include DC and DB elements where the employer contributes a specified share of earnings for each employee into a hypothetical account. Some of the pensionable income would be guaranteed while other income would depend on the investments earnings. In Australia, there is a compulsory superannuation scheme where employers are required to make contributions on behalf of their employees while individuals can add personal contributions. Each Australian state has unique plans most of which are DB based or a hybrid of a DB and DC.[16] France has an unfunded DB plan in addition to complementary fully funded DC (voluntary) and DB plans. German plans are based on a DB arrangement and other partially funded pension arrangements. In the Netherlands, there is a funded DB plan for government and educational and health care workers. Sweden's plans include DB and DC arrangements, and the United Kingdom has DB plans for central and local government.

The financial crisis magnified the pension challenges in Europe and OECD countries, resulting in several policy changes. For example, in Finland, the pensionable age rose from 62 to 68, and France increased the rate of required pension contributions from 2 to 20 per cent in 2012. The reforms in Greece, Italy, Spain and Portugal illustrate reforms of altering the pension mix to include DB and DC elements, increasing contributions, curtailing the benefits through more strict calculation, reducing administrative costs by combining pension authorities and lowering the level of payments.[17] Some of the reforms in Finland, France, Germany, Italy, Portugal and Sweden lowered the generosity of public sector pension plans. Even with the pressures, Canada has maintained most of its DB pension plans for federal and provincial workers, teachers and health care workers.[18]

Social security systems. Most countries have a social safety net, originally thought of as income assistance, as a last resort when all else fails. Social security systems can be part of pension earning, for example, the United States has a three-tiered pension system for federal employees which includes social security, an unfunded DB plan and a DC thrift savings plan, whereas the state government plans are generally DB based. Employees receive many pension and health benefits as part of their country's social safety net, but employers also provide many benefits to assist employees and their families. Most people enjoy many social, health and quality-of-life benefits whether they work or not. Beyond this, many employers provide a range of medical, extended health insurance, vacation and quality-of-life and retirement benefits for employees to attract them to stay with an organization.

Many benefits come from the public purse, but others are supported by employer and employee payments in the same way that a person contracts with an insurance company. Many of these benefits assist employees if they are sick or injured or need to change jobs; others help them make adjustments during retirement; and others provide them with paid vacations and educational leave.

Australia has become a recognized example of how to reform a pension plan. In 1972, less than 20 per cent of women had pensions. Today, more than 90 per cent of men and women are covered by a mandatory retirement savings programme, the Superannuation Guarantee programme, which began in 1992. Because of the 1992 legislation, all employers have to contribute 9 per cent of earnings to a retirement plan, although employees are not required to contribute (and only 20% do make extra contributions). Since the introduction of the Superannuation Guarantee, many existing DB plans were closed, including those in the public sector.[19]

Another example of a unique retirement savings plan is Singapore's Central Provident Fund (CPF), a mandatory savings plan originally designed for the purpose of retirement savings but which has evolved to provide financing for a wide range of participants' needs. All temporary, part-time and full-time employees who are Singaporean citizens and permanent residents are required to participate in the CPF. Since July 1988, those above age 55 contribute at a lower rate of wages, a policy designed to partly de-link wages from seniority and to reduce the cost of hiring elderly workers. CPF contributions are credited into three accounts: (i) an ordinary account – these savings can be used to buy a home, pay for CPF insurance and for investment and education; (ii) a special account – these savings are for old age, contingency purposes and investment in retirement-related financial products; and (iii) a Medisave account – these savings can be used for hospitalization expenses and approved medical insurance. Participants can withdraw their CPF savings at the age of 55 while setting aside the CPF minimum sum for their retirement account, which they can start withdrawing at 62 years old. A philosophy of self-reliance encourages individuals to take care of themselves and their family members. There is minimal direct public expenditure in the plan as Singapore views the state's role as only providing the guiding framework.[20]

Social assistance programmes have grown to be a front-line set of programmes for replacement, supplementation and support programmes to assist employable recipients. **Income replacement programmes** include employment insurance, workers' compensation and paid parental leave and social assistance for those not expected to work. The employment insurance programme provides temporary financial assistance to those who are unemployed and are looking for work or upgrading their skills. Support is also provided to people who are sick, pregnant or caring for a newborn or adopted child. Workers' compensation programmes protect employees from financial hardships associated with work-related injuries and occupational diseases. The key objective is to return employees to work as quickly as possible and provide them with income support, medical care and rehabilitation. Earning supplementation programmes add to a person's basic wage through wage supplementation, tax benefits and supplementation of child benefits. Employment support programmes include child care, employment services and training, disability support and supplemental health care, and are intended to break down the welfare wall when people try to get off social assistance. These programmes are usually supported by general tax revenues.[21] You can review various social security systems at www.ssa.gov/international/links.html.

As pension plans are being challenged, employees are encouraged to take more responsibility in investigating other options to finance their retirement.

CO 2: THE NEW WORLD OF FUNDING HEALTH CARE BENEFITS

In addition to testing the sustainability of the pension system, the financial crisis had profound effects on the lives of citizens around the world and tested the resilience of health care plans and the general wealth of citizens. Group benefit plans in some countries in 1994 were estimated to be 3.7 per cent of payroll, but by 2006, they had increased to 7.3 per cent of payroll. The crisis resulted in health care reforms, expenditure cuts and general uncertainty. In 2014, the average health spending in OECD countries was 9.35 of GDP and consumed over 15 per cent of public expenditures. Health spending in the United States is the highest at 16.9 per cent of GDP. It is the only country with a greater share of private versus public spending on health care. Other countries higher than average include the Netherlands (11.8%), France (11.6%), Switzerland (11.4%), Germany (11.4%), Austria (11.1%), Denmark (11.0%), Canada (10.9%), Belgium (10.0%), New Zealand (10.0%) and Sweden (9.6%). The United Kingdom is at 9.3 per cent, and Australia is 9.1 per cent.[26]

Governments already spend a significant part of their revenue on health care, and there is a growing debate to shift some of these costs to private plans and limit health care services. Most developed countries, with the exception of the United States, have a fully funded or partially funded health care system, either from a form of compulsory social insurance or taxation.

A RELEVANT POINT OF VIEW: TAKING PERSONAL CONTROL OF YOUR RETIREMENT

As a young adult, you probably have not thought much about retirement benefits or your retirement. Why should you? It is 30 or 35 years away. Or you might think that you love your work so much that you never want to retire. The fact is that you can significantly improve your retirement benefits by making certain decisions now rather than waiting until you are older or trusting that the organization will design a retirement package that will meet your needs.

How much should you set aside for your retirement? There is no standard answer to this question as the answer depends on so many variables such as whether you have a pension plan from the organization you work in, the age you want to retire, your possible health care costs when you retire, the rate of return you can assume your investments will make and when you will die and not need a retirement income.

In answering this question, David Chilton, in *The Wealthy Barber*,[22] offers the 10 per cent solution which is a recommendation to put aside between 10 and 15 per cent of your gross income for your retirement. The book investigates the lives of three young individuals who regularly visit the local barber for financial advice. David Chilton's point is that average people, like your barber, can be very wealthy people in their retirement if they invest wisely.

Even if you do not invest 10 per cent, one important lesson offered relates to the principle of compound interest. If you invested £1,582 ($2,400) for the next 30 years, you would have invested £47,446 ($72,000), which is £1,582 ($2,400) × 30 years, not considering compound interest.

But, considering how compound interest enhances your benefits, if you invested £1,582 ($2,400) each year (or £132 [$200] a month), you would have £331,779.33 ($503,474.82) in your account based on 10 per cent interest and £215,028.00 ($326,304.79) at 8 per cent. From 1950 to 2009, the Standard and Poor's 500 index averaged 7 per cent. From 1982 to 1999, the index surged to 18 per cent a year on average. Even though forecasts for future returns are much lower, at 7 to 8 per cent, there are still gains to be made.

Getting started is as easy as setting up an online investing account with your bank or meeting with a broker to discuss your plan of putting aside a specific amount. This is akin to developing your own personal DC plan. Chilton's book and Warren Buffet books[23] offer ideas for investing and savings, from picking stocks in the stock market to using a tax-free retirement savings plan. It is far beyond the scope of this book to offer advice for investing, except to encourage people to ask whether developing a personal retirement savings plan is a useful strategic objective.

Many countries (like Canada) have tax-free saving accounts, educational savings planning or registered retirement savings plans. The United States has what is called a 401(k) defined contribution plan that allows employees to deduct a defined percentage of their income and place the money in a personal tax-free savings account. A tax-free savings account is a registered general-purpose account to encourage savings and investments, and a registered education saving plan allows a person tax savings in setting aside money for a child's post-secondary education. Some countries have a registered retirement savings plan (RRSP), which is an individually directed retirement savings plan that allows you to develop a pension fund to supplement your retirement income. Within specific contribution limits, you can save money, tax free, until you retire. Income is not taxed until money is withdrawn, and for this reason, investments grow faster than those held outside an RRSP plan. When you are in a lower income bracket during your retirement, you can withdraw the money you have.

Chilton's book also talks about the conventional wisdom for some people that their best investment was the house or condominium they owned. People often say this because their home was their only investment.

There are several good reasons for owning a house. You are paying into a mortgage rather than paying rent, and you will own something rather than paying into someone else's property. When you retire, you have assets you can sell for cash, tax free. You can also sell a higher-priced home and move into a lower-priced accommodation and, possibly, gain a little extra cash to supplement retirement needs.

As in the stock market, there have been ups and downs, or dramatic fluctuations, in housing prices. For example, in the 1970s, there was a major slump in the market, and interest rates climbed to over 20 per cent. Housing prices increased in the 1980s because of the demand from baby boomers, and by the end of the decade housing prices were relatively high before declining significantly in the 1990s. And then there was the subprime crisis in 2008, when housing prices in several countries dropped dramatically.

In general, housing prices follow inflation, but don't add a great deal of real returns (income beyond inflation).[24] As in the stock market, there are exceptions where housing prices have shown 'windfall gains' and have shown appreciable gains over other investment earnings. However, most academic experts point to data that suggests that, on average, 'housing prices follow inflation'.

Real estate investments might be risky, but so are stock market investments. The subprime crisis that saw housing and stock prices fall, beginning in November 2008, is an example of the risks that exist in both sectors. When considering a housing investment, other factors have to be taken into consideration: (i) Investing in housing creates a 'forced savings' effect. Instead of spending money eating out, you spend it to pay your mortgage. (ii) Any appreciation on your primary dwelling, even if it only follows inflation, is tax free. (iii) There is also the psychological satisfaction from pride of ownership versus renting. For some people, it is welcome work to fix and improve things you own or maintain a garden.[25]

The scare in health care comes from increased expenditures due to demographic changes and increases in benefit levels. Over the next decades, OECD countries will continue to age. In 1950, less than 1 per cent of the global population was over 80 years old, but by 2050, this is expected to reach 4 per cent. For OECD countries, by 2050, almost 9.5 per cent will be significantly older, and the proportion will be about 15 per cent in Japan, Germany, Korea and Italy. An individual's cost to the health system begins to rise dramatically in his or her mid- to late 70s. This growth in the percentage of older people will affect future costs because of demands for more care.[27]

The cost of benefits also relates to expensive improvements in diagnostic tests, drugs and treatments that have entered the market and have reduced mortality and extended lives. A high proportion of the increased costs of health care relate to the increased demands for medications related to treating cancer, depression, rheumatoid arthritis and cardiovascular ailments. There are also higher expectations among health professionals and family members to improve wellness and even to prolong life of the terminally ill.

After the financial crisis, growth in health care spending had slowed considerably until 2013, especially in countries hit hardest by the economic crisis. Governments targeted wages and medical goods such as pharmaceuticals, prevention and public health. In several countries, patients are expected to assume a greater share of health costs.[28] In 2014, health spending started to rise again, although the pace of growth was below pre-crisis rates.

Most countries have both publicly and privately funded health care systems which are managed and funded in different ways. Publicly funded universal health care systems, such as those in Canada and the United Kingdom, might still allow for private services. In Canada, patients have the freedom to choose their medical providers (doctors and facilities), and most people receiving care do not pay directly for the care provided. In the United Kingdom, the National Health Service (or NHS) provides universal coverage while private health care (used by a very small percentage of the population) can be provided by private insurance to supplement the coverage.

In responding to the financial pressures on universal public health systems, managers are searching for ways to reduce costs and improve efficiencies. One tactic is to set priorities and focus on those in need, and give elective procedures – those which are less serious and not life threatening – lower priority. For some, this has led to longer wait lists to see specialists and undergo elective surgery. The frustrations over waiting lists have stirred criticism about the sustainability of universal public health care and led to proposals for private health insurance or for allowing individuals to pay for private health care treatments.

Two-tiered health systems are now more common in various countries. They allow patients to use private medical insurance or personal finances to pay for treatment and comforts not available to those dependent on a state system. For example, Singapore's two-tiered system allows for personal and insurance funding. The government-subsidized hospitals accept all patients while a parallel system provides services with extra amenities (such as private rooms).

The strategic alternatives: Different types of benefits

In managing costs, as with retirement costs, managers are seeking ways to control or manage the increasing costs of health benefits and have begun implementing a number of initiatives including shifting costs to consumers, educating consumers on costs, taking steps to improve employee education and wellness and using flexible benefit programmes.

Managing health care costs by shifting towards consumer-directed health care. The shift towards individuals taking more responsibility for health care costs has resulted in employees paying larger amounts of health premiums and deductibles. In the United States, legislation allows for the creation of health savings accounts (HSAs) that can be combined with high-deductible insurance policies. In addition, it has resulted in the creation of consumer-directed health care (CDHC), where an employer's tax deductible contribution to health benefits is put in a health spending account from which employees purchase services. CDHC differs significantly from traditional insurance as the employee has a defined amount of money to spend from the HSA and is encouraged to seek price information and be more frugal in using health services.

Cost control through education. One option for controlling costs is to educate employees about the cost of health care, based on the assumption that lack of awareness may have led to over-utilization of health services. Given that health services were a part of the benefits package, most employees viewed health care coverage and insurance, along with other benefits such as paid time off, as a standard benefit. Such plans offered a great deal of freedom to employees to go directly to the doctor of their choice, and they often requested services that they may not have needed. Even as the costs of health care rose in the 1980s and 1990s, employers continued to offer generous health care coverage.[29] Educating employees about health costs as well as the benefits of seeking lower-cost preventative health care should facilitate the development of a more consumer-driven health care system.

Promoting health and wellness. Another tactic for managing and reducing costs includes education on workplace health and wellness.[30] During tough economic times, seemingly non-essential programmes such as health and wellness initiatives are cut. However, these programmes are most valuable to organizations in turbulent times when stress is higher and employee wellness is lower. When workplace education on wellness and health are a priority, there is often less absenteeism among employees as they are more mentally and physically healthy. These organizations are also more attractive to prospective employees.

Promoting health and wellness in the workplace conceivably has an impact on the bottom line. Some estimates put the cost of absenteeism to be about 1.2 per cent of payroll annually.[31] If we assume a country's total annual wage bill to be about £403.9 billion ($612.9 billion), a reduction of 0.1 percentage point (from the 1.2% to 1.1%) would be a £402 million ($610 million) saving.[32] In addition to reducing the costs of absenteeism, health and wellness programmes can reduce the need for employee benefits and for employee assistance programmes. Strategies for enhancing the 'return on investment' on workplace wellness include (i) encouraging insurance companies to recognize wellness options, creating benefit plans so wellness is cost-neutral (where employees receive money back for improving their health) and (ii) developing and implementing workplace policies and environmental changes that support healthy living.[33]

Flexible benefit programmes. Flexible benefit plans can allow employers to keep costs in control while letting employees tailor their plans to their specific needs and select benefits that are most valued. Flexible benefit plans, also called *cafeteria benefits plans*, recognize the need to craft a mixture of benefits to meet the needs of an increasingly diverse workforce. Employees can opt for some benefits over others in a menu of benefits rather than a 'one-size-fits all' benefit approach which is often more costly. For example, for a single employee with good teeth, a dental package may provide some benefit, but for a mother of four children who all need orthodontic work, the benefit could be a major incentive.

One flexible benefit plan, for example, included a core plan with life, accidental death and dismemberment, and long-term disability (LTD) insurance, each of which has options that provide for more coverage. The plan can be purchased for the employees, spouse and/or children. An employee can also opt for an LTD with a cost-of-living adjustment for an extra cost. This plan also has flex credit valued at 6.25 per cent of the basic salary that employees can select. Some of the options include supplemental health (e.g. travel coverage and plans for prescriptions, psychologists, vision, etc.), dental health (with different options), optional critical illness, health spending account (non-taxable health spending account for health-related expenses), personal spending account (taxable personal spending for expenses related to wellness, professional development and family care) and group savings plan (credits can be used to purchase a retirement saving for self or spouse).[34]

CO 3: THE NEW WORLD OF WORK–FAMILY BENEFITS

Over the last few decades, we saw dramatic changes in organizational and family life, involving a changed gender balance in the workplace, increases in dual-earner households and single-parent families, and more people caring for elderly relatives. The result is that employees are facing more problems juggling work and family responsibilities, often leading to more stresses on how they function at work or in their families. In response, many OECD countries have responded with public policies and interventions designed to reduce the work–family conflict or support employees' lives outside of their work and educational benefits or time off and financial assistance for employee development. There is wide acknowledgement that the spheres of work and family are interdependent. To help reduce the pressure of work–life imbalance and the associated costs of health care, employers are turning to family-friendly policies that have 'been shown empirically to decrease job-family conflicts among employed parents'.[35] These include policies or benefits such as flexible arrangements, family leaves and dependant care.[36] Other benefits include spousal hiring, assistance with mortgages and educational assistance for employees and their families.

In a style similar to their health care programming, the US strategy treats employers as key providers in responding to their employee family needs, while government provides minimal or targeted public problems for the most needy. In an OECD study that ranked its 34 member countries on work–life balance, the United States was 29th, a ranking attributed to long work hours and a lack of social activities. Japan, Austria, Canada, Australia, New Zealand and the United Kingdom were in the lower third while the top countries were Denmark, Spain, Belgium, Netherlands, Norway, Sweden and Germany. The OCED Better Life Index ranking is based on three criteria: percentage of employees working more than 50 hours a week, employment rate of women with children and the time spent on 'leisure and personal care'.[37]

Although the benefits themselves are important, their meaning to an employee depends on whether they reduce work–family conflict. Work–family conflict is a type of conflict when role demands in one sphere (work or family) are not compatible with demands in another.

Adopting work–family benefits, such as child care and flexible schedules, can be seen as a practical response to the increasing proportion of women in the workplace; however, the evidence is that these programmes are relied on as heavily in non-female-intensive organizations. Instead, the logic for work–family practices is used to enhance satisfaction and attract and retain people in an organization[38] in addition to giving workers more flexibility in balancing the demands of work and home.

Studies assessing the impact of work–family practices on work–family conflict and family enrichment are mixed.[39] At best, such work–family benefits are considered to be extrinsic job characteristics that might promote job satisfaction, but not commitment or intrinsic motivation.[40] That is, people are happier with these benefits as they reduce some of the problems they experience in their work and in balancing life's pressures.

The value of work–family programmes might be partially related to the employee's perception of the relationships in their work environment. Four areas of research provide a framework for understanding whether family-centred programmes are likely to reduce work–family conflict. These include the supportiveness of the supervisor, the perceptions of the organizational culture, the perceived control over work time and perceived overload.[41]

- **Supportiveness of the supervisor:** An employee's perception of the supervisor's support with regard to work and family issues is positively related to perceived success in work and life, loyalty to the organization, job satisfaction and turnover intentions.[42]
- **Supportiveness of the work culture:** Dimensions such as career penalties, time demands and managerial support for work and family issues are used to measure the supportiveness of the work–family culture.[43] Using these measures, there is a positive relationship between the work–family culture and work–family conflict for mothers, but not for fathers. However, it is not clear whether the role of the manager, the work–family policies or informal organizational supports are most helpful in developing a supportive work culture.[44]
- **Control over work time:** The more that employees perceive that they have control of the timing of their work, the less they are likely to have work–family conflicts and the more they are likely to experience work–family balance. Control over work time generally describes employees' ability to schedule when they work, the hours they work and where they work. Research on parents working in health care organizations (mainly mothers), suggests that flexible schedules and supervisor support increases perceived control, and perceived control predicts the degree of work–family conflict, which

is significantly linked to depressive symptoms, somatic complaints, high cholesterol and degree of job satisfaction.[45]
- **Perceived overload:** Longer work hours affect work–family conflict, especially if employees do not expect them. Often workload is affected by the perception that individuals should do more to demonstrate their commitment or protect their job.[46]

Overall, the findings in this area suggest that increased work–family conflict is linked to lower job satisfaction and organizational commitment, and higher intention to quit and absenteeism. That is, 'relationships' are key in whether work–family conflict is reduced. These relationships are those with the supervisor and work culture; another important factor is whether people can control their work and work time.[47]

> MANAGERIAL IMPLICATIONS: An employee's pensions and benefits, often called indirect forms of compensation, include pension benefits, health care and dental plans and paid holidays. Their importance is defined by the fact that they can represent up to 30 per cent of the total compensation package as well as by the realization that their sustainability is being challenged. For managers, pensions and benefits will be contentious issues that will likely be an important part of future collective bargaining negotiations. As pensions and benefits are costly and potentially challenging issues for organizations, there might be a need to explore ways to reduce costs and encourage employees to take more personal responsibility.

BEFORE APPLYING, LET'S REVIEW

CO 1: Review the new world of employee retirement plans.

In the new world of employee pension plans, fears exist that pension plans do not have the financial resources to pay retirees during their years of retirement. In the emerging landscape following the financial crisis, many defined benefit (DB) plans, a stalwart of retirement plans since the early twentieth century, have been terminated or adjusted to include defined contribution components. Even with these adjustments, employees are being asked to take more responsibility in funding their retirement and to consider their own investment plans.

CO 2: Review the new world of health benefits provided by the government and employers.

The financial crisis also had profound effects on the lives of citizens around the world and tested the resilience of the health care plans. The scare over health care comes from increased expenditures due to demographic changes and increases in benefit levels. Most developed countries, with the exception of the United States, have a fully funded or partially funded health care system, either from a form of compulsory social insurance or taxation. Governments already spend a large part of their revenue on health care, and there is a growing debate to shift some of these costs to private plans and limit health care services. In seeking ways to control or manage the increasing costs of health benefits, employers are implementing a number of initiatives, including shifting costs to consumers, educating consumers on costs, taking steps to improve employee education and wellness and using flexible benefit programmes.

CO 3: Illustrate the new world of family-friendly organizational practices.

Studies assessing the impact of work–family practices on work–family conflict and family enrichment are mixed. The value of work–family programmes might be partially related to the employees' perceptions of the relationships in their work environment. Four areas of research provide a framework for understanding whether family-centred programmes are likely to reduce work–family conflict: the supportiveness of the supervisor, perceptions of the organizational culture, perceived control over work time and perceived overload.

DISCUSSION AND REVIEW QUESTIONS

1. The new world of employee benefits illustrates the increased costs of health benefits and retirement benefit programmes and the need to, perhaps, 'share costs and share risks'. What are the philosophies underlying the old world and new world of pension and health benefits, and what do they mean to pensions, health care, work–family and educational benefits?
2. Unique lives and needs of twenty-first-century families are creating a corollary need to think of new types of work–family-centred benefits. The importance of these depends on the extent to which they reduce work–family conflict. Define objectives and initiatives you think are important for reducing work–family conflict.
3. Consider the fact that many public organizations are shifting from defined benefit retirement plans to defined contribution plans and encouraging employees to take more financial risk for saving for their retirements. In addition to gaining the tax advantages of tax free saving, what are some of the other strengths and weaknesses of younger people taking the initiative in developing a self-directed pension plan which includes savings and investments? What are some of the forces encouraging and inhibiting their willingness to develop self-directed plans? How can we overcome the forces inhibiting them from taking action?
4. Benefit programmes seek to attract and retain employees by providing financial protections during retirement or from risks of ill health in addition to providing ways to reduce work–family conflict. Given this as a strategic theme, identify strategic objectives within each perspective of the SHRM BSC. (i) In achieving the organization's vision, what do we want internal customers (employees) and other stakeholders to say about the retirement, health and work–family benefit programmes? (ii) What internal processes should the organization excel at to make these programmes work effectively? (iii) To satisfy our internal clients how do we add value in meeting financial objectives for the organization and employees? (iv) To achieve our customer, internal process and financial objectives, what HR and personal practices improve our ability to learn and grow?

CASE: CHANGING A WORK SCHEDULE AT PROVINCIAL HEALTH[48]

There was one agenda item on Tuesday's Board meeting. Staff wanted to discuss the report: *Staff Satisfaction at Provincial Health: Suggestions for Improvement*. Katie Thomas, Director of Provincial Health, had let herself be talked into doing a survey of employees, and she was questioning that decision now. Sure, there was some expression of dissatisfaction. But a little dissatisfaction was okay, right?

Now, she had a report in front of her on a job satisfaction survey at Provincial Health. Staff satisfaction was at an all-time low, with 30 per cent of the staff saying they were either dissatisfied

(21%) or very dissatisfied (9%). Although 49 per cent indicated they were very satisfied (10%) or satisfied (39%), a large number of employees (21%) were ambivalent about their work and the organization, and generally wanted to just do their job and go home.

One of the many reasons for the dissatisfaction pointed to the difficulties of getting things done in the organization and the inflexible work schedule. Katie felt the results were a foregone conclusion because she knew that some staff had been lobbying for a change in the work schedule.

The survey drew attention to different types of schedules and the fact that health organizations generally used a regular work schedule with set hours. It also highlighted other scheduling options, shown in Table 15.1.

Table 15.1 Different Scheduling Options

Option	Impact
Regular (full-time)	Set hours each week, arriving and departing at the same time each day.
Flexitime	Varying arrival and departure times around a 'core' time at work.
Compressed workweek (CWW)	Working days off in exchange for longer hours each day (e.g. working a 10-hour day for four days and getting three rather than two days off each week).
Part-time	Reduced workweek.
Job sharing	Sharing a job with another employee on a part-time basis.
Work from home/telework	Working part or all of the workweek from home.

Most of the employees at Provincial Health wanted a change, but staff opinions diverged as to how this should be achieved, as indicated in Table 15.2.

Table 15.2 Schedules Most Used in Various Health Organizations and Desired by Staff

Type of Schedule	Schedule Used in Various Health Organizations	Schedule That Provincial Health Employees Wanted
Regular workday	58.9%	25%
Flexitime	23.1%	45%
Compressed workweek	14.2%	25%
Part-time	3.9%	5%
Formal telework in addition to other schedule	1.1%	25%
Shift work	23.3%	0%
Guerilla telework	16.1%	0%

The results suggested that employees were juggling competing responsibilities and commitments daily, making the achievement of an effective work–life balance a challenge. There was no time for family or for pursuing education to improve one's career. The report suggested that most employees felt the traditional nine-to-five work schedule was inflexible. Some employees wanted a flexitime schedule to accommodate their diverse work and family priorities. Others wanted a compressed workweek, telecommuting, job-sharing or working part-time.

Employees seemed to be calling for more flexible schedules, but the administrative group hated the idea. Teresa, a co-ordinator in the administrative group, was most vocal: 'Flex schedules are systems from hell. We never know where people are. Half the time, they're probably not even working.'

Janal, a supervisor in Healthy Communities, had no problem with it: 'I don't care where they are or when they take their breaks. I trust them. We meet once a week and set out the priorities. And then, their jobs are to get the work done.'

One of Katie's concerns was the impact of scheduling changes on motivation of employees. She felt that flexitime and flexible schedules reduces a person's time at work and commitment to the organization and profession. In the long run, she felt that work motivation would decrease.

The meeting went on for another two hours before they agreed that they would have to evaluate it in more detail. They could keep the current schedule and figure out better ways to help employees with their competing priorities, or they could contemplate different types of schedules such as flexitime, compressed workweeks or telework. The problem is that different groups of employees and different employees within each group seemed to want different things.

After the meeting, Katie wrote a note asking you to prepare a presentation which assesses the different options.

Memo Re: Flexible Scheduling at Provincial Health

To: HR Specialist

From: Katie Thomas

At a recent meeting with our employees, we agreed to assess the implications of different scheduling options – maintaining the current schedule, two different flexitime options and a compressed workweek. Some people also talked about including telework in these options. Based on a recent job satisfaction survey, some employees indicated that they wanted us to consider adopting new schedules. I would appreciate it if you could prepare a briefing note presentation which assesses the strengths and weaknesses of different options (see the book's website for briefing note structure).

Thank you,
Katie

16 Paying for Performance and Recognizing Employees

Chapter Outline

- Chapter objectives (COs)   305
- A driving issue focusing managerial action: Seeing how different countries place more emphasis on pay for performance (PFP)   305
- CO 1: PFP in public organizations   306
- CO 2: Recognizing and providing feedback on employee contributions   313
- Before applying, let's review   315
- Discussion and review questions   316
- Case: Reviewing bonus systems in a quasi-government agency   316

CHAPTER OBJECTIVES (COs)

After reading this chapter, you will be able to implement the following objectives:

CO 1: Assess the implications of different pay-for-performance (PFP) incentive programmes.

CO 2: Design a process for recognizing and providing feedback on employee contributions.

A DRIVING ISSUE FOCUSING MANAGERIAL ACTION: SEEING HOW DIFFERENT COUNTRIES PLACE MORE EMPHASIS ON PAY FOR PERFORMANCE (PFP)

The topics of variable pay and pay-for-performance (PFP) financial incentives often ignite a great deal of controversy. Although researchers point to the importance of a distinct public service motivation in performance,[1] governments have rapidly adopted incentive plans that link compensation directly to some tangible measure of individual, group or organizational productivity or profitability.

Researchers point out that some people place a higher importance on certain types of rewards: Some favour equity rewards (defining rewards based on an individual's performance), while others are concerned with equality (distributing rewards equally throughout the workforce), or recognizing individuals' needs in providing rewards. In a survey of five countries – West and East Germany, the United Kingdom, New Zealand, the United States and Brazil – researchers found that organizations in nations embracing hierarchical structures are more likely to favour equity (or rewarding people based on individual performance), while organizations in egalitarian countries favoured equality and recognizing needs. Organizations in countries that favoured more harmonious relationships were more inclined to use equality rather than equity allocating rewards. Social and economic factors also play a role in understanding why certain organizations favour certain rewards. People who work in high performing private sector organizations are more likely to favour equity rewarding individual performance than those in public sector organizations, perhaps, because of greater imperative to perform economically.[2]

Wages and bonuses are said to be the most important motivational factor for Koreans and the second most important for Japanese managers. Korean and Japanese managers viewed opportunity and speed of promotion and career development (growth) as very important. There were three important differences: (i) Employment stability was much more important for Korean than Japanese managers (a hygiene factor). (ii) There are distinct differences relating to the need to have a clear company policy and job objectives (a hygiene factor). While this was important to both Korean and Japanese managers, it was much more important for the Japanese. (iii) Unique to Japanese managers, there seems to be a higher need for esteem and praise for job performance.[3]

One main argument for PFP is that it acts as a motivator in providing extrinsic rewards and plays a significant role in attracting and retaining people who want to work in environments where their contribution is recognized.[4] However, some countries have other objectives, such as the Nordic countries that focus more on personnel development, and Westminster countries that are concerned more with motivation. Others, such as France and Italy, seem more concerned with accountability of top managerial employees.[5]

> STRATEGIC CONTEXT: *This chapter reviews the fourth component of the total compensation package: incentive pay.*
>
> *The introductory perspective reviews different preferences for PFP practices. As mentioned, PFP is controversial, particularly in public organizations as it is seen to challenge traditional ideas of public sector motivation. Given an overall strategic theme of attracting and retaining top quality managers and staff, this chapter provides information on strategic objectives and initiatives related to effectively and fairly motivating and rewarding people for their performance and contribution to the organization or team. Key strategic objectives include the design and implementation of a merit or bonus programme that balances motivation and performance. Other objectives might include the design of jobs that are more intrinsically motivating.*

CO 1: PFP IN PUBLIC ORGANIZATIONS

In the private sector, PFP is a way to share the gains of extra profit and reward people based on their performance. They describe initiatives in 'how a company differentiates among employees on the basis of performance for purposes of compensation – how bonuses and merit increases are allocated, for example'.[6] These plans summarize a variety of compensation options including bonuses, profit sharing, gain sharing, stock options, employee ownership programmes, commissions and merit-based pay. These practices are implemented to respond to financial pressures in business to be more competitive by encouraging desired behaviours in employees, attracting high performers and distracting those that don't fit or don't want to perform to expectations. There is a substantial body of research supporting these practices.[7] However, scholars have pointed to a number of unintended consequences. Detractors point out that these programmes have destructive effects on intrinsic motivation and teamwork[8] – in other words, that employees sometimes focus specifically on what they need to do to gain the reward at the expense of other activities that can be helpful to the organization.[9] In addition, scholars point to the fact that stresses from PFP practices may outweigh the gains from their incentive value.[10]

Examples of forms of PFP existed as early as 1946 in France, which allowed for the periodic granting of individual and group bonuses, and in the 1950s, in Japan, where there were provisions to grant employees a 'diligence allowance'. An official system of merit increases was introduced in Canada in 1964; and in the United States, the 1978 Civil Service Reform Act introduced a system of performance pay for the senior executive service.

PFP ideas are now very common in public sector organizations and exist in a majority of countries in the OECD and developing world. The general trends across governments in OECD countries illustrate an increasing number of PFP programmes in both managerial and non-managerial groups, and team and organizational incentives. There is more decentralization of PFP decision-making and an increased diversity of criteria that recognize competencies and social skills, in addition to restrictions on the number of people who can receive bonuses. The merit increments allocated are usually below 5 per cent, and bonuses are less than 10 per cent of base salary.[11]

The PFP programmes launched in the 1980s (starting in Canada, Denmark, the Netherlands, Spain, the United Kingdom and the United States) were more systematic than previous approaches where many merit increases seemed to be given to employees regardless of performance, often reflecting length of service or general career progress. The programmes in the 1980s and 1990s set out ways to link performance criteria to pay rewards. Presently, most OECD countries have a formal performance appraisal programme that generally links performance to the organization's overall goals or strategies. Most countries have a different performance management system for senior people than for other staff, and although incentives are common in promoting good performance, there are few ways to link incentives to bad performance.[12]

PFP ideas in government were stirred on by worldwide weak economic growth, low productivity, high unemployment and inflation. These economic difficulties triggered calls for reform in governments to limit pay costs, as the public sector wage bill is the largest budget item of most OECD countries. 'Doing more with less' became a mantra for developing more programmes to define performance objectives, measures and incentives to improve public sector performance and productivity.

The emphasis on performance was inspired by private sector management methods and New Public Management (NPM), which recommended organizational structural changes, privatizing many government services and devolving financial and personnel services to provide better accountability. Within this context, the adoption of PFP practices assumed that the private sector culture of incentives and accountability works more effectively in encouraging productivity than that in the public sector, an assumption which has been challenged.[13] Another important emphasis of reform was an attempt to relax rigid, seniority-based pay systems by creating more decentralized and flexible pay systems linked to performance.[14]

The strategic advantages of different PFP plans

A variety of individual, team or organization-wide PFP exist. **Merit systems** provide employees with an increase in pay based on individual performance, usually measured by an immediate supervisor's appraisal.[15] Merit pay is different than other bonus programmes because the yearly merit increments add to an employee's base salary, whereas most incentives and bonuses are a one-time payment. Merit increments tend to be smaller than lump-sum bonuses, and generally lower than 5 per cent of the base salary. Their advantage to the employee is that the pay increment becomes part of the base salary.[16]

Merit pay is arguably a very popular form of incentive pay because of its goal of rewarding high performers. Sceptics point to several reasons why merit pay plans can be problematic. One of the most famous sceptics of merit systems was management guru Dr. W. Edward Deming. He indicated that although the idea of merit rating is alluring, much of a person's performance depends on interactions with others, many of whom are not directly controllable by the employee.[17] Given that many organizations have difficulty implementing an objective performance appraisal system, and one that motivates people to improve performance, tying merit increases to faulty appraisals might be counterproductive.[18] Added to this, many supervisors resist performance appraisals, and few are trained in the art of providing feedback and developing a collaborative relationship to motivate people to improve their performance.[19] Other problems relate to the fact that merit pay can detract from a person's perception of doing well in an organization[20] and from public service motivation.[21] Because almost all employees feel they are above average performers, being paid an average or below average merit increase is demoralizing and affects their self worth. Not surprisingly, the percentage of unionized employees covered by individual PFP programmes generally is low, and merit pay provisions appear in under 10 per cent of all collective agreements.[22]

Lump-sum bonuses are pay increments given to employees on the basis of employee or group performance and are generally more cost-effective than other merit systems because the bonus does not become an ongoing part of the base salary. Some countries rely only on bonuses, such as is the case for France, Italy, Spain and the United States (senior executive service). Canada, Finland, Germany, Korea, New Zealand and Switzerland are OECD countries that use a combination of bonus and merit increments.

The most important disadvantages of individual plans are that they can harm co-operative team relationships, increasing unnecessary competition and hindering the working relationships between employees and supervisors. Added to this, managers or supervisors experience many difficulties in applying individual pay plans, partially because of a human tendency of not wanting to make hard judgements by rewarding one person and not another. Some of these difficulties reflect managers' reluctance to evaluate people given that there are so many inherent problems in measuring performance.

Many **team incentive plans** emerged in response to competitive pressures to improve productivity and involve workers in production decisions, ideas which grew from their success in Japanese companies and public organizations. The building blocks of team-based incentive systems are similar to all plans: (i) explicitly stated departmental or organizational level goal(s) to be achieved through teamwork, (ii) an incentive system based on the achievement of the goal(s), (iii) rewards that employees perceive as resulting from their contribution, (iv) rewards that are perceived to be fair and (v) rewards offered which clearly signal what is meant by 'good performance'.[23]

Teams don't always work as intended, especially in cultures that are individually oriented. As a result, when managers introduce team compensation systems, they can encounter difficulties such as lack of cohesiveness and complaints about free riders. These difficulties give rise to the expression 'A camel is what results when you try to design a horse with a committee or a team'. Given the problems of teamwork, generally, placing a team-based incentive system on the team experience is likely to add to any difficulties that already exist.

The most recognized **organizational PFP** plans are generally gain-sharing programmes which reward employees for reducing costs and improving performance and, in the private sector, for the organization's improved profits (employee stock ownership plans). This encourages employees to think of the organization before they think of themselves as individuals or team members.

In the private sector, gain-sharing programmes have existed in various formats over the years, and key plans are the *Scanlon Plan*, the *Rucker Plan*, *Improshare* (improved productivity through sharing) and other customized plans. The Scanlon Plan is legendary in illustrating labour management co-operation focused on productivity improvement. It is also a useful template to use in designing individual and group plans.

After a shutdown caused by the Great Depression, Joseph N. Scanlon (who was the president of a local union in an Ohio steel company) asked management to reopen its doors, stating that the union would work with management in reducing costs through production committees.[24] The Scanlon Plan's commitment to employee participation sets it apart from other gain-sharing programmes and illustrates principles that highlight this unique employee participation philosophy:

- *Identity:* Meaningful involvement of all people who are working for the organization means that employees must understand how the business operates, the customer demands and needs and how the organization seeks to achieve competitive advantage.
- *Competence:* Employees must be competent in their jobs and must also have the competence to identify and implement productivity improvements.
- *Participation:* Given that knowledgeable employees can improve productivity, they must be given the opportunity to provide ideas and participate.
- *Equity:* Organizational success is based on partnerships with employees who provide labour, customers who purchase goods and services, and investors who provide capital.[25]

Production committees in each department are the main mechanism for employee participation in addressing production problems and offering ideas for improvement. These ideas are considered by an organization-wide screening committee, made up of equal numbers of employees and managers, which consults with top management and is responsible for reviewing and acting on suggestions as well as reviewing how monthly bonuses are to be allocated. Financial incentives are based on a formula using productivity compared to the norm. The norm, which is reviewed regularly, is based on the relationship between labour costs and sales value. The plan also has a reserve fund where 25 per cent of the bonuses are set aside for labour costs which might exceed the norm. At the end of the year, any surplus is distributed to employees.

As an example of a gain-sharing programme in the public sector, government workers in Singapore receive an annual bonus based on the GDP growth of the country. The bonus in 2014 was 1.8 extra months of salary, and if you include a mid-year bonus of 0.5 a month's salary, Singapore civil servants will get 2.3 months of bonus this year, down 0.2 from the previous year's.

Table 16.1 reviews the general advantages and disadvantages of individual, team and organizational incentive plans. Although a key advantage of individual and team incentive plans is in encouraging employees to focus on specific objectives and initiatives which are deemed important, such a focus might encourage employees to avoid other important work which is not being rewarded. Team plans, in encouraging people to work together, are very appropriate for public sector organizations where it is important to get people from different specialized areas to work together.

A key advantage of an organizational-wide gain-sharing programme is encouraging the use of labour management committees to work together on productivity issues. Although most of these plans have been applied in the private sector, Singapore's Annual Wage Supplement is a bonus system where the formula is set based on the employment contract between labour and management. The annual bonus is a one-time payment based on the rise and fall of the country's GDP. Singapore might be one of the few countries that explicitly link bonuses to growth.

Reviewing the motivational assumptions of PFP

In a variety of ways, PFP seeks to enhance motivation and performance in the public sector. These pay practices are used to boost public sector efficiency,[26] motivation[27] and accountability of civil servants. They also change the traditional compensation system where pay is seen as an entitlement; benefits are given because of tenure; merit increases do not differentiate performance sufficiently; and even

Table 16.1 The Pros and Cons of Individual, Team and Organizational Plans

Advantages	Disadvantages
Individual-based Incentive Plans	
Employees tend to improve performance on objectives or initiatives where there is a clear link to pay.	Individual performance plans may create competition and destroy co-operation among peers and can sour relationships between employees and supervisors.
Rewarding performance helps to achieve individual equity. Equity theory suggests that high performers may leave the company if they do not receive rewards equal to their efforts.	People might focus too narrowly on only achieving the goals rewarded and avoid other important tasks which are not as easily measured.
Individual plans encourage competition in an individualistic culture, which may motivate employees to perform better than their colleagues.	Rewards for individual pay plans are generally controlled by supervisors or managers promoting a possible hierarchical relationship.
	Individual merit plans are more costly in the long term because increases add to the base salary.
Team-based Incentive Plans	
Team rewards can be useful in encouraging teamwork among different specialized groups working on complex problems.	Some groups experience free rider effects, where some people contribute little to the team because of low motivation or ability. Other problems include 'group think' and the difficulty of establishing cohesive, heterogeneous groups who work well together.
Team plans are useful when it is more difficult to single out individual performance and when the organizational structure encourages teamwork. These might be cases where the task or technology allows for natural team formations, or there is a need to pull together people with diverse skills and backgrounds.	One of the most serious problems of teams is that they can encourage team performance and team rivalry at the expense of organizational goals.
Organization-wide Incentive Plans	
Of the organizational-wide incentive plans, **gain sharing** is unique in that it is not based on the idea that pay incentives motivate people. Instead, gain sharing assumes that cost savings and productivity improve by treating employees better and empowering them in company management. As such, gain sharing can provide a way to elicit employee involvement and co-operation across workers and teams.	Although the formulas for calculating bonuses in gain sharing programme are clearly established, problems can occur in adjusting measures and managing the plan.
	Gain sharing programmes introduce labour management committees and an integrative approach to labour relations, an atmosphere which can be resisted by managers or union executives.
The most macro type of organization-wide incentive programme is a gain sharing programme, which rewards employees on the basis of organizational profits. Rewards are given to employees as a share of profits, something which, in principle, is a fair distribution of wealth.	Gain sharing results sometimes occur from several factors that have nothing to do with employee effort (economic conditions, new trends).
	Employees cannot see the linkage between efforts and rewards received.

executive bonuses become an entitlement.[28] As a tool, they are seen as important for improving performance, rewarding valuable employees, promoting customer relationships and helping focus on strategic objectives like safety, cost control and service delivery.

PFP is supported by various theories such as principal-agent theory, expectancy theory and equity theory. Principal-agent theory supports the idea that monetary incentives can resolve conflicting interests and provide a closer symmetry between the interests of the rational principal (e.g. supervisor) and agent (employee).[29] Based on expectancy theory, people are generally motivated to pursue rewards they find attractive and are discouraged from rewards they find unattractive. A person's motivation to exert effort depends on (i) **expectancy** (the probability that it will happen), that the effort will lead to performance; (ii) **instrumentality** (perceived connection between performance and the rewards); and (iii) **valence** (the preference or value of the reward for the person). Motivation = E × I × V where E is expectancy, I is instrumentality and V is valence.[30]

Like many other theories highlighting the linkage between pay, motivation and performance, Adams' Equity Theory recognizes how many subtle, contextual factors can affect an employee's relationship with work and the employer. The theory suggests that each person has an inherent sense of fairness which is a fine balance between an employee's inputs (e.g. work put in, skill demonstrated, tolerance and enthusiasm) and outputs (e.g. salary or incentives, benefits, recognition).[31] In other words, if employees feel that pay and incentives do not justify the work they are putting in, they are likely to be less enthusiastic and motivated to perform. Further, employees demotivated by their perception of a lack of equity can become disgruntled or even disruptive.

These theories generally suggest that the effectiveness of a PFP programme depends on factors such as (i) establishing a close link between pay and performance, (ii) fairly discriminating between levels of performance and (iii) offering an incentive that is sufficiently high to motivate performance. Despite the strong theoretical support for PFP ideas, several implementation issues have been identified,[32] including employee perceptions of supervisor arbitrariness and inconsistency in rating performance, union opposition and reluctance of central agencies to monitor performance systems.[33]

PFP plans generally are accused of assuming a model of the self-interested *homo economicus*, where extra money rewards top performers and secures their long-term commitment.[34] This is sometimes seen as a carrot-and-stick approach to motivation, based on assumptions that people need to focus their efforts to achieve rewards and avoid pain. Pundits suggest that money is less available as a motivator in public organizations and is less important as a motivator, whereas managers in private sector organizations placed a higher value on the use of pay as a motivator and tended to use pay more often.[35]

Assessing the advantages of different individual, team and organizational plans is difficult to do objectively, as each plan can be implemented with many variations. It is also important to recognize that the use of incentives and money can be overstated in importance in solving motivation and performance problems. People are motivated by many things other than money, including recognition, fair treatment, a sense of justice and learning. **Monetary or compensable factors** include direct payments (salary) in addition to indirect payments such as the benefits, bonuses and health plans. **Non-monetary factors** (which are not always seen as compensable) include aspects of the work environment that enhance a person's competence and self-respect. These factors include recognition and status, support, training and development, learning and growth, and a sense of personal accomplishment.

In critiquing PFP ideas, many public administration scholars point to their effect on public service motivation (PSM) that describes an individual's public sector–oriented predisposition.[36] PSM is defined as 'a motivational force that induces individuals to perform meaningful public, community and social service',[37] and involves the 'beliefs, values and attitudes that go beyond self-interest and organizational interest, that concern the interest of a larger political entity and that motivates individuals to act accordingly whenever appropriate.'[38] Individuals with a greater public service motivation are likely to perform better in public service work that is generally characterized as having higher task significance.[39] Such jobs allow public service–motivated employees more opportunities to fulfil their values and to be intrinsically motivated.

A review of 57 studies of PFP in the public sector concluded that 'performance-related pay continues to be adopted but persistently fails to deliver its promise'.[40] In this meta-analysis of public sector organizations, researchers point out that pay is less useful for motivating people who are intrinsically motivated to work. On the other hand, pay can enhance performance for non-interesting tasks.

A follow-up vignette study suggests that PFP might change a person's motivational orientation and encourage people to make a cognitive shift in strengthening extrinsic motivation and weakening their intrinsic motivation. The research helps explain some of the modest success of PFP in public organizations, in addition to guiding any application.[41]

Other researchers warn us about the fact that an over-reliance on extrinsic rewards might distract from a person's **intrinsic motivational** needs, which are internal to the person.[42] Financial incentives are not as effective in focusing the efforts and performance of people who are motivated by the job itself and the challenge and growth it provides (e.g. artists, computer software designers, woodworkers, novelists). Incentive pay for highly motivated people might distract from general interest and motivation. Herzberg's motivation-hygiene theory helps us understand that a number of extrinsic factors, such as incentive pay, salary and working conditions, might be useful in reducing job dissatisfaction but might not contribute to motivation.[43] A person's motivation involves an entirely different set of factors focused on enriching the job, developing relationships with customers and improving the level of challenge in the job. Herzberg's point is that relying on salary, incentives and other financial measures can have some unintended consequences unless we link them to motivational factors (recognition for achievement, challenge).

Performance metrics: Making PFP work better

Many of the suggestions for improving the effectiveness of a PFP programme depend on establishing a clear link between pay and performance; however, it is useful to pay attention to the process of implementation. That is, a PFP programme might be improved with (i) supervisorial relationships that link incentives and performance to feedback and recognition and (ii) a review process that is perceived to be fairly administered.

PFP plans work best when they build on supervisorial relationships and the collaborative problem-solving practices discussed in Chapter 8. The practices highlight planning, setting goals, problem-solving discussions, providing clear feedback aimed at helping employees improve their performance and motivating them to improve.[44] In illustrating how these practices can be usefully linked to PFP, researchers implemented four types of incentive plans in field settings. In using a routine PFP plan, supervisors simply communicated the specifics of the plan when it started and provided no coaching or feedback after the initial communication. Supervisors implementing the monetary performance plan were trained, and provided workers with ongoing help and coaching throughout. Supervisors in a third group were trained in providing recognition and attention if they observed specific behaviours. In the performance feedback intervention, supervisors developed charts and objective information on performance. Unlike the recognition group, these supervisors did not add personal comments, but simply charted the information they collected. Productivity improved least in the routine PFP group (12%), where no coaching and feedback was provided, and most within the monetary incentive plan (32%), where coaching and feedback was provided, followed by recognition (24%) and performance feedback (20%). These results point to the importance of interpersonal feedback and recognition and the role of the supervisor.[45] A PFP plan works much better if the supervisor makes it work. On the other hand, good supervisorial feedback and recognition-driven performance improvement does not seem to rely on providing monetary incentives.

The procedural justice literature argues that the perceived fairness of procedures used in making decisions is an important facet of a PFP programme. Justice researchers call for allocation processes where there is consistency across people and time, no personal bias, a sharing of accurate information, representation of interests and values of people involved and opportunities to change an unfair decision.[46] In a meta-analysis of 148 field studies and 42 laboratory studies, procedural justice was a better predictor of performance than other forms of justice. Procedural justice is concerned with the fairness and transparency of the process by which decisions are made.[47]

Reviews of PFP point out that other HR practices are just as useful in improving performance.[48] That is, higher performance is linked to empowerment initiatives which provide meaningful work, a sense of competence in making sure that people can perform a task, self-determination in giving people freedom to choose their work activities and methods, and a belief that one's actions will make a difference.[49] Also, higher performance is connected to initiatives described in Chapters 4 and 8, such as designing jobs with higher levels of task significance[50] and performance systems involving employees in setting goals which are clear and challenging.[51]

CO 2: RECOGNIZING AND PROVIDING FEEDBACK ON EMPLOYEE CONTRIBUTIONS

Recognition and appreciation programmes are valuable ways to send signals to employees and avoid some of the possible difficulties of PFP systems.

Recognition can be given at the individual, group or organizational level. Examples of individual awards might be medals, titles, luncheons, gift certificates or plaques. An Emeritus Professorship is an example of a long-service award, and a medal is a form of recognition given to a soldier for taking part in a combat mission. Team awards might include trophies or gift certificates for a team that achieved a performance objective. At the organizational level, the Beacon scheme in the United Kingdom attempts to commend best practices in local government.

Recognition programmes have many features that are unique from PFP programmes. They are less costly but are highly visible in comparison with merit awards or bonuses, which are often given in secret. As they recognize overall performance, and because the criteria are not defined specifically for certain objectives, they do not encourage people to focus only on objectives where there are rewards. Recognition programmes put less emphasis on extrinsic motivation at the expense of intrinsic motivation because the recognition is given for overall performance as opposed to attaining specific objectives; these include supporting others, positive attitudes, customer service, productivity and achieving the organization's strategic objectives.[52]

Employees consistently say they want more recognition and indicate it is one of the most important things that managers can do to thank them and show appreciation for a job well done. Employee recognition from supervisors and peers is highly correlated with organizational commitment and performance.[53]

As with many incentive programmes, formal recognition programmes have detractors who argue that they 'are perceived as stale and irrelevant by employees, a by-product of a bygone era'. 'Employees no longer hang up their certificates', and some people even feel embarrassed at being singled out as a managerial favourite.[54]

How do we explain the apparent inconsistency that employees want recognition, yet they don't seem to appreciate many of the forms of formal recognition they receive? To begin with, certain awards are of less value to employees. For example, achievement awards (years of service, employee of the month, certificates for achievement), cash substitutes (such as gift certificates or entertainment tickets, vouchers), nominal gifts (mementos, coffee mugs, lunch or dinner with manager, pens) and perks (preferred parking spots, special privileges) are ranked on the bottom of employee preferences. The top forms of recognition are support, involvement (information, involvement and support if a mistake is made) and

QUIZ 16.1 – WHAT DO EMPLOYEES WANT IN BEING RECOGNIZED?

Before implementing any recognition programme, it is often a good idea to develop a better understanding of how employees want to be recognized. Perhaps employees like some forms of recognition more than others. Individually, rank the following list of 13 factors in their order of importance to you. Place the number 1 beside the item you think that the greatest number of employees would include in their list of things as important in a job. Place the number 2 beside the items which the next largest numbers of employees would include, and so on, to the number 13.

Factors	Your Ranking
1. Public praise (public sharing of customer letters, praising employee in organizational meetings, recognition in organization's awards ceremony, acknowledgement in organizational newsletter)	
2. Flexible working hours (being allowed to leave work early when necessary, time off from work, being allowed compensatory time for extra hours worked)	
3. Written praise (letters of praise placed on employee's personal file, written notes of praise, thank-you card)	
4. Public perks (special privileges, preferred parking, 'employee of month' award, pass-around trophy)	
5. Support and involvement (providing information needed, support when making a mistake, involving employee in decision-making, manager asking for opinion)	
6. Cash or cash substitutes (a nominal cash award, gift certificate or voucher, dinner out for two, entertainment tickets)	
7. Achievement awards (years of service award, gift certificate, certificate of achievement, entertainment tickets)	
8. Learning and development (manager support in learning new skills, manager discussing career options, being allowed a learning activity, manager discussing learning after completing a project)	
9. Nominal gifts or food (manager providing food to celebrate success, being given flowers, receiving coupons for food, car wash, movies, manager buying lunch or dinner)	
10. Electronic praise (letters of praise sent by e-mail, being copied on positive e-mail message, being given praise by e-mail or voice mail)	
11. Autonomy and authority (being allowed to decide best way to do work, being given more job autonomy or more choice of assignment)	
12. Personal praise (being thanked, receiving verbal praise)	
13. Manager's availability and time (manager being available to answer questions, manager taking the time to get to know employee, manager spending time with employee, manager listening to employee on non-job issues)	

personal praise (of various forms when a job is well done), preferring such praise to occur 'immediately' or 'soon after' something is accomplished.[55]

There are two basic forms of recognition: achievement recognition and compensatory recognition. Recognition for achievement acknowledges accomplishments: 'You have done a great job, and because you showed a lot of talent, we are going to give you the opportunity to use more of your talents.' Rewards like support, autonomy and authority, learning and development, and sincere praise attached to this achievement are examples of this form of recognition.

Compensatory, or hygiene, forms of recognition, are rewards given to a person for 'going along' or as an attempt to make people feel good as they perform according to expectations. This form of recognition is not tied to the job achievement and is a reward for long service, completing a course or doing what a manager wanted done, rather than for accomplishing something unique or for using special talents. Frederick Herzberg's motivation-hygiene theory suggests that recognition for achievement is a motivator, whereas compensatory recognition is only useful for making people feel good. As a result, these hygiene rewards have less value over a period of time.[56]

Recognition for achievement is a cost-effective way to reward employees, increasing their commitment to an organization, and most forms of recognition don't require formal recognition programmes. Informal or spontaneous recognition that is sincere is one of the best ways to recognize employees.[57] A job well done can also be recognized by providing additional support or empowering the employee in ways such as greater choice of assignments, increased authority or naming the employee as an internal consultant to other staff. Symbolic recognition such as plaques or coffee mugs with inscriptions can also be effective, provided they reflect sincere appreciation for achievements. The bottom line is that the method of recognition should highlight achievements and should be sincere, meaningful and immediate.

Successful implementation of recognition plans hinges on a manager's positive working relationship with employees. In establishing a positive relationship, managers should ensure that employees understand the goals of the recognition plan, that is how it can enhance employee motivation, in addition to designing and administering plans with clear standards and measures. The building blocks of a recognition programme include (i) explicitly stated departmental or organizational level goal(s); (ii) a clear understanding of the importance and use of informal, sincere and immediate recognition; (iii) a clear signal of what is meant by outstanding achievements; and (iv) fairness in the administration of any formal programme (possibly by having a staff committee administering the programme so it is not seen as a programme administered by management).

BEFORE APPLYING, LET'S REVIEW

CO 1: Assess the implications of different PFP incentive programmes.

PFP is a controversial topic in all organizations. In government, PFP proponents see it as a way to boost efficiency, motivation and accountability of civil servants, but public administration scholars see it as a challenge to public sector motivation. Programmes for PFP can be more effective if there is a clear link between pay and performance. Beyond this, most important facets of PFP involve supervisorial relationships that link incentives and performance to feedback and recognition, and a review process that is perceived to be fairly administered. PFP should be seen in relation to other practices which are very useful in improving performance, such as employee empowerment, designing jobs with higher levels of significance, and performance management systems that encourage employee goal setting.

CO 2: Design a process for recognizing and providing feedback on employee contributions.

Employees consistently say they want more recognition while indicating it is one of the most important things that managers can do to thank them and show appreciation for a job well done. Recognition and appreciation programmes are valuable ways to send signals to employees and avoid some of the possible difficulties of PFP systems. Successful implementation of recognition plans hinge on a manager's positive working relationship with employees. In establishing a positive relationship, managers should ensure that employees understand the goals of the recognition plan and how it can enhance employee motivation, in addition to designing and administering plans with clear standards and measures.

DISCUSSION AND REVIEW QUESTIONS

1. Define some of the key reasons that incentive systems don't work well. Define the most important characteristics of a successful incentive plan and how it might work in a unionized environment.
2. Divide the class into groups of three or four students. Half of the groups will defend the position that incentives and PFP programmes are important for motivating employees and reinforcing goals and preferred behaviours. The other groups will take the stance that incentives promote narrow attitudes – 'Let's do what we have to and nothing more' – and reduce intrinsic motivation and corporate responsibility. Each group should defend its position against a group that is taking a different stance. Each group should have five minutes to articulate their position, four minutes for the rebuttal and two minutes for concluding statements. All members of each group should have the opportunity to speak.
3. Public sector organizations represent a large part of our workforce, and motivation and recognition are critically important in these organizations. However, it is not easy to identify performance criteria or measure the impact of employee efforts. Working individually or with other people, consider the adoption of incentive, merit or recognition programmes for public sector organizations. Develop a recognition programme for public sector workers such as police officers, nurses and teachers. Define the principles for administering the plan, the motivational objectives that are important and the form of recognition.
4. Incentive programmes seek to attract and retain people who want to work in organizations where they have the ability to improve their pay for performing well. Given this as a strategic theme for rewarding people in a quasi-public agency like a university, identify strategic objectives within each perspective of the SHRM BSC for implementing a bonus system for top university administrators: (i) In achieving the organization's vision, what do we want internal customers (managers, employees) and external stakeholders to say about the incentive programme? (ii) What internal processes should the organization excel at to make these programmes work effectively? (iii) To satisfy our internal and external clients, how do we use the bonus system in meeting financial objectives for the organization and employees? (iv) To achieve our customer-related, internal process and financial objectives, what HR practices improve our ability to learn and grow?

CASE: REVIEWING BONUS SYSTEMS IN A QUASI-GOVERNMENT AGENCY

In recognizing the rising costs of higher education, legislators are questioning a trend where university presidents and heads of quasi-government agencies are receiving bonus packages which, in many cases, more than double already high salaries. Some university presidents, for example, make more than £658,979 ($1,000,000), and the bonuses make up about half of the total salary base. To get their bonuses, presidents need to meet a series of goals such as increasing research funding, undergraduate enrolments and student retention rates.

The justification for the bonuses is based on a trend where top university administrators are benchmarking their salaries and bonuses against those in giant business organizations. In these organizations, there has also been a growth in salaries paid to top people, where the distance between the average salaries has increased substantially. At the same time that bonuses are rising, so are tuition fees. Criticism from the public encouraged legislators to ask a government salary review committee to investigate compensation practices. At the conclusion of its work, the committee identified three potential avenues of change:

- *Option 1:* In our review of practices, the current bonus structure seems to have evolved because universities have tended to follow practices of others,[58] even though there is no conclusive evidence the university system is more effective now than before bonuses were introduced. While recognizing that the bonuses are costly, there are worse problems in many agencies that are a higher priority. It would be difficult to implement changes in the current incentive systems without a great deal of dissatisfaction from top university people, and we might end up losing some of them. We suggest that the legislators may wish to leave the existing system intact and wait until timing is right for making changes.
- *Option 2:* We suggest a tighter system for allocating performance bonuses. While bonuses of our four major universities add up to more than £1,317,958 ($2 million) each year, student tuition has increased significantly. The proposal is to restrict bonuses to 20 per cent of the president's base salary and allocate bonuses once every four years. We suggest that you also introduce legislation to use the money saved for funding higher-education tuitions to help families struggling to pay for university.
- *Option 3*: In defining a better system for allocating bonuses, create criteria that are more specific and clearly tied to performance of the university as a whole. In the present system, it is too easy for university presidents to achieve their bonuses while ignoring responsibilities and activities they should be doing as part of their job. This option calls for a two-tiered system. The first tier identifies criteria and expected goals – related research funding, undergraduate enrolments and student retention rates – which are part of the basic contract. The second tier focuses on high-level strategic goals, and the criteria are more difficult to achieve and might allow for a 20–30 per cent increase.

Task. As a team of senior policy advisers reporting to legislators who are seeking to respond to this issue, assess the strengths and weaknesses of each option and make a decision on which of the three options to follow.

References

Preface

1. Lienhard, A. (2006) Public private partnerships (PPPs) in Switzerland: Experiences risks – potentials. *International Review of Administrative Services*, 72: 547–563.
2. Meyer, M.W. (1979) *Change in public bureaucracies*. Cambridge: Cambridge University Press.
3. Simon, H.A. (1995) Why public administration? *Journal of Public Administration Research and Theory*, 8: 1–12.
4. Thompson, J.D. (1962) Common and uncommon elements in administration. *Social Welfare Forum*, 89: 181–201.
5. Savoie, D.J. (2003) *Breaking the bargain: Public servants, ministers and parliament*. Toronto: University of Toronto Press.
6. Gruening, G. (2001) Origin and theoretical basis of New Public Management. *International Public Management Journal*, 2: 1–25.
7. Ingraham, P.W. (1994) *New paradigms for government: Issues for the changing public services*. San Francisco: Jossey-Bass.
8. Rainey, H.G. (2009) *Understanding and managing public organizations*. 4th ed. San Francisco: Jossey-Bass.
9. Bozeman, B. (1987) *All organizations are public: Bridging public and private organization theories*. San Francisco: Jossey-Bass, p. xi.
10. Dahl, R.A., & Lindblom, C.E. (1953) *Politics, economics and welfare*. New York: Harper and Brothers.
11. Downs, A. (1967) *Inside bureaucracy*. Boston: Little, Brown; Lindblom, C.E. (1977) *Politics and markets*. New York: Basic Books.
12. Rainey, H.G. (2009) op. cit., p. 67.
13. Moore, M.H. (1995) *Creating public value: Strategic management in government*. Cambridge, Mass: Harvard Business School Press.
14. Bozeman, B. (2007) *Public values and public interest*. Washington, DC: Georgetown U. Press, p. 17.
15. Ibid.
16. Rainey, H.G. (1999) Using comparisons of public and private sector organizations to assess innovative attitudes among members of organizations. *Public Productivity and Management Review*, 23: 130–149; Lewis, G.B., & Frank, S.A. (2002) Who wants to work for the government? *Public Administration Review*, 62: 395–404.
17. Ulrich, D. (1998) A new mandate for human resources. *Harvard Business Review*, November: 123–134.
18. Kaplan, R., & Norton, D.P. (2004) *Strategy Maps: Converting intangible assets into tangible outcomes*. Boston: Harvard Business School Press.
19. Kaplan, R., & Norton, D.P. (1992) The Balanced Scorecard: Measures that drive performance. *Harvard Business Review*, January–February: 71–79.
20. Hong, Y., Liao, H., Hu, J., & Jiang, K. (2013) Missing link in the service profit chain: A meta-analysis review of the antecedents, consequences, and moderators of service climate. *Journal of Applied Psychology*, 98: 239, 237–267.

21. Becker, B.E., Huselid, M.A, & Ulrich, D. (2001) *The HR Scorecard: Linking people, strategy, and performance*. Boston: Harvard Business School Press; Becker, B.E., Huselid, M.A., & Beatty, R.W. (2005) *The Workforce Scorecard: Linking people, strategy, and performance*. Boston: Harvard Business School Press.

Chapter 1

1. Pilichowski, E., Arnould, E., & Turkisch, E. (2007) Ageing and the public sector: Challenges for financial and human resources. *OECD Journal on Budgeting*, 7: 1–40.

2. Truss, C. (2013) The distinctiveness of human resource management in the public sector. In *Human resource management in the public sector*, R.J. Burke, A.J. Noblet, & C.L. Cooper (eds.), pp. 17–36. UK: Edward Elgar Publishing.

3. Kim, S.H., & Taylor, D. (2013) Intellectual capital vs. the book value of assets. *Journal of Intellectual Capital*, 15: 65–82; Blair M.M., & Wallman, S.M.H. (2001) *Unseen wealth: Report of the Brookings Task Force on intangibles*. Washington, DC: Brookings Institution Press. In a previous study by the Brookings Institute, tangible assets in 1982 represented 62% of industrial organizations' market value. By 1992, the figure had dropped to 38%. See: Blair, M.B. (1995) *Ownership and control: Rethinking corporate governance for the 21st century*, Washington, DC: Brookings Institution Press.

4. Paterson, T.A., Luthans, F., & Wonho, J. (2014) Thriving at work: Impact of psychological capital and supervisor support. *Journal of Organizational Behavior*, 35: 434–446.

5. Nafukho, F.M., Hairston, N.R., & Brooks, K. (2004) Human capital theory: Implications for human resource development. *Human Resource Development International*, 7: 545–551.

6. Lepak, D.P., & Snell, S.A. (1999) The human resource architecture: Toward a theory of human capital allocation and development. *Academy of Management Review*, 24: 34, 31–48.

7. Boxall, P., & Steeneveld, M. (1999) Human resource strategy and competitive advantage: A longitudinal study of engineering consultancies. *Journal of Management Studies*, 36: 443–463; Schultz, T.W. (1961) Investment in human capital. *American Economic Review*, 51: 1–17.

8. Jiang, K., Lepak, D.P., Hu, J., & Baer, J.C. (2012) How does human resource management influence organizational outcomes? A meta-analytic investigation of mediating mechanisms. *Academy of Management Journal*, 55: 1264–1294.

9. Carmeli, A., & Tishler, A. (2004) The relationship between intangible organizational elements and organizational performance. *Strategic Management Journal*, 25: 1257–1278.

10. Truss, C. (2013) op. cit.; Marciano, V.M. (1995) The origins and development of human resource management. *Academy of Management Proceedings*, 1: 223–227.

11. Brown, K. (2004) Human resource management in the public sector. *Public Management Review*, 6: 303–309.

12. OECD (2005) *HRM working party report*. Paris, OECD; OECD (2009) *Fostering diversity in the public service. Public employment and management working party report*. Paris: OECD.

13. Drucker, P.F. (1954) *The practice of management*. New York: AMACOM.

14. Ibid., p. 263.

15. Ibid., p. 264.

16. Bakke, E.W. (1958) *The human resources function*. New Haven, CT: Yale Labor Management Center, p. 5.

17. Ibid., p. 6.

18. Miles, R. (1965) Keeping Informed: Human relations or human resources. *Harvard Business Review*, 43: 148–163.

19. Robbins, S.P. (1978) *Personnel: The management of human resources*. Englewood Cliffs, NJ: Prentice-Hall; Werther, W.B., Davis, K., Schwind, H., & Das, H. (1990) *Canadian human resource management*. 3rd ed. Toronto: McGraw-Hill Ryerson.
20. Marciano, V.M. (1995) op. cit.
21. Stone, R. (1995) *Human Resource Management*. Brisbane: Wiley, pp. 10–13.
22. Burke, R.J., Allisey, A.F., & Noblet, A.J. (2013) The importance of human resource management in the public sector, future challenges and the relevance of the current collection. In *Human resource management in the public sector*, R.J. Burke, A.J. Noblet, & C.L. Cooper (eds.), pp. 1–13. UK: Edward Elgar Publishing.
23. Truss, C. (2013) op. cit.; Marciano, V.M. (1995) op. cit.
24. Brown, K. (2004) op. cit.
25. Truss, C. (2013) op. cit.; Marciano, V.M. (1995) op. cit.
26. Brown, K. (2004) op. cit.; Combs, J., Liu, Y., Hall, A., & Ketchen, D. (2006) How much do high-performance work practices matter? A meta-analysis of their effects on organizational performance. *Personnel Psychology*, 59: 501–528; Lepak, D., & Shaw, J. (2009) Strategic HRM in North America: Looking to the future. *International Journal of Human Resource Management*, 19: 1486–1499; Becker, B., & Huselid, M. (2006) Strategic human resources management: Where do we go from here? *Journal of Management*, 32: 898–925; Wright, P.M., & McMahan, G.C. (1992) Theoretical perspectives for strategic human resource management. *Journal of Management*, 18: 295–320.
27. Marciano, V.M. (1995) op. cit.; see also: Tichy, N.S., Fombrun, C.J., & Devanna, M.A. (1982) Strategic human resource management. *Sloan Management Review*, 22, Winter: 47–60.
28. Beer, M., Spector, B., Lawrence, P.T., Mills, D.Q., & Walton, R.E. (1984) *Managing human assets*. Cambridge, MA: Free Press.
29. Lengnick-Hall, C.A., & Lengnick-Hall, M.L. (1988) Strategic human resource management: A review of the literature and proposed typology. *Academy of Management Review*, 13: 454–470.
30. Schuler, R.S. (1992) Strategic human resource management: Linking people with the strategic needs of the business. *Organizational Dynamics*, 21: 18–32.
31. Wright, P.M., & McMahan, G.C. (1992) op. cit.
32. Guest, R. (1989) Personnel and HRM: Can you tell the difference? *Personnel Management*, 21: 48–51.
33. Gowing, M.K., & Lindholm, M.L. (2002) Human resource management in the public sector. *Human Resource Management*, 41: 283–295.
34. Wright, P.M., & Snell, S.A. (1998) Toward a unifying framework for exploring fit and flexibility in strategic human resource management. *Academy of Management Review*, 23: 756–772; Wright, P.M., & McMahan, G.C. (1992) op. cit.
35. Becker, B.E., & Huselid, M.A. (2010) Strategic human resource management: Where do we go from here? *Journal of Management*, 32: 899, 898–925.
36. Ulrich, D. (1997) A new mandate for Human Resources. *Harvard Business Review*, January–February: 124–134; Ulrich, D., Younger, J., Brockbank, W., & Ulrich, M. (2012) *Six competencies for the future of human resources*. New York: McGraw-Hill.
37. Ulrich, D. (1997) op. cit., pp. 130, 132, 124–134.
38. Emery, F.E., & Trist, E.L. (1965) The causal texture of organizational environments. *Human Relations*, 18: 21–31.
39. Rittel, H.W.J., & Webber, M.M. (1973) Dilemmas in a general theory of planning. *Policy Sciences*, 4: 155–169.

40. Pressman, J.L., & Wildavsky, A. (1973) *Implementation: How great expectations in Washington are dashed in Oakland*. Berkeley: University of California.

41. Cascio, W.F., & Aguinis, H. (2008) Staffing twenty-first-century organizations. *Academy of Management Annals*, 2: 135, 133–165.

42. Internet live stats (2015) These statistics come from internetlivestats.com on 2 September 2015. Use any search engine using a term like 'Internet users in the world' to get updated statistics.

43. Mishra, A., & Akman, I. (2000) Information technology in human resource management: An empirical assessment. *Public Personnel Management*, 39: 272, 271–290.

44. Garavan, T.N., et al. (2001) Human capital accumulation: The role of human resource development. *Journal of European Industrial Training*, 25: 49; Luthans, F., & Youssef, C.M. (2004) Human, social, and now positive psychological capital management: Investing in people for sustainable competitive advantage. *Organizational Dynamics*, 33: 143–160.

45. Zula, K.J., & Chermack, T.J. (2007) Human capital planning: A review of literature and implications for human resource development. *Human Resource Development Review*, 6: 245–262.

46. Ibid.; Nafukho, F.M., Hairston, N.R., & Brooks, K. (2004) op. cit.

47. Gary S. Becker (1993) *Human capital: A theoretical analysis with special reference to education*. Chicago: University of Chicago Press, p. 16.

48. Luthans, F., & Youssef, C.M. (2004) op. cit.; Perez, J.R., & de Pablos, P.A. (2003) Knowledge management and organizational competitiveness: A framework for human capital analysis. *Journal of Knowledge Management*, 7: 82–91.

49. Stiles, P., & Kulvisaechana, S. (2003) *Human capital and performance: A literature review*. University of Cambridge: Judge Institute of Management.

50. Nufakho, F., Hairston, N., & Brooks, K. (2004) Human capital theory: Implications for human resource development. *Human Resource Development International*, 7: 547, 545–551.

51. Lepak, D.P., & Snell, S.A. (1999) op. cit., p. 34.

52. Boxall, P., & Steeneveld, M. (1999) Human resource strategy and competitive advantage: A longitudinal study of engineering consultancies. *Journal of Management Studies*, 36: 443–463; Schultz, T.W. (1961) Investment in human capital. *American Economic Review*, 51: 1–17.

53. Jiang, K., Lepak, D.P., Hu, J., & Baer, J.C. (2012) How does human resource management influence organizational outcomes? A meta-analytic investigation of mediating mechanisms. *Academy of Management Journal*, 55: 1264–1294.

54. Cascio, W.F., & Aguinis, H. (2008) op. cit.

55. Lawler III, E.E. (1994) Total quality management and employee involvement: Are they compatible? *Academy of Management Executive*, 8: 68–76.

56. Boudreau, J.W., & Ramstad, P.M. (2008) Beyond HR: The new science of human capital. *Harvard Business School Press*, p. 9.

57. Becker, T.E., Billings, R.S., Eveleth, D.M., & Gilbert, N.L. (1996) Foci and bases of employee commitment: Implications for job performance. *Academy of Management Journal*, 39: 464–482.

58. Steigenberger, N. (2013) Power shifts in organizations: the role of high performance work systems. *The International Journal of Human Resource Management*, 24: 1165–1185.

59. Guthrie, J.P., Flood, P.C., Liu, W., Mac Curtain, S., & Armstrong, C. (2011) Big hit, no cattle? The relationship between use of high performance work systems and managerial perceptions of HR departments. *International Journal of Human Resource Management*, 22: 1672–1685.

60. House, R., Javidan, M., Hanges, P., & Dorfman, P. (2002) Understanding cultures and implicit leadership theories across the globe: An introduction to project GLOBE. *Journal of World Business*, 37: 5, 3–10.
61. Hofstede, G. (1980) Motivation, leadership, or organization: Do American theories apply abroad? *Organizational Dynamics*, Summer, 43: 42–63.
62. House, R., Javidan, M., Hanges, P., & Dorfman, P. (2002) op. cit.
63. Ibid.; Hofstede, G. (1993) Cultural constraints in management theories. *Academy of Management Executive*, 7: 81–94.
64. House, R., Javidan, M., Hange, P., & Dorfman, P. (1999) Understanding cultures and implicit leadership theories across the globe: An introduction to project GLOBE. *Journal of World Business*, 37: 3–10. These grew from the first GLOBE research conference at the University of Calgary, where 54 researchers from 38 countries convened to begin a project to gather information in 61 countries.
65. Caza, A., Barker, B.A., & Cameron, K.S. (2004) Ethics and ethos: The buffering and amplifying effects of ethical behavior and virtuousness. *Journal of Business Ethics*, 52: 169–178.
66. Cameron, K.S. (2006) Good or not bad: Standards and ethics in managing change. *Academy of Management Learning and Education*, 5: 317–323.
67. The Universal Declaration of Human Rights. New York: United Nations.
68. Mawhinney, A., & Griffiths, I. (2011) Ensuring that others behave responsibly: Giddens, governance, and human rights. *Social and Legal Studies*, 20: 481–498.
69. Kaufman, B.E. (2012) Strategic human resource management research in the United States: A failing grade after 30 years. *Academy of Management Perspectives*, 26: 12–36.
70. Rynes, S., Giluk, T., & Brown, K. (2007) The very separate worlds of academic and practitioner periodicals in human resource management: Implications for evidence based management. *Academy of Management Journal*, 50: 987–1008.
71. Ferlie, E., Fitzgerald, L., Wood, M., & Hawkins, C. (2005) The nonspread of innovations: The mediating role of professionals. *Academy of Management Journal*, 48: 117–134.
72. Guest, D.E. (2007) Don't shoot the messenger: A wake-up call for academics. *Academy of Management Journal*, 50: 1020–1026.
73. Mintzberg, H. (1994) *The rise and fall of strategic planning: Reconceiving the roles of planning, plans, and planners*. New York: Free Press.
74. Kaplan, R.S., & Norton, D.P. (2008) *The strategy premium: Linking strategy to operations for competitive advantage*. Boston: Harvard Business School Press, Chapter 1. (60 to 80 per cent of companies fall far short of the targets expressed in their strategic plans.)
75. Deming, W.E. (1982) *Quality, productivity, and competitive position*. Cambridge, MA: Center for Advanced Engineering Study, MIT.
76. Connor, P.E. (1997) Total quality management: A selective commentary on its dimensions, with reference to its downside. *Public Administration Review*, 57: 502, 501–509.
77. The 42 Canadian airports with NAV CANADA air traffic control towers reported 4.85 million aircraft take-offs and landings in 2007, up 8.4 per cent compared to 2006 (4.48 million). This marks the second consecutive annual increase in total aircraft movements; movements had shown a declining trend since the last peak in 1999 (5.3 million).
78. Henneman, T. (2005) Measuring the true benefit of human resources outsourcing. *Workforce Management*, July: 76–77.
79. Mallory, T. (2008) May I handle that for you? Companies that will take payroll – and the rest of the HR department – off your plate. *Inc. Magazine*, March: 40–42; Gelman, L., & Dell, D. (2002) *HR Outsourcing Trends*. New York: Conference Board.

80. Greer, C.R., Youngblood, S.A., & Gray, D.A. (1999) Human resource management outsourcing: The make or buy decision. *Academy of Management Executive*, 13: 85–96.

81. Shen, J. (2005) Human resource outsourcing: 1990–2004. *Journal of Organisational Transformation & Social Change*, 2: 275–296.

82. Klass, B.S., McClendon, J., & Gainey, T.W. (1999) HR outsourcing and its impact: The role of transaction costs. *Personnel Psychology*, 52: 113–136. This perspective has been called the transaction costs economics perspective.

83. Goldman, N.M. (2003) *Outsourcing trends*. New York: Conference Board.

84. Colbert, B.A. Ed., Schuler, R.S., & Jackson, S.E. (2007) The complex resource-based view: Implications for theory and practice in strategic human resources management. *Strategic Human Resource Management*, 2nd ed. New York: Blackwell Publishing, pp. 98–123.

85. Klass, B.S., McClendon, J., & Gainey, T.W. (1999) op. cit.

86. Tremblay, M., Patry, M., & Lanoie, P. (2008) Human resources outsourcing in Canadian organizations: An empirical analysis of the role of organizational characteristics, transaction costs and risks. *International Journal of Human Resource Management*, 19: 686, 683–715.

87. Ibid.

88. Woodall, J., Scott-Jackson, W., Newham, T., & Gurney, M. (2009) Making the decision to outsource human resources. *Personnel Review*, 38: 236–252; Klaas, B.S., McClendon, J.A., & Gainey, T.W. (2001) Outsourcing HR: The impact of organizational characteristics. *Human Resource Management*, 40: 125–138.

89. Stroh, L.K., & Treehuboff, D. (2003) Outsourcing HR functions: When – and when not – to go outside. *Journal of Leadership & Organizational Studies*, 10: 19–28.

90. Klaas, B.S. (2008) Outsourcing and the HR function: An examination of trends and developments within North American firms. *International Journal of Human Resource Management*, 19: 1503, 1500–1514.

91. Tremblay, M., Patry, M., & Lanoie, P. (2008) op. cit.

92. Delmotte, J., & Luc, S. (2008) HR outsourcing: Threat or opportunity. *Personnel Review*, 37: 543–563.

93. Hesketh, A. (2006) *Outsourcing the HR function possibilities and pitfalls*. Lancaster University Management School. London: Corporate Research Forum.

94. Beaman, K. (2007) *Common cause: Shared services for human resources*. Austin, TX: International Association for Human Resource Information Management.

95. Ulrich, D. (1995) Shared services: From vogue to value. *Human Resource Planning*, 18: 12–23.

96. Reilly, R., & Williams, T. (2003) *How to get best value from HR: The shared services option*. Burlington, VT: Gower Publishing Limited; Wilson, D. (2005) *Implementing shared services in the public sector*. Washington, DC: National Association of State Comptrollers; Farquhar, C., Fultz, J.M., & Graham, A. (2005) Implementing shared services in the public sector: Lessons for success. Ottawa, Ont.: The Conference Board of Canada.

97. Tushman, M.L., & O'Reilly III, C.A. (1996) Ambidextrous organizations: Managing evolutionary and revolutionary change. *California Management Review*, 38: 8–30.

98. Ibid.

99. Patel, P.C., Messersmith, J.G., & Lepak, D.P. (2013). Walking the tightrope: An assessment of the relationship between high-performance work systems and organizational ambidexterity. *Academy of Management Journal*, 56: 1420–1442.

Chapter 2

1. Kellough, J.E. (1999) Reinventing public personnel management: Ethical implications for managers and public personnel systems. *Public Personnel Management*, 28: 655–671.
2. Pablo, A.L., Reay, T., Dewald, J.R., & Casebeer, A.L. (2007) Identifying, enabling and managing dynamic capabilities in the public sector. *Journal of Management Studies*, 44: 687–708.
3. Osborne, D., & Gaebler, T. (1993) *Reinventing government: How the entrepreneurial spirit is transforming the public service*. New York: Plume.
4. Osborne, D., & Plastrick, P. (1997) *Banishing bureaucracy: The five strategies for reinventing government*. New York: Penguin Putnam.
5. Moynihan, D.P. (2005) Goal-based learning and the future of performance management. *Public Administration Review*, 65: 203–216.
6. Kellough, J.E. (1999) op. cit.
7. Savoie, D.J. (2003) *Breaking the bargain: Public servants, ministers and parliament*. Toronto: University of Toronto Press; Hood, C. (1991) A Public Management for All Seasons? *Public Administration*, 69: 3–19; Gruening, G. (2001) Origin and theoretical basis of New Public Management. *International Public Management Journal*, 2: 1–25; Diefenbach, T. (2009) New Public Management in public sector organizations: The dark sides of managerial 'enlightenment'. *Public Administration*, 87: 892–909.
8. Kellough, J.E. (1999) op. cit.
9. Diefenbach, T. (2009) op. cit.
10. Hays, S.W., & Kearney, R.C. (1997) Riding the crest of a wave: The national performance review and public management reform. *International Journal of Public Administration*, 20: 11–40.
11. Savoie, D.J. (1995) What is wrong with the New Public Management? *Canadian Public Administration*, 23: 113, 112–121.
12. Llewellyn, S., & Tappin, E. (2003) Strategy in the public sector: Management in the wilderness. *Journal of Management Studies*, 40: 955–982.
13. Kelman, S. (2007) Public administration and organizational studies. *The Academy of Management Annals 1*: 225–267.
14. Porter, M.E. (1985) *Competitive advantage: Creating and sustaining superior performance*. NY: Free Press.
15. Moore, M.H. (1995) *Creating public value*. Cambridge, MA: Harvard University Press, p. 55.
16. Colbert, B.A. (2004) The complex resource-based view: implications for theory and practice in strategic human resource management. *Academy of Management Review*, 29: 341–358.
17. Wright, P.M., & Snell, S.A. (1998) Toward a unifying framework for exploring fit and flexibility in strategy human resource management. *Academy of Management Review*, 23: 756–772; Delery, J.E., & Doty, D.H. (1996) Modes of theorizing in strategic human resource management: Tests of universalistic, contingency, and configurational performance predictions. *Academy of Management Journal*, 39: 802–835.
18. The effect is such that a one standard deviation change in the HR system is 10–20 per cent of a company's market value; see: Huselid M.A., & Becker B.E. (2000) Comment on measurement error in research on human resources and firm performance: How much error is there and how does it influence effect size estimates? *Personnel Psychology*, 53: 835–854.
19. Marchington, M., & Grugulis, I. (2000) Best practice Human Resource Management: Perfect opportunity or dangerous illusion. *International Journal of Human Resource Management*, 11: 1104–1124; Becker, B.E., & Huselid, M.A. (1999) Overview: Strategic human resource management in five leading firms. *Human Resource Management*, 38: 290, 287–301.

20. Pfeffer, J. (2007) Human resource from an organizational behaviour perspective: Some paradoxes explained. *Journal of Economic Perspectives*, 21: 119, 115–134; Pfeffer, J. (1995) Producing sustainable competitive advantage through the effective management of people. *Academy of Management Executive*, 9: 55–69.

21. Pfeffer, J. (1998) Seven practices of successful organizations. *California Management Review*, 40: 96–124; Pfeffer, J. (1995) op. cit.

22. Huselid, M.A., & Becker, B.E. (2000) op. cit.

23. Kehoe, R.R., & Wright, P.M. (2013) The impact of high-performance human resource practices on employees' attitudes and behaviours. *Journal of Management*, 39: 366–391; Schuler, R.S., & Jackson, S. (1987) Linking competitive strategies with human resource management practices. *Academy of Management Executive*, 1: 207–219; Baird, L., & Meshoulam, I. (1988) Managing two fits of strategic human resource management. *Academy of Management Review*, 13: 116–128.

24. Gould-Williams, J. (2003) The importance of HR practices and workplace trust in achieving superior performance: A study of public-sector organizations. *International Journal of Human Resource Management*, 14: 28–54.

25. Miles, R.E., & Snow, C.C. (1984) Designing strategic human resources systems. *Organizational Dynamics*, 13: 36–52.

26. Wright, P.M., & McMahan, G.C. (1998) op. cit. They use the terms *vertical* and *horizontal fit*.

27. Huselid, M.A. (1995) The impact of human resource management practices on turnover, productivity, and corporate financial performance. *Academy of Management Journal*, 38: 635–672. They use the terms *external* and *internal fit*.

28. Sun, L.Y., Aryee, S., & Law, K.S. (2007) High performance human resource practices, citizen behavior, and organizational performance: A relational perspective. *Academy of Management Journal*, 50: 558–577.

29. Bowen, D.E., & Ostroff, C. (2004) Understanding HRM-firm performance linkages: The role of the 'strength' of the HRM system. *Academy of Management Journal*, 29: 203–221.

30. Baird, L., & Meshoulam, I. (1988) Managing two fits of strategic human resource management. *Academy of Management Review*, 13: 116–128.

31. Gould-Williams, J. (2003) op. cit.; Lee, J.W., & Kim, S.E. (2012) Searching for strategic fit: An empirical analysis of the conditions for performance management implementation in U.S. federal agencies. *Public Performance & Management Review*, 36: 31–53; Westerman, J.W., & Vanka, S. (2006) A cross-cultural empirical analysis of person-organization fit measures as predictors of student performance in business education: Comparing students in the United States and India. *Academy of Management Learning and Education*, 4: 409–420.

32. Wernerfelt, B. (1984) A resource-based view of the firm. *Strategic Management Journal*, 5: 171–180; Wernerfeit, B. (1995) The resource-based view of the firm: Ten years after. *Strategic Management Journal*, 16: 171–174; Barney, J.B. (1991) Firm resources and sustained competitive advantage. *Journal of Management*, 17: 99–120; Barney, J.B. (1996) The resource-based theory of the firm. *Organizational Science*, 1: 469.

33. Bryson, J.M., Ackermann, F., & Eden, C. (2007) Putting the resource-based view of strategy and distinctive competencies to work in public organizations. *Public Administrative Review*, 67: 702, 702–717.

34. Colbert, B.A. (2004) op. cit.

35. Ibid.

36. Crook, T.R., Ketchen, Jr., D.J., Combs, J.G., & Todd, S.Y. (2008) Strategic resources and performance: A meta-analysis. *Strategic Management Journal*, 29: 1141–1154.

37. Stewart, J. (2004) The meaning of strategy in the public sector. *Australian Journal of Public Administration*, 63: 16–21.
38. Bryson, J. M. (2011) *Strategic planning for public and nonprofit organizations*, 4th ed. San Francisco: Jossey-Bass, p. 8.
39. Grigoroudis, E., Orfanoudaki, E., & Zopounidis, C. (2010) Strategic performance measurement in a health care organization: A multiple criteria approach based on the balanced scorecard. *Omega*, 40: 104–119.
40. Kaplan, R.S., & Norton, D.P. (1992) The Balanced Scorecard: Measures that drive performance. *Harvard Business Review*, January–February: 71–79; Kaplan, R.S., & Norton, D.P. (1996) *The Balanced Scorecard: Translating strategy into action*. Boston: Harvard Business School Press, pp. 1–2; Kaplan, R.S., & Norton, D.P. (2001) *The Strategy-focused organization: How balanced scorecard companies thrive in the new business environment*. Boston: Harvard Business School Press; Kaplan, R.S., & Norton, D.P. (1997). *The Balanced Scorecard: Translating strategy into action*. Boston: Harvard Business School Press.
41. Kaplan, R.S., & Norton, D.P. (1992) op. cit.; Kaplan, R.S., & Norton, D.P. (1996) op. cit.; Kaplan, R.S., & Norton, D.P. (2001) op. cit.
42. Niven, P.R. (2003) *Balanced Scorecard: Step-by-step for government and nonprofit organizations*. New York: John Wiley & Sons.
43. Bryson, J. M. (2011) op. cit., p. 48.
44. STEER analysis involving (Social Technological, Economic, Ecological, and Regulatory factors), PEST analysis (Political, Economic, Social, and Technological analysis) or STEEP analysis (Socio-cultural, Technological, Economic, Ecological or environmental, and Political).
45. Scott, R.W. (1987) *Organizations: Rational, natural, and open systems*. 2nd ed. Englewood Cliffs, NJ: Prentice Hall.
46. These definitions represent terminology used by the Balanced Scorecard Institute.
47. Bryson, J.M. (2011) op. cit.
48. Grigoroudis, E., Orfanoudaki, E., & Zopounidis, C. (2010) op. cit.; Butler, A., Letza, S.R., & Neale, B. (1997) Linking the balanced scorecard to strategy. *Long Range Planning*, 30: 242–253.
49. Gunn, E., Cunningham, J.B., & MacGregor, J.N. (2013) Developing benchmarks for CAO performance. *Local Government Studies*, 40: 851–868.
50. Niven, P.R. (2003) op. cit., p. 17.
51. Salge, T.O., & Vera, A. (2012) Benefiting from public sector innovation: The moderating role of customer and learning orientation. *Public Administration Review*, 72: 554, 550–560.
52. Hong, Y., Liao, H., Hu, J., & Jiang, K. (2013) Missing link in the service profit chain: A meta-analysis review of the antecedents, consequences, and moderators of service climate. *Journal of Applied Psychology*, 98: 237–267.
53. Rohit, D., Farley, J.U., & Webster, Jr., F.E. (1993) Corporate culture, customer orientation, and innovativeness in Japanese firms: A quadrad analysis. *Journal of Marketing*, 57: 23–37.
54. Kaplan & Norton (1996) op. cit., pp. 24–25.
55. Quinn, R.E., Faerman, S.R., Thompson, M.P., McGrath, M.R., & St. Clair, L.S. (2007) *Becoming a master manager: A competing values approach*. 4th ed. New York: John Wiley and Sons.
56. Kaplan, R.S., & Norton, D.P. (2004) *Strategy maps: Converting intangible assets into tangible outcomes*. Boston: Harvard Business School Press, pp. 3–17.
57. Ibid.
58. This was Cool Aid's first strategy map in 2004. See https://coolaid.org or search on 'Cool Aid Victoria' and link to strategic planning for more recent strategy maps.

59. Alford, J. (2002) Defining the client in the public sector: A social-exchange perspective. *Public Administration Review*, 62, 337, 337–346.

60. Ibid.

61. Jos, P.H., & Tompkins, M.E. (2009) Keeping it public: Defending public service values in a customer service age. *Public Administration Review*, 69, 1077–1086.

62. Ibid.

63. Chrisman, J.J., Hofer, C.W., & Boulton, W.R. (1988) Toward a system for classifying business strategies. *Academy of Management Review*, 13: 414, 413–428.

64. Boyatzis, R.E. (1982) *The Competent Manager*. New York: John Wiley & Sons, p. 21.

65. Ibid.

66. For examples of these theme areas and objectives, insert 'Saanich Strategic themes' into a search engine.

Chapter 3

1. Horton, S. (2000) Competency management in the British civil service. *International Journal of Public Sector Management*, 13: 354–368.

2. McClelland, D.C. (1973) Testing for competence rather than for intelligence. *American Psychologist*, 28: 1–14.

3. Ibid.

4. Boyatzis, R.E. (1982) *The Competent Manager*. New York: John Wiley & Sons, p. 21.

5. Ibid., p. 21.

6. Ibid., p. 230; Boyatzis, R.E. (2007) Competencies in the 21st century. *Journal of Management Development*, 27: 5–12.

7. Ibid., p. 230; Getha-Taylor, H. (2008) Identifying collaborative competencies. *Review of Public Personnel Administration*, 28: 106, 103–119; Spencer, L.M., McClelland, D.C., & Spencer, S.M. (1994) *Competency assessment methods: History and state of art*. Boston: Hay McBer Research Press.

8. Ibid.; Daley, D.M. (2002) *Strategic human resource management: People and performance management in the public sector*. Upper Saddle River, NJ: Prentice Hall.

9. Drucker, P.F. (1994) *The practice of management*. New York: Evanston.

10. Anderson, J.C., Rungtusanatham, M., & Schroeder, R.G. (1994) A theory of quality management underlying the Deming method. *Academy of Management Review*, 19: 472–509.

11. Hammer, M., & Champy, J. (1993) *Reengineering the corporation: A manifesto for business revolution*. New York: Harper Business.

12. Deming, W.E. (1986) *Out of crisis*. Cambridge, Massachusetts Institute of Technology, Center for Advanced Engineering Study.

13. Horton, S. (2000) op. cit.

14. Bartram, D. (2005) The great eight competencies: A criterion-centric approach to validation. *Journal of Applied Psychology*, 90, 1185–1203.

15. Horton, S. (2000) op. cit.

16. Daley, D.M. (2002) op. cit.

17. Flanagan, J.C. (1954) The critical incident technique. *Psychological Bulletin*, 51: 328, 327–358.

18. Ibid., 327–358.
19. DiNisi, A.S., Cornelius, E.T., III, & Blencoe, A.G. (1987) Further investigation of common knowledge effects on job analysis ratings. *Journal of Applied Psychology*, 72: 262–268.
20. Morgeson, F.P., Delaney-Klionger, K., Ferrara, P., Mayfield, M.S., & Campion, M.A. (2004) Self-presentation processes in job-analysis information: A field experiment investigating inflation abilities, tasks, and competencies. *Journal of Applied Psychology*, 89: 674–686.
21. Dierdorff, E.C., & Wilson, M.A. (2003) A meta-analysis of job analysis reliability. *Journal of Applied Psychology*, 88: 635–646. The intra-rater reliability of the PAQ reported in the meta-analysis was 82.
22. Daley, D.M. (2002) op. cit.
23. Bonder, A., Bouchard, C., & Bellemare, G. (2011) Competency-based management – An integrated approach to human resource management in the Canadian public sector. *Public Personnel Management*, 40: 1–10.
24. Prahalad, C., & Hamel, G. (1990) The core competences of the corporation. Harvard Business Review, May–June: 79–91; Prahalad, C., & Hamel, G. (1995) *Competing for the future*. Boston: Harvard Business School Press; Wright, P.M., McMahan, G.C., McCormick, B., & Sherman, W.S. (1998) Strategy, core competence, and HR involvement as determinants of HR effectiveness and refinery performance. *Human Resource Management*, 37: 17–29.
25. US Office of Personnel Management (OPM). (2007) Executive core qualifications.
26. Horton, S. (2000) Introduction – the competency movement: Its origins and impact on the public sector. *International Journal of Public Sector Management*, 13: 306–318; Horton, S. (2000) op. cit., 354–368.
27. Boyatzis, R.E. (1982) op. cit.; Goleman, D., Boyatzis, R., & McKee, A. (2002) *Primal leadership: Realizing the power of emotional intelligence*. Boston: Harvard Business School Press.
28. Leslie, J.G., & Van Velsor, E. (1996) *A look at derailment today: North America and Europe*. Greensboro, NC: Center for Creative Leadership.
29. Posner, B.Z., & Kouzes, J.M. (1988) Development and validation of the Leadership Practices Inventory. *Educational and Psychological Measurement*, 48: 483–496; Posner, B.Z., & Kouzes, J.M. (1993) Psychometric properties of the Leadership Practices Inventory—updated. *Educational and Psychological Measurement*, 53: 191–199.
30. Kouzes, J.M., & Posner, B.Z. (1995) *The leadership challenge: How to keep getting extraordinary things done in organizations*. San Francisco: Jossey-Bass.
31. Bartram, D. (2005) op. cit.
32. Borman, W.C., & Motowidlo, D.J. (1993) Expanding the criterion domain to include elements of contextual performance. In *Personnel selection in organizations*, N. Schmitt & W. C. Borman (eds.), pp. 71–98. San Francisco: Jossey-Bass.
33. Hogan, J., & Holland, B. (2003) Using theory to evaluate personality and job-performance relations: A socioanalytic perspective. *Journal of Applied Psychology*, 88: 100–112.
34. Russell, C.J. (2001) A longitudinal study of top-level executive performance. *Journal of Applied Psychology*, 86: 560–573.
35. Gunn, E., Cunningham, J.B., & MacGregor, J.N. (2013) Developing benchmarks for CAO performance. *Local Government Studies*, 40: 851–868.
36. Russell, C.J. (2001) op. cit.; Boyatzis, R.E. (1982) op. cit.
37. Getha-Taylor, H. (2008) op. cit.
38. Gundry, L. (1994) Critical incidents in communicating culture to newcomers: the meaning is the message. *Human Relations*, 47: 1063–1088.

39. Herzberg, F., Mausner, B., & Snyderman, B.B. (1959) *The motivation to work*. New York: Wiley.
40. Darou, W. (1990) Training the people who help troubled kids. *Training and Development Journal*, March, 44: 54.
41. Daniel, T. (1992) Identifying critical leadership competencies of manufacturing supervisors in a major electronics corporation. *Group and Organizational Management*, 17: 57–71.
42. Kelly, G. (1955) *The psychology of personal constructs*. Vol. 1. New York: Norton.
43. Cunningham, J.B. (2001) *Researching organizational values and beliefs*: The Echo approach. Westport, CT: Quorum Books, p. 4.
44. Wilson, J. (1997) Australian nurses' personal constructs about effective nurses – A repertory grid study. *Journal of Professional Nursing*, 13: 193–199.
45. Ibid.
46. Fournier, V. (1994) Change in self construction during the transition from university to employment: a personal construct psychology approach. *Journal of Occupational and Organizational Psychology*, 67: 297–314.
47. Burnett, D. (1994) Exercising better management skills. *Personnel management*, 26: 42–46.
48. Brown, S. (1992) Cognitive mapping and repertory grids for qualitative survey research. *Journal of Management Studies*, 29: 287–307.
49. Cunningham, J.B. (2001) op. cit.

Chapter 4

1. Perry, J.L., & Wise, L.R. (1990) The motivational bases of public-service. *Public Administration Review*, 50: 367–373.
2. Perry, J.L., & Porter, L.W. (1982) Factors affecting the context for motivation in public organizations. *Academy of Management Review*, 7: 89–98; Perry, J.L., & Wise, L.R. (1990) op. cit., p. 4.
3. Brewer, G.A., & Selden, S.C. (1998) Whistle blowers in federal civil service: New evidence of the public service ethic. *Journal of Public Administration Research and Theory*, 8: 417, 413–439.
4. Rainey, H.G., & Steinbauer, P. (1999) Galloping elephants: Developing elements of a theory of effective government organizations. *Journal of Public Administration Research and Theory*, 9: 23, 1–32.
5. Vandenabeele, W. (2007) Toward a public administration theory of public service motivation: An institutional approach. *Public Management Review*, 9: 547, 545–556.
6. Perry, J.L. (1996) Measuring public service motivation: An assessment of construct reliability and validity. *Journal of Public Administration Research and Theory*, 6: 5–22; Waldner, C. (2012) Do public and private recruiters look for different employees? The role of public service motivation. *International Journal of Public Administration*, 35: 70–79.
7. Perry, J.L., & Hondeghem, A. (2008) Building theory and empirical evidence about public service motivation. *International Public Management Journal*, 11: 3–12.
8. Gruening, G. (2001) Origin and theoretical basis of New Public Management. International Public Management Journal, 4: 1–25; Diefenbach, T. (2009) New public management in the public sector organizations: The dark side of manageralistic 'enlightenment'. *Public Administration*, 87: 892–909.
9. Lyons, S.T., Duxbury, L.E., & Higgins, C.A. (2006) A comparison of the values and commitment of private sector, public sector, and parapublic sector employees. *Public Administration Review*, 66: 605–618.

10. Kahn, W.A. (1990) Psychological conditions of personal engagement and disengagement at work. *Academy of Management Journal*, 33: 694, 692–724.

11. Vigoda-Gadot, E., Eldor, L., & Schohat, L.M. (2012) Engage them to public service: Conceptualization and empirical examination of employee engagement in public administration. *The American Review of Public Administration*, 43: 518–538.

12. Deci, E.L., & Ryan, R.M. (2000) The 'what' and 'why' of goal pursuits: Human needs and the self-determination of behavior. *Psychological Inquiry*, 11: 227–268; Moran, C.M., Diefendorff, J.M., Kim, T.Y, & Liu, Z.Q. (2012) A profile approach to self-determination theory motivations at work. *Journal of Vocational Behavior*, 81: 354–363.

13. Herzberg, F., Mausner, B., & Snyderman, B.B. (1959) The motivation to work. New York: Wiley; Herzberg, F. (1976) *The managerial choice: To be efficient and to be human*. Homewood, IL: Dow Jones-Irwin, p. 55.

14. Ibid. p. 25.

15. Ibid. p. 25.

16. Salary can be both a motivator and a hygiene factor, although mainly a hygiene factor. It can take on properties of a motivator because it is linked to recognition.

17. Ibid.

18. Ibid.

19. Grant, A.M. (2007) Relational job design and the motivation to make a prosocial difference. *Academy of Management Review*, 32: 393–417.

20. Grant, A.M., & Parker, S.K. (2009) Redesigning work design theories: The rise of relational and proactive perspectives. *The Academy of Management Annals*, 3: 317–375.

21. Taylor, J. (2012) Public service motivation, relational job design, and job satisfaction in local government. *Public Administration*, 92: 902–918.

22. Hackman, J.R., & Oldham, G.R. (2010) Not what it was and not what it will be: The future of work design. *Journal of Organizational Behavior*, 31: 463–479.

23. Hackman, J.R., & Oldham, G.R. (1980) *Work Redesign*. Menlo Park: Addison Wesley.

24. Hackman, J.R., & Oldham, G.R. (1975) Development of the Job Diagnostic Survey. *Journal of Applied Psychology*, 60: 159–170; Pierce, J., & Jussila, I. (2009) Psychological ownership within the job design context: Revision of the job characteristics model. *Journal of Organizational Behavior*, 30: 477–496.

25. Hackman, J.R., & Lawler III, E.E. (1971) Employee Reactions to Job Characteristics, *Journal of Applied Psychology Monograph*, 55: 259–286; Hackman, J.R., & Oldham, G.R. (1980) op. cit.; Turner, A.N., & Lawrence, P.R. (1965) *Industrial Jobs and the Worker: An Investigation of Response to Task Attributes*. Boston: Harvard University Graduate School of Business Administration.

26. Hackman, J.R., & Oldham, G.R. (1980) op. cit.

27. A number of researchers might point out some of the limitations of the JDS. These limitations have primarily to do with the lack of independence among measures of the job characteristics, the relative ease with which respondents who are so inclined can 'fake' their scores by deliberately distorting their answers to JDS items, restricted reliabilities of some scales, and an absence of firm evidence about the validity of some of the JDS measures. The risk of overreliance on available paper-and-pencil instruments, we believe, far exceeds the risk that users will be excessively conservative and cautious in interpreting and applying findings from such instruments. Hackman and Oldham recognize these limitations, although encourage careful and appropriate application of what they believe is 'a good, but flawed and incomplete, diagnostic tool'. Hackman, J.R., & Oldham, G.R. (1980) op. cit., p. 108.

28. Two concepts in the theory are not assessed by the JDS – the level of employee knowledge and skill, and employee work effectiveness – as they are not possible to measure across organizations. Also, two characteristics that are not measured in the motivational theory are measured by the JDS: feedback from agents and dealing with others.
29. Grant, A.M., & Parker, S.K. (2009) op. cit.; Fried, Y., & Ferris, G.R. (1987) The validity of the job characteristics model: A review and meta-analysis. *Personnel Psychology*, 40: 287–322.
30. Grant, A.M. (2007) op. cit.; Grant, A.M., & Parker, S.K. (2009) op. cit.
31. Taylor, J. (2012) op. cit.
32. Grant, A.M. (2007) op. cit.
33. Hackman, J.R., & Oldham, G.R. (1976) Motivation through the design of work: Test of a theory. *Organizational Behavior and Human Performance*, 16: 250–279.
34. Gutek, B.A., Bhappu, A.D., Liao-Troth, M.A., & Cherry. B. (1999) Distinguishing between service relationships and encounters. *Journal of Applied Psychology*, 84: 218–233; Kanfer, R. (2009) Work motivation: Advancing theory and impact. *Industrial and Organizational Psychology: Perspectives on Science and Practice*, 2: 118–227.
35. Getha-Taylor, H. (2008) Identifying collaborative competencies. *Review of Personnel Administration*, 28: 103–119.
36. Davis, L.E., & Cherns, A.B. (1975) *The quality of working life. Vols. I & II*. New York: Free Press; Davis, L.E., & Taylor, J. (1979) *Design of jobs*. 2nd ed. Santa Monica: Goodyear.
37. Grant, A.M., & Parker, S.K. (2009) The quality of work life: Is Scandinavia different? *European Sociological Review*, 19: 61–79; Katz, D., & Kahn, R.L. (1978) *The social psychology of organizations*. John Wiley and Sons.
38. Cunningham, J.B., & White, T.H. (1984) (with a foreword by Eric Trist). *Quality of working life: Contemporary cases*. Ottawa: Canadian Government Printing Centre; Mansell, J., & Rankin, T. (1983) *Changing organizations: The quality of working life process*. Toronto, Ontario: Ontario Ministry of Labour, Quality of Working Life Center.
39. Cunningham, J.B., & White, T.H. (1984) op. cit.
40. Katz, D., & Kahn, R.L. (1978) op. cit, p. 702.
41. Trist, E.L., & Bamforth, K.W. (1951) Some social and psychological consequences of the longwall method of coal getting. *Human Relations*, 4: 3–38; see also Jacques, E. (1951) *The changing culture of a factory*. London: Tavistock. In this project in the Glacier Metal Company, the researchers studied the psychological and social forces affecting group behaviour, and then, working with group members, focused on resolving social systems issues in the organization of work.
42. Trist, E.L., Higgin, G.W., Murray, H., & Polluck, A.B. (1963) *Organizational choice*. London: Tavistock.
43. Rice, A.K. (1958) *Productivity and social organization: The Ahmedabad experiment*. London: Tavistock.
44. Trist, E.L., Trist, B., & Murray, H. (1997) *The social engagement of social science: A Tavistock anthology: The social-ecological perspective*. University of Pennsylvania; Katz, D., & Kahn, R.L. (1978) op. cit.
45. Halpern, N. (1984) Socio-technical systems design: The Shell Sarnia experience. In J.B. Cunningham & T.H. White, *Quality of Working Life*. Ottawa: Labour Canada, p. 67.
46. Gaille, D. (2003) The quality of work life: Is Scandinavia different? *European Sociological Review*, 19: 61–79.
47. Pot, F.D., & Koningsveld, E.A.P. (2009) Quality of working life and organizational performance: Two sides of the same coin? *Scandinavian Journal of Work*, 35: 421–428.

48. Jokinen, E., & Heiskanen, T. (2013) Is the measured quality of working life equivalent to strategically strong HRM system. *World Congress On Administrative And Political Sciences, Book Series*, 81: 131–141; Tuula, H., & Esa, J. (2014) Stability and change of the quality of working life in restructuring municipalities. *Social Indicators Research*, 118: 579–599.

49. Redmond, R., Curtis, E., Noone, T., & Keenan, P. (2008) Quality in higher education: The contribution of Edward Deming's principles. *International Journal of Educational Management*, 22: 432–441.

50. Schroeder, R.G., Linderman, K., Liedtke, C., & Adrian, S.C. (2008) Six Sigma: Definition and underlying theory. *Journal of Operations Management*, 26: 534–544.

51. Anderson, J.C., Rungtusanatham, M., & Schroeder, R.G. (1994) A theory of quality management underlying the Deming method. *Academy of Management Review*, 19: 472–509; Rungtusanatham, M., Ogden, J.A., & Wu, J. (2003) Advancing theory development in total quality management: A Deming management method. *International Journal of Operations & Production Management*, 23: 918–936; Fisher, C.M., Barfield, J., Li, J., & Mehta, R. (2005) Retesting a model of the Deming management method, *Total Quality Management*, 16: 401–412.

52. This is based on Anderson, J.C., Rungtusanatham, M., & Schroeder, R.G. (1994) op. cit.

53. Ibid.

54. Ouchi, W.G. (1982) *Theory Z: How American business can meet the Japanese challenge*. New York: Avon; Daft, R.L. (2004) Theory Z: Opening the corporate door for participative management. *The Academy of Management Executive*, 18: 117–121.

55. Oxborne, D., & Gaebler, T. (1993) *Reinventing government: How the entrepreneurial spirit is transforming the public service*. New York: Plume.

56. Gore, A. (1993) *Creating a government that works better and costs less: The report of the national performance review*. New York: Plume.

57. Deming, W.E. (1993) *Out of the crisis*. Cambridge, MA: MIT Press; Saint-Martin, D. (2001) When industrial policy shapes public sector reform: Total quality management in Britain and France. *West European Politics*, 24: 105–124; Hsieh, A.-T., Chou, C.-H., & Chen, C.-M. (2002) Job standardization and service quality: A closer look at the application of total quality management to the public sector. *Total Quality Management*, 13: 899–912; Mansour, A., & Ateeq, J. (2013) Is total quality management feasible in a developing context? The employees' perspective in the United Arab Emirates Public Sector. *International Journal of Public Administration*, 36: 98–111.

58. Holzer, M., & Charbonneau, Kim, Y. (2009) Mapping the terrain of public service quality improvement: Twenty-five years of trends and practices in the United States. *International Review of Administrative Sciences*, 75: 403–418.

59. Hackman, J.R., & Oldham, G.R. (2010) op. cit.; Steers, R.M., Mowday, R.T., & Shaprio, D.L. (2004) The future of work motivation theory Academy of Management. *The Academy of Management Review*, 29: 379–387.

60. Morgeson, F.P., & Humphrey, S.E. (2006) The work design questionnaire (WDO): Developing and validating a comprehensive measure for assessing job design and the nature of work. *Journal of Applied Psychology*, 91: 1321–1339; Parker, S.K., & Wall, T. (1998) Job and work design: Organizing work to promote wellbeing and effectiveness. London: Sage; Parker, S.K., Wall, T.D., & Cordery, J.L. (2001) Future work design research and practice: Towards an elaborated model of work design. *Journal of Occupational and Organizational Psychology*, 74: 413–440.

61. Grant, A.M., & Parker, S.K. (2009) op. cit.

62. Cummings, T. (1978) Self-regulating work groups: A sociotechnical synthesis. *Academy of Management Review*, 3: 625–634; Katz, D., & Kahn, R.L. (1978) op. cit.

63. Kirkman, B.L., & Rosen, B. (1999) Beyond self-management: Antecedents and consequences of team empowerment. *Academy of Management Journal*, 42: 58–74.
64. Strubler, D.C., & York, K.M. (2007) An Exploratory Study of the Team Characteristics Model Using Organizational Teams. *Small Group Research*, 38: 670–695.
65. Hackman, J.R., & Oldham, G.R. (2010) op. cit.
66. Kirkman, B.L., & Rosen, B. (1999) op. cit.; Erkutlu, H., & Chafra, J. (2012) The impact of team empowerment on proactivity. *Journal of Health Organization and Management*, 26: 560–577; Proenca, E.J. (2007) Team dynamics and team empowerment in health care organizations. *Health Care Management Review*, 32: 370–378.
67. Guzzo, R.A., Yost, P.R., Campbell, R.J., & Shea, G.P. (1993) Potency in groups: Articulating a construct. *British Journal of Social Psychology*, 32: 87–106.
68. Kirkman, B.L., & Rosen, B. (1999) op. cit.; Hackman, J.R., & Oldham, G.R. (1980) op. cit.
69. Ibid.
70. Lewin, K. (1947) Quasi-stationary social equilbria and the problem of permanent change. In *Readings in social psychology*, T.M. Newcomb & E.L. Hartley (eds.), 340–344. New York: Henry Holt.

Chapter 5

1. Colley, L. (2014) Understanding ageing public sector workforces: Demographic challenge or a consequence of public employment policy design. *Management Public Review*, 16: 1030–1052; Pilichowski, E., Arnould, E., & Turkisch, E. (2007) Ageing and the public sector: Challenges for financial and human resources. OECD *Journal on Budgeting*, 7: 1–40.
2. United Nations. (2013) *World Population Ageing*. New York: Department of Economic and Social Affairs Population Division.
3. Ibid.
4. By 2031, about 25 per cent of Canadians will be aged 65 years or older, up from 13 per cent in 2006; Government of Canada. (2006) *The demographic time bomb: Mitigating the effects of demographic change in Canada*. Report of the Standing Committee on Banking, Trade, and Commerce.
5. Anderson, G.F., & Hussey, P.S. (2000) Population aging: A comparison among industrialized countries. *Health Affairs*, 19: 191–203.
6. Collins, B.K. (2008) What's the problem in public sector workforce recruitment? A multi-sector comparative analysis of managerial perceptions. *International Journal of Human Resource Management*, 31: 1592–1608; Conference Board of Canada (2006) *The strategic value of people: Human resource trends and metrics*. Ottawa: The Conference Board of Canada, p. 5.
7. Foote, D., & Stoffman, D. (1986) *Boom, bust, and echo: How to profit from the coming demographic shift*. Toronto: McFarlane, Walter, and Ross.
8. Colley, L. (2014) op. cit.
9. Kulik, C.T., Ryan, S., Harper, S., & George, G. (2014) From the editors: Aging populations and management. *Academy of Management Journal*, 57: 929–935.
10. Cunningham, J.B., Campbell, D., & Kroeker-Hall, J. (2015) Motivational goals and competencies of older workers who re-engaged in the workforce. In *The Multi-generational and aging workforce*, R.J. Burke, C.L. Cooper, & A.G. Antoniou (eds.), pp. 183–211. UK: Edward Elgar Publishing.
11. Ng, T.W.H., & Feldman, D.C. (2012) Evaluating six common stereotypes about older workers with meta-analytical data. *Personnel Psychology*, 65: 821–858.

12. Colley, L. (2014) op. cit.
13. Goodman, D., French, P.E., & Battaglio, R.P. Jr. (2015) Determinants of local government workforce planning. *American Review of Public Administration*, 5: 135–152.
14. Colley, L., & Price, R. (2010) Where have all the workers gone? Exploring public sector workforce planning, *Australian Journal of Public Administration*, 69: 202–213; Anderson, M. (2004) The Metrics of Workforce Planning. *Public Personnel Management*, 33: 363–378.
15. Colley, L., & Price, R. (2010) op. cit.
16. Belcourt, M., & McBey, K.J. (2016) *Strategic Human Resource Planning*. 6th ed. Toronto, Canada: Nelson Education; Cotten, A. (2007) *Seven Steps of Effective Workforce Planning*. Washington: IBM Center for the Business of Government, p. 4.
17. Anderson, M. (2004) op. cit.
18. There are various terms used to plan for staffing needs, including *succession planning, human resource planning, human capital planning, employment planning, personnel planning, manpower planning* and *workforce planning*, among others. Succession planning has been used to describe the process of grooming staff to fill executive positions. See for example: Young, M.B. (2006) Strategic workforce planning: Forecasting human capital needs to executive business strategy. *Conference Board, Inc.*, p. 9.
19. Chew, L.L. & Suliman, A.-H. (2001) Government initiatives and the knowledge economy: Case of Singapore. In *The Human Society and the Internet-related socio-economic issues*, G. Goos, J. Hartmanis & J. van Leeuwen (eds.), pp. 19–32. Heidelberg: Springer Berlin.
20. Choudhury, E.H. (2007) Workforce planning in small local governments. *Review of Public Personnel Administration*, 27: 264–280.
21. Anderson, M. (2004) op. cit.
22. Ibid.
23. The term is sometimes used to describe generations in most countries born between 1965 and 1982. In the United States, it was referred as the 'baby bust' generation because of the small number of births following the baby boom. The term was used by a Canadian novelist Douglas Coupland in *Generation X: Tales for an Accelerate Culture* (1991). He describes the angst of the generation born between roughly 1960 and 1965, as they had no connection to what was important to the baby boom generation.
24. These three myths and evidence underlying them were described in: Dube, R. (2008) Gen Y wants to work it out. *Globe and Mail*, April 14: 1–2; Moses, B. (2006) *Dish: Midlife women tell the truth about work, relationships, and the rest of life*. Toronto: McClelland & Stewart.
25. These four myths and evidence underlying them were described in: Moses, B. (2008) Oh why the outcry about Gen Y. *Globe and Mail*, March 28; Moses, B. (2006) op. cit.
26. Napen, D. (2008) *Workforce planning models*. Public Service Agency, B.C. Government.
27. Overview of Ontario Employment Patterns. (2004) *Ontario Job Futures*. Ministry of Training, Colleges and Universities. This forecast was constructed from data from the Statistics Canada Labour Force Survey and the Conference Board of Canada's Macroeconomic Models, Occupational Projection Systems (COPS), Fall 2004.
28. Teaching and health care jobs are not included in this category.
29. Senge, P.M., Kleiner, A., Roberts, C., Ross, R.B., & Smith, B.J. (1994). The fifth discipline fieldbook: Strategies and tools for building a learning organization. New York: Currency Doubleday, p. 277.
30. Kahn, H., & Weiner, A. (1967) The Year 2000: A framework for speculation on the next thirty-three years. New York: Macmillan.
31. Ibid.

32. Neiner, J.A., Howze, E.H., & Greaney, M.L. (2004) Using scenario planning in public health: Anticipating alternative futures. *Health Promotion Practice*, 5: 69–79.

33. Rosell, S.A., Meridian International Institute & Parliamentary Centre. (1995) *Changing maps: Governing in a world of rapid change*. Ottawa: Carleton University Press in collaboration with the Meridian International Institute.

Chapter 6

1. Ewoh, A.I.E. (2013) Managing and valuing diversity: Challenges to public managers in the 21st century. *Public Personnel Review*, 42: 107–122.

2. Thomas, D.A., & Ely, R.J. (1996) Making differences matter: A new paradigm for managing diversity. Harvard Business Review, September–October: 79–90.

3. Ibid.

4. Ibid.

5. Sue, D.W., & Sue, D. (1990) Counseling the culturally different: Theory and practice. New York: John Wiley, p. 35.

6. Collins, B.K. (2008) What's the problem in public sector workforce recruitment? A multi-sector comparative analysis of managerial perceptions. *International Journal of Human Resource Management*, 31: 592–1608; Breaugh, J.A., & Starke, M. (2000) Research on employee recruitment: So many studies, so many remaining questions. *Journal of Management*, 26: 405–434.

7. Latham, V.M., & Leddy, P.M. (1987) Source of recruitment and employee attitudes: An analysis of job involvement, organizational commitment, and job satisfaction. *Journal of Business and Society*, 1: 230–235.

8. Sabharwal, M. (2014) Is diversity management sufficient? Organizational inclusion to further performance. *Public Personnel Management*, 43: 197–217.

9. Thomas, D.A., & Ely, R.J. (1996) Making differences matter: A new paradigm for managing diversity. *Harvard Business Review*, September–October: 79–90.

10. Andrews, R., & Ashworth, R. (2014) Representation and inclusion in public organizations: Evidence from the UK civil service. *Public Administration Review*, 75: 279–288.

11. Ibid.

12. Meier, K.J., Wrinkle, R.D., & Polinard, J.L. (1999) Representative bureaucracy and distributional equity: Addressing the hard question. *The Journal of Politics*, 61: 1025–1039.

13. Shore, L.M., Randel, A.E., Chung, B.G., Dean, M.A., Erhart, K.H., & Singh, G. (2011) Inclusion and diversity in work groups: A review and model for future research. *Journal of Management*, 37: 1262–1289.

14. Meier, K.J., Wrinkle, R.D., & Polinard, J.L. (1999) op. cit.

15. Choi, S., & Rainey, H.G. (2010) Managing diversity in US federal agencies: Effects of diversity and diversity management on employee perceptions of organizational performance. *Public Administration Review*, 70: 109–121.

16. Selden, S.C., & Selden, F. (2001) Rethinking diversity in public organizations for the 21st century: Moving toward a multicultural model. *Public Administration Review*, 66: 911–923.

17. Truss, C. (2013) The distinctiveness of human resource management in the public sector. In *Human resource management in the public sector*, R.J. Burke, A.J. Noblet, & C.L. Cooper (eds.), pp. 17–36. UK: Edward Elgar Publishing.

18. Treasury Board of Canada Secretariat. (2013) *Demographic snapshot of the federal public service*. Ottawa: Government of Canada.

19. Truss, C. (2013) op. cit.; Evans, M., Edwards, M., Burmester, B., & May, D. (2015) 'Not yet 50/50' – Barriers to progress of senior women in the Australian public service. *Australian Journal of Public Administration*, 73: 501–510.
20. Ibid.
21. Truss, C. (2013) op. cit.
22. Canada's Top 100 Employers website. http://www.canadastop100.com/national/.
23. The Conference Board of Canada. (2014) Business benefits of accessible workplaces. Ottawa: Conference Board of Canada.
24. McLean, D. (2003) Workplaces that work – creating a workplace culture that attracts, retains and promotes women. Centre for Excellence for Women's Advancement. Report prepared for Federal/Provincial/Territorial Ministers Responsible for the Status of Women.
25. Äijälä, K. (2001) *Public sector – An employer of choice*. Paris: OECD Public Management Service Report; Davidson, G., Lepak, S., & Newman, E. (2007) Recruiting and staffing in the public sector: Results from the IPMA-HR research series. IPMA-HR; Lowe, G.S. (2001) *Employer of choice? Workplace innovation in government*. Ottawa: Canadian Policy Research Network.
26. Canada's Top 100 Employers website, op. cit.
27. Groeneveld, S., & Verbeek, S. (2012) Diversity policies in public and private sector organizations: An empirical comparison of incidence and effectiveness. *Review of Public Personnel Administration*, 32: 353–381.
28. Andrews, R., & Ashworth, R. (2014) op. cit., p. 279.
29. Zhang, Y., & Rajagopalan, N. (2004) When the known devil is better than an unknown God: An empirical study of the antecedents and consequences of relay CEO succession. *Academy of Management Journal*, 47: 483–500.
30. Hope Pelled, L., Ledford Jr., G.E., & Mohrman, S.A. (1999) Demographic Dissimilarity and Workplace Inclusion. *Journal of Management Studies*, 36: 1014, 1013–1031.
31. Andrews, R., & Ashworth, R. (2014) op. cit.
32. Ibid.
33. New Zealand police website. http://www.police.govt.nz.
34. Redman, T., & Mathews, B.P. (1997) What do recruiters want in a public sector manager? *Public Personnel Management*, 26: 245–256.
35. Ng, W., & Gossett, C.W. (2013) Career choice in Canadian public service: An exploration of fit with the millennial generation. *Public Personnel Management*, 42: 337–358.
36. Connerly, M.L., Carlson, K.D., & Mecham III, R.L. (2003) Evidence of difference in applicant quality. *Personnel Review*, 32: 22–39.
37. Griffeth, R.W., Horn, R.W., Fink, L.S., & Cohen, D.J. (1997) Comparative tests of multivariate models of recruiting sources effects. *Journal of Management*, 23: 19–26.
38. Zottoli, M.A., & Wanous, J. P. (2000) Recruitment sources and post-hire outcomes for job applicants and new hires: A test of two hypotheses. *Journal of Applied Psychology*, 78: 163–172.
39. Breaugh, J.A., Greising, L.A., Taggart, J.W., & Chen, H. (2003) The relationship of recruiting sources and pre-hire outcomes: Examination of yield ratios and applicant quality. *Journal of Applied Social Psychology*, 33: 2267–2287; Zottoli, M.A., & Wanous, J.P. (2000) Recruitment source research: Current status and future directions. *Human Resource Management Journal*, 10: 353–382.
40. Vecchio, R.P. (1995) The impact of referral sources on employee attitudes: Evidence from a national sample. *Journal of Management*, 21: 953–965.

41. Taylor, M.S., & Schmidt, D.W. (1983) A process-oriented investigation of recruitment source effectiveness. *Personnel Psychology*, 36: 343–354.
42. Collins, C.J. (2007) The interactive effects of recruitment practices and product awareness on job seekers' employer knowledge and application behavior. *Journal of Applied Psychology*, 92: 180–190.
43. Breaugh, J.A., Greising, L.A., Taggart, J.W., & Chen, H. (2003) op. cit.
44. Collins, C.J. (2007) op. cit.
45. Canada's Best Diversity Employers website. http://www.canadastop100.com/diversity/.
46. Pfeffer, J. (1998) Seven practices of successful organizations. *California Management Review*, 40, Winter: 96–124.
47. Van Hoye, G., & Lievens, F. (2007) Investigating Web-based recruitment sources: Employee testimonials vs. word-of-mouse. *International Journal of Selection and Assessment*, 15: 372–382.
48. Canada's Top Employers for Young People website. http://canadastop100.com/young_people/.
49. Canada's Top Employers for Older Workers website. http://www.canadastop100.com/older_workers/.
50. Ibid.
51. Gray, J. (1992) *Men are from Mars, Women are from Venus*. New York: Harper Collins.
52. De Cooman, R., De Gieter, S., Pepermans, R., DuBois, C., Caers, R., & Jegers, M. (2008) Freshmen in nursing: Job motives and work values of a new generation. *Journal of Nursing Management*, 16: 15–64.
53. Simmon, B.A., & Betschild, M.J. (2001) Women's retirement, work and life paths: Changes, disruptions and discontinuities. *Journal of Women and Aging*, 12: 53–70.
54. Rowe, R., & Snizek, W.E. (1995) Gender differences in work values. *Work and Occupations*, 22: 215–229.
55. Cappelli, P. (2001) Making the Most of Online Recruiting. *Harvard Business Review*, 79: 139–146.
56. Delong, B., & St. Clair, S. (1990) An analysis of recruitment strategies in public and private organizations. *Applied HRM research*, 1: 43–50.
57. Federal legislation in Canada and the United States ensures equal opportunity and non-discrimination in organizations within the federal government's jurisdiction, such as banks, airlines, television and radio stations, interprovincial and interstate communications and telephone companies, buses and railways that travel between provinces or states, Aboriginal populations and other federally regulated industries. Each province or state has its own human rights commission focusing on organizations within their jurisdictions, organizations like schools, universities, businesses and provincial and local governments.
58. International commissions: United Nations Human Rights Council, African Commission on Human and Peoples' Rights, Inter-American Commission on Human Rights (Americas), ASEAN intergovernmental Commission on Human Rights (AICHR), Asian Human Rights Commission, International Society of Human Rights (Europe).
59. OECD (2009) *Central government recruitment system*. *Government at a Glance*, OECD Publishing.
60. Zhang, Y., & Rajagopalan, N. (2004) op. cit., pp. 483–500.
61. Lorsch, J.W., & Khurana, R. (1999) Changing leaders: The board's role in CEO succession. *Harvard Business Review*, 77: 96–106.
62. OECD (2009) op. cit.
63. Helton, K.A., & Jackson, R.D. (2007) Navigating Pennsylvania's dynamic workforce: Succession planning in a complex environment. *Public Personnel Management*, 36: 335–347.
64. Sekiguchi, R. (2006) How organizations promote person-environment fit: Using the case of Japanese firms to illustrate institutional and cultural differences. *Asia Pacific Journal of Management*, 23: 47–69.

65. Lee, S., & Kingsley, G. (2009) The impact of relational factors on contracting management in public organizations. *Review of Public Personnel Administration*, 29: 270–292.

66. Lindholst, A.C., & Bogetoft, P. (2011) Managerial challenges in public service contracting: Lessons from green-space management. *Public Administration*, 89: 1036–1062.

67. Kessler, I., Coyle-Shapiro, J., & Purcell, J. (1999) Outsourcing and the employee perspective. *Human Resource Management Journal*, 9: 5–19.

68. Greer, C.R., Youngblood, S.A., & Gray, D.A. (1999) Human resource management outsourcing: The make or buy decision. *Academy of Management Executive*, 13: 93, 85–96.

69. Marvel, M.K., & Marvel, H.P. (2007) Outsourcing oversight: A comparison of monitoring for in-house and contracted services. *Public Administration Review*, 67: 512–530.

70. Barbieri, D., & Salvatore, D. (2010) Incentive power and authority types: Toward a model of public service delivery. *International Review of Administrative Studies*, 76: 347–365.

71. Conklin, D.W. (2005) Risks and rewards in HR business process outsourcing. *Long Range Planning*, 38: 579, 579–598; Stroh, L.K., & Treehuboff, D. (2003) Outsourcing HR functions: When – and when not – to go outside. *Journal of Leadership and Organizational Studies*, 10: 19–28.

72. Aubert, B.A., Rivard, S., & Patry, M. (1996) A transactional cost approach to outsourcing behaviour: Some empirical evidence. *Information and Management*, 30: 51–64.

73. Marvel, M.K., & Marvel, H.P. (2007) op. cit.

74. Lee, S., & Kingsley, G. (2009) op. cit.

75. Breaugh, J.A., Greising, L.A., Taggart, J.W., & Chen, H. (2003) op. cit.

76. Boudreau, J.W., Boswell, W.R., Judge, T.A., & Bretz Jr., R.D. (2001) Personality and cognitive ability as predictors of job search among employed managers. *Personnel Psychology*, 54: 25–50.

77. Creed, P., Buys, N., Tilbury, C., & Crawford, M. (2013) The relationship between goal orientation and career striving in young adolescents. *Journal of Applied Psychology*, 43: 1480–1490.

78. Fitzgerald, G.E., (1989) Report of a commission of inquiring pursuant to orders in council. Brisbane: Government Printer.

Chapter 7

1. Carbonara, P. (1996) Hire for attitude: Train for skill. *Fast Company*, August–September: 73–80.

2. Graham, L. (1995) *On the line at Subaru-Isuzu*. Ithaca, NY: ILR Press.

3. Wright, B.E., & Christensen, R.K. (2010) Public service motivation: A test of the job attraction-selection-attrition model. *International Public Management Journal*, 13: 155–176; Perry, J.L., & Wise, L.R. (1990) The motivational bases of public-service. *Public Administration Review*, 50: 367–373.

4. Schneider, B. (1987) The people make the place. *Personnel Psychology*, 40: 437–454.

5. O'Reilly, C.A. Chatman, J.A., & Caldwell, D.E. (1991) People and organizational culture: A profile comparison approach to assessing person-organizational fit. *Academy of Management Journal*, 34: 487–516; Chatman, J.A. (1991) Managing people and organizations: Selection and socialization in public accounting firms. *Administrative Science Quarterly*, 36: 459–484.

6. O'Reilly, C.A., Chatman, J.A., & Caldwell, D.F. (1991) op. cit.

7. Hackman, J.R., & Oldham, G. (1980) *Work Redesign*. Reading, MA: Addison Wesley.

8. Werbel, J.D., & Johnson, D.J. (2001) The use of person-group fit for employment selection: A missing link in person-environment fit. *Human Resource Management*, 40: 227–240.

9. Rokeach, M. (1973) *The nature of human values*. New York: Free Press.

10. Ibid.

11. Meir, E., & Hasson, R. (1982) Congruence between personality type and environment type as a predictor of stay in an environment. *Journal of Vocational Behavior*, 21: 309–317.

12. This was based on a revised version of the original OCP instrument. See: Cable, D.M., & Judge, T.A. (1997) Interviewers' perceptions of person-organization fit and organizational selection decisions. *Journal of Applied Psychology*, 82: 546–581.

13. Schein, E. (2010) *Organizational culture and leadership*. 4th ed. San Francisco: John Wiley and Sons, p. 18.

14. Perry, J.L. (1996) Measuring public service motivation: An assessment of construct reliability and validity. *Journal of Public Administration Research and Theory*, 6: 5–22; Waldner, C. (2012) Do public and private recruiters look for different employees? The role of public service motivation. *International Journal of Public Administration*, 35: 70–79.

15. Godwin, A. (2011) Merit and its merits in the public service: Are we confusing the baby with the bathwater? *Australian Journal of Public Administration*, 70: 318–326.

16. Matheson, C. (2001) Staff selection in the Australian public service: A history of social closure. *Australian Journal of Public Administration*, 60: 43, 43–58.

17. Truss, C. (2013) The distinctiveness of human resource management in the public sector. In *Human resource management in the public sector*, R.J. Burke, A.J. Noblet, & C.L. Cooper (eds.), pp. 17–36. UK: Edward Elgar Publishing.

18. OECD (2005) *HRM Working Party Report*, Paris: OECD.

19. Stone, T.H. (1982) *Understanding personnel management*. Hinsdale, IL: Holt-Saunders.

20. Scroggins, W.A., Thomas, S.L., & Morris, J.A. (2008) Psychological testing in personnel selection, Part II: The refinement of methods and standards in employee selection. *Public Personnel Management*, 37: 185–186, 185–198.

21. Phillips, J.M. (1998) Effect of realistic job previews on multiple organizational outcomes: A meta-analysis. *Academy of Management Journal*, 41: 673–690; Breaugh, J.A. (1983) Realistic job previews: A critical appraisal and future research directions, *Academy of Management Review*, 8: 612–619.

22. Dugoni, B.L., & Ilgen, D.R. (1981) Realistic job preview and the adjustment of new employees, *Academy of Management Journal*, 24: 579–591.

23. Source for validity coefficients: Schmidt, F.L., & Hunter, J.E. (1998) The validity and utility of selection methods in personnel psychology: Practical and theoretical implications of 85 years of research findings. *Psychological Bulletin*, 124: 262–274. Validity coefficients for the situational judgement test are from McDaniel, M.A., Morgeson, F. P., Finnegan, E.B., Campion, M.A., & Braverman, E.P. (2001) Use of situational tests to predict job performance: A clarification of the literature. *Journal of Applied Psychology*, 86: 730–740. Validity coefficients range from 0 to 1.0, with higher numbers indicating better prediction of job performance.

24. The labels 'high' and 'low' are designations relative to other tools rather than based on specific expense level. These are estimates, some of which are consistent with Ryan, A.M., & Tippins, N.T. (2004) Attracting and selecting: What psychological research tells us. *Human Resource Management*, Winter, 43: 305–318.

25. Klimoski, R.J. (1993) Predictor constructs and their measurement. In N. Schmitt & W.C. Borman (eds.), *Personnel selection in organizations*. San Francisco: Jossey Bass, pp. 99–134.; Hunter, J.E., & Hunter, R.F. (1984) Validity and utility of alternative predictors of job performance. *Psychological Bulletin*, 96: 72–98.

26. Aamodt, M.G., Bryan, D.A., & Whitcomb, A.J. (1993) Predicting performance with letters of recommendation. *Public Personnel Management*, 52: 287–297.

27. Miedema, A., & Hall, C. (2012) Are you fact-checking the résumés of your new hire? You should. *The Globe and Mail*. August 15. Accessed at theglobeandmail.com.

28. Muchinsky, P.M. (1979) The use of reference reports in personnel selection: A review and evaluation. *Journal of Occupational Psychology*, 52: 287–297.

29. Aamodt, M.G., Bryan, D.A., & Whitcomb, A.J. (1993) op. cit.

30. Wessel, D. (1989) Evidence is skimpy that drug testing works, but employers embrace the practice. *Wall Street Journal*, B1, B9.

31. Cunningham, J.B. (1993) Action research and organizational development. Westport, CT: Praeger; Jick, T.D. (1979) Mixing qualitative and quantitative methods: Triangulation in action. *Administrative Science Quarterly*, 24: 602–611.

32. Randall, R., Davies, H., Patterson, F., & Karrell, K. (2006) Selecting doctors for postgraduate training in paediatrics using a competency based assessment centre. *Archives of Disease in Childhood*, 91: 444–448.

33. Sekiguchi, T. (2006) How organizations promote person-environment fit: Using the case of Japanese firms to illustrate institutional and cultural influence. *Asia Pacific Journal of Management*, 23: 47–69.

34. Ibid.

35. Morishima, M. (1995) The Japanese human resource management: A learning bureaucracy. In *Human resource management on the Pacific Rim: Institutions, practices, and attitudes*, L.F. Moore & P.D. Jennings (eds.), pp. 119–150. Berlin: Walter de Gruyter.

36. Sekiguchi, T. (2006) op. cit.

37. Ibid.

38. Redman, T., & Mathews, B.P. (1997) What do recruiters want in a public sector manager? *Public Personnel Management*, 26: 245–256.

39. Scroggins, W.A., Thomas, S.L., & Morris, J.A. (2008) Psychological testing in personnel selection, Part I: A century of psychological testing. *Public Personnel Management*, 37: 99–109.

40. Scroggins, W.A., Thomas, S.L., & Morris, J.A. (2008) Psychological testing in personnel selection, Part II: The refinement of methods and standards in employee selection. *Public Personnel Management*, 37: 185–186, 185–198.

41. Ibid.

42. Digman, J.M. (1990) Personality structure: Emergence of the five factor model. *Annual Review of Psychology*, 41: 417–440.

43. Behling, O. (1998) Employee selection: Will intelligence and conscientiousness do the job? *Academy of Management Executive*, 12: 80, 77–86.

44. Barrick, M.R., & Mount, M.K. (1991) The big five personality dimensions in job performance: A meta-analysis. *Personnel Psychology*, 44: 1–26.

45. Haaland, D.E. (2005) Who's the safest bet for the job? Find out why the fun guy in the next cubicle may be the next accident waiting to happen. *Security Management*, 49: 49–51.

46. Fortune. (1996) Microsoft's big advantage – hiring only the supersmart. November 25: 159–162.

47. Thurstone, L.L. (1941) *Factorial studies of intelligence*. Chicago: University of Chicago Press.

48. Behling, O. (1998) op. cit.

49. Scroggins, W.A., Thomas, S.L., & Morris, J.A. (2009) Psychological testing in personnel selection, Part III: The resurgence of personality testing. *Public Personnel Management*, 38: 67–77.

50. Royal Canadian Mounted Police website. http://www.rcmp-grc.gc.ca/en.

51. Ones, D.S., Viswesvaran, C., & Schmidt, F.L. (1993) Comprehensive meta-analysis of integrity tests validities: Findings and implications for selection and theories of job performance. *Journal of Applied Psychology*, 78: 679–703.

52. Huffcutt, A.I., Conway, J.M., Roth, P.L., & Stone, N.J. (2001) Identification and meta-analytic assessment of psychological constructs measured in employment interviews. *Journal of Applied Psychology*, 86: 897–913; Cortina, J.M., Goldstein, N.B., Payne, S.C., Davison, H.K., & Gilliland, S.W. (2000) The incremental validity of interview scores over and above cognitive ability and conscientiousness scores. *Personnel Psychology*, 53: 325–351.

53. Way, S.A., & Thacker, J.W. (1999) Selection practices: Where are Canadian Organizations? *HR Professional Research Forum*, 16: 33–37.

54. Arvey, R.D., & Campion, J.E. (1982) The employment interview: A summary and review of recent research. *Personnel Psychology*, 3: 281–322; Harris, M.M. (1989) Reconsidering the employment interview: A review of recent literature and suggestions for future research. *Personnel Psychology*, 42: 691–726.

55. Springbett, B.M. (1958) Factors affecting the final decision in the employment interview. *Canadian Journal of Psychology*, 12: 13–22.

56. Hackett, R.D., Lapierre, L.M., & Gardiner, H.P. (2004) A review of the Canadian human rights cases involving the employment interview. *Canadian Journal of Administrative Sciences*, 21: 215–228; Campion, M.A., Palmer, D.K., & Campion, J.E. (1997) A review of structure in the selection interview. *Personnel Psychology*, 41: 25–42.

57. Hackett, R.D., Lapierre, L.M., & Gardiner, H.P. (2004) op. cit.

58. Ibid.

59. Ibid.

60. Latham, G.P., Saari, L.M., Pursell, E.D., & Campion, M.A. (1980) The situation interview. *Journal of Applied Psychology*, 65: 422–427.

61. Janz, T. (1982) Initial comparisons of pattern behavioural descriptions interviews versus unstructured interviews. *Journal of Applied Psychology*, 67: 577–580.

62. Hackett, R.D., Lapierre, L.M., & Gardiner, H.P. (2004) op. cit.

63. Hackett, R.D., Lapierre, L.M., & Gardiner, H.P. (2004) op. cit.; Campion, M.A., Palmer, D.K., & Campion, J.E. (1997) A review of structure in the selection interview. *Personnel Psychology*, 41: 25–42.

64. Janz, T., Hellervik, L., & Gilmour, D.C. (1986) *Behaviour Description Interviewing: New, Accurate, Cost Effective*. Toronto: Allyn & Bacon, p. 32.

65. Ibid., p. 33.

66. Dillman, D.A. (1978) *Mail and Telephone Surveys; The Total Design Method*. New York: John Wiley.

67. Janz, T., Hellervik, L., & Gilmour, D.C. (1986) op. cit., p. 33.

68. Ibid.

69. Ibid.; Dillman, D.A. (1978) op. cit.

70. Angus Reid Survey for William M. Mercer Ltd., cited in Eric Atkins (1999) Talent rules. *Workplace News*, 5 (May): 1–2.

71. Perry, J.L., & Porter, L.W. (1982) Factors affecting the context for motivation in public organizations. *Academy of Management Review*, 7: 89–98; Perry, J.L., & Wise, L.R. (1990) The motivational bases of public service. *Public Administration Review*, 50: 367–373.

72. Waldner, C. (2012) Do public and private recruiters look for different employees? The role of public service motivation. *International Journal of Public Administration*, 35: 70–79.

Chapter 8

1. Elicker, J.D., Levy, P.E., & Hall, R.J. (2006) The role of leader-member exchange in the performance appraisal process. *Journal of Management*, 32: 531–551.

2. Keeping, L.M., & Levy, P.E. (2000) Performance appraisal reactions: Measurement, modeling, and method bias. *Journal of Applied Psychology*, 85: 708–723.

3. Lawler, III, E.E. (1994) Performance management: The next generation. *Compensation and Benefits Review*, May–June: 26, 16–19.

4. Canadian Business Online, [cited March 16, 2006] Best Practices: Performance reviews that actually improve performance. Available from www.canadianbusiness.com.

5. Posthuma, R.A., & Campion, M.A. (2008) Twenty best practices for job employee performance reviews. *Compensation and Benefits Review*, 40, January–February: 47–55.

6. Cho, Y.J., & Lee, J.W. (2012) Performance management and trust in supervisors. *Review of Public Personnel Administration*, 3: 239, 236–259.

7. Bach, S., Givan, R., & Forth, J. (2009) The public sector in transition. In *The evolution of the modern workplace*, W. Brown, A. Bryson, J. Forth, & K. Whitfield (eds.), pp. 307–331. Cambridge, Cambridge University Press; OECD (2005) HRM working party report. Paris: OECD.

8. Jawahar, I.M. (2006) Correlates of satisfaction with performance appraisal feedback. *Journal of Labor Research*, 27: 213–236.

9. Jung, S.J., & Ritz, A. (2014) Goal management, management reform, and affective organizational commitment in the public sector. *International Public Management Journal*, 17: 463–492; Rainey, H.G. (2009) *Understanding and Managing Public Organizations*. 4th ed. San Francisco: Jossey-Bass; Jung, C.S. (2011) Organizational goal ambiguity and performance: Conceptualization, measurement, and relationships. *International Public Management Journal*, 14: 193–217.

10. Soloman, E.E. (1986) Private and public sector managers: An empirical investigation of job characteristics and organizational climate. *Journal of Applied Psychology*, 71: 247–259.

11. Jung, S.J., & Ritz, A. (2014) op. cit.

12. Jung, C.S. (2011) op. cit.; Lipsky, M. (1980) *Street-level bureaucracy: Dilemmas of the individual in public services*. New York, NY: Russell Sage Foundation.

13. Giauque, D., Anderfuhren-Biget, S., & Varone, F. (2013) HRM practices, intrinsic motivators, and organizational performance in the public sector. *Public Personnel Management*, 42: 123–150.

14. Kalleberg, A.L., Marsden, P.V., Reynolds, J., & Knoke, D. (2006). Beyond profit? Sectoral differences in high-performance work practices. *Work and Occupations*, 33: 271–302; Lindorff, M. (2009) We're not all happy yet: Attitudes to work, leadership, and high performance work practices among managers in the public sector. *Australian Journal of Public Administration*, 68: 429–445.

15. Locke, E.A., & Latham, G.P. (2002) 'Building a practically useful theory of goal setting and task motivation: A 35-year odyssey.' *American Psychologist*, 57: 705–717.

16. Wright, B.E. (2004) The role of work context in work motivation: A public sector application of goal and social cognitive theories. *Journal of Public Administration Research and Theory*, 14: 59–78; Pandey, S.K., & Wright, B.E. (2006) Connecting the dots in public management: Political environment, organizational goal ambiguity and the public manager's role ambiguity. *Journal of Public Administration Research and Theory*, 16: 511–532.

17. Deming, W.E. (1986) Out of crisis. Cambridge, MA: MIT Center for Advanced Engineering Study. 102. Referenced in Walton, M. (1989) *The Deming management method*. Melbourne: The Business Library, p. 89.

18. Schmitt, N., Pulakos, E.D., Nason, E., & Whitey, D.J. (1996) Likability and similarity as potential sources of predictor-related criterion bias in validation research. *Organizational Behavior and Human Decision Processes*, 68: 272–286.

19. Avolio, B.J., & Barrett, G.V. (1987) The effects of age stereotyping in a simulated interview. *Psychology and Aging*, 2: 56–63.

20. Jung, C.S. (2011) op. cit.

21. Beehr, T.A., Glazer, S., Fischer, R., Linton, L.L., & Hansen, C.P. (2009). Antecedents for achievement of alignment in organizations. *Journal of Occupational and Organizational Psychology*, 82: 1–20; Kaplan, R.S., & Norton, D.P. (1996) The balanced scorecard: Translating strategy into action. Boston, MA: Harvard Business School Press.

22. Drucker, P. (1954) *The Practice of Management*. New York: Harper and Brothers.

23. Odiorne, G. (1965) *Management by Objectives*. New York: Pitman.

24. Meyer, H.H., Kay, E., & French, Jr. J.R.P. (1965) Split Roles in Performance Appraisal. *Harvard Business Review*, XLIII, January–February: 123–129.

25. Latham, G.P., & Yukl, G.A. (1975) Assigned versus participative goal setting with educated and uneducated wood cutters. *Journal of Applied Psychology*, 60: 299–302.

26. Kaplan, R.S., & Norton, D.P. (1996) *The Balanced Scorecard: Translating strategy into action*. Boston: Harvard Business School Press.

27. Locke, E.A., & Latham, G.P. (2002) op. cit.

28. Tosi, H.L., & Carroll, S.J. (1968) Managerial reaction to management by objectives. *Academy of Management Journal*, 13: 415–426.

29. Jamieson, B.D. (1973) Behavioral problems with management by objectives. *Academy of Management Journal*, 16: 496–505.

30. Cunningham, J.B., & MacGregor, J.N. (2006) The Echo approach in developing items for student evaluation of teaching performance. *Teaching of Psychology*, 33: 96–100.

31. Adapted from Millard, C.W., Luthans, F., & Ottemann, R.L. (1976) A new breakthrough for performance appraisal. *Business Horizons*, August: 69: 66–73.

32. Adapted from Millard, C.W., Luthans, F., & Ottemann, R.L. (1976) A new breakthrough for performance appraisal. *Business Horizons*, August: 69: 66–73.

33. Carroll, J.D., & Messenger, J.C. (2008) Medical simulation: A new tool for training and skill assessment. *Perspectives in Biology and Medicine*, 51, Winter: 47–60.

34. Flanagan, J.C. (1954) The critical incident technique. *Psychological Bulletin*, 51: 327–358.

35. Conway, J.M., Lombardo, K., & Sanders, K.C. (2001) A meta-analysis of incremental validity and nomological networks for subordinate and peer ratings. *Human Performance*, 14: 267–303.

36. Drexler J.A. Jr, Beehr, T.A., & Stetz, T.A. (2001) Peer appraisals: Differentiation of individual performance on group task. *Human Resource Management*, 40: 333–345; Viswesvaran C., Ones, D.S., & Schmidt, F.L. (1996) Comparative analysis of the reliability of job performance ratings. *Journal of Applied Psychology*, 81: 557–560.

37. Conway, J.M., Lombardo, K., & Sanders, K.C. (2001) op. cit.

38. Greguras, G.J., Robie C., & Born, M. (2001) Applying the social relations model to self and peer evaluations. *The Journal of Management Development*, 20: 508–525; Viswesvaran C, Schmidt F.L., & Ones, D.S. (2002) The moderating influence of job performance dimensions on convergence of supervisory and peer ratings of job performance: Unconfounding construct level convergence and rating difficulty. *Journal of Applied Psychology*, 87: 345–354.

39. London, M., & Smither, J.W. (1995) Can multisource feedback change perceptions of goal accomplishment, self-evaluations, and performance-related outcomes? Theory-based applications and directions for research. *Personnel Psychology*, 48: 803–839.

40. Miller, C.C. (2006) Peer review in the organizational and management sciences: Prevalence and effects of reviewer hostility, bias, and dissensus. *Academy of Management Journal*, 49: 425–431.
41. Kane, J.S., & Lawler, E.E. (1978) Methods of peer assessment. *Psychological Bulletin*, 88: 80–81.
42. McEvoy, G.M., & Buller, R.J. (1989) User acceptance of peer appraisals in an industrial setting. *Personnel Psychology*, 40: 785–787.
43. Kane J.S., & Lawler, E.E. (1978) op. cit.
44. Druskat, V.U., & Wolf, S.B. (1999) Effects and timing of developmental peer appraisals in self-managing work groups. *Journal of Applied Psychology*, 84: 58–74.
45. Reilly, R.R., Smither, J.W., & Vasilopoulos, N.L. (1996) A longitudinal study of upward feedback. *Personnel Psychology*, 49: 599–612.
46. Greguras, G.J., Robie, C., Schleicher, D.J., & Goff, M. (2003) A field study of the effects of rating purpose on the quality of multisource ratings. *Personnel Psychology*, 56: 1–21.
47. Walker, A.G., & Smither, J.W. (1999) A five-year study of upward feedback: What managers do with the results matters. *Personnel Psychology*, 52: 393–423; Atwater, L.E., Waldman, D.A., Atwater, D., & Cartier, P. (2000) An upward feedback field experiment: Supervisors' cynicism, reactions, and commitment to subordinates. *Personnel Psychology*, 53: 297, 275–297.
48. Crotts, J.C., Dickson, D.R., & Ford, R.C. (2005) Aligning organizational processes with mission: The case of service excellence. *Academy of Management Executive*, 19: 54–68.
49. Shore, T.H., Adams, J.S., & Tashchian, A. (1998) Effects of self-appraisal information, appraisal purpose, and feedback target on performance appraisal ratings. *Journal of Business and Psychology*, 12: 283–298.
50. Levy, P.E. (1993) Self-appraisals and attributions: A test of a model. *Journal of Management*, 19: 51–62.
51. Ghorpade, J. (2000) Managing five paradoxes of 360-degree feedback. *Academy of Management Executive*, 14: 140–150.
52. Antonioni, A. (1996) Designing an effective 360-degree appraisal feedback process. *Organizational Dynamics*, Autumn: 24–38; London, M., & Smither, J. (1995) Can multisource feedback change perceptions of goal accomplishment, self-evaluations, and performance related outcomes? *Personnel Psychology*, 48: 803–839; Waldman, D.A., Atwater, L.E., & Antonioni, D. (1998) Has 360-degree feedback gone amok? *Academy of Management Executive*, 12: 86–94.
53. Ibid.
54. Shipper, F., Hoffman, R.C., & Rotondo, D.M. (2007) Does the 360 feedback process create actionable knowledge equally across cultures. *Academy of Management Learning and Education*, 6: 33–50.
55. Lepsinger, R., & Lucia, A.D. (1997) *The art and science of 360-degree feedback*. San Francisco: Jossey-Bass, p. 17.
56. Scullen, S.E., Mount, M.K., & Goff, M. (2001) Understanding the latent structure of performance ratings. *Journal of Applied Psychology*, 85: 956–970.
57. DeNisi, A.S., & Kluger, A. (2000) Feedback effectiveness: Can 360-degree appraisals be improved? *Academy of Management Executive*, 14: 129–139.
58. Rosenthal, R. (1973) The Pygmalion effect lives. *Psychology Today*, 7: 56–63; Rosenthal, R., & Jacobson, L. (1968) *Pygmalion in the Classroom: Teacher Expectations and Pupils' Intellectual Development*. New York: Holt, Reinhart and Winston.
59. Livingston, J.S. (1969) Pygmalion in management. *Harvard Business Review*, 47: 81–89.
60. Rowe, G.W., & O'Brien, J. (2002) The role of Golem, Pygmalion, and Galatea on opportunistic behaviour in the classroom. *Journal of Management Education*, 26: 612–628: Collins, H., & Pinch, T. (1998)

The Golem: *What you should know about science*. 3rd ed. Cambridge, England: Cambridge University Press.

61. McNatt, D.B. (2000) Ancient pygmalion joins contemporary management: A meta-analysis of the result. *Journal of Applied Psychology*, 85: 314–322; Reynold, D. (2007) Restraining Golem and harnessing Pygmalion: A laboratory study of managerial expectations and task design. *Academy of Management Learning and Education*, 6: 475–483.

62. Eden, D. (1990) *Pygmalion in management: Productivity as a self-fulfilling prophecy*. Lexington, MA: Lexington Books.

63. Kierein, N.M., & Gold, M.A. (2000) Pygmalion in work organizations: a meta-analysis. *Journal of Organizational Behaviour*, 21: 913–928.

64. Lewin, K. (1936) *Principles of Topological Psychology*. New York: McGraw-Hill; Tolman, E.C. (1932) *Purposive Behavior in Animals and Men*. New York: Century.

65. Vroom, V.H. (1964) *Work and Motivation*. New York: Wiley; Deci, E.L., & Ryan, R.M. (2000) The 'what' and 'why' of goal pursuits: Human needs and the self-determination of behavior. *Psychological Inquiry*, 11: 227–268.

66. Locke, E.A., & Latham, G.P. (2006) New directions in goal setting theory. *Current Directions in Psychological Science*, 15: 265, 265–268.

67. Locke, E.A., & Latham, G.P. (2002) op. cit.

68. Ibid.

69. Posthuma, R.A., & Campion, M.A. (2008) op. cit.

70. Maier, N. (1976) *The appraisal interview: Three basic approaches, a revision of the appraisal interview: objectives, methods, and skills*. La Jolla, CA: University Associates; Maier, N. (1952) *Principles of Human Relations*. New York: John Wiley.

71. Levy, P.E., & Williams, J.R. (2004) The social context of performance appraisal: A review and framework for the future. *Journal of Management*, 30: 881–905; Graves, L.M. (1993) Sources of individual differences in interviewer effectiveness: A model and implications for future research. *Journal of Organizational Behavior*, 14: 349–370.

72. Graen, G.B., & Uhl-Bien, M. (1995) Relationship-based approach to leadership: Development of Member Exchange (LMX) theory of leadership over 25 years: Applying a multi-level multi-domain perspective. *Leadership Quarterly*, 6: 219–247.

73. Mayer, R.C., & Davis, J.H. (1999) The effect of performance appraisal system on trust for management: A field quasi-experiment. *Journal of Applied Psychology*, 84: 123–136.

74. Levy, P.E., & Williams, J.R. (2004) The social context of performance appraisal: A review and framework for the future. *Journal of Management*, 30: 892, 881–905.

75. Graen, G.B., & Uhl-Bien, M. (1995) op. cit. p. 237.

76. Levy, P.E., & Williams, J.R. (2004) op. cit.; Elicker, J.D., Levy, P.E., & Hall, R.J. (2006) op. cit.

77. Ilgen, D.R., Mitchell, T.R., & Frederick, J.W. (1981) Poor performers: Supervisors' and subordinates' responses. *Organizational Behavior and Human Performance*, 27: 386–410.

78. Baron, R.A. (1988) Negative effects of destructive criticism: Impact on conflict, self-efficacy, and task performance. *Journal of Applied Psychology*, 65: 355–356.

79. Burke, R.J., Weitzel, & Weir, T. (1978) Characteristics of effective employee performance review and development interviews: Replication and extension. *Personnel Psychology*, 31: 903–919; Maier, N.R. (1976) op. cit.; Posthuma, R.A., & Campion, M.A. (2008) op. cit.

80. Blanchard, K. & Johnson, S. (1996) *The one minute manager*. London: HarperCollins Business.

81. These forms were designed and used by Pauline Brandes who was an executive director in a provincial government human resource agency.
82. This process was developed by Pauline Brandes in her capacity as Associate VP, Human Resources & Leadership Development, when she worked in the post-secondary sector in Alberta. It was called PEP: Performance Enhancement and Development Program.
83. O'Reilly III, C.A., & Weitz, B.A. (1980) Managing marginal employees: The use of warnings and dismissals. *Administrative Science Quarterly*, 25: 467–484.
84. Schermerhorn, J.R., Gardner, W.L., & Martin, T.N. (1990) Management dialogues: Turning on the marginal performer. *Organizational Dynamics*, 18: 47–59.
85. O'Reilly, C.A.III, & Weitz, B.A. (1980) op. cit.
86. Guffey, C.J., & Helms, M.M. (2001) Effective employee discipline: A case of the Internal Revenue Service. *Public Personnel Review*, 30: 111–127.
87. Ibid.
88. Kleiner, B.H. (2003) Principles and techniques for rightful termination. *Equal Opportunities International*, 22: 74–79.
89. Termination of Employment, Ontario Ministry of Labour, Accessed from www.labour.gov.on.ca.
90. Schweiger, D.M., Ivancevich, J.M., & Power, F.R. (1987). Executive actions for managing human resources before and after acquisitions. *Academy of Management Executive*, 1: 127–138.
91. Coleman, D.T. (2001). *Ending the employment relationship without ending up in court*. Alexandra, MA: Society for Human Resource Management.

Chapter 9

1. Bolles, R.N. (2004) *What color is your parachute? A practical manual for job-hunters and career changers*. Berkeley: Ten Speed Press.
2. Wong, C. (2009) Did you make the right career choice? *Globe Careers, Globe and Mail*, June 10, accessed from www.theGlobeandMail.com.
3. Holland, J.L. (1994) *The self-directed search*. Odessa, FL: Psychological Assessment Resources, accessed from http://www.self-directed-search.com/.
4. Nauta, M.M. (2007) Career Interests, self-efficacy, and personality as antecedents of career exploration. *Journal of Career Assessment*, 15: 162–180; Amit, A., & Sagiv, L. (2009) Where have the investigative occupations gone? *Journal of Career Assessment*, 17: 214–231.
5. O'Reilly, C.A., Chatman, J.A., & Caldwell, D.F. (1991) People and organizational culture: A profile comparison approach to person-organization fit. *Academy of Management Journal*, 34: 487–516.
6. Holland, J.L. (1996) Exploring careers with a typology: What we learned and some new directions. *American Psychologist*, 51: 397–406; Helms, S.T. (1996) Some experimental tests of Holland's congruency hypothesis: The reactions of high school student to occupational simulations. *Journal of Career Assessment*, 4: 253–268.
7. Rottinghaus, P.J., Hees, C.K., & Conrath, J.A. (2009) Enhancing job satisfaction perspectives: Combing Holland's themes for basic interests. *Journal of Vocational Behavior*, 75: 139–151; Holland, J.L. (1996) op. cit.; Holland, J.L., Johnston, J.A., & Asama, N.F. (1994) More evidence of the relationship between Holland's personality types and personality variables. *Journal of Career Assessment*, 2: 331–340.
8. Perry, J.L. (1996) Measuring public service motivation: An assessment of construct reliability and validity. *Journal of Public Administration Research and Theory*, 6: 5–22; Waldner, C. (2012) Do public

and private recruiters look for different employees? The role of public service motivation. *International Journal of Public Administration*, 35: 70–79.

9. Vigoda-Gadot, E., & Meiri, S. (2008) New Public Management values and person-organization fit: A social psychological approach and an empirical examination among public sector personnel. *Public Administration*, 86: 111–131.

10. Kernaghan, K. (1991) Career public service 2000: Road to renewal or impractical vision? *Canadian Public Administration*, 34: 551–572.

11. Hall, D.T. (1996) Protean careers of the 21st century. *Academy of Management Executive*, 10: 8–10.

12. E.H. (1965) *Organizational psychology*, 2nd ed. Englewood Cliffs, NJ: Prentice Hall; Argyris, C. (1957) *Understanding organizational behavior.* Homewood, IL: Irwin Dorsey; Levinson, H. (1962) *Men, management, and mental health.* Cambridge, MA: Harvard Business School Press; Schein, E.H. (1996) Career anchors revisited: Implications for career development in the 21st century. *Academy of Management Executive*, 10: 80–88; Schein, E.H. (1971) The individual, the organization, and the career. A conceptual scheme. *Journal of Applied Psychology*, 7: 401–426; Schein, E.H. (1970) *Career dynamics: Matching individual and organizational needs.* Reading, MA: Addison Wesley.

13. Perry, J.L., & Wise, L.R. (1990) The Motivational Bases of Public-Service. *Public Administration Review*, 50: 367–373.

14. Rousseau, D.M. (1995) *Psychological contracts in organizations: Understanding written and unwritten agreements.* Thousand Oaks, CA: Sage; Rousseau, D.M. (1990) New hire perceptions of their own and their employer's obligations: A study of psychological contracts. *Journal of Organizational Behavior*, 11: 389–400.

15. Lemire, L., Saba, T., & Gagnnon, Y.C. (1999) Managing career plateauing in the Quebec public sector. *Public Personnel Management*, 28: 375–391.

16. Sing, P., & Burke, R.J. (2013) Managing human resource management in the public sector during economic downturn. In *Human resource management in the public sector*, R.J. Burke, A.J. Noblet, & C.L. Cooper (eds.), pp. 17–36. UK: Edward Elgar Publishing.

17. In the 1985 budget, the Canadian federal government planned to reduce the 15,000 employees by 1990/1991 and although they were unsuccessful, they continued. For example, in the budget speech of 1995, the finance minister announced plans to reduce 45,000 positions over the next three years; Frater, T. (2004) *Public sector modernization and downsizing.* Ontario Institute for Studies in Education/University of Toronto.

18. Budros, A. (1997) The new capitalism and organizational rationality: The adoption of downsizing programs, 1979–1994. *Social Forces*, 76: 229–250.

19. Hall, D.T. (1996) op. cit., p. 8.

20. Arthur, M.B., & Rousseau, D.M. (1996) *The boundaryless career: A new employment principle for a new organizational era.* Oxford, UK: Oxford University Press.

21. Hall, D.T. (2002) *Careers in and out of organizations.* Thousand Oaks, CA: Sage, p. 23, pp. 17–47.

22. Ibid.

23. Hughes, E.C., & Coser, L.A. (eds.) (1994) *On work, race, and the sociological imagination.* Chicago: University of Chicago press. Careers can be defined in both objective and subjective terms according to these authors.

24. Schein, E.H. (1996) op. cit.

25. Hall, D.T. (1996) op. cit.

26. Arthur, M.B., Khapova, S.N., & Wilderom, C.P.M. (2005) Career success in a boundaryless career world. *Journal of Organizational Behavior*, 26: 177–202.

27. Greenhaus, J.H., Parasuraman, S., & Wormley, W.M. (1990) Effects of race on organizational experiences, job performance evaluations, and career outcomes. *Academy of Management Journal*, 33: 64–86.
28. Arthur, M.B. (1994) The boundaryless career: A new perspective for organizational inquiry. *Journal of Organizational Behavior*, 5: 295–306; O'Mahony, S., & Bechky, B.A. (2006) Stretchwork: Managing the career progression paradox in external labor markets. *Academy of Management Journal*, 49: 918–941.
29. Wanca-Thibault, M. (2009) Assessing high potentials earlier. *Talent Management*, October 16.
30. National Defence and Canadian Forces website. See also Lang, K. (1972) Military career structure: Emerging trends and alternatives. *Administrative Science Quarterly*, 17: 487–498.
31. Graen, G., Dharwadkar, R., Grewal, R., & Wakabayashi, M. (2006) Japanese career progress: An empirical examination. *Journal of Business Studies*, 37: 148–161.
32. London, M., & Smither, J.W. (1999) Career-related continuous learning: Defining the construct and mapping the process. *Research in Personnel and Human Resources Management*, 17: 81, 83, 82–121.
33. London, M., & Smither, J.W. (1999) Empowered self-development and continuous learning. *Human Resources Management Journal*, 38: 3–16.
34. Homer, *The Odyssey*, E.V. Rieu (transl.) (January 1946 edition). Penguin Books, UK, 1961 edition.
35. Cunningham, J.B., & Eberle, T. (1993) Characteristics of the mentoring experience: A qualitative study. *Personnel Review*, 22: 54–66, 54. This definition was based on Vance, C.N. (1982) The mentor connection. *Journal of Nursing Administration*, 12: 7–13; Roche, G.R. (1979) Much ado about mentors. *Harvard Business Review*, 5: 14–24; Levinson, D.J., Darrow, C.N., Klein, E.F., Levinson, M.A., & McKee, B. (1978) *Seasons of a man's life.* New York: Alfred A. Knopf.
36. Cunningham, J.B. (1994) Using mentoring for professional development. *1994 Annual: Developing Human Resources.* La Jolla, CA: Pfeffer, pp. 227–241.
37. Kram, K.K., & Isabella, L.A. (1985) Mentoring alternatives: The role of peer relationships in career development. *Academy of Management Journal*, 28: 122–123, 110–132; Levine, H.Z. (1985) Consensus on career planning. *Personnel*, 63: 67–72.
38. Allen, T.D., Eby, L.T., Poteet, M.L., Lentz, E., & Lima, L. (2004) Career benefits associated with mentoring for protégés: A meta-analysis. *Journal of Applied Psychology*, 89: 127–136; Roche, G.R. (1979) op. cit.
39. Kram, K.K., & Isabella, L.A. (1985) op. cit.
40. Ibid.
41. Ibid.
42. Feldman, D.C., & Ng, T.W.H. (2007) Careers: Mobility, embeddedness, and success. *Journal of Management*, 33: 350–377.
43. De Caluwé, C., Van Dooren, W., Delafortry, A., & Janvier, R. (2014) Mind-sets of the boundaryless careers in the public sector: The vanguard of a more mobile workforce? *Public Personnel Management*, 43: 490–519.
44. Cunningham, J.B., & Hillier, E. (2012) Informal learning in the workplace: Key activities and processes. *Education and Training*, 55: 37–51; Bednall, T.C., Sanders, K., & Runhaar, P. (2014) Stimulating informal learning activities through perceptions of performance appraisal quality and human resource management system strengths: A two-wave study. *Academy of Management Learning and Education*, 13: 45–61; Hughes, P.D., & Campbell, A. (2009) *Learning and development outlook 2009: Learning in tough times.* Conference Board of Canada, August 4.
45. Lent, R.W., Brown, S.D., & Hackett, G. (1994) Toward a unifying social cognitive theory of career and academic interest, choice, and performance. *Journal of Vocational Behavior*, 45: 79–122.

46. Bandura, A. (1986) *Social foundations of thought and action: A social cognitive theory.* Englewood Cliffs, NJ: Prentice Hall; Bandura, A. (1989b) Human agency in social cognitive theory. *American Psychologist*, 77: 122–147.

47. Zimmerman, B.J., Bandura, A., & Martinez-Pons, M. (1992) Self-motivation for academic attainment: The role of self-efficacy beliefs and personal goal setting. *American Educational Research Journal*, 29: 663–676.

48. Latham, G.P., & Locke, E.A. (1991) Self-regulation through goal setting. *Organizational Behavior and Human Decision Process*, 50: 212–247; Hollenbeck. J.R., & Brief, A.P. (1987) The effects of individual differences and goal origin on goal setting and performance. *Organizational Behavior and Human Decision Process*, 40: 393–362.

49. Latham, G. P. (2004) The motivational benefits of goal-setting. *Academy of Management Executives*, 18: 126–129; Locke, E.A., & Latham, G.P. (2002) Building a practically useful theory of goal setting and task motivation: A 35-year odyssey. *American Psychologist*, 57: 705–717.

50. Elliot, A.J., & Murayama, K. (2008) On the measurement of achievement goals: Critique, illustration, and application. *Journal of Educational Psychology*, 100: 614, 613–628.

51. Dweck, C.S. (1986) Motivational processes affecting learning. *American Psychologist*, 41: 1040–1048; Payne, S.C., Youngcourt, S.S., & Beaubien, J.M. (2007) A meta-analytic examination of the goal orientation nomological net. *Journal of Applied Psychology*, 92: 128–150.

52. McClelland, D.C. (1961) *The Achieving Society.* Princeton, NJ: Van Nostrand; McClelland, D.C. (1965) Achievement motivation can be developed. *Harvard Business Review*, 43: 6–24.

53. Dweck, C.S. (1986) op. cit.

54. Elliot, A.J., & Murayama, K. (2008) On the measurement of achievement goals: Critique, illustration, and application. *Journal of Educational Psychology*, 100: 613–628. Elliot, A.J., & Church, M.A. (2003) A motivational analysis of defensive pessimism and self-handicapping. *Journal of Personality*, 71: 369–396.

55. Dweck, C.S., & Leggett, E.L. (1988) A social-cognitive approach to motivation and personality. *Psychological Review*, 95: 256–273.

56. Elliot, A.J., & Murayama, K. (2008) op. cit.

57. DeShon, R.P., & Gillespie, J.Z. (2005) A motivated action theory account of goal orientation. *Journal of Applied Psychology*, 90: 1105, 1096–1127.

58. Ibid.

59. Igbaria, M., & Baroudi, J.J. (1993) A short-form of career orientations: A psychometric evaluation. *Journal of Management Information Systems*, Fall, 10: 131–154.

60. Hogan, R.C., & Champagne, D.W. (1980) Personal style inventory. In J.W. Pfeiffer and J.E. Jones (eds.), *The 1980 Annual Handbook for Group Facilitators.* San Diego: University Associates; McCrae, R.R., & Costa Jr., P.T. (1989) Reinterpreting the Myers-Briggs Type Indicator from the perspective of the Five-Factor Model of Personality. *Journal of Personality*, 57: 17–40.

61. Costa Jr., P.T., & McCrae, R.R. (1992) Revised NEO Personality Inventory (NEO-PI-R) and NEO Five-Factor Inventory (NEO-FFI) manual. Odessa, FL: *Psychological Assessment Resources*; McCrae, R.R., & Costa Jr., P.T. (1987) Validation of the five-factor model of personality across instruments and observers. *Journal of Personality and Social Psychology*, 52: 81–90; McCrae, R.R., & John, O.P. (1992) An introduction to the five-factor model and its applications. *Journal of Personality*, 60: 175–215.

Chapter 10

1. Dolezalek, H. (2006) 2006 Industry Report. *Training*, 43: 20–32. The 2006 industry estimate was $70 billion (£46.1 billion) in 2006 for formal training, products and services in the US and $100 million (£65.9 million) in 2008. The 2013 data are based on estimates from the American Society for Training Development (ASTD) and TrainingIndustry.com.

2. Salas, E., Cannon-Bowers, J.A., Rhodenizer, L., & Bowers, C.A. (1999) Training in organizations: Myths, misconceptions, and mistaken assumptions. *Research in Personnel and Human Resource Management*, 17: 123–161.

3. Cunningham, J.B. (1994) Using mentoring for professional development. 1994 Annual: *Developing Human Resources*. La Jolla, CA: Pfeffer, pp. 227–241. The ideas underlying Action Learning were developed from Professor R.W. Revans' management experience after World War II in Britain's newly nationalized coal industry. He sought to establish programmes which encouraged colleagues to meet and work together in groups for the purpose of solving organizational problems within the British coal industry. These Action Learning groups, or 'sets', are described as 'the heart of the Action Learning process'. The model was successfully used in resolving problems in hospital and community environments. In the early 1960s, he tried to start an experienced-based management development programme with the Management Business School, and later moved to the Foundation Industrie-Université of Belgium, which was connected with the University of Brussels. Some of the history of this work is contained in McNulty, N.G. (1979) Management development by action learning. *Training and Development Journal*, 33: 12–18. See also: MacNamara, M., & Weekes, W.H. (1982) The action learning model of experiential learning for developing managers. *Human Relations*, 35: 879–901. The approach was that of General Electric and the University of Michigan. See: Garratt, B. (1977) Don't call me teacher. In *More than Management Development: Action Learning at GEC*, D. Casey, & D. Pearce (eds.), pp. 79–90. London: Gower Press.

4. Senge, P.M. (1990) *The fifth discipline: The art and practice of the learning organization*. Toronto, Currency Doubleday, pp. 12–14.

5. Wu, J.L. (2013) The study of competency-based training and strategies in the public sector: Experience from Taiwan. *Public Personnel Management*, 42: 259–271.

6. Naquin, S.S., & Holton, E.F. (2003). Redefining state leadership and management development: A process for competence-based development. *Public Personnel Management*, 32: 23–46.

7. Dubois, D., & Rothwell, W. (2004) Competency-based or a traditional approach to training? *T+D Magazine*, 58: 46–57.

8. Pfeffer, J. (2007) Human resources from an organizational behaviour perspective. Some paradoxes explained. *Journal of Economic Perspectives*, 21: 119, 115–134; See also: Shaw, K. (2006) The value of innovative human resource practices. In *America at work: Choices and Challenges*, E. Lawler III & J. O'Toole (eds.), pp. 227–239. New York: Palgrave Macmillan; Pfeffer, J. (1998) Seven practices of successful organizations. *California Management Review*, 40: 96–124.

9. MadDuffie, J.P., & Kochan, T.A. (1995) Do U.S. firms invest less in human resources? Training in the world auto industry. *Industrial Relations*, 34: 153, 147–168.

10. Developing business leaders for 2010. (2003) New York: The Conference Board.

11. Truss, C., Gratton, L., Hope-Halley, V., McGovern, P., & Stiles, P. (1997) Soft and hard models of human resource management: A reappraisal. *Journal of Management Studies*, 34: 60, 53–73.

12. Cannon-Bowers, J.A., Rhodenizer, L., Salas, E., & Bowers, C.A. (1998) A framework for understanding pre-practice conditions and their impact on learning. *Personnel Psychology*, 51: 291–320.

13. Wexley, K.N., & Latham, G.P. (2002) *Developing and training human resources in organizations*. 3rd ed. Upper Saddle River, NJ: Prentice Hall.

14. Salas, E., & Cannon-Bowers, J.A. (2001) The science of training: A decade of progress. *Annual Review of Psychology*, 52: 471–499.

15. Latham, G.P. (2004) The motivational benefits of goal-setting. *Academy of Management Executives*, 18: 126–129; Locke, E.A., & Latham, G.P. (2002) Building a practically useful theory of goal setting and task motivation: A 35-year odyssey. *American Psychologist*, 57: 705–717.

16. Martacchio, J.J., & Baldwin, T.T. (1997) The evolution of strategic organizational training: New objectives and research agenda. In *Research in personnel and human resource management*, G.R. Ferris (ed.), 15, 1–46. Greenwich, CT: JAI Press.

17. Holton III, E.F., Bates, R.A., & Naquin, S.S. (2000) Large-scale performance-driven training assessment: A case study. *Public Personnel Management*, 29: 249–267.

18. Ibid.; Chang, J.C., Chiang, T.C., & Yi, C.K. (2012) The systematic construction and influential factors of training needs assessment. *International Journal of Business and Social Science*, 3: 31–41; Swanson, R.A. (1994) *Analysis for improving performance: Tools for diagnosing organizations and documenting workplace expertise.* San Francisco: Berrett-Kohler; Rummler, G.A., & Brache, A.P. (1995) *Improving performance: How to manage the white space on the organization chart.* San Francisco: Jossey-Bass.

19. Bassi, I.J., & Cheney, S. (1996) *Results from the 1996 benchmarking forum.* Alexandria, VA: American Society for Training and Development.

20. McGehee, W., & Thayer, P.W. (1961) *Training in business and industry.* New York: John Wiley & Sons. p. 25.

21. Ibid.

22. Ibid.

23. McClelland, D.C. (1973) Testing for competence rather than 'Intelligence' *American Psychologist*, Jan: 1–14.

24. Boyatzis, R.E. (1982) *The Competent Manager.* New York: John Wiley & Sons.

25. Goldstein, I.L., & Gilliam, P. (1990) Training system issues in the year 2000. *American Psychologist*, 45: 134–143; Goldstein, I.L. (1990) Training in work organizations. *Annual Review of Psychology*, 31: 229–272.

26. Kraigen, K., Ford, J.K., & Salas, E. (1993) Application of cognitive, skilled-based, and affective theories of learning outcomes to new methods of training evaluation. *Journal of Applied Psychology Monograph*, 78: 311–328.

27. Heinrich, C.J. (2002) Outcome-based performance management in the public sector: Implications for government accountability and effectiveness. *Public Administration Review*, 62: 712–725.

28. Kirkpatrick, D.L. (1994) *Evaluating training programs: The four levels.* San Francisco: Berrett-Koehler. Philipps suggests including a fifth level to assess the return on investment in training; Kirkpatrick, D.L., & Kirkpatrick, J.D. (2005) *Transferring learning to behaviour: Using the four levels to improve performance.* San Francisco: Berrett-Koehler; Kirkpatrick, D.L., & Kirkpatrick, J.D. (2006) *Evaluating training programs.* San Francisco: Berrett-Koehler. See: Phillips, J.J. (1997) *Handbook of training evaluation and measurement methods.* Houston, TX: Gulf Publishing; Phillips, J.J. (2003) *Return on investment in training and performance improvement programs.* Boston: Butterworth-Heineman.

29. Alliger, G.M., & Janak, E.A. (1989) Kirkpatrick's levels of training criteria, Thirty years later. *Personnel Psychology*, 42: 331–342.

30. Gagne, R.M. (1984) Learning outcomes and their effects: Useful categories of human performance. *American Psychologist*, 39: 377–385; Kraigen, K., Ford, J.K., & Salas, E. (1993) op. cit.

31. Kraiger, K. (2002) Decision-based evaluation. In K. Kraiger (ed.), *Creating, implementing, and maintaining effective training and development: State-of-the-art lessons for practice.* San Francisco: Jossey-Bass, pp. 331–375.

32. Vyas, L. (2010) Balancing outlook: Assessment of public service training in Hong Kong by providers and clients. *Public Personnel Management*, 39: 149–167.

33. Kolb, D.A. (1984) *Experiential learning: Experience as the source of learning and development.* Englewood Cliffs, N.J. Prentice Hall; Kolb, D.A., Rubin, I., & McIntyre, J.M. (1971, 1979) *Organizational Psychology: An experiential approach.* Englewood Cliffs, NJ: Prentice Hall, pp. 27–54; Kolb, D.A., & Kolb, A.Y. (2005) Learning styles and learning spaces: Enhancing experiential learning in higher education. *Academy of Management Learning and Education*, 4, 193–212.

34. Armstrong, S.J., & Mahmud, A. (2008) Experiential learning and the acquisition of managerial tacit knowledge. *Academy of Management Learning and Education*, 7: 190, 189–208.

35. Ibid.

36. Kolb, David A. (1984) op. cit.

37. Salas, E., & Cannon-Bowers, J.A. (2001) The science of training: A decade of progress. *Annual Review of Psychology*, 52: 471–499.

38. Taylor, P.J., Russ-Eft, D.F., & Taylor, H. (2009) Transfer of management training from alternative perspectives. *Journal of Applied Psychology*, 94: 104–131.

39. Donovan, J.J., & Radosevich, D.J. (1999) A meta-analytic review of the distribution of practice effective: Now you see it, now you don't. *Journal of Applied Psychology*, 84: 795–805.

40. Driskell, J.E., Willis, R.P., & Copper, C. (1992) Effect of overlearning on retention. *Journal of Applied Psychology*, 77: 615–622.

41. Donovan, J.J., & Radosevich, D.J. (1999) op. cit.

42. Senge, P.M. (1990), op. cit., pp. 79–80. Reinforcing feedback can also be negative or generate decline.

43. Richman-Hirsch, W.L. (2001) Posttraining interventions to enhance transfer: The moderating effects of work environments. *Human Resource Development Quarterly*, 12: 105–120.

44. Tracey, J.B., Tannebaum, S.I., & Kavanagh, M.J. (1995) Applying trained skills on the job: The importance of the work environment. *Journal of Applied Psychology*, 80: 239–252.

45. Brower, H.H. (2003) On emulating classroom discussion in a distance-delivered OBHR course: Creating an on-line learning community. *Academy of Management Learning and Education*, 2: 22–36.

46. Blunt, R. (2001) How to build an e-learning community. *Learning & Training Innovations Magazine*.

47. Brower, H.H. (2003) op. cit.

48. Proserpio, L., & Gioia, D.A. (2007) Teaching the virtual generation. *Academy of Management Learning and Education*, 6: 69–80.

49. Van Velsor, E., & Leslie, J.B. (1995) Why executives derail: Perspectives across time and cultures. *Academy of Management Executive*, 9: 62–72.

Chapter 11

1. CBC. Dying for the job. (2006) CBC Indepth: Workplace Safety. This was from a three-year study by a CBC Investigative Unit who used freedom-of-information laws and other methods to gather data from workplace insurance boards across Canada.

2. World Health Organization (WHO) website. http://www.who.int/en/.

3. Takala, J., Hämäläinen, P., Saarela, K.L., Yun, L.Y., Manickam, K., Jin, T.W., Heng, P., et al. (2014) Global estimates of the burden of illness at work in 2012. *Journal of Occupational and Environmental Hygiene*, 11: 326–337; Hämäläinen, O., Saarela, K.L., & Takala, J. (2009) Global trend according to estimated number of occupational accidents and fatal work-related diseases at region and country level. *Journal of Safety Research*, 40: 125–139.

4. Becker, A.E., & Kleinman, A. (2013) Mental health and the global agenda. *The New England Journal of Medicine*, 369: 66–73.

5. Ibid.

6. World Health Organization (WHO), op. cit.

7. Cameron, C.M., Purdie, D.M., Kliewer, E.V., & McClure, R.J. (2006) Mental health: A cause or consequence of injury: A population based match cohort study. *BMC Public Health*, 6: 114.

8. Macklin, D.S., Smith, L.A., & Dollard, M.F. (2006) Public and private sector work stress: Workers compensation, levels of distress and job satisfaction, and the demand-control-support model. *Australian Journal of Psychology*, 58: 130–143.

9. Moorehead, A., Steele, M., Alexander, M., Stephen, K., & Duffin, L. (1997) *Changes at work: The 1995 workplace industrial relations survey*. Melbourne: Longman.

10. Noblet, A., Rodwell, J., & McWilliams, J. (2006) Organizational change in the public sector: Augmenting the demand control model to predict employee outcomes under new public management. *Work & Stress*, 20: 335–352.

11. Giauque, D., Anderfuhren-Bigetn, S., & Varone, F. (2013) Stress perception in public organizations: Expanding the job-demands-job resources model by including public service motivation. *Review of Public Personnel Administration*, 33: 58–83.

12. Hsieh, C.W. (2012) Burnout among public service workers: The role of emotional labor requirements and job resources. *Review of Public Personnel Administration*, 34: 379–402.

13. Becker, A.E., & Kleinman, A. (2013) op. cit.

14. Macklin, D.S., Smith, L.A., & Dollard, M.F. (2006) op. cit.

15. Stansfeld, S., & Candy, B. (2006) Psychological work environment and mental health – A meta-analytic review. *Scandinavian Journal of Work Environment and Health*, 32: 443–462.

16. Lazarus, R.S. (1991) Psychological stress in the workplace. *Journal of Social Behavior and Personality*, 6: 1–13; Lazarus, R.S., & Folkman, S. (1984) *Stress, appraisal and coping*. New York: Springer Publishing.

17. Karasek, R. (1979) Job demands, job decision latitude and mental strain: Implications for job redesign. *Administrative Science Quarterly*, 24: 285–308.

18. Macklin, D.S., Smith, L.A., & Dollard, M.F. (2006) op. cit.

19. Ibid.; Marmot, M.G., Bosma, H., Hemingway, H., Brunner, E., & Stansfeld, S. (1997) Contribution of job control and other risk factors to social variations in coronary heart disease incidence. *Lancet*, July 26; 350: 235–239.

20. Siegrist, J., & Klein, D. (1990) Occupational stress and cardiovascular reactivity in blue-collar workers. *Work and Stress*, 4: 295–304; Siegrist, J., Dagmar Starke, D., Chandola, T., Godin, I., Marmot, M., Niedhammer, I., & Peter, R. (2004) The measurement of effort-reward imbalance at work: European comparisons. *Social Science and Medicine*, 58: 1483–1499.

21. Bosma, H., Perter, R., Siegrist, J., & Marmot, M. (1998) Two alternative job stress models and the risk of coronary heart disease. *American Journal of Public Health*, 88: 68–74.

22. Byrne, D.G., & Espnes, G.A. (2008) Occupational stress and cardiovascular disease. *Stress and Health*, 24: 231–238.

23. Caverley, N., Cunningham, J.B., & MacGregor, J.N. (2007) Sickness presenteeism, sickness absenteeism, and health following restructuring in a public service organization. *Journal of Management Studies*, 44: 304–319.

24. Bosma, H., Perter, R., Siegrist, J., & Marmot, M. (1998) op. cit.

25. Giauque, D., Anderfuhren-Bigetn, S., & Varone, F. (2013) op. cit.

26. Noblet, A., Rodwell, J., & McWilliams, J. (2006) op. cit.

27. Cooper, C.L., & Marshall, J. (1976) Occupational sources of stress: A review of the literature relating to coronary heart disease and mental health. *Journal of Occupational Psychology*, 49: 11–28; Rees, D.W., & Cooper, C.L. (1992) Occupational stress in health service workers in the U.K. *Stress Medicine*, 8: 79–90; Chen, W.Q, Wong, T.W., & Yu, T.S. (2001) Reliability and validity of Occupational Stress

Scale for Chinese off-shore oil installation workers. *Stress and Health*, 17: 175–183; Based on Cooper, C.L., Sloan, S.J., Williams, S. (eds.) (1998) *Occupational Stress Indicator Management Guide*. Windsor, England: ASE a division of NFER-Nelson.

28. William, S., & Cooper, C.L. (1998) Measuring occupational stress: Development of the Pressure Management Indicator. *Journal of Occupational Health Psychology*, 3: 306–321.

29. Noblet, A., Rodwell, J., & McWilliams, J. (2006) op. cit.

30. Bakker, A.B., Van Emmerik, H., & Van Riet, P. (2008). How job demands, resources, and burnout predict objective performance: A constructive replication. *Anxiety Stress and Coping*, 21: 309–324.

31. Giaque, D., Anderfuhren-Biget, S., & Varone, F. (2013) Stress perception in public organizations: Expanding the job demands-job resources model by including public service motivation. *Review of Public Personnel Administration*, 33: 75–76, 58–83. The items are from the survey in the appendices of this article.

32. Seyle, H. (1956) *The stress of life*. New York: McGraw-Hill.

33. Cunningham, J.B. (2000) *The stress management sourcebook*. 2nd ed. New York: McGraw-Hill.

34. Ibid.; Cooper, C.L., & Marshall, J. (1976) op. cit.

35. Cunningham, J.B. (2000) op. cit.

36. Ibid.

37. William, S., & Cooper, C.L. (1998) op. cit.

38. Brown, J.A., Shannon, H.S., Mustard, C.A., & McDonough, P. (2007) Social and economic consequences of workplace injury: A population-based study of workers in British Columbia, Canada. *American Journal of Industrial Medicine*, 50: 633–645.

39. Caverley, N., Cunningham, J.B., & MacGregor, J.N. (2007) op. cit.; MacGregor, J.N., Cunningham, J.B., & Caverley, N. (2008) Factors in absenteeism and presenteeism: Life events and health events. *Management Research News*, 31: 607–615.

40. The Statistics Canada survey indicated that 38.8 per cent of Canadians between the ages of 15 and 75 are slightly stressed at work, 25 per cent are relatively stressed at work, and 5.4 per cent are extremely stressed at work. *Statistics Canada, 2002* – updated in September 2004.

41. Australian Government Productivity Commission (2010). Performance benchmarking of Australian business regulation: Occupational health & safety; McTernan, W.P., Dollard, M.F., & LaMontange, A.D. Depression in the workplace:an economic cost analysis of depression related productivity loss attributable to job strain and bullying. *Work &Stress: International Journal of Work, Health & Organizations*, 27: 21–338.

42. Satyanarayana, S., Cox, B.J., & Sareen, J. (2009) Prevalence and correlates of chronic depression in the Canadian community health survey: Mental health and well-being. *Canadian Journal of Psychiatry*, 52: 389–398.

43. Patten, S.B., Williams, J.V.A., Lavorato, D.H., & Eliasziw, M. (2010) Major depression and injury risk. *Canadian Journal of Psychiatry*, 55: 313–318.

44. Marshand, A., Demers, A., & Durand, P. (2005) Do occupations and work conditions really matter? A longitudinal analysis of psychological distress experiences among Canadian workers. *Sociology of Health and Illness*, 27: 602–627.

45. Satyanarayana, S., Cox, B.J., & Sareen, J. (2009) op. cit.

46. Caron, J., & Liu, A. (2010) A descriptive study of prevalence of psychological distress and mental disorders in the Canadian population: Comparison between low-income and non-low-income populations. *Chronic Diseases in Canada*, 30: 84–95.

47. Dibben, P., James, P., & Cunningham, I. (2010) Development: Absence management in the public sector: An integrative model. *Public Money and Management*, 21: 55–60; Hughes, L. (2010) Benefits II: Disability programs and absence management in Canadian workplaces. Ottawa: The Conference Board of Canada.

48. Hughes, L. (2010) *Benefits II: Disability programs and absence management in Canadian workplaces*. Ottawa: The Conference Board of Canada.

49. Ibid.

50. Parks, K.M., & Steelman, L.A. (2008) Organizational wellness programs: A meta-analysis. *Journal of Occupational Health Psychology*, 13: 58–68.

51. Ibid.

52. Bachmann, K. (October, 2002) *Health promotion programs at work: A frivolous cost or a sound investment?* (Available from The Conference Board of Canada, 255 Smyth Rd., Ottawa, ON, K1H 8M7).

53. Parks, K.M., & Steelman, L.A. (2008) op. cit.

54. Bachmann, K. (October, 2002) op. cit.

55. Brun, J.P., & Lamarche, C. (2006) *Assessing the costs of stress*. Research report. Université Laval, Quebec, Canada.

56. Shumway, S.T., Wampler, R.S., Dersch, C., & Arredondo, R. (2004) A place for marriage and family services in employee assistance programs (EAPs): A survey of EAP client problems and needs. *Journal of Marital and Family Therapy*, 30: 71–79. The authors, who also asked 800 individuals who had used EAPs, revealed that family problems and emotional problems were prevalent.

57. Macdonald, S., Csiernik, R., Durand, P., Rylett, M., & Wild, T.C. (2006) Prevalence and factors related to Canadian workplace health programs. *Canadian Journal of Public Health*, March–April: 121–125.

58. Macdonald, S., Lothian, S., & Wells, S. (1997) Evaluation of an employee assistance program at a transportation company. *Evaluation and Program Planning*, 20: 495–505.

59. James, C., Southgate, E., Kable, A., Rivett, D.A., Guest, M., & Bohatko-Naismith, J. (2011) The return-to-work coordinator role: Qualitative insights for nursing. *Journal of Occupational Rehabilitation*, 21: 220–227.

60. Ibid., 224.

61. Ahlstrom, L., Hagberg, M., & Delive, L. (2013) Workplace rehabilitation and social supportive conditions at work: A prospective study. *Journal of Occupational Rehabilitation*, 23: 248–260.

62. Dewa, C.S., & Hoch, J.S. (2014) Estimating the net benefits of a specialized return-to-work program for workers on short-term disability related to mental disorder: An example exploring investment in collaborative care. *Journal of Occupational and Environmental Medicine*, 56: 628–631.

63. Hoffman, H., Jäckel, D., Glauser, S., Muese, K.T., & Kupper, Z. (2014) Long-term effectiveness of supported employment: 5 year follow-up of a randomized controlled trial. *American Journal of Psychiatry*, 171: 1183–1190.

64. Even though there has been a resurgence in some 'blue-collar' jobs (in construction, oil and gas), there has been a long-term shift from manufacturing and resources jobs to service jobs.

65. Holmann, D.A., & Stetzer, A. (1998) The role of safety climate and communication in accident interpretation: Implications for learning from negative events. *Academy of Management Journal*, 41: 644, 644–657.

66. Ibid.

67. Ibid.

68. Holmamn, D.A., & Stetzer, A. (1996) A cross-level investigation of factors influencing unsafe behaviors and accidents. *Personnel Psychology*, 49: 331, 307–339.

356 References

69. Wright, C. (1986) Routine deaths: Fatal accidents in the oil industry. *Sociological Review*, 4: 265–289.
70. McCarthy, S., & Waldie, P. (2010) Perils and profit of offshore oil. *Globe and Mail*. Report on Business.
71. Lang, T.A., Hodge, M., Olson, V., Romano, P.S., & Kravitz, R.L. (2004) Nurse-patient ratios: A systematic review on the effects of nurse staffing on patient, nurse employee, and hospital outcomes. *Journal of Nursing Administration*, 34: 326–337.
72. Janis, I.L. (1972) *Victims of groupthink: A psychological study of foreign-policy decisions and fiascoes*. Boston: Houghton Mifflin.
73. Dr Kelsey is one of America's more celebrated public servants and was given the Order of Canada by her home country in 2015. Her Order of Canada award comes 'for her efforts to protect public health, notably by helping to end the use of thalidomide, and for her contributions to clinical drug trial regulations'.
74. Holmanm, D.A., & Stetzer, A. (1996) op. cit.
75. Beus, J.M., Payne, S.C., Bergman, M.E., Arthur Jr., W. (2010) Safety climate and injuries: An examination of theoretical and empirical relationships. *Journal of Applied Psychology*, 95: 713–727. The term was introduced by Zohar, D. (1980) Safety climate in industrial organizations: Theoretical and applied implications. *Journal of Applied Psychology*, 65: 96–102.
76. Zhang, H., Wiegmann, D.A., von Thaden, T.L., Sharma, G., & Mitchell, A.A. (2002) Safety culture: A concept in chaos. *Proceedings of the 46th Annual Meeting of the Human Factors and Ergonomics Society*. Santa Monica, Human Factors and Ergonomics Society.
77. Wiegmann, D.A., Zhang, H., von Thaden, T.L., Sharma, G., & Mitchell, A.A. (2002) *A synthesis of safety culture and safety climate research*. Technical report ARL-02-3/FAA-02-2 for Federal Aviation Administration, Atlantic City International Airport, NJ.
78. McIntyre, R.M., & Salas, E. (1995) Measuring and managing for team performance: Emerging principles from complex environments. In *Team effectiveness and decision making in organizations*, R.A. Gum & E. Salas (eds.), 945. San Francisco: Jossey-Bass.
79. Statistics Canada Criminal Victimization in the workplace. Based on police and self-reported data from 2004 statistics.
80. Vickers, M.H. (2010) Introduction – Bullying, mobbing, and violence in public service workplaces: The shifting sands of 'acceptable' violence. *Administrative Theory & Praxis*, 32: 7–24; International Labour Organization (ILO) (2002) *Framework guidelines for addressing workplace violence in the health sector*.
81. Corney, B. (2008) Aggression in the workplace: A study of horizontal violence utilising Heideggerian hermenutic phenomenology. *Journal of Health Organization and Management*, 22: 164–177.
82. Rhodes, C., Pullen, A., Vickers, M.H., Clegg, S.R., & Pitsis, A. (2010) Violence and workplace bullying: What are an organization's ethical responsibilities? *Administrative Theory & Praxis*, 32: 97, 96–115.
83. McTernan, W.P., Dollard, M.F., & LaMontange, A.D. (2013) op. cit.

Chapter 12

1. Robert, Y. (2012) The women changing Britain's unions. *The Guardian*, August 5; Akyeampong, E.B. (1998) The rise of unionization among women. *Perspectives on Labour and Income* (Statistics Canada, Catalogue 75-001-XPE) 10: 30–43.
2. Eaton, J.K. (1976) Union growth in the sixties. *Economics and Research Branch, Canada Department of Labour*. Ottawa.
3. Bronfenbrenner, K., & Juravich, T. (1998) It takes more than house calls: Organizing to win a comprehensive union building strategy. In *Organizing to win: New research on union strategies*,

K. Bronfenbrenner, S. Friedman, R.W. Hurd, R.A. Oswald, & R. Seeber (eds.), pp. 19–36. Ithaca, NY: ILR Press; Kearney, R.C. (2014) Public sector labor-management relations: Change or status quo? *Review of Public Personnel Administration*, 30: 89–111; Simpson, J. (2013) When politicians campaign against public-sector unions. *The Globe and Mail*. Accessed from theglobeandmail.com; US Bureau of Labor Statistics. In 2009, there were 7.9 million in the public sector unions and 7.4 in private sector unions.

4. Organization for Economic Co-operation and Development (OECD). StatExtracts from the OECD's library; there is a higher percentage of people in public sector unions in some countries (Australia at 40%, Germany at 30%).

5. Statistics Canada. (2009) Perspectives on Labour and Income. Accessed from statcan.gc.ca.

6. The metaphor is a personal statement by some labour negotiators. See also: Potter, G. (2005) *Sui Generis* social structures: The heuristic example of poker. *Canadian Journal of Sociology*, 28: 171–202.

7. Alberta Labour Relations Board. (2003) *Bad faith bargaining*.

8. Moran, R.T. (1987) *Getting the yen's worth: How to negotiate with Japan, Inc.* Houston: Gulf.

9. Chandler, T.D., & Judge, T.A. (1998) Management chief negotiators, bargaining strategies, and the likelihood of impasse in public sector collective bargaining. *American Review of Public Administration*, 28, 160: 146–165.

10. Walton, R.E., & McKersie, R.B. (1965) *A behavioral theory of labor negotiations*. New York: McGraw-Hill.

11. Nierenberg, G.I. (1986) *The complete negotiator*. London: Souvenir Press.

12. Craig, A.W.J. (1986) *The system of industrial relations in Canada*. 2nd ed. Scarborough, Prentice Hall.

13. Hüffmeier, J., Freund, P.A., Zerres, A., Backhaus, K., & Hertel, G. (2014) Being tough or being nice? A meta-analysis on the impact of hard- and soft-line strategies in distributive negotiations. *Journal of Management*, 40: 866–892.

14. Stevens, C.M. (1963) *Strategy and collective bargaining negotiations*. New York: McGraw-Hill. The ZOPA is also called the bargaining zone or contract zone.

15. Based on Statistics Canada. (2009) Perspectives on Labour and Income. Accessed from statcan.gc.ca.

16. Buttigieg, D.M., Deery, S.J., & Iverson, R.D. (2007) An event history analysis of union joining and leaving. *Journal of Applied Psychology*, 92: 829–839; See: Statistic Canada (2002) Unions and fringe benefits. Perspectives on Labour and Income.

17. Hinchey, G. (2014) University of Victoria faculty members embrace union. *The Globe and Mail*. Accessed from theglobeandmail.com.

18. Lowe, G.S., & Krahn, H. (1989) Recent trends in public support for unions in Canada. *Journal of Labor Research*, 10: 391–410; Fiorito, J., Gall, G., Martinez, A.D. (2010) Activism and willingness to help in union organizing: Who are the activists? *Journal of Labor Research*, 31: 263–284; Bamberger, P.A., Kluger, A.N., & Suchard, R. (1999) The antecedents and consequences of union commitment: A meta-analysis. *Academy of Management Journal*, 42: 304–318.

19. Buttigieg, D.M., Deery, S.J., & Iverson, R.D. (2007) op. cit.

20. Kelly, J. (1998) *Rethinking industrial relations: Mobilization, collectivism, and long waves*. London: Routledge.

21. Badigannavar, V., & Kelly, J. (2005) Why are some union organizing campaigns more successful than others? *British Journal of Industrial Relations*, 43: 515–535.

22. Flood, P., Turner, T., & Willman, P. (2000) A segmented model of union participation. *Industrial Relations*, 39: 108–114; Kessler, I, & Heron, P. (2001) Steward organization in a professional union: The case of the Royal College of Nursing. *British Journal of Industrial Relations*, 39: 367–391.

23. Juravich, T., & Bronfenbrenner, K. (1998) op. cit.
24. Caverley, N., Cunningham, B., & Mitchell, L. (2006) Reflections on public sector-based integrative collective bargaining. *Employee Relations*, 28: 62–75.
25. Follett, M.P. (1942) *Dynamic administration: The collected papers of Mary Parker Follett*. New York: Harper.
26. Walton, R.E., & McKersie, R.B. (1965) op. cit.
27. Fisher, R., & Ury, W. (1981) *Getting to yes: Negotiating agreements without giving in*. 1st ed. New York: Penguin Books; Fisher, R., Ury, W., & Patton, B. (1991) *Getting to yes: Negotiating agreements without giving in*. (rev. ed.) New York: Penguin Books.
28. Caverley, N., Cunningham, J.B., & Mitchell, L. (2006) op. cit.; Beil, M., & Litscher, J.E. (1998) Consensus bargaining in Wisconsin State Government: A new approach to labor negotiation. *Public Personnel Management*, 27: 39–50; Brainerd, R. (1998) Interest-based bargaining: Labor and management working together in Ramsey County, Minnesota. *Public Personnel Management*, 27: 51–68.
29. Wheeler, M., Ghazzawi, I.A., & Palladini, M. (2011) The Los Angeles County Metropolitan Transportation Agency: Interest based bargaining as an alternative approach to collective bargaining. *Journal of the International Academy of Case Studies*, 17: 99–116.
30. Fisher, R., & Ury, W. (1981) op. cit., p. 11.
31. Maier, N.R. (1976) *The appraisal interview: Three basic approaches*. La Jolla, CA: University Associates, p. 168.
32. Caverley, N., Cunningham, B., & Mitchell, L. (2006) op. cit.; Cutcher-Gershenfeld, J., Kochan, H., & Well, J.C. (2001) In whose interest? A first look at national survey data on interest-based bargaining in labor relations. *Industrial Relations*, 40: 1–21.

Chapter 13

1. International Labour Organization. (2014) Rules of the game: A brief introduction to international labour standards. ILO, first published in 2005; revised in 2014.
2. International Labour Organization. (2014) ILO Declaration of fundamental principles and rights at work.
3. Martinez, A.D., & Fiorito, J. (2008) General feelings toward unions and employers as predictors of union voting intent. *Journal of Labor Research*, 30: 120–134.
4. Fisher, R., & Ury, W. (1981) *Getting to yes: Negotiating agreements without giving in*. 1st ed. New York: Penguin Books; Fisher, R., Ury, W., & Patton, B. (1991) *Getting to yes: Negotiating agreements without giving in*. (rev. ed.) New York: Penguin Books.
5. Deery, S.J., Erwin, R., & Iverson, R.D. (1999) Industrial relations climate, attendance behaviour and the role of trade unions. *British Journal of Industrial Relations*, 37: 533–558.
6. Deery, S.J., & Iverson, R.D. (2005) Labor-management cooperation: Antecedents and impact on organizational performance. *Industrial and Labor Relations Review*, 58: 588–609.
7. Undy, R. (2001) New labour and new unions, 1997–2001: But is it the same old story? *Employee Relations*, 24: 638–656.
8. Guest, D.E., & Peccei, R. (2001) Partnership at work: Mutuality and the balance of advantage. *British Journal of Industrial Relations*, 39: 207–236; Deery, S., Erwin, R., & Iverson, R.D. (1999) op. cit.
9. Badigannavar, V., & Kelly, J. (2005) Why are some union organizing campaigns more successful than others?, *British Journal of Industrial Relations*, 43: 515–535.

10. Ibid.

11. Frege, C., & Kelly, J. (2004) Analyzing social partnership: A tool of union revitalization? In *Varieties of unionism: Strategies for union revitalization in the globalizing economy*, C.M. Frege & J. Kelly, (eds.), pp. 71–92. Oxford, UK: Oxford University Press.

12. Deery, S.J., Iverson, R.D., & Erwin, P.J. (1994) Predicting organizational and union commitment: The effective of industrial relations climate. *British Journal of Industrial Relations*, 32: 581–596.

13. Guest, D.E., & Dewe, P. (1991) Company or trade union: Which wins workers allegiance? A study of commitment in the UK electronic industry. *British Journal of Industrial Relations*, 29: 75–96; Sherer, P.D., & Morishima, M. (1989) Roads and roadblocks to dual commitment: Similar and dissimilar antecedents of union and company commitment. *Journal of Labor Research*, 10: 311–330.

14. Deery, S.J., Iverson, R.D., & Erwin, P.J. (1994) op. cit.

15. Dastmalchian, A., Blyton, P., & Abdollahian, R. (1982) Industrial relations climate and company effectiveness. *Personnel Review*, 11: 35–39; Deery, S.J., Iverson, R.D., & Erwin, P.J. (1994) op. cit.

16. Dastmalchian, A. (2008) Industrial relations climate. In *The SAGE Handbook of Industrial Relations*, P. Blyton, N. Bacon, J. Fiorito, & E. Heery (eds.), pp. 548–571. London: Sage; see also: Blyton, P., Dastmalchian, A., & Adamson, R. (1987) Developing the concept of industrial relations climate, *Journal of Industrial Relations*, 29: 207–216.

17. Dastmalchian, A., Blyton, P., & Adamson, R. (1991) *The climate of workplace relations*. London: Routledge. The wording of the example measures has been slightly altered from the original scale; Dastmalchian, A., Blyton, P., & Abamson, R. (1989). Industrial relations climate: Testing a construct. *Journal of Occupational Psychology*, 62: 21–32.

18. Deery, S.J., & Iverson, R.D. (2005) Labor-management cooperation: Antecedents and impact on organizational performance. *Industrial and Labor Relations Review*, 58: 588–609.

19. Deery, S.J., Erwin, R., & Iverson, R.D. (1999) op. cit.; Fullagar, C., & Barling, J. (1991) Predictors and outcomes of different patterns of organizational and union loyalty. *Journal of Occupational Psychology*, 64: 129–143.

20. Frege, C. (2005) Discourse of industrial democracy: Germany and the US revisited. *Economic and Industrial Democracy*, 26: 151–175.

21. Thorsrud, E., & Emery, F.E. (1970) Industrial democracy in Norway. *Industrial Relations*, 9: 187–196.

22. Deutsch, S. (2005) A researcher's guide worker participation, labor and economic and industrial democracy. *Economic and Industrial Democracy*, 26: 645–656.

23. Ibid., p. 649.

24. Peterson, R.B. (1987) Swedish collective bargaining – A changing scene. *British Journal of Industrial Democracy*, 25: 31–48; Peterson, R.B. (1968) Swedish experience with industrial democracy. *British Journal of Industrial Democracy*, 6: 185–203.

25. Jirjahn, U. (2010) Work councils and employment growth in German establishments. *Cambridge Journal of Economics*, 34: 475–500; Poole, M., Lansbury, R., & Wailes, N. (2001) A comparative analysis of developments in industrial democracy. *Industrial Relations*, 40: 490–525; Frege, C. (2005) Discourse of industrial democracy: Germany and the US revisited. *Economic and Industrial Democracy*, 26: 151–175.

26. Poole, Lansbury & Wailes (2001) op. cit.

27. Kalliola, S. (2005) Confronting a changing economy: Union responses in Finland. *Economic and Industrial Democracy*, 26: 269, 257–287.

28. Rolfsen, M., & Johansen, T.S. (2012) The silent practice: Sustainable self-managing teams in a Norwegian context. *Journal of Organizational Change Management*, 27: 175–187.

29. Forsyth, A. (2003) The retreat of government support for social dialogue in the Australian public service. *Australian Journal of Public Administration*, 62: 52–64.

30. Swimmer, G. (ed.) (2001) *Public sector labour relations in an era of restraint and restructuring Don Mills, ON*. Oxford, UK: Oxford University Press.

31. National Labor Relations Act or Wagner Act of 1935.

32. Rose, J.B. (2008) Regulating and resolving disputes in Canada. *Journal of Industrial Relations*, 50: 545–559.

33. Rose, J.B. (2004) 'Public Sector Bargaining: From Retrenchment to Consolidation', *Relations Industrielles/Industrial Relations*, 59: 271–294.

34. Rose, J.B. (2008) op. cit.

35. Ibid.

36. Fryer, J. (chair) (2001) Working together in the public interest. Ottawa: Treasury Board of Canada; the original idea came from a previous task force: Woods, H.D. (chair) (1968) *Canadian industrial relations: The report of the task force on labour relations*. Ottawa: Privy Council Office.

37. Susskind, L., & Ozawa, C. (2001) Mediated negotiation in the public sector; Mediator accountability and the public interest problem. *American Behavioral Science*, 27: 255–279; Rubin, J.Z (ed.) (1981) *Dynamics of third party intervention: Kissinger in the Middle East*. New York: Praeger.

38. Rosenthal, R., & Cross, S. (1999) Three models of conflict resolutions: Effects on intergroup expectancies and attitudes. *Journal of Social Issues*, 55: 561–580; Kelman, H.C. (1992) Informal mediation by the scholar/practitioner. In *Mediation in international relations*, J. Bercovitch & J. Rubin (eds.), pp. 64–96. New York: St Martin's Press.

39. Rose, J.B. (2008) op. cit.

40. Adell, B., Grant, M., & Ponak, A. (2001) *Strikes in Essential Services*. Kingston: IRC Press, Queen's University.

41. Rose, J.B. (2008) op. cit., 50: 558.

42. Vander Veen, S. (2014) Dispute resolution and design. MediateBC.com: Vander Veen Research and Evaluation; CPP Inc. (July, 2008). Global human capital report: Workplace conflict and how businesses can harness it to thrive. Author CPP Inc.

43. Brett, J.M., Barsness, Z.I., & Goldberg, S.B. (1996) The effectiveness of mediation: An independent analysis of cases handled by four major service providers. *Negotiation Journal*, July: 259–269.

44. Colquitt, J.A., Conlon, D.E., Wesson, M.J., Portern, C.O.L.H., & Ng, K.Y. (2001). Justice at the millennium: A meta-analytic review of 25 years of organizational justice research. *Journal of Applied Psychology*, 86: 524–445.

45. Kim, W.C., & Mauborgne, R.A. (2005) *Blue ocean strategy: How to create uncontested market space and make competition irrelevant*. Cambridge, MA: Harvard Business School Press.

46. Kelman, S. (2007) Public administration and organizational studies. *Academy of Management Annals*, 1: 225–267.

47. Cropanzano, R., Bowen, D.E., & Gilliland, S.W. (2007) The management of organizational justice. *Academy of Management Perspectives*, 21: 34–48.

48. Elovainio, M., Kivimaki, M., & Helkama, K. (2001) Organizational justice evaluation, job control, and occupational strain. *Journal of Applied Psychology*, 86: 418–424.

49. Greenberg, J. (2010) Organizational injustice as an occupational health risk. *The Academy of Management Annals*, 4: 205–243.

50. Graen, G.B., & Uhl-Bien, M. (1995) Relationship-based approach to leadership: Development of Member Exchange (LMX) theory of leadership over 25 years: Applying a multi-level multi-domain perspective. *Leadership Quarterly*, 6: 219–247, p. 237.

51. Ibid., 6: 219–247; See also: Hooper, D.T., & Martin, R. (2008) Beyond personal leader member exchange (LMX) quality: The effects of perceived LMX variability on employee reactions. *Leadership Quarterly*, 19: 20–30.

52. Wilkinson, A., & Fay, C. (2011) Guest editor's note: New times for employee voice. *Human Resource Management*, 50: 65–74.

53. Farndale, E., Van Ruiten, J., & Kelliher, C. (2011) The influence of perceived employee voice on organizational commitment: An Exchange perspective. *Human Resource Management*, 50: 113–129.

54. Wilkinson, A., Dundon, T., Marchington, M., & Ackers, P. (2004) Changing patterns of employee voice: Case studies from the UK and Republic of Ireland. *Journal of Industrial Relations*, 46: 298–322.

55. Mowday, R., Steers, R.M., & Porter, L. (1979) The measurement of organizational commitment. *Journal of Vocational Behavior*, 14: 224–247.

56. Hagedoorn, M., Van Yperen, N.W., Van De Vliert, E., & Buunk, B.P. (1999) Employees' reactions to problematic events: A circumflex structure of five categories of responses, and the role of job satisfaction. *Journal of Organizational Behavior*, 20: 309–331.

57. Klass, B.S., Olson-Buchanan, J.B., & Ward, A. (2012) The determinants of alternative forms of workplace voice: An integrative perspective. *Journal of Management*, 38: 314–345.

58. Craig, A.W.J. (1986) *The system of industrial relations in Canada*. 2nd ed. Scarborough, Prentice Hall, pp. 232–252.

59. Ibid.

Chapter 14

1. Easterbrook, G. (2005) The real truth about money. *Time*, January 17: A32–A34.

2. Currall, S.C., Towller, A.J., Judge, T.A., & Kohn, L. (2005) Pay satisfaction and organizational outcomes. *Personnel Psychology*, 58: 613–640.

3. Nunnally, J.C., & Bernstein, I.H. (1994) *Psycho-metric theory*. 3rd ed. New York: McGraw-Hill.

4. Rynes, S.L., Gerhard, B., & Minette, K.A. (2004) The importance of pay in employee motivation: Discrepancies between what people say and what they do. *Human Resource Management*, 43: 381–394.

5. Williams, V.L., & Sunderland, J.E. (1999) New pay program boost retention. *Workforce*, 78: 36–40.

6. Rynes, S.L., Gerhard, B., & Minette, K.A. (2004) op. cit.; Rynes, S.L., Golbert, A., & Brown, K.G. (2002) HR professionals' beliefs about effective human resource practices: Correspondence between research and practice. *Human Resource Management*, 41: 149–174.

7. Nelson, M.F., Frye, C.M., & Chown, D.W. (2008) Pay me more: What companies need to know about employee pay satisfaction. *Compensation & Benefits Review*, 40: 35–42.

8. Currall, S.C., Towller, A.J., Judge, T.A., & Kohn, L. (2005) op. cit.

9. Easterbrook, G. (2005) op. cit.

10. Nelson, M.F., Frye, C.M., & Chown, D.W. (2008) op. cit.; Judge, T.A. (1993) Validity of dimensions of the pay satisfaction questionnaire: Evidence of differential prediction. *Personnel Psychology*, 46: 331–355; Heneman, H.G., & Schwab, D.P. (1985) Pay satisfaction: Its multidimensional nature and measurement. *International Journal of Psychology*, 20: 129–141; Heneman, R.L., Greenberger, D.B., & Strasser, S. (1988) The relationship between pay-for-performance perceptions and pay satisfaction. *Personnel Psychology*, 41: 745–759.

11. Pandey, N., & Martocchio, J.J. (2008) Health care and retirement costs in North America spiraling uncontrollably: What are employers to do? *The International Journal of Human Resource Management*, 19: 1515–1533.

12. Fortin, N.M., & Huberman, M. (2002) Occupation gender segregation and women's wages in Canada: A historical perspective. Montreal, CIRANO (Center for Interuniversity Research and Analysis of Organizations).

13. Reese, C.C., & Warner, B. (2012) Pay equity in the states: An analysis of the gender-pay gap in the public sector. *Review of Personnel Administration*, 32: 312–331.

14. Arulampalam, W., Booth, A.L., & Bryan, M.L. (2007) Is there a glass ceiling over Europe? Exploring pay gap across the wage distribution, *Industrial and Labor Relations Review*, 60: 163–186; Smith, M. (2011) Limits and possibilities: Rights-based discourses in Australian gender pay equity reform 1969–2007. *Gender, Work and Organization*, 18: e180–e201; Jain, H.C., Horwitz, F., & Wilkin, C.L. (2011) Employment equity in Canada and South Africa: A comparative review. *The International Journal of Human Resource Management*, 23: 1–17.

15. Pillinger, J. (2006) Pay equity now! Gender mainstreaming and gender pay equity in the public services. *International Feminist Journal of Politics*, 7: 591–599.

16. Convention on the elimination of all forms of discrimination against women. (1979) *UN Women*. New York, United Nations; Equal Remuneration Convention (1951). Declaration of fundamental principles and rights of work. International Labour Office.

17. See: The Constitution Act 1982 C.11 (I.K.) Section 12 of Canadian Charter of Rights and Freedoms after 15 April 1985.

18. Faundez, J. (1995) *Affirmative Action: International Perspectives*. Geneva: International Labour Office.

19. Henderson, R.I. (1979) *Compensation management: Rewarding performance*. 3rd ed. Reston, VA: Reston Publishing.

20. Employment Equity Review (2001) A report on the standing committee on the human resource development and the status of persons with disabilities. Human Resources and Skills Development Canada.

21. Hills, F.S. (1986) *Compensation decision-making*. Chicago: Dryden Press.

22. McHabb, R., & Whitfield, K. (2001) Job evaluation and high performance work practices: Compatible or conflictual? *Journal of Management Studies*, 38: 293–312.

23. CUPE Job Evaluation Department (2008) CUPE, *Gender – Neutral Job Evaluation Plan*. Canadian Union of Public Employees.

24. Universal Classification Standard, UCS 2.0, Factors and Elements, Treasury Board of Canada, Secretariat, October 1999.

25. Connect to haygroup.com/ca/.

26. Kilgour, J.G. (2008) Job evaluation revisited: The point factor method. *Compensation and Benefits Review*, July–August: 37–46.

27. A way to implement this rule of thumb is to take the highest paid job covered by the plan and divide its wage rate with the lowest paid job's wage rate, and then multiple by 100.

28. Henderson, R.I. (1979) op. cit., p. 207.

29. Van de Ven, A., Delbecq, A., & Gustafson, D. (1975) *Group techniques for program planning: A guide to nominal group and Delphi processes*. Glenville, IL: Scott Foreman.

30. Kilgour, J.G. (2008) op. cit.

31. Dierdorff, E.C., & Surface, E.A. (2008) If you pay for skills, will they learn? Skill change and maintenance under a skill-based pay system. *Journal of Management*, 34: 721–743; Shaw, J.D., Gupta, N., Mitra, A., Ledford, Jr., G.E. (2005) Success and survival of skill-based pay plans. *Journal of Management*,

31: 28–49; Murray, B., & Gerhart, B. (1998) An empirical analysis of a skill-based pay program and plan performance outcomes. *Academy of Management Journal*, 41: 68–78.

32. Ledford Jr., G.E. (1991) Three case studies on skill-based pay: An overview. *Compensation and Benefits Review*, 23: 11–23.

33. Lawler III, E.E., & Ledford Jr., G.E. (1986) Skill-based pay: A concept that's catching on. *Compensation and Benefits Review*, 18: 135–161; Ledford Jr., G.E. (1991) op. cit.

34. Lawler III, E.E., & Ledford Jr., G.E. (1986) op. cit.

35. Lawler & Ledford, op. cit.; Lawler III, E.E., Ledford Jr., G.E., & Chang, L. (1993). Who uses skill-based pay, and why. *Compensation and Benefits Review*, 25: 22–26.

36. Adams, J.S. (1963) Toward an understanding of inequity. *Journal of Abnormal and Social Psychology*, 67: 422–436; Adams, J.S. (1965) Inequity in social exchange. In L. Berkowitz (ed.), *Advances in Experimental Social Psychology*, 2: 267–299; Huseman, R.C., Hatfield, J.D., & Miles, E.W. (1987). A new perspective on equity theory: The equity sensitivity construct. *Academy of Management Review*, 12: 222–234.

Chapter 15

1. Johnson, A.A. (1995) The business case for work-family programs. *Journal of Accountancy*, 180: 53–59.

2. Griffeth, R.W., Hom, P.W., & Gaertner, S. (2000) A meta-analysis of antecedents and correlates of employee turnover: Update, moderator tests, and research implications for the next millennium. *Journal of Management*, 26: 463–488; Griffeth, R.W., Steel, R.P., Allen, D.G., & Bryan, N. (2005) Reducing voluntary, avoidable turnover through selection. *Journal of Applied Psychology*, 90: 159–166; Guthrie, J.P. (2001) High-involvement work practices, turnover, and productivity: Evidence from New Zealand. *Academy of Management Journal*, 44: 180–190.

3. Hedge, J.W., Borman, W.C, & Lammlein, S.E. (2006) *The aging workforce*. Washington, DC: American Psychological Association.

4. Frone, M.R., & Yardley, J.K. (1996) Workplace family-supportive programmes: Predictors of employed parents' importance ratings. *Journal of Occupational and Organizational Psychology*, 69: 351–366.

5. Thompson, L.F., & Aspinwall, K.R. (2009) The recruitment value of work/life benefits. *Personnel Review*, 38: 195–210.

6. Meisenheimer, J.R., & Wiatroeski, W.J. (1989) Flexible benefits plans: Employees who have a choice. *Monthly Labour Review*, 112: 17–23.

7. Anderson, L.B., Eriksson, T., Kristensen, N., & Pederen, L.H. (2012) Attracting public service motivated employees: How to design compensation packages. *International Review of Administrative Sciences*, 78: 615–641.

8. The remaining 29 per cent of the benefits costs were for disability and casual absence plans, extended health-care, dental plans, life and accident insurance plans and wellness programs (in order of amount spent). See Thorpe, K. (2010) Benefits benchmarking 2009: Balancing bompetitiveness and bost. *The Conference Board of Canada*. Accessed at conferenceboard.ca on 10 October 2012.

9. Pandey, N., & Martocchio, J.J. (2008) Health care and retirement costs in North America spiralling uncontrollability: What are employers to do? *The International Journal of Human Resource Management*, 19: 1515–1533.

10. Yermo, J., & Severinson, C. (2010) *The impact of the financial crisis on defined benefit plans and the need for counter-cyclical funding regulations*. Paris: OECD Working papers on Finance, Insurance & Private Pensions No. 3.

11. Stalebrink, O.J. (2014) Public pension funds and assumed rates of return: An empirical examination of public sector defined benefits plans. *American Review of Public Administration*, 44: 92–111.

12. Ponds, E., Severinson, C., & Yermo, J. (2011) *Funding in public sector pension plans – International evidence*. Paris: OECD Working papers on Finance, Insurance & Private Pensions No. 8.

13. McNish, J. (2009) Retirement lost. October 16. Accessed from GlobeandMail.com.

14. Ponds, E., Severinson, C., & Yermo, J. (2012) Implicit debt in public sector pension plans: An international comparison. *International Social Security Review*, 65: 75–101; Hammouya, M. (1999) *Statistics on public employment: Methodology, structures, and trends*. Geneva: International Labour Office.

15. The Public Employees Pension Plan (PEPP). Accessed as the Government of Saskatchewan website.

16. Ponds, E., Severinson, C., & Yermo, J. (2012) op. cit.

17. Natail, D., & Stamati, F. (2014) Reassessing South European pensions after the crisis: Evidence from two decades of reforms. *South European Society and Politics*, 19: 309–330.

18. Ponds, E., Severinson, C., & Yermo, J. (2012) op. cit.

19. Brown, R.L., & McInnes, C. (2014) *Shifting public sector DB plans to DC: The experience so far and implications for Canada*. Canadian Public Pension Leadership Council.

20. Pai, Y. (2006) Comparing individual retirement accounts in Asia: Singapore, Thailand, Hong Kong, and PRC. Social Protection: *The World Bank. Discussion Paper No. 0609*.

21. Torjman, S. (2007) *Repairing Canada's social safety net*. Ottawa: Caledon Institute of Social Policy, May.

22. Chilton, D. (1989) *The wealthy barber*. Toronto: Stoddart; see also: Chilton, D. (2011) *The wealthy barber returns*. Toronto: Stoddart.

23. Buffet, M., & Clark, D. (2008) *Warren Buffett and the interpretation of financial statements*. New York: Scribner.

24. Richard, D. (2010) Appreciate your house, but don't expect it to appreciate a lot. Globe Investor, Real Estate. *Globe and Mail*, April 26, B8. Based on data from: Eichholtz, P.M.A. (1997) A long run house price index: The Herengracht Index, 1628–1973. *Real Estates Economics*, 25: 175–192.

25. Park, J. (2011) Retirement, health and employment among those 55 plus: Perspective on Labour and Income. *Statistics Canada*. Accessed from Statistics Canada website.

26. OECD health statistics (2014) OECD.

27. OECD (2011) Help Wanted? Providing and paying for long term care. *OECD*, 61–84.

28. OECD (2013) Health at a glance 2013. *OECD*. See also: OECD health data at www.oecd.org/health/healthdata.

29. Pandey, N., & Martocchio, J.J. (2008) Health care and retirement costs in North America spiraling uncontrollably: What are employers to do? *The International Journal of Human Resource Management*, 19: 1515–1533.

30. Ibid.

31. Watson Wyatt, *Staying@work: Effective Presence at work*, p. 10.

32. Stewart, N. (2010). *Beyond benefits: Creating a culture of health and wellness in Canadian organizations*. Ottawa: Conference Board of Canada. Accessed from conferenceboard.ca website.

33. Ibid.

34. *Alberta Health Plan*. Accessed from healthservice.ca website.

35. Glass, J., & Estes, S.B. (1997) The family responsive workplace. *Annual Review of Sociology*, 23: 382, 289–313.

36. Kelly, E.L., Kossek, E.E., Hammer, L.B., Durham, M., Bray, J., Chermack, K., Murphy, L.A., et al. (2008) Getting there from here: Research on the effects of work-family initiatives on work-family conflict and business outcomes. *The Academy of Management Annals*, 2: 305–349.

37. OECD better life index. OECD website. www.oecd.org.
38. Lambert, S.J. (2000) Added benefits: The link between work-life benefits and organizational citizenship behavior. *Academy of Management Journal*, 43: 801–815.
39. Wood, S.J., & de Menezes, L.M. (2010) Family-friendly management, organizational performance and social legitimacy. *The International Journal of Human Resource Management*, 21: 1575–1597; Kelly, E.L., et al. (2008) op. cit.
40. Herzberg, F., Mausner, B., & Snyderman, B.B. (1959) *The motivation to work*. New York: Wiley; Herzberg, F. (1968) One more time: How do you motivate employees? *Harvard Business Review*, 90: 53–62.
41. Kelly, E.L., et al. (2008) op. cit.
42. Ibid.
43. Thompson, C.A., Beauvais, L.M., & Lyness, K.S. (1999) When work–family benefits are not enough: The influence of work-family culture on benefit utilization, organizational attachment, and work-family conflict. *Journal of Vocational Behavior*, 54: 392–415; Thompson, C.A., & Prottas, D.J. (2006) Relationships among organizational family support, job autonomy, perceived control, and employee well-being. *Journal of Occupational Health Psychology*, 10: 100–118.
44. Kelly, E.L., et al. (2008) op. cit.
45. Thomas, L.T., & Ganster, D.C. (1995) Impact of family-supportive work variables on work–family conflict and strain: A control perspective. *Journal of Applied Psychology*, 80: 6–15.
46. Ibid.
47. Kelly, E.L., et al. (2008) op. cit.
48. This case was written by Soo Myong and J. Barton Cunningham.

Chapter 16

1. Moynihan, D.P., & Sanjay, J.P. (2010) The big question for performance management: Why do managers use performance information?' *Journal of Public Administration Research and Theory*, 20: 849–866.
2. Fischer, R., Smith, P.B., Richey, B., Ferreira, M.C., Assmar, E.M.L., Maes, J., & Stumpf, S. (2007) How do organizations allocate rewards? *Journal of Cross-Cultural Psychology*, 38: 3–18.
3. Usugami, J., & Park, K.Y. (2006) Similarities and differences in employee motivation viewed by Korean and Japanese executives: Empirical study of employee motivation management of Japanese-affiliated companies in Korea. *International Journal of Human Resource Management*, 17: 280–294.
4. Atkinson, M.M., Fulton, M., & Kim, B. (2014) Why do governments use pay for performance? Contrasting theories and interview evidence. *Canadian Public Administration*, 57: 444, 436–458.
5. OECD (2005) *Performance-related pay policies for government employees*. Paris; OECD (2008) *The state of the public service*. Paris.
6. Muson, H. (2007) Designing the high-performance compensation plan that works. *The Conference Report Executive Action Series*, No. 220: 2.
7. Gerhart, B., Rynes, S., & Fulmer, I.S. (2009) Pay and performance: Individuals, groups, and executives. *Academy of Management Annals*, 3: 251–315; Guzzo, R.A., Jette, R.D., & Katzell, R.A. (1985) The effects of psychologically based intervention programs on worker productivity: A meta-analysis. *Personnel Psychology*, 38: 275–291; Pohler, D., & Schmidt, J.A. (2015) Does pay-for-performance strain the employment: The effect of manager bonus eligibility on non-management employee turnover. *Personnel Psychology*, Wiley online library. 10.1111/peps.12106.
8. Pfeffer, J. (1998) *The human equation: Building profits by putting people first*. Boston, MA: Harvard Business School Press.

9. Beer, M., & Cannon, M.D. (2004) Promise and peril in implementing pay-for-performance. *Human Resource Management*, 43: 3–48.
10. Pohler, D., & Schmidt, J.A. (2015) op. cit.
11. OECD (2005) op. cit.; OECD (2008) op. cit.
12. OECD (2005) op. cit.; OECD (2008) op. cit.
13. Downs, G.W., & Patrick, D.L. (1986) *The Search for Government Efficiency*. New York: Random House; Goodsell, C.T. (2004) *The Case for Bureaucracy: A Public Administration Polemic*. 4th ed. Washington, DC: CQ Press.
14. Nielen, P.A. (2013) Performance management, managerial authority, and public service performance. *Journal of Public Administration Research and Theory*, 24: 431–458.
15. Hallamore, C. (2005) *Merit pay in unionized environments*. Ottawa: Conference Board of Canada.
16. OECD (2005) op. cit.; OECD (2008) op. cit.
17. Deming, W.E. (1986) *Out of crisis*. Cambridge, MA: Productivity Press.
18. Campbell, D.J., Campbell, K.M., & Chia, H. (1998) Merit pay, performance appraisal, and individual motivation: An analysis and alternative. *Human Resource Management*, 37: 131–146.
19. Ibid.
20. Scott, K.L, Shaw, J.D., & Duffy, M.K. (2008) Merit pay raises and organizational-based self-esteem. *Journal of Organizational Behavior*, 29: 967–980.
21. Marsden, D., & Richardson, R. (1994) Performing for pay? The effects of 'merit pay' on motivation in a public service. *British Journal of Industrial Relations*, 32: 243–261.
22. Hallamore, C. (2005) op. cit.
23. Taylor, J., & Beh, L. (2013) The impact of pay-for-performance schemes on the performance of Australian and Malaysian government employees. *Public Management Review*, 15: 1090–1115; Ost, E.J. (1990) Team-based pay: New wave strategic initiatives. *Sloan Management Review*, 31: 19–29.
24. Henderson, R.I. (1979) *Compensation management*. Reston, VA: Reston Publishing, pp. 360–362.
25. Markham, S.E., Scott, K.D., Cox, Jr. W.G. (1992) The evolutionary development of a Scanlon Plan. *Compensation and Benefits Review*, 24: 50–56.
26. Lavy, V. (2007) Using performance-based pay to improve the quality of teachers. *Future of Children*, 17: 87–10; Swiss, J.E. (2005) A framework for assessing incentives in results-based management. *Public Administration Review*, 65: 592–602.
27. Soloman, E.E. (1986) Private and public sector managers: An empirical investigation of job characteristics and organizational climate. *Journal of Applied Psychology*, 7: 247–325.
28. Beer, M., & Cannon, M.D. (2004) op. cit.
29. Eisenhardt, K.M. (1989) Agency Theory: An Assessment and Review. *Academy of Management Review*, 14: 57–74; Weibel, A., Rost, K., & Osterloh, M. (2010) Pay for Performance in the Public Sector – Benefits and (Hidden) Costs. *Journal of Public Administration Research and Theory*, 2: 387–412.
30. Vroom, V. H. (1964) *Work and motivation*. New York: Wiley.
31. Adams, J.S. (1963) Toward an understanding of inequity. *Journal of Abnormal and Social Psychology*, 67: 422–436; Adams, J.S. (1965) Inequity in social exchange. In *Advances in experimental social psychology*, L. Berkowitz (ed.), vol. 2, pp. 267–299. New York: Academic Press; Huseman, R.C., Hatfield, J.D., & Miles, E.W. (1987) A new perspective on equity theory: The equity sensitivity construct. *Academy of Management Review*, 12: 222–234.

32. Park, S., & Berry, F. (2014) Successful diffusion of a failed policy: The case of pay-for-performance in the US federal government. *Public Management Review*, 16: 763–781; Kellough, J.E., & Nigro, L.G. (2002) Pay for performance in Georgia state government: Employee perspectives on Georgia gain after 5 years. *Review of Public Personnel Administration*, 22: 146–166.

33. Taylor, J., & Beh, L. (2013) op. cit.

34. Weibel, A., Rost, K., & Osteroh, M. (2010) op. cit.

35. Ibid.

36. Perry, J.L., & Wise, L.R. (1990) The motivational bases of public service. *Public Administration Review*, 50: 368, 367–373.

37. Brewer, G.A., & Selden, S.C. (1998) Whistle blowers in the federal civil service: New evidence of the public service ethic. *Journal of Public Administration Research and Theory*, 8: 417, 413–439.

38. Vandenabeele, W. (2007) Toward a public administration theory of public service motivation: An institutional approach. *Public Management Review*, 9: 547, 545–556.

39. Taylor, J., & Beh, L. (2013) op. cit.

40. Perry, J.L., Engbers, T.A., & Jun, S.Y. (2009) Back to the future? Performance-related pay, empirical research, and the perils of persistence. *Public Administration Review*, 46: 39–51; Perry, J.L., & Petrakis, B.A. (1988) Can pay for performance succeed in government? *Public Personnel Management*, 17: 359–367.

41. Weibel, A., Rost, K., & Osteroh, M. (2009) op. cit.

42. Deci, E. (1975) *Intrinsic motivation*. New York: Plenum; Stajkovic, A.D., & Luthan, F. (2001) Differential effects of incentive motivators on worker performance. *Academy of Management Journal*, 44: 580–590.

43. Ibid.

44. Burke, R.J., Weitzel, & Weir, T. (1978) Characteristics of effective employee performance review and development interviews: Replication and extension. *Personnel Psychology*, 31: 903–919. This research is partially based on groundbreaking research by: Maier, N.R. (1976) *The appraisal interview: Three basic approaches*. La Jolla, CA: University Associates; originally published as: Maier, N.R.F (1958) *The appraisal interview: Three basic approaches*. New York: John Wiley.

45. Stajkovic, A.D., & Luthan, F. (2001) op. cit.

46. Leventhal, G.S. (1980) What should be done with equity theory? New approaches to the fairness in social relationships. In *Social exchange theory*, K. Gergen, M. Greenberg and R. Willis (eds.), pp. 27–55. New York: Plenum; Taylor, J., & Beh, L. (2013) op. cit.

47. Cohen-Charash, Y., & Spector, P. E. (2001) The role of justice in organizations: A meta-analysis. *Organizational Behavior and Human Decision Processes*, 86: 78–321.

48. Taylor, J., & Beh, L. (2013) op. cit.

49. Spreitzer, G.M. (1995) Psychological empowerment in the workplace: Dimensions, measurement, validation. *Academy of Management Journal*, 38; 1442–1465; Sigler, T.H., & Pearson, C.M. (2000) Creating an empowering culture: Examining the relationship between organizational culture and perceptions of empowerment. *Journal of Quality Management*, 5: 27–52.

50. Hackman, J.R., & Oldham, G.R. (1980) *Work redesign*. Menlo Park, CA: Addison Wesley.

51. Locke, E.A., & Latham, G.P. (2002) Building a practically useful theory of goal setting and task motivation: A 35-year odyssey. *American Psychologist*, 57: 705–717.

52. Frey, B., Homberg, F., & Osterloh, M. (2013) Organizational control systems and pay-for-performance in the public service. *Organizational Studies*, 34: 949–972.

53. Wayne, S.J., Shore, L.M., Bommer, W.H., & Tetrick, L.E. (2002) The role of fair treatment and rewards in perceptions of organizational support and leader-member exchange. *Journal of Applied Psychology*, 87: 590–598.

54. Nelson, B. (2004) Formal recognition programs do not work. *Industrial and Commercial Training*, 36: 243–246.

55. Ibid.

56. Herzberg, F. (1976) *The managerial choice: To be efficient and to be human.* Homewood, IL: Dow Jones-Irwin. pp. 325–326.

57. Nelson, R.B. (2001) Factors that encourage or inhibit the use of non-monetary recognition by U.S. managers. *Claremont Graduate Faculty of Executive Management*, Doctoral dissertation.

58. Atkinson, M.M., Fulton, M., & Kim, B. (2014) Why do governments use pay for performance? Contrasting theories and interview evidence. *Canadian Public Administration*, 57: 444, 436–458; Perry, J.L., Engbers, T.A., & Jun, S.Y. (2009) Back to the future? Performance related pay, empirical research, and the perils of persistence. *Public Administration Review*, 69: 39–51.

Glossary

1. Holtz, L. 2006 Entrepreneur reveals secrets of success. Insidemyprofile, Accessed at www.myprofile.com.au

2. Dweck, C. S. (1986) Motivational processes affecting learning. *American Psychologist*, 41: 1040–1048; Payne, S. C., Youngcourt, S. S., & Beaubien, J. M. (2007) A meta-analytic examination of the goal orientation nomological net. *Journal of Applied Psychology*, 92: 128–150.

3. Graen, G.B., & Uhl-Bien, M. (1995) Relationship-based approach to leadership: Development of Member Exchange (LMX) theory of leadership over 25 years: Applying a multi-level multi-domain perspective. *Leadership Quarterly*, 6: 72, 219–247.

4. Graen, G.B., & Uhl-Bien, M. (1995) Relationship-based approach to leadership: Development of Member Exchange (LMX) theory of leadership over 25 years: Applying a multi-level multi-domain perspective. *Leadership Quarterly*, 6: 219–247, p. 237.

5. Rokeach, M. (1973) *The nature of human values.* New York: Free Press.

6. Graen, G.B., & Uhl-Bien, M. (1995) Relationship-based approach to leadership: Development of Member Exchange (LMX) theory of leadership over 25 years: Applying a multi-level multi-domain perspective. *Leadership Quarterly*, 6: 219–247, p. 237.

7. McBey, K.J. (2000) *Strategic Human Resource Planning.* Scarborough, Ontario: Thomson Nelson Learning; Cotten, A. (2007) *Seven Steps of Effective Workforce Planning.* Washington: IBM Center for the Business of Government, p. 4.

Glossary

A

ABILITIES The sum of one's expertise (knowledge and skills). A person's abilities are illustrated by their mastery or level of performance.

ABSENTEEISM The failure of an employee to report to work as scheduled for various reasons. Absenteeism can be of various types: casual absences, short-term disability and long-term disability. In some plans, *casual absences* usually involve incidental or non-consecutive absences of up to nine days, whereas *short-term disability* is a prolonged absence of up to six months, usually with full pay. If a disability keeps a person away from work for more than six months, employees will receive a continuing source of income as defined in the *long-term disability* plan.

ACCIDENTS ATTRIBUTION ERRORS Two types of errors occur in understanding the causes of accidents: the *fundamental attribution error* describes the tendency of an investigator to blame, overestimate or use as a scapegoat the individuals who are closest to the accident and to underestimate the influence of the context or the behaviour of others. At the worker level, the *defensive attribution error* is the tendency to empathize with the victim and to attribute the accidents to external factors.

ACTION LEARNING In action learning, projects become the central learning experience, where participants, working in groups, are charged with developing a solution for an important organizational task. After initial training, the participants manage the project by carrying out a diagnosis and developing a solution that they present to management.

AFFECTIVE COMMITMENT An emotional attachment (affective energy) to work based on values; more committed than being involved through consultation and input.

AFFIRMATIVE ACTION Programmes and initiatives directed at overcoming past and present discriminatory practices, policies or other barriers to equality in employment in the United States and Australia. Other countries use terms such as *employment equity* and *diversity management* for similar programmes.

ARBITRATION An arbitration process comes into effect when informal bargaining to settle the grievance has not been effective, and the steps to the grievance process have been systematically followed without satisfaction. *Interest arbitration* is a slightly different process to resolve potential disputes as an alternative to taking strike action. This comes into effect when parties agree on an independent arbitrator to resolve a dispute by considering the positions of both parties.

ASSESSMENT CENTRE PROCESS A process that uses a variety of techniques – job-related simulations, interviews, psychological tests, group exercises, and in-basket problems – to assess a candidate's potential for promotion or selection on a wider range of competencies.

ATTRITION The normal separation of people leaving through resignation, retirement and mortality.

B

BABY BOOMERS A group of people born in the post–World War II baby boom, between 1946 and 1964. In Europe and North America, they are associated with privilege, as many grew up during a time when there were generous government subsidies for education and housing.

BALANCED SCORECARD (BSC) Provides a framework for viewing the strategic themes, objectives and initiatives (use of resources) within different perspectives – customer, internal process, financial, and learning and growth – that need to be addressed in implementation. The BSC is more than a measurement system; it is a management system to help facilitate the implementation of strategic objectives. An assumption is that organizations that are able to align objectives within these various perspectives are more effective in implementing their strategies. In the public sector, the BSC is focused less on competition and profit than on implementing the mission and service relationship.

BEHAVIOURAL ANCHORED RATING SCALES (BARS) Graphic rating scales that use critical incidents to define behavioural terms for different levels of performance.

BEHAVIOURAL DESCRIPTION The goal of behaviour description questions in a selection interview is to seek examples (both positive and not so positive) of what actually happened in a person's experience, based on the assumption that the best prediction of future behaviour is past behaviour which illustrates similar circumstances.

BEHAVIOURAL EVENT INTERVIEW (BEI) A focused, clinical-type, recorded interview that uses the critical incident technique to evoke examples.

BENCHMARK JOBS In developing a compensation plan, benchmark jobs are key jobs which are representative of those in the organization. These key jobs can be compared to other jobs in other organizations in helping managers establish external equity. They are also used to design a wage profile or hierarchy to assess the internal equity of what one key job is paid in relationship to others.

BENEFITS Different types of remuneration to employees, including retirement, health care, social and work-family benefits. *Retirement benefits* involve financial support for employees when they are no longer earning income from employment. There include basic *health care benefits* which protect employees and their families when they are ill or injured, as well as provide preventative health, dental and optical health. There are also *social benefits* such as unemployment insurance and social assistance provided by federal, provincial, state and territorial laws. *Work-family benefits* provide flexibility in balancing work and non-work and in supporting employees in their personal development.

'BIG FIVE' PERSONALITY FACTORS A renewed interest exists in the potential of personality testing because of meta-analysis research which has helped develop a synthesis around five key personality factors: extroversion, emotional stability, agreeableness, conscientiousness and openness. Research has illustrated how some of these factors are correlated with outcome measures like performance, motivation and safety.

BOUNDARY-LESS A characteristic of many careers where an employee has no defined career path within an organization.

BOUNDARY-LESS CAREER A career that has no set career path and moves across the boundaries of different employers, indicating that it is no longer based on lifetime employment with an organization, but is a 'boundary-less' career that includes both subjective and objective reference points.

BROAD BANDING A job grading process where salary grades are consolidated into fewer, but broader, pay ranges. This can allow for more latitude for pay increases and career growth.

BULLYING As a form of aggression and/or violence, it is illustrated when one employee creates a hostile work environment for another, through verbal and non-verbal behaviours.

BURNOUT A stage of exhaustion or overload where continuing exposure to the stressors may eventually overtax various organs in the body. Long-term damage might occur because the glands (especially the adrenal gland) and the immune system are exhausted. This is when the person feels burned out, exhausted or lacks enthusiasm to work and even to get up in the morning. It is possible that this is when psychosomatic diseases emerge, such as emotional exhaustion, elevated blood pressure, weight loss or gain and insomnia.

C

CAREER Positions occupied by a person during a lifetime, also known as one's objective career.

CAREER-BASED SYSTEMS Systems which encourage competitive recruitment and selection in attracting public servants and then developing and grooming them for higher level positions in a career path.

CAREER DEVELOPMENT Describes the way people manage and structure their career paths within and outside organizations, and 'who develops whom, when and how'.

CAREER PATH A logical, planned progression of development that is usually associated with organizationally directed career development.

CAREER-RELATED CONTINUOUS LEARNING (CRCL) Career development which is self-initiated and where an individual takes responsibility for applying knowledge from formal and informal learning activities.

CAREER SATISFACTION A summary of one's perceptions of success in career, career progress in meeting career goals and success in meeting goals for income, advancement and development of new skills.

CAREER SUCCESS A measure of career satisfaction and development over a period of time.

CASCADING A review of strategic or work plans in order to translate or diffuse them to lower levels.

CENTRALIZATION OF AUTHORITY Exists when all decisions in an organization come from a centralized source.

CHARACTERISTICS Usually referred to as personal characteristics or 'other' characteristics such as attitude, motivation, values, and beliefs. They are harder to measure but have a high impact on performance and positive working relationships.

COGNITIVE ABILITY A description of a person's intelligence or aptitude.

COGNITIVE ABILITY TESTING Tests that measure a range of general mental abilities (GMAs) from verbal and quantitative skills to aptitude, cognitive ability and cognitive style.

COGNITIVE STYLE Generally described as the way people think, gather, remember and use information in problem solving.

COLLECTIVE BARGAINING The process of negotiating a formal collective agreement or contract on issues such as wages and benefits, hours of work, working conditions, health and safety, overtime, grievance mechanisms and the right to participate in workplace decisions.

COLLECTIVE BARGAINING IMPASSE A deadlock in a negotiation between union and management, where parties are staled in their ability to move forward in reaching any further agreements.

COLLECTIVE BARGAINING STANCES Different bargaining activities – distributive bargaining, integrative, attitudinal structuring and intra-organizational bargaining – that occur at different times during the course of negotiating a collective bargaining contract. *Distributive bargaining* is generally thought to be positional and competitive in bargaining how to divide up the 'fixed pie'. *Integrative bargaining* activities are attempts to work together on common problems as equal partners. *Attitudinal structuring* describes activities involved in shaping relationships between the parties by increasing friendship and reducing hostility. *Intra-organizational bargaining* illustrates activities that try to shape and influence constituents – such as the public – that their position is more central.

COLLECTIVE BARGAINING UNIT A group of employees identified as eligible to vote in a certified bargaining unit.

COMMUNITY OF PRACTICE A group of people who are bound by a shared practice and who have a context for learning from each other.

COMPARABLE WORTH Determination of a job's worth by validly and accurately making comparisons between dissimilar jobs.

COMPENSABLE FACTORS Common job dimensions, involving skill, effort, responsibility and working conditions, that the organization identifies as important to pay.

COMPENSATION Payment involving four components: fixed salaries, pensions, benefits and incentives.

COMPETENCY An underlying characteristic of an individual which is causally related to effective or superior performance in a job and which illustrates the human resource talents needed to implement strategic objectives. *Core or distinctive* competencies are those which are important for an organization's success or uniqueness. *Threshold or foundation* competencies are more general as a baseline. A competency is defined by knowledge, skills, abilities and other characteristics. *Knowledge* is the 'know-how' or ability to do something as defined through experience, a degree or a certification. A *skill* is the 'can do' and is the expertise which the person demonstrates in practice. *Abilities* represent the sum of one's expertise (knowledge and skills) and are illustrated by their mastery or talent which allows people to perform at a higher level. The *'other'* characteristics in defining a competency describe a range of characteristics such as motivation, attitude and ability to change. A large part of performance is related to a person's willingness and motivation to do something. For some managers, 'ability is what you're capable of doing, whereas motivation determines what you do, and attitudes determine how well you do it'.[1]

COMPETENCY-BASED MANAGEMENT (CBM) Involves identifying a profile of competencies distinguishing high and average performers in various areas of organizational activity and using it as a framework for planning, work design, recruitment, selection, training and career development, and compensation.

COMPETENCY FRAMEWORK A framework of competencies and principles for hiring, paying, rewarding and promoting people, and guiding their performance and learning in career development.

CONGRUENCE THEORY Suggests that when people choose an occupation that is consistent with their vocational preferences, they are more likely to be satisfied and successful in that occupation.

CRITERION TESTING Involves understanding the job skills that predict proficiency on the job, observing actual performance and comparing superior performers with less successful performers.

CRITICAL INCIDENTS Positive and not-so-positive examples of employee behaviours which are often linked to performance or motivation.

CRITICAL INCIDENT TECHNIQUE (CIT) The critical incident interviewing process can be used as a job analysis method for understanding a job's critical requirements and the competencies that employees need to be effective and efficient in meeting strategic objectives. The interviewer usually seeks critical incident examples that exemplify effective and ineffective behaviours or desirable and undesirable behaviours. This technique has been used in a variety of settings to uncover the types of events that new employees see as critical in communicating an organization's culture, understanding motivational characteristics, discovering the training needs for youth and identifying critical leadership competencies of manufacturing supervisors.

CRITICAL SUCCESS FACTORS Intangibles which contribute, in combination, to the success of public or private organizations. Success factors important to public organizations include culture, reputation, geographical location and environmental stability, as well as labour relations, human capital, internal auditing, and managerial capabilities.

CULPABLE ACTIONS Errant actions where the employee knows or can be expected to know what is required, is capable of carrying out what is required but chooses to perform in a manner which is inconsistent with this.

CULTURE A reflection of the preferences and shared motives, values and beliefs, in addition to shared identities and interpretation learned over the history of relating to others. Culture is present at different levels: *visible artefacts* which can be easily discerned, *espoused beliefs and values* which are conscious strategies and goals, and *basic assumptions* that people share (these are the core unconscious assumptions which are difficult to discern and which are often taken for granted as beliefs and values. A *societal culture* is a collective mental programming describing what people have in common. Beyond being diverse and multigenerational, the *workforce culture* comprises a range of values, attitudes, traits and behaviours.

CUSTOMER In public sector organizations, the customer or client relationship is not an economic exchange where a person buys a product for a price, but something that is enjoyed collectively, and the decisions about preferences are made in the democratic political process. Public organizations have different relationships with a customer such as being a professional (e.g. drug treatment), guardian (e.g. corrections officer), facilitator/citizen (e.g. brokering information) and regulator (e.g. environment protection). *External customers* are those constituents to whom the organization seeks to respond, whereas *internal clients or customers* are other managers. For example, HR's job is to align the HR system to be responsive to the line managers who are internal customers.

CUSTOMER-CENTRED JOB DESIGNS Focus on customer needs in designing and implementing services to achieve the organization's strategic objectives.

CUSTOMER SERVICE CLIMATE Attitudes within an organization for satisfying customers and developing customer loyalty to products and services.

D

DECERTIFICATION Revoking a union's status to bargain exclusively for workers.

DEFINED BENEFIT PLANS Pension benefits where an employer promises to pay a retiree a stated pension, often defined as a percentage of preretirement earnings.

DEFINED CONTRIBUTION PLANS A type of pension plan that establishes a rate of contribution to a pension fund and where future benefits depend on how fast the fund grows.

DELPHI METHOD A series of questionnaires (three or more) to a panel of experts who are asked for anonymous comments or forecasts of future events. The group interaction in the Delphi is anonymous, as one of the goals of the approach is to guard against group biases or strong personalities when developing a consensus.

DEMAND/CONTROL MODEL This model of stress suggests that stress results from the demands in the job which creates tension which results from the perceptions of inabilities to control the demands.

DISABILITY A physical or mental impairment that limits one or more life activities.

DISCIPLINARY DISCHARGE A termination resulting from a culpable performance problem or from a gross breach of conduct such as fighting, theft, fraud, or wilful destruction of property.

DISCRIMINATION Giving of unfair advantage (or disadvantage) to members of a specific group.

DISSATISFIERS (HYGIENE FACTORS) Job characteristics (such as improving the administration, working conditions and pay) which are said to focus on lower order human needs and are deemed important to reducing job dissatisfaction. They may not be highly correlated with improving internal motivation.

DISTRIBUTIVE BARGAINING A bargaining posture that assumes goals of parties are irreconcilable and what one party loses, the other wins.

DIVERSITY When addressing workplace diversity, emphasis is on responding to groups of people that, for historical, cultural and systemic reasons, have faced barriers that have inhibited their full participation in the workforce. A broader perspective on managing diversity involves creating a positive environment where all people feel 'included' and using recruitment, selection and performance management in attracting and retaining diverse individuals into a culture that values their individuality.

DIVERSITY-BASED RECRUITMENT Recruitment strategies that systematic favour designated groups.

DIVISION OF LABOUR The separation of a work process into a number of tasks, where each task is performed by different groups or people.

DUE PROCESS Using fair proceedings to determine employee wrongdoings so that employee rights are maintained. Requiring that a treatment of an individual is not unfair, arbitrary, or unreasonable.

E

EFFORT/REWARD MODEL This model suggests that stress is related to the imbalance in the degree of effort put into the job and level of reward resulting from that effort. This is based on the assumption that stressors are less harmful if there are rewards or pleasures associated with them.

EMPLOYEE ASSISTANCE PROGRAMMES (EAP) These programmes are the most common health and wellness services for employees and their family members to help with emotional, family, stress and substance abuse problems that might ultimately impact work performance and health.

EMPLOYEE-CENTRED JOB DESIGNS Designs which use principles that encourage worker responsibility, learning, and empowerment.

EMPLOYEE NEEDS ANALYSIS (ENA) Focuses on the competency gaps (in separating learning from non-learning needs) and determines who needs to be trained and the competencies that should be focused on in the training. This identifies performance objectives and benchmarks and the competencies needed.

EMPLOYER OF CHOICE A designation in Canada and Australia of employers that are attractive places to work because they are supportive, inclusive environments. These designations include employers who are inclusive of *designated groups of workers* (e.g. females, aboriginal, disadvantaged people) or of *older or younger workers*, or who illustrate *family-friendly practices*. Such employment practices are correlated with improvement on the organization's bottom line in that they illustrate positive retention, attendance, safety, performance and work quality.

EMPLOYMENT EQUITY Programmes in some countries which encourage special measures and accommodation of differences.

ENGAGEMENT The identification of a person's 'self' to one's work roles. In engagement, a person employs and expresses oneself physically, cognitively, and emotionally in work in being 'fully present'. In disengagement, a person is withdrawn and their 'self' finds no connection. Engagement captures how employees experience their work in being 'fully there'. This is more than *affective commitment* or the emotional attachment based on values (affective energy). It is also more than *job involvement* which implies consultation and input (cognitive energy).

EQUITY The fairness of a pay system in terms of the relative worth of the jobs to the organization and competitive rates outside the organization.

ETHICAL BEHAVIOUR Calls for more ethical behaviour are demonstrated in expectations for public organizations to be socially responsible and to balance the dual interest of economic development and quality of life of the workforce, families and the community at large.

EVALUATION Most often viewed as a management directed process for 'evaluating' performance whereas a performance 'review' is seen as a joint management-employee process.

EXPECTANCY In expectancy theory, it is defined by the probability that a person's effort will lead performance.

EXPECTANCY THEORY A theory of motivation which suggests that people are generally motivated to pursue rewards they find attractive and are discouraged from rewards they find unattractive. A person's motivation depends on expectancy, instrumentality or perceived connection between performance and rewards, and valence (the preference or values of the reward to the person).

EXPEDITED ARBITRATION Fixed fee arbitrations with strict time frames and limitations on the number of documents, length of briefs, and time for the hearing. In this process, the appointed arbitrator or grievance commissioner proceeds more informally.

EXPERIENTIAL LEARNING Learning through immersing learners in an experience and encouraging them to reflect on it to develop new skills, attitudes and ways of thinking.

EXTERNAL CUSTOMERS OR CLIENTS Those external constituents who departments provide services for as, for example, a fire department provides services for different groups in the community.

EXTERNAL EQUITY Fairness of wages paid in comparison with what other organizations are paying.

EXTERNAL RECRUITING Looking outside the organization in identifying and recruiting qualified people.

EXTERNAL SUPPLY OF CANDIDATES The shortage or abundance of people with different skills as a reflected in the labour market.

F

FACT FINDER A neutral third-party mechanism commonly used in the public sector to resolve an impasse. In this process, each party submits whatever information it thinks is relevant to the resolution of the dispute.

FACTOR COMPARISON A job evaluation plan which compares or ranks jobs relative to each other, on the basis of a set of compensable factors like job knowledge, mental effort, physical effort, working conditions, supervision and responsibility. After ranking the job on each factor, money values are assigned to each level on each factor.

FACTORS Yardsticks or dimensions for measuring jobs, these are the heart of the point method of job evaluation.

FAIRNESS A driving criterion for judging procedural justice in public organizations; its importance is underlined in many decisions such as those relating to merit pay, promotion and performance appraisal: 'Was the decision fair?'

FALSE-NEGATIVE ERROR Occurs when an employer rejects a person who could have been a talented staff member.

FALSE-POSITIVE ERROR Occurs when an employer hires a person who does not perform as expected or who does not fit with the public sector culture.

FINANCIAL MEASURES A set of measure within the financial perspective of the SHRM BSC which focus *on* the costs of providing services and adding value.

FITNESS WITHIN AN ORGANIZATION People tend to stay with organizations where their values, motives and needs 'fit' best. Other ideas of fitness include person–organizational (P–O) or the degree to which individuals (their values, skills and needs) match those of the workplace. Person–job (P–J) fit is the match between a person's growth needs (e.g. need for challenge, job security) and the job's ability to meet these needs, and person–group (P–G) fit is the match between individuals and work groups (i.e. co-workers, team and supervisors).

FORMATIVE ASSESSMENTS The goal of formative assessments is encourage feedback from peer groups, clients or customers rather than summative evaluation.

401(K) PLAN A defined-contribution plan in the United States in which the employee deducts a certain amount of income from taxes and places this in a personal retirement account. Sometimes, employers match the contribution and the combined sums grow tax-free until they are withdrawn at retirement.

FUTURE SHOCK The suggestion that the changes which are occurring in many parts of society will be rapid and transformational, like the cultural shift of moving rapidly from communal to industrial or virtual societies. *Future shock* is like culture shock that leaves people disconnected because they are disoriented from what they know and value, because there is too much change in too short a period of time.

G

GAIN SHARING PLANS A form of organizational PFP plan which rewards employees for reducing costs and improving performance.

GENERAL (GENERIC) A job description which includes a larger range of duties and responsibilities.

GENERAL ADAPTATION SYNDROME A definition of stress as essentially the body's nonspecific response to the demands placed upon it.

GENERAL MENTAL ABILITIES (GMAs) Quantitative and qualitative measures of cognitive ability and intelligence.

GENERATION X AND Y Generation X follows the Baby Boomers and consists of people born between the mid 1960s and early 1980s. These people are shaped by events that occurred during this period, such as the Vietnam War, the end of the Cold War and the Thatcher-era government in the United Kingdom. Generation Y people were born between the 1980s and the year 2000, and are sometimes referred to as Gen Y, the Millennial Generation, or simply Millennials. Gen Y people grew up with technology and are said to be connected and tech savvy.

GLASS CEILING The barrier women face in breaking into senior management positions, so called because these jobs are visible, but there is an barrier to reaching them.

GOAL ORIENTATION 'Dispositional or situational preferences in achievement situations.'[2]

GOALS Broad, long term aims which provide the basis for an organization's vision and strategic themes. Within the SHRM BSC, strategic themes are the main, high-level conceptual streams that are the basis for the organization's strategic framework.

GOAL THEORY This theory posits that if employees can see how their work contributes to achieving organizational goals, they are more likely to perceive that their work is meaningful and adjust their performance accordingly.

GOLEM EFFECT The dark side of the Pygmalion effect, where low or negative expectations lower subordinates' performance. In management, the Golem effect describes the destructive and performance-restricting effects of supervisors with low expectations of a person's performance. If we have low expectations, we are likely to get what we expect.

GREEN-CIRCLED POSITIONS Those paid below the policy line. In these cases, it might be appropriate to increase the annual adjustments until they fall within guidelines.

GRIEVANCE A written complaint against action or inactions relating to terms and conditions of employment as part of the collective bargaining agreement. *Individual grievances* concern the complaint of one individual, whereas *group grievances* are concerns of the work team or group. A *policy grievance* can be filed against management because of a misapplication or misinterpretation of the collective agreement on a range of issues like scheduling or overtime payments.

GROUP CONSENSUS A method of decision making that seeks to get agreement among participants by using the diversity of perspectives in coming up with insightful ideas or solutions.

GROUP GRIEVANCES A complaint by two or more employees relating to terms and conditions of employment as part of the collective bargaining agreement.

H

HEALTH CARE BENEFITS Benefits which protect employees and their families when they are ill or injured, as well as provide preventative health, dental and optical health.

HIERARCHICAL ORGANIZATION Pyramid-like organization structure where one person is in charge of functional areas and where higher level positions imply a chain of command.

HIGH NEED FOR ACHIEVEMENT A description of a person's needs or motives as illustrated in being more goal oriented and persistent in the need to accomplish goals.

HIGH-PERFORMANCE PRACTICES Work practices that maximize fit between an organization's social system and its technology and strategies.

HIRING FREEZE A tactic to reduce costs by not hiring people except in areas where critical skills are needed.

HOMO ECONOMICUS This motivation assumption – that people are motivated to achieve rewards and avoid pain – is said to be the underlying assumption of PFP plans.

HUMAN CAPITAL An organization's human capital defines the competencies – the knowledge, skills, abilities and other characteristics – that individuals gain through experience, education and innate talent. It is a key component of an organization's general 'intellectual capital' that includes human capital (competencies), social capital (relationships and networks among people) and organizational capital (the structures, processes and culture of the organization).

HUMAN RELATIONS Although scientific management sought to apply scientific principles in reducing costs and improving efficiency, the human relations movement suggested that management should treat workers as individuals and recognize their needs. The human relations movement is often linked to Elton Mayo and his protégé Fritz J. Roethlisberger and the Hawthorne studies in the 1920s. These studies generally observed that productivity gains are often associated with taking an interest in employees and making decisions based on their natural needs and motivations. These ideas were also foundational in academic writers Abraham Maslow, who suggested that individuals have higher level self-actualization needs, and Douglas MacGregor, who advocated a Theory Y approach to motivation based on recognizing that individuals seek responsibility, are self-motivated and pursue higher level goals to realize their potential.

HUMAN RESOURCE Comparable to all other resources but for the fact that human resources have specific properties that are not present in other resources. Human resources have the ongoing ability to make decisions and act, whereas other resources are consumed.

HUMAN RESOURCE INFORMATION SYSTEM (HRIS) The HRIS provides capabilities for collecting, storing, maintaining, retrieving and validating the data needed by the organization for its human resource management. It can track attendance, pay raises and history, pay grades and positions held, performance management goals and ratings, training desired and received, disciplinary actions received, succession plans for key employees and applicant tracking and selection.

HUMAN RESOURCE MANAGEMENT (HRM) HRM's role focuses on delivering core activities such as training, recruitment, selection and classification in addition to technical expertise. HRM's role began to shift in recognizing employees as human resources.

HUMAN RIGHTS In the Universal Declaration of Human Rights, adopted in 1948 by the United Nations, human rights was defined as rights concerning equity and equality, such as the right to life and liberty, freedom from slavery and torture, freedom of opinion and expression, the right to work and education and many more.

HYBRID PENSION PLANS Pension plans which combine the features of defined benefit and defined contribution plans.

I

INCOME REPLACEMENT PROGRAMMES Include employment insurance, workers compensation, and paid parental leave and social assistance for those unable to work.

INDIVIDUALLY DIRECTED PERSPECTIVE ON CAREER DEVELOPMENT   Individuals are encouraged to be more proactive in their career development and to assume responsibility for developing their careers through experiences inside and outside of organizations.

INDUSTRIAL DEMOCRACY   The term industrial democracy (ID) has varied meanings, depending on the country, from workers' direct participation in the work setting in worker councils and shop-floor programmes, to worker's participation and co-management at the management and board level, to worker's self-governance as semiautonomous work groups. It is an organizational model for involving employees in managing and operating the workplace.

INFORMAL LEARNING   Learning that goes beyond formal classroom courses and takes place without an externally imposed curriculum. It can take place during ad hoc problem-solving, incidental conversations, coaching and mentoring, group problem solving, lunch-and-learns and communities of practice.

INFORMATIONAL JUSTICE   Describes a person's feeling about the information supplied and whether it is truthful, accurate and adequate when things don't go well, as when a person is receiving feedback on why he or she did not get promoted.

INITIATIVES   The change projects or programmes that are being used to implement a strategic objective.

INSTRUMENTALITY   In expectancy theory, this is the perceived connection between performance and possible rewards.

INSTRUMENTAL VALUES   Are the standards of conduct that we might have for attaining a goal or methods for attaining an end. There are two types of instrumental values: *morality* (behaving appropriately or being honest) and *competence* (being logical, obedient or helpful).

INTANGIBLE ASSETS   Reputation, name recognition and intellectual property such as knowledge and know-how, in addition to motivation.

INTERACTIVE PROBLEM SOLVING   A process that emphasizes analytical dialogue and joint problem solving and is designed to go deeper in researching the problems or issues driving a conflict.

INTEREST ARBITRATION   A dispute resolution mechanism whereby a neutral third party hears the different positions and decides on binding settlement terms.

INTEREST-BASED BARGAINING   Focuses on each party's interests as a way of getting beyond strongly held positions. Interest-based bargaining has also been called principled negotiations, integrative bargaining, mutual gains bargaining or consensus bargaining in which parties collaborate in finding a solution where both parties can win. Negotiators jointly engage in a problem-solving process in recognizing common interests and resolving the problems they need to address.

INTERNAL CUSTOMERS OR CLIENTS   Other managers within an organization that a department is providing services for. For example, HR's job is to be responsive to the line managers who are internal customers and to work as partners with them.

INTERNAL MOTIVATION   A self-directed or autonomous behaviour that manifests intrinsic or other higher-level needs or callings. Frederick Herzberg's motivational theory suggests that internal motivation is the catalyst within oneself which is driven by intrinsic motivational factors. Hackman and Oldham's job characteristic model suggests that people experience high internal motivation when they exhibit three critical psychological states: (i) experienced meaningfulness, (ii) experienced responsibility and (iii) knowledge of results.

INTERNAL PROCESSES   Within the internal process perspective of the SHRM BSC, these processes focus on the efficiencies of the way we deliver services.

INTERNAL RECRUITMENT   The real emphasis of an internal recruitment strategy, or recruiting from within, is a commitment to training and development of employees for a career in the organization. Internal recruitment is most critical for developing higher-level or specialized jobs in rounding out an employee's tacit and contextual knowledge.

INTERPERSONAL JUSTICE   Describes the quality of the interpersonal treatment amongst employees and between their supervisor and employees. A positive interpersonal climate is one which is free from public harassment and humiliation, criticism, and abusive action by supervisors and co-workers.

INTERVIEW QUESTION YIELD HIERARCHY Summarizes the potential yield of different interview questions. The hierarchy summarizes different types of questions: personal attributes, qualifications, specialized knowledge, self-reflective questions and behavioural description questions. It is suggested that the interview questions at the top of hierarchy might provide lower predictive power.

INTRINSIC CHARACTERISTICS Job characteristics that are internal to the individual and focus on higher level needs like meaningfulness, responsibility for results, and knowledge of results.

INVOLVEMENT Consultation, participation and input into decision making.

J

JOB ANALYSIS PROCESS The process of obtaining information about jobs and their requirements and the skills needed for performing them.

JOB CLASSIFICATION METHOD The once-dominant job evaluation plan in governmental organizations, it involves fitting jobs into established job classifications or a hierarchy of classes and grades. Each classification describes a group of jobs, and each grade defines different levels of difficulty, responsibility and education required.

JOB DESCRIPTION The job description summarizes the information collected in a job analysis and provides an overall summary of the job's key requirements and specifications. *Generic* job descriptions apply to a wide range of jobs and positions in various parts of the organization. Job descriptions can illustrate *customer-centred job designs* which focus on customer needs and designing and implementing services to achieve the organization's strategic objectives. They can also capture *employee-centred job designs* principles (e.g. job enrichment) and can be used for improving effectiveness and productivity by improving employee satisfaction and commitment.

JOB ENLARGEMENT Involves horizontally loading a job by increasing the number of tasks and variety of tasks at the same level. It is useful in reducing some of the monotony associated with doing the same thing day-in and day-out.

JOB ENRICHMENT Involves vertically loading a job or giving it higher level tasks and responsibilities which match the skills, knowledge and abilities of an employee.

JOB EVALUATION A process for establishing the worth of jobs or positions with respect to their value or worth to the organization to meet equity objectives. Job evaluation approaches are both non-quantitative and quantitative in nature. The *non-quantitative methods* include *ranking* whole jobs from highest to lowest and *job classification methods* which put jobs into classes or grades of professional, technical, managerial, clerical and sales. *Quantitative methods* include the *factor comparison method* – a variation of the ranking and point method – where evaluators rank jobs within specific factors. In the *point job evaluation system*, evaluators rate jobs and assign points to factors which are weighted in terms of their importance.

JOB HIERARCHY Levels of compensation given to a range or hierarchy of grades, bands or job family levels. A listing of the relative assessed value of jobs from highest to lowest.

JOB INVOLVEMENT This implies consultation and input in work (cognitive energy) and is a facet of engagement at work.

JOB SHARING A tactic of sharing the duties of a job between one or more employees.

JOB SPECIFICATION A written summary of worker requirements for a given job.

JUST CAUSE Usually requires employers to be 'just', make fair judgements and provide evidence to illustrate an employee's liability and negligence. Other requirements include warning the employee, giving the employee a fair hearing and being fair and reasonable in making sure the rules are enforced evenly and without discrimination. Just-cause dismissals involve cases such as theft, sexual harassment, fraud and dishonesty, intoxication and wilful disobedience.

JUST-IN-TIME MANAGEMENT Production, service, or inventory control system in the private sector which purchases materials which are needed only for customer demands.

K

KEY JOBS Also known as benchmark jobs in job evaluation, these jobs are representative of the types of jobs in an organization.

KNOWLEDGE The 'know how' and the ability to understand and explain something. This might be defined by a degree or diploma.

KNOWLEDGE-BASED (COMPETENCY-BASED) PLAN Compensation plans which pay people according to the skills people possess rather than just the skills they perform.

KNOWLEDGE, SKILLS, ABILITIES AND OTHER CHARACTERISTICS (KSAOS) Describe the elements of a competency that an individual might require to effectively achieve objectives and respond to clients.

L

LABOUR RELATIONS CLIMATE The degree of positivity and the quality of union management relationships among employees, their unions and management.

LAY-OFF Permanently or temporarily reducing the number of employees for business reasons such as a reorganization or recession.

LEADERSHIP ACTION PLAN (LAP) The LAP encourages you to define performance and learning goals in implementing a career plan that is based on your initiative. It illustrates a philosophy of self-directed career development where the individual is directly responsible for his or her career development.

LEADERS-MEMBER RELATIONS (LMX) The quality of the relationship between the leader and subordinates, LMX is described by three factors: respect, trust and obligation. Respect is the mutual respect that one person has for the capabilities of other people and is not an indication of personal friendship or liking. *Trust* is defined by ability, benevolence and integrity. *Obligation* is the 'expectation that interacting obligation will grow over time as career-oriented social exchanges blossom into a partnership'.[3]

LEARNING AND GROWTH A perspective within the SHRM BSC that focuses on learning and improvement and is an enabler of the other perspectives. It focuses on tapping into the energy and enthusiasm of individuals and groups in the way we motivate people and design their work so that it engages them in responding to customer or clients.

LEARNING GOALS Generally intrinsically motivating, learning goals encourage people to develop skills and involve themselves in ongoing learning and development.

LOCKOUT Describes the closing of a place of employment or suspension of work by an employer, to compel employees to agree to conditions of employment.

LOW YIELD The potential of various questions or selection tools in their ability to predict job behaviour or success.

M

MACRO-ENVIRONMENT The external environment of an organization which is described by political, economic, social and demographic, technological, environmental or ecological, and legal forces.

MANAGEMENT BY OBJECTIVE (MBO) An approach for defining objectives so that employees can compare their performance against objectives that are important for the organization.

MASS PRACTICE Conditions under which individuals practise a task for longer active practice with fewer rest periods in order to learn a new procedure.

MEDIATION A process by which a neutral third party assists two factious parties to come to an agreement on the issues that divide them.

MENTOR Someone who serves as a career model and who actively advises, guides and promotes another's career and training in a relationship of trust. Terms such as *role model, guide, guru, counsellor, confidante, teacher* and *adviser* are also used in connection with mentoring.

MERIT Although defined in different ways in different countries, merit within public organizations generally means that people are hired and promoted based on competencies (merit) rather than because of political connections.

MERIT PAY Provides for pay increases based on individual performance. Merit pay is different from other bonus programmes because the yearly merit increments add to an employee's base salary, whereas most incentives and bonuses are a one-time payment.

MERIT SYSTEMS Provide employees with an increase in pay based on individual performance usually measured by their immediate supervisor's appraisal.

META-ANALYSIS A statistical summary of research across different studies.

MOBBING A more sophisticated tactic than bullying as it involves cliques of people working collectively to control others.

MONETARY OR COMPENSABLE FACTORS People are motivated by both monetary and non-monetary factors. *Monetary factors* are the direct payments (salary) in addition to indirect payments such as the benefits, bonuses and health plans. *Non-monetary factors* (which are not always seen as compensable) include aspects of the work environment that enhance a person's competence and self-respect. These factors include recognition and status, support, training and development, learning and growth, and sense of personal accomplishment.

MOTIVATION The catalyst for action within an individual. That which is 'internal' to the individual and is a self-generated process that causes behaviour to be energized, directed and sustained.

MOTIVATIONAL FACTORS Frederick Herzberg suggests that motivation is best understood with two sets for factors: dissatisfiers and motivational factors. Focusing on the *dissatisfiers* (such as improving the administration, working conditions and pay) will not improve motivation, but will only reduce the level of dissatisfaction to a point of no dissatisfaction. If we want to motivate people and create the self-sustained internal energy, it is important to focus on *motivational factors* in designing one's work to encourage achievement, recognition, advancement and growth.

MULTIPLE-HURDLE STRATEGY Involves a series of steps or hurdles (pre-screening, testing, interviewing, background reference checks) in the selection process.

MULTI-RATER SEQUENTIAL INTERVIEWING In this style of interviewing, potential applicants participate in several interviews with different interviewers who assess applicants at different stages of the process.

N

NEED FOR ACHIEVEMENT The need for achievement (N-Ach) describes a person's desire or motive for success. Individuals with a high need for achievement tend to be more goal oriented and to take on moderately difficult tasks, and are more persistent in their need to accomplish them.

NEW PUBLIC MANAGEMENT (NPM) NPM attempted to apply private sector, competitive-based strategies theories in developing public organizations in quasi-markets with clients or customers. The NPM emerged in the 1990s at a time when the public had little faith in public institutions as a result of their inability to manage their finances. In part, NPM was a reaction to the traditional model of bureaucratic organizations and its monopolistic forms.

NOMINAL GROUP METHOD Combines individual generation of ideas with the group's consensual judgement in making a decision.

NON-MISCONDUCT TERMINATION Results for reasons such as lack of work and are not the fault of an employees.

NON-MONETARY FACTORS Aspects of the work environment that enhance a person's competence and self-respect including recognition and status, support, training and development, learning and growth, and sense of personal accomplishment.

O

OBJECTIVES Strategic objectives are more specific things that need to be accomplished to execute a strategic theme They represent a result that a person or organization seeks to achieve within a time frame.

OBLIGATION The expectation that through a career, obligations will grow over time as career-oriented social exchanges blossom into a partnership.

ONE-MINUTE GOAL SETTING This principle suggests that the most important aspect of goal setting is taking a few minutes to engage employees in an ongoing way. That is, problems occur on a regular basis, and as they do, they can be resolved in discussions in quick one-minute meetings. An important part of this one-minute goal-setting process is a relationship which provides ongoing, honest feedback on a continual basis.

OPERATIONAL ANALYSIS OR TASK ANALYSIS Focuses on the performance gaps and is used to decide what the training should consist of. This involves a study of what a person should be taught in performing the tasks effectively and in pinpointing the capabilities that need to be focused on in improving performance. This focuses on the job description and job requirements and reviews whether the job is effectively designed and the appropriate tasks to be performed.

ORGANIZATIONAL ANALYSIS   Assesses the strategic needs and the training which should occur in an organization as it seeks to achieve its strategic themes. This is aimed at the objectives and initiatives that an organization is using to achieve its strategic themes in order to find out if the proper objectives and initiatives are being used.

ORGANIZATIONAL COMMITMENT   A willingness to engage at a higher level and engage oneself in the work.

ORGANIZATIONAL PFP   Plans are generally gain-sharing programmes which reward employees for reducing costs and improving performance and, in the private sector, for the organization's improved profits (employee stock ownership plans).

'OTHER' CHARACTERISTICS   In defining a competency, these describe a range of characteristics such as motivation, attitude and ability to change. A large part of performance is related to a person's willingness and motivation to do something.

OUTCOMES   The impact or results of a set of initiatives or program.

OUTPUTS   Described by the quantity of the reports or other deliverables produced. These outputs might be important for the department in achieving *outcomes* like improved accounting services and customer satisfaction which might enhance the organization's long-range outcomes of improving the organization's customer base.

OUTSOURCING   Seen as contracting out specific functions of an organization – and sometimes entire divisions of an organization. IT resources and services were once very commonly associated with the practice of outsourcing, due in large part to the rapid and radical evolution that occurred in IT during the latter part of the twenty-first century, which required an equally rapid and radical response on the part of business and industry. The practice has now become common in nearly all organizational divisions.

OVERLEARNING   Deliberate overtraining to encourage the transfer of a skill as a strategy to improve.

P

PAIRED COMPARISON   A rating method in which an employee is compared to every other member.

PARADIGM SHIFT   In management philosophy, a dramatic or transformational shift in the way of thinking about an issue.

PAY EQUITY   Concerned with establishing gender equity in pay, using principles such as equal pay for equal work and equal pay for work of equal value.

PAY SATISFACTION   An attitude about one's pay compared with what others are paid or what one feels he or she should be paid.

PAY-FOR-PERFORMANCE (PFP)   Variable pay or financial incentives which are linked to performance.

PEER MENTORING   A mentoring relationship based on different types of peer relationships, including relationships which provide information, emotional support and feedback.

PENSION   Money paid at a regular basis to a person who has retired from work.

PERFORMANCE APPRAISAL   Most often viewed as a management directed process for 'appraisal' performance whereas a performance 'review' is seen as a joint management-employee process.

PERFORMANCE GOALS   Focus on outcomes and goals that are clearly linked to performance improvement.

PERFORMANCE MANAGEMENT   Broadly defined at the strategic level to describe a managerial process involving the collection, interpretation and utilization of performance information, with the goal of improving performance.

PERFORMANCE PLANNING AND REVIEW   The performance planning and review process builds on many of the assumptions of MBO and other goal-setting approaches. In the process, employees develop their annual plan, including organizational and personal goals and objectives. They might also define personal development goals and objectives related to the competencies for the job, as well as those supporting personal well-being and life balance.

PERFORMANCE REVIEW Usually a face-to-face meeting between the manager and employee for the purpose of solving personal and organizational problems, linking to organization priorities and encouraging employee learning, development and motivation to improve. The word *review* suggests a process of jointly reviewing performance and encouraging development and improvement, whereas words like *appraisal* and *evaluation* suggest a managerial-directed process.

PERSONAL CHARACTERISTICS AND ATTITUDES AND BEHAVIOURAL MEASURES OF PERFORMANCE Characteristics such as conscientiousness, reliability, customer orientation, leadership ability and team attitude. They are measured with graphic rating scales, behavioural checklists and behavioural anchored rating scales (BARS).

PERSONNEL MANAGEMENT Personnel was traditionally thought of as a staff responsibility in the administration of compensation, occupation health and safety, and collective bargaining, in addition to ensuring compliance with regulations, laws and collective agreements. The traditional public sector personnel system was highly centralized and run by central agencies responsible for hiring, setting employment policies, and training and career development. Public sector employment was based on a 'career service' model of security and tenure based on lifelong employment.

PESTEL An acronym for the (P) political, (E) economic, (S) social, (T) technological, (E) environmental and (L) legal factors. These factors are involved in scanning the macro environment.

PHILOSOPHY STATEMENT Identifies an organization's core values and what it cherishes; values which can be the cornerstone for strategic planning and its implementation.

POINT JOB EVALUATION SYSTEM A job evaluation technique which involves defining the jobs by several compensable factors, giving each job a numerical score on each of the factors, and summing the scores to obtain the value of the job. The rating scales are carefully worded and include a definition of the compensable factor; several divisions or degrees of each factor, carefully outlined; and a point score for each degree. Evaluators assign a numerical value for each factor, and money values are assigned.

POLICY GRIEVANCE Complaint filed because of a misapplication or misinterpretation of the collective agreement on a range of issues like scheduling or overtime payments.

POSITIONAL BARGAINING A negotiation that is generally competitive in holding on to a fixed idea, or position, and arguing for it within the stance that there is a 'fixed pie' of what I lose, you will gain.

POSITION-BASED SYSTEM Systems which open the recruitment and selection process to all internal and external candidates, placing less emphasis on internal employee development and more on finding the best person.

POSITIVE DISCIPLINE A participatory process which encourages the employee to recognize his or her deficiencies, take responsibility for improving and recommit to the organization's goals and mission.

PRACTICE The opportunity to apply training in real settings. *Active practice* involves giving individuals the chance to demonstrate their sills in an applied way. *Mass practice* conditions are when individuals practise a task continuously for longer periods of time, and *spaced practices* involves intervals between practice.

PRESENTEEISM Behaviour where people come to work even though, under normal conditions, their illness justifies an absence.

PROCEDURAL INJUSTICE Conflict or disagreement relating to procedural injustice describes an employee's perception of the unfairness of procedures – whether they are perceived to be biased or as not recognizing any prevailing ethical and moral codes.

PROGRESSIVE DISCHARGE Results from a progressive disciplinary process where there have been several attempts to corrective breaches of conduct or negligence such as problems in performance, violation of work rules, disobeying a supervisor and general personal behaviour.

PROGRESSIVE DISCIPLINE A process where increasingly severe disciplinary measures are applied with the objective of ensuring that employees understand the errant behaviour and have a reasonable time period to improve their performance.

PROSOCIAL VOICE A form of citizen behaviour and allows individuals to show their value to their managers.

PROTEAN A metaphor for a career that is driven by the person, not the organization, and that will be reinvented by the person from time to time as the person and the environment change. The metaphor is based on Proteus, a mythical sea god and one of the several deities described in Homer's *Odyssey*, who had the power of assuming different shapes and being flexible, versatile and adaptable.

PUBLIC SECTOR ORGANIZATIONS Organizations in the public arena which carry out a wide variety of public-related tasks in providing social services (e.g. education, health care and social services), regulations (e.g. gaming, housing, transportation), safety and justice (e.g. police, courts, fire, military) and common services (e.g. transportation, utilities) and which establish planning guidelines (e.g. development, education, safety). The differentiation of what is public and private is confounded by several factors, including the growing involvement of businesses in carrying out many governmental services and the adoption of business management practices in some public organizations. The uniqueness of public organizations is partially shaped by their raison d'être, their special role in society, the people who work in them and the prominence of public sector unions.

PUBLIC SERVICE MOTIVATION (PSM) A unique predisposition or motivational dimension that goes beyond self-interest and organizational interest and motivates people to perform meaningful public service and to serve the interests of a community of people, a state, a nation or humanity. It is illustrated by four factors: attraction to public policy making, commitment to the public interest, compassion in showing empathy for the welfare of others, and self-sacrifice in being willing to substitute service for others for personal rewards.

PUBLICNESS Given the growth of hybrid forms of public and private organizations, organizations might be defined by their publicness, where one end of the continuum defines the extent to which an organizations is constrained primarily by political authority, and at the other end is the degree to which an organization is constrained by economic authority.

PYGMALION EFFECT A self-fulfilling prophecy where a person or group of people internalize higher expectations placed on them and act in ways to fulfil these expectations. Pygmalion was a Cypriot sculptor who carved a woman out of ivory and, according to the legend, his statue was so fair and realistic that he fell in love with it. Pygmalion quietly wished for a bride who would be the living likeness of his ivory girl. As the legend goes, his beliefs and expectations encouraged Aphrodite to come to the rescue and transform the statue into a real person.

Q

QUALITY MOVEMENT In the early days of Taylor's scientific management, quality goals sought to reduce errors to a minimum. The quality movement in public and private organizations today comes with new expectations that suggest rather bluntly, '*Quality means refusing to accept error*' in the delivery of products or services.

QUALITY OF WORKING LIFE (QWL) QWL designs are implemented through open dialogues over the way the work is organized and managed. Individuals should be able to make judgements about what is desired and not desired. The 'choices' can lead to the development of jobs and organizations that enable people to develop their abilities and to fulfil their needs through new schedules, new ways of working, cooperative labour relations and work-group designs.

QUOTAS A set number of people whom an organization must hire or promote to comply with obligations in addressing employment gaps within certain groups.

R

RANKING A basic and rudimentary job evaluation technique where jobs are evaluated and ordinally ranked by order of importance.

REALISTIC JOB PREVIEW (RJP) A summary of realistic information about job demands, expectations, the customer environment and strategic objectives of the organization.

REASONABLE ACCOMMODATIONS Adjustments in the work environment to allow for the special needs of individuals with disabilities.

RECENCY ERROR A rating error when a person assigns a rating on the basis of an employee's more recent performance rather than overall performance.

REENGINEERING Reviewing and redesigning work processes to make them more efficient and to improve quality.

RELIABILITY The degree to which an interview, test or other selection procedure gives consistent results over a period of time. Just as a thermometer is reliable when we are confident that it is calibrated correctly, reliability in selection is the consistency of our measurement device. Reliability is also concerned with the consistency of different interviewers in producing the same ratings of applicants.

REPERTORY GRID INTERVIEW (REPGRID) The RepGrids were originally created as a way to help psychotherapists, but they have since been adapted for a variety of studies, especially in identifying skills and characteristics of people and organizations. The interview process encourages interviewees to define a set of constructs by comparing different people, tasks or organizations. For example, in comparing three people, the interviewee will be asked to define a characteristic which two of the people have in common but which is different in the third. After the construct is identified, the interviewer probes to have it described more fully with questions such as 'What does this mean? Could you give me an example of this?' More than one characteristic might emerge from each set of comparisons.

RESISTANCE POSITION (OR BOTTOM LINE) The absolute minimally acceptable position, where a person might be willing to strike or lockout before giving any more than this resistance point.

RESPECT Within the LMX instrument, it is defined as the mutual respect that one person has for the capabilities of other people and is not an indication of personal friendship or liking.[4]

RETIREMENT BENEFITS Financial benefits to support employees when they are no longer earning income from employment.

RETURN-TO-WORK (RTW) PROGRAMMES Programmes that facilitate the process of returning people to work after a long-term or short-term disability absence. RTW coordinators assist by advocating and supporting people in easing the transition.

S

SAFETY CLIMATE Key elements of the safety climate include management's commitment to safety, the priority of safety, co-worker safety behaviour, general safety policies, procedures and practices, safety training, safety communication, safety reporting and employee safety involvement.

SAFETY CULTURE Reflects the enduring attitudes, beliefs, perceptions and values that employees share in relation to safety.

SCENARIO PLANNING A forecasting tool which defines a set of contrasting scenarios as a way of creating a dialogue about what might occur in the future.

SCIENTIFIC MANAGEMENT An early theory of management linked to Frederick Taylor and his attempts to apply scientific principles in analyzing and designing jobs to improve efficiency. The designs often applied principles of specialization, division of labour and work simplification. Although scientific management is seen as an obsolete theory of management, its themes of efficiency, elimination of waste, and standardization of work procedures are still alive in industrial engineering and management today.

SEGREGATED OCCUPATIONS Often called gender segregation, as when there is an unequal distribution of men and women in some occupations. *Vertical segregation* is illustrated by the clustering of men at the top of occupational hierarchies and women at the bottom, whereas *horizontal segregation* is exemplified when one gender group is dominate in one occupation or set of tasks.

SELECTION RATIO The percentage of people hired, which is used in evaluating the usefulness of a predictor.

SELECTION TESTING A number of tests that have been used in selection which focus on personality, general intelligence, aptitude and integrity. Some of the characteristics assessed by these tests are correlated with job performance.

SELF-DISCIPLINE Managers encourage people to take responsibility in addressing their problems or unproductive work behaviours.

SEVERANCE PAY Payment based on length of service, organizational level and reason for termination.

SEVERITY The tendency to rate a person low on all criteria being evaluated.

SEXUAL HARASSMENT Unwelcome sexual advances, requests for sexual favours or other unwanted verbal or physical conduct of a sexual nature, which are made in relation to an individual's employment, education or living environment.

SHRM-BALANCED SCORECARD (SHRM BSC) The SHRM BSC builds on the BSC to show how various HR strategic objectives can be aligned to the organization's strategic objectives. The SHRM BSC framework is based on the assumption that HR strategic objectives are aligned to help line managers responds respond to the organizational strategic objectives. As such, strategies are initially aligned to respond to interests or needs of the line managers or the internal customers or clients that HR is responding to. As in the general Balanced Scorecard framework, the SHRM BSC summarizes four perspectives arranged in a semi-causal chain and encourages HR to develop objectives and initiatives within each of the different perspectives.

SITUATIONAL INTERVIEWS Interview questions which ask candidates how they would respond in a certain job-related situation.

SKILL-BASED PAY OR KNOWLEDGE-BASED PAY (OR COMPETENCY-BASED) Pay people according to the skills people possess rather than just the skills they perform.

SOCIOTECHNICAL PERSPECTIVES The sociotechnical perspective suggests that all effective systems need to recognize the requirements of both the social system (the people) and a technical system (the tools, knowledge, techniques). The technology can put demands and limits on the way the work is organized, but the employees have social and psychological requirements of their own in any job. Major needs for people include closure, or a sense of finishing a meaningful unit of work; some control over these tasks; some challenge; and satisfactory relationships.

SPACED PRACTICES Designing intervals or time periods (spaces) during practice. There is evidence that 5 different spaced sessions of learning are more likely to achieve better results than one longer session.

SPAN OF CONTROL The number of subordinates for whom a manager or supervisor is directly responsible.

SPECIALIZATION A principle of organization involving the division of general operations into more specialized operations in order to improve efficiencies.

STRAIN Although stress is a response to demands, strain is the result of applied stress and is the deformation which results. Strain might be manifested initially in burnout, depression and high blood pressure. Other impacts might be seen in relationship difficulties, substance abuse and performance.

STRATEGIC HUMAN RESOURCE MANAGEMENT (SHRM) SHRM argued for a more proactive role in linking HRM to an organization's strategic framework to improve performance in achieving outcomes like commitment, competence, congruence and cost-effectiveness. SHRM emphasized the importance of organizing HR activities and other activities affecting the behaviour of individuals so they 'fit' in a more strategic direction. As such, SHRM is a process of aligning human resource objectives so that HR resources, activities and initiatives assist internal clients to achieve the organization's strategies and goals. Thus, SHRM manager seeks to act as a partner to assist the organization's line managers in their strategic management in implementing objectives related to external clients and customers.

STRATEGIC MANAGEMENT In the private sector, the strategic management focus is concerned with goals of being more effective in a competitive environment, such as improving profit, product quality, market share and customer satisfaction. Strategy is a tool for being more effective than one's competitors. In the public arena, a strategy helps to identify priorities and engage the community in addressing important policy problems, challenges or needs for change. It involves identifying strategic themes (those that an organization is pursuing in relation to its vision) in responding to pressures from various stakeholders or clients. In public organizations with social goals, strategy can be a tool for the activist manager in focusing his or her programme and engaging others in the cause.

STRATEGIC OBJECTIVES Specific things that need to be accomplished to execute a strategy. Strategic objectives represent a result that a person or organization seeks to achieve within a time frame.

STRATEGIC PLANNING A process that often includes an analysis to identify the stakeholders and how to respond to them and whether different aspects of the mission statement and strategies might be important to different groups.

STRATEGIC RECRUITING PERSPECTIVE Calls for managers to be creative in attracting an external or internal pool of qualified applicants in a changing and social environment.

STRATEGY In the public arena, a strategy helps to identify priorities and engage the community in addressing important policy problems, challenges, or needs for change. It involves identifying strategic themes (strategic themes that an organization is pursuing in relation to its vision) in responding to pressures from various stakeholders or clients. In public organizations with social goals, strategy can be a tool for the activist manager in focusing their programs and engaging others in the cause.

STRATEGY MAP A visual tool for representing the cause-and-effect relationship among the strategic objectives and other components of a strategy.

STRESS Dr. Hans Selye, an endocrinologist at the University of Montreal, is frequently referred to as the 'Father of Stress.' He introduced the term *stress* as a *general adaptation syndrome*, as essentially the body's nonspecific response to the demands placed upon it. *Occupational stress* suggests that stress can be caused from stressors like workload, relationships, lack of recognition, organizational climate, personal responsibility, managerial responsibilities or lack of opportunity, home and work balance, as well as by daily hassles.

STRESS REACTION As a result of the appraisal of a situation, the body mobilizes its forces. Three distinct phases are part of the stress response: alarm, frustration and exhaustion.

STRESSORS The outside forces or agents acting on an organism which can potentially wear it down. A stressor is any stimulus or condition that has the potential to be appraised as challenging, threatening or harmful.

STRIKE A cessation or refusal to work or a slowdown of work activities on the part of employees in an effort to restrict or limit output.

STRUCTURED INTERVIEW Such interviews apply a series of job-related questions with predetermined answers across all interviews for a particular job. A traditional structured interview, although more reliable and valid, can be very restrictive, and many interviewers reject it because it was too confining and stressful for the candidate.

SUCCESSION PLANNING Manages the development and promotion of employees from one set of jobs to another. The planning recognizes the timing of when positions will need replacing, identifying the initial competencies, designing developmental opportunities, developing and maintaining a talent pool and reassessing the progress in meeting competencies and placement. This puts the onus on the organization to develop training opportunities to develop employees for key positions.

SUMMATIVE TOOLS Provide feedback and reviews which focus on the outcomes of a person's performance and what the person has achieved.

SWOT ANALYSIS A strategic plan can also include a review of the organization's (S) strengths and (W) weaknesses, (O) opportunities and (T) threats.

SYSTEMIC DISCRIMINATION A practice that appears, on the surface, to be fair and neutral and applied equally to all individuals, but which results in one group being treated in a different way.

SYSTEMIC RATER ERRORS Biases of the performance review process – unclear benchmarks, halo effect, recency effect, leniency tendencies and societal stereotypes – which produce reviews or ratings that are consistently too high or low in relationship to performance.

SYSTEMS THEORY An interdisciplinary theory in nature and society which is used as a framework to illustrate the connections between groups of objects. Organizational theorists using the system metaphor say that organizations are like living organisms and exhibit lifelike qualities of survival and growth. In the same way, systems theory can be a framework to integrate the various components of an HRM system to respond to larger organizational needs of survival and growth.

T

TACIT KNOWLEDGE Tacit knowledge is believed to be a product of learning from experience that affects performance in real-life situations. It is described as knowledge which is personal, profound and non-scientific; derives from experience and analogical reasoning; and which forms intuitions and instincts.

TARGET GOAL What you want to achieve and would regard as a 'win' in the bargaining plan.

TEAM INCENTIVE PLANS Emerged in response to competitive pressures to improve productivity and involve workers in production decisions, ideas which grew from their success in Japanese companies and public organizations. The building blocks of team based incentive systems are similar to all plans: (i) explicitly stated departmental or organizational level goal(s) to be achieved through team work, (ii) an incentive system based on the achievement of the goal(s), (iii) rewards that employees perceive as resulting from their contribution, (iv) rewards that are perceived to be fair and (v) rewards offered which clearly signal what is meant by good performance.

TELEWORK Work carried out in remote locations away from the central facilities, where workers connect virtually with others.

TEMPORARY A characteristic of many jobs where an employee remains in a position for a short term basis.

TERMINAL VALUES Describe outcomes or goals for an individual. According to Rokeach, there are few of these but they are easier to identify in society. They are either personal (e.g., desire for peace of mind, happiness, or excitement) or social (e.g., equality, security, national security, world peace).[5]

TERMINATIONS There are three types of terminations. A *non-misconduct termination* results for reasons such as lack of work and is not the fault of an employee. A *disciplinary discharge* results from a gross breach of conduct such as fighting, theft, fraud or wilful destruction of property. A *progressive discharge* results from more minor breaches of conduct or negligence such as problems in performance, violation of work rules, disobeying a supervisor and general personal behaviour.

THIRD-PARTY DISPUTE RESOLUTION Third-party dispute settlement processes, such as mediation, interactive problem-solving, fact finding and interest arbitration.

TOTAL QUALITY MANAGEMENT (TQM) The Deming-inspired quality movement and total quality management (TQM) called for shaping organizational activities on meeting or exceeding customer expectations for products and services. The idea is to redesign the organization's entire service delivery and production system to meet customer needs.

TRAINING EVALUATION Training evaluators focus on one of two questions: whether learning objectives are achieved (learning issues) or whether the accomplishment of the training objectives enhanced job performance or helped the organization achieve its strategic objectives. Learning outcomes are usually assessed at four levels (i) reaction of learners, (ii) learning, (iii) behaviour and (iv) results.

TRAINING NEEDS ASSESSMENT A comprehensive training needs assessment reviews organizational, operational and personal needs for training. The organizational analysis assesses the strategic needs, and the organizational analysis focuses on performance gaps in effectively carrying out the necessary tasks. The employee needs analysis (ENA) identifies competency gaps and determines the competencies that should be addressed in training.

TRANSFER A statement of whether or not the training received is easily practised in a real setting.

TRIANGULATION This principle suggests that, given the potential biases of different methods, it is useful to triangulate or use multiple selection tools in gaining data and information from a variety of perspectives and viewpoints.

TRUST Defined within the LMX scale by measures of ability, benevolence, and integrity.[6]

U

UNEMPLOYMENT RATE The percentage of the total labour force that is unemployed but is actively looking for employment or willing to work.

UNION SHOP A provision stipulating that, as a condition of employment, an individual must belong to the union that represents the employees.

UNITY OF COMMAND A term suggesting the need to ensure unity of focus where one person has the responsibility for completing a task.

V

VACANCY RATE The ratio of vacancies in comparison with the percentage of all job openings (both filled and unfilled).

VALENCE In expectancy theory, this is preference or the value of the reward for the person.

VALIDITY The degree to which the characteristics measured in a test are related to the requirements of some aspect of the job performed. Because a goal in using a selection test is to determine a person's motivation or performance, the validity of a test or interview is the extent to which the information gathered corresponds to actual motivation or job performance.

VALUES Values describe the preferences that individuals have, their perceived rights and benefits and obligations. According to Rokeach, there are two types of values: instrumental and core. *Instrumental values* are the standards of conduct that we might have for attaining a goal or methods for attaining an end. There are two types of instrumental values: morality (behaving appropriately or being honest) and competence (being logical, obedient or helpful). *Terminal values* are easier to identify in society as they are illustrated as goals and outcomes. They are either personal (e.g. desire for peace of mind, happiness or excitement) or social (e.g. equality, security, national security, world peace).

VIRTUAL A non-physical, digital organizational structure characterized in a spider-like web rather than a hierarchical organizational chart.

VIRTUAL PUBLIC ORGANIZATIONS Geographically distributed organizations where members are connected by goals, interests, or contracts, and who work together digitally.

VISION STATEMENT A statement of the future, like an architect's vision of a development, a vision statement illustrates a value-based sketch of the future which pulls the organization in a certain direction.

VOICE The term *voice* is generally used to describe how employees are able and willing to have a say in work activities and in the way they work. Organizations might introduce voice systems as a way to increase employee perceptions of fairness such as allowing for engagement and input into decision making.

W

WA (HARMONY) Expresses a quality of relationship, a form of teamwork or group consciousness of the employees. Individual employee action is not dominant in Japanese organizations, and may be discouraged because of the competition and possible antagonisms it might generate among team members.

WAGE GROWTH An indicator of labour supply which illustrates an upward trend in the average hourly rate.

WICKED PROBLEMS In the public arena, many problems – like nutritional deficiencies, drug use, poverty and global warming – are called wicked problems. A wicked problem is difficult or impossible to solve because of contradictory or changing requirements which are difficult to recognize.

WIN–LOSE BARGAINING A bargaining posture that assumes that the goals of the parties are irreconcilable (also known as distributive bargaining).

WIN–WIN BARGAINING A bargaining posture that assumes that the goals of the parties are reconcilable and that parties can work together in responding to common interests (also known as integrative bargaining).

WORKFORCE FORECASTING Seeks to forecast or predict labour requirements by understanding future organizational and environmental demands affecting human resources.

WORKFORCE PLANNING (WFP) Seeks to align an organization's human resources with the mission and strategic objectives of its strategic plan and ensure that the 'right people with the right skills are in the right place at the right time to help their organizations perform'.[7]

Index

A
Affective commitment, 70
Arbitration, 261–262, 266
Assertiveness, 14
Assessment centers, 143–144

B
Bakke, E.W., 6
Balanced Scorecard (BSC), xviii, 31–34
Balanced Scorecard (BSC) template and terms, *see also* SHRM-Balanced Scorecard
   Competency, *see* Competency
   Goals and vision, 41–42
   Initiatives, 33, 42
   Measures or markers, 33, 42
   Resources, 42
   Strategic objectives, 33, 41
   Strategic themes, 33, 41
Behavioural event interview (BEI), 50
Blanchard, K., 175
Bolles, R.N., 187
Boundary-less, temporary organization, 11, 189–190
Boseman, B., xv
Boyatzis, R., 50
Bryson, J., 31

C
Career development
   Activities to enhance a boundary-less career, 192–194
   Informal learning, 194
   Performance metrics defining career success, 190–191
   A strategic shift to a boundary-less career contract, 189–190
   Traditional organizationally directed career, 192
Career development planning
   Leadership action plan (LAP) template for self directed planning, 195–197
   Theoretical logic for self-directed career development, 195
   Writing a LAP, 197
Centralization of authority, 11, 190–191
Challenges affecting SHRM, *see* Strategic Pressures
Change pressures, 7, 9–12Collective bargaining
   Dynamics in negotiating a collective agreement, 241–242
   Interest-based bargaining, 246–249
   Linking to the strategic context, 241–242
   Performance metrics in negotiating a collective agreement, 243
   Positional bargaining, 244–246Collectivism, 14
Compensation systems for funding different types of employee benefits
   Challenges of funding health care benefits, 297–298
   Challenges of funding pensions benefits, 291–292
   Challenges of providing work-family benefits, 299–301
   Different types of employee benefits, 289–290
   Strategic alternatives of different employee benefits, 298–299
   Strategic alternatives of different pensions for public employees, 292–295
   Taking personal control of retirement plans, 296–297
Compensation systems in establishing fixed salaries
   Approaches for evaluating jobs in assessing their value, 277–279
   Knowledge or skill-based pay systems, 284
   Linking to the strategic context surrounding pay equity and equality, 275–276
   Performance metrics in relation to pay equity, 276–277
   Using a point job evaluation plan for meeting pay equity objectives, 279–285
Competency, 50–52
   Competence-based management (CBM), 49–50
   Core requirements, 54
   Distinguishing and threshold competencies, 50–51, 54
   Identifying competencies using critical incidents, 62–64
   Identifying competencies using repertory grid, 63–65
   Job analysis methods for defining competencies, 54–57
   KSA, 512, 54
   KSAO, 54, 58
Competency models and frameworks, 55, 58–64
   Competencies based on meta-analysis, 59–60
   Competencies defining executive failure, 59
   Competency Scorecard model, 60–61
   Posner and Kouzes model, 59
   Russell's model, 60
   UK and US perspectives, 58
Cooper, C., 217
Critical incident technique, 50–51, 55–56, 57, 62–63, 65, 168–169, 204
Criterion testing, 50
Critical success factors, 4
Culture, 4, 14–15
Customers in public organizations
   Customer relationship in public arena, 41, 47
   Customer requirements in TQM, 19
   Definition, xviii, 41
   External and internal customer, 41

D
Dahl, R.A., xv
Dastmalchian, A., 256
Deming, W., 18, 79, 82, 160
Disciplinary procedures, 178–180
   Positive discipline, 178
   Progressive discipline, 179
   Termination interview, 179–180
Diversity, 1, 14, 109
   Different paradigms of diversity, 109–111</test>
   Designated groups within a diversity perspective, 109, 114–115
   Evolving context defining diversity, 114–115
Diversity strategies in recruiting
   Becoming an employer of choice for designated groups, 115–116, 123
   Developing an inclusive culture for designated groups, 116
   Developing an inclusive culture for older and younger workers, 123
   Employers of choice for younger and older workers, 123
   The strategic recruiting perspective in diversity, 113–114
Drucker, P., 6, 163

E
Employee assistance programme (EAP), 20
Employee engagement, 12–14, 69–70
   Job designs to improve engagement, *see* Job enrichment
   Linking to the strategic context, 70
   Performance metrics in linking a job design to engagement, 71–72
Employment equality, 15
Employment equity, 15, 109, 275–277
Ethical behaviour, 15

F

Fact finding, 261
Fitting into an organization, *see* SHRM as fit; Vocational preferences
Forecasting, *see* Workforce planning (WFP)
Future orientation, 14
Future-shock, 9–10
Friedman, M., 221

G

Gabler, T., 26, 80
Gender equalitarian, 14–15
General mental ability (GMA), 17
Gilmore, D., 153
Global economic crisis, 9
Globe Leadership and Organizational Behavior Effectiveness (GLOBE), 14
Goal setting, *see* Performance reviews (PR)
Golem effect, 172
Gore, A., 80
Grant, A., 84, *see also* Job design, relational perspective
Grievance, 265

H

Hackman, J., 74–76, 82, *see also* Job enrichment
Hall, D., 190
Health promotion
  Assisting employees through employee assistance programs, 225
  Developing a culture to support health, *see* Workplace safety and health
  Health promotion in reducing absenteeism, 224–225
  Managing absenteeism in returning people to work, 224–226
  Return-to-work programmes, 226–227
Hellervick, L., 153
Herzberg, F., 70–74, 82, 312, *see also* Job enrichment
Hierarchical organization, 11
Hoftstede, G., 15
Human capital, 4, 12–13
Human relations, 6
Human resource (HR), 1, 6–7
  Strategic role, 36–37
Human resource information system (HRIS), 12
Human resource management (HRM), 1, 5–9
Human rights, 15
Humane orientation, 14

I

Implementation, 17, 37
Industrial democracy, 258
Informational justice, 263
Intangibles, 3–5
Interactive problem-solving, 261
Interpersonal justice, 263
Involvement, 13–14

J

Janz, T., 153
Job analysis process, 51–54
  Job analysis methods, 54–57
  Linking to the strategic context, 54–55
  Performance metrics related to job analysis, 55
  Traditional job analysis, 53, 55
Job description, 52–54
  Generic job descriptions, 52
  Template for writing a job description, 53–54
Job design, 52–53
  Customer-centered job designs, 52
  Early history, 70–71
  Employee-centered job designs, *see* Job enrichment
  Relational job design perspective, 82, *see also* Teams
Job enlargement, 70
Job enrichment, 52–53, 70
  Elaborate JCM, 83
  Herzberg's job enrichment, 71–74
  Herzberg's motivators and dissatisfiers, 71–74
  JCM key factors, 75
  Job characteristics model (JCM), 74–76
  Job JCM internal motivation, 74
Job evaluation plans, 277–279
  Point job evaluation plan, 279–284
Job requirements, 51–52
Johnson, S., 175

K

Kahn, H., 101
Kaplan, R.S., 17, 31
Kirkpatrick, D.L., 205–206
Kirkman, B., 83, 84
Kouzes, J., 59

L

Labour relations climate, 4, 256
  International laws, 253–254
Latham, G., 171, 173
Leader member exchange (LMX), 263
Lewin, K., 84, 171
Leader member relations (LMX), 174
Lindblom C.E., xv
Locke, E., 171, 173
Lockout, 259

M

Managerial roles, 9
MacArthur, D., 18, 79
Maier, N., 173, 174
McClelland, D.C., 50, 195
Mediation, 261
Merit principle, 137
Miles, R., 6
Mintzberg, H., 17
Motivators and satisfiers, *see* Job enrichment, Herzberg's motivators and satisfiers
Motivation, 70, 71, *see also* Job enrichment

N

New public management (NPM), xiv, 1, 6, 7, 25–27, 52, 137
Norton, D.P., 17, 31

O

Older workers
  Changing age profile, 89–90
  Employers of choice for older workers, 123
Oldham, G., 74–76, 82, *see also* Job enrichment
Osborne, D., 26, 80
Outsourcing, 19–20, 128–130

P

Parker, A., 82, *see also* Job design, relational perspective
Pay equity and equality, *see* Compensation systems in establishing fixed salaries
Pay satisfaction, 274–275
Performance orientation, 14
Performance reviews (PR)
  Difficulties in assessing progress in meeting goals, 161
  Design and implementation principles, 158
  Linking to the strategic context, 159–160
  Performance metrics in using goal setting in PR, 160–161
  Problems with PR, 157–158
Performance review approaches
  Competencies approaches, 161, 167–168
  Goals and objectives, 162–163
  Personal characteristics or behavioural approaches, 161, 163–167
  Results oriented approaches, 161, 168–169
Performance reviews (PR) for employee development, 169–171
Performance reviews (PR) in linking to strategic themes
  Goal setting in PR, 171–173
  Encouraging problem solving in PR, 173–174
  Implementing the goal setting approach, 174–178
  One minute goal setting, 175
  Performance planning and review, 175–176

Index

Personnel management, 5–6
Point job evaluation system, 279–284
Plastrick, P., 26
Posner, B., 59
Power distance, 14
Public arena, xiv,xv, 1, 11
Publicness, xv
Public organization's purpose, xiv-xvii
Public private partnerships (PPP), xiv, chap 13
Public sector motivation (PSM), 68–69, 76
Public sector values, xv–xvi, 68–69
Procedural justice, 262–263
   Procedural justice in guarding employee rights, 264–265
   Voice systems to improve procedural justice, 264
Prosocial voice, 264
Pygmalion effect, 172

Q

Quality of working life (QWL), 76–79
   Early history of QWL, 76
   QWL key factors, 76–77
Quality requirements, 18–19

R

Recruiting, *see also* Diversity
   Career-based and position based recruiting, 126
   External recruiting, 117–127
   Identifying markets for recruiting different groups, 118–119
   Internal recruiting, 127–128
   Linking to the strategic context, 114–116
   Outsourcing, 19–20, 128–130
   Performance metrics related to recruitment, 116–117
   Recruiting to meet diversity objectives, 122–123
   Recruiting from an employee perspective in the job search, 130–131
Recruiting process
   Assessing different recruiting sources, 119–121
   Being creative in developing a larger pool of applicants, 122–12
   Designing the application process, 124–127
   On-line recruiting, 123–124
Resource-based view of strategy, 29–30
Rosen, B., 83, 84
Rosenman, R., 221
Russell, C., 60

S

Scanlon, J.N., 309
Scenario planning, *see* Workforce planning tools
Segregated occupations, 275–276

Selection
   Employee value fitness in public organizations, 135–137
   Linking to the strategic context, 138
   Performance metrics related to selection, 139–145
   Selection errors, 138–145
   Triangulation principle in improving selection, 142–144
Selection interviewing
   Advantages and disadvantages, 148–149
   Developing behavioural description interviews, 150–153
   Principles of effective interviews, 149–150
Selection testing
   Aptitude tests, 147
   Big five personality factors, 54, 145–146
   Cognitive ability tests, 146
   General intelligence tests, 147
   Integrity tests, 147
Selye, H., 218
SHRM, xiii–xvii, 5–9
SHRM-Balanced Scorecard, xviii-ix, 34–39
   Customer perspective, 35–36, *see also* Customers in public organizations
   Definition and perspectives, 27–30, 33, 34–37
   Financial perspective, 37–38
   Internal process perspective, 36
   Learning and growth perspective, 37–38
   Logic for using SHRM-BSC, 37–39
   Strategy mapping, xviii, 38–39, 40
SHRM BSC applications
   Define competencies for perspectives of the SHRM-BSC, 65
   Define competencies in responsibility for career development, 198–199
   Define learning initiatives for managerial career development, 212–213
   Develop a strategy map for a 'social well-being' strategic theme, 44
   Develop a personal strategy map for improving life quality, 44
   Identify pressures affecting HR's strategic context, 23–24
   Identify initiatives and markers for getting recruited, 105
   Identify initiative and markers for recruitment objectives, 132
   Identify initiative and markers for diversity and inclusive objectives, 132
   Identify employee objectives which link to strategic objectives, 182
   Illustrate the linkage of objective to strategy themes, 44–46
   Use How-why questions in defining objectives, 198–199

   Use the SHRM BSC for attracting and retaining younger workers, 212–213Use the SHRM BSC for defining pay equity objectives, 287
   Use the SHRM BSC for designing attractive benefits programs, 287
   Use the SHRM BSC for more effectively negotiating, 250
   Using a strategy map to assist line managers implement improve QWL, 86
   Use a strategy map to define workplace health and safety objectives, 234
SHRM as fit
   SHRM best practicefit, 28–29
   Strategy-employee behaviour fit, 28
   Strategy-employee skills fit, 28
Simon, H., xiv
Smith, A., 12
Social system, 12, 77
Sociotechnical perspective, 78
Strategic Human Resource Management (SHRM), *see* SHRM
Strategic management, 27, 41
   Resource-based view of strategy, 29–30, 58
Strategic planning, 17, 31–33
   Goals, 41
   Macro-environment, 32
   Mission statement, 32
   PESTEL, 32
   Philosophy statement, 32
   Strategy, 41
   SWOT analysis, 32
   Vision, 41
   Vision statement, 32Strategic pressures or forces, 7–20
Strategic themes, 33
   Direct approach, 34
   Goals approach, 34
   Visions of success approach, 34
Stress causes and effects
   Framework for understanding the causes and effects, 220
   Stress effects, 223–224
Stress profile
   Burnout, 222–223
   Type A personality, 221–222
Strikes, 259–260
Succession planning, 127–128
Systemic discrimination, 276

T

Tactic knowledge, 12
Tavistock researchers, 78, 82
Taylor, F., 18
Teams
   Self-managed, autonomous teams, 78, 82
   Team design as a relational perspective, 82
   Team empowerment model, 83–84
   Types of teams, 82–83

Thatcher, M., 6, 26, 190
Third party dispute settlement
  Fact finding, 261
  Interactive problem-solving, 261
  Interest arbitration, 261–262
  Mediation, 261
Thompson, J., xiv
Toffler, A., 9
Tolman, E., 171
Total quality management (TQM), 19, 52
  Deming and other TQM proponents, 79
  Early history of TQM, 79
  Just-in-time management (JIT), 79
  TQM key factors, 79–80
  Wa (harmony), 80
Training
  Competency based training, 203
  Linking to the strategic context, 203–204
  Performance metrics in assessing training, 205–206
  Types of training, 202
Training within an experiential model
  Experiential learning in acquiring tacit knowledge, 208
  An experiential learning model, 207–208
  Experiential learning in training and development, 207–210
  Using experiential learning with E-technology, 210–211
Training needs, 203–204
Trist, E., 82

U

Uncertainty avoidance, 14–15
Unity of command, 11
Universal Declaration of Human Rights, 15
Ulrich, D., 8
Union membership changes and strength, 238–239, 243

V

Values, *see* Public sector values; Selection, employee value fitness
Virtual organizations, 11–12
Vocational preferences, 187–188

W

Weber, M., xiv
Weiner, H., 101
White, L., 71
Wicked problem, 10–11
Willoughby, W., 71
Workforce planning (WFP), 91–92
  Charting progress of WFP, 95
  General WFP model, 92–94
  Initiatives for implementing WFP, 94–95
  Linking to the strategic context, 92–95
  Performance metrics related to selection, 95
  WFP at the national level, 93
Workforce planning tools
  Qualitative tools for forecasting, 99–101
  Quantitative tools for forecasting, 96–97
  Scenario planning, 99, 101–104
  Uncertainties of WFP forecasting, 97–99Workplace safety and health
  Demands causing occupational stress, 218–219
  Developing a culture to support workplace safety and health, 226–233
  Linking to the strategic context of workplace stress, 217–218
  Major causes and key challenges, 214–216
  Models explaining the impact of stress, 216–217
  Performance metrics in understanding the effects of stress, 219–214
Workplace accidents
  Causes of accidents, 227–228
  Communicating positive safety norms, 230–231
  Developing a climate and culture for encouraging safety, 229–230
  Making a commitment to a joint management approach, 230
  Underlying causes, 228–229
Workplace violence and bullying, 231

Manufactured by Amazon.ca
Bolton, ON